Analyzing the Economics of Financial Market Infrastructures

Martin Diehl
Deutsche Bundesbank, Germany

Biliana Alexandrova-Kabadjova
Banco de México, Mexico

Richard Heuver
De Nederlandsche Bank, The Netherlands

Serafín Martínez-Jaramillo
Banco de México, Mexico

A volume in the Advances in Finance, Accounting, and Economics (AFAE) Book Series

BUSINESS SCIENCE Reference
An Imprint of IGI Global

Managing Director: Lindsay Johnston
Managing Editor: Keith Greenberg
Director of Intellectual Property & Contracts: Jan Travers
Acquisitions Editor: Kayla Wolfe
Production Editor: Christina Henning
Development Editor: Courtney Tychinski
Cover Design: Jason Mull

Published in the United States of America by
Business Science Reference (an imprint of IGI Global)
701 E. Chocolate Avenue
Hershey PA, USA 17033
Tel: 717-533-8845
Fax: 717-533-8661
E-mail: cust@igi-global.com
Web site: http://www.igi-global.com

Library of Congress Cataloging-in-Publication Data

Analyzing the economics of financial market infrastructures / Martin Diehl, Biliana Alexandrova-Kabadjova, Richard Heuver, and Serafin Martinez-Jaramillo, editors.

pages cm

Includes bibliographical references and index.

ISBN 978-1-4666-8745-5 (hbk. : alk. paper) -- ISBN 978-1-4666-8746-2 (ebk.) 1. Financial institutions--United States. 2. Financial institutions--Law and legislation--United States. I. Diehl, Martin, editor.

HG181.A595 2016

332'.04150973--dc23

2015019504

This book is published in the IGI Global book series Advances in Finance, Accounting, and Economics (AFAE) (ISSN: 2327-5677; eISSN: 2327-5685)

British Cataloguing in Publication Data

A Cataloguing in Publication record for this book is available from the British Library.

Advances in Finance, Accounting, and Economics (AFAE) Book Series

Ahmed Driouchi
Al Akhawayn University, Morocco

ISSN: 2327-5677
EISSN: 2327-5685

Mission

In our changing economic and business environment, it is important to consider the financial changes occurring internationally as well as within individual organizations and business environments. Understanding these changes as well as the factors that influence them is crucial in preparing for our financial future and ensuring economic sustainability and growth.

The **Advances in Finance, Accounting, and Economics (AFAE)** book series aims to publish comprehensive and informative titles in all areas of economics and economic theory, finance, and accounting to assist in advancing the available knowledge and providing for further research development in these dynamic fields.

Coverage

- Economics of Innovation and Knowledge
- Economics of Intellectual Property Rights
- Theoretical Issues in Economics, Finance, and Accounting
- Economics Geography
- E-Accounting
- Public Finance
- Field Research
- Statistical Analysis
- Borrowing and Lending
- Health Economics

IGI Global is currently accepting manuscripts for publication within this series. To submit a proposal for a volume in this series, please contact our Acquisition Editors at Acquisitions@igi-global.com or visit: http://www.igi-global.com/publish/.

The Advances in Finance, Accounting, and Economics (AFAE) Book Series (ISSN 2327-5677) is published by IGI Global, 701 E. Chocolate Avenue, Hershey, PA 17033-1240, USA, www.igi-global.com. This series is composed of titles available for purchase individually; each title is edited to be contextually exclusive from any other title within the series. For pricing and ordering information please visit http://www.igi-global.com/book-series/advances-finance-accounting-economics/73685. Postmaster: Send all address changes to above address.

Titles in this Series

For a list of additional titles in this series, please visit: www.igi-global.com

Contemporary Global Perspectives on Gender Economics
Susanne Moore (The Centre for Gender Economics and Innovation, Australia)
Information Science Reference • copyright 2015 • 357pp • H/C (ISBN: 9781466686113) • US $195.00 (our price)

Green Accounting Initiatives and Strategies for Sustainable Development
Chiraa Caraiani (Bucharest University of Economic Studies, Romania) Camelia I. Lungu (Bucharest University of Economic Studies, Romania) Cornelia Dascălu (Bucharest University of Economic Studies, Romania) and Florian Colceag (Bucharest University of Economic Studies, Romania)
Business Science Reference • copyright 2015 • 382pp • H/C (ISBN: 9781466687202) • US $205.00 (our price)

Handbook of Research on Globalization, Investment, and Growth-Implications of Confidence and Governance
Ramesh Chandra Das (Katwa College, University of Burdwan, India)
Information Science Reference • copyright 2015 • 526pp • H/C (ISBN: 9781466682740) • US $345.00 (our price)

Handbook of Research on Sustainable Development and Economics
Ken D. Thomas (Auburn University, USA)
Business Science Reference • copyright 2015 • 512pp • H/C (ISBN: 9781466684331) • US $325.00 (our price)

Green Economic Structures in Modern Business and Society
Andrei Jean-Vasile (Petroleum-Gas University of Ploiesti, Romania) Ion Raluca Andreea (Bucharest Academy of Economic Studies, Romania) and Turek Rahoveanu Adrian (University of Agronomic Sciences and Veterinary Medicine, Bucharest, Romania)
Business Science Reference • copyright 2015 • 325pp • H/C (ISBN: 9781466682191) • US $195.00 (our price)

Handbook of Research on Behavioral Finance and Investment Strategies Decision Making in the Financial Industry
Zeynep Copur (Hacettepe University, Turkey)
Business Science Reference • copyright 2015 • 525pp • H/C (ISBN: 9781466674844) • US $245.00 (our price)

Agricultural Management Strategies in a Changing Economy
Gabriel Popescu (Bucharest Academy of Economic Studies, Romania) and Andrei Jean-Vasile (Petroleum - Gas University of Ploiesti, Romania)
Business Science Reference • copyright 2015 • 439pp • H/C (ISBN: 9781466675216) • US $225.00 (our price)

Handbook of Research on In-Country Determinants and Implications of Foreign Land Acquisitions
Evans Osabuohien (Covenant University, Nigeria & German Development Institute, Germany)
Business Science Reference • copyright 2015 • 430pp • H/C (ISBN: 9781466674059) • US $265.00 (our price)

IGI GLOBAL
DISSEMINATOR OF KNOWLEDGE
www.igi-global.com

701 E. Chocolate Ave., Hershey, PA 17033
Order online at www.igi-global.com or call 717-533-8845 x100
To place a standing order for titles released in this series, contact: cust@igi-global.com
Mon-Fri 8:00 am - 5:00 pm (est) or fax 24 hours a day 717-533-8661

Editorial Advisory Board

List of Reviewers

Table of Contents

Detailed Table of Contents

Like a human being's backbone, well-functioning financial market infrastructures contribute to the stability of the financial system. They enable fast and smooth movements, channel relevant information, protect the channels for transmission and reduce risk. Problems in financial market infrastructures may lead to dysfunctions of financial markets, a lack of options for transaction and, therefore, to limited movability, misleading information or disturbed information channels and in the worst case to systemic risk. The chapter explains the role of financial market infrastructure within the wider definition of a financial system. Based on the historical emergence of payment systems, central clearing and central securities depositories, the special advantage of financial market infrastructures for the productivity of intermediaries, for the efficiency of financial markets and for the welfare of an economy is explained. The chapter shows the economic and analytical importance and specificity of financial market infrastructures.

Financial Market Infrastructures (FMIs) are essential for the well-functioning of the financial system, as they play a central role in facilitating clearance and settlement of financial transactions such as payments, securities, and derivatives contracts. Nowadays, it is widely acknowledged that the proper functioning of systemically important FMIs is also vital to maintain financial stability; their failure for solvency

been applied in other econometric areas such as VAR models but not in payment system simulations. In this empirical paper, a reduction in total execution times of payment system simulations is studied by exploiting computational parallelization in a one multicore PC environment. The preliminary results of parallel simulations are reported and the possible benefits of analyzing financial market infrastructures using this technique are discussed. This information can be very useful for choosing a parallelization strategy and designing the next generation platforms for parallel processing of payment and securities settlement system simulations. This is the first time parallel computing techniques have been applied to payment system simulations.

In this chapter the authors provide a method to aggregate large value payment system transaction data for executing simulations with the Bank of Finland payment simulator. When transaction data sets get large, simulation may become too time consuming in terms of computer power. Therefore, insufficient data from a statistical point of view can be processed. The method described in this chapter provides a solution to this statistical problem. In order to work around this problem the authors provide a method to aggregate transaction data set in such a way that it does not compromise the outcome of the simulation significantly. Depending on the type of simulations only a few business days or up to a year of data is required. In case of stress scenario analysis, in which e.g. liquidity position of banks deteriorates, long time series are preferred as business days can differ substantially. As an example this chapter shows that aggregating all low value transactions in the Dutch part of TARGET2 will not lead to a significantly different simulation outcome.

This chapter examines the network of Colombian sovereign securities settlements. With data from the settlement market infrastructure we study financial institutions' transactions from three different trading and registering networks that we combine into a multi-layer network. Examining this network of networks enables us to confirm that (i) studying isolated single-layer trading and registering networks yields a misleading perspective on the relations between and risks induced by participating financial institutions; (ii) a multi-layer approach produces a connective structure consistent with most real-world networks (e.g. sparse, inhomogeneous, and clustered); and (iii) the multi-layer network is a multiplex that preserves the main connective features of its constituent layers due to positively correlated multiplexity. The results highlight the importance of mapping and understanding how financial institutions relate to each other across multiple financial environments, and the value of financial market infrastructures as sources of data for working on multi-layer financial networks.

High credit card debt default has been symptomatic for the U.S. and other countries in the last decades. Different explanations for this situation exist in the literature. One explanation is overconfidence, which has become a key concept in behavioural economics for explaining anomalies in financial markets such as excessive trading volume. There is also the idea that overconfidence is to blame for high credit card debt. In this paper, an agent-based model is presented that examines the effects of overconfidence on credit card usage. Overconfidence is used here to explain why people who never intend to borrow on their credit card(s) do so anyway. The model contains consumption, two means of payment (credit card and cash), and a distortion to agents' income expectations via overconfidence. It was found that overconfidence leads to more "accidental" borrowing and higher interest rates.

Timing analysis in an RTGS payment system offers input to operators, overseers and supervisors about the behavior of the system or individual participants. Timing related indicators can be used as a monitoring tool to identify liquidity circulation problems. Study of the behavior of participants may help identify changes due to business practices shifts, reactions to unexpected events or even to various types of stress. Furthermore, the indicators can be used in simulation studies, where the impact to timing of different levels of induced stress to a system or changes of its institutional features may be measured and compared. This chapter explores the experiences and challenges while setting up and evaluating two payments timing indicators for the European RTGS TARGET2. The indicators are the "value weighted average settlement time" as well as a form of payments "delay" indicator. The goal is to present specific aspects of a methodological framework for implementing such indicators, for possible replication based on granular transaction level data of other RTGS payment systems.

In this chapter, the authors present a methodology to study the flow of funds in large-value payment systems (LVPSs). The algorithm presented differentiates the flow of payments into two categories: 1) external funds, i.e. funds transferred from other financial market infrastructures (FMIs) or provided by the central bank, and 2) the reuse of incoming payments within the same FMI. Using individual transaction data, the algorithm evaluates to what extent incoming payments are used to cover obligations. The method also studies the flow of intraday liquidity under the framework of its provision within Mexican FMIs. The aim is to evaluate the impact of intraday liquidity provision, and understand how liquidity is transmitted to participants in the Mexican Large Value Payment System, or SPEI®.

Section 3
Economics of Single Types of Financial Market Infrastructures

This chapter develops a framework to analyse the factors influencing central counterparties' (CCPs') risk controls and the role of regulation. The framework illustrates the importance of sound regulation of CCPs and helps to explain why different CCPs may make different risk management choices. Key factors include ownership, governance and the profile and preferences of participants. International standards for the design and operation of CCPs and other financial market infrastructures (FMIs) are reflected in the Principles for Financial Market Infrastructures (PFMIs). Modelling key elements of these standards, the chapter demonstrates the importance of a flexible regulatory framework that achieves the desired level of stability while allowing the mix of risk controls applied by each CCP to vary according to its particular incentives and operating environment. The chapter goes on to discuss the emerging trends towards competition and interoperability between CCPs and cross-border provision of clearing services, and consider the implications for CCPs' risk management choices.

We provide estimates of the collateral gap in the global and Canadian OTCD markets. Using the latest available data as of December 31 2011, it is estimated that current exposures after netting are \$3.9T globally and \$71B in Canada. The estimated amount of available collateral after correcting for re-hypothecation in each market is \$767B and \$48B, respectively. Thence, the current gap in variation margins stands at \$3.1T globally and at \$23B in Canada. The initial margin that would be required to centrally clear OTCD is estimated at \$4T globally and \$104B in Canada. The rate of collateralization has increased globally, but specially in Canada. In 2001, 92% of global and 72% of Canadian current exposures were undercollateralized; currently, the figures are 80% for global and 30% for Canadian current exposures. The high level of collateralization and the lack of re-hypothecation could make the Canadian market more resilient to systemic shocks. Further, it is likely that the upcoming regulatory reforms will have a more subtle impact on Canadian banks than on banks elsewhere.

In this chapter Central Securities Depositories (CSDs) are analyzed, in playing an essential role in the European post-trade market. The background is presented, describing their services both on domestic level, and in a cross border context in Europe. CSDs have introduced (self) regulation and this chapter outlines the efforts they are making to remove existing barriers in a still fragmented European post-trade market, in order to achieve more efficiency. Particular attention is given to the changes and challenges the CSDs face with respect to the Central Security Depository Regulation (CSDR) and Target2-Securities (T2S), which is an initiative of the Eurosystem and is expected to go live as of June 2015. T2S will connect CSDs within the European area, performing as a cross border securities settlement engine.

Foreword

Payment transactions have been fundamental to business activities from time immemorial. Today, payment and financial transactions stand at the core of economic activities. Nevertheless, the ultimate goal is for agents' business decisions not to be affected by the way they pay. This implies that effective payment methods should become smoothly integrated into complex logistics processes. Four determinant factors play a crucial role here: price, processing and settlement speed, simplicity, and availability. With the evolution of institutional frameworks, the development of technology, and the advantages of economies of scale and network economies, modern integrated and complex financial market infrastructures (FMIs) are getting closer to the goal of transforming payments so that they are transparent to the user.

To that end, solid research on FMIs is essential and should proceed further to consider design, the establishment of operations rules, and the development of regulation for those infrastructures, as is the case in Mexico. Research is made easier by detailed data on a wide variety of financial transactions, from money market operations to repos. Mexico is among the few countries in a position to use real data from long time series to study the complex structure of the backbone of the financial system. There are two reasons for that development – the 1994 crisis and significant volumes of retail payments, which are settled in real time, since 2004, by the large value payment system, SPEI, operated by Banco de México.

In recent years, regulation has been designed on a worldwide scale to ensure financial stability as a result of the 2007-2008 financial crisis. In this context, the present book is particularly timely because FMIs are an element critical to studying the effect of this regulation and possibly mitigating some of the risks stemming from potential future financial crises. This volume advances the scope of studies integrating economic research related to FMIs, such as payment systems (PSs), securities settlement systems (SSSs), central securities depositories (CSDs), central counterparties (CCPs), and trade repositories (TRs). For the first time, stress testing, monitoring and early warning indicators, network studies and simulations are combined to form a comprehensive overview of the tools and applications available for analysing and monitoring FMIs. I would like to congratulate the editors and authors for this wonderful effort, which will be very useful to academics, central banks, and other financial authorities throughout the world as they face ever-changing payment systems, induced by economic development and technological innovation.

Agustín Carstens
Governor of Banco de México

***Agustín Carstens** was named Governor of Banco de México starting January 1, 2010, a position he currently holds. Since July 1, 2013, he has been chairman of the Economic Consultative Council (ECC) and the Global Economy Meeting (GEM) at the Bank for International Settlements (BIS) and from March 23, 2015 he chairs the IMF's International Monetary and Financial Committee.*

Foreword

The economic analysis of financial market infrastructures has been given a boost in recent years, not least because of the financial crisis. While financial market infrastructures have certainly proven to be stable and robust, it was vital that they be further developed. Firstly, following the crisis, measures were taken to further bolster the stability of financial market infrastructures and to create greater transparency. The specific requirements developed for this purpose are contained in the Principles for Financial Market Infrastructures. Implementing these requires a series of analyses, including stress tests and simulations, for which some techniques are still being developed. Secondly, today we have a much clearer understanding of the interdependencies between financial market infrastructures, such as systems for securities settlement and payment transactions. Here it is crucial to look at feedback loops between the systems and to keep interdependencies in mind without focussing too much on details. It is in this spirit that the efforts of the Eurosystem to create a single European platform for securities settlement are to be seen. Together with Banco de España, Banca d'Italia, and Banque de France, the Deutsche Bundesbank is developing the new TARGET2-Securities platform on behalf of the Eurosystem. This will lead to a single securities settlement system in Europe linked directly to TARGET2, the European real-time gross settlement system. In the context of the increased importance of analysis, the third point I would like to mention is the use of transaction data from financial market infrastructures for other central banking tasks such as monetary policy analysis or macro-prudential supervision.

The Deutsche Bundesbank has therefore continually expanded its analysis activities in the area of financial market infrastructures in recent years. The focus here is on applied analysis, which provides decision-makers with background information and data to back-up their decisions. In addition, the Bundesbank also benefits from the participation of its experts in academic debates at conferences or via publications. I therefore very much welcome the fact that this book on "Analyzing the Economics of Financial Market Infrastructures" has been produced with the significant involvement of Bundesbank staff. I hope that this book reaches a wide audience and that readers gain valuable ideas for their own work.

Carl-Ludwig Thiele
Member of the Executive Board of the Deutsche Bundesbank

Carl-Ludwig Thiele *is a member of the Executive Board of the Deutsche Bundesbank and is responsible for Payments and Settlement Systems, Cash Management, Economic Education, the Bundesbank's University of Applied Sciences and Technical Central Bank Cooperation.*

Foreword

In previous years the analysis of financial networks was focused largely on a topology of bilateral relationships among a group of credit institutions as a model for a single market. A drawback of such research is that it tends to neglect the crucial role of Financial Market Infrastructures. In fact, one can say that it takes the functioning of market infrastructures for granted. More recently and certainly since the default of Lehman Brothers, it has been widely recognized that such assumptions are not very realistic. Market infrastructures worldwide absorbed the shock of the Lehman default well, but only little imagination is needed to come up with more adverse scenarios.

It is therefore desirable to broaden the scope of analysis beyond single markets or single infrastructures in order to obtain a comprehensive view of the whole financial system in your economy and worldwide. Three elements for this research task are important in this respect: institutional knowledge of financial market infrastructures, network theory and granular data availability. It is a pleasure to observe that these three topics received broad attention in the book in front of you.

Institutional knowledge of relevant market infrastructures is essential when carrying out research as trading and routing of financial transactions strongly depends on the specific aspects of these infrastructures.

Network theory will enable overseers to analyze financial market infrastructures both from a micro perspective, analyzing the network of participants, as well as analysis at a higher level, aiming to study the interconnectivity between these infrastructures.

As data availability and computer processing capabilities are rapidly increasing, focus of research can also be directed towards the combination of several infrastructures. An example of newly available highly granular data is the formation of trade repositories. In 2009 the G20 countries decided that, in order to increase market transparency, all standardized over-the-counter derivatives were to be cleared through central counterparties and reported to trade repositories, thus making individual trade data on over-the-counter derivatives available to central banks and other authorities.

It is the unique position of central banks with their mandate to pursue financial stability in combination with the ability to obtain highly granular data that enables them to perform the aforementioned research task. The results of that research can benefit several areas next to financial stability, such as monetary policy, financial markets, payments policy, prudential supervision and oversight.

I would like to thank the authors and editors for this splendid cross-border initiative and wish the readers pleasure while their knowledge is enriched.

Job Swank
Member of the Executive Board of De Nederlandsche Bank

***Job Swank** is a member of the executive board of De Nederlandsche Bank and is responsible for economic policy and research, financial stability, financial markets, payments and statistics.*

Preface

Financial Market Infrastructures (FMIs) are the backbone of financial systems in modern societies. They form an essential link between financial intermediaries and they are of critical importance for the efficiency and stability of financial systems. Being the mainstays of financial transactions in the modern world, FMIs reflect the ongoing an unprecedented change in market forces, regulations and technical developments. Regulatory changes are predominantly reactions to the ongoing financial crisis. Market forces are adjusted business strategies by market participants and impacts of further market integration. Finally, technical developments affect the emergence of transactions to be settled (e.g. induced by a rising number of embedded electronic devices), the information processing technology (e.g. see the next generation of internet), and the potential data management and analysis tools ("Big Data").

These ongoing changes are the background for this book on Analyzing the Economics of Financial Market Infrastructures. The volume provides a comprehensive collection of works, covering the newly established areas of economic research related to FMIs, which includes, but is not limited to payment systems (PSs), central counterparties (CCPs), central securities depositories (CSDs), securities settlement systems (SSSs) and trade repositories (TRs). Given the multifaceted developments in FMIs there is a need to have a compound description of how to deal with these FMIs from the analytical perspective. This book is not intended to describe single FMIs which would be the focus of institutional economics and which would be of limited interests outside the regional reach of the FMI in question. Neither does this book intend to cover the aspects of operations research of FMIs which is a subject of informational economics. However, we aspire to deliver an overview of state-of-the-art analytical tools and applications for the economic analysis of FMIs.

This said we have already outlined the structure of the book. In part I we start from a functional analysis of the role the FMIs play in modern financial systems and economies and the risks they imply. Special regulatory aspects as well as the specific view of participants are also covered in separate chapters. Part II is devoted to the tools and applications for analyzing FMIs. We provide chapters on simulations, network analysis, agent-based modeling, monitoring indicators and transactional analysis. The approach by authors have been different: some deal explicitly with methodological questions about how to apply or improve a tool, whereas others demonstrate a fully developed application of a certain tool on a specific research question. In part III we provide a facts and evidence-based economic analysis of each type of FMI covering PSs, CCPs, CSDs including a special chapter on the newly established European platform for the settlement of securities and trade repositories, TARGET2-Securities. For each type of FMI we highlight the topics of interest for management, risk analysis and functional development.

According to the definition given by the Committee on Payment and Settlement Systems[1] (CPSS) of the Bank for International Settlements and the Technical Committee of the International Organization of Securities Commissions (IOSCO) the main purpose of FMIs is to facilitate the clearing, settlement, and recording of monetary and other financial transactions. The prime elements that nowadays form part of the FMIs are PSs, CSDs often in combination with securities settlement systems (SSSs), and CCPs, as well as TRs. In the aftermath of the financial crisis and not least due to the multifaceted regulatory efforts around the world, financial analysis has gained new prominence and progress. Much attention has been paid to the micro-level – the banks and requirements for their stability – and to the macro-level – the so-called macro-prudential approach. However, the meso-level, meaning the level of FMIs, deserves attention in its own right.

The economics of FMIs differs from both the micro- and the macro-level. FMIs are complex systems and single institutions at the same time. The common theme of FMIs is clearing, settlement and recording of transactions. Their economic rationale deals with institutional efficiency and stability of large-scale processing. Their business models build on (low) transaction fees for a large number of standardized transactions. They do not earn on market developments (e.g. changing asset prices) while at the same time they are being subject to risks stemming from market developments. In comparison to financial institutes which deal predominantly with discretionary risks FMIs mainly deal with rule-based risks. A bank may grant a loan and incur by doing so a principal risk. The settlement of the payment by the FMI, however, is independent of the discretionary risk by the underlying loan. It is like the settlement of all other payments only a rule-based risk (mainly: operational risk) of a highly standardized transaction.

This fact, that the degree of discretionary risks in FMIs is limited and that the main risk in everyday business is of operational nature may have contributed to the perception of limited economic rationale in FMIs. However, as the development of economic analysis of FMIs has shown, the economic considerations for the functional development of FMIs and for stability analysis do by no means lack any intellectual sophistication. The analytical approaches for analyzing FMIs have to cover features of two-sided markets, economies of scale and network externalities. FMIs are themselves complex systems. In order to be properly modelled sophisticated computational techniques have to be applied (e.g. as agent-based models). For solving more detailed questions still simulations are the tool of choice and substitute for modelling for the sake of manageability. In a similar way to the methodological progress in the field of financial stability, there is still no consensus for the economic analysis of FMIs. However, this opens the opportunity to approaches which are not fully recognized as mainstream economics, making the task of analyzing the economics of FMIs a challenging but an innovative one. The majority of FMIs are of systemic importance to the whole financial system and this leads us to the situation in which financial authorities and in particular central banks are incorporating their oversight and research efforts into their financial stability mandates. FMIs serve different financial institutes and in doing so they determine the efficiency, stability and overall reliability of financial systems.

Given the critical role in financial stability, the body of research focused on economics of financial market infrastructure has grown significantly over the last decade displaying various analytical approaches usually highly specialised for the institution in focus. It has grown to the point where an overview of the state-of-the-art analytical tools and applications is warranted providing benchmarks for analysts and guidelines for practitioners. Moreover, it is time to sum up the known stylised facts about FMIs and provide thereby a basis for a more systematic and interchangeable analysis.

Hitherto, there are only limited sources dedicated purely to the study of FMIs from the analytical perspective. In fact, there is only one scientific journal - the Journal of Financial Market Infrastructures (http://www.risk.net/static/about-the-journal-financial-market-infrastructures) that provides a high quality discussion forum for the field based on quantitative analysis. Further, the proceedings of the Bank of Finland Payment System Simulator seminars are another source. They provide a biennial snapshot of current analytical work with a focus on payment systems. In addition, central banks increasingly devoted conferences to the research on FMIs in the recent years and created therefore additional incentives for researchers to enter this field.

The readers of this book will find a mix of institutional and tool-specific chapters. This is intended to enable a broad access for readers with different knowledge background and different interests. It was our aim that every single chapter could be read and understood independently. In compiling different approaches we allow for a multifaceted perspective on FMIs showing that there is not a single possible approach. This is also related to the fact that analyzing FMIs involves a high degree of technical knowledge specific to the type of FMI under scrutiny. This situation promotes multidisciplinary research as well given that in some cases the object of study is a sophisticated and complex machinery resisting to be treated as a typical economic topic.

As already stated Part I of the book comprises four articles all dealing with the role of Financial Market Infrastructures. Chapter 1 "Financial Market Infrastructures – The Backbone of Financial Systems" gives an overall introduction into the functions of FMIs within financial systems. The interplay of basic financial institutions, financial intermediaries, financial markets and Financial Market Infrastructures is depicted, both in a theoretical and historical perspective giving reason for the description of FMIs as backbone of financial systems. Moreover, based on the historical emergence of FMIs the functions of themselves are explained. This forms the ground for a common economic analysis of FMIs which broadly follow similar rationales. The chapter concludes with the preeminent economic questions relating to FMIs and the welfare aspects.

Chapter 2 is organized in two parts: the first part provides an overview of financial market infrastructures (FMIs) in the context of financial stability; the second part gives a general view on the Principles for Financial Market Infrastructures (PFMIs) issued jointly by the Committee on Payment and Settlement Systems (CPSS) and the International Organisation of Securities Commissions (IOSCO). More specifically, in the first part of this chapter the authors provide concrete examples of the interaction between FMIs and financial stability. Among such examples, the authors describe the following ones: i) the case of payment systems in monetary policy implementation and systemic liquidity usage, ii) the importance of securities settlement systems failures, iii) the differences of Over the Counter and centrally-cleared repo transactions, iv) the introduction of Central Counterparties (CCPs) in the derivatives markets, v) the increasing interconnectedness of CCPs, and vi) the role played by Trade Repositories (TRs) in the so called Data Gaps Initiatives of the Financial Stability Board (FSB). Meanwhile, the second part of the paper deals with a condensed description of the PFMIs; in there, the authors provide a non-exhaustive revision of the approaches followed by different jurisdictions and institutions regarding the compliance with such principles. In this part the authors call for international coordination on the implementation of the principles and also to avoid over-reliance on the PFMIs as there are still many aspects which deserve further study under the new international regulatory landscape.

Chapter 3 studies the implications of the arising systemically important FMIs and examines the different regulations, both domestic and international which apply to such entities. The author argues that despite of the progress being made more international coordination is needed in order to guarantee the stability and efficiency of such global entities. In particular, this chapter focusses on the implications of the commitments of the G-20 in promoting the use of TRs and CCPs. The author also argues that the implementation of such reforms faces important challenges given that some FMIs operate on a cross-border environment. In addition, the author points to the impact of the regulatory structure on the operational efficiency of cross-border FMIs.

Chapter 4 has been written by authors from a market participant. Looking differently at the role of FMIs they explain how FMIs contribute to the changing needs of financial intermediaries both in using FMIs as well as in managing own business. The authors lay out the benefits of FMIs for financial intermediaries and the possible drawbacks as well as means to counter them. In addition, they point to the inherent dynamics of financial markets caused by the changing role of FMIs in combination with new regulatory efforts. The dynamic is most pronounced in liquidity needs (especially intraday liquidity management), collateral management and risk management. The authors outline the implications for the business case in transaction banking as well as possible strategies for financial intermediaries to cope with it.

Part II is going one step further to focus on tools and applications for analyzing FMIs. The chapters 5 through 10 cover simulations, network analysis, agent-based modeling, monitoring indicators and transactional analysis. In chapter 5 the authors ask themselves whether it is possible to implement parallelization during simulations, and if so, to what extent the speed of simulations can be increased. After going into the concepts of parallelization in general, they focus on the ways it can be implemented in the Bank of Finland Payment and Settlement Simulator. Simulation runs require time for a number of tasks and their performance depends highly on the number of transactions and accounts, the scenario to be simulated, the topology of the payment network, the scarcity of liquidity leading to queue management and the complexity of the netting algorithms. The authors conclude form their experiments that parallelization is possible and increases simulation speed; the highest gain in speed is found at full liquidity level and database operations ignored. The experiment is also interesting for a possible future implementation of parallelization over a network of computational environments (distributed computers), as opposed to the current implementation of parallel computers within one multicore PC.

Chapter 6, also focusing on simulations elaborates on the possibility to skip some of the transaction data in simulations for the sake of faster simulation runs. It is called "Using FMI Transaction Data in Simulations - Less is More". As multi day simulations take more and more time and computer power is limited, researchers often have to limit the time span in simulations. The authors, therefore, test if it is possible to speed up simulations by aggregating the lower value transactions, and still maintaining the same reliable simulation outcome. In order to test this the authors set up a set of benchmark simulations and compared this to simulations in which the lower value transactions between two participants within the day were aggregated. The set of benchmark and aggregation simulations was then repeated for ten different levels of liquidity, as often simulations are focusing on situations in which the liquidity decreases. The outcome was compared at four different statistics; percentage of value settled, lower bound of liquidity, balance drop within the day and the average queue value. The comparison of the benchmark simulations to the outcome leads the authors to the conclusion that aggregation of low value transactions is indeed possible without disturbing the reliability of simulations. The authors have observed features about the duration of simulations: the decrease in the number of transactions leads to a linear decrease in duration; the decrease in liquidity leads to an exponential increase in duration.

In chapter 7 – "A Multi-layer Network of the Colombian Sovereign Securities Market" the Colombian sovereign securities settlement network is analyzed. The transactions in the Central Bank owned system for clearing and settlement of local sovereign securities have been broken down into three trading platform networks; SEN, MEC and MEC-R. Using granular transaction datasets, these three networks have been analyzed individually as well as their aggregated total and compared using modern network analysis statistics. Statistics used are density, degree, power-law exponent, mean geodesic distance and clustering coefficient. After this comparison the importance of individual participants across the networks is analyzed using a correlation matrix containing the degree, strength, hub centrality and authority centrality. The authors conclude that the total network is similar to the underlying three monoplex networks, according to both the global statistics as well as the measures at individual participant level. The participants that are too connected to fail appear to have that characteristic in all three underlying networks. Using a multi-layer approach by studying the individual networks as well as their aggregated total can give important added information. Analyzing one monoplex network does not provide a full view of the market, nor does analyzing the aggregated total network as diversions from one layer to the other are not visible.

In chapter 8, an agent-based model is presented that examines how overconfidence impact the usage of credit card. The authors use the concept of overconfidence to explain why people who never intend to borrow on their credit card(s), do so anyway. Agents' decisions are model based on their propensity to buy. Further, these decisions are effected by two factors - their friends' consumption behavior and their expectations about future income, which may be distorted due to overconfidence. In addition, credit card issuers can compete for customers by changing the conditions in the market. Under this rich framework the authors have created a model, which contains consumption, two means of payment (credit card and cash), and a distortion to agents' income expectations via overconfidence. The model allows the analysis of how consumer overconfidence can influence consumer behavior and the dynamics of the credit card market. Despite several strong simplifications by the model, it can be seen as a method to analyze behavior of credit card users with and without overconfidence. The authors found that overconfidence leads to more "accidental" borrowing and higher interest rates.

Chapter 9 provides a detailed conceptual view of how timing indicators in payment systems can be constructed. Being a prima facie simple measure the authors provide empirical and theoretical explanation why the basic construction of an indicator matters for results. The chapter provides empirical examples of the relevant measures based on data from TARGET2. However, the chapter goes well beyond the TARGET2 specific aspects and derives in great detail the implications of specific features of timing indicators. The chapter is written with utmost care for traceability in order to facilitate reproduction of the indicators proposed.

For more than a decade liquidity issues have been one of the strongest lines of research in payment systems. This reveals the significant role of liquidity for the sound functioning not only of the payment system, but for financial market infrastructures overall. Under this line of research follows the aim of chapter 10, which presents a methodology to study the flow of funds in large-value payment systems (LVPSs). With data from the Mexican Real Time Payment System SPEI, the authors study how intraday liquidity is distributed through different FMIs in Mexico. The presented algorithm splits payment transactions into two categories: 1) external funds, which are funds transferred from other financial market infrastructures (FMIs) or are provided by the central bank, and 2) the use of incoming payments to cover payment obligations within the same FMI. The algorithm uses individual transaction data, in order to evaluate to what extent incoming payments are recycled. The method also studies the interdependency among FMIs towards the flow of intraday liquidity. More specifically, this analysis involved another three FMIs, which are – the security settlement system DALÍ, the Continuous Link Settlement (CLS) system and SIAC, the system in charge to provide intraday liquidity provision within Mexican FMIs. The aim is to evaluate the level of efficiency of intraday liquidity distribution, and understand how liquidity is transmitted to participants within FMIs in Mexico.

Finally, the Part III of the book provides chapters which do not focus on a particular tool, but rather on a particular type of FMI. Since many different questions in economic analysis of FMIs are of interest the most important types of FMIs are covered by more than one chapter.

The Part III starts in chapter 11 with a first look at payment systems analysis. Central banks play the most prominent role in the analysis of PS, since they have unique responsibilities, which consequently creates a unique opportunities. Chapter 11 systematizes the different aspects of payment system analysis and presents their importance from a central bank perspective. This is performed by theoretical and practical points of view by giving examples of actual work in the field. The structure of the chapter is determined to three different types of payment system analysis, which the author defined as: analysis of PS in the broad sense of the term; specific PS analysis and finally the use of payment system data. The first definition relates to the entire set of instruments, banking procedures and interbank funds transfer systems employed to facilitate the circulation of money in an economy; in the context of the second type of analysis, interbank funds transfer systems is synonymous to "payment systems" and the research is focused on a more technical aspects. In the third case, payment transactional data is used for purposes beyond the functioning of the PS.

Chapter 12 - Liquidity-saving Mechanisms in Payment Systems and Settlement Liquidity: From the Experience of Japan's Next-Generation RTGS Project – deals with stability and safety vs efficiency. Not a trivial dilemma, given that from economic perspective both sides contribute to a harmonious and integrated social development. In this regard, chapter 12 makes an important contribution and focuses on the evolutionary process of PS, starting by explaining the DNS scheme and following with the development on RTGS system. Further, much more sophisticated designs of PS have been put in place, which include "Hybrid System," and "RTGS system with Liquidity Saving Mechanism (LSM)." To finalize, the chapter include a discussion on the experience from the "Next-Generation Real-Time Gross Settlement" (RTGS-XG) project of BOJ-NET. BOJ-NET is the large-value payment system operated by Bank of Japan (BOJ). BOJ-NET added an LSM in 2008. The impact of the LSM's introduction is analyzed, which includes the liquidity-saving effect, the average waiting time in the queue, the turnover ratio, and the volume of idle liquidity.

Chapter 13 is one of three chapters dealing with CCP. Here CCPs are viewed from the perspective of practical oversight. The paper starts with a short summary of the historical development of CCPs, followed by an outline of the concept and core functions CCPs. Then an illustration of the main risk management safeguards of CCPs is provided. This includes an excursus regarding the hierarchical structure of clearing and regarding procyclical considerations with respect to CCPs. The outline of CCP counterparty risk management is complemented by a brief overview of other risks, including liquidity risk, legal risk, and operational risk. The consideration of the risk profile of CCPs is concluded with some insight into the main factors determining the oversight of CCPs' governance. The full picture of CCPs from an oversight perspective is given by placing the CCPs in the clearing process and the outlining the resulting challenges for regulatory oversight. The chapter concludes with a description of the manifold layers of today's oversight of CCPs.

In the context of the financial crisis starting in 2008, studying how effectively CCPs deal with the risks associated with trading in financial markets is the aim of chapter 14. This chapter presents a framework to analyze the role of regulation and the factors influencing the risk controls CCPs have in place. Without a clear assessment method, authorities would face difficulties to figure out the motivation behind the management choices of different CCPs. The framework developed in this chapter illustrates the importance of sound regulation of CCPs and helps to explain why different risk management choices could make sense. The authors incorporate key factors into their approach, which include ownership, governance and the participants' profile and preferences. Furthermore, as Principles for Financial Market Infrastructures (PFMIs) incorporate international standards for the design and operation of CCPs, the chapter also considers these standards. Modelling key elements of the standards, the authors demonstrate the importance of a flexible regulatory framework that allows for the mix of risk controls applied by each CCP to vary according to its particular incentives and operating environment and it is able to achieve the desired level of stability. The chapter goes on to discuss the emerging trends towards competition and interoperability between CCPs. The authors argue that, the market structure of clearing and the robustness of CCP risk management will determine the extent to which increased central clearing contributes to greater financial stability.

Chapter 15 discusses an all important issue in the new international financial landscape: the problem of undercollateralization in the global OTC derivatives market as well as in the specific case of Canada. The chapter starts providing estimates of the collateral gap by using data from several sources. The author estimates the collateral gap under two definitions: the first one is the amount of additional assets needed to collateralize current exposures in the OTCD market; the second one is the amount of assets needed to collateralize potential future exposures. The author also highlights that after the 2007-2008 global crisis, the amount of collateral has increased relative to gross credit exposures. However, such an increase is partially due to the reuse of collateral (known as re-hypothecation). After controlling for the double counting due to re-hypothecation the author arrives at the important conclusion that the level of undercollateralization currently stands (in terms of current exposures) at \$3.1 trillion globally and \$23 billion in Canada, meaning that 80% of global and 30% of Canadian current exposures are undercollateralized. Moreover, the author also estimates that \$4 trillion and \$104 billion of collateral would be needed to centrally clear the global and Canadian OTCD markets, respectively. Finally, the author arrives at the conclusion that given the recent trends and the current levels of collateralization, Canadian banks would face fewer difficulties in closing the collateral gap than banks elsewhere.

Chapter 16 – The changing Role of CSDs in the Post-Trade Industry in Europe – focusses on the current introduction of TARGET2-Securities. This moment is used by the author to describe past, present and future of the European post-trade market in which the position of CSDs and cross-border securities settlement is changing. Cross border securities settlement in the EU is still complex and complicated. In the past years, more efficiency was achieved by market participants, resulting in lower costs and prices of domestic and cross-border transactions. CSD-R and T2S will however enforce the speedup of efficiency, safety, transparency and market integration. T2S, which has gone live in June 2015, will deliver securities settlements for the entire euro area, to the 24 committed CSDs which will outsource their securities settlement business. This way settlement volumes will be consolidated on one single platform, bringing efficiency and economies of scale, with the aim to lower the settlement fees in Europe, to economize on liquidity and collateral. The concentration of activities does however also introduce a concentration of risk in the financial system.

Chapter 17 describes from an historic perspective well into modern times the evolution of securities settlement systems and central securities depositories (CSDs) in various jurisdictions. The author also examines liquidity and clearing and settlement risks in the context of CSDs. The author starts by describing how the important concept of ownership has evolved from paper based systems and how nowadays ownership is recorded and transferred in modern global financial markets by means of securities accounts; then he explains the main risks and costs involved in securities clearing and settlement: i) principal risk, ii) replacement and operational risk, iii) the provision of liquidity for securities market transactions, and

iv) settlement failures. An important element of the paper is that disentangles some of the concepts in the FMIs parlance like multi-tiered ownership, fungibility, custodian bank, etc. This chapter includes a section in which the interesting topic of failed trades is examined, including opposite views on the systemic implications of these failures. Then, the author discusses systemic implications for securities settlement systems and CSDs; in his discussion the authors points to the increasing complexity faced by securities settlement systems in a cross border context and he also shares his concerns about how contagion like cascade effects after a trade fails which may be exacerbated by the widespread use of re-hypothecation.

Finally, in chapter 18 – Undressing the Global Derivatives Market: Trade Repositories: Past, Present and Future – the author first gives a description of the history of trade repositories. Starting 2009, due to the initiative of the G20 meeting in Pittsburg all standardized OTC derivatives were required to be cleared through Central Counterparties and reported to Trade Repositories, in order to enhance market transparency. TRs in Europe are overseen by the European Securities and Market Authority (ESMA) under the European Market Infrastructure Regulation (EMIR), starting with DTCC (UK), KDPW (Poland), Regis-TR (Luxembourg) and Una-Vista (UK) in November 2013 and soon followed by ICE Trade Vault (UK) and CME Trade Repository (UK). Nowadays the interoperability and proper data reporting of the individual TRs remains a big challenge. In the United States the reporting mandate is single sided, meaning that only one side of the transaction is obliged to report, leading to higher data integrity. The landscape in Asia Pacific differs hugely from the others, caused by the high number of different jurisdictions. Looking ahead, regulators should be able to supervise at macro and micro level.

The editors are grateful having edited this book. We would like to acknowledge all authors who contributed and incorporated their respective contributions to the overall structure of the book. All of them experts in the field share with generosity their insights, accumulated over a good deal of years. We thank all reviewers, and the members of the editorial advisory board. In addition we are grateful to our central banks granting us some freedom to work on this project. Freedom was also granted by our spouses and families who equally deserve a warm thank you. The book is jointly edited by four researchers from three central banks. We are proud having brought together some outstanding experts and researchers from around the world to write or review high quality chapters in our book. All chapters have undergone a double-blind review process by two anonymous reviewers and have been substantially revised afterwards. The overwhelming majority of reviews has been very considerate and well worked-out, some of them even being worth to be published independently, because of the expertise of their authors and the profoundness of their considerations. Finally, we thank IGI Global for publishing our book and for supporting us over the last year and beyond.

Martin Diehl
Deutsche Bundesbank, Germany

Biliana Alexandrova-Kabadjova
Banco de México, Mexico

Richard Heuver
De Nederlandsche Bank, The Netherlands

Serafín Martínez-Jaramillo
Banco de México, Mexico

Section 1

The Role of Financial Market Infrastructures

Chapter 1
Financial Market Infrastructures:
The Backbone of Financial Systems

Martin Diehl
Deutsche Bundesbank, Germany

ABSTRACT

Like a human being's backbone, well-functioning financial market infrastructures contribute to the stability of the financial system. They enable fast and smooth movements, channel relevant information, protect the channels for transmission and reduce risk. Problems in financial market infrastructures may lead to dysfunctions of financial markets, a lack of options for transaction and, therefore, to limited movability, misleading information or disturbed information channels and in the worst case to systemic risk. The chapter explains the role of financial market infrastructure within the wider definition of a financial system. Based on the historical emergence of payment systems, central clearing and central securities depositories, the special advantage of financial market infrastructures for the productivity of intermediaries, for the efficiency of financial markets and for the welfare of an economy is explained. The chapter shows the economic and analytical importance and specificity of financial market infrastructures.

WHAT IS THE BACKBONE?[1]

This book deals with financial market infrastructures, referring to payment systems, central counterparties, central securities depositories, securities settlement systems, and trade repositories, as well as to TARGET2-Securities, which is not an infrastructure in the pure sense, but rather a platform. According to the CPSS-IOSCO Principles for Financial Market Infrastructures, a "financial market infrastructure is defined as a multilateral system among participating institutions, including the operator of the system, used for the purposes of clearing, settling, or recording payments, securities, derivatives, or other financial transactions." (CPSS, 2012b, p. 7). Although the existing financial market infrastructures reveal a striking plurality of details (CPSS, 2011 and 2012a; Manning et alii, 2009), their basic functions for the economy are rather similar in nature, since they deal with standardized forms of transactions (Berndsen, 2010).

Financial market infrastructures could be considered the backbone of financial systems in a modern society with reference to metaphorical similarities to the backbone's features such as its stabilizing effect,

DOI: 10.4018/978-1-4666-8745-5.ch001

being the central axis for all parts of the body, facilitating movability, cushioning against vibrations, and channeling and protecting the nerve cords. Like a human being's backbone, well-functioning financial market infrastructures contribute to the stability and growth of the financial system (CPSS, 2012b, p. 18; Martinez-Jaramillo et al. 2014). Financial market infrastructures are linked to all relevant parts of the financial system and are in network topology central to the financial system regardless of the centrality measure applied. This unmatched centrality results from three types of links they provide (Berndsen, 2011 and 2012). First, the institution-based links of a financial market infrastructure to its members (e.g. banks). Second, the systemic links between different types of financial market infrastructures which are necessary to channel liquidity, securities and information. And third, the common links of financial market infrastructures to external service providers. Financial market infrastructures at the same time enable fast and smooth movements, i.e. re-allocation of funds and liquidity across regions, durations, risk levels and currencies. They channel relevant information about payment streams, investment trends, risk perceptions, liquidity status and systemic risk. This makes them a prime subject of interest for all overseers and analysts. In addition, modern research has shown that the analysis of pure payment streams can yield significant insights for other seemingly unrelated research topics, e.g. business cycle forecasting (SWIFT, 2012). They protect the channels for transmission and reduce operational risk. Just as a backbone is robustly designed to prevent any harm to the sensible nerve cords the financial market infrastructures are – as required by overseers and for the purpose of convincing participants – specially designed to withstand operative problems and to resume operations quickly without loss of data after operational failures.

In addition, in recent years publicly operated financial market infrastructures in particular have contributed significantly to the understanding of flows and operations therein by increasingly allowing research and publication of aggregated results of this research. Therefore, providing information has become a new function for financial market infrastructures. Without breaking any confidentiality rule they can by publishing aggregated and anonymized research results, contribute to a better understanding of clearing and settlement by market participants. Moreover, and surely not the last parallel, problems in financial market infrastructures could be critical for the financial system just as injuries to a backbone are to a human being. Operational problems in financial market infrastructures may lead to dysfunctions of financial markets, a lack of options for transaction and, therefore, to limited movability, misleading information or disturbed information channels and, in the worst case, to systemic risk. The analogies to the devastating impact of backbone problems for the life of vertebrates are obvious.

Using the metaphor of the backbone merely serves an illustrative and explanatory purpose. The analogies are striking, but are by no means perfect. The analogy also has its shortcomings, especially when we consider the development perspective. Unlike invertebrates, which of course have no backbone, a financial system is well capable of establishing new and other financial market infrastructures. Indeed, although some financial market infrastructures like payment systems have a history spanning centuries, most financial market infrastructures have in recent years undergone a significant amount of change in functions, scope, and scale.

FUNCTIONS IN FINANCE

To understand the importance of financial infrastructure for the financial system a brief look at the functions of a financial system and its development process is useful. The financial system provides important functions for an economy: it facilitates allocation, diversification and management of capital and risks, and it produces information on investment opportunities, financial instruments and participants.

As an economy develops, the need for more complex financial services arises. The growing sophistication of financial services encompasses:

- A growing number of cases to be settled (scale),
- A broadening of cases to serve different needs (scope),
- A widening differentiation leading to new cases (function),
- A growing average amount per case (size),
- A widening of time dimensions from spot trading to long-term financing (time),
- A widening of regional outreach (space),
- A growing number of participants and different interests to be served simultaneously in single contracts or bundles of contracts (complexity).

The stages of development of financial systems are the subject of the research on financial inclusion (IFC, 2013). We can distinguish between a basic financial infrastructure, financial intermediaries, financial markets and financial market infrastructures. The functioning of the first is the precondition for the second and so on. Sometimes, however, they develop in co-movements to support a growing and increasingly more complex financial system.

Figure 1 depicts the stages of development of a financial system. The basic financial infrastructure enables the effective operation of financial intermediaries which trade for the sake of more transparency

Figure 1. Stages of development of a financial system with growing complexity

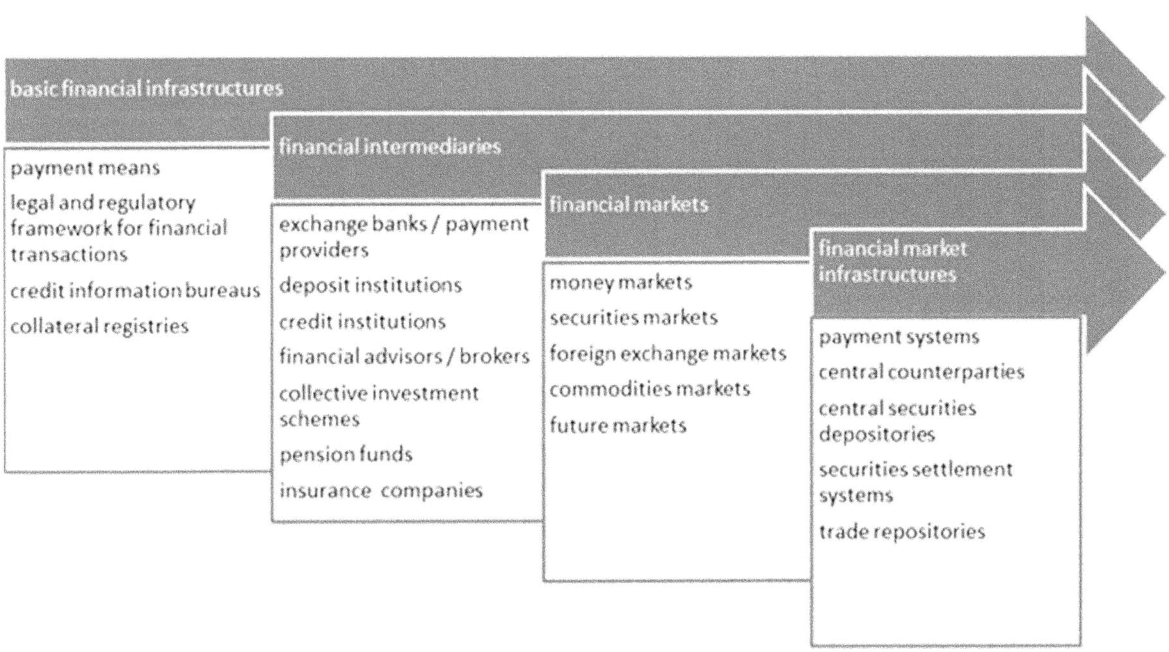

and economies of scale on financial markets. Finally, financial market infrastructures enable the transaction and settlement of financial products (money, claims) after trading has taken place. With regard to payment systems, it is obvious that even at the earliest stage of a simple financial system a basic payment means is necessary. Moreover, the emergence of financial intermediaries requires the function of financial transactions (e.g. by an exchange bank or a payment provider). Therefore, those institutions could be seen as predecessors of modern payment systems serving similar needs.

The direction of the arrows in Figure 1 corresponds to the development of an economy and its growing need for more sophisticated financial products. More sophisticated means growing in scale, scope, function, size, time, space and complexity. The arrows do not stop, because the further development of a financial system requires financial infrastructure, intermediaries, markets, and market infrastructures to adapt to changing needs, technology, and regulations. Somewhat beyond the pure realm of financial markets are other foundations for a well-functioning financial system such as the rule of law, a proper set of civil rights and at least a basic level of financial literacy on the part of individuals. It goes without saying that concomitant to the increasing sophistication of a financial system, informational and technical infrastructure also has to be developed further.

The focus of financial market infrastructures is on facilitating transactions and not on price formation. For this reason, exchanges are structurally different from financial market infrastructures. The various functions in finance are depicted in Figure 2.

Functions of Various FMIs

The functions of the various FMIs are defined in the Principles of Financial Market Infrastructures (CPSS, 2012a, pp. 8-9) as follows:

"A payment system is a set of instruments, procedures, and rules for the transfer of funds between or among participants; the system includes the participants and the entity operating the arrangement."

Figure 2. Functions in finance[2]

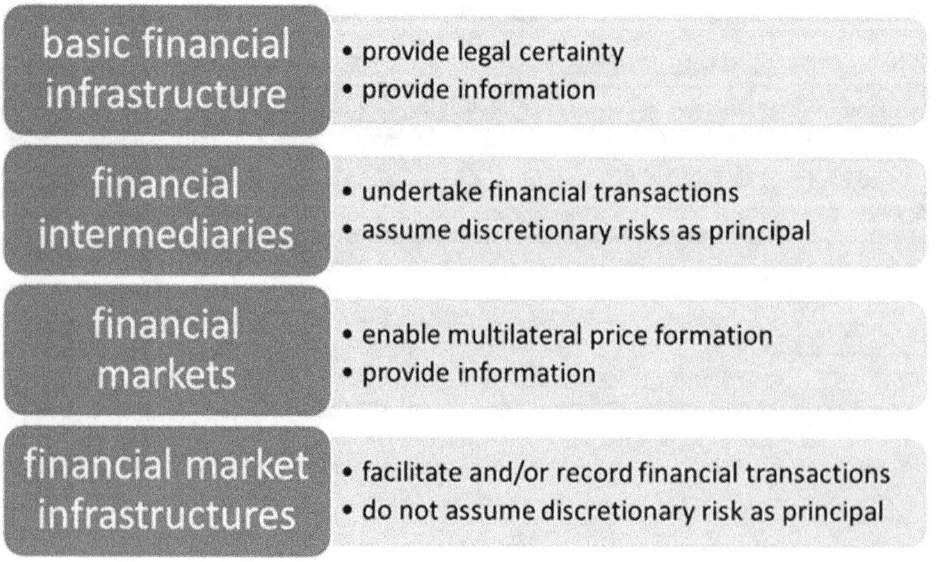

"A central securities depository provides securities accounts, central safekeeping services, and asset services, which may include the administration of corporate actions and redemptions, and plays an important role in helping to ensure the integrity of securities issues [...]." "A securities settlement system enables securities to be transferred and settled by book entry according to a set of predetermined multilateral rules." "A central counterparty interposes itself between counterparties to contracts traded in one or more financial markets, becoming the buyer to every seller and the seller to every buyer and thereby ensuring the performance of open contracts." "A trade repository is an entity that maintains a centralized electronic record (database) of transaction data." A more detailed description in a functional perspective as well as figures of importance can be found in some of the chapters in this volume (e.g. Goerlach et alii, van Wageningen, Milne and Massarenti).

HISTORICAL EMERGENCE OF FINANCIAL MARKET INFRASTRUCTURES

The historical emergence of financial market infrastructures is closely related to the growing sophistication of banking. In some cases new developments were driven by new services offered in the market. In other cases, new developments were driven by public action like regulation or central bank action.[3]

From the Tally to Coins to Exchange Bankers

In the times when commerce was locally confined such that creditors and debtors had a personal relationship, the tally[4] could still serve as the principal instrument of commerce. Purchases or debts would be notched in the tally, a stick of squared hazel-wood or instruments of similar nature. The oldest tallies are recorded from 1000 and 2000 B.C. which was around 1,000 years before the introduction of coins (Innes, 1913). Tallies were still in use in the late 15th century (North, 2009, p. 66). The tally bore the names of the debtor and the creditor and was used to document bilateral obligations, but was not designed for trading.

With the advent of coins, debt became tradable and it became possible for means of payments to leave the local area. Coins were minted by the monarch and some feudal lords or seigniors. For a long time precious metals (gold, silver, copper and related alloys) were used to make the coins durable. The intrinsic value of the coin was lower than the face value or the value assigned to the coin, since many coins did not have a nominal value (North, 2009, p. 11). The residual – the seigniorage – accrued to the minter. The people were forced to accept the coins as payments (legal tender) and were able to pay their debt or taxes with them. From time to time the ruler needed more money and decreed a reduction of the nominal value of the coins – a form of taxation. Or they called in the coins in circulation and exchanged them for coins with a lower intrinsic value.

Over times and with increasing spatial widening of trades, more and more different coins from other mints, from former times, in other denominations and of different weights and materials circulated (North, 2009, p. 95). Thus, a need for exchange bankers emerged. Records of banking business in Greece go as far back as around 500 B.C. (Fellmeth, 2008, p. 39). The word for banker used in old Greek is τραπεζίτης (see e.g. Matthew 25:27) which comes from τραπεζα, which was the table on which the exchange took place. This indicates that exchange was among the first services, if not the original service, that bankers supplied. Clearly, coins made claims tradable and it was not a great step from exchanging different coins to accepting deposits and giving credits was not far.

The concurrent circulation of many different coins was quite common during antique and medieval times (Danmarks Nationalbank, 2005, chapter 2.2), e.g. in medieval France, besides the royal monies 80 different coinages are recorded, belonging to more than 20 different monetary systems. All had as its unit the Livre, but the value of the Livre differed in different parts of the country (e.g. Livre Parisis, Livre Tournois, Livre Estevenante), and their relative value (exchange rate) varied over time (Innes, 1913).

Bills of Exchange – The First European Payment Instrument

Concomitantly the profession performed by moneychangers or exchange bureaus grew in importance as long-distance trading flourished. Their comparative advantage was the knowledge they possessed about coins and their value. They exchanged foreign coins for domestic ones and contributed to the regional expansion of trade by facilitating the flow of payments across different coinages. It is commonly attributed to Italy in the late Middle Ages that those exchange bureaus started serving as deposit banks and issued bills of exchange for the surplus of coins not withdrawn. This bill of exchange basically became the first European payment instrument (Danmarks Nationalbank, 2005, box 2.2).

Bills of exchange were far more convenient than coins as a payment instrument for international trade than coins because of the lower weight and the tailored denomination. In addition, the circulating volume of coins was too small to settle the volumes of trade. Within the proximity of a merchant's office, the bills accepted could be immediately encashed with the exchange bureau serving as a local clearinghouse. Supra-regional clearing took place at fairs, prominent examples being St. Giles in Winchester and the fairs in the Champagne region in France (North, 2009, p. 28; Innes, 1913; Danmarks Nationalbank, 2005, box 2.3). Merchants and bankers from many countries gathered there. Some bilateral credit and debit was cleared between the merchants directly, leaving only the bilateral netted claim to the bankers' clearing. Bankers established booths where debts and credits were cleared in bilateral and multilateral clearing, thus reducing the necessary liquidity and facilitating large amounts of trade.

Public Exchange Banks as Central Banks

We clearly see transaction banking as a source of welfare-enabling trade, reducing the liquidity costs of an economy and reducing risks, but it was still in the hands of single bankers based on the trust placed in them. An important step towards a payment system was the emergence of clearing banks and central banks acting as public banks or under public supervision.[5] One prominent example is the Bank of Amsterdam or the Amsterdam Wisselbank, founded in 1609. The purpose of the Wisselbank was to reduce the transaction costs in clearing stemming from a chaotic monetary system with multiple coins from different coinages and to solve the debasement problem. The Dutch economy suffered not only from a plurality of coins stemming from eight Dutch coinages, but was also flooded with foreign coins which, due to incremental debasement, aggravated the uncertainty in the value of payments (Quinn and Roberds, 2005, 2006). The Wisselbank was set up as an exchange bank. It accepted all sorts of coins and valued them according to their true value. Illegal coins were only valued at their intrinsic value, thus leading to a significant loss against their face value. Withdrawals, however, were possible in a coin of consistent weight and value. This coin was called the trade coin ("negotiepenningen"). In this way, creditors paid through the exchange bank were protected against debasement (Quinn and Roberds, 2006, p. 18). To enforce the central role of the Wisselbank in the payment system, the City of Amsterdam stipulated that all bills of exchange above 600 guilders had to be settled through the Wisselbank, and cashiers (the private exchange bureaus) were outlawed. Over time, the Wisselbank proved to be a successful innovation for Dutch trade and finance. It not only contributed to the stabilization of the circulation of money: it became the central hub for large value payments in Europe. In addition, it even had an immense positive effect on local Dutch commerce, which benefitted from a stable currency and a reliable clearing institution.

Similarly successful for an even longer time-span was the Hamburger Bank, which was founded as an exchange bank in 1619 and in 1875 finally became part of the German Reichsbank to continue the exchange service for the newly founded larger state (Denzel, 2014).[6] The same principle was applied as with the Wisselbank. Merchants were required to leave the exchange service to the Hamburger Bank, which created a new currency, the "Marc Banco", as a stable payment device. The Hamburger Bank contributed likewise to the economic and financial flourishing of Hamburg and the whole surrounding region. Its reputation as a credible clearing bank operating a fast and reliable giro network facilitated international trade and regional trade alike. The efficient and stable giro network was a reason why Danish merchants kept using the Hamburger Bank for their settlement until the mid-19th century (Danmarks Nationalbank, 2005, chapter 2.4). This giro network became the core of the giro network of the later founded Reichsbank. Therefore, the function as an exchange bank for payments can be considered one of the origins for modern central banks; others are the right to issue bank notes (issuing bank)[7] and the function as a lender of last resort.

A stable, reliable and cheap giro network remained an asset for the competitiveness of banks. Access to a centrally provided network proved to be especially helpful for small and regionally confined banks. Take as an example the German savings and loans banks, which were originally (19th century) restricted to local business. They used only a limited number of correspondents for their transactions. However, trade increasingly became supra-regional and the small savings and loans banks faced competition from larger private banks, some of which offered their clients a nation-wide giro network. Those large banks attracted more and more companies as customers, which were able to economize on liquidity and costs by using their payment network. This was a driving motivation for the smaller local savings and loans banks to establish their own nationwide giro network in 1908 (Birninger, 2014, p. 217).

The Emergence of Clearinghouses

To some extent the central clearing mechanism deployed for money became a role model for the clearing and custody of securities, first developed for futures markets. However, the clearing and settlement of futures is more complicated and subject to higher risks. Therefore, risk reduction can be seen as the main driver of the evolution of clearing mechanisms independently of reducing transaction costs.

The first clearinghouses served more basic functions compared to present-day central counterparties (Kroszner, 2006).[8] Three clearing methods can be distinguished (Moser, 1998): direct, ringing and complete. Direct clearing refers to simple bilateral contracts where the exchanges merely served as mediators. Ringing is the next step in the evolution towards a clearinghouse. Ring settlements were initially rather informal arrangements for a simultaneous multilateral settlement. The preconditions for that to happen were standardized contracts and fungibility. The advantages were a reduction in the exposure to counterparty risk and reduced costs of maintaining open positions (Moser, 1998, p. 15). However, substitutes for original counterparties had to be accepted and the counterparty risk shifted, as all the parties involved in a ringing settlement could affect the risks of all the others. The third step is the complete clearing, whereby a clearinghouse acts as counterparty to each party to the contract (Moser,

1998, p. 31). The credit risk assumed by the clearinghouse substitutes for the credit risk of individual counterparties. Clearly, this requires the complete fungibility of contracts and the clearinghouse playing a strong role in all governance questions such as margining and loss allocation.

An early example of a clearinghouse is the London Clearing House (LCH) which, according to Spahr (1926, pp 70-71, quoted in Moser, 1998, p. 23), was established in 1773 to clear commodities contracts in London.[9] Other examples are the New York Clearinghouse founded in 1853 (Moser, 1998, p. 23) and the clearing house of the Chicago Board of Trade, founded in 1883. The latter is taken as *pars pro toto* here to illustrate the historic reasoning.[10] The purpose of the clearinghouse was to create and impose incentives for adherence to the rules of the Chicago Board of Trade, including the contractual obligations. The Chicago Board of Trade had the right to bar a member from the trading floor. This threat was quite important for all solvent members; however, it meant little to an insolvent institution. For this reason, the Chicago Board of Trade in 1873 began to require members to open their accounts to enable a solvency check, and introduced the initial and variation margins. As a next step, the Chicago Board of Trade founded a clearinghouse in 1883. This clearinghouse, not yet a true central counterparty, served as a mechanism to reduce transaction costs. It calculated the net deliverables for each member, posted margins and settled. If a member defaulted, the clearinghouse did not assume any responsibility for settlement of open trades. This did not come about until 1925 with the foundation of the Board of Trade Clearing Corporation, a central counterparty in the modern sense.

The Emergence of Central Securities Depositories

In contrast to central counterparties and payment systems, the emergence of central securities depositories was more a question of reducing transaction costs than of managing risk.[11] Prior to the existence of central securities depositories, banks acted as custodians for the securities deposited by their customers. The securities had to be separated from the bank's own securities. This was done by way of jacket custody,[12] whereby a jacket or banderole was put around the securities (which still existed physically as papers) to separate them and guarantee the ownership of the customer. Trading these securities was cumbersome and costly, since the jacket had to be opened for every trade, the securities physically delivered or new securities added to the bundle. Therefore, significant simplification of handling procedures and reduction of transaction costs were to be expected of a centralization of that business which would reduce the transport of papers/securities. An early example of this centralization was the founding of the "Bank des Berliner Kassen-Vereins" in Berlin in 1882 (Frankfurter Kassenverein, 1963). The bank's services remained for another 40 years restricted to the banks using the Berlin exchange. As securities trading grew in volume and importance, other local "Kassenvereine" were set up at the other stock exchanges in Germany and started later on to cooperate with each other to enable national central securities depository services (Schmidt, 2014, p. 423). In the meantime, the business has assumed international dimensions and international central security depositories are also common.

Summing Up Early Developments

What can we learn from this short history of transaction banking for the role of financial market infrastructures? First of all, it remains a fact that increasing complexity of economic business and trades required more sophisticated tools for clearing and settlement. Second, the successful operation of an effective and stable clearing mechanism contributed to economic growth and facilitated further economic development. Third, the function of an exchange bank can be operated independently of the issuance of money or any other function of modern central banks; although settling in central bank money is safer. Fourth, the function of an exchange bank does not require public ownership.

When explaining the emergence of financial market infrastructure, we can clearly refer to the transaction cost approach (Williamson, 1981, p. 555). Exchange banks and clearinghouses enjoyed both lower transaction costs and lower production costs compared to exchange bureaus or normal banks. The transaction costs for banks in dealing with exchange banks were lower, because the exchange banks were able to reduce uncertainty by using a single currency of consistent weight and value. The transaction costs for banks in dealing with clearinghouses were lower due to central collateral holding and the central counterparty's deeper insights into the solvency situation. Financial market infrastructures specialized in exchange and clearing transactions and refrained increasingly from competing in other bank services. They were able to make use of transaction-specific investments and knowledge, and benefited from the economies of scale and the network externalities inherent in a giro or clearing network. Thus, their production costs were also lower in their core business. The banks and merchants dealing with the financial market infrastructures benefited from these cost advantages.

ECONOMICS AND IMPLICATIONS FOR WELFARE

Historical reasoning gives plenty of insights into the intended functions of financial market infrastructures. This chapter draws on the examples given above and tries to make the case for an abstract explanation of the impact of financial market infrastructures on economic welfare.

Defining Infrastructure

An examination of the implications of financial market infrastructures for economic welfare should start by qualitatively listing their various economic impacts. At the very beginning, we used the CPMI definition for the term financial market infrastructures. For the economic explanation of infrastructures in general, it makes sense to broaden the definition somewhat.

Let us define as infrastructure an *institution which facilitates the exchange of goods, services, information and rights between others*. The infrastructure facilitates the exchange after the contract between the participants has been agreed upon; it does not exchange on its own behalf. It helps, for example, to exchange money between banks, but it is separate from the users of the system. Therefore, a newspaper, which facilitates the exchange of information, is not an infrastructure; however, an electronic network to facilitate news can be.[13] In the case of a financial market infrastructure, facilitating the exchange means that the contract has been agreed upon and only clearing and settlement are to be carried out. Therefore, those institutions which are involved in price formation (e.g. exchanges) and those which are involved in finding counterparties (e.g. platforms for crowd financing) are different in nature from financial market infrastructures as defined in this chapter.

Costs and Externalities of Infrastructures and Business Model

The outstanding feature of an infrastructure is its economic externality. The costs for the infrastructure are mostly fixed and high, and they by far exceed the benefits for a single user of that infrastructure, which in turn are far smaller than the positive externalities of the infrastructure. The service provided by an infrastructure is of high specificity, being able to serve usually only one purpose and of limited divisibility. Take a road as an example of traffic infrastructure. The cost of building a road is high compared to the savings for a single user who uses that road for a single trip. However, since the marginal costs for using that road are rather small, the positive externalities for repeated use and for other users are huge. The road connecting two cities cannot serve another city (high specificity) and must be at least of a capacity that enables a single user to pass (limited divisibility). An infrastructure in the sense of our definition is not a public good. This holds even for the given economies of scale which have been used to argue for at least temporary public subsidies to newly created financial market infrastructures (Bolt and Humphrey, 2005). An infrastructure is not a public good since it incorporates a rivalry in consumption. There is a capacity limit and we face increasing costs for higher consumption, albeit mostly step costs.

Problems of Growth Accounting

The contribution of financial market infrastructures to economic welfare cannot be the simple sum of value added by all financial market infrastructures, no matter how impressive they may be. Two major problems would arise. First, as we have seen, the purpose of introducing financial market infrastructures was to reduce transaction costs and risks. Therefore, measuring the current value added of those infrastructures would understate the true impact which would be the difference in the social costs for transactions when comparing the situation with financial market infrastructures with the virtual situation without them. Second, since only a few financial market infrastructures operate privately and/or under competitive pressure, we cannot estimate the value added of all financial market infrastructures at market prices.

The economic literature on growth has tried to calculate the impact of infrastructure on economic growth. Two lines of research stand out (Conrad and Seitz, 1994, p. 303): In the first approach the stock of public infrastructure would be incorporated as an additional explanatory variable to explain the productivity of private inputs. Most studies found significant positive effects. The second approach tried to calculate the cost savings for private industry when using public services based on a presumed growth model. Both approaches yielded valuable insights into the growth contribution of infrastructure in general. However, both are far from perfect. The latter, the cost savings approach, works only in a given growth model and depends on the validity of the model. The empirical productivity explanation cannot capture the structural break in the industry that occurs after introducing an infrastructure. This introduction has the potential to change whole industries, since the relative cost situation may be fundamentally altered.

Given the intricacies in the general measurement of impacts of infrastructure in general on growth, it is not surprising that the understanding of the impact of financial market infrastructure in particular is even less developed.[14] There is great interest in the impact of finance on growth, which gained strength during the recent financial crisis. However, financial market infrastructures seem to be of less interest to research. Levine (2005) in his extensive survey article "Finance and Growth" in the Handbook of Economic Growth states that financial instruments or institutions that lower transaction costs could promote specialization, technological innovation and growth (Levine, 2005, pp 24f). However, he did not explicitly mention the terms "infrastructure", "transaction banking", "payment system", "clearing" or any other infrastructure-related term. Therefore, it remains inconclusive whether he refers to financial services provided by infrastructures at all, beyond the distinction between market-based and bank-based supply.

Business Model

The business model for a financial market infrastructure reveals some special features in the production function, the cost function, the revenue function and the expected risk function:

The production consists of a large one time effort to set up a settlement engine including all procedural rules and some relatively minor maintenance actions. The same structure applies to customer care efforts. After a first intensive effort to link a customer to the system and obtain agreement on all contractual issues, the business of providing ongoing service is, ideally, rather routine. The day-to-day business is rules-based rather than of a discretionary nature. The critical success factor with regard to acquiring (and keeping) customers is the credibility of the financial market infrastructure. The critical success factor with regard to risks stemming from ongoing production is a high level of stability and institutional efficiency in settling large numbers of transactions.

The cost function of a financial market infrastructure consists of high fixed costs for the initial setting-up process and further improvements and rather low marginal/incremental costs for every transaction settled. The cost function is a step function, whose steps are mainly based on the incremental IT costs for raising the capacity.

Revenue from financial market transactions mainly stems from the collection of relatively low transaction fees for a large number of transactions. In addition, some infrastructures charge participants a fixed connection fee. Financial market infrastructures do not earn on price developments in financial markets, but on a possible subsequent jump in the number of transactions because of a need to reallocate.

With regard to risks, all financial market infrastructures face a significant operational risk. The ongoing operations for vast numbers of transactions and their proper recording have to be assured on all accounts. For this reason, the Principles for Financial Market Infrastructure explicitly require an operational risk management framework and a business continuity plan (CPSS, 2012b, p. 94). In addition, liquidity, credit and general business risks need to be dealt with. In particular, those financial market infrastructures which do not operate with immediate finality or which offer credits (e.g. intraday credits) for participants arc subjcct to increased liquidity and credit risks. In addition, they could be subject to risks stemming from price developments in financial markets. Therefore, financial market infrastructures are asymmetrically exposed to market developments: they are exposed to some risks stemming from price movements, but they cannot earn on them directly. This asymmetry requires them to practice rather rules-based risk-taking, meaning risk avoidance and risk coverage in substance. If an institution cannot earn on market developments, but only lose, then the expected outcome of deliberate risk-taking is always negative. Therefore, the natural strategy for them is to avoid risks and to cover against potential losses (e.g. by requiring participants to put up collateral).

Social Benefits

Almost all contributions of financial market infrastructures to the welfare of a society have been explicitly or implicitly mentioned so far. We just need to phrase them in economic terminology. The following *economic benefits* accrue because of the introduction of financial market infrastructures.[15]

Financial market infrastructures enable interconnectedness and contribute to a widening division of labor. This is a foundation for greater specialization of producers, wider diversification of investors and more choice for consumers. Without financial market infrastructures banks would need to transact with all counterparts directly. They would have many more links to take care of. Every link involves the need for monitoring and regular checks with regard to functionality. Financial market infrastructures reduce costs even more significantly nowadays than in the times of non-electronic banking. In former times a link was just the regular exchange of some papers and the subsequent booking on nostrum and lore accounts. A link in modern finance is a technical interface that is capable of automatically processing certain information and data, and it may require some degree of harmonization of operating procedures. In addition, more sophisticated links helpful in meeting the requirements of digital banking allow for some degree of interoperability and straight-through processing at the transaction level of the underlying technical platforms. The number of links (L) in a system with central clearing is equal to the number of participants (N), since all participants have one link to the central clearer. With central clearing: L_c=N

Without central clearing, the number of possible links is much larger. For three banks, we already arrive at three links; for four banks, six; and for five banks we have ten possible links: Without central clearing: L_{nc}=N(N-1)/2.

Therefore, central clearing reduces complexity by a factor of $F = L_c/L_{nc} = 2 / (N-1)$. F will be lower than unity for all N > 3. Therefore, central clearing reduces complexity if we assume more than three participants. To provide a few figures based on the numbers of direct participants (CPSS, 2013, pp 486f): complexity as measured by the total number of possible links decreases due to the payment system for CHAPS Sterling (UK) from 135 to 18; for the SIC (Switzerland), from 3,212 to 380; and for BESP (Russia) from 29,214 to 3,248. The numbers are more impressive if we include the indirect participants using the service via a direct participant.

Financial market infrastructures enable economies of scale as they involve (high) fixed costs and specialized knowledge requirements for clearing operations. This holds for pure economies of scale within a payment system (Adams et alii, 2002) as well as for operation costs in general. A detailed study covering 2,810 U.S. banks for the period 2001 to 2012 reveals significant economies of scale in banking (Kovner et alii, 2014). The authors found a strong negative relationship between bank size and the ratio of noninterest expenses to the sum of net interest income and noninterest income. A ten percent increase in assets contributes to a reduction of noninterest expenses (relative to income) by 0.3-0.6 percent. Moreover, scrutinizing the details they found that compensation costs, corporate overheads and information technology in particular contributed to the economies of scale.

Financial market infrastructures enable network externalities, since the marginal benefit of joining the network rises for new participants with increasing participation. The new participant installs one link to the central clearer and can transact to all existing participants. A system like TARGET2 offers around 40,000 addressable BICs worldwide to every participant (direct or indirect) to exchange money with – quite a sizable network to join.

Central clearing reduces the costs of liquidity for settlement. The degree of synchronized payments increases with rising participation in central clearing, and the level of net liquidity to be transferred is lower. The net claim stemming from a bilateral exchange may experience certain fluctuations from day to day. The net claim for participants in a large payment system reveals, however, a striking stability. This is simply due to the fact that the net claim is reduced in multilateral netting. Therefore, the overall cost for liquidity in an economy needed for settlement is significantly lower with central clearing, and the management of intraday liquidity is disburdened. Reduced costs, i.e. transaction or liquidity costs, will contribute to a more balanced income distribution. Since a large fraction of transaction costs are fixed for the buyer or seller of securities, lowering them will disproportionately benefit the participants with small value transactions and it will facilitate diversification of investments.

Financial market infrastructures allow for a deeper specialization by the operating unit since their core business is limited to the function of the infrastructure. Risk treatment, operative functions and consultancy to the participants should all benefit from the specialization of the financial market infrastructure. The impact of specialization can be gauged by the size of the User Detailed Functional Specification for TARGET2, an admittedly rather complex payment system. In the current version, these specifications comprise some 2,972 pages (3CB, 2014).

Financial market infrastructures will facilitate overall higher standards for transaction management if the procedural rules and techniques of the central clearer become a generally accepted benchmark for clearing. The standards set and agreed by the infrastructure may over time have an effect on other forms of settlement, e.g. correspondent banking. An increasing speed of transactions will make compatibility of systems a top priority.

Financial market infrastructures contribute to more competition between intermediaries for all services outside the transaction business since they can level the transaction costs between banks of a different size. They contribute to financial integration and help to limit segregation in financial services (Cirasino et alii, 2014, p. 122). The financial markets in a region served by a financial market infrastructure become deeper and broader due to enhanced market liquidity.

Not least, financial market infrastructures provide a rich data source for research on stability and efficiency as well as on all aspects related to financial transactions (see Müller in this volume). Exploiting this data source is and must be subject to strict confidentiality rules to protect the customers' interest. However, aggregated data of financial market infrastructures can be used to support public functions like monetary policy, financial stability and banking supervision.

Social Costs

The introduction of financial market infrastructures also has some drawbacks beyond the pure cost of the institution:[16]

Reduced competition in transaction banking and clearing. Over time this can lead to fewer innovations, supernatural profits for the clearer, organizational slack, and the risk of corruption. Clearly, strong competitors would be a factor to drive innovation. However, a financial market infrastructure enjoys a larger volume of transactions than a bilateral exchange. Therefore, the potential scope for innovations is wider, and we can reasonably assume the central clearer to implement some innovations which, in pure bilateral clearing, would not have been profitable due to lacking economies of scale. Moreover, most financial market infrastructures still face some sort of direct competition from another financial market infrastructure besides bilateral clearing, as in correspondent banking. The number of payment systems or central counterparties or other financial market infrastructures around the world is still large enough to facilitate a fruitful benchmarking for state-of-the-art technology.

Reduced knowledge of financial intermediaries about clearing and transaction banking and the risk involved. In combination with a possible propensity to assign risk management in clearing to the financial market infrastructure, this may lead to a loss in risk awareness. Indeed, banks have come to rely more and more on central clearing mechanisms, and ongoing professionalization through the use of more advanced technology has made it almost impossible for people who are not full-time professionals in this business to keep track. As a consequence, the role for public oversight has increased. The general public's interest in a stable, reliable and efficient financial market infrastructure must be pursued by people serving as full-time expert overseers. It is in this sense that the task of analyzing financial market infrastructures is of systemic importance.

Concentration of settlement and other risks. This is indeed a danger related to the emergence of financial market infrastructures, notably with regard to central counterparties. Central clearing concentrates clearing risks. This is the main reason why financial market infrastructures are subject to particular oversight requirements. In general, the form of risk-taking differs between financial intermediaries and financial market infrastructures. Intermediaries predominantly engage in discretionary forms of risk-taking. In contrast, financial market infrastructures have a much more standardized service and act primarily with rules-based forms of risk-taking. The degree of risk-taking inherent in the business of a central counterparty is much more pronounced than with other forms of financial market infrastructures. However, compared to financial intermediaries, under current requirements even central counterparties have a limited scope for risk-taking, e.g. limited discretion over the ways in which collateral is invested (Duffie, 2014). The concentration of risks with central counterparties remains a central issue in analyzing, overseeing and political arguing.[17] The difference between systemically important financial intermediaries and systemically important financial market infrastructures is that the latter typically facilitates transactions and does not typically assume discretionary risk as principal, whereas an intermediary (a bank, say) conducts transactions typically assuming risk as principal. A financial market infrastructure will – leaving aside the case of operational failure – typically not trigger financial risk, but it may well amplify financial stress triggered by participants.

Analytical Approaches

The economics of financial market infrastructures differs from both the economics of banks (micro level) and the economics of a financial system (macro level). Financial market infrastructures are systems and single institutions at the same time. As single institutions, they differ significantly from intermediaries in terms of business model, risk exposition and the production function. As systems, they encompass not only their own technical service but also their relations to many participants with different needs and behaviors. They could be called the meso level: they are central nodes in the overall financial system channeling transactions from many single institutions. Therefore, they are essentially of higher systemic importance than an average bank, because of the possibility of financial stress being amplified by them. However, since they contribute "only" certain functions, they are much less than the financial system as a whole. This meso level is subject to specific theoretic particularities and deserves analytical attention. The analytical approach to the subject financial market infrastructures has to cover features of two-sided markets, economies of scale and network externalities. With regard to methodological considerations, the modeling of these complex systems proves extremely difficult because of the sequential nature of multi-step processing. The outcome of a clearing process for a day depends on all the steps of that day and may change as a result of a different outcome of a single step at the very beginning of this process. Therefore, simulation rather than modeling has been the predominantly applied analytical method when analyzing clearing systems (Diehl, 2012, p. 32).

FUTURE TRENDS FOR FINANCIAL MARKET INFRASTRUCTURES

History will not stop in the foreseeable future; and so the development of financial market infrastructures will continue to undergo a change process, the detailed outcome of which is unpredictable, although some detailed thought-provoking forecasts have been made (Berndsen, 2011, p. 23). However, some forces that will shape the future landscape of financial market infrastructures are clearly identifiable.

Ongoing pressure to streamline transactions. As financial systems are developed further and more and more countries enter a stage of modern finance, the need for lower transaction costs and easier processing rises. Let us consider payments: according to estimates by Cap Gemini, the number of cashless payments more than doubled in the decade starting in 2001, a period including a serious financial crisis. They estimate that in 2011, 307 billion cashless payments were settled (DB Research, 2014, p. 20).

Consolidation of financial market infrastructures. The powerful leverage of economies of scale and network externalities does not stop at current institutional boundaries. Different currencies will only hamper, but not stop, the process of consolidation as clearing and settlement can take place in multi-currency infrastructures.

The average speed of settlement will be further increased by advancements in technology. As settlement cycles fade away, the need for net settlement systems and the concurring risk measures may disappear. The same may hold for central counterparties as soon as the speed of settlement exceeds the implementation of related risk measures. Notwithstanding this trend in the case of intertemporal trading central counterparties may retain a business case.

Immediate settlement 24 hours a day and seven days a week will become the new standard. The economy does not stop on weekends, therefore settlement needs arise continuously. This trend, which is already visible in quite a few markets (Fundtech, 2013), may contribute to an integration of large value payment systems and retail payment systems.

Integration of different financial market infrastructures. The various financial market infrastructures will grow closer together if not actually integrate. Drivers for integration are the ongoing growth of inter-regional trade and investment activities, the demand from customers who are themselves expanding their spatial reach and the business considerations of infrastructures which want to economize on economies of scale and network externalities (Cirasino et alii, 2014, p. 121). With regard to the integration of different infrastructures, there are also significant economies of scope to deal with; for example settlement of a security also involves a cash leg which has to be channeled through a payment system. TARGET2-Securities, which is not an infrastructure but a platform, will integrate securities and cash settlement on a single platform and pave the way for further integration. In addition, the increasing need to save on collateral has already brought about tendencies to link securities management and payments as in auto-collateralization. Central securities depositories could also partner with custodians (Dubrau, 2014, p. 217). Trade repositories, collecting and providing data on trade are increasingly fed by data streams from infrastructures. Therefore, an integration of trade repositories into a real clearing infrastructure could at some point of development appear more natural than not. In fact, the introduction of trade repositories and preceding institutions like the Trade Information Warehouse were based on the support and efforts of the Depository Trust and Clearing Corporation (Bodson, 2013, p. 92).

The ongoing digitalization of economic processes (DB Research, 2014) will demand compatibility of data formats for further use in upstream and downstream processes. Payment and settlement processes have to be linked to preceding (e.g. billing) and succeeding processes (e.g. bookkeeping) and to related tasks (e.g. customer care). Therefore, the pressure to accept general standards and provide compatible tools will rise.

Financial market infrastructures will increasingly be used to carry out analyses of transactions and all kinds of financial developments. This is necessary to support oversight and functional development, and will equally be relevant for other public tasks. In addition, big market players will pay to use these data bases to improve their understanding of market forces and bank behavior.

REFERENCES

Adams, R. M., Bauer, P. W., & Sickles, R. C. (2002). Scope and Scale Economies in Federal Reserve Payment Processing. *Federal Reserve Bank of Cleveland Research Department Working Paper,* 02-13.

Berndsen, R. (2010, March). Toward a Uniform Functional Model of Payment and Securities Settlement Systems. *De Nederlandsche Bank Working Paper*, No. 243.

Berndsen, R. (2011, February 25). *What is happening at Scrooge Digiduck's Warehouse?* Inaugural address at Tilburg University.

Berndsen, R. (2012). Letter from the editor. *The Journal of Financial Market Infrastructures*, 1(2), Winter 2012/2013.

Bodson, M. C. (2013). New Infrastructures for a sounder financial system (trade repositories). *Banque de France. Financial Stability Review*, *17*, 91–99.

Bolt, W., & Humphrey, D. (2005, July). Public Good Issues in TARGET: Natural Monopoly, Scale Economies, Network Effects and Cost Allocation. *ECB Working Paper Series*, 505.

Buhr, W. (2003). *What is Infrastructure*? University Siegen Discussion Paper, No. 107-03.

Cirasino, M., Garcia, J. A., & Tumpel-Gugerell, G. (2014). Materialising the expected benefits from financial infrastructure integration: The "Guidelines for the Successful Regional Integration of Financial Infrastructures. *Journal of Payments Strategy & Systems*, *8*(2), 119–128.

Conrad, K., & Seitz, H. (1994). The economic benefits of public infrastructure. *Applied Economics*, *26*(4), 303–311. doi:10.1080/00036849400000077

CPSS. (2011, September). Payments, clearing and settlement systems in the CPSS countries, 1, BIS.

CPSS. (2012a November). Payments, clearing and settlement systems in the CPSS countries, 2, BIS.

CPSS (2012b, April). *Principles for financial market infrastructures*, BIS.

CPSS (2013). *Statistics on payment, clearing and settlement systems in the CPSS countries – Figures for 2011*, BIS, January 2013.

DB Research (2014, September). Fintech – Die digitale (R)evolution im Finanzsektor. *Deutsche Bank Research*, 23.

Denzel, M. A. (2014). Die Errichtung der Hamburger Bank 1619. In Lindenlaub et alii, 38-50.

Diehl, M. (2012). The Use of Simulations as an Analytical Tool for Payment Systems. In B. Alexandrova-Kabadjova, et al. (Eds): *Simulation in Computational Finance and Economics: Tools and Emerging Applications*, 29-45. Retrieved from http://www.igi-global.com/book/simulation-computational-finance-economics/64901

Dirninger, C. (2014). Der bargeldlose Zahlungsverkehr der Sparkassen 1908. In: Lindenlaub et al., 216-228.

Dubrau, F. (2014). CSD regulation: A major change for the post-trade arena. *Journal of securities operations & custody*, 6(3), 212-219.

Duffie, D. (2014). Financial Market Infrastructure: Too Important to Fail. In M. Bailey & J. Taylor (Eds.), *The U.S. Financial System – Five Years After the Crisis. Hoover Institution and Brookings Institute, 2014.*

Frankfurter Kassenverein (1963). *Der Frankfurter Kassenverein.* Überblick über seine Geschichte und Funktionen.

Fundtech (2013). Immediate Payments – Innovation is Knocking [White Paper]. *Fundtech.*

Gutheil-Knopp-Kirchwald, G. (2012). Infrastruktur – ein Begriff im Wandel der Zeiten. Lecture at the IFIP-Jahrestagung "Öffentliche Infrastruktur im Wandel", Vienna, June 15, 2012.

IFC. (2013). *Progress in Responsible Financial Inclusion.* Washington: International Finance Corporation.

Innes, A.M. (1913, May). What is Money? *The Banking Law Journal.*

Innes, A. M. (1914, Dec./Jan.). *The Credit Theory of Money. The Banking Law Journal,* 31, 151–168.

Kovner, A., Vickery, J., & Zhou, L. (2014). Do Big Banks Have Lower Operating Costs? Federal Reserve Bank of New York Economic Policy Review, 20(2).

Kroszner, R. S. (2006, April 3). *Central Counterparty Clearing: History, Innovation, and Regulation.* Proceedings of of Chicago joint conference on issues related to central counterparty clearing, Frankfurt, Germany.

Levine, R. (2005). Finance and growth: Theory, evidence, and mechanisms. In P. Aghion & S. Durlauf (Eds.), *The Handbook of Economic Growth.* Amsterdam: North Holland.

Lindenlaub, D., Burhop, C., & Scholtyseck, S. (Eds.). (2014). *Schlüsselereignisse der deutschen Bankengeschichte.* Stuttgart: Franz Steiner Verlag.

Manning, M., Erlend, N., & Schanz, J. (Eds, 2009). The Economics of Large-Value Payments and Settlement: Theory and Policy Issues for Central Banks. Oxford: Oxford University Press.

Martinez-Jaramillo, S. & Molina-Borboa, J.L., Bravo-Benitez, B. (2014). The Role of Financial Market Infrastructures in Financial Stability: An overview. *In this volume.*

Moser, J. T. (1998). Contracting Innovations and the Evolution of Clearing and Settlement Methods at Futures Exchanges. *Federal Reserve Bank of Chicago Working Papers Series Research Department* (WP-98-26).

Norman, P. (2007). *Plumbers and Visionaries: Securities Settlement and Europe's Financial Market.* Chichester: John Wiley & Sons.

Norman, P. (2011). *The Risk Controllers: Central Counterparty Clearing in Globalised Financial Markets*. Chichester: John Wiley & Sons.

North, M. (2009). *Kleine Geschichte des Geldes: Vom Mittelalter bis heute*. München: C.H. Beck.

Payment Systems in Denmark, Chapter 2: Payment Systems in a Historical Perspective. (2005). Danmarks Nationalbank. København: Danmarks Nationalbank.

Quinn, S., & Roberds, W. (2005). The Big Problem of Large Bills: The Bank of Amsterdam and the Origins of Central Banking. *Federal Reserve Bank of Atlanta Working Paper,* 16.

Quinn, S., & Roberds, W. (2006). An Economic Explanation of the Early Bank of Amsterdam, Debasement, Bills of Exchange, and the Emergence of the First Central Bank. *Federal Reserve Bank of Atlanta Working Paper,* 13.

Schmidt, H. (2014). Die Entstehung der Deutschen Terminbörse 1988. In: Lindenlaub et al 414-440.

Single shared platform: user detailed functional specifications (Version 8.0). (2014). Deutsche Bundesbank, Banque de France and Banca d'Italia.

Skyrm, S. E. D. (2012). *The history of central counterparties*. Retrieved from http://scottskyrm.com/2012/11/the-history-of-central-counter-parties/

Steigerwald, R.S. (2014). *Financial Market Infrastructure: Selected References*. An Introduction to the Literature on Payment Systems, Trade Execution Facilities and Post-Trade Clearing and Settlement Systems. Federal Reserve Bank of Chicago, Financial Markets Group, mimeo.

SWIFT. (2012). *The SWIFT Index*. Mimeo.

Thier, A. (2014). Die Gründung der Königlichen Giro- und Lehnbanco 1765. In: Lindenlaub et al, 63-78.

Williamson, O. E. (1981, November). The Economics of Organization: The Transaction Cost Approach. *American Journal of Sociology*, *87*(3), 548–577. doi:10.1086/227496

ENDNOTES

1 This paper represents the judgments and views of the author and does not necessarily reflect the opinion of the Deutsche Bundesbank.

2 Obviously, CCPs, unlike other infrastructures, assume some form of discretionary risk. Therefore, CCPs' functions go well beyond the depicted functions of financial market infrastructures in general.

3 Steigerwald (2014) provides a selective reading list which focuses particularly on public reaction to crisis in the last century.

4 Latin: talea. German: Kerbholz. French: taille.

5 It must be noted that the term "central bank" stems from the central position in the clearing network. The central banks at that time did not act as issuers of money or lenders of last resort, which are often cited as the most prominent tasks of a modern central bank; rather, they facilitated clearing.

6 The following paragraph draws on Denzel, 2014.

7 In German the words "Zentralbank" and "Notenbank" are often used as synonyms.

8 The term "clearinghouse" was more widely used, e.g. also for the clearing institutions for check clearing founded as early as 1853 (Skyrm, 2012).

9 For a history of central counterparties see Norman (2011).

10 The rest of the paragraph draws on Kroszner, 2006.

11 For a history of central securities depositories see Norman (2007).

12 German: Streifbandverwahrung.

13 The term infrastructure was rarely used before the 20th century and has undergone significant changes in meaning during history. See Gutheil-Knopp-Kirchwald (2012).

14 Even the somewhat extensive enumeration of examples of infrastructures in Conrad and Seitz (1994) or in Buhr (2003) does not list financial market infrastructures.

15 The following reasoning is not intended to refer in detail to trade repositories, which do not engage in financial transactions.

16 The following reasoning is not intended to refer in detail to trade repositories, which do not engage in financial transactions.

17 See the detailed considerations of Manning et alii, Pliquett and Cruz in this volume.

Chapter 2
The role of Financial Market Infrastructures in Financial Stability:
An Overview

Serafin Martinez-Jaramillo
Banco de Mexico, Mexico

Jose Luis Molina-Borboa
Banco de Mexico, Mexico

Bernardo Bravo-Benitez
Banco de Mexico, Mexico

ABSTRACT

Financial Market Infrastructures (FMIs) are essential for the well-functioning of the financial system, as they play a central role in facilitating clearance and settlement of financial transactions such as payments, securities, and derivatives contracts. Nowadays, it is widely acknowledged that the proper functioning of systemically important FMIs is also vital to maintain financial stability; their failure for solvency reasons or operational disruptions could almost certainly lead to systemic instability. As a consequence, the adequate supervision of FMIs is inherent to the function of preserving financial stability. The aim of this chapter is to provide a general overview of the different FMIs; discuss their role in financial stability and to give an overview of the efforts made by some financial authorities towards the supervision, risk assessment and reinforcement of FMIs.

INTRODUCTION

Financial market infrastructures (FMIs) are essential in modern economies as they represent the platforms and interfaces through which financial operations are performed. In order to avoid threats to the stability of the system as a whole, their adequate supervision is of the utmost importance. The aim of this chapter is to provide a general overview of the different FMIs; discuss their role in financial stability

DOI: 10.4018/978-1-4666-8745-5.ch002

by presenting specific cases, and to describe efforts made by some jurisdictions in the supervision, risk assessment and reinforcement of FMIs under the framework provided by the Principles for Financial Market Infrastructures (PFMIs).

It is important to state that although in this chapter we review the relationship between FMIs and financial stability and we focus more specifically on the risks that FMIs may pose to financial stability, FMIs were designed in the first place to provide and improve upon the stability of the financial system. In the absence of such key infrastructures, financial stability would be much more difficult.[1]

The reader will find many definitions of Financial Market Infrastructures (FMIs) in the current growing literature. Nevertheless, for the purpose of this chapter, it is enough to say that FMIs are composed of the organisations and entities in charge of the registration, clearing and settlement of financial transactions. Among them can be found: payment systems (PSs), central securities depositories (CSDs), securities settlement systems (SSSs), central counterparties (CCPs), and trade repositories (TRs).

This chapter turns on two important axes: the first is the rationale for the strong relationship between financial stability and the proper functioning of FMIs, including significant cases on the role played by FMIs in financial stability; the second axis provides the reader with a general view of the Principles for Financial Market Infrastructures (PFMIs), jointly issued by the Committee on Payment and Settlement Systems (CPSS) and the International Organisation of Securities Commissions (IOSCO).

Financial Stability, Systemic Risk and FMIs: Important Definitions

In order to provide an ordered discussion on the role FMIs play in financial stability, we use this section to make some important definitions. For further details on some of the concepts introduced in this chapter, we refer the reader to the references mentioned throughout this section. The following are simple definitions for some FMIs as stated in CPSS-IOSCO (2013a):

- **Payment System.** Set of instruments, infrastructures, procedures, and rules for the transfer of funds between or among participants; the system includes the participants and the entity operating the arrangement.
- **Central Securities Depository.** Provides securities accounts, central safekeeping services, and asset services, which may include the administration of corporate actions and redemptions. This FMI plays an important role in helping to ensure the integrity of securities issues (that is, it ensures that securities are not accidentally or fraudulently created, destroyed, or have their features changed). A CSD can hold securities either in physical form (but immobilised) or in dematerialised form (that is, they exist only as electronic records).
- **Securities Settlement System.** Enables securities to be transferred and settled by book entry according to a set of predetermined multilateral rules. Such systems allow transfers of securities either free of payment or against payment.
- **Central Counterparties.** Interposes itself between counterparties to contracts traded in one or more financial markets, becoming the buyer to every seller and the seller to every buyer; therefore ensuring the performance of open contracts.
- **Trade Repository.** A trade repository is an entity that maintains a centralised electronic record (database) of transactional data.

As is widely acknowledged, there are many definitions of financial stability and systemic risk; here we provide simple yet useful definitions of financial stability and systemic risk in relation to FMIs.

The European Central Bank (ECB) on its Internet page[2] defines financial stability as follows:

"Financial stability can be defined as a condition in which the financial system – intermediaries, markets and market infrastructures – can withstand shocks without major disruption in financial intermediation and in the effective allocation of savings to productive investment."

From the above definition the importance of FMIs to the stability of the financial system is clear. Moreover, in the same way individual banks may pose large risks to the system while pursuing their own interests, FMIs may also impose large risks on the system as a whole in case of failure or disruption. For this reason, their existence within the financial system must be evaluated from a systemic point of view.

Another significant concept in the context of FMIs and financial stability is that of systemic risk. This concept can be broadly defined as the risk of an event which threatens the proper functioning of the financial system. This definition is shared by Martinez-Jaramillo et al. (2010) and in Kane (2009). In Allen and Carletti (2013), the authors identify four types of systemic risk:

1. Banking crises due to multiple equilibria
2. Banking crises due to asset price falls
3. Contagion
4. Foreign exchange mismatches in the banking system

On the other hand, Manning et al. (2009) identify four sources of systemic risk in payment and settlement systems, which are closely related to the concept of FMIs:

- **Credit risk.** This type of risk is associated with the failure of a counterparty in the system, causing other participants to suffer losses. This risk is driven by the settlement process and has been mitigated by the introduction of real time gross settlement (RTGS) systems, in contrast to systems which delay settlement at the end of the business day, when a netting process is applied.
- **Liquidity risk.** This type of risk is associated with the introduction of RTGS systems. RTGS systems require relatively high levels of liquidity, which is costly for banks. On the other hand, banks have an incentive to delay payments in order to reduce their liquidity usage by reusing incoming payments in order to fund outgoing payments. This behaviour might lead to gridlock in the payment system.
- **Operational risk.** This risk is related to possible technical failures of the system itself and external events (such as power failures, violence-related events, or other types of disasters). In order to mitigate this risk, appropriate technical arrangements and contingency plans are needed.
- **Business risk.** This risk is related to the insolvency of the provider of the payment system. The requirement of adequate solvency levels for the provider can help to mitigate this risk.

THE ROLE OF FINANCIAL MARKET INFRASTRUCTURES IN FINANCIAL MARKETS

Financial markets can be defined as a group of institutions with the main purpose of facilitating the exchange of assets. The assets to be traded depend on the specific type of each financial market. Some examples are: stock markets, bond markets, money markets, commodity markets, foreign exchange markets, and derivatives markets. Financial market infrastructures provide the means to conduct this exchange of assets in a secure and cost-efficient way.

In Diehl (in press) the author analyses how many of the activities developed in modern financial systems result in financial transactions which are settled or cleared in any of the FMIs within a single jurisdiction or multiple jurisdictions. In addition, some FMIs are responsible for money and securities transactions within or across countries. Furthermore, different FMIs provide important specific services for financial markets; for example, payment systems facilitate the transmission of money related to loans between market participants, whereas securities settlement systems do likewise for equities and securities. Central counterparties, by acting as a buyer for all sellers and as a seller for all buyers, protect participants in the event of the default of either. Finally, central securities depositories provide services with the purpose of safekeeping securities.

FMIs and Financial Stability: Rationale and Relevant Cases

In this section we provide a few concrete examples of the function of FMIs in financial (in)stability. The relevant cases provided are: i) monetary policy implementation and payment systems, ii) systemic liquidity and payment systems, iii) securities settlement systems failures, iv) centralized vs. OTC re-purchase agreement (repo) markets in Europe and in the U.S., and v) recent reforms of the OTC derivatives market. The first and second cases are rather generic descriptions of the impacts of payment systems on financial stability and vice versa, the third case illustrates the relationship between securities settlement systems and financial stability, and the fourth is a clear illustration of the concrete impact that the presence of a CCP has on the stability of a particular market. The fifth case presents the impact of the new regulation on CCPs on the stability of the global financial system. Finally, the last case describes the problem of too-interconnected-to-fail for CCPs.

In the recent subprime and European debt crises, interconnectedness is acknowledged as a crucial factor in the widespread impact on the world economy of what would otherwise be considered local events. The concept of too-interconnected-to-fail has become part of the new economic and financial parlance. However, determining how interconnected a financial system is remains difficult since banks and other financial institutions interact across markets using different instruments involving financial transactions performed on different platforms.

Nevertheless, despite the fact that apparently, a number of interactions takes place bilaterally, it is almost certain that such interactions will be performed, cleared and settled by one or more FMIs. For example, an OTC repo agreement implies, in the first place, a cash transfer between the lending and the borrowing institution, which could be performed through the payment system; the second part of the repo involves transferring the ownership of a security from the cash-borrowing institution to the cash-lending institution, which would go through a securities settlement system and, in some cases, with the intervention of a CCP.

Along this line of argumentation, it is clear that increased interconnectedness between market participants implies at the same time increased reliance on FMIs. Therefore, it is crucial to incorporate into our notion of interconnectivity the fact that FMIs should be considered the vehicle that allows interconnection to take place. In Leon et al. (2014) the authors study the way in which the FMIs should be integrated in the financial network and analyse the resulting structure and the implications to financial stability.

Monetary Policy Implementation and Payment Systems

In recent times, financial authorities around the world have sought to strengthen infrastructures not only to prevent them from posing a risk to financial stability, but also to contribute to the efficiency, adequate management of risk, and fostering of liquidity in financial markets. In addition to these goals, there are some specific cases in which FMIs have a very important function in maintaining financial stability.

An example of this is given by payment systems. In a broad sense, payment systems ensure the distribution of a central bank's money from institutions with excess liquidity to those in need of it. However, there is another important reason for the close link between financial stability and payment systems: the implementation of monetary policy.

In many countries, central banks implement monetary policy by manipulating the short-term interbank rate. At the end of the day, some banks have a liquidity deficit while others have a surplus; in order to level out liquidity, banks lend to each other through overnight loans. The corresponding rate on these loans is called the interbank overnight rate. Most central banks establish a target for the interbank overnight rate, with the aim of keeping inflation low and predictable. This influences other short-term interest rates, thus transmitting the policy stance to the broad economy.

As described in detail by Schmitz (2006), the institutional framework of a payment system can have an impact on the implementation of monetary policy, which can be categorized under one of the following:

1. The institutional arrangements of the payment system affect the structural liquidity deficit. Specifically: if the payment system can settle payments in real time rather than using a netting procedure at the end of the day, then the demand for liquidity from the central bank is different, with the demand for liquidity being higher in the former than in the latter settlement process. If a payment system has a tiered structure, only a few banks have direct access to the central bank's liquidity, thereby reducing the number of counterparties in open market operations at the cost of increasing credit risk for the system.
2. The settlement mechanism and the tiered structure of the payment system have an impact on the level of reserves and on the amount of intraday credit given by the central bank.
3. An operational disruption to the payment system can be a source of a liquidity shock to the system. This can, in turn, lead into greater volatility for the interbank overnight rate, making it more difficult for the central bank to assess the system's liquidity needs.

The link between payment systems and financial stability goes in both directions. In Schmitz (2006) the other side of the equation (the impact of the monetary policy framework on payment systems) is also described, and more aspects of this complex interaction are examined.

Systemic Liquidity Usage and Payment Systems

In order to operate smoothly, payment systems require participants to have adequate levels of liquidity, as described in Benos et al. (2012). Some banks reuse incoming payments to different degrees to fund outgoing payments, consequently facing smaller or larger liquidity pressure. In Benos et al. (2012), the authors observe payments delays in CHAPS two months after the collapse of Lehman Brothers. The implications for financial stability come from the fact that, instead of reusing incoming payments to fund the outgoing payments, banks had to resort to their own sources of liquidity, putting pressure on the liquidity available in the system.

Benos et al. (2012) conduct an empirical study to determine if the greater payments delay after Lehman's default was driven, at least partially, by an increased perception of counterparty and system-wide risk. The authors use two approaches to measure default risk: the credit default swap (CDS) price and the spread between the expected market overnight bank borrowing rate and the Bank of England's policy rate. The authors find that part of the greater delay can be explained by counterparty and system-wide risks. According to Benos et al. (2012), this increased payments delay not only made the system more vulnerable to disruptions caused by operational outage, but also led to an increased expected impact on the system's liquidity in such an operational outage.

Securities Settlement Systems Failures

The previous case presented the implications for the payment system of an important disruptive event. In contrast, securities settlement systems possess different characteristics and pose different risks to the stability of the financial system. Some examples of FMI failures which led to threats to financial stability are presented in Manning, Nier and Schanz (2009). In particular, the failure of the Hong Kong Futures Exchange clearing house in 1987 had dramatic consequences for Hong Kong's financial system, including a two-stage 4 billion HKD rescue package.

In Fleming and Garbade (2002), the authors describe clearly how the settlement process for the Treasury market after 9/11 suffered an enormous increase in the number of failed transactions (from US$1.7 billion to US$190 billion a day). These settlement failures were associated with the destruction of trade records and communication facilities. A securities transaction fails in the settlement process if the securities are not delivered or paid on the agreed date. According to Fleming and Garbade (2005), securities transactions do fail in the settlement process, with these failures persisting through time with varying patterns. However, there are limits to what the financial system is able to tolerate before these failures present a threat to the stability of the financial system as a whole. The failures have an impact on market liquidity due to increasing costs faced by brokers and, as a consequence, they affect financial stability. Therefore, it is important to take a closer look at such settlement failures, both in terms of amounts and how they develop. The right incentives to market players should also be put in place to avoid failures during the securities settlement process.

In Fleming and Garbade (2002), the story is different: a huge increase in settlement failures is caused by a major operational disruption, namely, the destruction of the records located physically at the World Trade Center and the collapse of communications after the 9/11 attacks. Given the impact on market liquidity of a sudden increase in settlement failures, the Treasury Department took an important remedial action: it sold additional 10-year notes despite the fact there was no need for the additional income from the sales. This measure certainly works for government securities, but it may not work for corporate securities.

Additionally, it is widely acknowledged that repo markets have seen their importance rise as one of the primary sources of funding for financial institutions, including banks. If the number of failures increases beyond a financial system's absorption capacity, cascading effects could exacerbate such negative events to threaten the stability of the financial system as a whole.

Our arguments are more anecdotal than analytical, but further research, like that presented in Devriese and Mitchell (2005), is needed on this hypothetical contagion mechanism. Although contagion in payment systems and interbank markets has been extensively studied, there are no empirical studies on contagion in securities settlement systems with the exception of Devriese and Mitchell (2005), where the authors study the systemic implications of failures of large participants in such settlement systems via simulations. The conclusions in Devriese and Mitchell (2005) are very important from the perspective of financial stability. First, the authors find that settlement failures would last more than two days after the initial default of a large institution due to the continuation of the contagion process. Second, the net trade position of the defaulting institution would have an impact on the severity of the contagion process that follows the initial failure.

Finally, in Iori (2004) and Iori & Deissenberg (2008), the authors compare two different securities settlement architectures in the presence of external delays: gross versus net. The authors find that, even if netting systems are generally acknowledged to be more stable than gross systems, netting systems are more severely affected by contagious defaults.

The Repo Markets in Europe and the U.S.

Repo markets have recently become important sources of wholesale funding for banks and other financial institutions. These markets represent a huge portion of the financial system in many jurisdictions and are, without a doubt, crucial for the stability of the financial system and economy as a whole. The recent crises provided evidence of the importance of the presence or absence of one specific type of FMI in the repo market: a CCP.

It has been well documented in Gorton & Metrick (2012) that, during the subprime crisis in the U.S., the financial system suffered a new kind of run: a repo run. The authors document an increase in the repo rates and haircuts of securitised bonds which lead to what they call a run on the repo and to a massive liquidity deficit for the financial system. This, in turn, was an important source of financial instability for the U.S. financial system.

In contrast, in Mancini et al. (2014) the authors find that the European repo market was resilient during the different crises. Furthermore, the authors claim that, in addition, the European repo market served as a shock dampener, and the central counterparty repo market was used to hoard liquidity. The authors identify trading through a central counterparty, in addition to using healthy collateral, as a key factor for the resilience of the European repo market.

The idea that a CCP is a way to avoid a run on OTC repo markets is too simplistic. The run on the U.S. repo market might be related to many other factors, such as the quality of collateral. However, these two cases serve as clear examples of the impact of CCPs under stressful situations in which market liquidity for certain securities dries, asset values decline, and securities used as collateral on repos experience higher haircuts. Nevertheless, a word of caution is necessary here: in Gorton & Metrick (2012), the authors report their findings on the repo market backed by securitised assets. This market was very important in the U.S., unlike in Europe. However, in Mancini et al. (2014), the authors report that the segment of the repo market that was centrally cleared performed better than other segments.

The evidence provided in this example is by no means complete and rather anecdotal but opens the door to new studies on the impact of having central counterparties for repo and other OTC markets. Could the U.S. run on the repo have been avoided if repos were settled by a CCP? The question remains unanswered, but the next case provides a good example of how the impact of CCPs can be assessed.

The International Reform of Derivatives Traded in OTC Markets

In the BIS-MAGD (2013) document, it is argued that the 2007-2008 crisis was propagated to an as-before unseen scale because of exposures associated with derivatives traded in OTC markets. Moreover, the uncertainty on counterparties (and their size) involved in such trades led to the so-called credit crunch as trust evaporated in several markets. Since then, international regulation has pushed to reduce counterparty risk in the OTC derivatives markets. Among the many aspects of such reforms, two are deemed crucial: i) the establishment of collateral requirements against current and potential future exposures; and ii) requiring that standardised OTC derivatives be cleared through CCPs. Our concern is obviously related to the second major reform.

The BIS-MAGD (2013) paper rigorously evaluates the impact and the costs that the implementation of CCPs on the clearing of OTC derivatives would have. The paper points to a long-term benefit of a reduction in losses originating from financial crises in which the OTC derivatives play a central role. On the costs side, economic activity can be reduced due to higher risk transfer prices and increased capital and collateral holdings. The study's main findings are that under different cost scenarios (low, central and high), the net benefits of the reforms, measured as the change in expected annual GDP, are between 0.13 percent for the low-cost scenario and 0.9 percent for the high-cost scenario. The benefits are measured as the reduction in output losses from financial crises, and the costs are estimated as the effect on GDP of higher prices for financial services.

Unlike the previous case, the study presented here is supported by comprehensive research involving FSB members in collaboration with the IMF, academics, the private sector, and infrastructure providers. The assessment faced technical and data challenges, but in the end, the results provide clear guidance for similar impact studies on related topics such as repo markets.

CCPs and the Too-Interconnected-to-Fail Problem

Markets in which CCPs cleared an important part of the transactions rose from the recent financial crisis in good shape. In contrast, other OTC markets, showed tremendous structural vulnerabilities, some of them to the point of total meltdown. The contagion-stopping capacity of CCPs has put them in the spotlight: they have been used more often and international regulators and institutions such as the FSB and the IMF have even encouraged their use. Nevertheless, despite all the good characteristics of such FMI, popularity comes with an important associated risk: CCPs are highly interconnected with other participants, markets and CCPs. For instance, figure 1a shows the network of OTC derivatives in Mexico, and figure 1b shows an estimation of the same network after considering the new regulation of the OTCD market. From this figure, it is straightforwardly seen that the introduction of CCPs considerably changes the structure of the derivatives exposures network, with the CCPs playing a central role in the new structure.

In order to study interconnectedness of CCPs and potential risks to the financial system, network analysis has become a prominent tool allowing evaluating the impact of a CCP's failure on the rest of the

Figure 1. The derivatives exposure network for the Mexican financial system a) Before reforms b) After the introduction of CCPs

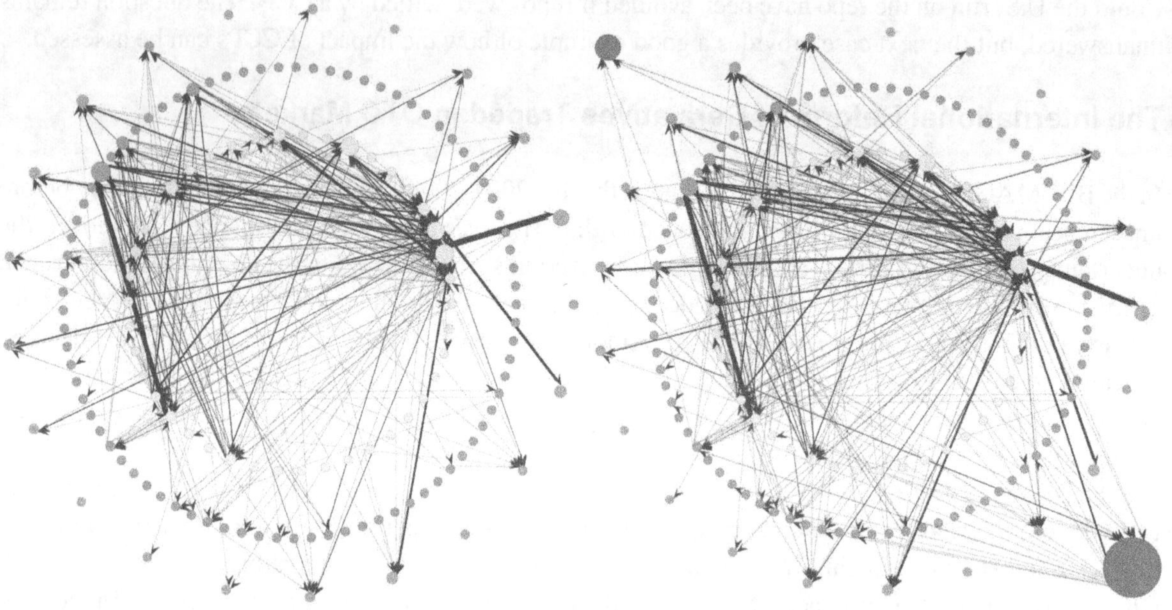

system. Some recent studies that have used a network-based approach to study CCPs include Anderson et al (2013), Garratt and Zimmerman (2013), Duffie et al (2014) and Wendt (2015).

Network modelling has become popular in studying CCPs because it allows to explicitly model the structure of the interconnections between CCPs, participants, markets, and other CCPs; likewise, network analysis allows extracting relevant information from network structures in order to identify possible threats from a systemic perspective. For instance, in Anderson et al. (2013) the authors provide a framework to study different connectivity patterns between domestic CCPs and global CCPs; the main result of the study is that high connectivity between domestic and global CCPs may lead to higher exposures for the domestic CCPs and lower netting efficiency.

In Garratt and Zimmerman (2013), the authors use a simple network growth mechanism to generate (scale-free) networks in order to evaluate the impact that the introduction of CCPs would have on netting efficiency. Duffie et al. (2014), using CDS data, evaluate the impact that new regulations on margin requirements and the introduction of CCPs would have on the demand for collateral; the authors find that the system-wide demand for collateral associated to margin requirements increases, but the introduction of CCPs, under specific circumstances, would lower such demand for collateral.

Finally, Wendt (2015) acknowledges that despite the benefits that CCPs bring to the market, their high interconnectedness causes them to be too-important-to-fail (or too-interconnected-to-fail, as we say). Wendt (2015) goes further in suggesting that, given their highly connected nature and their growing importance, it is vital to correctly manage the risks that can be associated with them. One important suggestion in the paper is that CCPs and authorities should conduct network analysis in order to estimate potential losses.

Data Gaps and Transparency Issues

In April 2009 the G-20 asked the IMF and FSB to explore the existing data gaps and make proposals in order to strengthen data collection around the globe. The IMF and the FSB issued 20 recommendations to Ministers for Finance and central bank Governors to ensure consistency on the implementation of the objectives of the data gaps initiative group (DGI). In this initiative, the G-20 and the FSB acknowledged that important data gaps were present during the 2007-2008 crisis, something that had to be addressed.

In addition to this important global initiative, more initiatives were launched by the FSB, the BCBS and the IOSCO, recognizing the existence of relevant data gaps. Trade repositories (TRs) are explicitly considered to be important pieces in these new initiatives aiming to help ensuring the stability of the global financial system. Particularly, TRs were given an important place in the FSB policy framework to address shadow banking risks in securities lending and repos (FSB, 2013). This framework attempts to address important issues in the securities lending and repo markets, as it is very difficult to accurately compute the size of counterparty exposures and estimate the number of times a security has been rehypothecated.[3]

TRs, in addition to CCPs, are expected to play a central role in the OTC derivatives market reform due to the current lack of adequate data to estimate exposures arising from derivatives contracts. This situation became clear during the recent financial crises, with the implications for financial stability being evident nowadays. Additionally, TRs will also be useful to identify cross-border risks by closing the data gap on foreign currency exposures. The most important goals of the global initiatives presented in this section are to improve market transparency and provide authorities and the public with the necessary data to monitor and detect possible threats to financial stability; for that purpose, TRs are perceived as the key FMI. However, despite the existence and creation of new TRs around the world, data aggregation and data compatibility between repositories remain an issue. Fortunately, the FSB has become aware of this problem and has even published a study on different approaches to the aggregation of OTC derivatives data (FSB, 2014b).

THE PRINCIPLES FOR FINANCIAL MARKET INFRASTRUCTURES

In this section, we provide an extremely condensed description of the principles borrowed from the PFMIs document, which will be useful for further discussion. However, before a general description of the principles is addressed, it is important to remember the main reasons behind the development of the initiative. According to the PFMIs document, the main public policy objectives of the issuance of these principles were "to enhance safety and efficiency in payment, clearing, settlement, and recording arrangements, and more broadly, to limit systemic risk and foster transparency and financial stability."

In April 2012, the Committee on Payment and Settlement Systems (CPSS) and the International Organisation of Securities Commissions (IOSCO) issued the Principles for Financial Market Infrastructures (PFMIs),[4] which consolidate international standards for FMIs and update the responsibilities of the authorities that regulate, supervise or oversee FMIs.

In addition to this document, the CPSS and the IOSCO published the document "Principles for financial market infrastructures: Disclosure framework and Assessment methodology" in late 2012. In this document, a more detailed description is given of the form and content of the expected disclosure from FMIs. Additionally, detailed guidance is provided for the evaluation of compliance with the 24 principles.

The Principles

The principles fall in the following categories:

- General organisation, principles 1-3
- Credit and liquidity risk management, principles 4-7
- Settlement, principles 8-10
- Central securities depositories and exchange-of-value settlement systems, principles 11-12
- Default management, principles 13-14
- General business and operational risk management, principles 15-17
- Access, principles 18-20
- Efficiency, principles 21-22
- Transparency, principles 23-24

The Principles: A Critical View

The principles provide a solid starting point. However, further work is required by regulators and FMIs. Moreover, issuance and compliance with such principles should not provide regulators and FMIs with a false sense of security, keeping them from further work on pending topics. This is the case for the reforms of the OTC derivatives markets. Under them lies the implicit assumption that CCPs reduce systemic risk. Furthermore, the study discussed previously evaluates the impact of such reforms on the costs involved in systemic crises, and the results are encouraging. However, there are still implications which deserve a more careful examination when all the proposed reforms are considered. For example, since we are moving into a more collateralised financial system, there is the need to study the global implications of this transition on the stability of the financial system, as has been pointed out in Cruz et al. (2013).

Another important factor which merits further examination is the way interconnectedness in the financial system is changing. In addition to the reforms in the OTC derivatives markets, there is also more regulation which will transform the network structures where financial institutions interact, such as the framework for large exposures (BIS, 2014). The principles are silent in this regard, and there is a strong implicit assumption that CCPs are beneficial in dealing with interconnectedness. Again, in our opinion, there is a risk of overreliance on the principles. We would emphasize that the financial landscape will be changing dramatically as a result of all these new regulations, and financial authorities must be alert to new risks, arising in particular from the interaction of FMIs and financial stability.

Furthermore, the PFMIs do not make a distinction between the purposes of stabilizing a single FMI versus stabilizing the financial system as a whole. More importantly, it is not clear whether full compliance with all the PFMIs is enough to ensure the correct operation of FMIs and as a consequence sufficient to ensure financial stability.[5]

Finally, it should be noted that the principles lack clarity on the definition of systemic importance, and they rely mainly on financial authorities' own rationales to decide whether their FMIs are systemically important, and consequently, adhere to the PFMIs. The lack of an internationally coherent definition of systemic importance and coordinated application of such a definition may lead to regulatory arbitrage.

THE ROLE OF FINANCIAL AUTHORITIES REGARDING FMIS

As the variety of institutions, systems and entities that conform FMIs would imply, many authorities are involved in the supervision, regulation and monitoring of FMIs. Among such institutions, central banks, supervisory agencies, and market regulators are those with the highest degree of responsibility to ensure the proper functioning of FMIs. Financial authorities' responsibilities regarding FMIs are described in CPSS-IOSCO (2012a) and CPSS-IOSCO (2012b). Appendix B provides a brief summary of them.

Special attention should be paid to the process of globally adopting the PFMIs. Despite growing consensus on the benefits that adopting the principles would bring to financial stability, lack of coordination or the presence of inconsistencies among regulatory regimes can lead to arbitrage and other risks. To avoid this, cooperation on oversight of international links among FMIs has been important in assuring a smooth process of acceding to the principles. Several countries have made efforts to comply with the principles, each acting differently according to self-assessment studies leading to tailored policies and actions. Consequently, various countries have faced unique challenges in this process, each country working towards mitigating systemic risk. In countries where FMIs were already present, self-evaluation exercises have been useful in ensuring that existing FMIs to adopt the PFMIs by taking actions that improve these FMIs, such as strengthening OTC derivatives markets or encouraging the use of delivery-vs.-payment in settlement systems. In the case of countries in which some specific FMIs were not present, studying threads to financial stability according to the PFMIs has led to the creation of new FMIs aiming to meet the standard. Some examples include new payment systems, clearing services and houses (CLS Bank), and OTC trade repositories, all of which were designed with the conditions established by the principles taken into consideration.

Various countries and industry members have adopted the principles to different degrees and under their respective circumstances. In this section some public positions will be described.

The U.S. Federal Reserve System

With the objective of fostering the safety and efficiency of payment and settlement systems and seeking to mitigate systemic risk, the Federal Reserve Board maintains its Policy on Payment System Risk (PSR), which incorporates the recommendations issued prior to the PFMIs by the CPSS and the IOSCO.

The two main payment and settlement systems operated by the Federal Reserve Banks are the Fedwire Funds Service and the Fedwire Securities Services. Under the Federal Reserve Act, the Board has authority over the Reserve Banks' provision of payment and settlement services and promises to meet the requirements for similar private-sector systems. The policy applies to both Reserve Banks and certain private-sector systems. Enhanced regulation and supervision is applicable to financial market utilities (FMUs, including some FMIs) considered by the Financial Stability Oversight Council to be systemically important. This is all conducted under application of robust risk-management standards, followed by an examination process and a review of ongoing operations.

In the case of FMIs interacting with U.S. institutions or clearing U.S. dollar transactions, efforts are made to share important information with the relevant authorities to accurately assess risks to the U.S. financial system. There is also cooperation on the oversight of SWIFT (the Society for Worldwide Interbank Financial Telecommunication), on which many financial institutions depend for daily messaging.

The Bank of England

The Bank of England's supervision of FMIs seeks to enhance the stability of the financial system and ensure that FMIs are managed in a way that reduces systemic risk. Taking the PFMIs as the main guide for its supervisory approach, the Bank assumed responsibilities for supervising CCPs and securities settlement systems. One consequence was the improvement of margin models for CCPs. Additionally, Bacs and FPS retail payment systems eliminated settlement risk using a prefunding approach and the continuity of essential services if a drastic financial shock occurs. This has been ensured thanks to arrangements for allocating losses in the event of the default of a clearing member exceeding a certain threshold. Furthermore, efforts have been made to assess operational risk in the presence of external events, in particular, cyber-attacks on the U.K. financial sector.

On international cooperation, the Bank of England promises to surpass the requirements of European Market Infrastructure Regulation (EMIR) for U.K. FMIs considered important to the international financial system, exceeding expectations for international cooperation as described in the PFMIs.

The Bank of Mexico

In the Mexican case, the central bank is taking measures to strengthen the FMIs of systemic importance in the aim of mitigating systemic risk. The measures include reforms to strengthen the Over-the-Counter (OTC) derivatives market and the adoption of the PFMIs for the country. The central bank is in the midst of an assessment of the Mexican Large Value Payment System, SPEI, to determine PFMIs compliance and has requested that private FMI administrators conduct a self-assessment of their own infrastructures: DALI (the securities settlement system operated by INDEVAL, the central securities depository), CCV (the equities CCP), and Asigna (the derivatives transactions CCP).

The Bank of Canada

Four FMIs have been determined by the Bank of Canada to meet the standards introduced by the PFMIs. Through self-evaluation against the principles, a robust risk control level has been reached, and plans are being developed to attend to underdeveloped areas. These FMIs are: the Large Value Transfer System (LVTS, settling payments denominated in CAD); CDSX (made up of a securities settlement and depository system, and central counterparty); the Canadian Derivatives Clearing Service (CDCS, a central counterparty for certain fixed-income securities, repos, and derivatives); and finally the CLS Bank (a worldwide payments-vs.-payment settlement service for FX transactions).

The Reserve Bank of New Zealand

NZClear is a delivery-vs.-payment system between wholesale counterparties (bearing on 19 out of the 24 Principles for FMIs) and is owned and operated by the Reserve Bank of New Zealand (RBNZ). Complying with the Principles for FMIs, the NZClear system acts as a payments system, a central securities depository, and a securities settlement system. In consequence, principles related to being a CCP do not apply to NZClear. The New Zealand Clearing and Depository Corporation Limited (NZCDC) acts as a CCP for trades on some derivatives and the NZX (New Zealand Exchange).

The Hong Kong Monetary Authority (KKMA)

In order to maintain Hong Kong's role as an international financial centre (which is one of the HKMA's objectives), it is important to strengthen and develop Hong Kong's FMIs. To guarantee compliance with the Clearing and Settlement Systems Ordinance (CSSO), the HKMA can appoint clearing and settlements systems and supervise them. FMIs (owned and operated by the HKMA) being developed include the Hong Kong Dollar Clearing House Automated Transfer System (Hong Kong dollar CHATS), the Central Money markets Unit (CMU), and the OTC Derivatives Trade Repository (HKTR). These FMIs are expected to have made necessary changes to comply with the PFMIs, and be generally observant of the Principles by December 31, 2015 (although most of the relevant principles are already observed or broadly observed by the FMIs). As a CLS Oversight Committee member, the HKMA cooperates in CLS oversight arrangements. Likewise, the HKMA cooperates on oversight of cross-border links installed by FMIs abroad.

IBERCLEAR

IBERCLEAR is Spain's central securities depository (CSD), part of the BME Group (Bolsas y Mercados Españoles), overseen by the Spanish securities market regulator (CNMV), and acts under the European Central Securities Depositories Association (ECSDA) framework. Thus is has open connections with CSDs abroad and the central counterparty clearing house in London. Risk management and control is carried out by the BME's Risk Committee. IBERCLEAR keeps accounting records of securities traded in organised or OTC markets and manages the settlement and clearing of securities and cash via SCLV platforms (the Securities Clearing and Settlement Service) and the CADE (the Spanish public debt book-entry system), which allows for settling differences in real time.

The Monetary Authority of Singapore

Singapore has a well-developed payment, clearing, and settlement infrastructure, including two CCPs for financial products (the Central Depository Limited and the Singapore Exchange Derivatives Clearing Limited), a large value payment system operated by the central bank and securities and derivatives clearing and settlement systems operated by the Singapore Exchange Limited (SGX). The FMIs are subject to regulation and supervision by the Monetary Authority of Singapore (MAS), which has publicly announced the adoption of the PFMIs. Risk-management frameworks enable CCPs to maintain sufficient financial resources to cover the default of the clearing member with the largest exposure as well as the default of the two weakest clearing members. Models are subject to back testing, sensitivity analysis and in-depth reviews by the internal risk management unit and the MAS.

Areas that may benefit from further development include: encouraging CCPs to prefer government securities as collateral; enhancing the SGX's recovery plan in line with international policy developments to ensure continuation in extreme circumstances; mitigating risks related to conflict among laws, to which the SGX-DC (the Singapore Exchange Derivatives Clearing Limited) is exposed given the global regulatory reforms for OTC derivatives clearing, and dealing with competition from foreign CCPs, especially for OTC derivatives.

The Bank of France

The Banque de France has a long-standing practice of overseeing infrastructures on a cooperative basis. It is responsible for overseeing the three FMIs based in France: the clearing system operated by the CCP (LCH.Clearnet SA), the ESES France settlement system (managed by the CSD Euroclear France), and the CORE retail payment system (based on multilateral clearing, run by STET). It also takes part in cooperative oversight of other FMIs active in France that operate throughout the euro area (large value payment systems TARGET2 and EURO1) and worldwide (SWIFT, CLS, among others). TARGET2 is a real-time gross settlement system for transactions in euros, developed and operated by the Eurosystem.

The European Central Bank

According to the ECB, the use of FMIs across markets has been growing, in part, after the G20 OTC derivatives reform and the growing use of CCPs for products such as repos. It should be ensured that FMIs are prepared for stress scenarios even more severe than the ones experienced during the recent crisis. The CPSS and the IOSCO have strengthened their international standards by raising minimum requirements including those for managing financial risks. The principles for FMIs include new requirements such as addressing business risk, the need to protect indirect participants through segregation, and the need to address risks relating to tiering.

Regarding credit risk, the strongest new requirement for a CCP is to maintain at least the financial resources needed to cover the default of the two participants (and their affiliates) that would cause the largest credit exposure to the CCP. Principles also require payment systems to employ a deferred net settlement mechanism (DNS), as well as requiring contingency planning for credit losses that are not covered by the resources which are part of regular risk management practices.

For liquidity risk, FMIs should maintain sufficient liquid resources in all relevant currencies to effect same-day (and sometimes intraday and multi-day) settlements while contemplating a wide range of stress scenarios. For collateral requirements, stable and conservative haircuts should be applied, calibrating periods of stressed market conditions.

One of the biggest risks would be the overlapping and inconsistency between authorities' rules for OTC derivatives given that, domestic requirements may be applied to foreign FMIs.

The Bank of Japan

The Bank of Japan oversees FMIs in order to ensure compliance with the principles. Some improvements in payment and settlement systems include the establishment of new securities clearing and settlement systems, as well as the dematerialisation of major types of securities. The use of delivery-vs.-payment has been encouraged in the settlement of securities. This has been complemented with government action affecting the legal framework. To prevent disturbances on the yen funding of Japanese institutions, the scope of the legislation covers FMIs that settle transactions in foreign currency. In the oversight process, the Bank of Japan first analyses various aspects of each FMI in order to guarantee safety and efficiency, taking into consideration the systemic importance of each FMI so as to not to disturb "smooth settlement of funds among institutions," and decides whether to treat a relevant FMI as an exception if the risk of not achieving smoothness is posed. Finally, the Bank determines whether the objectives have been met for a particular FMI, promoting resolution if the objectives have not been achieved.

International Coordination on the Regulatory Reforms for FMIs

In addition to the coordination efforts within countries suggested by the PFMIs, there is the need to coordinate efforts across countries of the adoption process in order to avoid regulatory arbitrage. Cross-border cooperation is particularly important in cases in which an FMI has cross-border activities. For example, in the case of the Continuous Linked Settlement (CLS) there exists a cooperative oversight arrangement between the 17 central banks of all the currencies which are settled via CLS. International bodies like the Financial Stability Board (FSB) are heavily involved on the implementation of the OTC derivatives reforms. However, to the best of our knowledge, little has been done on the coordination of the adoption process of the PFMIs across jurisdictions.

In Russo (2013), the author makes the case for the elaboration of realistic recovery and resolution plans in order to avert moral-hazard-related problems. In the case of globally active FMIs, by definition these plans involve the collaboration of many supervisors and regulators across jurisdictions. However, more recently the Financial Stability Board (see FSB (2014)), the European Commission and the U.K. Treasury, among other institutions, have been making progress on this topic.

CONCLUSIONS AND FUTURE RESEARCH DIRECTIONS

This chapter presents a clear and simple explanation of the relationship between FMIs and financial stability and introduces the reader to the very important initiative of the issuance of the PFMIs by the CPSS and the IOSCO.

Despite the fact that the purpose of this paper is to be merely introductory, it is possible to enumerate some promising lines of future research on FMIs form the perspective of financial stability. The field has been only recently opened; therefore, there are many opportunities to innovate from the methodological point of view or to perform relevant empirical studies.

One of the most important aspects to study in the future is the emergent architecture of interconnectivity between FMIs. For this purpose, network theory can be a critical tool to characterise the structure, identify relevant components, and to study possible threats to the stability of the system as a whole, with a systemic view. Some interesting progress has already been made in León & Pérez (2014); however, the analysis is limited to identifying important players, and more can be done on contagion transmission and assessing the robustness of particular architectures under regular and stressful scenarios.

In Leon et al. (2014), the authors use data from Colombia to study the way in which FMIs should be incorporated into the financial network. A study on a global scale or from different jurisdictions would be welcome. However, these studies would face formidable data-collecting challenges.

Regarding CCPs, new lines of research are open for the estimation of collateral requirements for such institutions. This is of particular importance given that, by construction, some of the CCPs will be systemically important institutions. As pointed out in Goyal and Vigier (2010), it is possible to design robust networks in the presence of random and directed attacks. A very intuitive result is that centralised networks are more robust to random attacks but in the case of directed attacks, the robustness of the networks depends heavily on the "defence" budget. In the context of CCPs this means that a necessarily sufficient budget (monitoring, risk management, collateral requirements, etc.) must be allocated in order to preserve the robustness of the new financial architecture incentivised by the new proposed regulation.

As mentioned, important studies have been done on the possible implications of changes to the regulatory landscape, such as in Macroeconomic Assessment Group on Derivatives (2013), where the macroeconomic impact of the OTC derivatives reform is assessed. Nevertheless, the availability of the necessary data to perform this study was one of the most important challenges. On the bright side, this study required close cooperation among many jurisdictions and international institutions both from the methodological point of view and on data collection.

Another source of concern comes from the reforms on OTC derivatives together with the changes on liquidity regulation, which might lead to the scarcity of high-quality collateral. There is also concern on the pro-cyclicality of the initial margins and capital requirements associated with such reforms. Hence, more studies on these topics would be welcomed by academia, industry and regulators alike. Moreover, interconnectedness through the use and reuse of collateral will increase. Given that little information is available on the underlying collateral network, it will be very difficult to predict possible cascade effects under stressful conditions.

There is also a strong need to understand the new emerging network structures in which financial institutions will interact. This has been done in Garratt and Zimmerman (2013) for CCPs, while in Cont and Kokholm (2012), Cont and Minca (2014) the authors study the differences between bilateral and multilateral netting for OTC derivatives. It has been argued that during the recent financial crisis, interconnectedness played a very important role. New regulation is changing the conditions under which financial institutions operate, stressing the need to study and understand the new emerging network structure from the perspective of financial stability. More of this type of research would be welcome, especially if it includes other FMIs besides CCPs.

Finally, in addition to close monitoring and tight regulation;[6] there is an urgent need to elaborate realistic recovery and resolution plans in order to prevent moral-hazard-related problems, as pointed out in Russo (2013) and as the FSB has also emphasized. This is especially so since, due to the way they have been designed, several of such infrastructures will become systemically important financial institutions. Finally, there is always the challenging issue of the endogenous nature of systemic risk: an important part of the feedback mechanism which further destabilizes the financial system is related to the market participant behavioural response.[7]

ACKNOWLEDGMENT

The authors are in great debt to Martin Diehl, Marco Massarenti and anonymous readers for their valuable comments. Without them, the chapter would have had many significant defects. All the remaining errors are ours. The opinions expressed here are those of the authors and do not represent the views of the institution that employs them.

REFERENCES

Allen, F., & Carletti, E. (2013). What Is Systemic Risk? *Journal of Money, Credit and Banking*, *45*(1).

Benos, E., Garratt, R., & Zimmerman, P. (2012). Bank behaviour and risks in CHAPS following the collapse of Lehman Brothers. *Bank of England Working Paper, 451*.

Macroeconomic impact assessment of OTC derivatives regulatory reforms BIS- MAGD. (2013). Bank for International Settlements and the Macroeconomic Assessment Group on Derivatives.

Supervisory framework for measuring and controlling large exposures - final standard. (2014BIS. Basel Committee on Banking Supervision.

Cont, R., & Kokholm, T. (2014). Central Clearing of OTC Derivatives: Bilateral vs multilateral netting. *Statistics & Risk Modeling, 31*(1), 3–22. doi:10.1515/strm-2013-1161

Cont, R., & Minca, A. (2014). Credit default swaps and systemic risk. *Available at SSRN 2487947.*

A glossary of terms used in payments and settlement systems. CPSS. Bank for International Settlements.

Principles for financial market infrastructures. (2012a). CPSS-IOSCO. Bank for International Settlements.

Principles for financial market infrastructures: Disclosure framework and Assessment methodology. (2012b). CPSS-IOSCO. Bank for International Settlements.

Cruz Lopez, J., Mendes, R., & Vikstedt, H. (2013). The Market for Collateral: The Potential Impact of Financial Regulation. *Bank of Canada, Financial System Review.*

Devriese, J., & Mitchell, J. (2006). Liquidity risk in securities settlement. *Journal of Banking & Finance, 30*(6), 1807–1834. doi:10.1016/j.jbankfin.2005.09.008

Diehl, M. (in press). FMI: The backbone of financial systems. *Analyzing the Economics of Financial Market Infrastructures.*

Duffie, D., Scheicher, M., & Vuillemey, G. (2015). Central clearing and collateral demand. *Journal of Financial Economics, 116*(2), 237–256. doi:10.1016/j.jfineco.2014.12.006

Fleming, M. J., & Garbade, K. (2002). When the back office moved to the front burner: Settlement fails in the Treasury market after September 11. *Economic Policy Review, 8*(2).

Fleming, M. J., & Garbade, K. (2005). Explaining settlement fails. *Current Issues in Economics and Finance, 11*(9).

Strengthening Oversight and Regulation of Shadow Banking. (2013). FSB. *Policy Framework for Addressing Shadow Banking Risks in Securities Lending and Repos,* 20 -21.

Key Attributes of Effective Resolution Regimes for Financial Institutions. (2014a). Financial Stability Board.

Feasibility Study on Approaches to Aggregate OTC Derivatives Data. (2014b). Financial Stability Board.

Garratt, R., & Zimmerman, P. (2013). Does a CCP Reduce Counterparty Risk in a Scale-Free Network? [Unpublished manuscript].

Gorton, G., & Metrick, A. (2012). Securitized banking and the run on repo. *Journal of Financial Economics, 104*(3), 425–451. doi:10.1016/j.jfineco.2011.03.016

Goyal, S., & Vigier, A. (2010). Robust networks. Retrieved from http://www.econ.cam.ac.uk/faculty/goyal/wp10/robustnet-works55.pdf

Iori, G. (2004). An analysis of systemic risk in alternative securities settlement architectures, *European Central Bank, Working paper, 404*.

Iori, G., & Deissenberg, C. (2008). An Analysis of Settlement Risk Contagion in Alternative Securities Settlement Architectures. In *Computational Methods in Financial Engineering* (pp. 299–315). Springer Berlin Heidelberg.

León, C., & Pérez, J. (2014). Assessing financial market infrastructures' systemic importance with authority and hub centrality. *Journal of Financial Market Infrastructures*, *2*(3), 67–87.

León, C., Berndsen, R., & Renneboog, L. (2014). Financial Stability and Interacting Networks of Financial Institutions and Market Infrastructures. *CentER Discussionpaper Series*, 69.

Macroeconomic impact assessment of OTC derivatives regulatory reforms. (2013). Bank for International Settlements.

Mancini, L., Ranaldo, A., & Wrampelmeyer, J. (2014). The Euro interbank repo market. *Swiss Finance Institute Research Paper*, 13-71.

Manning, M., Nier, E., & Schanz, J. (Eds.). (2009). *The economics of large-value payments and settlement: theory and policy issues for central banks*. Oxford University Press.

Martínez-Jaramillo, S., Pérez, O. P., Embriz, F. A., & Dey, F. L. G. (2010). Systemic risk, financial contagion and financial fragility. *Journal of Economic Dynamics & Control*, *34*(11), 2358–2374. doi:10.1016/j.jedc.2010.06.004

Martinez-Jaramillo, S., Alexandrova-Kabadjova, B., Bravo-Benitez, B., & Solórzano-Margain, J. P. (2014). An empirical study of the Mexican banking system's network and its implications for systemic risk. *Journal of Economic Dynamics & Control*, *40*, 242–265. doi:10.1016/j.jedc.2014.01.009

Kane, E. J. (2009). Discussion of "An Industrial Organization Approach to the Too Big to Fail Problem" by Jean-Charles Rochet. In *Prepared for Federal Reserve Bank of Boston 54th Economic Conference in Chatham, MA (October)*.

Schmitz, S. (2006). How payment systems affect monetary policy. *Central Banking*, *17*(2), 65.

Russo, D., (2013). CPSS-IOSCO Principles for financial market infrastructures: vectors of international convergence, Banque de France, *Financial Stability Review*, 17.

Wendt, F. (2015). Central Counterparties: Addressing their Too Important to Fail Nature. *International Monetary Fund Working Paper 15/21*.

KEY TERMS AND DEFINITIONS

Financial Contagion: Is the process by which financial difficulties are transmitted from one country or financial intermediary to other countries or financial counterparties.

Financial Derivative: A financial derivative (generally known only as derivative) is a contract between at least two parties whose price is determined by an underlying asset. There are four main types of derivatives: options, swaps, futures and forwards.

Financial Market Infrastructure: Set of organisations and entities in charge of the recording, clearing and settlement of financial transactions.

Financial Network: Mathematical object used to determine and study the performance and structural aspects of a system.

Financial Security: A financial security is a document that represents the ownership over a specific asset (like a stock) or a loan from an investor to the owner of an asset (like a corporate or government bond).

Financial Stability: The state in which the financial system is capable of allocating investors' resources to the most productive investments, facilitating risk sharing, under the well-functioning of markets and FMIs.

Repurchase Agreement: A repurchase agreement (repo) is a money-market financial transaction used to obtain short-term funding. A repo is a form of collateralised lending. In a typical bilateral repo agreement, two parties participate: the cash borrower (securities seller) and the cash lender (securities buyer). The cash borrower agrees to re-purchase the securities (collateral) in the future, whereas the cash lender performs a reverse repo transaction agreeing to sell the securities back at an agreed-upon future date.

Systemic Risk: Risk of occurrence of an event which threatens the well-functioning of the financial system.

ENDNOTES

1 The authors would like to thank one of the readers for pointing this out.

2 https://www.ecb.europa.eu/pub/fsr/html/index.en.html

3 Rehypothication refers to the use of securities that have been used by an institution (A) as collateral with another institution (B), and are used again by institution B as collateral for other transactions.

4 CPSS-IOSCO (2012a), Principles for financial market infrastructures, Bank for International Settlements.

5 We want to thank Martin Diehl for suggesting this line of argument.

6 However, as Martin Diehl suggests, it is also important to distinguish the oversight from the macroprudential perspective on the identification of risks and on the elaboration of relevant indicators.

7 We appreciate Martin Diehl's remark on this topic.

APPENDIX: RESPONSIBILITIES OF CENTRAL BANKS, MARKET REGULATORS, AND OTHER RELEVANT AUTHORITIES FOR FINANCIAL MARKET INFRASTRUCTURES

Responsibility A: Regulation, Supervision, and Oversight of FMIs

FMIs should be subject to appropriate and effective regulation, supervision, and oversight by a central bank, market regulator, or other relevant authority.

Responsibility B: Regulatory, Supervisory, and Oversight Powers and Resources

Central banks, market regulators, and other relevant authorities should have the powers and resources to carry out their responsibilities effectively in regulating, supervising, and overseeing FMIs.

Responsibility C: Disclosure of Policies with Respect to FMIs

Central banks, market regulators, and other relevant authorities should clearly define and disclose their regulatory, supervisory, and oversight policies with respect to FMIs.

Responsibility D: Application of the Principles for FMIs

Central banks, market regulators, and other relevant authorities should adopt the CPSS-IOSCO Principles for financial market infrastructures and apply them consistently.

Responsibility E: Cooperation with Other Authorities

Central banks, market regulators, and other relevant authorities should cooperate with each other, both domestically and internationally, as appropriate, in promoting the safety and efficiency of FMIs.

Chapter 3
Regulating Global FMIs:
Achieving Stability and Efficiency across Borders

Aaron Unterman
Ontario Securities Commission, Canada

ABSTRACT

A key regulatory response to the 2008 financial crisis has been to greatly enhance the role of financial market infrastructures (FMIs) including central counterparties and trade repositories in the global OTC derivatives market. This chapter analyses the implications, from a regulatory perspective, of reliance on internationally active FMIs that can be systemically important to multiple jurisdictions by examining the multiple sources of domestic and international laws applicable to such entities. This chapter argues that, although achievements have been made, greater international coordination is necessary to ensure that global FMIs operate in a stable and efficient manner.

INTRODUCTION

Lack of transparency, transmission of counterparty risk and the inability of regulators and market participants to understand the network of over-the-counter (OTC) derivatives transactions and relationships between global financial institutions played a central role in the 2008 financial crisis. Prior to the crisis, the OTC derivatives market flourished in a largely borderless and unregulated environment and involved many of the world's largest and most systemically important institutions. Although the market proliferated, the vast majority of transactions involved a relatively limited number of large interconnected international dealers. Leading up to the crisis, OTC derivatives played an increasingly important role in most developed economies and created systemic cross border links that were opaque to both regulators and market participants. The predominance of cross border transactions in this market facilitated the global contagion of credit risk to an extent not previously witnessed.

Traditional methods of credit evaluation became unreliable due to opaque chains of counterparty exposures as well as underdeveloped record keeping and processing systems. Even prior to the crisis, vulnerabilities of the OTC market were recognized with a view emerging that: "(i) there should be a clear

DOI: 10.4018/978-1-4666-8745-5.ch003

system for aggregating individual exposures across intermediaries through timely, consistent reporting using common identifiers and (ii) credit enhancement through central counterparty clearing potentially could mitigate the potential for contagion, runs, and other systemic ills" (Corcoran, 2013, p. 4).

In order to address the vulnerabilities of the OTC market, a key aspect of the global regulatory response to the 2008 crisis was to greatly enhance the role of financial market infrastructures (FMIs) in the global economy, for the purposes of increasing transparency and mitigating counterparty risk. FMIs facilitate the payment, clearing, settlement and recording of monetary and other financial transactions. They can be systemically important and perform a crucial role during and post transaction. The G-20 leader's statement from the Pittsburgh Summit (2009) laid out the roadmap for the derivatives market reform in the following statement:

All standardized OTC derivative contracts should be traded on exchanges or electronic trading platforms, where appropriate, and cleared through central counterparties by end-2012 at the latest. OTC derivative contracts should be reported to trade repositories. Non-centrally cleared contracts should be subject to higher capital requirements. We ask the FSB and its relevant members to assess regularly implementation and whether it is sufficient to improve transparency in the derivatives markets, mitigate systemic risk, and protect against market abuse.

This chapter will focus on the regulatory implications of the G-20 commitments to mandate the use of trade repositories (TRs) and central counterparties (CCPs), as well as the international reform efforts to implement these commitments. As this chapter will explain, the implementation of these reforms challenges the traditional construct of market infrastructure regulation and highlights the difficulties of efficiently regulating FMIs that operate on a cross-border basis. This chapter argues that the two main objectives of international FMI regulation should be market stability and market efficiency. Market stability includes monitoring and mitigating systemic risk and providing protection to market participants who use FMIs. To achieve market efficiency, there must be a regulatory structure that functions seamlessly across-borders, promotes innovation and does not create unnecessary costs. In the wake of the financial crisis, the focus on market stability has largely displaced efficiency concerns. However, in this chapter, the author argues that in order to facilitate the cross-border nature of OTC derivatives activity, the need for efficiency presents the more pressing regulatory challenges.

OVER-THE COUNTER DERIVATIVES MARKET REFORM: RATIONALE, ACHIEVEMENTS, AND REGULATORY IMPLICATIONS

Benefits and Challenges of International FMIs

Prior to the financial crisis, the OTC derivatives market was essentially unregulated in most jurisdictions, which created a major gap in international financial regulation and an opaque market fraught with risk. The regulatory goals of increasing transparency and mitigating systemic risk in the OTC derivatives market, in response to the lack of oversight revealed by the 2008 financial crisis, are uncontroversial. FMIs such as TRs and CCPs can play an important role in achieving these goals. However, the growing importance of these FMIs also introduces important new risks by centralizing credit risk and trade information.

A well-designed CCP can reduce the counterparty risk of its clearing members and has the potential to mitigate systemic risk in the OTC market through the multilateral netting and novation of trades, the imposition of risk controls, and the mutualisation of default risk. In particular, OTC derivatives CCPs require participants to post collateral to cover participant exposures. This collateral protects the CCP and its participants from the failure of a participant. Further, CCPs serve to mutualize risk through mechanisms such as default funds, which represent the collective resources of the CCP members.

TRs, in their current form, are largely regulatory creations that seek to address the lack of transparency in the OTC derivatives market. They are centralized facilities where OTC derivative transaction data is collected and stored electronically. Trade repositories provide essential information to regulators and will also provide the public with a new measure of transparency.

From a market efficiency and regulatory standpoint, there are advantages to FMIs operating internationally. For CCPs, international participation diversifies risks by including geographically diverse participants, which can help to insulate a CCP from a crisis affecting clearing members from a particular jurisdiction or region. Further, to the extent that an international crisis occurs, systemically important CCPs may have mechanisms in place to receive assistance on an internationally coordinated basis (for example, see the LCH.Clearnet Limited (a multi-national clearing house) college of regulators), thus mitigating the risk of a disorderly wind down of the nature experience by certain systemically important institutions during the financial crisis. For TRs, data collection on a multinational basis can reduce fragmentation and duplicative reporting, given that cross-border transactions are the norm in the OTC derivatives market. Operating on an international basis has the potential to provide regulators with a comprehensive global view of risk exposure.

Characteristics of OTC Derivative FMIs

FMIs such as securities or futures exchanges offering products or services to foreign markets are not a new phenomenon. Such entities are typically primarily regulated in their home jurisdiction and may operate on a partially or fully exempt basis in foreign jurisdictions. Although these FMIs operate internationally, they tend to have a domestic focus with a high percentage of domestic participants. A key difference between OTC derivatives FMIs and ones servicing traditional markets is that the OTC derivatives market is fundamentally borderless. Because counterparties to OTC derivative transactions are so frequently located in different jurisdictions, FMIs servicing this market need to have the ability to operate on a cross border basis to attract sufficient liquidity to their marketplaces. Consistent with the international nature of the OTC derivatives market, global TRs and CCPs thus provide services to geographically diverse market participants and, in many cases, have become critical infrastructures in multiple jurisdictions. OTC CCPs present greater systemic risk to the global economy than other CCPs or other infrastructures because of their role in concentrating counterparty risk and the large aggregate notional amounts of transactions cleared. There is also a much longer period of potential exposure that OTC CCPs must manage. For example, securities typically settle three days after they are traded exposing a securities based CCP to a small window of potential risk exposure. In contrast, OTC CCPs experience much longer periods where they guarantee payments to clearing members, which can leave them exposed to larger obligations. The failure of an OTC CCP or one or more significant clearing members could have far-reaching international consequences, potentially damaging the economies of multiple nations. In particular, the failure of an OTC CCP could disrupt the operation of critical derivatives markets, leaving major market participants without access to financial services that are essential to their operation.

As experienced during the financial crisis, this can cause funding markets to become illiquid which can have a significant impact on the broader economy. The internationally coordinated effort to increase the use of OTC CCPs has also lead to a situation where these FMIs hold extremely large amounts of market participants' collateral. Rapid liquidation of such collateral in the event of an OTC CCP failure could distort global asset prices, creating widespread market turmoil. The risks posed by OTC CCPs thus make it crucial that these infrastructures are properly regulated and economically resilient.

Although OTC TRs do not pose the same level of direct economic risk as CCPs, they maintain data which is critical to regulatory oversight in multiple jurisdictions and provide important transparency to market participants. An abrupt cessation of operations by an OTC TR would impair a crucial source of information for regulators and force users of that TR to find replacement service providers – an extremely costly and resource-intensive endeavour. The failure of either of these infrastructures would have a severely disruptive effect on the global derivatives market and regulators ability to oversee this market. These characteristics have led regulators to apply heightened regulatory standards to both domestic and foreign OTC derivative FMIs.

Regulatory Considerations

There are a variety of important considerations and fundamental trade-offs that must be analysed in determining a jurisdiction's approach to regulating international FMIs. While it is clear that systemically important FMIs should be subject to robust and effective regulation in order to ensure market stability, heightened regulation can come at the expense of efficiency and these goals must be balanced in order to achieve a stable and liquid market. From an international perspective the need to balance regulatory sovereignty versus the need for international cooperation and deference is a crucial consideration. Cooperation can take the form of agreed upon deference to a FMIs home country regulatory regime or through the adoption of principles or recommendations of international working groups dealing with FMI regulation. In both cases cooperation reduces the likelihood of FMIs being subject to duplicative or conflicting regulations. There is a great emphasis on achieving international harmonization in regulating international FMIs and as discussed throughout this chapter there are a range of international groups working towards this end. However, there can also be benefits to diverse regulatory approaches and requirements that are tailored to the specific needs of local markets and regulatory environments. These important considerations will be discussed through the examination of the domestic and international rules applicable to FMIs that follows in this chapter.

While the benefits to international operation are clear, the evolving multi-jurisdictional reliance on systemically important FMIs challenges the traditional construct of financial market regulation. Depending on the geographic scope of their operations, the laws of multiple jurisdictions will impact both TR and CCP operations. For international FMIs to effectively and efficiently operate in multiple jurisdictions and fulfill their roles as envisioned by the G-20, it is essential that consistent legal and regulatory outcomes be achieved in the global market, notwithstanding the application of more than one jurisdiction's laws. From the regulatory perspective, a key question, which will be the focus of this chapter, is how these infrastructures should be regulated to ensure that the stability and efficiency goals are met.

This chapter describes the challenges associated with regulating international infrastructures through domestic law and examines the achievements in regulatory harmonization and cooperation that have helped to mitigate these challenges. Indeed, in the wake of the international financial crisis, a great deal of progress has been made in the area of international coordination in regulating FMIs. However, in order to efficiently regulate FMIs at the international level, individual nations will need to become more flexible in their adoption of and adherence to international norms and processes of coordination.

Regulation of International FMIs

FMIs operating on an international basis are subject to a myriad of regulation and standards at the domestic and international levels. Regulation of FMIs involves a complicated network of international principles, domestic laws and bilateral and multilateral agreements between jurisdictions. Navigating this complex and interconnected regulatory landscape in an efficient manner is a daunting task for international FMIs. Although standard setting at the international level has made significant advancements, the rules and regulations applicable to international FMIs are fundamentally domestic or regional. Without harmonized regulations, it is inefficient, and in the case of conflicting laws and regulations, impossible to comply with multiple laws and regulations. Industry groups have consistently stressed the need for greater international harmonization, highlighting the impediments to OTC markets caused by the lack of coordination between jurisdictional rulemaking. This section will discuss the implications of the regulatory environment in which international FMIs operate.

Domestic Regulation

Fundamentally, international FMIs are regulated at a domestic or regional level. There is no supra-national entity with legal authority to impose regulations across global jurisdictions. Domestically, FMIs are regulated through, and overseen in accordance with a variety of laws, regulations, policies, guidelines and approval processes. Moral suasion, the use of influence and pressure to influence the behaviour of an FMI or its participants, can also play an important role in guiding an FMI's operations. However, the effectiveness of the domestic regulatory model is significantly challenged by the rapid globalization and borderless operation of the markets. Particularly in the case of derivatives FMIs, like CCPs or TRs offering important services to multiple jurisdictions, a coordinated set of rules would greatly enhance efficiency. This is not to say that all international FMIs need be structured in a similar manner, but rather that the shared international regulatory objectives of protecting market participants and promoting financial stability should be sufficiently coordinated, such that an FMI can operate seamlessly from a regulatory perspective. This efficiency does not need to come at the expense of regulatory objectives and would reduce regulatory arbitrage opportunities. However, achieving a level of consensus whereby jurisdictions are willing or able to delegate their regulatory obligations to a joint rulemaking authority does not appear realistic in the near term.

The terms home and host regulator or country are used throughout this chapter and refer to, respectively, the country where an entity is formed or located and a country in whose markets a foreign entity operates in. An FMI's home jurisdiction generally plays the lead role in determining the rules and requirements applicable to an FMI located within its borders. However, in many cases, in order for an internationally active FMI to gain access to a foreign market, it must submit to the jurisdiction and rules of host jurisdictions. This overlapping jurisdiction can impede the effectiveness of an FMI when the rules applicable to it are not harmonized. In recognition of the limitations of domestic regulation and importance of harmonization of laws across jurisdictions, greater emphasis has been placed on the development of international agreements to implement harmonized regulations domestically. This section discusses the application of domestic laws to international FMIs, from the perspectives of both home and host regulators.

The G20 commitments to mandate trade reporting and central clearing are generally being implemented through domestic or regional legislation (for example, see the Commodity Exchange Act (U.S.) section 2 and the European Markets Infrastructure Regulation Article 4). Former U.S. Commodity Futures Trading Commission (CFTC) Chairman Gary Gensler, one of the driving forces behind the global derivatives reform effort, has stated that, "Effective reform cannot be accomplished by one nation alone. It will require a comprehensive, international response. The response to the global financial crisis lies in efforts by governments to bring about a harmonious global regime of financial regulations" ([CFTC], 2011, March 22). Achieving a harmonious global regime requires willingness for home and host country jurisdictions to compromise and defer to international standards.

Nonetheless, there is a near uniform aversion to sacrificing national lawmaking sovereignty to the implementation of binding international rules. This stems in large part from regulators' desire and, in some cases, legal obligation to maintain authority over their domestic economy. It also relates to the strong preference of regulators to operate with their own domestic standards rather than incur the costs of adopting another standard (Brummer, 2010, p. 330). However, these desires no longer reflect the realities of financial markets. In lieu of the development of binding international rules, a variety of approaches involving deference to home country regulations have evolved.

Impediments to Reliance

Before examining the methods by which jurisdictions open their markets to foreign infrastructures, it is important to understand the reluctance of jurisdictions to allow foreign FMIs unfettered access to domestic markets. A first issue is that there is a concern that exclusively relying on a foreign regime may increase the risk of domestic market failure because the host country regulator may not be in a position to detect risks and must trust that the home country regulator will succeed in preventing any failures (Tafara & Peterson, 2007, p. 49). Reliance risks are complicated by uncertainty with respect to how a foreign regulator would behave in a crisis situation involving a systemically important FMI. Would that regulator focus equal attention on all interested jurisdictions or prioritize its domestic market to which it is primarily accountable? Home country regulators can also implement requirements, which are not appropriate for the host country market. For example, any limits on the acceptability of foreign collateral such as sovereign debt can disadvantage a host country and its market participants. It is unrealistic to expect a home country regulator to take into account the specific needs of all participating jurisdictions in the same way it does for its domestic market.

The second major issue is economic competitiveness. The higher the regulatory standards are set, the greater likelihood that market activity will gravitate to more lightly regulated jurisdictions. This creates a situation whereby creating a robust regime could put domestic infrastructure at a competitive disadvantage if foreign infrastructures with lower standards are able to operate in the jurisdiction. Regulatory arbitrage opportunities occur when a jurisdiction defects from an efficient regulatory strategy and adopts a riskier regulatory approach. (Griffith, 2014, p. 1326). Particularly with respect to systemically important FMIs, any prospect of jurisdictions competing for business through reduced regulatory standards would be a recipe for systemic failure and is an important consideration to determining market access.

In some cases, jurisdictions have focused their efforts on having their domestic approaches to derivatives regulations exported through foreign adoption of harmonized rules. At a more extreme level, jurisdictions may seek to impose their authority outside of their borders through the extraterritorial approach to regulation. In this regard, section 722(d) of the U.S. Dodd-Frank Wall Street Reform and Consumer

Protection Act (2010) requires the regulation of foreign entities that "have a direct and significant connection with activities in, or effect on, commerce in the United States." Clearly then, any foreign FMI offering services in the U.S. would meet this test. If all jurisdictions in which an FMI operated adopted this approach, the cross border model of operation would face significant efficiency challenges.

The main approaches to facilitate the operation of international FMIs, which will be discussed in the following sections, are comparability determinations, bilateral or multilateral agreements and collectively developed international standards.

Deference to Home Country Rules

The G-20 Finance Ministers and Central Bank Governors have affirmed that "jurisdictions and regulators should be able to defer to each other when it is justified by the quality of their respective regulatory and enforcement regimes, based on similar outcomes, in a non-discriminatory way, paying due respect to home country regulatory regimes." (2014). Moving from the domestic approach to regulation to a more internationalized system will require jurisdictions to overcome discomfort with deferring to foreign regulators.

The practice of treating foreign market participants subject to regulations in their home country jurisdiction differently from local participants is not new. Most jurisdictions are likely to have the flexibility to exempt market participants from regulatory requirements and, in the case of cross border FMIs, exemptions based on home country regulations are common. The practice of exempting requirements is evolving into more formalized conceptual systems of deference. New approaches to cross-border regulation including the concepts of substituted compliance and equivalency may offer opportunities to streamline regulation. This section discusses these approaches.

Substituted Compliance

Domestic regulatory structures are evolving to facilitate cross-border operation of FMIs. Recognizing the impediments to efficient operation presented by applying different sets of rules to a single FMI, host countries have incorporated varying levels of deference to home country regulation of FMIs.

The U.S. concept of substituted compliance represents a hybrid approach to regulation of foreign infrastructure permitting an FMI to adhere to home country regulations exclusively in certain situations. Tafara and Peterson, authors of *A Blueprint for Cross-Border Access to U.S. Investors: A New International Framework* (2007), recommend an approach that balances the protection of domestic market participants while ensuring that access to foreign infrastructure is available. As the name suggests, this approach allows a non-U.S. entity to substitute compliance with the requirements of its home country regulations in lieu of compliance with U.S. rules. Although substituted compliance requires an FMI to register with the relevant U.S. authority, the burden of registration on foreign entities is reduced, as the oversight of the foreign entity would remain the primary responsibility of its home regulator. (Tafara & Peterson, 2007, p. 57). An FMI may also be granted an exemption from formal registration; for example, a CCP may be exempt from registration if the Securities Exchange Commission (SEC) "determines that the derivatives clearing organization is subject to comparable, comprehensive supervision and regulation by the Securities and Exchange Commission or the appropriate government authorities in the home country of the organization." (7 U.S.C. 7a-1(h)). The burden of compliance is thereby significantly reduced.

In order for substituted compliance to be available, a number of preconditions must be satisfied. The primary requirement, as explained in Commodity Futures Trading Commission's (CFTC) policy—*Interpretive Guidance and Policy Statement Regarding Compliance with Certain Swap Regulations* (2013)—is that a home jurisdiction's relevant rules and requirements must be comparable to those of the CFTC. Comparability analysis involves assessments of the comprehensiveness of the foreign jurisdictions rules and requirement(s), the scope and objectives of the relevant regulatory requirement(s), the comprehensiveness of the foreign regulator's supervisory compliance program, as well as the home jurisdiction's authority to support and enforce its oversight of the registrant (Interpretive Guidance and Policy Statement Regarding Compliance with Certain Swap Regulations, 2013). Comparability allows the host country regulator to ensure that it is adhering to its regulatory mandate and that opportunities for regulatory arbitrage or reduction in transparency are reduced. (Tafara & Peterson, 2007, p. 60).

Both the SEC and CFTC subscribe to this approach, and have indicated that home country rules need not be identical. A comparability analysis is intended, on an outcomes based approach, to determine whether the home jurisdiction's regulatory requirement is comparable to and as comprehensive as the corresponding U.S. regulatory requirement(s). Certain commentators have pointed out that interpretations of substituted compliance differ: Griffith maintains that the structure of the rules between the CFTC and the SEC are identical, yet the approach of the CFTC differs from that of the SEC in that the SEC's approach is "more principles-based and less focused on rule-by-rule comparability," which means that the SEC's more flexible middle-ground approach "contemplates that jurisdictions that are partially, but not fully comparable might receive a substituted compliance determination for specific requirements rather than on a regime-wide basis" (2014, pp. 1337-1338). In adopting Exchange Act rule 0-13, the SEC explained that it would ultimately focus on regulatory outcomes rather than a rule-by-rule comparison and that substituted compliance determinations may be made even with differences between regulatory regimes when the differences accomplish "comparable regulatory outcomes" ([SEC], 2014).

As a precondition to a substituted compliance determination, both the SEC and CFTC require that a Memorandum of Understanding (MOU) or similar arrangement be in place with the relevant foreign regulator. Such an MOU would need to include a high degree of "prudential and enforcement information-sharing" (Tafara & Peterson, 2007, p. 56). With respect to CCPs, the CFTC would also require that the CCP be assessed to be in compliance with the Committee on Payment and Settlement Systems (CPSS) and International Organization of Securities Commission (IOSCO) *Principles for financial market infrastructures* (2012) (PFMIs). The CFTC believes that the use of the PFMIs, an international standard, is substantially similar to the requirements for registered CCPs under the CFTC's regulations.

Substituted compliance represents a balance between reducing duplicative regulations on FMIs creating a more efficient system of regulation while ensuring that the host country is satisfied that its regulatory mandate is being met. However, substituted compliance is most efficient where rules are harmonized, either through international standards or where a jurisdiction has made a decision to converge with U.S. requirements. Where regulatory regimes differ it can be extremely challenging to evaluate whether a rule framework is comparable. Much depends on the prerogative of the regulator responsible for the comparability analysis. Where comparability is not found the full extent of the rule is applied.

Equivalency

The concept of equivalency, championed primarily by the European Union, provides a different framework to facilitate the operation of foreign FMIs in the EU. While substituted compliance requires a granular assessment of rules and only provides exemptive relief for those rules that achieve an equivalent outcome, a positive equivalency assessment regarding a home country's legal framework as it pertains to FMIs allows FMIs from that jurisdiction to provide services to market participants established in the EU without adhering to EU law. In contrast to the substituted compliance approach, where an equivalency determination has been made, the EU will rely fully on a home country's rules and enforcement regime and will not require an FMI to register in the EU (European Securities and Markets Authority [ESMA], 2013). Where an equivalency determination is not reached, the FMI would be required to fully comply with EU law.

In order to determine foreign regime equivalence pursuant to the authority that the *European Markets Infrastructure Regulation* (EMIR) delegated to the European Commission (EC), the EC sought the technical advice of the European Securities and Markets Authority (ESMA) regarding the equivalence of the legal and supervisory frameworks of third countries (as a reference point, refer to p. 31 of ESMA's 2013 *Final report – Technical advice on third country equivalence under EMIR – US*). The analysis involves reviewing a third country's legal and supervisory arrangements with respect to TRs, CCPs and the countries clearing and reporting requirements for market participants, as well as, the legal, supervisory, and enforcement arrangements of a third country with respect to clearing and reporting requirements (ESMA, 2013, p. 31).

A positive equivalency determination thus results in the EC deferring to the legal and supervisory arrangements of a home country regime, thereby avoiding any overlapping or conflicting rules. This approach delegates traditional domestic or regional responsibilities and therefore requires a thorough upfront analysis of a home country regime.

Following the determination of equivalence, ESMA may recognise a CCP or TR established in a third country. In order to do so, ESMA (2013) requires that the following conditions be satisfied, in addition to a determination of equivalence:

- The third country CCPs and TRs "are subject to effective on-going supervision and enforcement" by thc third country,
- There are cooperation agreements in place with the competent authorities of the third country,
- With respect to CCPs, the third country legal framework offers an equivalent CCP recognition system, and
- With respect to TRs, there are guarantees of professional secrecy in the third country's framework that are at minimum equivalent to those required under EMIR.

Although determinations of equivalence concern the legal, supervisory and enforcement arrangements of a third country, they contemplate approval for each rulemaking area as a whole. Therefore, the level of equivalency required for a positive determination is key. If a foreign regime's rules are required to be substantively identical, then a foreign regime would have to harmonize its rules with EMIR or its resident FMIs would be subject to the full weight of EU law. However, ESMA (2013) has indicated that it will adopt a holistic outcome-based approach to assessment, focusing on a factual assessment but also assessing the consequences of an equivalence determination on the stability and protection of entities and investors in Europe. The EU approach is progressive in its reliance on home country law and oversight, reflecting the EU's multi-national makeup and greater comfort amongst its participants to deferring domestic authority.

Reconciling Domestic Approaches to International FMI Regulation

Both substituted compliance and equivalency provide a means of improving market efficiency through deference to home country regulation. However, in both cases, an overly strict interpretation could result in full extraterritorial application of domestic law. Deference to foreign regulation is contingent on the level of confidence not only in that regime's rules and oversight structure, but also based on whether equivalent protections are provided to domestic and foreign participants under the home country regime.

However, it is unclear whether home country regulatory regimes are fully equipped to monitor FMI activities in host country jurisdictions. Further, domestic laws, particularly those relating to bankruptcy and insolvency, can lead to unpredictable outcomes even where a regime's rules appear consistent. Finally, in real-time crisis situations, jurisdictions without direct oversight may lack the requisite information and input to support domestic interests.

In an effort to reconcile domestic approaches to OTC derivatives regulation, jurisdictions have been working on a bilateral and multilateral basis to address gaps, conflicts and inconsistencies. On July 11, 2013, the CFTC and EU published "A Path Forward", a document confirming the commitment of the jurisdictions with the two largest derivatives markets to coordinating regulation. The press release explained that CFTC and EMIR rules for CCPs are both based on international minimum standards and therefore there is a degree of harmonization for CCPs that operate in both the U.S. and EU. The jurisdictions further committed to "work together to reduce any prudential concerns or regulatory arbitrage opportunities and to reflect this in [their] respective decisions on registration and equivalence" (CFTC, 2013).

Ongoing Harmonization Challenges

Despite commitments to coordinate regulatory approaches, a continued lack of harmonization creates difficulties for the regulation and operation of CCPs and TRs that operate internationally. The Financial Stability Board (FSB) *OTC Derivatives Market Reforms Eight Progress Report on Implementation* (2014) highlights a number of instances where regulatory dis-harmonization is a contributing factor to delays in the progress of international OTC derivatives market reform. In particular, the report cites the unavailability of TRs and CCPs in certain jurisdictions as an impediment to implementing some of the G-20 commitments such as mandatory trade reporting and central clearing. In this regard, although the G-20 nations committed to mandating central clearing by the end of 2012, as of November 2014, only five jurisdictions reported having any central clearing requirements in effect ([FSB] 2014, p.3). Regulatory challenges relating to the authorization of internationally active FMIs in multiple jurisdictions are one of the causes of these delays. Generally, the regulatory burdens of complying with laws and requirements from multiple jurisdictions has led FMIs to focus their efforts on complying with the requirements of the largest trading markets. This has, in certain cases, left smaller markets without access to locally authorized infrastructure.

TR access issues have arisen with respect to foreign jurisdictions relying on international TRs, including the Dodd-Frank Act requirement that regulators indemnify TRs from whom they receive data. This has impeded certain regulators and central banks from accessing information necessary to fulfil their mandate and forced TRs to complicate their operating structures to accommodate participants from multiple jurisdictions. Further, the lack of international harmonization for data required by various jurisdictions to be reported has created operational difficulties for market participants, including TRs and their users, as well as significant data aggregation issues for regulators.

With respect to CCPs, there are significant differences between the initial margin requirements that the U.S. and EU require of CCPs. The holding period used by the CFTC to calculate initial margin for exchange-traded derivatives is one day, whereas EMIR standardizes a two-day holding period. Because the holding period is an assumption of the CCP's ability to liquidate the portfolio of a defaulting member, longer holding periods have been attributed to higher initial margin demands and therefore create an opportunity for regulatory arbitrage (Carr, 2013).

CFTC requirements that currently preclude foreign CCPs from offering services to U.S. customers that are not clearing members has threatened FMI market access in both the U.S. and EU. Although a non-U.S. CCP may qualify as an exempt CCP and allowed to take on U.S. clearing members, member firms are not allowed to take on U.S. customers. In retaliation, the EC has not recognized U.S.CCP rules as equivalent in its first proposed round of approvals for foreign CCPs. This rise in the spectre of U.S. CCPs not being deemed equivalent under EMIR, which requires a third country to have an effective equivalent system for recognition of CCPs authorized under foreign regimes, would result in significant market fragmentation (Becker, 2014; Becker & Madigan, 2014).

There are many similar examples of issues of regulatory conflict and though resolvable, they highlight the difficulties of coordinating domestic regimes on an ad hoc basis. As the global reform effort proceeds and more jurisdictions implement FMI regulations coordination will be increasingly complicated. Furthermore, derivatives regulation is in its early stages and regulatory approaches will need to be modified over time a process that will be extremely challenging given the current system of ad hoc comparability determinations. Without an internationally coordinated system for determining acceptable FMI legal regimes one can expect a continuous cycle of cross border issues to arise.

Bilateral/Multilateral Agreements

The traditional approach to coordinating regulation of cross-border entities has been through bilateral or multilateral agreements amongst regulators. However, given the large number of jurisdictions affected by systemically important FMIs and the limited scope of typical MOUs, these agreements may not be sufficient to coordinate regulation in internationalized markets.

Memorandums of understanding

Memoranda of understanding (MOUs) are the traditional means through which jurisdictions coordinate oversight and enforcement of financial market activity internationally. These bilateral or multilateral agreements generally focus on exchanges of information regarding internationally active entities or infrastructure. The *International Organization of Securities Commissions Multilateral Memorandum of Understanding Concerning Consultation and Cooperation and the Exchange of Information* was established in 2002 and represents an international benchmark for cross-border co-operation of market regulators (for more information, see http://www.iosco.org/library/index.cfm?section=mou_main). Recently, the process of updating the network of international MOUs with application to FMIs to reflect the evolution of financial markets and particularly the derivatives markets has begun; examples of recently updated MOUs include that of Canadian market regulators and the CFTC—*Memorandum of Understanding Concerning Cooperation and the Exchange of Information Related to the Supervision of Cross-Border Covered Entities* signed on March 25, 2014—and Japan and the CFTC—*Memorandum of Cooperation Related to the Supervision of Cross-Border Covered Entities* signed on March 10, 2014. Although these

MOUs are very useful to facilitate exchanges of information, they generally are not viewed as legally binding agreements and may not fully harmonize the regulation of FMIs that operate on a cross-border basis. For example, the MOU between the CFTC and the Financial Services Agency of Japan (2014), which applies to TRs or CCPs that operate in the U.S. and Japan, explicitly states that it "is not intended to limit or condition the discretion of an Authority in any way to discharge its regulatory responsibilities."

However, as MOUs are an established network between regulators, their traditional scope could be expanded to address overlapping regulation. Although it would require a significant divergence from current regulatory approach, MOUs have the potential to coordinate the regulation of internationally active FMIs. Within the current construct of cross-border regulatory arrangements, an expansion of bilateral and multilateral MOU's could improve efficiency and oversight without requiring jurisdictions to fundamentally alter domestic regulation.

MOUs could include common rules and protocols for the coordinated regulation of FMIs. For example, jurisdictions could include in their MOUs regulatory protocols with regards to the jurisdiction primarily responsible for regulating a cross-border FMI. This could significantly reduce burdens on FMIs by reducing duplicative regulation while increasing regulatory cohesion. MOUs are not legally binding documents and therefore improved efficiency would not come at the expense of regulatory sovereignty.

Colleges of regulators

Another method of international coordination applied to FMIs is known as a "college of regulators". Systemically important FMIs are sometimes overseen by a collection of regulators that coordinate oversight. An example of this is LCH.Clearnet Limited (LCH), an FMI that is overseen by a group of regulators led by the Bank of England. LCH is a major international CCP that clears a variety of exchange-traded and OTC products. LCH's college of regulators actively evaluates credit risk management models and monitors LCH's liquidity risk.

The CLS Group (CLS) serves as another example of a systemically important institution cooperatively overseen by a college of regulators. CLS operates a multicurrency cash settlement system to mitigate settlement risk in foreign exchange transactions. The college of regulators of CLS was created to monitor systemic risk arising from foreign exchange transactions. It maintains dialogue with regulators, government and industry groups in impacting the evolution of the foreign exchange industry. CLS regulated by the Federal Reserve and it participates in a cooperative oversight arrangement with 22 central banks from around the globe.

Prudential Regulators

Prudential regulators have long dealt with cross border institutions and have developed a set of home-host principles for internationally active financial institutions. The principles contained in the 1983 Basel Concordat of the Basel Committee on Banking Supervision (BCBS) allow for deference to home country regulations. The 1983 Basel Concordat, replacing that of 1975, is a guideline for best practices that "deals exclusively with the responsibilities of banking supervisory authorities for monitoring the prudential conduct and soundness of the business of banks' foreign establishments." (Basel Committee on Banking Supervision [BCBS], 1983, p. 1). The principles set out in the Basel Concordat are based on the presumption that the home supervisor is responsible for overseeing the activities and consolidated position of the bank incorporated under its jurisdiction.

The principles have been supplemented with formal mechanisms, such as supervisory colleges that facilitate cooperation between prudential supervisors from key jurisdictions of each banking group. In October 2010, the *Good practice principles on supervisory colleges* was published. The practices took into account the perspective of home supervisors, host supervisors and internationally active banks. The BCBS (2010) is clear that while the principles aim to encourage the effective operation of colleges, they should not be seen as a substitute for domestic regulation:

Colleges should not be seen as a substitute for effective national supervision nor undermine the legal and prudential responsibilities of respective supervisors. Colleges are not intended to be decision-making bodies but should provide a framework to enhance effective supervision of international banking groups on a consolidated and solo basis, and could inform decision-making in that regard. (p. 1)

Alongside with the good practices, the BCBS published its *Core Principles for Effective Banking Supervision* in September 2012, providing *de facto* minimum standards for sound prudential regulation and supervision. Principle 13 is of particular interest as it points out, "Supervisors require the local operations of foreign banks to be conducted to the same standards as those required of domestic banks." (BCBS, 2012, p. 37).

Limitations

Bilateral and multilateral agreements like MOU's and arrangements like regulatory colleges provide a flexible means of coordinated regulation for internationally active FMIs. However, they do not offer a comprehensive solution for FMIs due to the multiple jurisdictions and regulator types, many of which are not party to such arrangements. In response to the limitations of the domestic and bilateral/multilateral approaches international standards setters have undertaken significant regulatory efforts that will be discussed in the following section.

International Standard Setters

International standards are an essential means to achieving coordinated and harmonized rules for FMIs. International standard setting for derivatives market infrastructure is a crowded space. As a new frontier of regulation that encompasses market regulation, systemic oversight and banking regulation, there is no shortage of regulatory bodies and working groups contributing to the regulatory reform effort. Traditionally, international regulatory initiatives are derived from high level agreements that are translated into principles often referred to as "soft law", which are then implemented on an outcome-based approach through domestic laws. Principles are typically highly negotiated and drafted to ensure that they are compatible with the wide array of legal frameworks and market nuances of the participating jurisdictions. While international standards carry varying levels of persuasive weight, they generally do not have the force of law in any jurisdictions. As a result, the central criticism of international standards is that their impact on jurisdictional practice is limited. However, when such standards are widely adopted or adhered to they are an excellent tool for increasing cross border regulatory harmonization. This section examines the sources of international standards applicable to FMIs, how they are created and how they are applied.

OTC Derivatives Regulators Group

The OTC Derivatives Regulators Group (ODRG) is an international organization composed of leaders from regulatory authorities with responsibility for regulation of the largest OTC derivatives markets around the globe. It has targeted gaps in requirements or duplicative requirements as an area of concern. The ODRG (2014) has reached agreements and continues to coordinate on the application of substituted compliance and equivalence determinations on branches and affiliates, using an outcomes-based approach, to address cross-border implementation issues (for an example of a report, refer to *Report of the OTC Derivatives Regulators Group (ODRG) on Cross-Border Implementation Issues* available at http://www.esma.europa.eu/system/files/2014-03-odrg_odrg_report_to_the_g20_march_2014.pdf).

Whereas the international standards are typically high level and principles-based, the ODRG seeks to address specific problems of coordination that arise in connection with the implementation of derivatives reform. The ODRG has opted for member discussions, on a multilateral basis, aimed to allow access to and sharing of TR data in their respective jurisdictions. Additionally, the ODRG has considered the application of a stricter-rule approach to clearing obligations for transactions involving dually regulated branches and subsidiaries (ODRG, 2014).

Attempting to address issues as they arise at the international level on an ad hoc basis is not and will not be the most efficient means of coordinating regulation, but the ODRG provides an important venue to address cross-border issues. Some of the limitations of the ODRG are that there is no mandatory review mechanism and only those issues on which consensus can be reached are dealt with. Similar to other international groups, there is no force behind the decisions reached and it is challenging to achieve timely resolution of issues.

The FSB and its Four Safeguards

The G-20's edict for reform of the OTC derivatives market set in motion an unprecedented global reform effort that has been largely coordinated by the FSB. The FSB is comprised of national financial authorities and also standard setting bodies including the Bank for International Settlements (BIS) and its Committee, the CPSS (as of September 2014, renamed the Committee on Payment and Market Infrastructures (CPMI), as well as IOSCO, which are discussed separately later in this section. The FSB has been tasked by the G-20 leaders with the job of overseeing and monitoring implementation of financial reform and plays an oversight role pronouncing direction and timing for OTC derivatives reform. With respect to OTC derivatives, the FSB publishes progress reports outlining the status of implementation of related G-20 commitments. The FSB has no authority to sanction jurisdictions for non-compliance, but rather relies on the reputational consequences of public dissemination of non-compliance.

In addition to monitoring and publically disseminating derivatives reform progress, the FSB contributes, in certain circumstances, to international standard setting. For example, the FSB has identified and established four safeguards to facilitate a safe environment for the operation of globally active derivatives CCPs. These are:

(i) fair and open access by market participants to CCPs, based on transparent and objective criteria; (ii) cooperative oversight arrangements between all relevant authorities, both domestically and internationally, that result in robust and consistently applied regulation and oversight of global CCPs; (iii) resolution and recovery regimes that ensure the core functions of CCPs are maintained during times of

crisis and that consider the interests of all jurisdictions where the CCP is systemically important; and (iv) appropriate liquidity arrangements for CCPs in the currencies in which they clear. ([FSB], 2012, p. 19)

The four safeguards are focused on the international coordination essential to stable markets for clearing. The Bank of Canada purports that they "protect the stability of local markets and, in particular, address concerns that may arise when locally important markets are cleared through offshore CCPs" (Chande, Dion, McVanel, & Slive, 2012, pg. 43). The FSB's four safeguards do not have the force of law in any jurisdiction but the FSB participants promote their implementation through moral suasion and by conditioning FMI market access to their adoption.

CPMI AND IOSCO

With respect to FMIs, the major standard setters are CPMI (previously CPSS) and IOSCO. The CPMI, which reports to the G-10 central bank Governors, was established as a permanent forum for central banks to monitor and analyze developments in domestic payment, clearing and settlement systems, as well as, in cross-border and multicurrency settlement schemes. By 2009, CPMI (then CPSS) included 25 central bank members. It now focuses on "efficiency and stability of payment, clearing, settlement and related arrangements, and pays attention to issues related to these systems or arrangements and to their relation with the major financial markets that are relevant for the conduct of monetary policy" ("CPSS: History, organisation, cooperation", n.d.).

IOSCO is an organization that "develops, implements, and promotes adherence to internationally recognized standards for securities regulation, and is working intensively with the G-20 and the FSB on the global regulatory reform agenda" (International Organization of Securities Commission [IOSCO]). Its members, composed of 120 market regulators and 80 securities market participants, regulate over 95% of the global securities market. Its objectives revolve around cooperation in setting and adhering to international standards, enhancing investor protection and promoting investor confidence in the integrity of securities and derivatives markets and facilitating access to information to strengthen market infrastructure.

OTC Derivatives Regulators' Forum

The OTC Derivatives Regulators' Forum (ODRF) was formed "to provide regulators with a means to cooperate, exchange views and share information related to OTC derivatives CCPs and trade repositories" (OTC Derivatives Regulators' Forum [ODRF]). Its functional objectives include: providing mutual assistance for regulators to carry out their respective mandates; promoting the development, adoption, and implementation of consistent policies and standards; and coordinating and encouraging effective information sharing and communication. The ODRF is comprised of international financial regulators including governmental and non-governmental regulatory authorities, central banks and banking supervisors. Among nationally based representatives, international standard setters such as IOSCO and international organizations such as the European Union's banking authorities are also members. The ODRF, in an effort to meet its functional objectives, narrows its study focus through the use of subgroups and releases its conclusions (accessible to the public) in the form of plain language summaries.

Effectiveness of International Standards Setters

The traditional criticism of international standards setters is that they lack the power necessary to be effective. David Wright, former secretary general of IOSCO has publically commented on the organization's lack of power to compel members to abide by regulatory agreements; he has stated, "The reality is you do it if you like it and you probably don't if you don't like it. As the number of major interconnected capital markets grows, this problem will become more acute" (reported by Jones, 2013).

The most common tool to enforce the implementation of international standards is though assessments and issuing of progress reports regarding the implementation of internationally recognized standards. These assessments, in addition to the informational benefits they provide, are intended to encourage jurisdictions to implement agreements in a timely fashion lest they be exposed as laggards to their peers. However, while the reputational impact of these assessments carries a certain amount of weight, competing domestic political or economic interests can still prevail.

Nonetheless, some commentators argue that through the use of "international common law", powerful nations can unilaterally influence jurisdictions regulatory requirements through threats of action or inaction resulting in an increased cost of capital to other nations. Guzman and Meyer argue that "[a] lthough the cooperation-minded states give up some measure of control over the tribunal or [international organizations], they also create a body of soft legal rules that constrain, to some extent, the behavior of states not party to the creation of the tribunal or [international organization]" (2010, p. 178). By consenting to being bound by extraterritorial international institutions, powerful nations who are members of international organizations lose a level of control over standard setting but gain the advantage of an avenue to persuade standards on other non-members states (Guzman & Meyer, 2010, pp. 201-219). Although the only cost of deviation associated with soft law comes in the form of reputational damage, this damage can have serious implications for FMIs in non-compliant jurisdictions including loss of access to foreign markets.

Towards the more forceful side of the enforceability spectrum for international standards are principles whose implementation has economic implications to market participants of a jurisdiction. Examples, discussed below, include favourable capital treatment for CCPs in jurisdictions that have implemented the PFMI principles.

International Standards

Although there are a range of international standards with applicability to FMIs this section will discuss the main sources of standards.

CPSS-IOSCO Principles for financial market infrastructures

The Principles for financial market infrastructures (PFMIs) are a significant international achievement in coordination across jurisdictions and regulator types. The CPSS (now CPMI) and the Technical Committee of IOSCO have established these international risk-management standards to address the systemic risks associated with FMIs. In 2012, the PFMIs revised and replaced the three existing standards contained in the *Core principles for systemically important payment systems* (CPSS, 2001), the *Recommendations for securities settlement systems* (CPSS-IOSCO, 2001), and the *Recommendations for central counterparties* (CPSS-IOSCO, 2004) (the full report containing the 24 principles is available through the BIS and

IOSCO). The principles apply to FMIs that facilitate four main functions: payment, clearing, settling and recording of monetary and other financial transactions. While FMIs promote financial stability, they also concentrate risk by performing centralized activities that create interdependence between FMIs and other participating institutions. Because of this dual nature, if risk is not properly managed and regulated, FMIs can be a potential source of financial shock to the broader global economy.

The PFMIs, in an effort to ensure that global financial markets are better situated to withstand financial shock, strengthened and harmonized these standards by raising minimum requirements, providing more guidance, and broadening the scope of the standards. International implementation of the PFMIs has been successful to this point. CPMI-IOSCO continues to monitor the implementation of the PFMIs, and in their first level of assessment and its first update, assessed the steps taken by jurisdictions to adopt legislation and other policies that will enable them to implement the PFMIs. In CPMI-IOSCO's *Implementation monitoring of PFMIs: first update to the Level 1 report*, it is explained that, notwithstanding the large scale undertaking of implementing the PFMIs, jurisdictions have made significant progress toward implementation ([CPMI-IOSCO], 2014). Going forward, level 2 and 3 assessments will also examine whether each participating jurisdiction's reforms are complete and consistent with the PFMIs, and whether there is consistency in the outcomes of implementation of the principles by FMIs themselves.

The PFMIs generally do not prescribe specific arrangements to achieve their objectives, nor are they required to be implemented by regulatory authorities in a particular way; they allow for different means of implementing and satisfying the principles. Also, while the PFMIs set minimum requirements, authorities may impose higher standards for FMIs under their jurisdictional reach. All FMIs that are determined to be systemically important within each jurisdiction, a process that is jurisdiction specific, are expected by CPMI and IOSCO to comply with the PFMIs. To this end, CPMI-IOSCO is carrying out an assessment of member jurisdictions' implementation of the principles, and of each jurisdictions' FMIs adherence to the principles.

The PFMIs are necessarily high-level and principles-based because they are required to be implemented across a diverse set of regulatory regimes and FMI types. However, the PFMIs have had a meaningful impact on international FMIs and CCPs in particular. A distinguishing factor regarding the PFMIs is that, unlike many international principles or standards, the PFMIs are being integrated into the legal and regulatory regimes of participant jurisdictions. This allows the PFMIs to be enforceable in each such jurisdiction.

The principles contemplate flexibility and even include alternative approaches to compliance where a similar outcome is achieved. Importantly, the PFMIs include responsibilities for regulatory authorities intended to ensure that FMIs are appropriately and effectively regulated. For example, Responsibility E of the PFMIs calls on authorities to cooperate with each other, both domestically and internationally, to promote the safety and efficiency of FMIs.

Where international standards carry with them economic implications for market participants, their weight unsurprisingly increases significantly. Implementation of PFMI standards by jurisdictions carries significant economic implications for CCPs in that jurisdiction. The Basel Committee on Banking Supervision (BCBS), the global standard setter for prudential regulation of banks, has incorporated the PFMIs into its capital adequacy standards. In April 2014, the BCBS published its final policy framework for regulating capital requirements for bank exposures to CCPs. By implementing the standard, regulators will be in a better position to ensure that banks' exposures to CCPs, which consist of both trade and default fund related exposures, are adequately capitalized and appropriately measured, monitored and managed ([BIS], 2014).

The BCBS standard outlines that where a CCP is licensed and supervised by an appropriate regulator to operate as a CCP with respect to the products offered, and is subject to domestic rules and regulations that are consistent with the PFMIs, it is considered a qualified CCP (QCCP) (BIS, 2012). Exposures to the QCCPs are entitled to receive a preferential capital treatment from prudential regulators because they benefit from the multilateral netting and loss mutualisation mechanism provided by the QCCPs (BIS, 2012; BIS, 2010). This encourages the banks to deal with CCPs that are in compliance with the PFMIs. In April 2014, the BCBS, in collaboration the CPMI and IOSCO, developed and published the final standard for the capital treatment of bank exposures to CCPs (BIS, 2014).

In addition to the economic implications of preferable capital treatment, implementation of the PFMIs is a precondition to accessing key derivatives markets, in the U.S. and EU, where jurisdictional implementation of the PFMIs is a precondition for a substituted compliance or equivalency determination.

The success of the PFMIs demonstrates the importance of economic drivers to implement international standards. Market access and financial incentivization such as preferential capital treatment have provided a huge impetus to implementation. However, even in the case of the PFMIs, the high level nature of the principles which is generally necessary to garner broad support at the developmental stage has led to interpretive differences reducing the harmonization benefits of the principles.

CPSS-IOSCO Authorities' access to trade repository data

Trade repositories are an example of an international FMI where international coordination has not been particularly effective and provide an excellent case study for determining the characteristics of a successful international standard. Unlike CCPs, TRs are essentially a regulatory creation and play a central oversight role as opposed to an economic one. Coordinated oversight of TRs tests the willingness of jurisdictional compliance where economic incentives are not at play.

The CPSS-IOSCO report *Authorities' access to trade repository data* (2013) is an essential project to ensure that an international model for TRs can satisfy the needs of a wide range of international regulators. It is also an example of how the domestic laws of jurisdictions applied to internationally active FMI creates difficulties for the application of international agreements. Guided by PFMI principles (particularly, principle 24 related to disclosure of market data by TRs), the goal of the report is to promote broad access to TR data in accordance with a regulator's respective mandates or responsibilities. CPSS-IOSCO prescribes that relevant authorities should coordinate to ensure timely access to trade data recorded in a TR and states:

In general, it is not expected that a TR supervisor would seek to limit access levels beyond what is contemplated in this report, but such authority may seek to ensure that any policies and procedures of the TR are consistent with the applicable legal framework with due regard to confidentiality safeguards and mandates of requesting authorities. Specifically, the supervisor of a TR that maintains data pertaining to other jurisdictions should coordinate with other relevant authorities to ensure timely and effective access to trade data and establish an appropriate data access process that is fair and consistent with the responsibilities of the other relevant authorities, to the extent legally permissible. Consistent with the CPSS/IOSCO Responsibility E, all relevant authorities should mutually support each other's access to trade data in which they have a material interest in furtherance of their regulatory, supervisory, and oversight responsibilities, regardless of the particular organisational form or jurisdiction of a TR. (CPSS-IOSCO, 2013, p. 29).

This access should be based on a regulator's authority in its jurisdiction to require a TR to provide data regardless of TR location. For example, where a regulator has authority over a foreign TR operating in its jurisdiction, that regulator must be able to access relevant data held by the TR. Without such access, regulators would not be able to rely on foreign TRs, creating a situation where each country requires a domestic TR. Clearly, this may lead to fragmentation of data as well as an extreme duplication of effort. As stated in the report, "The multiplication of TRs for the same OTC derivatives class may actually increase the operational complexity for authorities in obtaining effective and practical access to information" (CPSS-IOSCO, 2013, p. 5). One can clearly see the difficulty of reconciling information from a plethora of TRs in a real-time crisis situation.

The report focuses on the issue of ensuring appropriate access to international TRs and provides specific instruction to home country regulators stating that "TR supervisors should avoid acting as gatekeepers and they should avoid actions that could hamper another authority's timely access" " (CPSS-IOSCO, 2013, p. 22).

However, the report acknowledges that domestic laws may hamper foreign authorities' access to TR data. A clear example of the limitations that international principles can have when faced with conflicting domestic legislation is the U.S. indemnity requirement for foreign regulator access to TR data. Sections 725, 728 and 763 of the Dodd-Frank Act require that swap data and security-based swap data repositories only make data available to non-U.S. regulators under certain conditions. These provisions insist that foreign regulators indemnify the data repository and the SEC or CFTC for litigation expenses arising from data sharing (The Library of Congress, 2012). The negative impacts of the indemnity requirements have been recognized to "(1) impede global regulatory cooperation, (2) risk fragmentation of a global data set for OTC derivatives, and (3) undermine efforts to increase market transparency and mitigate risk in this market" (The Library of Congress, 2012; quoting Larry Thompson, Managing Director and General Counsel for the Depository Trust & Clearing Corporation—accepted by the 112th Congress). The Swap Data Repository and Clearinghouse Indemnification Correction Act of 2013 (H.R. 742) was developed to address these concerns. This act is intended to resolve the issues created by the indemnity requirements of the Dodd-Frank Act by removing sections 725, 728 and 763 from American law ("Dodd-Frank Indemnification Briefing Paper", n.d.) however it is unclear whether there is any prospect for this to become law.

Without a more formalized approach, certain essential international infrastructures may not provide services effectively on an international basis, highlighting the difficulties of regulating international infrastructure on a domestic basis. As discussed above, without the force of law, international principles require economic incentivization to be effectively implemented. Unlike the PFMIs, which determine CCPs as qualified for capital and other regulatory purposes, adherence to the access guidelines contained in the report does not have direct economic consequences. Without direct economic incentives the most feasible form of incentivization would be market access restriction. For example, if adherence to the principles of the access report was an internationally agreed upon precondition for the licensing of a TR in all participating jurisdictions, implementation of the standards on TRs would be significantly more advanced. Although jurisdictions have agreed that non-substantive differences in regulation should not act as a barrier to market access, jurisdictional restrictions on the ability of foreign regulators to access information crucial to their mandate could be viewed as a substantive difference justifying this approach.

CPMI-IOSCO Recovery and resolution of financial market infrastructures

Large international FMIs act as critical infrastructure to multiple jurisdictions and one's failure has the potential to disrupt the operation of important sectors of the global economy. Therefore it is crucial that steps are taken to ensure that in a crisis situation there is an effective recovery and resolution regime that can mitigate the economic damage caused by a troubled FMI, ensuring that critical operations and services can continue to be performed as expected. Given the international nature of the FMIs discussed in this chapter, an orderly recovery or resolution is an extremely complex matter. The interaction of domestic bankruptcy and insolvency laws when dealing with cross border entities is unpredictable given the unique nature of such local laws, making it essential that international regulators have processes and understandings in place to deal with these situations in a coordinated manner and to avoid a disorderly wind-down.

In support of this objective, CPSS and IOSCO published a consultative report entitled *Recovery and Resolution of Financial Market Infrastructures* in 2012, which outlined the need for FMIs to have plans for dealing with and recovering from financial stress and also the need for jurisdictions to have modern and effective resolution regimes for failing FMIs. Drawing on the FSB's *Key Attributes of Effective Resolution Regimes for Financial Institutions* (2011) and the PFMIs, the report provided guidance on "[…] the essential features of recovery and resolution regimes necessary to ensure that the core functions of CCPs and other types of FMI can be maintained during times of crisis and in a manner that considers the interests of all jurisdictions where the CCP is systemically important" (CPSS-IOSCO 2012, p.1). The report explained that an FMI's detailed recovery plans should be evaluated and monitored on a continuous basis by its regulators.

The CPSS (now CPMI) and IOSCO finalized its recovery guidance in the report entitled *Recovery of financial market infrastructures* (2014), which builds on the consultative recommendations for recovery tools that FMIs should have in order to deal with financial viability issues. The report recommends tools, which include processes to allocate losses, to address uncovered liquidity shortfalls, to replenish financial resources and to allow a CCP to re-match its book (CPMI-IOSCO, 2014, p. 1). Importantly, the report explains that these processes should be transparent so that participants and stakeholders can identify any potential financial exposures they face in a recovery situation. In addition to recovery tools, FMIs are expected to have procedures to facilitate the wind-down of their operations when recovery is not feasible (CPMI-IOSCO 2014, p. 6).

The ability of an FMI to recover and avoid resolution proceedings is the best alternative to preventing a disorderly wind-down and the tools identified in the consultative report may allow FMIs facing financial difficulties to avoid failure. However, where recovery is not possible, it is crucial for the resolution of a failing FMI to occur in an orderly manner. The CPSS-IOSCO consultative report outlined the importance of jurisdictions having the necessary resolution powers incorporated into domestic law. These powers should allow a resolution authority to require the implementation of recovery measures and facilitate the continuation of an FMI's critical operations and services when possible. The insolvency of a systemically important internationally active FMI would represent perhaps the most complex interaction and application of jurisdictional bankruptcy laws ever in a proceeding. The consultative report also stressed the importance of cooperation and coordination amongst the various jurisdictions' authorities that oversee cross-border FMIs. The report identified the need for jurisdictions to have processes to facilitate foreign resolution measures and the importance of consistent recovery and resolution plans across jurisdictions. With respect to globally systemically important financial institutions, it was expected that crisis management groups be established to prepare for and manage the resolutions of these entities in a crisis situation (CPSS-IOSCO 2012, p. 17).

Further guidance on the resolution of systemically important FMIs and their participants has recently been provided in an annex to the FSB's *Key attributes of effective resolution regimes for financial institutions* document (FSB 2014, p. 57). The annex explains that resolution authorities should exercise their powers in a manner that promotes financial stability, facilitates the continuation of critical functions of the FMI and does not expose taxpayers to losses (FSB 2014, p. 59). It provides guidance on a wide range of recommended legal powers that resolution authorities should have to deal with failing FMIs. The annex also stresses the importance of cross-border cooperation and articulates that a resolution authority should consider the interests of and consult with all jurisdictions whose capital markets materially rely on the services of the FMI. Resolution processes should coordinate to achieve equivalent outcomes across jurisdictions for the resolution of an internationally active FMI. Additionally the guidance recommends that domestic laws should not automatically terminate an FMI's registrations or licences in one jurisdiction despite it entering into a resolution process in another jurisdiction, so that it may continue to provide critical services (FSB 2014, p. 65).

At this point it is unclear whether jurisdictions have successfully implemented these recommended resolution powers in a manner that would be effective in a crisis situation. Domestic bankruptcy and insolvency laws seek to balance a range of stakeholder interests and are notoriously difficult to amend. Further, there is always a level of uncertainty as to how bankruptcy and insolvency laws will be applied in a real time judicial proceeding. Nevertheless, the more tools domestic regulators have to deal with troubled FMIs in their jurisdiction the greater the likelihood that a resolution can be achieved without significant market disruption. However, no amount of planning can adequately prepare for the failure of a systemically important FMI. Such failure would be an unprecedented event with unpredictable consequences and would almost certainly result in economic instability and hardship. It is therefore crucial that authorities vigilantly monitor FMIs in a coordinated manner and attempt to create regulatory frameworks that reduce the likelihood of an FMI failure.

The recovery and resolution tools articulated collectively in these reports are extremely important for FMIs and it will be crucial for jurisdictions to monitor their implementation. These recommendations and guidance for FMIs and their regulatory authorities are particularly vital given that global OTC derivative reform measures have and will continue to significantly increase market reliance on FMIs. However, adherence to guidance of this nature can vary greatly across jurisdictions. In a crisis situation it remains to be seen whether domestic regulations applicable to cross-border FMIs will be applied in a coordinated manner or act as a barrier to the implementation of recovery plans. Where the resolution of a systemically important FMI becomes necessary it is likely that extended legal proceedings will take place in multiple jurisdictions. The interaction of jurisdictional bankruptcy and insolvency laws, while beyond the scope of this chapter, is an area in need of further research and development.

Summary

This section has outlined the key international working groups and standards applicable to FMIs. In doing so it has analyzed limitations and characteristics that correlate with successful implementation of standards. Building on this analysis the final section of this chapter will explore a range of recommendations for enhancing coordination, harmonization, market stability and efficiency for FMIs in the international derivatives market.

The Future of International FMI Regulation

The rapid internationalization of financial markets and the global impact of the financial crisis have required regulators to re-think the traditional model of market regulation. As should be expected, regulation of internationally active FMIs is a work in progress. While promising advancements in coordinated regulation are being achieved, a comprehensive framework for the regulation of international FMIs remains distant. In order to achieve the two pillars of international FMI regulation, market stability and market efficiency, more work needs to be done at the international level to achieve greater regulatory cooperation. This concluding section will explore a range of alternatives for a more formalized and efficient regulatory structure for international FMIs. It should be noted that the further an alternative departs from the status quo, the less the likelihood that such a measure is achievable in the short term. It is, however, this author's contention that we have entered a new era of financial regulation and that significant internationalization will, in time, occur.

Balancing market stability and market efficiency

As discussed, the joint pillars of promoting stability and efficiency can only be achieved through cross-border cooperation. However, even where cooperation has been achieved to varying degrees, it is not without its challenges, particularly with respect to the OTC market. Jurisdictions walk a fine line between implementing robust regulations and promoting their domestic derivatives markets. The mobile nature of the OTC market means that where regulation is comparatively burdensome, business can migrate, to the extent possible, to less stringently regulated jurisdictions. For example, it appears that certain non-U.S. derivatives market participants have avoided doing business with "U.S. Persons" in order to remain outside the scope of Dodd-Frank regulation (Bush & Hamilton, 2014; Madigan, 2014).

The financial crisis illustrated the essential need for baseline regulatory standards. Such standards are particularly important for internationally active systemically important FMIs. This is an area of significant achievement. There is a robust, relatively well implemented, body of baseline standards for FMIs that have been discussed throughout this chapter. Clearly, in the evolving OTC derivatives market there will be a need to refine and revisit standards but the achievements in coordination to date are impressive and will have a positive effect on the stability of FMIs. The area that requires further effort, in some cases, is ensuring that "soft law" standards are observed consistently across jurisdictions and as discussed, economic incentives like preferential capital treatment and market access requirements are a key characteristic of successful implementation.

In the wake of the financial crisis the focus on the regulatory world has rightfully been on market stability. Market efficiency has not garnered as prominent a position on the agenda. From an efficiency standpoint, if we are to facilitate cross-border activity, there must be certain limits to the requirements imposed for cross-border entities. International FMIs could not operate in an environment where they are subject to different rules and requirements in each jurisdiction that they are active. Although significant development in agreeing international minimums has been achieved, a system for coordinating where the line should be drawn with respect to requirements above these baseline standards has not been contemplated. If each jurisdiction that creates rules for FMIs above the baseline standards requires they be adhered to, the untenable situation of having to comply with different rules is largely unmitigated. As discussed, there is an international recognition that non-substantive differences in regulation should not present a barrier to market access, where similar outcomes are achieved and a variety of ad hoc methods such as substituted compliance and equivalency determinations are being developed to deal with the situation. Nonetheless, there are significant instances of disharmonization. Importantly, given the staggered pace of derivatives reform implementation, highlighted issues generally only involve the U.S. (and the CFTC in particular) and the EU. As the rules of other jurisdictions and regulators begin to take effect complications will multiply.

While jurisdictions should be free to implement standards as stringent as they determine appropriate, it should be recognized that there are legitimate policy motivations to limit regulatory burdens on market participants. The trade-off is between market stability and protection and the facilitation of a flexible and fast moving business environment. The more difficult question is whether the more stringent regulators should impose rules extraterritorially or whether market participants should be given the option to make their own prioritizations. Provided that a baseline standard is in force, it is not immediately obvious why market participants should not be able to choose between various levels of protections and costs.

Tafara and Peterson explain that regulatory competition can offer important benefits: "when different regulators share some overarching regulatory objectives, but, in implementing comparable regimes, compete with each other to develop the most effective and least costly ways to achieve these goals" (2007, p. 52). There are important diversification benefits to different operational models. Similarly, there can be benefits from heterogeneous regulations. Griffith argues that convergence of regulatory models can serve to increase systemic risk and that diversity of regulatory approaches should be encouraged (2014). Griffith theorizes that "uniform financial regulation can cause coordinated errors on the part of financial institutions thereby leading to multiple interconnected failures, potentially leading to the collapse of the financial system" (2014, 1356).

However, while homogeneity of regulatory models could potentially exacerbate a crisis, it is the concentration of counterparty risk in a relatively small number of large international dealers that is the true source of risk. Importantly, this concentration is not only amongst market participants, but spreads to the ownership of key international FMIs.

Although there can be cost saving incentives to move business to jurisdictions with lax regulatory standards, generally markets gravitate towards well-regulated environments because of the stability benefits. Given that baseline standards for FMIs are being well implemented, a strong argument can be made for facilitating cross-border FMI access where baseline standards are in place.

Enhancing the Status Quo

In order to enhance the current approach to regulation of FMIs, effort must be made to strengthen the implementation of international standards. As discussed, the most effective means of achieving this is through measures that create economic incentives and this approach could be more broadly utilized to encourage adoption of standards. The Basel requirement that financial institutions use PFMI compliant CCPs in order to receive favourable capital charges creates significant incentive to implement the PFMIs by jurisdictions and FMIs. If we consider the FSB's Four Safeguards, for example, tying these to capital charges would likely expedite their implementation significantly.

The more difficult scenario is where there is limited economic incentive which can be brought into play, as in the case of TRs. In this case market access could be preconditioned on implementation of internationally developed principles. The failure to comply with international agreements should result in a limitation on international operations for such market infrastructure. This is currently done on a nation by nation basis. For example a CCP that is not PFMI compliant by virtue of the agreement would not be able to operate in jurisdictions party to the agreement. If an agreement between FSB members could be reached to only permit compliant TRs to operate in FSB jurisdictions this would become a prerequisite for any TR seeking to operate on an international basis.

Much greater coordination can also be achieved internationally with respect to comparability analysis. The approach with which substituted compliance, equivalency or other form of comparative analysis between jurisdictional rules is undertaken has a large impact on market efficiency. As discussed, an overly rigorous analysis could always result in a determination of non-compliance resulting in extraterritorial application of host country laws. On the other hand, agreements could be reached that in addition to using an outcomes based approach comparisons should be done only at a very high level leaving total discretion to determine appropriate regulatory means to implement such standards to each jurisdiction. With respect to PFMIs, this could easily be done by deeming equivalent any jurisdiction that requires FMIs to follow the PFMIs. How in practice these high level requirements are implemented into rules would be left to the discretion of the jurisdiction. Further, to the extent that a particular jurisdiction chooses to create elevated standards for FMI located in their jurisdiction these would not be imposed on foreign FMIs.

With respect to coordinated oversight, the network of international MOUs could be enhanced for bilateral MOUs by including regulatory protocols to deal will applicable rules and oversight. A more significant approach would be the creation of a model multilateral MOU that outlines international protocols for regulation, including a jointly agreed upon regulatory roadmap for FMIs. Such a model would not seek to impose a particular operating model on FMIs but would rather incorporate baseline requirements (for example, the PFMIs) and principles for joint regulation and oversight. For example, agreements could be reached with respect to the obligations that apply to the home and host country regulator. For instance, the home country regulator could be responsible for day-to-day operational oversight of FMIs located in their jurisdiction. A multilateral MOU of this nature could be developed by IOSCO. This is a relatively modest proposal that essentially modernizes the status quo approach to cross-border regulation.

The International Model

For pragmatic reasons, the general recommendations of this chapter have focused on working within the current regulatory framework and strengthening existing coordination and harmonization mechanisms. The development of international model laws for the regulation of FMIs that could be adopted by interested jurisdictions would be a further step toward a more internationally harmonized framework. At the international level, model or uniform laws are a set of laws, usually developed by an international organization, that can be adopted in whole or part into the domestic laws of a jurisdiction. They can significantly increase harmonization though the use of shared language and concepts. Where effectively implemented, model laws can greatly reduce regulatory burdens for internationally active market participants by allowing them to refer to a common set of familiar rules. However, given the ongoing progress of implementing the PFMIs internationally, it is unlikely that jurisdictions would have an appetite for adopting the similar but more formalized mandate of developing model laws for the governance of FMIs any time in the near future, or perhaps until the PFMIs are truly adopted as international minimum risk management standards.

Further along the continuum of coordinated and harmonized international regulation would be the adoption of multilateral treaties applicable to the oversight and regulation of cross border FMIs. A treaty is a binding, written international agreement between two or more jurisdictions that is governed by international law. Multilateral treaties can have an associated organization to act as a tribunal to resolve any associated controversies. It is questionable whether a treaty governing oversight of cross-border FMIs would be appropriate given that such entities are typically primarily located in one jurisdiction and may not have a strong nexus to all jurisdictions where their services are offered. In any event, in addition to the cited reluctance of jurisdictions to formally bind themselves to any approach to regulating FMIs, to give effect to a treaty governing the oversight of internationally active FMIs would likely require extensive amendment to domestic legislation, including bankruptcy laws, to accommodate treaty agreements, and is likely not a feasible approach.

A less conventional but more radical proposal would be the establishment of an international organization (or expansion of mandate of a current one) to formally coordinate the regulation of international FMIs. This is not currently a feasible approach due to its impact on domestic regulatory sovereignty. However, it is this author's contention that regulatory models will be forced to evolve to effectively regulate international markets and this will require sacrificing a degree of domestic sovereignty.

An international organization could be developed and mandated with evaluating jurisdictional compliance with relevant international standards. Where a jurisdiction was found to be compliant, FMIs from that jurisdiction would be permitted to operate in participating jurisdictions without further substituted compliance or equivalency analysis. Mutualizing this analysis through an organization representing jurisdictions impacted by the PFMIs would greatly enhance regulatory efficiency. It would also be a superior means of avoiding regulatory arbitrage. Importantly, jurisdictions that attempt to attract business through lax standards would effectively be left out of the market. Clearly, any initiative of this sort would be very challenging to coordinate and gain acceptance. In order to incorporate such rules jurisdictions would likely need to amend legislation to permit the rules and equivalency determinations to be automatically incorporated into domestic law. Rather than the current system of ad hoc decisions on substituted compliance or equivalence, adherence to this determination would be the key to participation in the international market. Where implemented, this would operate as a jointly agreed upon comparability determination.

The development of an international organization empowered to make determinations on domestic market access would be a significant departure from the status quo and would face many hurdles before becoming a reality. A precondition would be the development of a mutually acceptable and democratic decision-making process that accommodates the needs of participating jurisdictions. This would be a difficult balancing act given that OTC derivatives market activity is dominated by a handful of jurisdictions but has important implications for the economies of a much broader group. Finding a middle ground between the interests of the dominant trading jurisdictions, who would likely be reluctant to cede control over any decision making power to an international organization, and those of smaller jurisdictions, who have unique circumstances and needs, would indeed be difficult but not unachievable.

The international nature of the OTC derivatives market, and FMIs that service this market, demands (not only from a market efficiency perspective but also a regulatory efficiency perspective) a more coordinated approach to cross border oversight and operation. This proposed organization could address one of the fundamental regulatory obstacles to cross-border activity: the current obligation to seek authorization and the application of unique domestic laws in each jurisdiction in which the FMI seeks to carry on business.

CONCLUSION

The regulatory response to the failures in the OTC derivatives market during the 2008 financial crisis has been to mandate the use of FMIs including CCPs and TRs. However, international coordination as to how these entities should be regulated on a cross-border basis to ensure market stability and efficiency remains incomplete. FMIs are subject to a complicated network of domestic laws and international principles that pose significant challenges to efficient cross-border operation.

We have entered a new era of internationalized markets that does not fit neatly within traditional domestic market regulation paradigm. As markets evolve so must the regulatory structures that oversee them. This evolution will require jurisdictions to move forward from traditional regulatory constructs and embrace systems that are better suited to truly global markets and institutions. Fundamental changes to longstanding approaches to regulation are difficult to achieve but the progress at the international level both by applying deference to home country regulation and development of international principles demonstrate that this regulatory evolution has begun.

ACKNOWLEDGMENT

The views expressed here are entirely those of the author and are not intended to represent those of the Ontario Securities Commission. The Author would like to thank Kevin Fine, Joshua Slive, Sina Akbari, Max Pare, Greg Toczylowski and Oren Winer for their insightful comments. A special thank you to Irene Fatehi for her valuable research assistance.

REFERENCES

G20 Leaders Statement: The Pittsburgh Summit. (2009). Proceedings of *G20 Information Centre*. Retrieved from http://www.g8.utoronto.ca/g20/2009/2009communique0925.html

About the International Organization of Securities Commissions. (n. d.). *The International Organization of Securities Commissions*. Retrieved from http://www.iosco.org/about/

Application of "Security-Based Swap Dealer" and "Major Security-Based Swap Participant" Definitions to Cross-Border Security-Based Swap Activities. (2014, June 25). U.S. Securities and Exchange Commission. Retrieved from http://www.sec.gov/rules/final/2014/34-72472.pdf

Authorities' access to trade repository data. (2013, April). *Committee on Payment and Settlement Systems and the Board of the International Organization of Securities Commission*. Retrieved from http://www.bis.org/publ/cpss108.pdf

Becker, L. (2014, May 23). EU regulators concerned by CFTC's foreign CCP rules. *Risk Magazine*. Retrieved from http://www.risk.net/risk-magazine/news/2346603/eu-regulators-concerned-by-cftcs-foreign-ccp-rules

Becker, L., & Madigan, P. (2014, June 16). EC to snub US in first wave of CCP equivalence decisions. *Risk Magazine.* Retrieved from http://www.risk.net/risk-magazine/news/2350239/ec-to-snub-us-in-first-wave-of-ccp-equivalence-decisions

Brummer, C. (2010). Post-American Securities Regulation. *California Law Review, 98*(2), 327–384.

Bush, S., & Hamilton, J. (2014, April 26). Banks' Overseas Swaps Moves Drawing CFTC Attention. *Bloomberg.* Retrieved from http://www.bloomberg.com/news/2014-04-25/banks-overseas-swaps-moves-said-to-draw-cftc-attention.html

Capital requirements for bank exposures to central counterparties. (2012, July). Bank for International Settlements. Retrieved from http://www.bis.org/publ/bcbs227.pdf

Capital requirements for bank exposures to central counterparties - final standard. (2014, April). *Bank for International Settlements.* Retrieved from http://www.bis.org/publ/bcbs282.htm

Carr, G. (2013, May 20). Emir futures margin rules create 'regulatory arbitrage'. *Energy Risk.* Retrieved from http://www.risk.net/energy-risk/news/2269032/emir-futures-margin-rules-create-regulatory-arbitrage

Chande, N., Dion, J.P., McVanel, D., & Slive, J. (2012, December). The Canadian Approach to Central Clearing for Over-the-Counter Derivatives. *Bank of Canada Financial System Review,* 43-49.

Committee on Payment and Market Infrastructures and the Board of the International Organization of Securities Commission [CPSS IOSCO]. (2014, October). *Recovery of financial market infrastructures.* Retrieved from http://www.bis.org/cpmi/publ/d121.pdf

Consultative Document - Capitalisation of bank exposures to central counterparties, 4. (2010, December). Bank for International Settlements. Retrieved from http://www.bis.org/publ/bcbs190.pdf

Corcoran, A. M. (2013). International Standards for Central Counterparties and Replumbing the Financial System: Retrofitting Listed Derivatives Infrastructure for the Global OTC Derivatives Market. *Futures and Derivatives Law Report, 33*(4), 1–29.

Core Principles for Effective Banking Supervision. (2012, September). *Basel Committee on Banking Supervision.* Retrieved from http://www.bis.org/publ/bcbs230.pdf

CPSS: History, organisation, cooperation. (n.d.). Bank for International Settlements. Retrieved from http://www.bis.org/cpss/cpssinfo01.htm

Dodd-Frank Wall Street Reform and Consumer Protection Act of 2010, H. R. 4173, 111th Congress (2010).

Communiqué. (2014, February 22-23). Finance Ministers and Central Bank Governors. Presented at the Meeting of Finance Ministers and Central Bank Governors, Sydney. Retrieved from https://www.g20.org/sites/default/files/g20_resources/library/Communique%20Meeting%20of%20G20%20Finance%20Ministers%20and%20Central%20Bank%20Governors%20Sydney%2022-23%20February%202014_0.pdf

Gensler, G. (2011, March 22). *Remarks, OTC Derivatives Reform, European Parliament, Economic and Monetary Affairs Committee, Brussels, Belgium* [Speech transcript]. Retrieved from http://www.cftc.gov/PressRoom/SpeechesTestimony/opagensler-75

Good practice principles on supervisory colleges. (2010, October). *Basel Committee on Banking Supervision*. Retrieved from http://www.bis.org/publ/bcbs177.pdf

Griffith, S. J. (2014). Substituted Compliance and Systemic Risk: How to Make a Global Market in Derivatives Regulation. *Minnesota Law Review*, *98*, 1291–1371.

House Report 112-471 - Part 1 - Swap Data Repository and Clearinghouse Indemnification Correction Act of 2012. (2012). The Library of Congress. Retrieved from http://thomas.loc.gov/cgi-bin/cpquery/?&dbname=cp112&sid=cp112jN8jw&refer=&r_n=hr471p1.112&item=&&&sel=TOC_3197&

Implementation monitoring of PFMIs: first update to the Level 1 report. (2014, May). *Committee on Payment and Settlement Systems and the Board of the International Organization of Securities Commission*. Retrieved from http://www.bis.org/cpmi/publ/d117.pdf

Implementing OTC Derivatives Market Reforms. (2010, October 25). *Financial Stability Board*. Retrieved from http://www.financialstabilityboard.org/publications/r_101025.pdf

Interpretive Guidance and Policy Statement Regarding Compliance with Certain Swap Regulations. 78 Fed. Reg. 144 (2013, July 26) (to be codified 17 CFR pt. 1).

Jones, H. (2013, November 5). Global watchdog says new body with teeth needed to police markets. *Reuters*. Retrieved from http://uk.reuters.com/article/2013/11/05/g20-regulation-idUKL5N0IQ2G820131105

Key Attributes of Effective Resolution Regimes for Financial Institutions. (2011, October) *Financial Stability Board*. Retrieved from http://www.financialstabilityboard.org/wp-content/uploads/r_111104cc.pdf?page_moved=1

Key Attributes of Effective Resolution Regimes for Financial Institutions. (2014, October 15) *Financial Stability Board*. Retrieved from http://www.financialstabilityboard.org/wp-content/uploads/r_141015.pdf

Madigan, P. (2014, June 19). Banks track US-facing business to avoid swap dealer tag. *Risk Magazine*. Retrieved from http://www.risk.net/risk-magazine/feature/2350345/banks-track-us-facing-business-to-avoid-swap-dealer-tag

Memorandum of cooperation related to the supervision of cross-border covered entities. (2014, March 10). U.S. Commodity Futures Trading Commission & Financial Services Agency of Japan. Retrieved from http://www.cftc.gov/ucm/groups/public/@internationalaffairs/documents/file/cftc-jfsamoc031014.pdf

Memorandum of understanding concerning cooperation and the exchange of information related to the supervision of cross-border covered entities. (2014, March 25). *U.S. Commodity Futures Trading Commission, Alberta Securities Commission, British Columbia Securities Commission, Ontario Securities Commission, & Autorite des marches financiers*. Retrieved from http://www.cftc.gov/ucm/groups/public/@internationalaffairs/documents/file/asc-bcsc-osc-amfmou032514.pdf

New developments in clearing and settlement arrangements for OTC derivatives. (2007, March). Committee on Payment and Settlement Systems. Retrieved from http://www.bis.org/publ/cpss77.pdf

OTC Derivatives Market Reforms Eighth Progress Report on Implementation. (2014, November 7). *Financial Stability Board*. Retrieved from http://www.financialstabilityboard.org/2014/11/eighth-progress-report-on-implementation-of-otc-derivatives-market-reforms/

Overview of Progress in the Implementation of the G20 Recommendations for Strengthening Financial Stability. Report of the Financial Stability Board to G20 Leaders. (2012, June 19). *Financial Stability Board*. Retrieved from http://www.financialstabilityboard.org/publications/r_120619a.pdf

Principles for financial market infrastructures. (2012, April). *Committee on Payment and Settlement Systems and the Technical Committee of the International Organization of Securities Commission*. Retrieved from http://www.bis.org/publ/cpss101a.pdf

Principles for the Supervision of Banks' Foreign Establishments. (1983, May). *Basel Committee on Banking Supervision*. Retrieved from http://www.bis.org/publ/bcbsc312.pdf

Recovery and resolution of financial market infrastructures. (2012, July). Committee on Payment and Settlement Systems and the Board of the International Organization of Securities Commission. Retrieved from http://www.bis.org/cpmi/publ/d103.pdf

Report of the OTC Derivatives Regulators Group (ODRG) on Cross-Border Implementation Issues. (2014). OTC Derivatives Regulators Group. Retrieved from http://www.esma.europa.eu/system/files/2014-03-odrg_odrg_report_to_the_g20_march_2014.pdf

Revised good practice principles for supervisory colleges. (2014, January). *Basel Committee on Banking Supervision*. Retrieved from http://www.bis.org/publ/bcbs276.pdf

Sheffield, H. (2014, July 7). Cross-border harmonisation threatened as MTF talks fall apart. *Global Capital*. Retrieved from http://www.globalcapital.com/article/m437mkgjc3p8/cross-border-harmonisation-threatened-as-mtf-talks-fall-apart

Tafara, E., & Peterson, R. J. (2007). A Blueprint for Cross-Border Access to U.S. Investors: A New International Framework. *Harvard International Law Journal*, *48*(1), 32–68.

Technical advice on third country equivalence under EMIR – US [Final report]. (2013, September 1). European Securities and Markets Authority. Retrieved from http://www.esma.europa.eu/system/files/2013-1157_technical_advice_on_third_country_regulatory_equivalence_under_emir_us.pdf

Dodd -Frank Indemnification Briefing Paper. (n.d.) The Depository Trust & Clearing Corporation. Retrieved from http://164.109.172.95/legal/government_relations/downloads/briefing/Indemnification.pdf

Union – A Path Forward. (n. d.). *Commodity Futures Trading Commission*. Retrieved from http://www.cftc.gov/PressRoom/PressReleases/pr6640-13

U.S. Commodity Futures Trading Commission. (2013, July 11). *Cross-Border Regulation of Swaps/ Derivatives Discussions between the Commodity Futures Trading Commission and the European*

7. U.S.C. §7a-1 (2011).

KEY TERMS AND DEFINITIONS

Colleges of Regulators: A collection of regulators that coordinate oversight of systemically important financial market infrastructures.

Equivalency: An approach that delegates traditional domestic or regional responsibilities to a foreign regulatory regime by relying fully on the home country's rules and enforcement mechanisms. It avoids any overlapping or conflicting rules and is championed by the EU.

Memorandums of Understanding: The traditional means through which jurisdictions coordinate oversight and enforcement of financial market activity internationally. These bilateral or multilateral agreements generally focus on exchanges of information regarding internationally active entities or infrastructure.

Principles for Financial Market Infrastructures (PFMIs): High-level and principles-based international risk-management standards that set a floor for compliance. They address the systemic risks associated with financial market infrastructures. Member jurisdictions of the International Organization of Securities Commission have initiated their integration into their legal and regulatory regimes.

Prudential Regulators: Regulate and supervise deposit-taking institutions in an effort to ensure financial stability. They have developed a set of home-host principles for internationally active institutions, which are contained in the Basel Concordat of the Basel Committee on Banking Supervision.

Soft Law: High-level agreements that are translated into international regulatory initiatives and implemented on an outcome-based approach through domestic law. Generally, this type of agreement does not have the force of law.

Substituted Compliance: A hybrid approach to domestic regulation of foreign infrastructures, permitting financial market infrastructures to adhere to home country regulations exclusively in certain situations. This approach often reduces duplicative regulations and is championed by the U.S.

Chapter 4
FMIs – Knights in Shining Armour?

Christian Goerlach
Deutsche Bank AG, Germany

Anne-Katrin Brehm
Deutsche Bank AG, Germany

Bradley Lonnen
Deutsche Bank AG, Germany

ABSTRACT

Great hope is being pinned on FMIs. They lie at the heart of the financial system and enable the post-trading business by successfully completing trades and concentrating as well as mitigating risks. This end of the payment and securities settlement business does not usually attract much attention: It is expected to be there and function. In this respect, it is comparable to oxygen in the air – most people do not think about it, however, if something is wrong with it, things can turn bad extremely quickly. Such was the case with the Lehman crisis of 2008, playing a major role in the unfolding of the global crisis of the late 2000s. It became apparent just how vital these FMIs were in enabling the continuation of the globe's securities & derivatives exchanges. In particular, CCPs played a major role in keeping transaction processing ticking over. It became evident which knock on effects the downturn of one institution can have on the global financial landscape. As such, we all depend on those markets and on the performance of what can only be described as 'knights in shining armour'.

Issue & Approach. Since the financial crisis, the role, composition and status quo of our 'knights in shining armour' has been intensively scrutinized from a regulatory and financial intermediary point of view. Despite the fact that FMIs operated well throughout the crisis, the unfolding events emphasized the need for more robust risk management. These needs together with the experience of implementing the existing international standards resulted in the Committee on Payment and Settlement Systems (CPSS) and the International Organization of Securities Commissions (IOSCO) reviewing and updating the standards for FMIs with the aim of strengthening core financial infrastructures and markets. (CPPS,

DOI: 10.4018/978-1-4666-8745-5.ch004

2012) This included technical infrastructure and a specialized risk management framework, appropriate to the risks they incur. These developments will lead to standardization of processes and risk management requirements. While the aforementioned measures are effectively increasing transparency and mitigating counterparty settlement risks, there are also potential adverse impacts stemming from mutualizing these processes – especially in the areas of liquidity and collateral. Risk tends to be like power – it is generally possible to convert it, but it is very hard to effectively eliminate it.

Structure. This chapter consists of four sections. The first section provides a short introduction to the different types of FMIs. The second section provides context and background regarding liquidity and collateral and explores the dynamics and power of FMIs as well as interdependencies among them. The third section outlines potential consequences for market participants with regards to liquidity and collateral as well as potential responses and enhanced product solutions for direct clearing members and third party access that will be essentially required in future. Finally, the fourth section provides a summary and conclusion of sections one to three.

INTRODUCTION TO FINANCIAL MARKET INFRASTRUCTURES

Types of Financial Market Infrastructures

FMIs are essentially the core of the financial payment and settlement ecosystem, either enabling the movement of cash and securities needed to settle transactions and/or intermediating exposures between market participants, thereby ensuring financial obligations are met. The fact that they help reduce and allocate inherent risks arising from transactions between market participants means they are an essential component in the functioning of the financial markets and wider economy (Rehlon, 2013).

In the past, clearing and settlement services were carried out through physical exchanges. Today it is a high-tech IT driven business. FMIs have had to adapt to those developments. To understand their increasing initial function within the financial market landscape globally, we need to have a look at each of them individually. The CPSS and IOSCO differentiate five types of FMIs: Payment Systems (PS), Securities Settlement Systems (SSS), Central Security Depositories (CSD), Central Counterparties (CCP) and Trade Repositories (TR).

Payment Systems

Concept. The PSs are of paramount importance for the smooth functioning of financial markets. A well-developed PS improves the interaction of markets and contributes to eliminating 'frictions in trade' (ECB, 2010). PSs are not accessible to everybody. Membership is governed by access criteria including minimum requirements to secure their robustness. Therefore, two basic access options exist: direct participation referring to full membership, or indirect participation making use of intermediaries (ECB, 2010).

Developments. Since the introduction of the PS there have been a multitude of developments. While in the early years these developments were more in the area of formats accepted and how the PSs could be accessed (including front ends), in recent years most large PSs have developed mechanisms and procedures that allow a more efficient payment processing. Such mechanisms include liquidity saving mechanisms, such as multilateral netting cycles.

Securities Settlement Systems

Concept. SSSs are just as important as PSs for the smooth functioning of financial markets. According to the Principles for Financial Market Infrastructures (PFMIs) published by the CPSS & IOSCO, "a securities settlement system enables securities to be transferred and settled by book entry according to a set of predetermined multilateral rules" (CPSS, 2012, p. 8). The CPSS and IOSCO are more precise in the classification and definition of SSSs. They exclude CSDs and CCPs from their SSS definition and narrow it to the primary function of providing security, clearing and settlement functions, such as the confirmation of trade and settlement instructions. CCPs and CSDs are treated as individual types of FMIs and explained in more detail below (CPSS, 2012).

Central Counterparties

Concept. CCPs are the most complex type of FMI when it comes to risk, liquidity and collateral management. Simplified, CCPs are clearing houses and interpose themselves between counterparties to arrange much simpler settlement options in a securities trade by becoming crucial nodes in the financial system worldwide (Rehlon, 2013). As described by Andrew Haldane, Executive Director for Financial Stability at the Bank of England, "a high-dimension web is instantly compressed to a sequence of bilateral relationships" so that overall "the lengthy network chain is condensed to a single link, effectively eliminating counterparty uncertainty" (Norman, 2012, p. 9).

Reasons for greater central clearing. CCPs "allow the city to sleep at night", was the description once used by Chris Tupker, former chairman of Euroclear and LCH.Clearnet, to describe a CCP's job (Norman, 2012, p. 8). And he is right: In 2008 the CCPs throughout the world worked together to protect global financial markets from the downturn of the world's securities and derivatives markets. The combination of insufficient collateral obligations and the lack of transparency over large bilateral positions between counterparties gathered intensity and led to the reduction of liquidity in financial markets worldwide. Central clearing made it possible to hedge all open positions within a week.

Access. CCPs usually limit direct participation in the clearing process to the most creditworthy subset of market participants. Only these key market participants have a principal-to-principal relationship with the CCPs and the possibility to intermediate directly in clearing. Those market participants that are not deemed as key clearing members have to establish an account relationship with a clearing member that acts as an approved settlement bank. Only then they can effect settlement. (ECB, 2010)

Benefits. CCPs facilitate various economic and risk-reducing benefits. One main benefit of central clearing is the 'multilateral netting' of transactions between market participants which leads to a substantial reduction in the number of settlements (ECB, 2010). 'Netting by novation' leads to a reduction in individual contract obligations and therefore facilitates more trading opportunities for participants. This means that a CCP has the potential to reduce liquidity risk by broadening the scope of payment clearing. Hence, market participants do not need to worry about the creditworthiness of other individual market participants due to the CCP's central function. Their management and redistribution makes it just more efficient than individual market participants 'could do in isolation' (ECB, 2010). In addition, the same level of risk protection can be achieved with a smaller amount of collateralization (Coeuré, 2014).

Case Study Box: Lines of defence against member defaults. One of the most important benefits of CCPs is the function they take in the event of a member's default. In contrast to non-centrally cleared markets, the CCPs 'multiple lines of defence' protect the clearing members in the case of a default (also

Figure 1. Default Waterfall

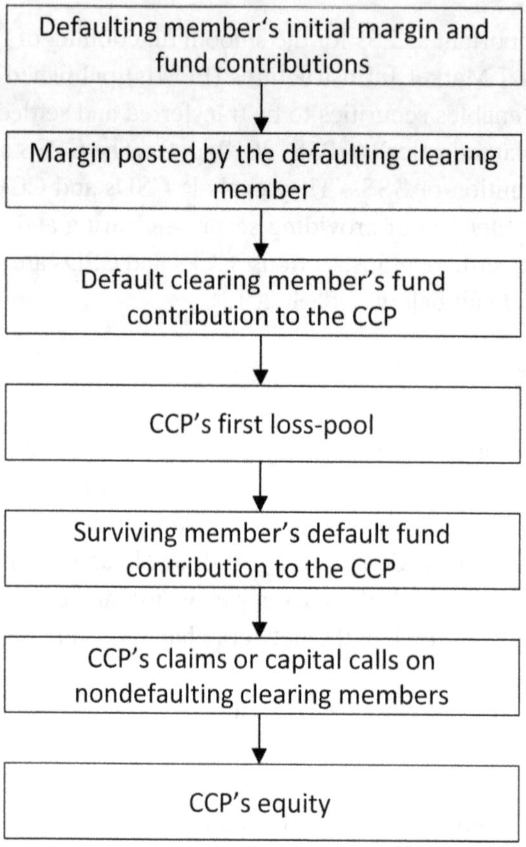

called 'default waterfall'). The default is managed in a structured way, based on rules and resources to respond quickly to member defaults. The lines of defence reflect the protection that a CCP gains in meeting the obligations of defaulting clearing members.

It is vital that a CCP finds the correct balance between initial margining and a guarantee fund. For example, a CCP that relies on a lower margining and a higher guarantee fund may inadvertently encourage some clearing members to assume higher risks, as their losses are mutualized among all clearing members. In addition, the CCP's own capital functions as the last layer of protection and is therefore always only a small portion of the overall risk exposure.

Although a number of lines of defence are in place, one needs to consider what the implications are in the event that there is not enough collateral (fund contributions and margins) to honor the members' claims. In turn, further questions then arise, e.g. which counterparties take the loss or is this then distributed to all members? –Furthermore, what would be the maximum amount of such losses and how is it reflected in the risk reporting and accounting of such member institutions? (Source: Deutsche Börse, Eurex Clearing, 2014; IMF, 2010; Rehlon, 2013)

Risks associated with CCPs. An unstable CCP could potentially act as a 'channel of contagion'. In the case of a downturn, solely covered markets would be required to close, at least for certain time. Thus as systemically important risk concentrators, they require comprehensive recovery rules and resolution regimes to keep any disruption to clearing services to an absolute minimum (Rehlon, 2013). As CCPs are effective 'shock absorbers', "markets would be very restricted and illiquid" without them (Norman, 2012, p. 13). We need to be well aware, however, that risks will never disappear completely.

Central Securities Depositories

Concept. CSDs function as a 'storehouse' and provide services for the safekeeping and transfer of securities for the whole market. A wide range of financial instruments for deposit and settlement services is accepted by CSDs – such as equities, corporate bonds and government securities and treasury bills (ECB, 2010; ECSDA, 2012). For CSDs, different holding structures exist. The CSDs can hold accounts for all final owners of securities in the form of a direct holding structure. Alternatively, custodians hold accounts (omnibus accounts) in a tiered structure as intermediaries with the CSDs for the indirect CSD participants (ECB, 2010). In this indirect holding structure, the CSDs hold fewer accounts as the final owners' accounts are held 'next tier down in a custody chain'. CSDs were basically set up to centralize the safekeeping and transfer of national securities markets and were typically domestic in scope. In addition to those national CSDs, international CSDs (ICSDs) arose: most notably the 'Euroclear Bank' based in Belgium and 'Clearstream Banking Luxembourg' (ECB, 2010).

Case Study Box: ICSDs. On its first day of business, Euroclear handled around 800 operations a day. Today they cover a volume of 480,000 transactions/operations on a daily basis. One of the breakthrough innovations was the 'electronic bridge' between Euroclear and Cedel (later Clearstream Banking Luxembourg). Until 1977 cars filled with physical securities had to cross the river Petrusse every day to enable the physical movement of securities between Euroclear and Cedel participants. In 1977 the two ICSDs "finally agreed to open cash and securities accounts with each other" to exchange securities electronically by book-entry transfers which was demanded by their participants. The first link was established worldwide. Today the two ICSDs have links with around 30 other local CSDs each; in addition to those that are members of Euroclear and Deutsche Börse respectively. (Source: Norman, 2014, Euroclear Webpage & Annual Review 2013)

Trade Repositories

Concept. A TR is a crucial tool for storing and aggregating relevant market information by ensuring that all key market intermediaries and the authorities have access to this data. As a central registry it enhances the stability of the financial system by providing up-to-date information of payment, clearing and settlement services over the life-time of a contract (ECB, 2010).

Developments. TRs services are a recent innovation. In 2006, they were used for the first time to record transaction data for credit derivatives. Given the lessons learned of the financial crisis, TRs services are now being introduced as central electronic record systems for a wider range of financial products - functioning as 'support infrastructures' for global markets worldwide (ECB, 2010).

General Considerations

FMI identification & classification. Each FMI has its clear function within the post-trading business. For many institutions around the world it is easy to identify them as a specific FMI, classifying them by their primary function. For others it is more difficult as they incorporate functions another type of FMI usually carries out (Lee, 2011). As for example in Spain, the local CSD "IBERCLEAR" is responsible for settling all equity transactions. However in this context, the CSD also fulfils certain tasks which would generally be attributed to a CCP, i.e. participants which want to trade on the exchange need to post collateral with the CSD. Within the current market environment, it has been recognized that a clear distinction of functionalities is required and the market is preparing the set up of a new CCP. Furthermore, there are institutions with the same functionality within the market. They appear similar to FMIs but were established with various different names and even in different contexts. Some of them call themselves proprietary trading systems (PTSs), electronic communication networks (ECNs), alternative trading systems (ATSs) or multilateral trading facilities (MTFs). This diverse FMI landscape has its origin mainly in the individual historical developments throughout the various countries. (Lee, 2011) As FMIs are so difficult to classify, it goes without saying that explicitly regulating them is extremely challenging.

Recent developments. As previously mentioned, everything was seemingly taking its course in the development of financial markets up until a few years ago. Needless to say, that was until the financial crisis and in particular the bankruptcy of Lehman Brothers which fundamentally changed the world. The crisis raised a number of issues ranging from excessive risk taking, its knock-on effects, the lack of liquidity buffers through to the lack of collateralization. The response has been the establishment of a new regulatory regime which, over the past six years, has progressively been implementing new risk requirements – also in the space of clearing and settlement. In 2009, for example, the G20 leaders declared the clearing obligation for bilaterally cleared ('over the counter' (OTC)) derivatives in Pittsburgh. In 2012, the CPSS and IOSCO presented their reviewed and updated principles for FMIs - including specified and stricter requirements to strengthen the resilience of financial markets globally (CPSS, 2012). Additionally, EMIR and the second Markets in Financial Instruments Directive (MiFID 2) in Europe but also the Dodd-Frank act in the US, covering almost all financial securities services, have contributed to the overall reform of financial markets globally (Barank, 2013). It is clear that regulation will continue to evolve. Consequently, the post trading landscape will, going forward, look fundamentally different to what we operate in today (Maijoor, 2014).

DYNAMICS OF FMIs

Liquidity

Liquidity requirements. The CPSS & IOSCO set up specific requirements for FMIs regarding liquidity risks. The new requirements prescribe, that FMIs "should maintain sufficient liquidity resources in all relevant currencies to affect same-day and, where appropriate, intraday and multiday settlement of payment obligations" (Russo, 2013, p. 72). They should be subject to potential stress scenarios that include the default of at least the two largest participants with the largest aggregate liquidity obligation. This is even more important for FMIs that are present in multiple jurisdictions. The PFMI have been even more forceful on the need of stress testing liquidity. The reason for this is that almost all market relationships and FMI links intensify liquidity risks and the probability of multiple failures among its participants' contagion effects (Russo, 2013). Almost all types of FMIs (except TRs) are concerned with liquidity risks. To be prepared against defaults of participants with the greatest exposures, FMIs should set up additional liquidity or collateral pools. CCPs already have default waterfalls in place. For CSDs, discussions are currently underway to set up similar liquidity buffers (ECB, 2010).

Settlement. Compared to the bilateral settlement of trades, the settlement via FMIs, therefore, comes with increased liquidity requirements. Liquidity management is a serious challenge for commercial banks – it is important for them to understand and interpret what increasing significant role FMIs will play in the context of (intraday) liquidity management in the near future. FMIs require and use liquidity, ideally central bank liquidity at pre-defined times within the day. Consequently, commercial banks have to ensure a sufficient level of liquidity is available at that defined point in time in order to meet the requirement of the FMI and complete settlement. Not meeting the requirements could lead to multiple underlying trades not settling with immediate visibility to the market (large commercial banks may settle thousands of underlying deals with one cash payment to an FMI). This marks a fundamental change to the OTC market, where there is often a 1:1 relationship of payment and settlement of underlying deal, where there is usually no hard intraday deadline and visibility is between the acting counterparties only. Furthermore, especially for large commercial banks participating in multiple FMI settlements each day, they have to manage multiple deadlines and the complexity of moving liquidity to different places - a dedicated intraday liquidity management has to be in place. Intraday liquidity management is different from the regular 'value date' liquidity management as a commercial bank could well be net cash long on a day. However, if this money only arrives in the afternoon, but a FMI requires a payment in the morning, a situation could arise where the commercial bank is liquid for the day, but still fails to meet the timed pay-in obligation from the FMI.

Collateral

Concept. Collateral is vitally important in financial markets due to the protection it offers against credit risk exposures. Moreover, it facilitates trading between parties that under normal conditions would not engage with each other due to their weaker creditworthiness. The posting of collateral should reflect anticipated worst-case losses. The amount of collateralized transactions has been steadily increasing, especially since the financial crisis – one reason for that is that more products are forced to settle via CCPs (ECB, 2010). Should a participant default, collateralized credit exposures protect an FMI and even its participants against resulting potential losses. Furthermore, collateralization encourages participants to manage the risks they potentially create for the FMI or other participants (CPSS, 2012, p. 46). As collateral will be used during stressed market conditions, the assets accepted as collateral need to be of highest quality (CPSS, 2012).

Collateral requirements. Additionally, an FMI should avoid concentrated holdings of certain assets where this would majorly reduce the capacity to liquidate such assets in an expedient manner without considerable adverse price effects ("slippage"). Concentration limits impede the ability of participants to provide certain collateral assets above a specific threshold as determined by the FMI (CPSS, 2012). It is evident, that collateral is becoming a more and more central function within the payment, clearing and settlement services. Therefore, the new PFMI also contain strengthened collateral requirements with the aim of avoiding concentration risks, wrong-way risk and procyclicality. "Procyclicality has been a source of concern in the recent financial crisis as it may cause or exacerbate financial instability" (Russo, 2013, p. 72). This is because additional collateral is required when asset prices decline and haircut levels increase in the event of a stressed market environment. Consequently a domino effect would be triggered whereby asset prices are driven down even further, requiring even further collateral obligations (Russo, 2013).

Systemic Risk

By completing settlement on time every day, FMIs are able to reinforce confidence of their functionality and enable continued trading and liquidity in the markets they operate. In the event that a systemically important system fails to settle correctly in a timely manner, not only will its participants be affected, but also wider markets risk being exposed to large systemic liquidity, market and credit risks. Thus, liquidity issues in payment, clearing and settlement systems can lead to an accumulation of far-reaching liquidity difficulties in financial markets (ECB, 2010). A lack of collateralization exacerbates systemic risk. If any given participant is unable to fulfil its obligation in a system, this will result in the failure of other participants to fulfil their due obligations. Systemic risks potentially arise from liquidity or credit issues in one institution and may adversely affect other systems or markets. "By their nature, networks such as payment, clearing and settlement systems are [...] a key institutional channel for the propagation of systemic crises, as they have the potential to increase, shift, concentrate or otherwise transform risks in unanticipated ways" (ECB, 2010, p. 128). As a consequence, financial institutions using FMIs for their payment, clearing and security settlement operations are confronted with higher levels of systemic risks. Given the concentration of clearing and transaction volume in a small number of direct participants, the financial and operational soundness of these upper-tier intermediaries becomes fundamental to the overall health of the entire system. Their unexpected unavailability can potentially trigger systemic downturns. Therefore, global financial institutions should have a particular interest in limiting systemic risk in the systems they operate. It is extremely important that all FMIs "identify their critical participants and set up appropriate business continuity measures" (ECB, 2010, pp. 129-130).

Market Power & Competition. To understand the full range of systemic risks, the FMIs' market power and competition level also needs to be taken into account. Most FMIs operate as monopolies in their respective local markets becoming crucial nodes in the financial system and thus, new competitors have not really been able to compete with a well established provider in the past. If there is more than one provider, each one normally focuses on a different asset class offering an unbeatable service and price. This monopolistic/oligopolistic situation is coupled with mergers and links between FMIs additionally (Lee, 2011).

FMI links. By establishing links, FMIs expand the services for their primary participants to other financial instruments, markets or institutions (CPSS, 2012). However, the configuration of links can influence and further increase the total system default exposure that may arise between participants and FMIs and/or between FMIs themselves. Furthermore, they can lead to oversight challenges by reducing the overall transparency. In other words, links can contribute to an outstanding enormous collapse of previously unknown magnitude (CPSS, 2012). Regulatory authorities already stepped in and now subscribe that FMIs "that establish a link with one or more FMIs should identify, monitor, and manage link-related risks" so that multiple links do not result in spill-over effects that would negatively influence the security of other linked FMIs and if nothing else, the entire financial market landscape (CPSS, 2012; Anderson, Dion, Perez-Saiz, 2013).

In summary, the likelihood that a system is subject to systemic risk increases due to the interconnection of FMIs that have a wide range of complex relationships among themselves which, in turn, leads to a higher vulnerability level of global financial markets (ECB, 2010).

Case Study Box: Fallen "knights in shining armour". Since their inception, there have only been a very small number of FMI failures. In fact, since 1974 only three CCP failures can be traced. The same applies to near-failures. Going back to 1974, the French Caisse de Liquidation clearing house had to close due to unmet margin calls by one large clearing member primarily caused by a downturn of sugar prices on futures exchanges. The main reason was the CCP's mistake of not requesting higher margin requirements, although market volatility was increasing as a first indication. The Malaysian Kuala Lumpur Commodity Clearing House failed in 1983 due to similar issues. The third failure was the closing of the Hong Kong Futures Exchange for four days and the later bail out by the government in 1987. Unmet margin calls on purchased equity futures followed the crash and led to the failure. In the aftermath of the October 1987 crash, two other exchanges were close to a failure. In both cases one of the largest clearing members faced challenges in meeting its margin obligations.

Due to the aforementioned experiences, the following conclusions can be drawn. First, margin requirements need to be adjusted on a regular basis and collected in a prompt manner thereby securing contract performance. Second, there needs to be a well coordinated approach with regards to the clearing and market oversight to enable efficient monitoring of exposures which, in turn, will allow for a faster action. Third, close scrutiny of the market and the ability to manage potentially dangerous exposures are essential. For CCPs, it is critical to be able to monitor positions, to ascertain whether limits need to be imposed as a result of daily price changes. They also need to impose exposure reductions when required.

The failure of an FMI can result in serious systemic disruptions in the event that it prevents markets from operating effectively. Even in the event of a financial crisis FMIs have to be able to carry out critical operations and as such this has to be fully considered when establishing Recovery and Resolution Plans (RRP). The CPSS & IOSCO and the FSB have significant headway with regards to this. Their RRPs now require FMIs to have on-going recovery procedures in place as well as a resolution planning process minimizing potentials for failure. One element that still has not been addressed however, relates to the implications of CCPs conducting 'additional business' that is potentially coupled with higher risk. In such a case, the logical conclusion to draw is, that the underlying transactions of their participants are no longer necessarily low in risk. Furthermore, such high risk related default exposures also need to be taken into consideration. (Source: IMF, 2010; Russo 2013; FSB, 2012)

CONSEQUENCES FOR MARKET PARTICIPANTS

Drivers of an Increased Liquidity and Collateral Requirement

There are various factors that result in potential consequences for market participants, especially in the need of higher liquidity requirements and increasing collateral demand. Those restrictions can be classified in FMI-related and external requirements.

Increased usage of FMI. More and more products are being settled via FMIs. This is driven both by regulation as well as market trends. Regulations for example, suggest mandatory CCP clearing for certain derivatives. Such market trends include, for instance, the shift of transactions from unsecured to secured money markets cumulating in a change in financial market behaviour. Consequently, a growing number of banks will participate in key CCPs across the globe. It is essential that the financial institutions that participate in and rely on CCPs are able to conduct effective due diligence to understand the risks they face as members and take appropriate steps to mitigate those risks (Levels, Capel, 2012).

Central bank collateral for FMI settlement. FMIs usually require cash settlement in central bank money at specified times within the day. In order to facilitate a settlement, participating members require intraday payment capacity in the form of central bank money or respective collateral (most central banks offer intraday settlement lines in return for the pledge of high quality collateral). This collateral is required to smoothen settlement – e.g. if the FMI requires payment at 8am and the cash cover from a client only arrives at 10am, the collateral can facilitate the 2 hour overdraft at the central bank. In contrast, bilateral settlement of trades could take place in central bank or commercial money and even for those trades settling in central bank money, there are usually no strict timing requirements – i.e. in the above example the bilateral settlement could queue up until 10am when funding arrives, mitigating or even eliminating the need for clearing collateral at the central bank for the settlement of this trade. With the increased usage of FMIs, the requirements on the central bank clearing portfolios will increase as well.

Stricter collateral requirements of FMIs. In addition, the regulatory requirements on FMIs, in the form of the latest PFMIs published by CPSS and IOSCO and additional regulation from EMIR and Dodd-Frank define and restrict the processing and procedures that need to be followed by FMIs and their participants when it comes to clearing and settlement. All those requirements prescribe that FMIs need to hold more collateral and cash in the form of margin and settlement payment capacity to have a more prudent setup and to cope with stress periods and to reflect possible future changes in the value of the underlying contracts (Deutsche Börse Group, Eurex Clearing, 2014).

Requirements in times of stress. CCP's primary liquidity sources are margin requirements and fund contributions of members. Those will rise in times of stress, as the CCP needs to make sure that it can cover potential member defaults (those clients will then need more collateral to participate in clearing). Even the clearing members rating can change in times of stress resulting in higher margin and fund contributions. Thus, CCPs remove liquidity from the markets at the worst possible point in time; during stress periods and shortly before potential market downturns (Financial News, 2012).

Basel III requirements. At the same time, there is an increased need of the same type of collateral in terms of Basel III, prescribed by the Liquidity Coverage Ratio (LCR) & the Net Stable Funding Ratio (NSFR). In fact, these additional 'external' restrictions have an adverse effect on the playing field of FMIs as they also result in additional collateral needs and liquidity buffers by all financial intermediaries.

Consequences and Challenges

Collateral scarcity. All of the above mentioned developments (increased usage of FMIs, stricter liquidity/collateral usage of FMIs, higher central bank clearing requirements and Basel requirements to hold buffers) lead to higher liquidity and collateral requirements for market participants. Furthermore, all of the aforementioned requirements need to be sourced with almost the same type of collateral, as all require to be of highest credit quality and highest market liquidity. Some of the increasing collateral requirements may not increase the overall collateral required in the system – an example is the variation margin, which one counterparty has to post, but the same amount will be released to the other counterparty. However, these transfers will add to the complexity of where collateral is located and moved between the counterparties and therefore requires participants to hold higher buffers. With an increased demand for collateral and demand potentially exceeding supply, collateral scarcity will be an issue going forward. Collateral scarcity will, in turn, negatively affect the ability of market participants to conduct financial transactions. Regulators and central banks also need to be aware of this issue as they must "safeguard the smooth operation of financial markets" (Levels, Capel, 2012, p. 30).

Levels and Chapel analyzed the expected developments in demand and supply of high quality collateral globally and as a result there is no absolute, but a relative shortage expected. In the time prior to the implementation of the additional regulatory requirements (2012) the global supply of high quality collateral was estimated to be three times the demand. It is expected that by the time this book is published the ratio will change to less than two. Hence, while the supply of high quality liquid assets is still more than twice the demand, the excess supply is expected to shrink by half. This is a considerable development as an absolute shortage will be experienced prior to a 1:1 relationship is achieved, given that there could be mis-allocations between currencies, countries etc. and also some market participants may choose to hold discretionary buffers over and above the regulatory requirements (Levels, Capel, 2012).

Balance sheet leverage. The balance sheet leverage regulation caps the maximum size of a bank's balance sheet at a defined multiple of the capital. This means that there is risk-independent maximum size of the balance sheet. Consequently balance sheet becomes a limited resource. In our context this has two implications. First, there is an absolute overall limit on how much collateral and liquidity a commercial bank could hold. Second, a commercial bank has to generate their profits with this defined amount of balance sheet and consequently there is a requirement to allocate the resource to areas and products where the return is most attractive (also taking into account other aspects such as credit risks and client relationships etc.).

The liquidity and collateral requirements discussed above all require high credit quality and high market liquidity. However, the return on such positions (e.g. the coupon of a government bond or the return from central bank deposits) is among the lowest in the industry – representing the low risk and high liquidity nature of these assets. Also, our analysis above regarding the scarcity of collateral suggests that with increased requirements for collateral and (relative) lower levels of supply, costs are expected to increase; i.e. the yields of such collateral is expected to reduce further. Consequently, within a bank, these assets are competing with other assets on the balance sheet, such as loans, mortgages, letters of credit and others.

Potential Responses: Efficiency

Due to the aforementioned challenges, market participants will require a more efficient use of collateral in future. Banks need to make sure they have a proper understanding of collateral allocation to gain more transparency in collateral usage. Furthermore, clearing enhancements are also required. Collateral needs to be made available more quickly to respond faster to possible open positions. One trend could be to prioritize CCPs that are covering different asset classes or are providing services in various markets, across borders. To use collateral in a more efficient way and to respond to scarcity, the following product enhancements are required. We would like to refer to four potential enhancements: re-use of collateral, cross-border collateral, auto-collateralization and improved management and operations of liquidity and collateral.

Collateral reuse. The reuse of collateral can be seen as a 'collateral multiplier' (Levels, Capel, 2012). According to Singh and Aitken, the reuse of collateral "occurs when the collateral posted by a prime broker is also used as collateral by the prime broker for its own purpose" (IMF, 2010, p. 3). Also the PFMIs define the reuse of collateral in a comparable manner. This is not the same practice when the FMI's use collateral in default scenario. In such an event, the collateral posted by the defaulter automatically becomes the property of the FMI, which can be used to cover other losses (see Case Study Box: Lines of Defence against Member Defaults) (CPSS, 2012). It should be noted that while collateral reuse helps efficiencies with regards to liquidity and collateral, it could add complexity on the credit aspects. The same piece of collateral can be used to collateralize exposure multiple times, but only one party could actually claim it in case of a default. Therefore, some regulation explicitly restricts the double usage of collateral as outlined e.g. in the Basel III requirements.

Cross-border / cross asset-class collateral. Making use of cross-border collateral can help when faced with a shortage of collateral in one specific currency or country. FMIs offering cross-border collateral services can enable quick transfer in other currencies to the location where a shortage has occurred (Capel, 2011). In effect, it provides a liquidity bridge across markets, easing collateral constraints and contributing to the efficiency of certain asset markets. The provisioning of this service would come from the (few) FMIs that operate in different currency areas and from global banks, that maintain an efficient network of security accounts and high class global operational services. On the downside, these linkages could create substantial interdependencies and risks to banks and FMIs which have to be taken into full consideration (CPSS, 2012). Especially in times of stress such liquidity mismatches are not so easy to resolve. The last financial crisis highlighted the limitations whereby numerous banks faced challenges in getting liquidity in foreign currency, even though they had ample domestic cash and securities." (Capel, 2011) Consequently a diligent management and transparent approach is required. As there are only a few FMIs that operate in different currency areas, such as CLS and some ICSDs they alone cannot completely solve banks' liquidity mismatches globally.

Auto-collateralization. Auto-collateralization can protect against liquidity risks in certain situations of stress. It allows the purchase of a security to settle, but at the same time moves the security into a repo (or repo-like) structure that generates the cash that is required to facilitate the settlement of the collateral. In other words, by immediately 'repo'ing' the security, the cash that is required to settle the transaction is generated. This mechanism allows a trade to settle even if the market participant does not have the (full) cash available to pay the purchase at that point in time. In such a case, the market participant can pay the cash at a later point within the day and therewith release the security. It de-couples the settlement of the security and the payment of cash by the market participant. Soren Koorsgrad summarizes this perfectly by stating that the "effect of auto-collateralization is to economize on collateral". (Korsgraad, 2012, pp. 4-5)

Improved management and operation of clearing liquidity and collateral. Most large banks already have dedicated teams and systems in place to identify idle collateral, collateral needs and how to match them in the most intelligent way. Intraday cash teams are also in place, identifying settlement and margin needs and ensure payment capacity is available when required (and where required). These functions and underlying systems will become even more important going forward, as operational efficiency directly translates into cost savings (for additional collateral). Furthermore, from a risk management perspective, strict collateral segregation solutions are key. Collateral segregation occurs when a direct member holds two or more separate collateral portfolios with the CCP; one usually for itself and others for its customers. All customers' collateral can be held in a customer omnibus account (consolidated account) or in an individualized (designated) account; in the name of the member tagged with customer. Both protect against the insolvency of other participants as clients' assets are segregated. (IMF, 2010) In the event of a clearing member defaulting, the CCP's clients' segregated positions and collateral will not bear losses as that collateral is not considered part of the insolvency estate. Hence, "a defaulting clearing member is 'ring-fenced' in centrally cleared markets so that its clients are not directly affected." (Deutsche Börse Group, Eurex Clearing, 2014, p. 13)

Potential Responses: Client Solutions

Third party access. In addition to the aforementioned responses that can be taken into account to stabilize a bank's own business, we need to have a look at potential consequences for (agent) banks' clients.

A number of clients of global financial institutions are indirect participants of FMIs requiring the use of direct participants as intermediaries and as such enhanced product solutions need to be developed for them. Banks should have already started identifying which particular challenges their clients potentially face in the new financial market environment and how those as direct members can help shape the FMI's current design so as to prevent any future issues.

Case Study Box: Third Party Access to Clearing Houses

The move from bilateral- to CCP-clearing changes the way market participants interact with each other and changes the risk profiles respectively. Picture1 depicts flows in a bilateral setup. It is more of a decentralized nature and consequently less transparent (if no other measures are taken to increase transparency). Taking out a single nod from the grid mostly impacts the nods that are directly linked. The dotted lines indicate that flows are non-timed, i.e. there is a low intraday liquidity risk attached to them. Picture 2 depicts the flow profile in a CCP-style setup. It is more of a centralized nature, with a central point (the CCP) and therefore more transparent. The impact of taking out a nod depends on which nod gets taken out: (1) Taking out the middle nod (the CCP) essentially stops the entire system, i.e. a central point of failure is created. (2) Taking out one of the directly linked institutions may impact the CCP and will impact the third party participants. Depending on how the third party market operates, this could also represent a significant risk to the third party participants in the event that there is only one link to the CCP with no back up. In this case, the exit of the direct participant will also remove the market access for the third party participant. (3) Taking out a third party participant usually only impacts the direct participant, i.e. no or mitigated impact to the CCP

The solid lines indicate that between the CCP and the direct participant there is a need to settle in a timed or collateralized fashion, whereas the settlement between the participant and the third party may remain non-timed. Compared to the bilateral clearing shown in picture1 this leads to a completely different liquidity/collateral risk-profile, especially for the direct participant; not only is it required to settle the own and the third parties position timed with the CCP, but the required sourcing of liquidity and collateral with the underlying third party may still be non-timed and hence time differences may require the direct participant to pre-fund the exposures intraday.

Figure 2. CCP access of third parties

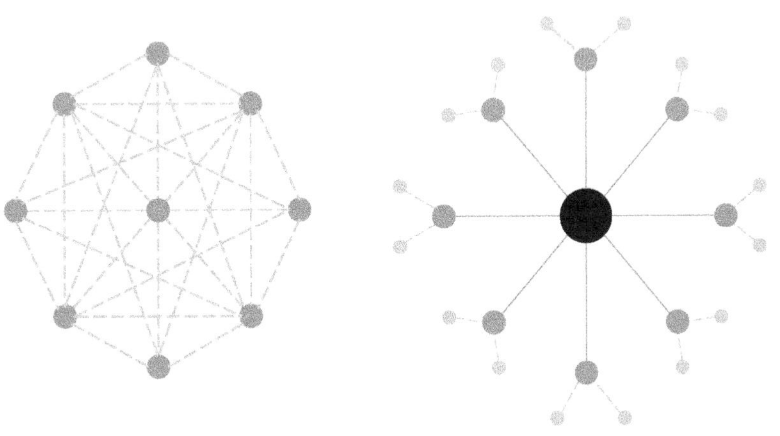

In summary, the centralized set-up in a CCP-style mode helps to improve transparency and find a more robust risk management among the direct participants. However, there are different risks introduced in the event of participants' exits (including a central point of failure). Additionally, the intraday liquidity risk increases. A further, subtle yet very important point is the visibility both of the direct participants flow towards the CCP as well as the direct participant vis-a-vis a third party participant: While in a decentralized set-up a delay or partial fulfilment of the required payment is usually only known by two parties, in a CCP environment the information of a participant not being able to honor the claims is visible immediately. This could be seen as an improvement to detecting issues, but could also increase nervousness in times of stress. Furthermore, in the event that a direct participant decides to no longer support a third party, this is no longer a bilateral conversation but a decision that will be shared with the entire market. Especially in times of stress, this can be seen as a signal that a former partner is now "pulling the plug". As outlined above, there are pro and cons for both solutions. One way to view this is to accept the advantages of the CCP approach and work on mitigating the potential shortcomings. Regarding the credit elements, especially when looking at CCP defaults, a wide-ranging debate is already ongoing. Regarding the liquidity and market visibility aspects, the risks could be mitigated by properly designing the relationships and introduce respective products with each other.

Collateral & liquidity transformation services. Collateral transformation involves the upgrading of collateral to meet CCP-eligible margin. Given the fact that clearing houses are not able to transform collateral, intermediaries will typically fund clients' cash margin requirements in return for lower quality collateral such as corporate bonds where a haircut is applied." (Deutsche Börse Group, Eurex Clearing, 2014, p. 15)

Especially banks that have a surplus in liquidity and high quality collateral could improve returns by transforming these surpluses into collateral of lesser quality through security lending with market participants that require these high quality assets to facilitate clearing and settlement with FMIs. The implications will also be different depending on the type of market participant. In particular, collateral transformation will be costly for participants with near-fully or fully-invested portfolios such as asset managers or pension funds if FMIs pose high restrictions on the collateral (e.g. variation margin in cash only). Furthermore, banks could offer transformation services for their clients, so that the bank faces the FMI with high quality collateral and the underlying client may provide lesser quality collateral (with a haircut), making it easier for smaller players to participate in such markets.

Case Study Box: Collateral transformation & Basel III. CCPs are not able to process collateral transformation on their own. This is carried out by clearing agent banks that transfer daily / intraday margins from and to the CCPs on their behalf. Although it is technically possible to make use of the cash accounts the clients are holding with the agent, the client usually deposits collateral in form of cash or securities with the agent in a separate manner. The agent bank transforms those securities via the repo market into 'CCP-eligible cash'. This kind of liquidity transformation has an impact on the agent bank's liquidity and balance sheet. As a result, additional equity is required by the agent banks in order to underwrite the residual risks. At the same time, they need to make sure that liquidity requirements (LCR and NSFR) are met. "Mandatory segregation of client accounts reduces the scope of collateral reuse, or the offsetting of margin flows from the agent's own trading activities." (DB, 2014, p. 18) Even an agent bank's exposures with their clients or CCPs they have a relationship with are to be considered part of the Basel III leverage ratio. Banks have to calculate these exposures deemed as replacement cost of the contract plus an add-on that reflects the potential change in future exposures of the contract. In other words, because of collateral transformation services, the clearing agent bank has margin cash and repo collateral on its balance sheet which needs to be reflected in the leverage ratio exposure. A potential outcome of this is the reluctance on behalf of clearing agent banks to onboard new clients that have low turnover (cost vs. efficiency). (Source: DB, 2014)

SUMMARY AND OUTLOOK

Summary

FMIs play an important role in the clearing and settlement ecosystem. The concepts have been developed over the last decades and cover a broad range of asset classes from cash, securities and derivatives. FMIs add value by increasing clearing and settlement efficiencies and transparency, while at the same time reducing counterparty settlement risks. The recent financial crisis unveiled how important it is to reduce counterparty settlement risks and improve the transparency in clearing and settlement to provide a sound basis for action in case it is required to unwind the trades of a market participant. Therefore, regulatory bodies around the globe scrutinized FMIs and published various rules that require more business to be traded and cleared via FMIs. At the same time, the FMIs themselves were classified and regulated in a harmonized manner. From a liquidity risk perspective, new standards have been published for FMIs to ensure there are sound liquidity frameworks among them. For their participants, usually commercial banks, the liquidity requirements are generally high for FMIs, especially in intraday liquidity management, as pay-in obligations are required to be fulfilled within a certain time period after the "intraday call". Collateral is generally used to mitigate credit risks and already plays an important role today.

Going forward, with all the focus on additional regulation and oversight, there will be even more emphasis on this topic for FMIs. This, in turn, means that clients of FMIs need to understand all aspects of these developments. Market trends and FMI regulation lead to an increased usage of FMIs and at the same time to tighter liquidity and collateral requirements of FMIs. This leads to a higher requirement of central bank clearing collateral for market participants. At the same time, Basel regulation requires banks to hold more liquid buffers. All these requirements (clearing liquidity, collateral, liquid buffers) are sourced from almost the same sources, as all require being of highest credit quality and highest market liquidity – increasing the demand for these types of assets. It is projected that the supply of such collateral will not cover the increase in demand, which will put pressure on price (i.e. reduce the yield of such collateral). At the same time, regulation on balance sheet leverage limits the usage of balance sheet and therewith turns it into a resource, which banks would want to deploy in the most efficient way. Consequently, clearing liquidity and collateral – with very low yields – are competing with other (potentially more profitable) usages of balance sheet. Potential responses from market participants include increases in efficiencies and client solutions. Efficiencies could be increased through the re-use, cross-border and cross-asset-class use of collateral. The improved management of intraday clearing liquidity and collateral will be key going forward. Improving client solutions could involve the further development of third-party access solutions and collateral transformation services.

Outlook

Focus. In order to determine where to focus next, it is important to understand what point of the "regulatory lifecycle" the industry currently finds itself in. The time since the financial crisis could be broadly clustered as follows: The quarters after the financial turmoil were used to stabilize the system. Thereafter, the situation was analyzed and potential areas of regulation identified. This phase was followed by an intensive global dialogue that led to many iterations of drafting regulation. These were finalized and are translated into legislation which determined implementation timelines. By the time of publication of this book (2015) the majority of regulation relevant for this topic will be either in the legislation process or in implementation, some with future timelines. Certainly we will see adoptions, fine-tuning and new iterations of existing regulation (soon Basel IV will be on the radar screen), but there are signs that the major aspects of regulation have now been dealt with. The industry now has to focus on three issues; (i) the effective and efficient implementation of the regulation, (ii) understanding how all of the different regulations interplay with each other on a global level (and deal with it) and (iii) identifying future client needs - especially when these clients are financial institutions and hence are impacted by the same or similar regulation.

Connecting all the dots. A growing number of banks will participate in FMIs across the globe, either directly or indirectly through clearing banks. It is essential that the financial institutions that participate in and rely on FMIs are able to conduct effective due diligence to understand the risks they face as members, as third parties or as providers of third party services. We have outlined in this chapter that risks do not only relate to credit, but could also include collateral and intraday liquidity implications. Appropriate steps have to be taken by all involved to understand and mitigate those risks. When all regulatory requirements have been translated into local law and are put to the test, it will become apparent if there is global consistency among all requirements or whether it causes regulatory disharmonies.

Collaboration. The solution lies in collaboration. Collaboration among all parties involved. It is the FMIs', banks', regulatory authorities' and policy makers' responsibility to shape the changes today to align and adapt efficiently to further prevent and mitigate future issues. We have seen that when banks face mutual industry-wide challenges, they frequently develop solutions jointly or come together as an advocating unit. This has brought material benefits that banks would otherwise have been unable to achieve independently. Considerable work has been undertaken by market players to demystify the complex playing field. Engagement and collaboration are not always easy. They require information sharing, debate and consensus amongst institutions that are often clients, competitors and peers at the same time. Collaboration is (almost) a pre-requisite to lower costs, to create greater efficiencies, mitigate risks and also to set new industry standards. This will not only build a healthier industry, but also deliver benefits for the clients of today and tomorrow. Nevertheless, further efforts are needed to be able to cope with defaults, to address risks associated with changes in market structures, and to remove cross-border differences in regulation to ensure cross-border consistency on a global level. (Coeuré, 2014) The dilemma is that financial market infrastructures have a high degree of independency and therefore, unless there is consistency and common purpose across various markets, the risk of dislocation will always prevail. And it is not unreasonable to suggest that what provides safety and security today may not be fit for purpose tomorrow in a rapidly changing market.

Knights in shining armour. Our "knights in shining armour" ensure the efficient and smooth functioning of financial markets. However, they are also a key institutional channel for risk concentration and market disruptions. In order for FMIs to be able to retain the title "knights in shining armour" it is fundamentally important to jointly ensure their right set-up and smooth functioning. FMIs are the latest chapter of the clearing and settlement saga, but they will not be the last. The re-positioning of FMIs addresses various issues experienced throughout the recent financial turmoil. However, as outlined in this chapter, these changes will create the need to focus on and improve other areas. Furthermore, new and developing types of financial products and instruments may lead to new payment, clearing and settlement operations and systems in the future. Consequently, there is a need to fully understand and manage the resulting risks. Stay tuned!

The chapter is published by the authors in their own capacity, i.e. it does not represent the view of the institution they are working in.

REFERENCES

Anderson, S., Dion, J.P., & Perez-Saiz, H. (2013, May). To link or not to link? Netting and exposures between central counterparties. *Journal of Financial Market Infrastructures,* 1(4), 3-29.

Baker, S. (2012). Clearing houses: failure not an option. *Financial News*. Retrieved from http://www.efinancialnews.com/story/2012-04-16/clearing-houses-failure-not-an-option?ea9c8a2de0ee11104560 1ab04d673622

Barank, J. (2013). *Financial Market utilities and Key Financial Market Infrastructure Elements*. Nova Science Publishers.

Capel, J. (2011, March). Banks' international liquidity management in the future: What role can financial market infrastructures play? *Journal of Payments Strategy & Systems*, *5*(1), 1.

Coeuré, B. (2014, January 23). Risks in CCPs. Proceedings of "Mapping and Monitoring the Financial System: Liquidity, Funding, and Plumbing". Financial Research & Financial Stability Oversight Council. http://www.ecb.europa.eu/press/key/date/2014/html/sp140331.en.html

CSD Factbook. (2013). ECSDA. Brussels, Belgium.

How Regulation Will Reshape FX and Rates Markets: Part 3. [Special Report]. (2014, July 24). *Deutsche Bank Markets Research.*

Deutsche Börse Group. Eurex Clearing (Eds.) (2014). How central counterparties strengthen the safety and integrity of financial markets.

Links between Security Settlement Systems. (2014). European Central Bank. Retrieved from http://www.ecb.europa.eu/paym/coll/coll/ssslinks/html/index.en.html

Recovery and Resolution Planning: Making the Key Attributes Requirements Operational. (2012, November). *Financial Stability Board.*

Making over-the counter-derivatives safer: the role of central counterparties. (April, 2010). *International Monetary Fund.*

Korsgraad, S. (2012, Fall). Auto-collateralization as a liquidity-saving mechanism. *Journal of Financial Market Infrastructures*, 1(1), 2-27.

Lee, R. (2011). *Running the World's Markets. The Governance of Financial Infrastructure.*

Levels. A& Capel, J. (2012, Fall). Is collateral becoming scarce? Evidence for the euro area. *Journal of Financial Market Infrastructures*, 1(1), 29-53.

Maijoor, S. (2014, May 7). Keynote *Speech. The reform of financial markets: halfway there*. Proceedings of AFME European Post-Trade Conference, London.

Norman, P. (2008). *Plumbers and Visionaries*. Securities Settlement and Europe's Financial Market.

Norman, P. (2012). *The Risk Controllers*. Central Counterparty Clearing in Globalised Financial Markets.

Principles for Financial Market Infrastructures. (2012Committee on Payment & Settlement Systems. Basel, Switzerland: Bank for International Settlements.

Rehlon, A. (2013). Central counterparties: What are they, why do they matter and how does the Bank supervise them? *Quarterly Bulletin*, Q2-2013.

Russo, D. (2013, April). CPSS-IOSCO principles for financial market infrastructures: vectors of international convergence. European Central Bank. Banque de France. *Financial Stability Review, 17.*

APPENDIX: ABBREVIATIONS

ATS Alternative Trading Systems
CCP Central Counterparties
CPSS Committee on Payment & Settlement Systems
CSD Central Securities Depositories
Dodd-Frank Act Dodd–Frank Wall Street Reform and Consumer Protection Act
ECB European Central Bank
ECN Electronic Communication Networks
ECSDA European Central Securities Depository Association
EMIR European Market Infrastructure Regulation
FMI Financial Market Infrastructures
FSB Financial Stability Board
ICSD International Central Securities Depository
IMF International Monetary Fund
IOSCO International Organization of Securities Commission
LCR Liquidity Coverage Ratio
MiFID 2 Markets in Financial Instruments Directive
MTF Multilateral Trading Facilities
NSFR Net Stable Funding Ratio
OCC Options Clearing Corporation
OTC Over the Counter
PFMI Principles for Financial Market Infrastructures
PS Payment System
PTS Proprietary Trading Systems
RRP Recovery & Resolution Plans
SSS Securities Settlement Systems
TR Trade Repositories

Section 2

Tools and Applications for Analyzing Financial Market Infrastructures

Chapter 5
Exploiting Parallelization to Increase the Performance of Payment Systems Simulations

Tatu Antero Laine
Bank of Finland, Finland

Kasperi Korpinen
Bank of Finland, Finland

ABSTRACT

The large amount of data and the need to perform large numbers of simulations of payment systems are a challenge and a starting point for this paper. Parallel and distributed simulation systems are widely used in many applications such as in military applications and entertainment. Parallel computing has been applied in other econometric areas such as VAR models but not in payment system simulations. In this empirical paper, a reduction in total execution times of payment system simulations is studied by exploiting computational parallelization in a one multicore PC environment. The preliminary results of parallel simulations are reported and the possible benefits of analyzing financial market infrastructures using this technique are discussed. This information can be very useful for choosing a parallelization strategy and designing the next generation platforms for parallel processing of payment and securities settlement system simulations. This is the first time parallel computing techniques have been applied to payment system simulations.

INTRODUCTION

Payment and settlement systems are a crucial part of financial market infrastructures (FMIs) (Kokkola, 2010; Manning, Nier & Schanz, 2009). Since 2000 the resilience of FMIs, including payment systems, has attracted increasing attention (BIS, 2001; BIS, 2011). A payment system is a network that links market players together and supports other FMIs such as securities settlement systems and central counterparties (BIS, 2008). It is important to study the effects of defaulting participants and how these effects spread in the network. The authorities also want to know how the resilience of payment systems can be

DOI: 10.4018/978-1-4666-8745-5.ch005

further improved. This is a challenging task, as payment system networks are often large and complex. Payment system simulations have proven their usefulness in testing and studying the robustness of payment systems (Diehl, 2013; Heijmans & Heuver, 2013; Laine, Korpinen & Hellqvist, 2013). Payment systems research covers stress testing in respect of participants in the payment system (Bedford, Millard, & Yang, 2005; ECB, 2013), liquidity saving mechanisms (LVMs) (Galbiati & Soramäki, 2013; Norman, 2010; McLafferty & Denbee, 2013), and development of new features in the payment system (Koponen & Soramäki, 1998; Imakubo & McAndrews, 2007).

There seems to be an increased interest in operative economical monitoring (BIS, 2012). Payment system simulations can assist in this work. As the number of scenarios to be run increases and the delivery time requirements shrink, something needs to be done to meet the growing challenges. Especially for stress testing, the set band of required scenarios and assessment frequencies tend to increase. This means that our simulation techniques need to be improved. In some of the largest large value payment systems (LVPS) a hundred thousand transactions are processed each day, and the participants amount to thousands. The overseers and operators of such a system are interested in liquidity issues, stress tests on participants, and the testing of new features of the payment system. Obviously, a critical payment system has high requirements for timely analysis and the large amount of data-specific challenges for simulations. The processing time of serial simulations increases rapidly with the number of simulation days and the number of stress test scenarios. The number of stress test scenarios can be in the thousands if they are performed for all participants individually, and the total simulation time can be several weeks.

Parallel and distributed simulation systems are widely used to speed up computation times in many communities such as in high-performance computing communities, defense communities and interactive gaming and internet communities (Fujimoto, 2000). In this study we explore the applicability of parallelization approaches to payment system simulations. The aim is to show that payment and securities settlement systems' total simulation times can be improved by parallelizing the execution of simulations. This is the first time the parallel computing technique has been applied to payment system simulations.

SIMULATING PAYMENT SYSTEMS

Factors Affecting Payment and Securities Settlement Simulation Performance

Except for communication protocols between participants and operators, the parts that consume the most processing time in simulations are likely to be the same as in live systems. This is because the phenomenon being simulated is physically analogous to the software used for the simulations. As the financial sector becomes digitalized, more and more of its occurrences in real life occur in computer software algorithmic form. In this context, simulating a payment system is analogous to running a live system. Specially, the core parts of the settlement processes in live systems are physically highly similar to their simulator models, depending on the replication accuracy and chosen method.

A general observation made based on the payment system simulation is that computational execution times increase as liquidity shrinks and netting algorithms are used more. This is not exactly the same phenomenon known as the liquidity delay tradeoff, discussed in the literature (Koponen & Soramäki, 1998; Leinonen & Soramäki, 1999; Arjani, 2007). In the context of the liquidity delay tradeoff, payment delay is observed because settlements in real time and gross bases are not possible due to liquidity constraints. It should be noted that increasing execution times for netting algorithms are also likely to cause delays in the settlement of payments. Here the extension of execution times of netting algorithms in the function of increasing amounts of queued payments is of interest. This is a natural outcome, as the most challenging computational tasks relate to netting algorithms. The concept of netting algorithm refers here to any transaction-settling algorithm that uses some form of netting when seeking a combination of queued transactions that can be settled. Netting algorithms may include eg gridlock resolution algorithms, partial net settlement algorithms, bilateral offsetting algorithms, and queue release algorithms.

The total processing time used by netting algorithms will depend on how often they are run, how they are implemented, and the number of queued payments included in the netting. Gridlock resolution problems (Güntzer, Jungnickel & Leclerc, 1998) are a form of the classic knapsack problem of combinatorial optimatization (Papadimitirou, 1994). The topology of the payment network of the payments involved also affects the performance of netting algorithms and define the complexity of the optimization problem. Different algorithms perform differently with different payment topologies (Renault & Pecceu, 2007). For example, in situations where relationships between accounts are mainly reciprocal, bilateral netting algorithms are likely to perform better. In cases where payment flows form rings involving more than two accounts, bilateral netting algorithms are likely to be less efficient. Netting algorithms can be optimized for certain kinds of payment topologies.

In regular scenario cases, where liquidity is abundant, payments are settled quickly, often directly at entry without any netting. In these cases Database (DB) operations account for a significant part of the total processing times. The time used by data base operations is however relatively stable by nature, as these are simple read-and-write operations. The number of rows to be fetched or written to the DB do not vary significantly as liquidity changes or between scenarios based on the same data.

The variables that increase processing time are the numbers of transactions and accounts involved in the scenarios to be simulated, the topology of the payment network, the scarcity of liquidity, and the complexity of the netting algorithms. For example, scarcity of liquidity leads to queuing of payments, thus putting pressure on queue resolution mechanisms. This is the case especially in stress scenarios. The performance of netting algorithms will depend on their optimality in computing netting solutions for the specific network topology of the transactions included in the simulation.

On Improving Simulation Execution Times

Computational through-put times can be shortened in many ways. It is possible to switch to more performing hardware, better processors or more memory, for example. These types of improvements, the computational burden being unchanged, naturally improve the execution times of simulations. However, there seem to be limits on how fast computers can be taken in to use. The faster a computer is, the more costly it is likely to be, and the technology also imposes its limits.

Data simplifications are also one approach that has been proposed. For example, Heuver proposes to omit small payments and concentrate more on aggregated values and volumes (Heuver, in press). This approach reduces computation times by reducing the number of transactions to be computed. Another example of data and model simplification are classical economic models in general, where the workings of the whole economy are simplified as a set of equations.

The main motivation for this study came largely from the results obtained in other projects at the Bank of Finland. In these other projects, computational parallelization was used in the estimation of empirical vector autoregression (VAR) models used at Bank of Finland (Gulan, Haavio & Kilponen, 2014; Luoto, 2014). For this purpose, a farm of distributed second-hand servers was built with almost zero hardware investment cost. The main costs were due to the Techila software solution managing the computer farm (Techila, 2009). In this solution the tasks were distributed over a farm of servers specially made available by the Bank of Finland for such purposes. In those applications the total time of the concurrent calculations is scaled down in line with CPU (Core Processing Unit) availability. The VAR model estimations showed that speed-up factors of several hundreds were achieved. This means that some computations that otherwise would have taken many hours actually, took only a few minutes. This naturally raised a strong incentive to try to apply a similar approach to payments and securities system simulations and to take advantage of the available cloud computing environment at the Bank of Finland.

Thus it seems that, instead of improving the processing speed of a processing unit, which after a certain limit is even technically impossible, it is more feasible to achieve faster performance by performing computational tasks in parallel. But the potential gains to be achieved via the parallelization approach depend on the share of parallelizable computational tasks in all the processes involved. This issue will be developed further in the next chapter

Identifying Parallelizable Parts of the Process

There are different alternatives as to how and on what level parallelization can be done, and in some cases where tasks are dependent on the order of results, parallelization cannot be applied. Actually, the BoF-PSS2 -simulator (Leinonen & Soramäki, 2003) used for this study, already uses parallelization to some extent. The database engine is naturally run in different computational threads, as the software is different, and the parallelism is then managed by the operating system. The simulator itself uses parallelism in its DB writing operations by executing them in separate threads. This is possible because the simulation processes are not logically dependent on the progress of the DB writing operations.

Payment system simulations belong to the field of analytic discrete events based simulations (Fujimoto, 2000). Further parallelization of the simulation processes requires first the identification of the parallelizable logical processes (LP) (Fujimoto, 2000). Parallelization can be separated into two types: data parallelism and task parallelism. Data parallelism is a form of parallelism in which the same tasks are performed on different data sets. Task parallelism is a form of parallelization where different tasks are performed in parallel, possibly on same data (Culler, Pal Singh & Gupta, 1997). Data parallelism is used here in the VAR model example.

Parallelization of individual procedures is possible if the procedures performed later in the simulation are not dependent on the output of the procedures performed in earlier stages of the simulation. The payment and securities settlement simulations seem to be non-parallelizable on an intraday level. This is because the intraday variables are dependent on the order of realization of prior events. For example the settlement of a payment will affect the account balance and thus will affect the prospects for further settlements occurring later. Theoretically at least a form of data parallelism is possible intraday if the payments form two or more disconnected independent networks. This option will not be investigated further here. Also some kind of task parallelism could be envisaged for searching for netting solutions. This would depend on the netting logics used. If the netting logics are such that several independent attempts are made to find a solution and they follow a predictable algorithmic path, it might be possible to parallelize the execution of these different attempts, and arrive at the solution faster. To our knowledge it is not easy to estimate whether some of the iterative atonement processes used in netting could be parallelized, but there is a chance that it might be.

The idea of parallelizing the execution of netting and gridlock resolution algorithms is novel to our understanding and has serious potential for real world applications. Accepting the fact that parallelization of existing netting logics is not self-evident, nothing prevents the designing of new ones or using old ones in a way that exploits parallelism. This approach would fall into the category of task parallelism. The idea would be to seek netting solutions for the same data set using different heuristics at the same time. At the end of an agreed netting period the different netting, solutions would be compared and the best ones would be booked.

As payment and securities system simulations can be multiday simulations, the parallelizability at day level will depend on whether the simulations are run with independence between days, e.g. the beginning-of-day balance might be set at the end-of-day balance of the previous day.

After parallelization of the processing by days inside an independent multiday simulation, the next level of parallelization would be the whole simulation, including one or multiple days. Parallelization of whole simulations can be done in two ways: either by running several simulator applications in parallel (the *replicated trials* approach) *(Fujimoto, 2000),* or by developing the BoF-PSS2 -simulator to enable the running of simulations in different threads at the same time inside one application. Here the form of parallelism is data parallelism - at the whole simulator level.

To implement the experiment of this study, a decision must be made on how to implement the parallelization. First the hardware options available were considered. Practically, the available options were the use of a multicore PC's or the cloud computing environment available at the Bank of Finland and used in the computing of VAR models. In other words, either one parallel computer with shared memory multiprocessors or distributed computers (Fujimoto, 2000). The difference in hardware costs was insignificant, as the cloud of computers was available free of charge and a new multiprocessor desktop PC would cost only a few thousand euros. Next the significant difference between these two hardware approaches in terms of needed code changes was evaluated. In this experiment a solution that would be compatible with the distributed computers hardware setup approach was also important, since the largest amount of CPU's is available only via clouds of computers. Another important factor to take into account, is that the simulations were to use the same database as in the final results of different scenarios. Otherwise, the results of the simulations would have to be brought back into the same analysis environment.

The code implementation cost analysis showed that the cheapest option was to perform the experiment by running simulator applications in parallel. This would leave the BoF-PSS2 -simulator code relatively unchanged compared to the approach where simulations would have been run in different threads inside the simulation application. Moreover, the running of several applications in the parallel approach is compatible with the approach that would have to be used with an infrastructure of distributed computers. Implementing the possibility to compute independent days of one multiday scenario in parallel is not at odds with the approaches above and could be implemented in addition. The implementation would have complicated the coding and from the experimental point of view would not have generated significant additional information at this point.

CONFIGURATION OF EXPERIMENTS

The parallel POC (proof of concept) was realized on a desktop PC with 32 CPUs with 64G of RAM. The hardware corresponds to the shared-memory multiprocessors environment described in (Fujimoto, 2000). The operating system was Windows 7 and the database was MySQL. Parallelization of simulations was implemented by running multiple instances of the payment system simulator in server mode. All simulator instances were configured to use the same project database for reading scenario data and writing the results. Only one database engine, MySQL, was running on the PC. The simulator instances were started one second before starting the execution of simulations. The simulator instances and simulations were started consecutively with a lag of 0.1 second between them.

The experiment was performed with artificial data and a system setup corresponding to fairly complex hybrid LVPS. The aim was to see how the total simulation time decreases when the scared liquidity limits direct settlement and a larger portion of payments go via netting logic. The amount of data written in output tables and files was minimized. As a reference, one simulation was executed in which the output statistics were not written at all, the reason being to separate the times between simulations and database operations.

One simulation included a transaction data set, participant data set, opening daily balances and intraday credit limits. Here the total initial liquidity is defined as the sum of opening daily balances and intraday credit limits. In the first experiment the simulations in serial and in parallel mode were executed with participants having unlimited access to intraday credit.

In the second experiment the same parallel simulation as described above was executed, but the output results are not written to the database (DB). In this way one can estimate the extent to which data base operations increase the total time of the simulations.

In the third experiment the upper bound (UB) of the liquidity was defined for the given setup (Leinonen & Soramäki, 2003). Then the liquidity corresponding to the upper bound was divided by a factor of two and a factor of four to see how the effect of the squeezed liquidity appears in the total simulation times of the concurrent simulations. The simulations (UB/2 and UB/4) were then executed in serial and in parallel mode. These results are compared with the unstressed situation, i.e. with the first experiment.

Even though the simulations used the same input data, for each concurrent simulation the transaction datasets were multiplied and given distinctive dataset ID's. This was to prevent the database engine from reusing results from previous executions of the same data base queries, which would have reduced the execution times.

These simulations were run in parallel with the different liquidity levels (see above) and by changing the number of simulations run at the same time.

RESULTS

We clocked 33 seconds for one simulation, which comes to nearly, 28 minutes if 50 independent simulations are run in a serial mode (black dots in Figure 1). The total simulation time is defined to be the time elapsed from the start of the first simulation to the end of the last simulation run in parallel.

In the first experiment the parallel simulations were run in increments of five parallel simulations. From Figure 1 (black squares) it can be seen that the total simulation times for different numbers of simulations run in parallel are better than in the serial simulations (black dots). With 50 parallel simulations, the total simulation time decreases to 12 minutes from 28 minutes of the serial execution. This linear increase of the total simulation times as a function of parallel simulations is due to serial database operations of concurrent simulations. The writing of simulation results to one database takes more time as the number of parallel simulations increases and more simulations try to write results to the same

Figure 1. Comparison between serial and parallel simulation total times. Simulations were run in parallel with the different liquidity levels and by changing the number of simulations run at the same time.

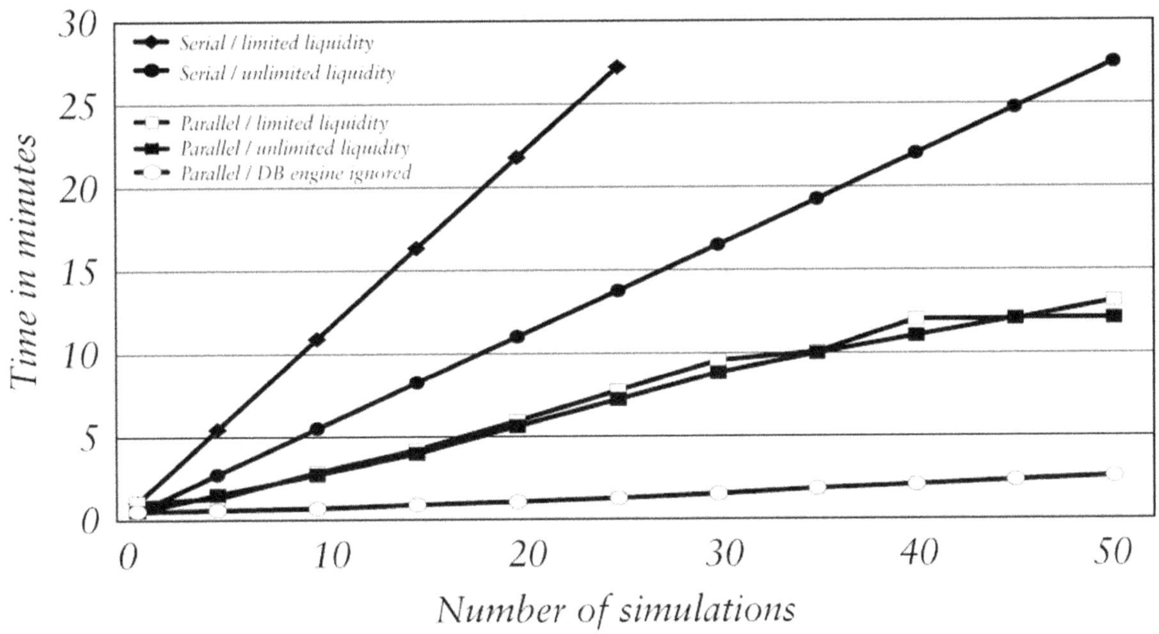

database at the same time. The improvement factor of the total simulation time between serial (black dots) and parallel (black squares) mode is two.

In the second experiment the database operations were instructed as in a normal runtime setup, but the write instructions were not executed (white dots in Figure 1). From the figure it can be seen that with 50 parallel simulations, one fifth of the total simulation time is spent on simulation execution (close to 3 minutes) and the rest (9 minutes) is used for writing results to the database. From the Figure 1 it can be concluded that without database writing operations the simulations benefit much more from parallelization.

The third experiment was the same as the first one except that the system liquidity was squeezed to half of the UB liquidity (not shown in figure 1) and to one quarter of the UB liquidity (white squares in figure 1). Both of these experiments (UB/2 and UB/4) were executed in serial and in parallel mode. From the point of view of the simulation setup this means that less payments are settled immediately and more payments are processed via netting algorithms. From our earlier experiments it is known that this usually leads to longer execution times of simulations, as there are more transactions in queues and burdening the netting algorithms. This experiment shows that the squeezing of total system liquidity from UB levels to one quarter differs only slightly (white squares in figure 1) from the case with unlimited liquidity (black squares in figure 1) in parallel mode. However, in the case of (UB/4) the improvement factor for the total simulation time between serial (black diamonds in figure 1) and parallel mode (white squares in figure 1) was four.

DISCUSSION

The main result of this work is that with the given hardware setup parallel simulations could be run approximately two times faster than in a serial mode in the benchmark case. In the case of squeezed liquidity, the improvement factor is actually four as between serial and parallel simulations. The database operations take 80% of simulation time and the execution of the simulations 20%, when the simulations are executed in parallel. The share of time used for database write operations seems to grow with the amount of parallel simulations. The experiment shows that when the initial liquidities (intraday credit values) are reduced to one-fourth of upper bound values the total simulation time remains same, i.e. close to 12 minutes in parallel mode. However, the total simulation time of the serial execution in the case of the squeezed liquidity is almost double compared with the benchmark case. This results in an overall improvement factor of four when the execution times are compared for serial and parallel simulations.

This novel experiment opens up further investigation paths. In the given hardware setup one could try to build and analyze simulations that are closer to real stress test exercises. The performance of the simulator is dependent on the network topology of the transaction datasets, the system setup, the hardware and the software environment in which the simulations are run. Therefore, the results obtained from this experiment must be taken as indicative. The speed-up factors differ from one environment to another. Also, the optimal amount of simulations allowed to be run in parallel is highly dependent on the environment and hardware setup. This means that for every specific environment and simulated system, the optimal setup should be evaluated separately. Earlier experiments indicate that more there are payments in queue, the larger the execution times for netting algorithms. In this experiment, even when the UB levels of liquidity were cut to one-fourth, the simulation execution times did not change significantly and the remaining total simulation time was dominated by database writing operations. This means that if this experiment is repeated with real data, with larger data amounts and a more realistic system setup, the execution times could react more strongly to a reduction in initial liquidity by reducing either the opening daily balances or intraday credit limits. From this novel experiment with artificial data it can be concluded that the benchmark simulation and the simulations with squeezed liquidity produce almost the same results and that the serial database writing operations seem to limit the achievable benefits of parallelization.

The next problem to resolve is how to manage large amounts of data in payment system simulations in parallel mode. It should be studied how to optimize the database structure used by the simulator. The first step is to minimize the amount of output data to be written. The output database should only contain information that is calculated during the simulation, otherwise indexes should be used and should link the output items to the input table and save only the indexes in order to minimize the amount of data to be written to the output database. The second step is to have only one master input database for transaction data. The different scenarios of the stress test exercise can be stored separately with a subset of the master data being used in an actual simulation execution phase. This means the multiplication of the original master transaction data is avoided.

The broader question is how to optimize the database structure of the payment system simulator to better serve reporting with large amounts of underlying data. The end-user often needs to send queries to the output database. These queries typically build an indicator across many simulation output tables. It is known from other large data applications that star base data structures provide a good foundation for reporting and analytical tools such as OLAP (Online Analytical Processing) cubes. It should be studied whether the OLAP cubes could assist end-users in utilizing the results of the simulations more efficiently.

CONCLUSION

This work shows that the payment system simulator can be run in concurrent mode if the parallelization is done via concurrent instances of the simulator. Fifty simulations can be run in parallel with the given hardware setup without any significant slowdown in performance. The total execution time is about two (benchmark case) to four (scarced liquidity case) times faster in parallel than in serial mode if the output statistics are written to the output database. The total execution time is around 10 times faster if the output statistics are not written to the database. The results show that writing the results to the output database is the next bottleneck if simulations are run in parallel mode. This result indicates that there is much room for improvement in the future. The data management of output results must be improved, and the possibility of moving the database server to a separate higher-performance machine should be studied.

This experiment is interesting also because it is technically analogous to the approach where parallelization is performed not only on one powerful multicore PC (parallel computers) but over a network of computational environments (distributed computers). This methodology can also be used to optimize the ratio of parallel simulations per amount of CPU, memory and hard disk space. The role of data base connections and the organization of data storage is another important and interesting topic. It can be concluded that the data storage model has a dominant effect on the performance of simulations, especially when the results of parallel simulations are written to a common database.

REFERENCES

Arjani, N. M. (2007). Examining the tradeoff between settlement delay and intraday liquidity in Canada's LVTS: a simulation approach. In H. Leinonen (Ed.), *Simulation studies of liquidity needs, risks and efficiency in payment networks* (pp. 87–121). Bank of Finland Publications.

Bedford, P., Millard, S., & Yang, J. (2005). Analysing the impact of operational incidents in large-value payment systems: a simulation approach. In H. Leinonen (Ed.), *Liquidity, risks and speed in payment and settlement systems – a simulation approach* (pp. 247–274). Bank of Finland Publications.

Core principles for systemically important payment systems. (2001, January). *Bank for International Settlements*. Retrieved from http://www.bis.org/publ/cpss43.pdf

The interdependencies of payment and settlement systems. (2008, June). *Bank for International Settlements.* Retrieved from http://www.bis.org/publ/cpss84.pdf

Principles for financial market infrastructures – consultative report. (2011, March). *Bank for International Settlements.* Retrieved from http://www.bis.org/publ/cpss94.pdf

Monitoring indicators for intraday liquidity management. (2012, July). *Bank for International Settlements.* Retrieved from http://www.bis.org/publ/bcbs225.pdf

Culler, D., Pal Singh, J., & Gupta, A. (1997). *Parallel computer architecture: A hardware / software approach.* Morgan Kaufmann Publishers.

Diehl, M. (2013). The Use of Simulations as an Analytical Tool for Payment Systems. In B. Alexandrova-Kabadjova, S. Martinez-Jaramillo, A. Garcia-Almanza, & E. Tsang (Eds.), *Simulation in Computational Finance and Economics: Tools and Emerging Applications* (pp. 29–45). Hershey, PA: Business Science Reference; doi:10.4018/978-1-4666-2011-7.ch002

The TARGET2 simulator. (2013, December). *Target Newsletter*, 7. Retrieved from https://www.ecb.europa.eu/paym/t2/shared/pdf/newsletter/TARGET_Newsletter_issue_number_7.pdf

Fujimoto, R. M. (2000). *Parallel and distributed simulation systems*. John Wiley & Sons, Inc Publications.

Galbiati, M., & Soramäki, K. (2013). Liquidity Saving Mechanisms and Bank Behavior in Payment Systems. In B. Alexandrova-Kabadjova, S. Martinez-Jaramillo, A. Garcia-Almanza, & E. Tsang (Eds.), *Simulation in Computational Finance and Economics: Tools and Emerging Applications* (pp. 103–119). Hershey, PA: Business Science Reference; doi:10.4018/978-1-4666-2011-7.ch006

Gulan, A., Haavio, M., & Kilponen, J. (in press). From Finnish great depression to great recession. *Bank of Finland Publications.*

Güntzer, M. M., Jungnickel, D., & Leclerc, M. (1998). Efficient algorithms for the clearing of interbank payments. *European Journal of Operational Research*, *106*(1), 212–219. doi:10.1016/S0377-2217(97)00265-8

Heijmans, R., & Heuver, R. (2013). Preparing Simulations in Large Value Payment Systems using Historical Data. In B. Alexandrova-Kabadjova, S. Martinez-Jaramillo, A. Garcia-Almanza, & E. Tsang (Eds.), *Simulation in Computational Finance and Economics: Tools and Emerging Applications* (pp. 46–68). Hershey, PA: Business Science Reference; doi:10.4018/978-1-4666-2011-7.ch003

Heuver, R. (in press). Compressing the number of transactions in order to increase performance of simulations. *Bank of Finland Publications.*

Imakubo, K., & McAndrews, J. J. (2007). Funding levels for the new accounts in BOJ-NET. In H. Leinonen (Ed.), *Simulation studies of liquidity needs, risks and efficiency in payment networks* (pp. 123–148). Bank of Finland Publications.

Kokkola, T. (Ed.). (2010). *The Payment System.* European Central Bank Publications.

Koponen, R., & Soramäki, K. (1998). *Intraday liquidity needs in a modern interbank payment system – a simulation approach.* Bank of Finland Publications. Retrieved from http://www.suomenpankki.fi/fi/julkaisut/tutkimukset/erillisjulkaisut/ Pages/E14.aspx

Laine, T., Korpinen, K., & Hellqvist, M. (2013). Simulation Approaches to Risk, Efficiency, and Liquidity Usage in Payment Systems. In B. Alexandrova-Kabadjova, S. Martinez-Jaramillo, A. Garcia-Almanza, & E. Tsang (Eds.), *Simulation in Computational Finance and Economics: Tools and Emerging Applications* (pp. 69–83). Hershey, PA: Business Science Reference; doi:10.4018/978-1-4666-2011-7.ch004

Leinonen, H., & Soramäki, K. (1999). Optimizing liquidity usage and settlement speed in payment systems. Bank of Finland Publications. Retrieved from http://www.suomenpankki.fi/fi/julkaisut/tutkimukset/keskustelualoitteet/Pages/dp1999_16.aspx

Leinonen, H., & Soramäki, K. (2003). Simulating interbank payment and securities settlement mechanisms with the BoF-PSS2 simulator. Bank of Finland Publications. Retrieved from http://www.suomenpankki.fi/fi/julkaisut/tutkimukset/keskustelualoitteet/Documents/0323.pdf

Luoto, J. (in press). An adaptive sequential Monte Carlo sampler for DSGE models. *Bank of Finland Publications.*

Manning, M., Nier, E., & Schanz, J. (2009). *The economics of large-value payments and settlement: theory and policy issues for central banks.* Oxford University Press.

McLafferty, J., & Denbee, E. (2013). Liquidity Saving in CHAPS: A Simulation Study. In B. Alexandrova-Kabadjova, S. Martinez-Jaramillo, A. Garcia-Almanza, & E. Tsang (Eds.), *Simulation in Computational Finance and Economics: Tools and Emerging Applications* (pp. 120–142). Hershey, PA: Business Science Reference; doi:10.4018/978-1-4666-2011-7.ch007

Norman, B. (2010). *Liquidity saving in real-time gross settlement systems – an overview. Bank of England Financial Stability Paper, 7,* 1–11. Bank of England Publications.

Papadimitriou, C. H. (1994). *Computational Complexity*. Addison Wesley.

Renault, F., & Pecceu, J. B. (2007). From PNS to TARGET2: the cost of FIFO in RTGS payment system. In H. Leinonen (Ed.), *Simulation studies of liquidity needs, risks and efficiency in payment networks* (pp. 43-85). Bank of Finland Publications.

TecHiLa Technologies. (2009). http://www.techila.fi/wp-content/uploads/2010/07/Tampere_University_of_Technology.pdf

Chapter 6
Using FMI Transaction Data in Simulations:
Less Is More?

Richard Heuver
De Nederlandsche Bank, The Netherlands

Ronald Heijmans
De Nederlandsche Bank, The Netherlands

ABSTRACT

In this chapter the authors provide a method to aggregate large value payment system transaction data for executing simulations with the Bank of Finland payment simulator. When transaction data sets get large, simulation may become too time consuming in terms of computer power. Therefore, insufficient data from a statistical point of view can be processed. The method described in this chapter provides a solution to this statistical problem. In order to work around this problem the authors provide a method to aggregate transaction data set in such a way that it does not compromise the outcome of the simulation significantly. Depending on the type of simulations only a few business days or up to a year of data is required. In case of stress scenario analysis, in which e.g. liquidity position of banks deteriorates, long time series are preferred as business days can differ substantially. As an example this chapter shows that aggregating all low value transactions in the Dutch part of TARGET2 will not lead to a significantly different simulation outcome.

INTRODUCTION

The financial crisis, starting in the summer of 2007, made it clear that the liquidity position of financial institutions (like banks and insurance companies) can deteriorate quickly. When Lehman Brothers collapsed in the fall of 2008 a severe shock went through the whole financial system. The impact was tangible way beyond the direct counterparties of Lehman Brothers. As a result of this collapse distrust in financial markets increased substantially, see e.g. Arciero, Heijmans, Heuver, Massarenti, Picillo and Vacirca (2013) for the European unsecured money market.

DOI: 10.4018/978-1-4666-8745-5.ch006

Financial institution settle many of their obligations in so called Financial Market Infrastructures (FMIs). These obligations can either be on behalf of their own business or of their customers (such as, businesses, consumers, governmental organizations or other financial institutions). In other words FMIs facilitate the settlement of many economic processes. Due to their importance for the economy FMIs have to live up to high standards. These standards are called the Principles For Financial Market Infrastructures (PFMIs), CPSS (2012).

An important sort of FMI are payment systems and among them is Real Time Gross Settlement (RTGS) systems.[1] These systems are often offered by central banks. The key features of an RTGS system are that each payment is executed individually and with finality. Finality means that as soon as a payment is processed by the system it cannot be revoked anymore, not even in case of bankruptcy. Each currency area in the industrialized world has its own system. In the euro area this system is called TARGET2, in the US this is Fedwire and in the UK this is CHAPS. The receiving institution can reuse the liquidity immediately again to fulfil its own financial obligations. Over the last years RTGS systems provide additional functionality, like sorting within waiting queues, re-entry of rejected payments, bilateral limits and so on. These features intend to speed up the settlement in case payments end up in the queue. This happens when insufficient liquidity is available. In a (pure) RTGS these payments would remain in the queue until sufficient liquidity is received from other financial institutions. The paying institutions could also bring in more collateral, which it can use for intraday credit.[2]

An often used method to analyze behavior, liquidity risk, credit risk and the efficiency of the payment system is simulation. The Bank of Finland developed a software tool that imitates several large value payment system, of which the RTGS is an example. As input the tool needs to know at least the system's characteristics, the participants that are active in the payment system and the individual transactions. Besides, it allows for setting the beginning of day balance (the available liquidity at the account at the beginning of the day) and the potential credit line (the maximum negative balance that is allowed). For a detailed description of the simulator tool see Leinonen and Soramäki (2005). In the remainder of this chapter the authors mean by "the simulator" and "simulations" the BoF simulator and simulations executed with the BoF simulator unless explicitly stated otherwise.

The main question of this chapter is to what extent it is possible to aggregate LVPS transaction data to be used in simulations without significantly changing the outcome of those simulations. The reason why researchers often limit their data sets is the amount of time required to run all simulations. Too often researchers are forced to settle for a very short time span or a too limited amount of days because running the simulations simply takes too much of their time.

The outline of this chapter is as follows. The authors first start with a background section containing an overview of simulation literature, then move on to the methodology section after which the results section contains the main findings. Finally the conclusion section shows the conclusions.

BACKGROUND

Focus of Simulation Research

Research in which FMI transaction data has been used as input for the simulator, can focus on a variety of aspects. The authors distinguish four main aspects, at the same time realizing that often a combination of multiple aspects occurs within the same research.

In the early years, often the payment system design was the main topic. An example of this was Arjani (2007), who showed that altering the queueing facility reduced the amount of intraday credit of the participants and could therefore lead to cost reduction.

An example of focusing on participant behavior and their liquidity positions is given by the research of Hellqvist and Snellman (2007), in which the effect of failure of a clearing participant in the securities settlement system to the liquidity position of other participants and the settlement process within the large value payment system was analyzed.

Third possible focus of research the authors see is the ability to withstand shocks. An example is the research by Andersen and Madsen (2009), who analyze the efficiency and need for contingency measures in RTGS systems and conclude amongst other that for the Kronos payment system it is sufficient that normal settlement is restored within 4 hours.

During the more recent years, looking at payments between participants as a network, opened the bridge to the field of network theory and therefore enabling researchers to investigate a large variety of system network measures and network positions of individual participants. An example of this is formed by the work of León, Machado, Cepeda and Sarmiento (2010) who use a variety of network measures to identify the most central participants and use simulations to investigate their contribution to systemic risk.

Limitation in the Time Span of Simulations

Depending on the focus of the analysis, the researcher will be required to choose the time span of the historical transaction data. When analyzing the system design, it is often sufficient to choose a few days, mostly weeks, to run and compare different scenarios. Focusing on participants liquidity positions after a system shock or failure of another participant might force the researcher to select a time span of several weeks, due to the fact that it can take a long time for participants to recuperate.

The longer the time span, the larger the transaction datasets will become and the longer it will take to run the simulation. In some cases the computing time becomes so large that the simulation would not be feasible anymore. Especially when the research focusses on participants' liquidity related issues, it is often required to have longer time series. An example of a simulation that would require more data is Heijmans (2009). He studies the potential impact when a single systemically important bank in the Dutch payment system reduces its outgoing payments. In his simulation two months of data is used while up to a year would have been statistically required. However, the processing time would have been unrealistically long.

Table 1. shows the list of publications in which the simulator was used to process FMI transaction data, including the main focus of the research as well as the time span used and the number of transactions processed.

How Can We Gain?

FMI transaction data usually show a certain distribution in terms of volume and value. As an illustration of how payment size is distributed, Figure 1 shows the cumulative share of the number and value of payments in the Dutch part of TARGET2 (i.e. the Lorenz curve). The tilting point divides all transactions into two groups; on the one hand the lower value transactions take only a small share in the value and a large share in the number of transactions, on the other hand the higher value transactions take a

Table 1. Overview of simulations based on FMI data using the BoF Simulator

Author	Year	Title	Focus of analysis	Country	System	Nr. of days	Nr. of transactions (* 1,000)
Andersen, K.S. & Madsen, I.	2009	A quantitative assessment of international best practice for business continuity arrangements in payment systems	System design, Participants behaviour, Shocks	Denmark	Kronos	22	64
Arciero, L.	2010	Evaluating the impact of shocks to the supply of overnight unsecured money market funds on the TARGET2-Banca d'Italia functioning: a simulation study	Participants behaviour, Shocks, Network theory	Italy	TARGET2-IT	28	3.605
Arculus, R.; Hancock, J. & Moran, G.	2010	The impact of payment system design on tiering incentives	System design, Participants behaviour, Network theory	Australia	RITS	21	624
Arjani, N. M.	2007	Examining the tradeoff between settlement delay and intraday liquidity in Canada's LVTS: a simulation approach	System design	Canada	LVTS	64	1.050
Bech, M. & Soramäki, K.	2005	Systemic Risk in a Netting System Revisited	System design, Participants behaviour, Shocks, Network theory	United States	Fedwire	21	10.314
Bech, M. & Soramäki, K.	2005	Gridlock Resoluation and Bank Failures in Interbank Payment Systems	System design, Participants behaviour, Shocks	Denmark	KRONOS	64	59
Bedford, P.; Millard, S. & Yang, J.	2005	Analysing the Impact of Operational Incidents in Large-Value Payment Systems: A Simulation Approach	System design, Shocks	United Kingdom	CHAPS	21	2.100
Clarke, A. & Hancock, J.	2010	Participant operational disruptions: the impact of system design	System design, Participants behaviour, Shocks	Australia	RITS	10	310
Denbee, E.; Garratt, R. & Zimmerman, P.	2010	Methods for evaluating liquidity provision in real-time gross settlement payment systems	System design, Participants behaviour	United Kingdom	CHAPS	102	12.750
Glaser, M. & Haene, P.	2009	Liquidity effects of a participant-level operational disruption in the Swiss Interbank Clearing System	Participants behaviour, Shocks	Switserland	SIC	18	2.950
Heijmans, R.	2009	Simulations in the Dutch interbank payment system: A sensitivity analysis	Participants behaviour, Shocks	Netherlands	TOP	22	405
Hellqvist, M. & Koskinen, J.	2005	Stress testing securities clearing and settlement systems using simulations	System design, Participants behaviour, Shocks	Finland	RM	22	2
Hellqvist, M. & Snellman, H.	2007	Simulation of operational failures in equities settlement	Participants behaviour, Shocks	Finland	HEXClear	19	906
Imakubo, K. & McAndrews, J. J.	2007	Funding levels for the new accounts in the BOJ-NET	System design, Shocks	Japan	BOJ-NET	10	1.200

continued on following page

Table 1. Continued

Author	Year	Title	Focus of analysis	Country	System	Nr. of days	Nr. of transactions (* 1,000)
Johnson, K.; McAndrews, J.J. & Soramäki, K.	2005	Economising liquidity with deferred settlement mechanisms	System design	US	Fedwire	10	4.031
Koponen, R. & Soramäki, K.	2005	Intraday Liquidity Needs in a Modern Interbank Payment System: A Simulation Approach.	System design, Participants behaviour, Shocks	Finland	PMJ, POPS	4	2.500
Lasaosa, A. & Tudela, M.	2007	Risks and efficiency gains of a tiered structure in large-value payments: a simulation approach	System design, Participants behaviour, Network theory	United Kingdom	CHAPS	21	2.500
León, C.; Machado, C.; Cepeda, F. & Sarmiento, M.	2010	Systemic risk in large value payments systems in Colombia: a network topology and payments simulation approach	Participants behaviour, Network theory	Columbia	CUD	22	162
Ledrut, E.	2007	How can banks control their exposure to a failing participant?	Participants behaviour, Shocks, Network theory	Netherlands	TOP	22	537
Leinonen, H. & Soramäki, K.	2005	Optimising Liquidity Usage and Settlement Speed in Payment Systems	System design	Finland	BoF-RTGS	100	179
Lovin, H.	2010	Systemically important participants in the ReGIS payment system	Participants behaviour, Shocks	Romaina	ReGIS	106	1.092
McVanel, D.	2007	The impact of unanticipated defaults in Canada's Large Value Transfer System	Participants behaviour, Shocks	Canada	LVTS	170	2.900
Oleschak, R. & Nellen, T.	2010	Does SIC need a heart pacemaker?	System design	Switserland	SIC	15	1.800
Petterson, J.	2005	Simulation of liquidity levels and delays in the Swedish RIX system	System design	Sweden	RIX	1	5
Renault, F. & Pecceu, J.B.	2007	From PNS to TARGET2: the cost of FIFO in RTGS payment systems	System design, Participants behaviour, Shocks	France	PNS	23	621
Schmitz, S. W. & Puhr, C.	2007	Risk concentration, network structure and contagion in the Austrian Real Time Interbank Settlement System	Participants behaviour, Shocks, Network theory	Austria	ARTIS	22	335
Lovin, H. & Pineta, A.	2010	Operational risk in ReGIS – a systemically important payment system	System design, Participants behaviour, Shocks	Romaina	ReGIS	85	850
Lublóy, A. & Tanai, E.	2009	Operational disruption and the Hungarian real time gross settlement system (VIBER)	Participants behaviour, Shocks, Network theory	Hungary	VIBER	41	141

Figure 1. Share in number and value of transactions in the TARGET2-NL payment system.

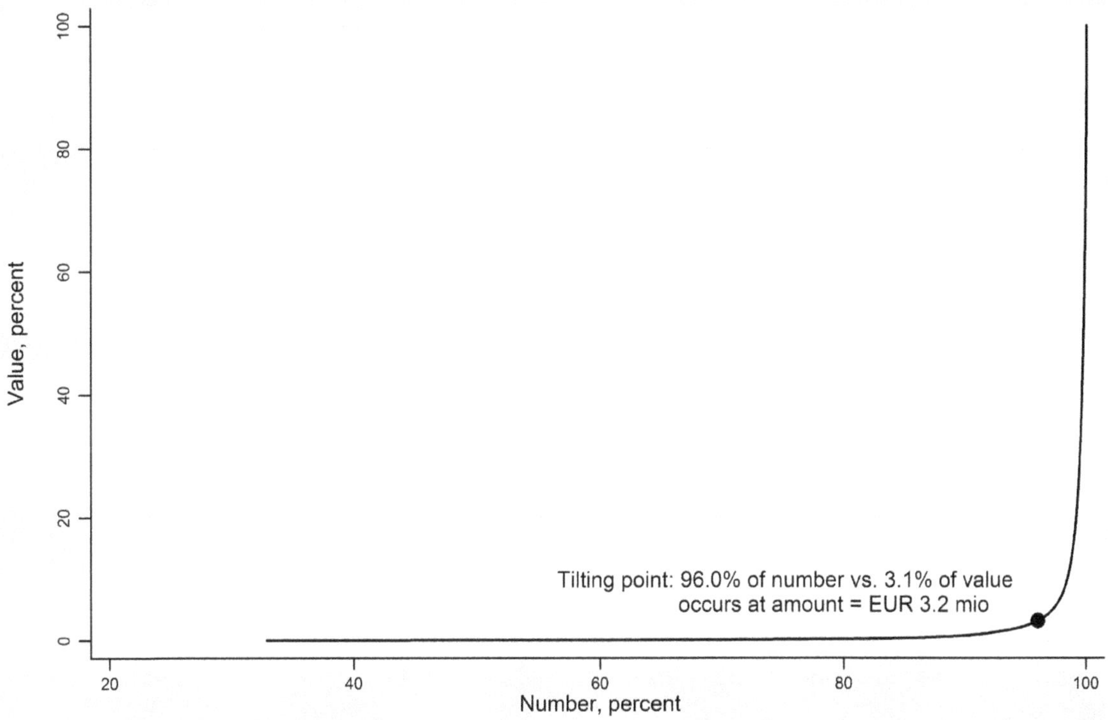

Based on the transactions of five representative days used in the simulations.

large share in the value and a small share in the number of transactions. At the tilting point all payments beneath EUR 3.2 million represent 96% of the number and only 3.1% of the value of payments.

Because there is a large group of payments of which the amount is almost negligible, the authors want to test if these transactions between participants can be totalized and still maintain a comparable simulation outcome. The aggregation amount is the payment size, below which all payments between two participants are aggregated to one value.

In order to test the level of possible aggregation the authors simulate the same data sets with different aggregation amount and different levels of liquidity. By changing the level of available liquidity it is possible to test whether the aggregation method is also valid in extreme liquidity cases. The reason for testing these extreme cases is that in scenario analysis often these extreme cases are of interest. Ten different liquidity levels are simulated between 0% and 100% of the original liquidity amount.

METHODOLOGY

When performing simulations using the Bank of Finland Payment and Settlement Simulator, each simulation input consists of three parts:

$SI = \{P, L, T\}$, where

P = list of Participants,

L = Liquidity at startup,

T = list of Transactions

The liquidity at startup consists of:

$L = AB + CL$, where

AB = Liquidity at Accounts Balances,

CL = Liquidity in Credit limits

The Simulator will start the simulation run, process the input, handle all the (transaction) events and calculate and store the outcome. From the outcome, that can be stored at several desired levels of detail, we will use the following measures that are stored at account level; percentage settled, lower bound of liquidity, balance drop and average queue value. These statistics are described in more detail in the results section.

In order to investigate to what extent the outcome of a simulation run remains the same when transactions below a certain size are aggregated, the simulation outcome containing the original transactions will be compared to the outcome of several simulations containing aggregated transactions below a ceiling amount:

$BS \approx AS$, where

BS = Benchmark Simulation using original transactions,

AS = Aggregation Simulation using aggregated transactions

Aggregation of transactions is simulated at ten levels, starting at zero (i.e. non-aggregation, i.e. the benchmark), up to the desired maximum "aggregation ceiling" value. This value was chosen at EUR 3.6 million, being well above the tilting point value (see Figure 1). Aggregation of transactions will be most effective when taking a low value transaction group, starting at zero and going up till the tilting point. Above this point the share in number of transactions is too small.

$BS = \{P, L, T_{aggr}\}$, where

$aggr = \{0\}$

$$AS = \left\{P, L, T_{aggr}\right\}, \text{ where}$$

$$aggr = \left\{\frac{1}{9}, \frac{2}{9}, \ldots, \frac{9}{9}\right\}$$

Aggregation of transactions is performed using the following approach:

- select all (outgoing) transactions from each participant to each other participant within the day and below the ceiling amount
- calculate the total value of these transactions
- calculate the value weighted average settlement time
- replace the selected transactions by the one that was calculated
- use the generated transactions together with the non-selected transactions (above the ceiling value) as input for the Simulator.

In order to investigate the outcome of simulations at different aggregation levels it was necessary to look at the full range of liquidity in the system. Whenever there is an abundance of liquidity in the payment system, it is certain that all transactions will be settled immediately, regardless of the used aggregation ceiling. Most often however, stress simulations are performed in situations where the level of liquidity decreases to the level at which waiting-queues and non-settlements may arise. We therefore look at the impact of each aggregation level in a range of ten "liquidity levels", ranging from maximum to zero liquidity.

$$BS, AS = \left\{P, L_{liq}, T\right\}, \text{ where}$$

$$liq = \left\{\frac{9}{9}, \frac{8}{9}, \ldots, 0\right\}$$

The maximum level of liquidity for a given participant is defined as the sum of all of its outgoing payments. This ensures us that payments will be settled, regardless of uncertainty of incoming payments or the order in which payments are processed.

We therefore come to a set of hundred simulations:

- ten simulations at different levels of aggregation, starting at zero (i.e. no aggregation, i.e. the benchmark simulations) up to the chosen maximum level of aggregation
- for each of these aggregation levels, again ten levels of available liquidity, starting at maximum liquidity and decreasing up to the point of zero liquidity.

RESULTS

Data Used

The authors chose 5 business days, from the Dutch part of TARGET2, from the period February 18 to 2008 to June 13, 2014.[3] The transaction data set of each business day contains the same percentage distribution of the share of the number and value of transactions as is shown in Figure 1. Therefore, any of the days could have been used for the simulations. The authors chose to repeat the series of hundred simulations on a five different business days ranging from the lowest to the highest number of transactions settled on that respective business day. The following 5 business days are used:

1. Lowest number (June 9, 2014, containing 25,408 transactions)
2. First quartile (November 12, 2012, containing 39,886 transactions)
3. Medium (May 11, 2010, containing 43,125 transactions)
4. Third quartile (July 18, 2008, containing 47,601 transactions)
5. Highest number of transactions (December 22, 2008, containing 96,898 transactions).

Statistics Used

For each simulation run four statistics were derived, available at individual account level, and are suitable for judging the liquidity flows within the system. The following four statistics are used: 1) percentage settled, 2) lower bound, 3) balance drop and 4) average queue value.

Percentage settled The percentage settled is composed of the ratio of two available statistics; the value of payments settled divided by the value of payments submitted. It is a good indicator of the throughput of payments and will drop if the liquidity in the system is decreased.

Lower bound The lower bound statistic gives the absolute minimum amount of liquidity necessary to settle all payments at the least by the end of the day, if necessary by using multilateral net settlement (BoF, 2013). This statistic is influenced directly by the amount of outgoing and incoming transactions. Waiting queues do not influence this statistic. Only the occurrence of unsettled transactions will alter this statistic.

$$LB_i = max\left(0, \sum_{k=1}^{d_i} a_{i,k} - \sum_{j=1}^{n}\sum_{k=1}^{d_j} a_{j,k} \mid \left(r_{j,k} = i\right)\right)$$

where

$a_{j,k} \in \mathbb{R}_+$ = the value of payment k of participant j

$r_{j,k} \in \left\{1, \ldots, j-1, j+1, \ldots, n\right\}$ = the receiver of the payment.

Balance drop The balance drop is the amount the balance dropped within the day, calculated as the difference between the account balance at the start of the day and the minimum balance. The balance drop is formed by incoming and outgoing payments and therefore forms a measure for the amount of liquidity that a participant attributed to the throughput of payments. This can only be the case when he total amount of outgoing payments up till that moment exceeds the amount of incoming payments. Decreasing the liquidity will lead to a decrease in the balance drop, as both the account balance decreases as well as the available collateral, therefore limiting the possible balance drop.

Average Queue Value The average queue value gives the average value of queued payments within the day, weighted by the time that the payments were in the waiting queue, and forms a good measure for liquidity problems. As liquidity decreases, it can be expected that waiting queues arise, therefore the average queue value will increase.

Outcome of Simulations

After running the simulations, the following output is available for analysis:

- For each of the five selected days
- At ten different levels of liquidity
- One benchmark simulation in which no aggregation has been performed
- Will be compared to nine simulations at increasing level of aggregation
- Using four different statistics.

In total this comes to 500 simulations, containing 50 benchmark simulations (5 days, 10 levels of liquidity) each being compared to 9 aggregation simulations (1+9). For each comparison the diversion from the benchmark is expressed as a percentage; the benchmark statistic therefore has been put at 100.

An overview of the outcome of the comparison is visualized in Figure 2, containing boxplots of diversions from the benchmarks. The graphs contain the box spanning the inter quartile range (i.e. IQR, the range from the first until the third quartile, therefore 50% of the data), whiskers that are 1.5 the size of the IQR (together with the box spanning 99.73% of data when normally distributed) as well as the remaining outer values. For a clear visibility of the boxes and whiskers, not all outer values are shown. The figures makes clear that, for all four statistics, the huge majority of simulations fall within the 99-101 range and are there fully comparable to the benchmark simulations. In order to take a closer look at the outer values and at which level of liquidity they arise, Figure 3 gives the same simulation outcome including all outer values and broken down into the ten levels of liquidity.

Figure 3 again shows the comparison to the benchmark simulations at four statistics, broken down into the ten used liquidity levels. The vertical axes all show the 97, 100 and 103 level of comparison. Showing all outer values containing the extreme diversions from the benchmark causes the IQR boxes and whiskers to be compressed. This means that the majority of simulations fall within very acceptable ranges, but at the same time few simulations show large diversions. These diversions occur mainly at the lowest liquidity levels 1 to 3. These are the liquidity levels where all participants are suffering from severe liquidity shortages, resulting in long waiting queues and many unsettled payments.

Taking a closer look at the breakdown into the levels of aggregation (in Figure 4) shows that there is no increasing level of diversions visible at increasing aggregation level. This means that even up to the highest level of aggregation, i.e. EUR 3.6 million, the percent share in the value of transactions is small enough for aggregation simulations to be fully comparable to the benchmark simulations.

Figure 2. Comparison of simulations containing aggregations to the benchmark values

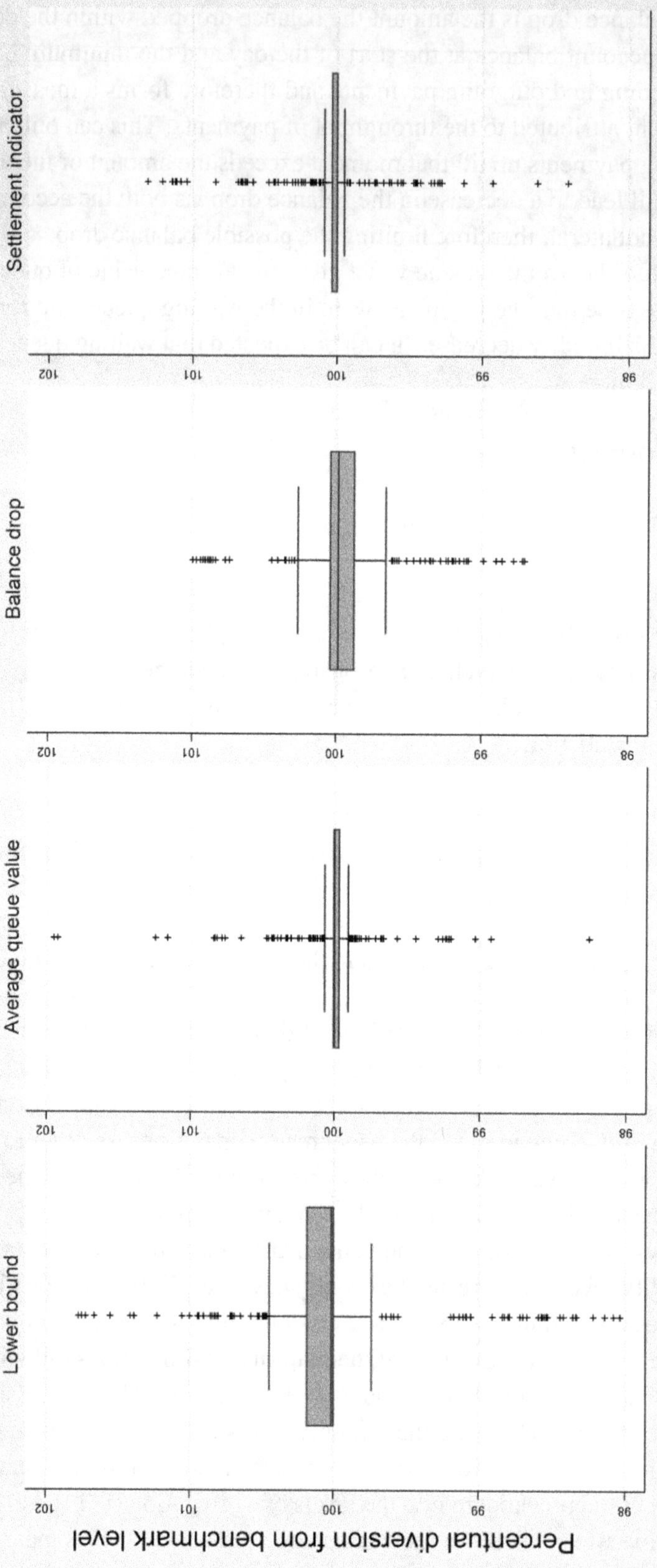

For each statistic the percentual diversion from the benchmark simulation (i.e. 100) was calculated.
For five days, ten benchmark simulations (at different liquidity levels) have each been compared to 9 simulations at different aggregation levels.

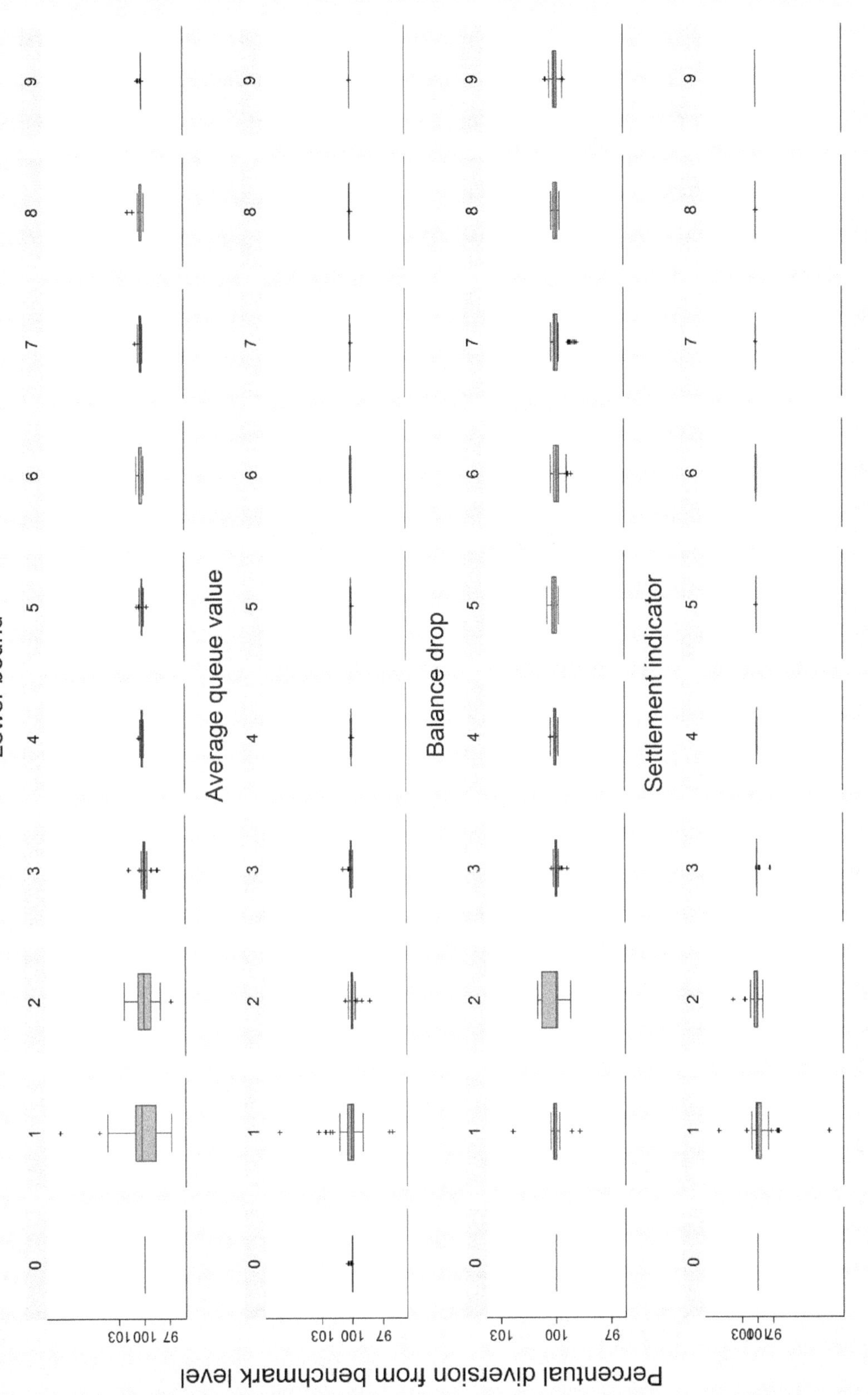

Figure 3. Comparison of simulations containing aggregations to the benchmark values, by liquidity level

Figure 4. Comparison of simulations containing aggregations to the benchmark values, by aggregation level

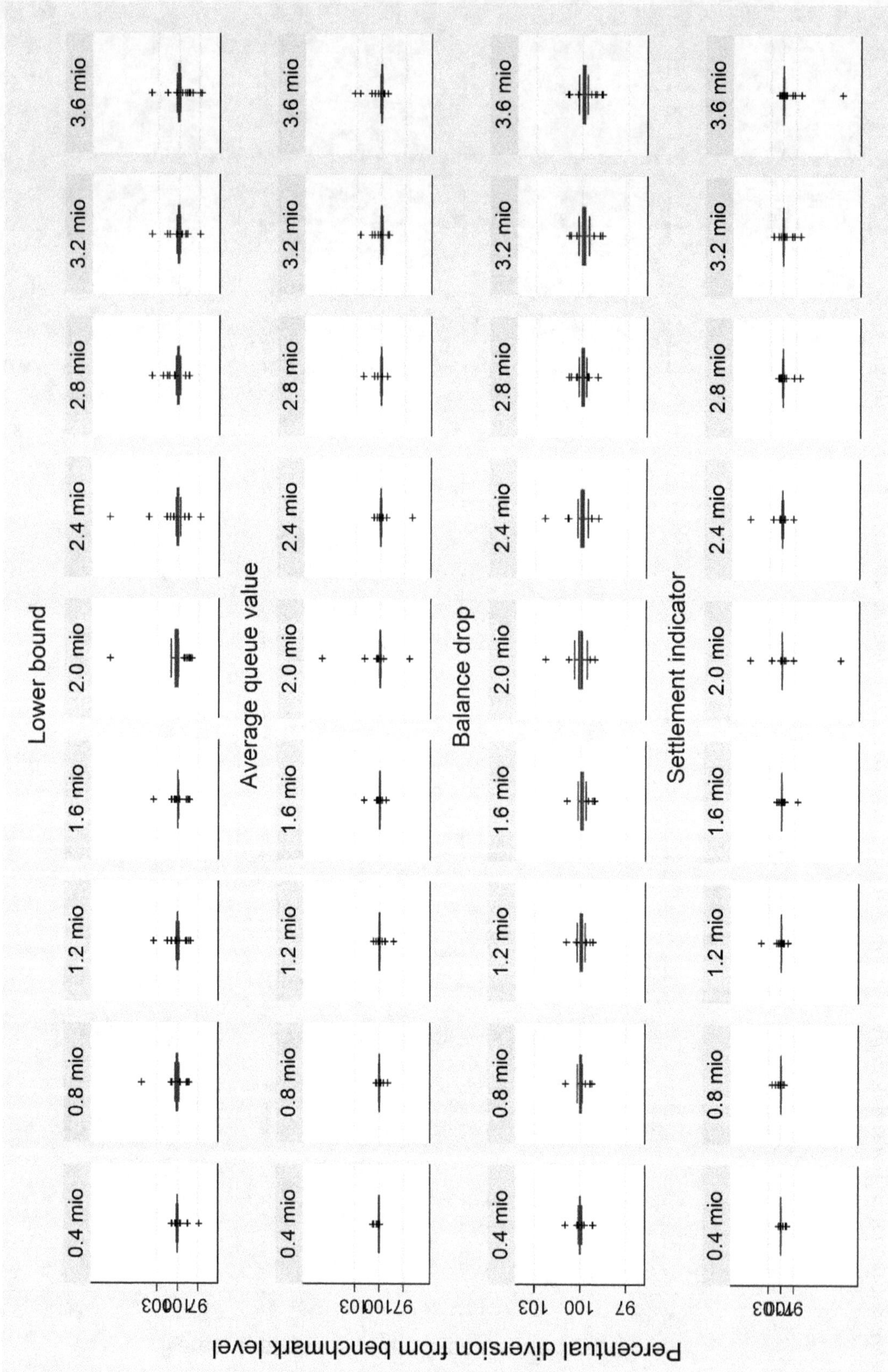

Increase in Speed Found

The aim of the simulation batches was to reduce the number of transactions by aggregating below the aggregation ceiling. As the simulator also saves performance statistics about each simulation run, these statistics were used to analyze the duration of simulations. The outcome is presented in Figure 5.

The figure shows all hundred simulations that were executed using day December 22nd, 2008, containing the largest number of transactions. Each aggregation level is gathered in one group, starting at no aggregation on the left, to the highest aggregation on the right. Within each group, a simulation duration is present for each liquidity level, starting at full liquidity on the left, to no liquidity on the right. The most left simulation on acts as the starting point, showing the full liquidity benchmark simulation duration of 15 seconds, followed by the other nine benchmark simulations, and ending at the benchmark simulation with no liquidity that took 44 minutes and 32 seconds. It becomes clear that there is gain of speed both at level of aggregation as well as at level of liquidity. This will be more explicitly analyzed hereafter.

How do the Levels of Aggregation and Liquidity Influence the Speed of Simulations

The duration of simulations are heavily influenced by aggregation of transactions as well as the level of liquidity. Aggregation of transactions below a certain ceiling value results in a decline of the number of

Figure 5. Duration of all simulation runs

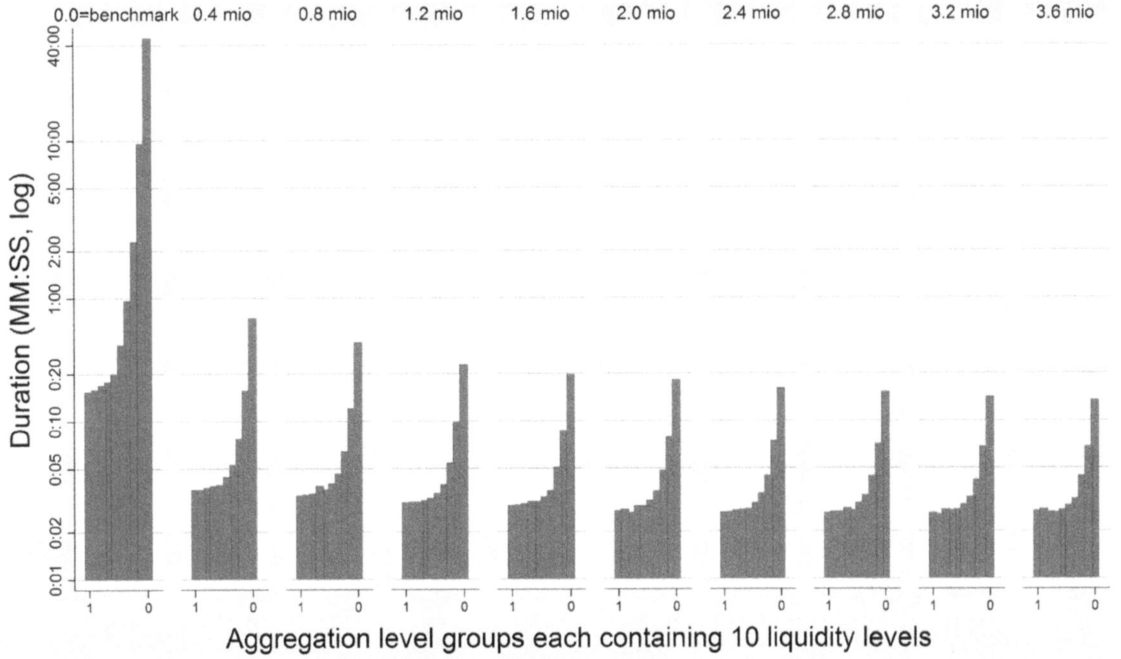

Most left graph - no aggregation; most right graph - highest level of aggregation (i.e. 3.6 million). Within each graph: most left - full liquidity; most right - none. Simulation dataset 22dec2008.

transactions, i.e. a compression level. Figure 6 shows the relation between the amount of compression (on the x-axis) and the resulting duration of simulations. As could be expected, there is a linear relationship between the two; the more compression, the more relative gain in speed.

Figure 7 shows how the level of liquidity influences the duration of simulations. The decreasing liquidity level is responsible for the largest growth in the duration of simulations, at a growth level beyond logarithmic. The growth of the duration booms at liquidity levels 0.3 (and less). The top line representing no compression (i.e. the benchmark) starts off at full liquidity level of 12 seconds, and after a relative comparable score of 30 seconds at the liquidity level of 44% starts growing to the highest measured duration of 44 minutes and 31 seconds at liquidity level zero.

CONCLUSION

Simulations carried out by researchers often use historical transaction data from FMIs. These transactions are than modified to simulate a certain (stress) scenario. The desired time span of simulations, from a statistical point of view varies from a few days up to a year, depending on the type of analysis the researcher has in mind. In case of testing technical features of a payment systems it may be sufficient to use just a few business days. However, when simulating liquidity stress scenarios much more days (e.g. up to a year) may be required. The reason for this is that business days vary during the year. However, it

Figure 6. How the level of compression influences speed of simulations

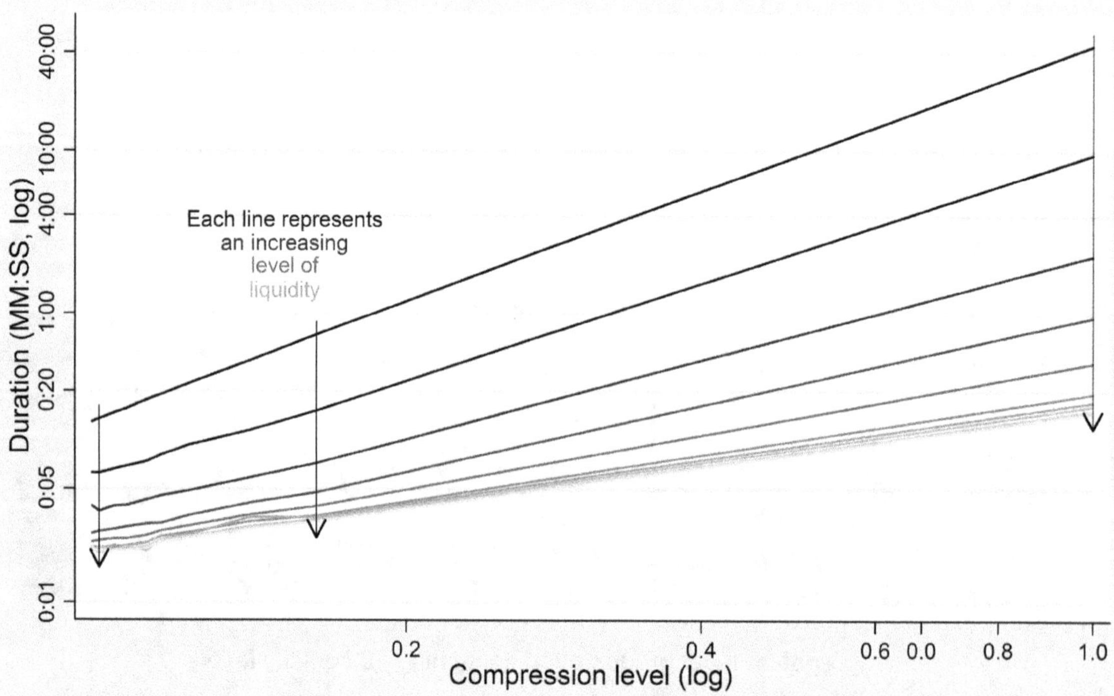

For each observed level of liquidity one line is drawn, showing the relation between compression and duration of simulation runs. Simulation dataset containing date 22dec2008.

Figure 7. How the level of liquidity influences speed of simulations

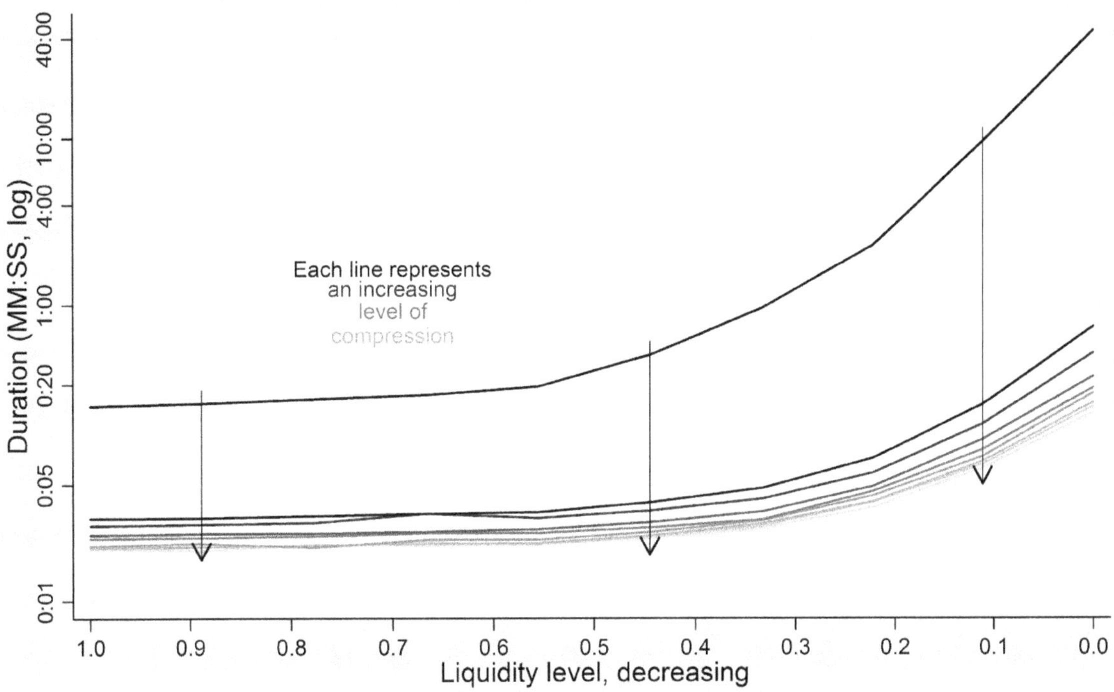

For each observed level of compression one line is drawn, showing the relation between liquidity and duration of simulation runs. Simulation dataset containing date 22dec2008.

is not always possible to choose the statistical ideal length of the time span, due to the lack of available computer performance. Even though business days vary significantly during the day, the distribution of the value of payments does not. Therefore it is possible to aggregate the low value transactions, without compromising the outcome of the analysis, significantly.

Our research consists of comparing benchmark simulations based on the original set of transactions, to a set of simulations for which transactions between participants beneath a certain value were brought down to one transaction containing the aggregated amount. This was done for a broad range of liquidity levels. The results show that the outcome of these simulations are comparable to the original simulation. However, when there are severe liquidity problems for all participants the diversions becomes larger. Furthermore, observed that the largest contribution to the duration of simulations is caused by the shrinking level of liquidity.

To conclude, aggregation of transactions below a ceiling value (in our case EUR 3.6 million) is a reliable approach in order to increase the desired time span of simulations. While the gain of simulation speed is the highest at the level of severe liquidity problems for all participants, the researcher must realize that diversions from the original simulation become larger and therefore the nature of diversions must first be analyzed.

REFERENCES

Andersen, K., & Madsen, I. (2009). A Quantitative Assessment of Interantional Best Practice for Business Continuity Arrangements in Payment Systems. In H. Leinonen, (Ed.), *Simulation analysis and stress testing of payment networks* (pp. 17–58). Proceedings from the Bank of Finland Payment and Settlement System Seminars 2007-2008.

Arciero, L. (2010). Evaluating the impact of shocks to the supply of overnight unsecured money market funds on the TARGET2-Banca d'Italia functioning: a simulation study (pp. 169–192). In M. Hellqvist & T. Laine (Ed.), Diagnostics for the financial markets–computational studies of payment system. Helsinki: Scientific Monographs.

Arculus, R., Hancock, J., & Moran, G. (2010). The impact of payment system design on tiering incentives (pp. 379–410). In M. Hellqvist & T. Laine (Ed.), Diagnostics for the financial markets–computational studies of payment system. Helsinki: Scientific Monographs.

Arjani, N. M. (2007). Examining the tradeoff between settlement delay and intraday liquidity in Canada's LVTS: a simulation approach (pp. 87–122). In H. Leinonen (Ed.), Simulation studies of liquidity needs, risks and efficiency in payment networks. Helsinki: Scientific Monographs.

Bech, M., & Hobijn, B. (2007). Technology Diffusion within Central Banking: The Case of Real-Time Gross Settlement. *International Journal of Central Banking*, *3*, 147–182.

Bech, M., & Soramäki, K. (2005a). Gridlock Resoluation and Bank Failures in Interbank Payment Systems (pages 151–178). In H. Leinonen (Ed.), Liquidity, risks and speed in payment and settlement systems: a simulation approach. Helsinki: Suomen Pankki.

Bech, M., & Soramäki, K. (2005b). Systemic Risk in a Netting System Revisited (pp. 277–298). In H. Leinonen (Ed.), Liquidity, risks and speed in payment and settlement systems: a simulation approach. Helsinki: Suomen Pankki.

Bedford, P., Millard, S., & Yang, J. (2005). Analysing the Impact of Operational Incidents in Large-Value Payment Systems: A Simulation Approach (pp. 247-274). In H. Leinonen (Ed.), Liquidity, Risks and Speed in Payment and Settlement Systems–A Simulation Approach. Helsinki: Suomen Pankki.

BoF. (2013). BoF PSS2 v3.2.1 User Manual. BoF.

Clarke, A., & Hancock, J. (2010). Participant operational disruptions: the impact of system design (pp. 193–218). In M. Hellqvist & T. Laine (Ed.), Diagnostics for the financial markets–computational studies of payment system. Helsinki: Scientific Monographs.

CPSS. (2012). *Principles for Financial Market Infrastructures: Disclosure Framework and Assessment Methodology*. Bank for International Settlements.

Denbee, E., Garratt, R., & Zimmerman, P. (2010). Methods for evaluating liquidity provision in real-time gross settlement payment systems (pp. 53–76). In M. Hellqvist & T. Laine (Ed.), Diagnostics for the financial markets–computational studies of payment system. Helsinki: Scientific Monographs.

Heijmans, R. (2009). Simulation in the Dutch Interbank Payment System: A Sensitivity Analysis. *DNB Working Paper*.

Hellqvist, M. (2009). Participants' internal intraday limits in large value payment systems, chapter 09, pp. 255–276. In Hellqvist (2009).

Hellqvist, M. (2012). *Diagnostics for the financial market - computational studies of payment systems. Proceedings from the Bank of Finland Payment and Settlement System Seminars 2009*-2011. Bank of Finland.

Hellqvist, M., & Koskinen, J. (2005). Stress testing securities clearing and settlement systems using simulations (pp. 324–350). In H. Leinonen (Ed.), Liquidity, risks and speed in payment and settlement systems: a simulation approach. Helsinki: Suomen Pankki.

Hellqvist, M., & Snellman, H. (2007). Simulation of operational failures in equities settlement (pp. 283–320). In H. Leinonen (Ed.), Simulation studies of liquidity needs, risks and efficiency in payment networks. Helsinki: Scientific Monographs.

Imakubo, K., & McAndrews, J. J. (2007). Funding levels for the new accounts in the BOJ-NET (pp. 123–148). In H. Leinonen (Ed.), Simulation studies of liquidity needs, risks and efficiency in payment networks. Helsinki: Scientific Monographs.

Johnson, K., McAndrews, J., & Soramäki, K. (2005). Economising liquidity with deferred settlement mechanisms (pp. 179–216). In H. Leinonen (Ed.), Liquidity, risks and speed in payment and settlement systems: a simulation approach. Helsinki: Suomen Pankki.

Koponen, R., & Soramäki, K. (2005). Intraday Liquidity Needs in a Modern Interbank Payment System: A Simulation Approach. (pp. 74–117). In H. Leinonen (Ed.), Liquidity, risks and speed in payment and settlement systems: a simulation approach. Helsinki: Suomen Pankki.

Lasaosa, A., & Tudela, M. (2007). Risks and efficiency gains of a tiered structure in large-value payments: a simulation approach (pp. 149–182). In H. Leinonen (Ed.), Simulation studies of liquidity needs, risks and efficiency in payment networks. Helsinki: Scientific Monographs.

Ledrut, E. (2007). How can banks control their exposure to a failing participant? (pp. 227–252). In H. Leinonen (Ed.), Simulation studies of liquidity needs, risks and efficiency in payment networks. Helsinki: Scientific Monographs.

Leinonen, H. (2005). *Liquidity, risks and speed in payment and settlement systems – a simulation approach. Proceedings from the Bank of Finland Payment and Settlement System Seminars 2003*-2004. Bank of Finland.

Leinonen, H. (2007). *Simulation studies of liquidity needs, risks and efficiency in payment networks. Proceedings from the Bank of Finland Payment and Settlement System Seminars 2005*-2006. Bank of Finland.

Leinonen, H., & Soramäki, K. (2005). Optimising Liquidity Usage and Settlement Speed in Payment Systems (pp. 117–151). In H. Leinonen (Ed.), Liquidity, risks and speed in payment and settlement systems: a simulation approach. Helsinki: Suomen Pankki.

León, C., Machado, C., Cepeda, F., & Sarmiento, M. (2010). Systemic risk in large value payments systems in Colombia: a network topology and payments simulation approach (pp. 267–314). In M. Hellqvist & T. Laine (Ed.), Diagnostics for the financial markets–computational studies of payment system. Helsinki: Scientific Monographs.

Lovin, H. (2010). Systemically important participants in the ReGIS payment system (pp. 219–234). In M. Hellqvist & T. Laine (Ed.), Diagnostics for the financial markets–computational studies of payment system. Helsinki: Scientific Monographs.

Lovin, H., & Pineta, A. (2010). Operational risk in ReGIS – a systemically important payment system (pp. 315–340). In M. Hellqvist & T. Laine (Ed.), Diagnostics for the financial markets–computational studies of payment system. Helsinki: Scientific Monographs.

McVanel, D. (2007). The impact of unanticipated defaults in Canada's Large Value Transfer System (pp. 253–282). In H. Leinonen (Ed.), Simulation studies of liquidity needs, risks and efficiency in payment networks. Helsinki: Scientific Monographs.

Oleschak, R., & Nellen, T. (2010). Does SIC need a heart pacemaker? (pp. 341–378). In M. Hellqvist & T. Laine (Ed.), Diagnostics for the financial markets–computational studies of payment system. Helsinki: Scientific Monographs.

Petterson, J. (2005). Simulation of liquidity levels and delays in the Swedish RIX system (pp. 218–228). In H. Leinonen (Ed.), Liquidity, risks and speed in payment and settlement systems: a simulation approach. Helsinki: Suomen Pankki.

Renault, F., & Pecceu, J. (2007). From PNS to TARGET2: the cost of FIFO in RTGS payment systems (pp. 41–86). In H. Leinonen (Ed.), Simulation studies of liquidity needs, risks and efficiency in payment networks. Helsinki: Scientific Monographs.

Schmitz, S. W., & Puhr, C. (2007). Risk concentration, network structure and contagion in the Austrian Real Time Interbank Settlement System (pp. 183–226). In H. Leinonen (Ed.), Simulation studies of liquidity needs, risks and efficiency in payment networks. Helsinki: Scientific Monographs.

KEY TERMS AND DEFINITIONS

Bank of Finlands Payment and Settlement Simulator: Software package that enables the user to simulate payment and/or settlement systems and is often used to analyze different scenarios.

Financial Market Infrastructure: A system that fulfills an important role in the payment and/or settlement of financial obligations.

Gridlock: Situation in which the combined payments between two or more participants cannot be released because of the lack of funds, while at the same time the value of these payments contain the necessary funds.

Liquidity: Often used term during analysis of FMIs to indicate the existence of funds that are available for generating payments.

Payment System: A system which enables participants to register funds and generate payments to other participants.

Principles for FMIs: The set of requirements, initiated by CPSS/IOSCO in 2012, that the most important FMIs have to meet in order to safeguard their robustness against shocks.

(Payment) Queue: Facility within a payment systems that stores payments until enough funds are available to the participant, immediately leading to release and finalization.

Real Time Gross Settlement: Immediate and irrevocable finalization of payments.

ENDNOTES

1 See Bech and Hobijn (2007) for the development of RTGS systems in the industrialized world over time.

2 In most systems banks have to provide collateral for intraday credit (e.g. TARGET2, CHAPS). However, in the United States it is also possible to obtain intraday credit without providing collateral.

3 The reason for choosing only the Dutch part of TARGET2, instead of the whole TARGET2 is data availability and confidentiality.

APPENDIX: USING THE PAYMENT AND SETTLEMENT SIMULATOR

The Payment and Settlement Simulator developed by the Bank of Finland is used worldwide mainly by central banks and manufacturers of payment systems. The simulator enables the user to mimic a large scale of payment and settlement systems in order to perform simulations.
The usual steps to run a simulation consists of (see also Figure 8):

- Defining the payment system.
- Loading participants, transactions, opening balances and (optionally) bilateral limits.
- Defining simulations.
- Running simulations.
- Exporting the generated statistics for further analysis.

In practice it is often the case that a large group of similar simulations have to be executed in sequence. As this is quite time-consuming, the Simulator has recently been enhanced with a command line interface (CLI). This feature enables the user to automatically start the most important functions using either

Figure 8. Actions and components using the Bank of Finland Simulator

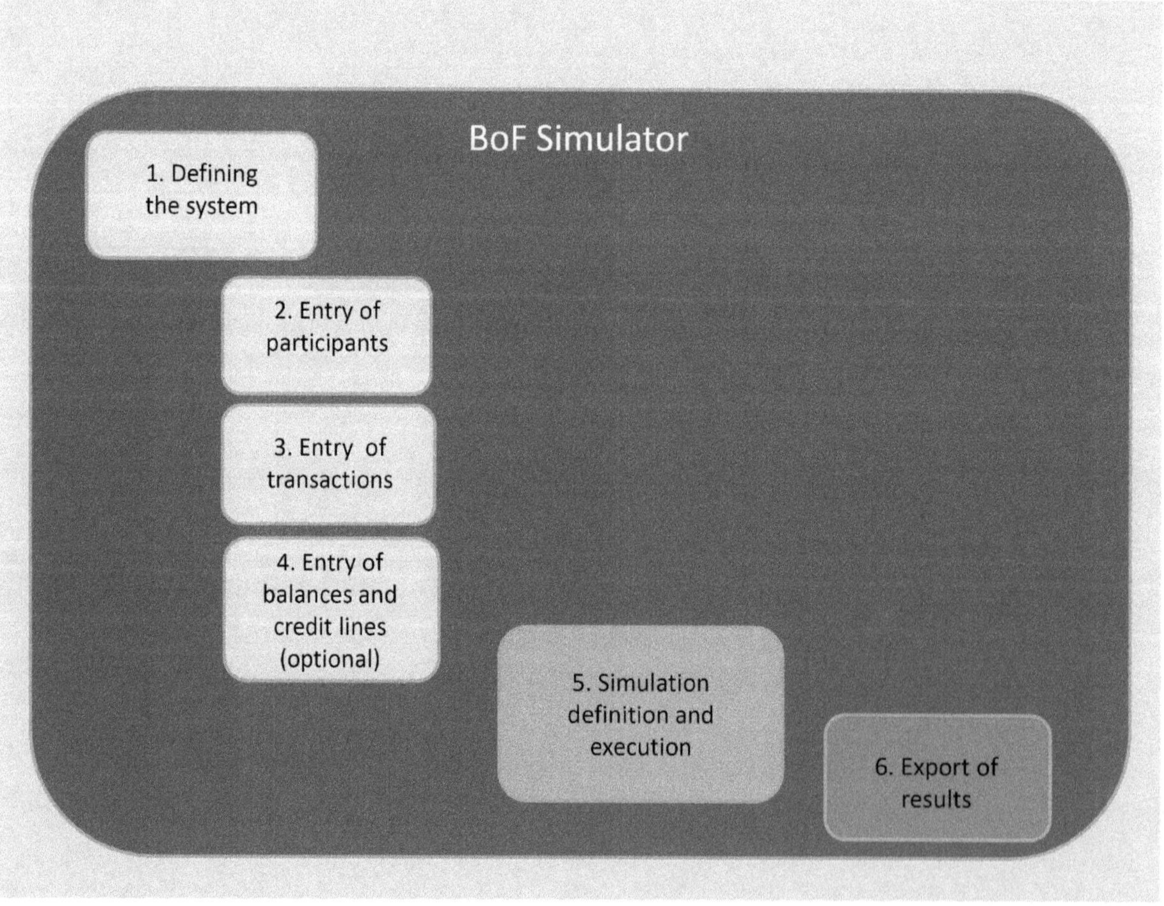

operating system commands, a script-file or directly from within other software. We used the Stata software to prepare data, start CLI-commands (in order to input data, define and start simulations and export the results) and afterward analyze the results.
Figure A2 shows how the series of simulations have been executed:

0 - Selection and altering of data from the payment system using Stata.
1 - Defining the payment system (one-time effort).
2 - Entry of participants.
3 - Entry of transaction data.
4 - Entry of start-of-day balances and credit lines.
5 - Defining and execution of a simulation batch.
6 - Export of statistics.
7 - Automatically repeating parts 2-7 using the command line interface.
8 - Analysis of exported statistics using Stata.

Once a payment system is defined, all other commands (2-7) can be executed through the command line interface (dark area) which enables the possibility of using the looping facility in Stata to generate series of simulations.

Figure 9. Automating simulation runs using the command line interface

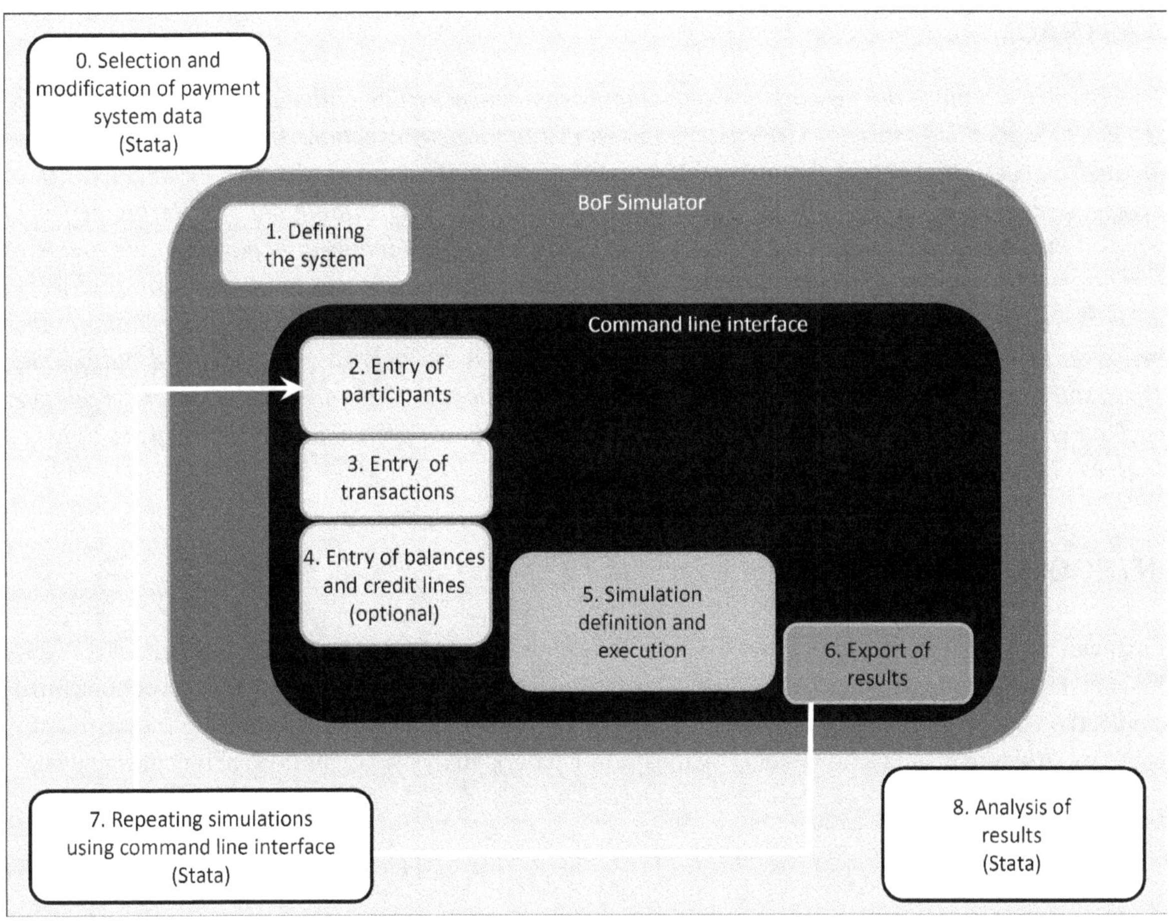

Chapter 7
A Multi-Layer Network of the Colombian Sovereign Securities Market

Carlos León
Banco de la República, Colombia

Jhonatan Pérez
Banco de la República, Colombia

Luc Renneboog
Tilburg University, The Netherlands

ABSTRACT

This chapter examines the network of Colombian sovereign securities settlements. With data from the settlement market infrastructure we study financial institutions' transactions from three different trading and registering networks that we combine into a multi-layer network. Examining this network of networks enables us to confirm that (i) studying isolated single-layer trading and registering networks yields a misleading perspective on the relations between and risks induced by participating financial institutions; (ii) a multi-layer approach produces a connective structure consistent with most real-world networks (e.g. sparse, inhomogeneous, and clustered); and (iii) the multi-layer network is a multiplex that preserves the main connective features of its constituent layers due to positively correlated multiplexity. The results highlight the importance of mapping and understanding how financial institutions relate to each other across multiple financial environments, and the value of financial market infrastructures as sources of data for working on multi-layer financial networks.

INTRODUCTION

Financial market infrastructures are considered the "plumbing" of financial systems (Bernanke, 2011). Financial market infrastructures responsible for settling transactions between financial institutions fulfill a pivotal position within that plumbing, thus they are of particular interest to disentangle and dissect this complex structure of financial systems by means of network analysis. Under this analytical framework,

DOI: 10.4018/978-1-4666-8745-5.ch007

this chapter studies the local sovereign securities settlement infrastructure in order to attain a more detailed and actual illustration of how financial intuitions organize themselves in the corresponding legal, operational, and economic contexts.

As transactions settled originate in different trading and registering platforms, a single network of settlements should necessarily aggregate networks from other financial market infrastructures. In this vein, the settlement network is a *network of networks*, which entails additional sources of complexity, critical for understanding financial markets. This is consistent with recent efforts to examine the consequences of considering financial systems as multi-layer networks, in which financial institutions interact across several environments or layers (e.g. markets, asset classes, trading and registering platforms, jurisdictions).

The theoretical development of multi-layer networks (and its empirical validation) is still in scaffolding, and consequently most literature on multi-layer financial networks is still preliminary. Nevertheless, there is a consensus regarding the need to examine how the basic assumptions of real-world networks are altered in a context of multi-layer networks or networks of networks. Most examinations have focused on how real-world networks' coupling affects their well-documented inhomogeneous connective architecture, in which connections being distributed in an extremely skewed fashion (presumably following a power-law distribution) contribute to their robustness; as most participants are weakly connected, most real-world networks, either biological or man-made, tend to be robust to the random failure of their constituents (see Newman, 2010, Barabási, 2003, Strogatz, 2003).

In this sense, studying networks of financial networks allows to confirm if their individual well-documented *robust-yet-fragile* feature (Haldane, 2009) is also valid within a financial multi-layer network. Moreover, studying how single-layer financial networks' couple allows understanding the rationale behind the main connective features of financial multi-layer networks.

Consequently, in the light of the above view of the transactions in a settlement market infrastructure as a network of networks, this chapter has two main purposes: First, it examines how Colombian sovereign securities' transactions that come from single-layer networks (corresponding to distinct trading and registering platforms) can be aggregated into a multiplex network of the sovereign securities settlement system. Second, it verifies whether or not viewing a financial system as a multiplex network is a superior view in that it preserves the main connective properties of its constituents, while revealing some additional layers of complexity.

This chapter contributes to the financial literature by examining the connective structure of financial institutions' interactions under different economic and operational environments, and by investigating how those interactions aggregate and result in the local sovereign securities' market. The examination of how financial networks' connective structure changes as a consequence of the overlap of financial institutions across different economic domains is significant for financial authorities pursuing or contributing to financial stability.

Moreover, in the context of the networks of networks literature, this chapter contributes to the study of financial market infrastructures by revealing that they critically depend on their interaction with other financial market infrastructures. In our case, the local sovereign securities settlement market infrastructure depends on its interaction with trading and registering platforms, but other types of interactions (i.e. with other settlement and clearing infrastructures) are also likely.

Finally, this chapter highlights that financial market infrastructures are a vital source of granular and timely data for examining single- and multi-layer networks as a way to better understand financial markets. In this vein, financial market infrastructures' data is essential for modeling contagion as a non-isolated effect that may affect several otherwise independent financial networks.

BACKGROUND

Most efforts to characterize the topology of complex systems by means of network analysis have assumed that each system is isolated (i.e. non-coupled) from other networks. In the case of single-layer networks (i.e. monoplex networks) such efforts have converged to an inhomogeneous connective structure, typically in the form of an approximate power-law distribution of links and their weights of real-world networks. The power-law or Pareto distribution of links is commonly referred as a *scale-free network* (Barabási & Albert, 1999), and it corresponds to the most documented type of network in social, biological, and man-made complex systems.[1] In the case of financial networks, most literature confirms their scale-free nature, whereas other papers confirm their inhomogeneity but report a divergence from a strict power-law distribution of links.[2]

Yet, as highlighted by Cardillo et al. (2013), "many biological and man-made networked systems are characterized by the simultaneous presence of different sub-networks organized in separate layers, with connections and participants of qualitatively different types" (p.1). This multi-layered nature of networks, also known as network of networks, has been the focus of network scientists rather recently, among whom Kurant and Thiran (2006) provided one of the most seminal contributions.

Research on multi-layer financial networks has recently emerged. The standard multi-layer framework in finance corresponds to the so-called *multiplex* network, which may be described as networks containing participants of one sort but with several kinds of connections between them (Baxter, Dorogovtsev, Glotsec, & Mendes, 2014).[3] The whole point of a multiple-network perspective is to superimpose multiple domains, with each plane or layer representing a different domain of activity (Padgett & Powell, 2012).

Figure 1 displays a two-layer network composed by layers X and Y, and the multiplex (Z) resulting from merging X and Y. Vertical lines connecting superimposed vertices are the participants, whereas each vertex has a function in the corresponding layer.

Montagna and Kok (2013) model interbank contagion in the US with a triple-layer multiplex network consisting of long-term direct bilateral exposures, short-term bilateral exposures, and common exposures to financial assets. Bargigli et al. (2013) examine the Italian interbank multiplex network by transaction type (i.e. secured and non-secured) and by maturity (i.e. overnight, short-term, and long-term).

This chapter examines the Colombian sovereign securities' market. It builds a triple-layer multiplex network corresponding to the three Colombian sovereign securities' trading and registering environments (i.e. SEN, MEC, and MEC-R), that altogether meet in the settlement market infrastructure for local sovereign securities: DCV.[4] As is the case in other countries, the sovereign securities settlement infrastructure is owned and operated by the central bank (Banco de la República), and works under a delivery versus payment setting, and it interacts with the large-value payment system within a real-time gross settlement framework.

As the network of networks deals with three different monoplex networks composed by a single type of participant (i.e. financial institutions) but distinct kinds of connections corresponding to different trading and registering platforms with divergent operational and economic features, it may be well defined as a multiplex network. Accordingly, the literature suggests that working on multi-layer networks may alter the basic assumptions that according to network theory lie at the basis of single networks (Kenett et al., 2014).

Contrary to what it is expected, the literature shows that the coupling of scale-free networks may yield a less robust network (Gao, Buldyrev, Stanley, & Havlin, 2012; Buldyrev, Parshani, Paul, Stanley, & Havlin, 2010). Exceptions to this finding would occur when the number of links (i.e. the *degree*) of

Figure 1. A multiplex network. Two networks, X and Y, and the multiplex (Z) resulting from merging X and Y. Vertical lines connecting superimposed vertices are the participants, whereas each vertex is a role in the corresponding layer.

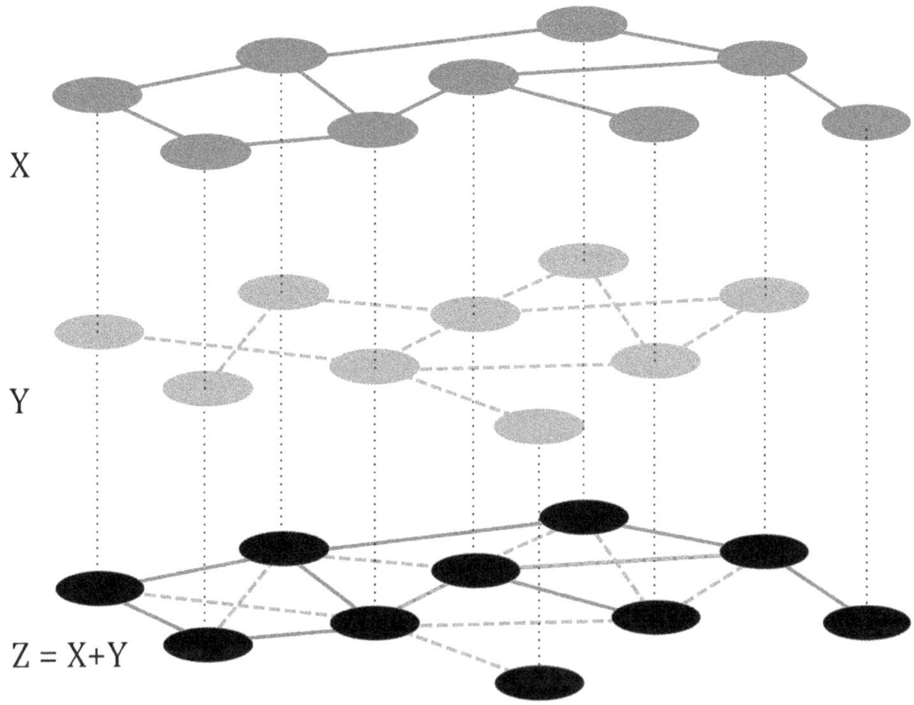

interdependent participants coincides across the layers. This is, scale-free networks' robustness is likely to be preserved if *positively correlated multiplexity* exists, such that a high-degree vertex in one layer likely is high-degree in the other layers as well (Lee, Kim, Lee, & Goh, 2014; Kenett et al., 2014).

Results in this chapter contribute to the related literature in two ways. First, results help to understand the economics of financial market infrastructures as the collective function of several layers of interaction between financial institutions. In this case, the settlement network is envisaged as a collection of the transactions routed via distinct trading and registering platforms with different economic and operational features. Second, the empirical analysis illustrates how the main features of individual networks aggregate into a multiplex network. As obtaining empirical data on multi-layer networks is particularly difficult (D'Souza, Brummit, & Leicht, 2014), and given the novelty of multi-layer network analysis, both these contributions could be valuable for financial authorities, market practitioners, and the academics.

THE DATA SET

As highlighted by León and Pérez (2014), the local sovereign securities market is the most important financial market in Colombia.[5] Not only this market is the most liquid and active by local standards, but it is also the most significant source of collateralized liquidity for financial institutions, either with the central bank (i.e. repos) or between financial institutions (i.e. repos and sell-buy backs).[6]

The clearing and settlement of local sovereign securities market takes place in DCV. Colombia's Central Bank owns and operates DCV, a financial market infrastructure that is both the local sovereign securities' clearing and settlement system, and also their central securities depository. Working on a real-time gross settlement system and a delivery-versus-payment mechanism, DCV clears and settles spot market transactions, repos, and sell-buy back transactions. DCV is the second most systemically important local financial market infrastructure according to León and Pérez (2014), only surpassed by the large-value payment system.

Most transactions in DCV result from three different Colombian sovereign securities' trading and registering platforms: SEN, MEC, and MEC-R.[7] SEN is the main local sovereign securities' trading platform, owned and operated by Colombia's Central Bank, in which a group of 14 market makers trade and settle anonymously, and free of any counterparty limit.[8] MEC is an anonymous trading platform privately owned and operated by the Colombian Stock Exchange (*Bolsa de Valores de Colombia*), which also serves as trading platform for other non-sovereign fixed income securities. SEN and MEC, are both multilateral trading platforms, but differ in particular issues. SEN is a "rich-club" of participants brought together by the Ministry of Finance into a market-maker scheme, in which they trade and settle anonymously without counterparty limits, whereas MEC is an open platform that allows participants to manage counterparty risk by imposing limits amid an anonymous trading environment.

Unlike MEC and SEN, MEC-R is not a multilateral trading platform; it is a facility provided by the Colombian Stock Exchange that enables local over-the-counter sovereign securities market transactions to be registered for settlement purposes. Transactions registered in MEC-R come from trades agreed outside the electronic trading systems (e.g. by phone), in which counterparty limits play a vital role due to its bilateral (i.e. non anonymous) nature.

DCV daily transactions corresponding to the third quarter of 2013 (i.e. from July 2 to September 30, 63 days) are used to construct the monoplex and multiplex networks analyzed in this paper. The choice of data is induced by practical reasons, such as that fact that it is a recent period that does not display seasonal effects (e.g. Easter, Christmas, end of the year, large firms' tax collection deadlines) and that can be considered typical according to the recent local sovereign securities' market dynamics.[9]

As highlighted by some authors (see Kyriakopoulos, Thurner, Puhr & Schmitz, 2009) the information conveyed in financial transactions from financial market infrastructures is particularly valuable due to their (i) granularity, with informative details such as sender, recipient, amount, type of transaction, underlying asset, etc.; (ii) completeness, because all financial transactions ineludibly involve the delivery of money or securities, or a trade; (iii) reliability from a supervisory perspective because payments and settlements cannot be –easily- falsified; and (iv) opportunity, with data usually available in real-time (or with a minimal lag). In this sense, the DCV sovereign securities' transactions database under analysis consists of 35,775 consolidated registers between 159 financial institutions, in which detailed information about the identity of the sender (seller) and receiver (buyer) of the securities, the source of the transactions (i.e. SEN, MEC, MEC-R), the amount of the transaction, and their time is readily available.

METHODOLOGICAL APPROACH

This chapter examines the main connective features of the monoplex networks and the resulting multiplex network. Particularly, it attempts to determine whether or not the monoplex and multiplex networks follow the sparse, scale-free, small-world, and clustered patterns that are ubiquitous in real-world networks. Therefore, each network is examined for its main connective features, while each participant is evaluated for its importance (i.e. centrality) within every network.

Main Connective Features of the Network

A network, or graph, represents patterns of connections between the parts of a system. Two concepts arise from this definition: parts and connections. The parts of the system correspond to the participants or elements, and are commonly referred to as vertices, whereas the connections correspond to the relations between the elements of the system, and are called edges. These concepts tend to have an equivalent when applied to specific networks, such as *nodes* and *links* in computer science, *actors* and *ties* in sociology, *neuron* and *synapse* in neural networks, *web page* and *hyperlink* in the World Wide Web network. In this chapter the participants or vertices correspond to financial institutions, whereas edges correspond to the delivery of local sovereign securities in the local settlement market infrastructure.

The most common mathematical representation of a network is the *adjacency matrix*. For an undirected network, in which the direction of the linkages between n elements or vertices is unimportant, the adjacency matrix (Ω) is a square matrix of dimensions $n \times n$, strictly symmetrical, with elements Ω_{ij} such that

$$\Omega_{ij} = \begin{Bmatrix} 1 \text{ if there is an edge between } i \text{ and } j, \\ 0 \text{ otherwise} \end{Bmatrix} \quad (1)$$

A network defined by the adjacency matrix in (1) is referred as an undirected graph, where the existence of the (i,j) edge makes both vertices i and j adjacent or connected, and where the direction of the link or edge is unimportant. However, the assumption of a reciprocal relation between vertices is inconvenient for some networks. For instance, the deliveries of money between financial institutions constitute a graph where the character of sender and recipient is a particularly sensitive source of information for analytical purposes, in which the assumption of a reciprocal relation between both parties is unwarranted. For a directed network, in which the direction of the linkages between n elements or vertices is relevant, the adjacency matrix (Ω) is a square matrix of dimensions $n \times n$, potentially non-symmetrical, with elements Ω_{ij} such that

$$\Omega_{ij} = \begin{Bmatrix} 1 \text{ if there is an edge between } i \text{ and } j, \\ 0 \text{ otherwise} \end{Bmatrix} \quad (2)$$

Moreover, networks may require edges to represent more information than that conveyed in a simple binary (0 or 1) relation; in the complex network context, edges are not binary, but are weighted according to the economic interaction under consideration (Schweitzer, Fagiolo, Sornette, Vega-Redondo, Vespignani, & White, 2009). Therefore, it may be useful to assign real numbers to the edges, where these numbers may represent distance, frequency or value, in what is called a weighted network and its corresponding weighted adjacency matrix. In this chapter, the weight is given by the market value of the delivery of local sovereign securities.

The simplest metric for approximating the connective pattern of a network is *density* (d), a statistic that measures its cohesiveness. Let n be the number of participants or vertices in the network, the density of a graph with no self-edges is the ratio of the number of actual edges (m) to the maximum possible number of edges (3).

$$d = \frac{m}{n(n-1)} \tag{3}$$

By construction, the density is restricted to the $0 < d \leq 1$ range. Formally, Newman (2010) states that a sufficiently large network for which the density (d) tends to a constant as n tends to infinity is considered as *dense*, whereas a network for which the density tends to zero as n tends to infinity is called *sparse*. However, as it is customary to works with non-sufficiently large networks, they are commonly characterized as sparse when the density is much smaller than the upper limit ($d \ll 1$), and as *dense* when the density approximates the upper limit ($d \cong 1$).

An informative alternative to density is to examine the degree's probability distribution (P_k), with degree (k_i) corresponding to the number of edges or links of the i-vertex. Such distribution provides a natural summary of the connectivity in the graph (Kolaczyk, 2009). Akin to density, the first moment of the distribution of degree (μ_k) measures the cohesion of the network, and is usually restricted to the $0 < \mu_k < n-1$ range. A sparse graph has an average degree that is much smaller than the size of the graph ($\mu_k \ll n-1$).

Most real-world networks display right-skewed distributions, in which the majority of vertices are of very low degree, and few vertices are of very high degree, hence inhomogeneous. Such right-skew of real-world networks' degree distributions has been found to approximate a power-law distribution, in what is commonly known as scale-free networks (Barabási & Albert, 1999).

The power-law (or Pareto-law) distribution suggests that the probability of observing a vertex with k edges obeys the potential functional form in (4), where z is a (arbitrary) constant, and γ is known as the *exponent* of the power-law.[10]

$$\mathrm{P}_k \propto z k^{-\gamma} \tag{4}$$

According to Newman (2010), values in the range $2 \leq \gamma \leq 3$ are typical of scale-free networks, although values slightly outside this range are possible and are occasionally observed. On the other hand, values much greater than 3 are considered typical of homogeneous or random networks.[11] As in in 't Veld and Lelyveld (2014), the power-law distribution of links is an asymptotic property, thus testing the scale-free features of a network is problematic. In this sense, a strict match between observed and expected theoretical properties for determining the scale-free properties of non-large networks –as those examined here- may be impractical.

Regarding the small-world feature (i.e. every vertex can be reached in a limited number of steps), the mean geodesic distance (l) reflects the global structure and measures how big the network is.[12] This average distance depends on the way the entire network is connected, and cannot be inferred from any local measurement (Strogatz, 2003). Let g_{ij} be the *geodesic distance* (i.e. the shortest path in terms of number of edges) from vertex i to j, the mean geodesic distance for vertex i (l_i) corresponds to the mean of g_{ij}, averaged over all reachable vertices j in the network, as in (5). Respectively, the mean geodesic distance or average path length of a network (i.e. for all pairs of vertices) is denoted as l (without the subscript), and corresponds to the mean of l_i over all vertices.

$$l_i = \frac{1}{(n-1)} \sum_{j(\neq 1)} g_{ij} \qquad l = \frac{1}{n} \sum_i l_i \tag{5}$$

The mean geodesic distance (l) of random or Poisson networks is small, and increases slowly with the size of the network. Therefore, as stressed by Albert and Barabási (2002), random graphs are *small-world* because, in spite of their often large size, in most networks there is relatively a short path between any two vertices. According to Newman, Barabási, and Watts (2006), l approximates $\ln n$ for random networks, where such slow logarithmic increase with the size of the network coincides with the small-world effect (i.e. short average path lengths). In the case of scale-free networks, the mean geodesic distance has been found to be smaller than $l \sim \ln n$, about $l \sim \ln \ln n$, which Cohen and Havlin (2003) refer to as *ultrasmall-world*

The clustering coefficient (c) corresponds to the property of network transitivity. It measures the average probability that two neighbors of a vertex are themselves neighbors; or, in other words, the frequency with which loops of length three (i.e. triangles) appear in the network. Let a *triangle* be a graph of three vertices that is fully connected, and a *connected triple* be a graph of three vertices with at least two connections, the calculation of the network's clustering coefficient is as follows: [13]

$$c = \frac{(\text{number of triangles in the network}) \times 3}{\text{number of connected triples}} \tag{6}$$

Hence, by construction, clustering reflects the local structure. It depends only on the interconnectedness of a typical neighborhood, the inbreeding among vertices tied to a common center, and thus it measures how incestuous the network is (Strogatz, 2003). Intuitively, the probability of connection of two vertices in a random or homogeneous graph tends to be the same for all vertices regardless the existence of a common neighbor. Therefore, the clustering coefficient is expected to be low in the case of random graphs, and tends to zero in the limit for large random networks.

Real-world complex networks tend to exhibit a large degree of clustering. Albert and Barabási (2002) report that in most –if not all- real networks the clustering coefficient is typically much larger then in comparable random networks, and that this factor slowly increases with the number of vertices. Accordingly, in inhomogeneous graphs, as those resulting from real-world networks, the probability of two neighbors of a vertex being themselves neighbors is reported to be in the 10% and 60% range in most cases (Newman, 2010). In this sense, a particularly low mean geodesic distance combined with high clustering in scale-free networks implies that a few too-connected vertices play a key role in bringing the other vertices close to each other. In the context of studies on robustness of and contagion in financial systems, it is important to identify those too-connected players that are central in a network and could threaten financial stability in case they would fail.

Importance within the Network

Regarding the importance of each participant within every network, *centrality* is the most prevalent and widely used concept. Centrality's most common and simple measure is degree centrality (k_i), which assesses how connected a vertex is to the network. For weighted networks, the strength (s_i) measures the total weight of connections for a given vertex and hence provides an assessment of the intensity of the interaction between participants.

Intuitively, the larger the degree or the strength, the more important the vertex is for the network. Nevertheless, the analytical reach of these two metrics as measures of the relative importance of a vertex is limited because they do not take into account the global properties of the network; this is, they are local measures of importance, and they do not capture neighbors' importance.

The simplest global measure of centrality is eigenvector centrality, whereby the centrality of a vertex is proportional to the sum of the centrality of its adjacent vertices; accordingly, the centrality of a vertex is the weighted sum of centrality at all possible order adjacencies. Hence, in this case centrality arises from (i) being connected to many vertices; (ii) being connected to central vertices; (iii) or both.[14] Alternatively, as put forward by Soramäki and Cook (2012), eigenvector centrality may be thought of as the proportion of time spent visiting each participant in an infinite random walk through the network.

Eigenvector centrality is based on the *spectral decomposition* of a matrix. Let Ω be an adjacency matrix (weighted or non-weighted), Λ a diagonal matrix containing the eigenvalues of Ω, and Γ an orthogonal matrix satisfying $\Gamma\Gamma' = \Gamma\Gamma = I_n$, whose columns are eigenvectors of Ω, such that

$$\Omega = \Gamma\Lambda\Gamma' \tag{7}$$

If the diagonal matrix of eigenvalues (Λ) is ordered so that $\lambda_1 \geq \lambda_2 \cdots \lambda_n$, the first column in Γ corresponds to the principal eigenvector of Ω. The principal eigenvector (Γ_1) may be considered as the leading vector of the system, the one that is able to explain most of the underlying system. The positive n-scaled scores corresponding to each element in the principal eigenvector may be considered as their weights within an index. Because the largest eigenvalue and its corresponding eigenvector provide the highest accuracy (i.e. explanatory power) for reproducing the original matrix and capturing the main features of networks (Straffin, 1980), Bonacich (1972) envisaged Γ_1 as a global measure of popularity or centrality within a social network.[15]

However, eigenvector centrality has some drawbacks. As stated by Bonacich (1972), eigenvector centrality works for symmetric structures only (i.e. undirected graphs); yet, it is possible to work with the right (or left) eigenvector (as in Markose et al., 2012), but this may entail some information loss. Nevertheless, the most severe inconvenience from estimating eigenvector centrality on asymmetric matrices arises from vertices with only outgoing or incoming edges, which will may result in zero eigenvector centrality, and may cause some other non-strongly connected vertices to have zero eigenvector centrality as well (Newman, 2010).

Among some alternatives to surmount the drawbacks of eigenvector centrality (e.g. PageRank, Katz centrality), the HITS (Hypertext Induced Topic Search) algorithm by Kleinberg (1998) has two main advantages that matter for this chapter's empirical design. First, it provides two separate centrality measures, *authority centrality* (a) and *hub centrality* (h), which correspond to the eigenvector centrality as recipient and as originator of links, respectively. Second, it avoids introducing inconvenient stochastic or arbitrary adjustments to the network –as in PageRank or Katz centrality.

The estimation of authority and hub centrality results from estimating standard eigenvector centrality (7) on two modified versions of the adjacency matrix, A and H, as in (8).

$$A = \Omega'\Omega \qquad H = \Omega\Omega' \tag{8}$$

Multiplying the adjacency matrix with a transposed version of itself enables one to identify directed (*in* or *out*) second order adjacencies. Regarding A, multiplying Ω' with Ω sends weights backwards –against the arrows, towards the pointing vertex-, whereas multiplying Ω with Ω' (as in H) sends scores forwards –with the arrows, towards the pointed-to vertex (Bjelland, Canright, & Engo-Mønsen, 2008). Thus, the HITS algorithm works on a circular thesis: the authority centrality of each participant is defined to be proportional to the sum of the hub centrality of the participants that point to it, and the hub centrality of each participant is defined to be proportional to the sum of the authority centrality of the participant it points to.

Therefore, authority (a) and hub (h) centrality provide global measures of participants' centrality that supplements traditional local measures such as degree (k) and strength (s). Together, local and global measures of centrality will be useful to comprehensively test the presence of positively correlated multiplexity in a system.

MAIN RESULTS

The multiplex network here analyzed consists of aggregating three different networks: SEN, MEC, MEC-R. In the sample period (third quarter of year 2013), SEN accounted for 52.6% of the value of transactions in DCV, whereas MEC and MEC-R accounted for 18.5% and 28.7%, respectively. The main connective features of SEN, MEC, MEC-R, and the resulting sovereign securities market multiplex are presented in Table 1. All statistics in Table 1 correspond to the mean of those estimated on daily networks; no serial aggregation of daily networks was implemented for estimating the statistics.

SEN, the largest contributor to the sovereign securities multiplex by market value of transactions, exhibits a rather odd connective structure. Against most documented real-world networks, SEN appears to be non-sparse, with a density about .60 and with participants directly connecting on average with more than half of their counterparties. Moreover, it appears to be homogeneous by degree, with the corresponding power-law exponent (6.05) well above typical values for scale-free networks (i.e. $\gamma_k \gg 3$) and inhomogeneous by strength. SEN is also non-clustered because the clustering coefficient is below the expected value for random networks of the same size ($\mu_k / n = .55$).[16] Yet, it is an approximately ultrasmall-world network due to the low mean geodesic distance ($l = 1.36$). Such a unique connective structure results from its design: it is a 14-vertex rich-club network created by the Ministry of Finance to foster sovereign securities market's liquidity, in which financial institutions agree to trade anonymously, free of any counterparty limit, while observing requisites that determine their permanence on the network.[17] Taken all together, these special features of SEN ultimately govern how participants relate to each other in the network.

Table 1. Main connective features of networks [a]

Statistics	SEN	MEC	MEC-R	Sovereign securities multiplex
Contribution (by value of transactions)	.53	.18	.29	1.00
Participants (n)	14	90	91	159
Density (d)	.60	.05	.02	.02
Mean degree (μ_k)	7.75	4.31	1.45	3.46
Degree power-law exponent (γ_k) [b,c]	6.05 [.45]	2.76 [.53]	2.99 [.53]	3.66 [.52]
Strength power-law exponent (γ_s) [b,c]	2.92 [.00]	2.43 [.01]	2.66 [.00]	2.40 [.00]
Mean geodesic distance (l)	1.36 [2.63]	2.23 [4.50]	3.11 [4.51]	2.78 [5.07]
Clustering coefficient (C)	.43 [.55]	.10 [.05]	.03 [.02]	.10 [.02]

This table shows that networks corresponding to MEC, MEC-R, and the sovereign securities multiplex display the conventional features of most real-world networks (e.g. sparseness, clustering, and inhomogeneity). SEN's network does not comply with those features. Despite some of the estimated power-law exponents do not make a strong case based on the goodness-of-fit tests of Clauset, Shalizi, and Newman (2009), the level of the exponent provides enough evidence of the alleged inhomogeneity in the distribution of degree for MEC, MEC-R and the multiplex. [a] All statistics in this table correspond to sample means estimated on daily statistics for the analyzed quarter (63 days). Expected values for homogeneous networks of n size appear in brackets for the mean geodesic distance (l) and the clustering coefficient (c). [b] The algorithm by Clauset, Shalizi, and Newman (2009) is used for estimating the power-law exponents. [c] The average goodness of fit p -value is reported brackets, with $p \leq 0.1$ corresponding to an implausible case for a power-law (Clauset, Shalizi, and Newman, 2009); however, ruling out a power-law does not mean that the distribution is not skewed, but that another skewed distribution (e.g. exponential) may provide a better fit.

Figure 2 presents the graph corresponding to SEN's network, in which the diameter of the vertices and the width of the arrows are determined by their strength and the market value of the sovereign securities' deliveries, respectively. The number of edges appears to be evenly distributed, but their width and the diameter of the vertices is inhomogeneous. Likewise, it can be easily observed that participants are well-connected and –therefore- the network is rather dense.

When examining the connective structure of the second network, MEC, its characteristics agree with what the literature considers a typical real-world network: it is sparse (the average density is about .05), scale-free (the average power law exponent estimated on degree and strength is around 2.76 and 2.43, respectively), and it is approximately ultrasmall-world (the mean geodesic distance averages to 2.23 edges).[18] Although the clustering level is not particularly high ($c = 0.10$), it is still higher than the probability of any two vertices in MEC being connected ($\mu_k/n = .05$), such that it could be considered as a clustered network. Figure 3 presents the graph corresponding to MEC's network, in which there is a high degree of agreement between the participants pertaining to SEN network (in black) and those vertices at which most edges are concentrated (i.e. with the highest degree) and which display the largest diameters (i.e. with the highest strength).

Akin to MEC, the connective structure of MEC-R, is very much like what one would expect of real-world networks. The MEC-R network is sparse, with average density about .02; scale-free, with the

Figure 2. SEN graph. Vertices correspond to participating financial institutions; the direction and width of each arrow represents the delivery of local sovereign securities and its market value, respectively; vertices' diameter correspond to their strength. The position of vertices results from the ForceAtlas2 algorithm (available in Gephi), which consists of two competing forces: nodes repulse each other, whereas edges attract nodes.

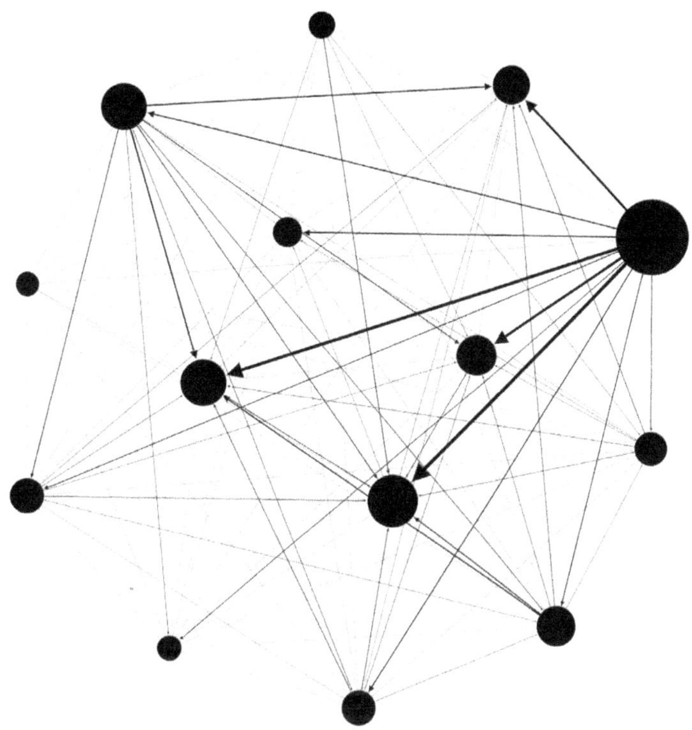

average power-law exponent estimated on degree and strength around 2.99 and 2.66, respectively; and approximately ultrasmall-world, with the mean geodesic distance averaging 3.11 edges. The clustering level is not particularly high ($c = .03$) , but it is slightly higher than the probability of any two vertices of MEC-R being connected ($\mu_k / n = .02$), and could thus be considered as somewhat clustered. Figure 4 presents the graph corresponding to MEC-R's network. As with MEC, there is a high degree of correspondence between the participants pertaining to SEN network (in black) and those vertices at which most edges are concentrated (i.e. vertices with the highest degree) and which display the largest diameters (i.e. vertices with the highest strength).

According to Table 1, the sovereign securities market multiplex network displays the sparse, inhomogeneous, approximately scale-free[19], approximately ultrasmall-world features documented in real-world networks. The clustering coefficient ($c = .10$) of the multiplex network is higher than the probability of any two vertices being connected within ($\mu_k / n = .02$), which indicates that significant clustering is present. Consequently, the multiplex reproduces the overall connective features of MEC and MEC-R, and ignores those of SEN, which is –paradoxically- its main contributor in terms of the market value of

Figure 3. MEC graph. Vertices correspond to participating financial institutions; the direction and width of each arrow represents the delivery of local sovereign securities and its market value, respectively; vertices' diameter correspond to their strength; SEN participants are in black. The position of vertices results from the ForceAtlas2 algorithm (available in Gephi), which consists of two competing forces: nodes repulse each other, whereas edges attract nodes.

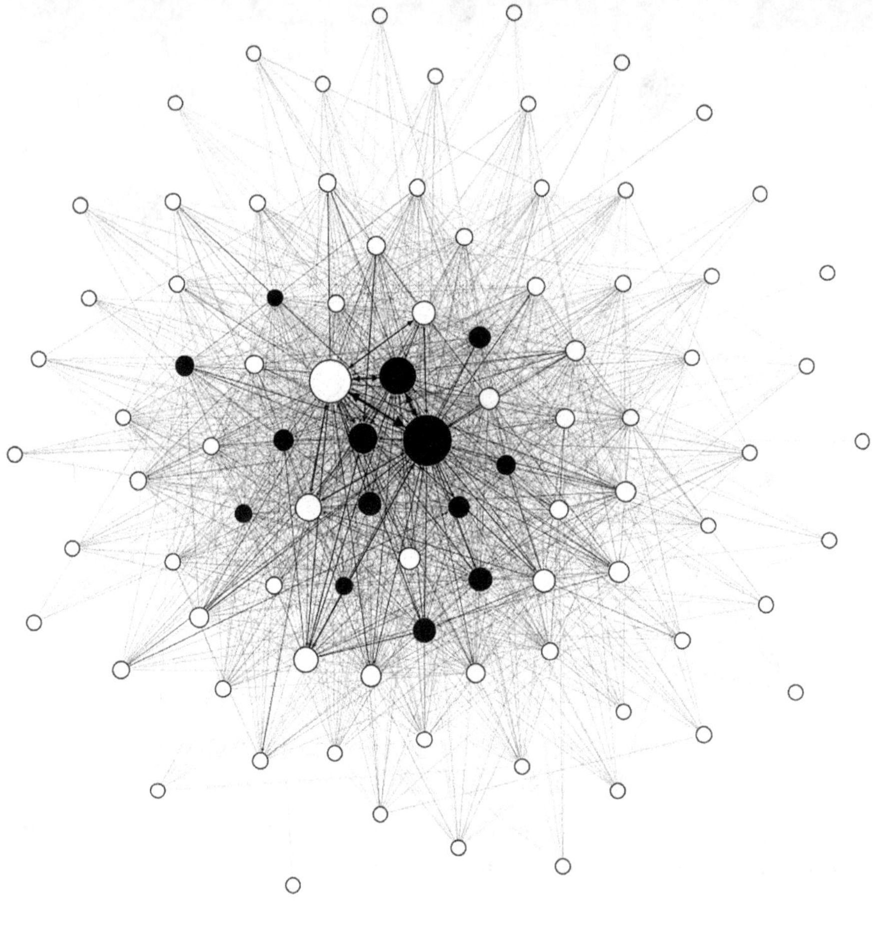

transactions. In this sense, the multiplex network of the Colombian sovereign securities market appears to largely preserve the robust-yet-fragile (Haldane, 2009) features of MEC and MEC-R.

Figure 5 presents the graph corresponding to the sovereign securities market multiplex, with the vertices filled out in black pertaining to the SEN network. As in MEC and MEC-R, there is a high degree of correspondence between the participants pertaining to SEN network and the participants with the highest concentration of edges (i.e. the highest degree) and with the largest diameters (i.e. the highest strength).

The main features of the multiplex of the sovereign securities market point out that it is a network of networks that preserves the main characteristics of the two networks that contribute the least (47%) to the total market value of sovereign securities transactions, whereas the most salient connective features of SEN appear to contribute less. Therefore, using SEN as a benchmark for the local sovereign securities market may be particularly misleading.[20]

Figure 4. MEC-R graph. Vertices correspond to participating financial institutions; the direction and width of each arrow represents the delivery of local sovereign securities and its market value, respectively; vertices' diameter correspond to their strength; SEN participants are filled in black. The position of vertices results from the ForceAtlas2 algorithm (available in Gephi), which consists of two competing forces: nodes repulse each other, whereas edges attract nodes.

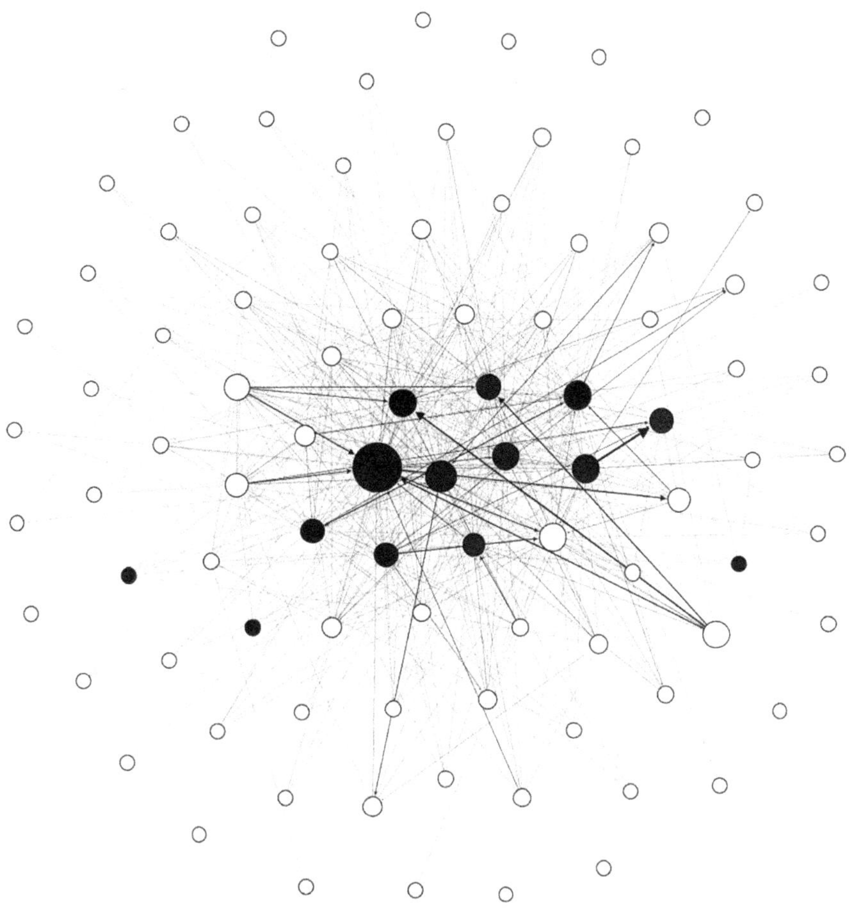

Interestingly, as the three monoplex networks result from different platforms with distinct economic settings and dissimilar operational frameworks, the multiplex network approach reveals how each of the monoplex networks shapes the multiplex one. First, the statistical and graphical resemblance between the multiplex, MEC and MEC-R monoplex networks is evident from Table 1 and the corresponding graphs, respectively. Second, when coupling SEN, MEC, and MEC-R, it is evident that SEN is no longer a rich-club network of 14-financial institutions densely interconnected, but a network in which there is a core of densely connected vertices surrounded by a vast periphery of non-linked participants, and with a connective structure approximating that of MEC and MEC-R. Under this comprehensive view revealed by the multi-layer approach, the SEN network is turned into a sparse, inhomogeneous and potentially scale-free network that preserves its ultrasmall-world and non-clustered nature.[21]

Figure 5. Sovereign securities market graph. Vertices correspond to participating financial institutions; the direction and width of each arrow represents the delivery of local sovereign securities and its market value in the three monoplex networks, respectively; vertices' diameter correspond to their strength; SEN participants are filled in black. The position of vertices results from the ForceAtlas2 algorithm (available in Gephi), which consists of two competing forces: nodes repulse each other, whereas edges attract nodes.

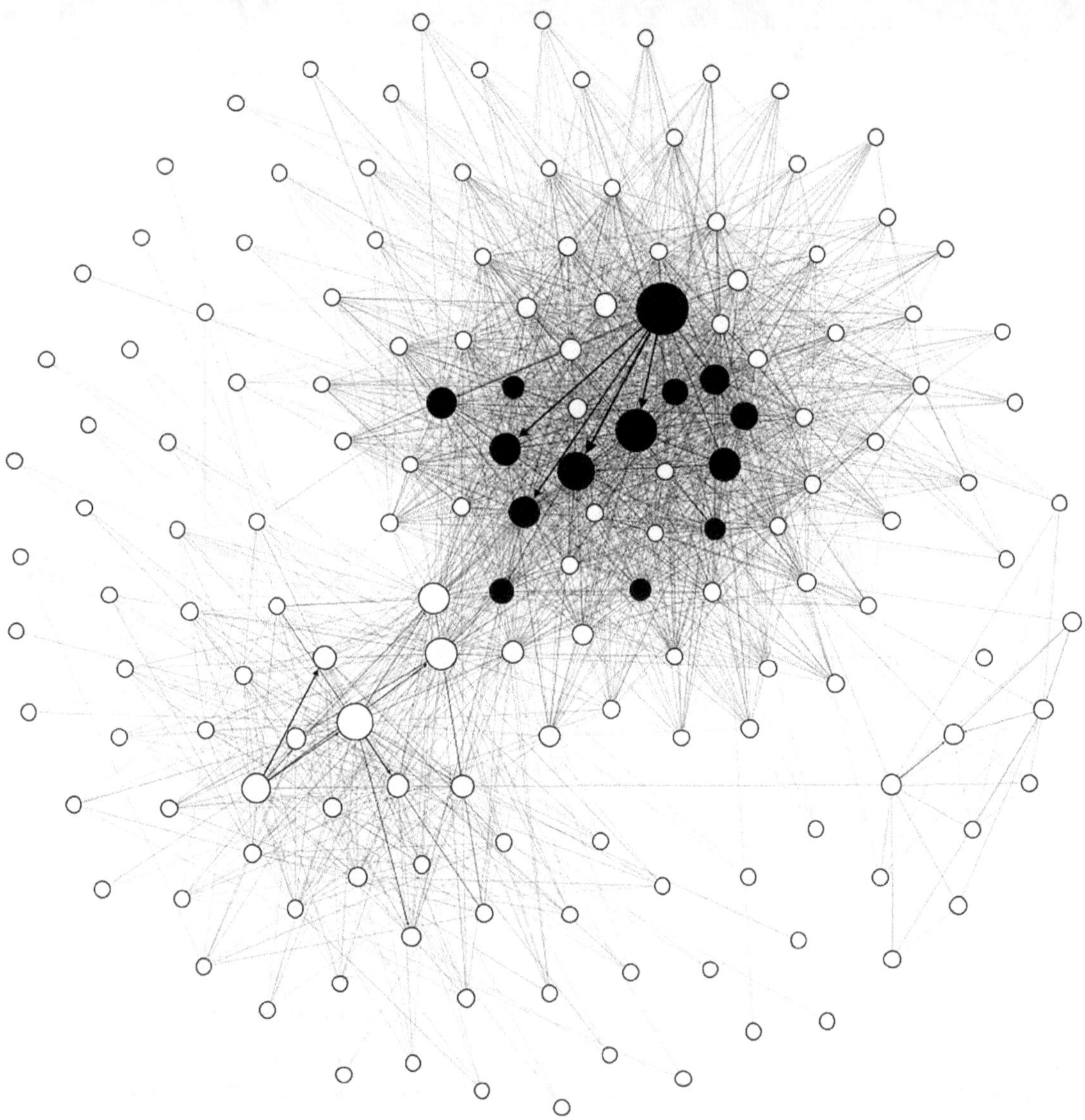

The connective coincidence across the layers in the sovereign securities multiplex network may suggest the presence of positively correlated multiplexity in the sense of Lee et al. (2014) and Kenett et al. (2014). This means that the main connective features of the constituent monoplex networks may be preserved as a consequence of consistency in the importance of participants across networks (i.e. vertices' centrality overlapping across layers). Table 2 contains the correlation matrix estimated on financial institutions' degree (k), strength (s), hub centrality (h) and authority centrality (a). The correlation matrix corresponds to the estimation of the (Pearson) correlation coefficient for selected pairs of the centrality measures. Let k_{SEN} and k_{MEC} be two vectors containing the contribution of each i -institution to the sum of degree in SEN and MEC, respectively, the correlation coefficient $\rho_{k_{SEN},k_{MEC}}$ is estimated as in (9). Non-participating financial institutions are assigned a contribution equal to zero.

$$\rho_{k_{SEN},k_{MEC}} = \frac{\operatorname{cov}\left(k_{SEN},k_{MEC}\right)}{\sigma_{k_{SEN}}\sigma_{k_{MEC}}} \tag{9}$$

The correlation matrix in Table 2 confirms that there is indeed a positive and non-negligible linear dependence in financial institutions' role and importance across the three different trading and registering platforms, either by local (i.e. degree and strength) or by global (i.e. hub and authority) measures of centrality.

Thus, evidence in this chapter confirms that the presence of positively correlated multiplexity prompts a multiplex network that tends to preserve the main features of its constituent monoplex networks. Moreover, unlike traditional literature on correlated multiplexity of real-world networks (Lee et al., 2014, Kenett et al. 2014), this chapter provides evidence of how different measures of centrality (i.e. degree, strength, authority centrality and hub centrality) agree about the overlapping of participants' roles within the studied multiplex network.

FUTURE RESEARCH DIRECTIONS

Some interesting research extensions are worth highlighting. Other types of multi-layer analysis can be implemented with the same database (i.e. from DCV) and with other data from different financial market infrastructures. In the first case, due to the granularity and great detail of transactions in DCV it is possible to build different multi-layer networks that may provide additional perspectives into the local sovereign securities market. For instance, the layers may relate to transactions' or participants' intrinsic characteristics which include – non-exhaustively - the maturity of the traded sovereign securities; the volatility of the securities; the ownership structures of the participating financial institutions; institutions' credit risk ratings; the types of institutions (e.g. banking, non-banking), and the final beneficiary of the transactions (e.g. proprietary or non-proprietary).

Likewise, data from other financial markets (such as foreign exchange, non-sovereign fixed income, derivatives, etc.) may profit from a multi-layer approach based on data provided by the corresponding financial market infrastructures. All these potential multi-layer networks may help understand how financial institutions relate into each other in distinct financial environments, and in the entire financial system.

It is also important to realize that the multiplex network is the standard case of multi-layer networks, but it is not the only one. It is possible to build multi-later networks with dissimilar participants, in which non-financial institutions are good candidates because of their usage of financial services. For instance, in the sovereign securities market analyzed in this chapter this would consist of identifying the end user

Table 2. Monoplex networks' degree, strength, authority and hub centrality correlation matrix [a]

Centrality measure	1	2	3	4	5	6	7	8	9	10	11	12
1. k_{MEC}	–											
2. k_{SEN}	.55	–										
3. k_{MEC-R}	.81	.71	–									
4. s_{MEC}				–								
5. s_{SEN}				.48	–							
6. s_{MEC-R}				.67	.70	–						
7. h_{MEC}							–					
8. h_{SEN}							.29	–				
9. h_{MEC-R}							.41	.49	–			
10. a_{MEC}										–		
11. a_{SEN}										.53	–	
12. a_{MEC-R}										.63	.70	–

[a] The correlation matrix is estimated based on the contribution of each financial institution to the total degree (k), strength (s), hub (h) and authority (a) centrality in the whole sample; non-participating financial institutions are assigned a contribution equal to zero. Correlations across centrality measures are omitted to enhance readability. Self-correlations in the main diagonal are replaced by a dash.

of each transaction (e.g. non-financial firms, households, government) and building the corresponding layers into the multi-layer network; due to the quality of the information of DCV this is attainable.

Furthermore, there is an unmapped source of complexity in the financial system worth exploring. Most literature on financial networks deals with a single type of participant: financial institutions. However, from the financial market infrastructures' perspective there is a critical role that has been absent of financial networks analysis, namely the unavoidable link between financial institutions and financial market infrastructures for the settlement of financial transactions. In this vein, as envisaged by Kurant and Thiran (2006), the edges or links between financial institutions are of a mere virtual or logical nature, with the network of financial market infrastructures and other physical networks (e.g. power, communications) providing the vital "plumbing" or "medium" for the functioning of financial systems; this is, financial systems' *critical infrastructures*[22] should be considered within the multi-layer network. As documented by León, Berndsen, and Renneboog (2014), the logical connective structure of the financial network changes when considering the "plumbing" role of financial market infrastructures, and is –therefore- crucial for understanding financial systems and for contributing to financial stability.

CONCLUSION

Financial markets are complex systems that can be better understood by examining how its constituents, the financial institutions, relate to one another. This type of research is particularly important to detect the pivotal players in a system whose robustness is vital for financial stability. Analyses on financial contagion enable us to chart systemic risks. The right approach to gain insight on the interrelated functioning of financial institutions is precisely by means of applying network science to financial data. The main objective is to get a comprehensive view of how financial institutions interact, and to avoid the pitfalls of traditional institution-centric analyses by means of a macro-prudential approach to financial systems.

As has been acknowledged rather recently, it is critical to go beyond single-layer networks to better understand how financial institutions interrelate without assuming that each financial network is isolated from the others. Data recorded in financial market infrastructures is a convenient source of information to take a step towards examining how financial institutions are linked across different financial environments.

This chapter has examined how financial institutions relate to each other in different trading and registering environments of sovereign securities (i.e. the platforms). It has also studied how those environments aggregate into a multiplex network that portrays the local sovereign securities as a network of networks. When the multiplex network is built, strong non-linear effects arise: the network characteristics of the most important monoplex network (i.e. SEN) in terms of the market value of its transactions do not hand over its characteristics to the multiplex network. SEN appears to be a non-sparse network with its participants directly connecting on average with more than half of their counterparties. It is also homogeneous by degree, inhomogeneous by strength, and non-clustered. In contrast, the multiplex resulting from the three constituting networks conforms to most real-world networks' features, i.e. sparse, inhomogeneous, scale-free, ultrasmall-world, and clustered, which are the traits of the lesser important networks MEC and MEC-R.

The unusual connective features of SEN actually reinforce the real-world networks' characteristics displayed by MEC and MEC-R by means of a strong linear dependence between most central participants across all networks. This important finding would have been omitted if one studies monoplex networks in isolation, and could have misled the perspective on the relations between and risks induced by participating financial institutions. Likewise, this finding would have been elusive without the data from the corresponding settlement market infrastructure (i.e. DCV).

Furthermore, the evidence of positively correlated multiplexity reveals some interesting characteristics of the local sovereign securities market. Three characteristics are worth reporting: First, the inhomogeneous and approximate scale-free connective structure, consistent with the robust-yet-fragile nature of financial networks (Haldane, 1999), is the result of structural similarity (i.e. positive correlated multiplexity) across networks within a multi-layer analytical framework. Second, due to the ultrasmall-world nature of all networks analyzed in this framework, it is evident that the role of too-connected financial institutions is critical for the efficiency of the market, not only at the single-layer level, but also for the whole market when the coupling of single-layer networks is considered. Third, notwithstanding the economic and operational differences of each monoplex network, financial institutions that are considered *too-connected to fail* tend to overlap across networks, and their role in financial stability is critical due to their contribution to *cross-system risk.*[23] These three characteristics are also an essential focus in order to better understand the local sovereign securities market and its contribution to financial stability.

This research has contributed to the literature by highlighting the relevance of network analysis on data from financial market infrastructures. First, data gathered by financial market infrastructures have the potential to overcome the main obstacles for working on multi-layer networks highlighted by D'Souza et al. (2014), namely the independent ownership and operation of layers, and the lack of data standardization and sharing. Second, unlike traditional balance sheet data, financial market infrastructures gather granular information from distinct financial environments, which may allow breaking down aggregated financial data into very different layers of complexity in order to reach a deeper understanding of financial markets.

Finally, this chapter has highlighted the convenience of taking a step ahead in the examination and understanding of financial markets' connective architecture, beyond single- and multi-layer financial institutions' networks. Building multi-layer networks with non-financial institutions as additional layers that couple with financial layers may reveal some other sources of complexity worth examining for understanding the functioning of financial systems and the economy as a whole. Furthermore, as recently documented by León, Berndsen, & Renneboog (2014), building and analyzing an interacting multi-layer network that reveals how financial institutions depend on the network of financial market infrastructures for the clearing and settlement of their transactions is a step forward in the study of financial networks and financial stability: some of the stylized facts documented in financial networks literature (e.g. clustering, modularity) vanish as the interaction between financial institutions and infrastructures is considered.

REFERENCES

Albert, R., & Barabási, A.-L. (2002). Statistical mechanics of complex networks. *Reviews of Modern Physics*, *74*(1), 47–97. doi:10.1103/RevModPhys.74.47

Barabási, A.-L. (2003). *Linked.* New York: Plume.

Barabási, A.-L., & Albert, R. (1999). Emergence of scaling in random networks. *Science*, *286*(5439), 509–512. doi:10.1126/science.286.5439.509 PMID:10521342

Bargigli, L., di Iasio, G., Infante, L., Lillo, F., & Pierobon, F. (2013). *The multiplex structure of interbank networks* (Working Paper Series – Economics No.26/2013). DISEI.

Baxter, G. J., Dorogovtsev, A., Glotsec, V., & Mendes, J. F. F. (2014). Avalanches in multiplex and interdependent networks. In G. D'Agostino & A. Scala (Eds.), *Networks of networks: the last frontier of complexity* (pp. 37–52). Cham, Switzerland: Springer. doi:10.1007/978-3-319-03518-5_2

Bech, M., & Atalay, E. (2008). *The topology of the Federal Funds Market* (Federal Reserve Bank of New York Staff Report No.354). New York: Federal Reserve Bank of New York.

Bernanke, B. (2011, April). *Clearinghouses, financial stability, and financial reform.* Remarks at the 2011 Financial Markets Conference, Federal Reserve Bank of Atlanta, Stone Mountain, Georgia.

Bjelland, J., Canright, G., & Engo-Mønsen, K. (2008). Web link analysis: Estimating document's importance from its context. *Telektronikk*, *1*, 95–113.

Bonacich, P. (1972). Factoring and weighting approaches to status scores and clique identification. *The Journal of Mathematical Sociology*, *2*(1), 113–120. doi:10.1080/0022250X.1972.9989806

Boots, B. N. (1984). Evaluating principal eigenvalues as measures of network structure. *Geographical Analysis*, *3*, 270–275.

Boss, M., Elsinger, H., Summer, M., & Thurner, S. (2004). The network topology of the interbank market. *Quantitative Finance*, *4*(6), 677–684. doi:10.1080/14697680400020325

Buldyrev, S. V., Parshani, R., Paul, G., Stanley, H. E., & Havlin, S. (2010). Catastrophic cascade of failures in interdependent networks. *Nature*, *15*(464), 1025–1028. doi:10.1038/nature08932 PMID:20393559

Cardillo, A., Gómez-Gardeñes, J., Zanin, M., Romance, M., Papo, D., del Pozo, F., & Boccaletti, S. (2013). Emergence of network features from multiplexity. *Scientific Reports*, *3*(1344), 1–6. PMID:23446838

Clauset, A., Shalizi, C. R., & Newman, M. E. J. (2009). Power-law distributions in empirical data. *SIAM Review*, *51*(4), 661–703. doi:10.1137/070710111

Cohen, R., & Havlin, S. (2003). Scale-Free Networks Are Ultrasmall. *Physical Review Letters*, *5*, 1–4. PMID:12633404

Committee on Payment and Settlement Systems – CPSS. (2008). The interdependencies of payment and settlement systems. Basel: Bank for International Settlements (BIS).

Council directive 2008/114/EC. (2008). *Official Journal of the European Union*. Retrieved from http://eur-lex.europa.eu/LexUriServ/LexUriServ.do?uri=CELEX:32008L0114:EN:NOT

Craig, B., & von Peter, G. (2014). Interbank tiering and money center banks. *Journal of Financial Intermediation*, *23*(3), 322–347. doi:10.1016/j.jfi.2014.02.003

D'Souza, R. M., Brummitt, C. D., & Leicht, E. A. (2014). Modeling interdependent networks as random graphs: connectivity and systemic risk. In G. D'Agostino & A. Scala (Eds.), *Networks of networks: the last frontier of complexity* (pp. 73–94). Cham, Switzerland: Springer. doi:10.1007/978-3-319-03518-5_4

Erdos, P., & Rényi, A. (1960). On random graphs. *Publicationes Mathematicae*, *6*, 17–61.

Estrada, D. & Morales, P. (2008, March). *La estructura del mercado interbancario y del riesgo de contagio en Colombia* (Reporte de Estabilidad Financiera). Bogotá, Colombia: Banco de la República.

Fricke, D., & Lux, T. (2014). Core-periphery structure in the overnight money market: Evidence from the e-MID trading platform. *Computational Economics*. doi:10.1007/s10614-014-9427-x

Gao, J., Buldyrev, S. V., Stanley, H. E., & Havlin, S. (2012). Networks formed from interdependent networks. *Nature Physics*, *8*(1), 40–48. doi:10.1038/nphys2180 PMID:23005189

Gómez-Gardeñes, J., Reinares, I., Arenas, A., & Floría, L. M. (2012). Evolution of cooperation in multiplex networks. *Scientific Reports*, *2*(620), 1–6. doi:10.1038/srep00620 PMID:22943006

Gould, P. R. (1967). On the geographical interpretation of eigenvalues. *Transactions of the Institute of British Geographers*, *42*(42), 53–86. doi:10.2307/621372

Haldane, A.G. (2009, April). *Rethinking the financial network*. Speech delivered at the Financial Student Association, Amsterdam, Netherlands.

in 't Veld, D., & van Lelyveld, I. (2014). Finding the Core: Network Structure in Interbank Markets. *Journal of Banking & Finance*, *49*, 27–40. doi:10.1016/j.jbankfin.2014.08.006

Inaoka, H., Ninomiya, T., Tanigushi, K., Shimizu, T., & Takayasu, H. (2004). *Fractal network derived from banking transaction* (Bank of Japan Working Paper Series No. 04-E04). Tokyo: Bank of Japan.

Ivanov, P. Ch., & Bartsch, R. P. (2014). Network physiology: mapping interactions between networks of physiologic networks. In G. D'Agostino & A. Scala (Eds.), *Networks of networks: the last frontier of complexity* (pp. 203–222). Cham, Switzerland: Springer. doi:10.1007/978-3-319-03518-5_10

Kenett, D. Y., Gao, J., Huang, X., Shao, S., Vodenska, I., & Buldyrev, S. V. et al. (2014). Network of interdependent networks: overview of theory and applications. In G. D'Agostino & A. Scala (Eds.), *Networks of networks: the last frontier of complexity* (pp. 3–36). Cham, Switzerland: Springer. doi:10.1007/978-3-319-03518-5_1

Kleinberg, J. M. (1998, January). Authoritative sources in a hyperlinked environment. *Proceedings of the 9th ACM-SIAM Symposium on Discrete Algorithms*, 668-677.

Kolaczyc, E. D. (2009). *Statistical analysis of network data*. New York: Springer. doi:10.1007/978-0-387-88146-1

Kurant, M., & Thiran, P. (2006). Layered complex networks. *Physical Review Letters*, *138701*(96). doi:10.1103/PhysRevLett.96.138701 PMID:16712049

Kyriakopoulos, F., Thurner, S., Puhr, C., & Schmitz, S. W. (2009). Network and eigenvalue analysis of financial transaction networks. *The European Physical Journal B*, *71*(4), 523–531. doi:10.1140/epjb/e2009-00255-7

Laverde, M., & Gutiérrez, J. (2012). *Cómo caracterizar entidades sistémicas?: medidas de Impacto Sistémico para Colombia (Temas de Estabilidad Financiera, No.65)*. Bogotá, Colombia: Banco de la República.

Lee, K.-M., Kim, J. Y., Lee, S., & Goh, K.-I. (2014). Multiplex networks. In G. D'Agostino & A. Scala (Eds.), *Networks of networks: the last frontier of complexity* (pp. 53–72). Cham, Switzerland: Springer. doi:10.1007/978-3-319-03518-5_3

León, C., & Berndsen, R. J. (2014). Rethinking financial stability: Challenges arising from financial networks' modular scale-free architecture. *Journal of Financial Stability*, *15*, 241–256. doi:10.1016/j.jfs.2014.10.006

León, C., Berndsen, R. J., & Renneboog, L. (2014). *Financial Stability and Interacting Networks of Financial Institutions and Market Infrastructures* (European Banking Center Discussion Paper Series No.2014-11). Tilburg: Tilburg University.

León, C., & Pérez, J. (2014). Assessing financial market infrastructures' systemic importance with authority and hub centrality. *Journal of Financial Market Infrastructures.*, *3*(2), 67–87.

Markose, S. M., Giansante, S., & Rais Shaghaghi, A. (2012). Too interconnected to fail financial network of US CDS market: Topological fragility and systemic risk. *Journal of Economic Behavior & Organization, 83*(3), 627–646. doi:10.1016/j.jebo.2012.05.016

Martí, J. R. (2014). Multisystem simulation: analysis of critical infrastructures for disaster response. In G. D'Agostino & A. Scala (Eds.), *Networks of networks: the last frontier of complexity* (pp. 255–278). Cham, Switzerland: Springer. doi:10.1007/978-3-319-03518-5_12

Martínez-Jaramillo, S., Alexandrova-Kabadjova, B., Bravo-Benítez, B., & Solórzano-Margain, J. P. (2012). *An empirical study of the Mexican banking system's network and its implications for systemic risk* (Working Papers No.2012-17), México: Banco de México.

May, R. M., Levin, S. A., & Sugihara, G. (2008). Ecology for bankers. *Nature, 451*(7181), 893–895. doi:10.1038/451893a PMID:18288170

Montagna, M., & Kok, C. (2013). *Multi-layer interbank model for assessing systemic risk* (Kiel Working Papers No.1873). Kiel, Germany, Kiel Institute for the World Economy.

Newman, M. E. J. (2010). *Networks: an Introduction*. Oxford: Oxford University Press. doi:10.1093/acprof:oso/9780199206650.001.0001

Newman, M. E. J., Barabási, A.-L., & Watts, D. J. (2006). *The structure and dynamics of networks*. Princeton: Princeton University Press.

Padget, J. F., & Powell, W. W. (2012). The Problem of Emergence. In J. F. Padget & W. W. Powell (Eds.), *The Emergence of Organizations and Markets* (pp. 2–29). Princeton: Princeton University Press.

Pahwa, S., Youssed, M., & Scoglio, C. (2014). Electrical networks: an introduction. In G. D'Agostino & A. Scala (Eds.), *Networks of networks: the last frontier of complexity* (pp. 163–186). Cham, Switzerland: Springer. doi:10.1007/978-3-319-03518-5_8

Pröpper, M., Lelyveld, I., & Heijmans, R. (2008). *Towards a network description of interbank payment flows* (DNB Working Paper, No.177). Amsterdam: De Nederlandsche Bank (DNB).

Renault, F., Beyeler, W. E., Glass, R. J., Soramäki, K., & Bech, M. L. (2007, November). *Congestion and Cascades in Coupled Payment Systems*. Paper presented at the joint European Central Bank-Bank of England conference on Payments and Monetary and Financial Stability, Frankfurt, Germany.

Rome, E., Langeslag, P., & Usov, A. (2014). Federated modeling and simulation for critical infrastructure protection. In G. D'Agostino & A. Scala (Eds.), *Networks of networks: the last frontier of complexity* (pp. 225–253). Cham, Switzerland: Springer. doi:10.1007/978-3-319-03518-5_11

Saade, A. (2010, September). *Estructura de red del Mercado Electrónico Colombiano (MEC) e identificación de agentes sistémicos según criterios de centralidad* (Reporte de Estabilidad Financiera). Bogotá, Colombia: Banco de la República.

Schweitzer, F., Fagiolo, G., Sornette, D., Vega-Redondo, F., Vespignani, A., & White, D. R. (2009). Economic networks: The new challenges. *Science, 325*, 422–425. doi:10.1126/science.1173644 PMID:19628858

Soramäki, K. & Cook, S. (2013). SinkRank: an algorithm for identifying systemically important banks in payment systems. *Economics: The Open-Access, Open-Assessment E-Journal, 2013-28 (7)*.10.5018/economics-ejournal.ja.2013-28

Soramäki, K., Bech, M., Arnold, J., Glass, R., & Beyeler, W. (2006). *The topology of interbank payments flow* (Federal Reserve Bank of New York Staff Report No 243). New York: Federal Reserve Bank of New York.

Straffin, P. D. (1980). Algebra in geography: Eigenvectors of networks. *Mathematics Magazine*, *5*(5), 269–276. doi:10.2307/2689388

Strogatz, S. (2003). *SYNC: how order emerges from chaos in the universe, nature and daily life*. New York: Hyperion.

Tinkler, K. J. (1972). The physical interpretation of eigenfunctions of dichotomous matrices. *Transactions of the Institute of British Geographers*, *55*(55), 17–46. doi:10.2307/621721

KEY TERMS AND DEFINITIONS

Centrality: A measure of the importance or popularity of a participant within a network.

Clustering: The average probability that two neighbors of a participant are themselves neighbors; it measures the transitivity in the network.

Multiplex Network: A type of multi-layer network containing participants of one sort but with several kinds of connections between them.

Network: A graphical representation of connections between the parts of a system.

Positively Correlated Multiplexity: overlapping of participants' importance (e.g. centrality) across layers in a multiplex network.

Scale-Free Network: A network displaying an inhomogeneous and skewed connective structure with a few heavily connected participants and many poorly connected participants, typically in the form of an approximate power-law distribution of links among its participants, in which there is no typical participant in the network, thus it has no scale (i.e. it is scale-free or scale-invariant).

Settlement: The completion of a transaction, by which the two parties exchange securities or financial instruments and money.

Small-World Effect: A feature of real-world networks by which every participant can be reached in limited number of steps despite the network's size.

Small-World Model: A model that reflects two salient features of real-world networks: small-world effect and high clustering or transitivity.

Sparse Network: A feature of real-world networks by which only a fraction of potential links are observed.

ENDNOTES

1 In scale-free networks the number of connections is distributed as in a power-law (i.e. extreme heterogeneity and skewness), with a few heavily connected participants and many poorly connected participants. Due to this particular type of inhomogeneity there is no typical participant in the network, thus it has no scale (i.e. it is scale-free or scale-invariant).

2 An incomplete list of articles that confirm the scale-free nature of financial networks is León & Berndsen (2014), Bargigli, di Iasio, Infante, Lillo, & Pierobon (2013), Fricke & Lux (2014), Bech & Atalay (2008), Pröpper, Lelyveld, & Heijmans (2008), May, Levin, & Sugihara (2008), Renault, Beyeler, Glass, Soramäki, & Bech (2007), Soramäki, Bech, Arnold, Glass, & Beyeler (2006), Inaoka, Ninomiya, Tanigushi, Shimizu, & Takayasu (2004), Boss, Elsinger, Summer, & Thurner (2004). An incomplete list of articles that confirm financial networks' inhomogeneity but report a divergence from a strict power-law distribution of links is Martínez-Jaramillo, Alexandrova-Kabadjova, Bravo-Benítez, & Solórzano-Margain (2012), in 't Veld and van Lelyveld (2014), Craig & von Peter (2014).

3 Several applications of multiplex networks have been documented for non-financial complex systems, such as transport systems (Kurant & Thiran, 2006; Cardillo et al., 2013), electrical networks (Pahwa, Youssed, & Scoglio, 2014), physiological systems (Ivanov & Bartsch, 2014), critical infrastructures (Martí, 2014; Rome, Langeslag, & Usov, 2014) and cooperation networks (Gómez-Gardenes, Reinares, Arenas, & Floría, 2012). Yet, other types of multi-layer networks are available, such as the multi-layer interacting network of financial institutions and financial market infrastructures in León, Berndsen, and Renneboog (2014). In the interacting networks the layers couple because their distinct participants connect across layers, whereas in the multiplex the layers couple because of participants' overlapping across layers.

4 *Sistema Electrónico de Negociación* (SEN, Electronic Trading System); *Mercado Electrónico Colombiano* (MEC, Colombian Electronic Market); *Módulo de Registro del Mercado Electrónico Colombiano* (MEC-R, Colombian Electronic Market Register Module); *Depósito Centralizado de Valores* (DCV, Centralized Securities Depository).

5 Most sovereign securities transactions refer to local currency denominated TES (*Títulos de Tesorería*), which are issued by the Central Government (i.e. Ministry of Finance).

6 Based on approximate figures, in 2012 79% of collateralized money market transactions (i.e. sell/buy backs and repos, excluding Central Bank's repos) used sovereign local securities (i.e. TES) as collateral, whereas 17% used other fixed income securities, and 4% used equities; if Central Bank's repos are considered, sovereign local securities represent about 93%.

7 Other trading platforms exist (i.e. GFI, Icap, and Tradition), but their contribution has always been practically nil, which is why they are excluded from the analysis.

8 SEN also provides an open trading platform for non-market makers and a registering platform for over-the-counter trades, but none of the market participants use it.

9 The local sovereign securities' market has not experienced structural shifts as a consequence of recent external events such as the Global Financial Crisis. With regard to the local market, the intervention of one of the largest and most connected broker dealers in the local financial market in November 2012 is the only recent event worth mentioning. Based on previous research on the Colombian sovereign securities' network the choice of the sample period for examining its main structural features is rather trivial as long as well-known seasonal effects are avoided.

10 The estimation of the power-law exponent was based on the maximum likelihood method proposed by Clauset, Shalizi, and Newman (2009); this method is preferred to the traditional ordinary least-squares due to documented issues regarding the latter.

11 Random networks correspond to those originally studied by Erdös and Rényi (1960), in which connections are homogeneously distributed between participants due to the assumption of exponentially decaying tail processes for the distribution of links –such as the Poisson distribution. This type of network, also labeled as "random" or "Poisson", was –explicitly or implicitly- the main assumption of most literature on networks before the seminal work of Barabási and Albert (1999) on scale-free networks.

12 The term "small-world" is used in two distinct but interrelated concepts (see Newman, Barabási, and Watts, 2006). First, "small-world effect" refers to the short average path length of a network. Second, "Small-world model" (also known as Watts-Strogatz model) refers to the conjunction of the "small-world effect" and clustering. Throughout the document we refer to small-world effects or features, meaning the former concept.

13 If three vertices (a, b, c) exist in a graph, a triangle exists when edges (a,b), (b,c) and (c,a) are present (i.e. the graph is complete), whereas a connected triple exists if at least two of these edges are present. In this sense, a triangle occurs when there is transitivity (i.e. two neighbors of a vertex are themselves neighbors). The factor of three in the numerator arises because each triangle is counted three times when connected triplets are counted (Newman, 2010).

14 For instance, Markose, Giansante, and Rais Shaghaghi (2012) use eigenvector centrality to determine the most dominant financial institutions in the US credit default swap market, and to design a super-spreader tax that mitigates potential socialized losses.

15 Straffin (1980) and Boots (1984) verify the convenience of estimating the largest eigenvalue for capturing the main features of networks (e.g. total connectivity, spread potential, equilibrium importance of vertices, degree of differentiation of vertices). Before Bonacich (1972), Gould (1967) and Tinkler (1972) suggested using the largest eigenvalue in Geography and Physics for similar reasons. It is worth noticing that if each entry of the eigenvectors is weighted by the square root of the corresponding eigenvalue, so that the elements of the eigenvectors associated with the smaller eigenvalues are successively reduced in scale, this is the conventional Principal Component Analysis (Gould, 1967).

16 Because the clustering coefficient for the SEN monoplex network is lower than the probability of two vertexes being connected in this dense network, the clustering level may be considered trivial.

17 The permanence in the SEN network is determined by means of a ranking revised each year. The score obtained by each participant depends on fulfilling requisites such as maximum bid-ask spreads; consistently quoting bid and ask prices; participating in primary auctions of sovereign securities; and maintaining a minimum level of capital.

18 Some aggregated statistics for MEC and MEC-R reported by Saade (2010) concur with ours regarding their sparseness, inhomogeneity and clustering.

19 As in Newman (2010), exponent values slightly outside the range are possible and are observed occasionally. Moreover, the level of the exponent is consistent with the inhomogeneous and skewed distribution of degree, a feature that may be easily verified by visual inspection of Figure 5. As before, the power-law distribution of links is an asymptotic property, thus a strict match between observed and expected theoretical properties for determining the scale-free properties of non-large networks may be impractical.

20 This is the case of Laverde and Gutiérrez (2012) and Estrada and Morales (2008).

21 As can be derived from equations 1, 4 and 3, respectively, a large number of non-participating financial institutions will turn the network sparse and less clustered, whereas the small-world effect will in this case remain the same because the mean geodesic distance considers reachable vertexes only.

22 Critical infrastructures are those systems that are essential for the maintenance of vital societal functions, health, safety, security, economy or social well-being of people (European Commission, 2008)

23 Cross-system risk corresponds to the potential effects caused by a financial institution experiencing problems across different markets or layers (CPSS, 2008).

Chapter 8
Overconfidence in the Credit Card Market

Susan Kriete-Dodds
University of Basel, Switzerland

Dietmar Maringer
University of Basel, Switzerland

ABSTRACT

High credit card debt default has been symptomatic for the U.S. and other countries in the last decades. Different explanations for this situation exist in the literature. One explanation is overconfidence, which has become a key concept in behavioural economics for explaining anomalies in financial markets such as excessive trading volume. There is also the idea that overconfidence is to blame for high credit card debt. In this paper, an agent-based model is presented that examines the effects of overconfidence on credit card usage. Overconfidence is used here to explain why people who never intend to borrow on their credit card(s) do so anyway. The model contains consumption, two means of payment (credit card and cash), and a distortion to agents' income expectations via overconfidence. It was found that overconfidence leads to more "accidental" borrowing and higher interest rates.

INTRODUCTION

In 2011, Americans had approximately $793.1 billion in credit card debt, equating to over $15,799 in credit card debt per card holder (Census, 2011).With average annual interest rates of 12.83%, varying between 4.25% and 22.99% (Consumer Action, 2010/2011), having the wrong credit card can be costly, especially if one borrows on it. It is therefore expected that consumers switch to credit card issuers offering lower rates, and by doing so "force" credit card issuers to compete for new customers by lowering interest rates.

A lack of banks and non-banks issuing credit cards in the U.S. cannot be the reason. Around 88% of credit card balances were held by the top 10 issuers, but in total there are over 6,000 potential issuers (GAO, 2009), even if some of these companies only operate in a small local area, there would still be enough to choose from, particularly since all credit card issuers offer an identical product. Several

DOI: 10.4018/978-1-4666-8745-5.ch008

authors (see for example Ausubel, 1991; Calem & Mester, 1995; or Stango, 2003) consider these – and the low entry barriers for new entrants in the credit card market – as evidence for a market with perfect competition, where issuers should, as economic theory suggests, try to attract new customers by lowering interest rates and therefore not be able to earn an economic profit in the long-run.

Empirical evidence proves this wrong: large issuers of credit cards have been, besides a steep decline during the financial crisis, among the most profitable banking institutions (GAO, 2009). Looking at the development of credit card interest rates compared to other interest rates in the last decades (Figure 1), credit card interest rates remained sticky and there is no sign of competing for new customers through competitive interest rates. Ausubel (1991) conjectured three reasons for the non-existing competition in the credit card market: consumers face switch and search costs when looking for and signing up with a different issuer, and credit card issuers face an adverse selection problem if they were to reduce their interest rates unilaterally.

The adverse selection problem can be described as follows: There are both customers who obtain a credit card solely for convenience usage and there are those who always intended to borrow on their credit card, the so-called "revolvers". Out of the first group of customers, there are some who accidental borrow on their credit card ("unintended borrowers"); this is the preferred customer group for credit card issuers, since they are more likely to repay their debt and since borrowing on their credit cards was not intended, they do not shop around for a credit card with low interest rates. Given these potential customers, banks will hesitate to compete by lowering interest rates, since this would mainly attract bad customers. Whereas, through improving credit card conditions like a low annual fee, enticements and bonus programs, more good customers are attracted (Ausubel, 1991). This is true in real-life: empirical studies suggest that bonus and enticement programs are indeed a crucial point for customers' credit card choice (Consumer Action, 2010/2011). Credit card companies also profit by charging the merchant commission and intercharge fees for accepting a credit card payment, leading true convenient users to accrue profit to the credit card company.

Figure 1. Development of various U.S. interest rates over time.

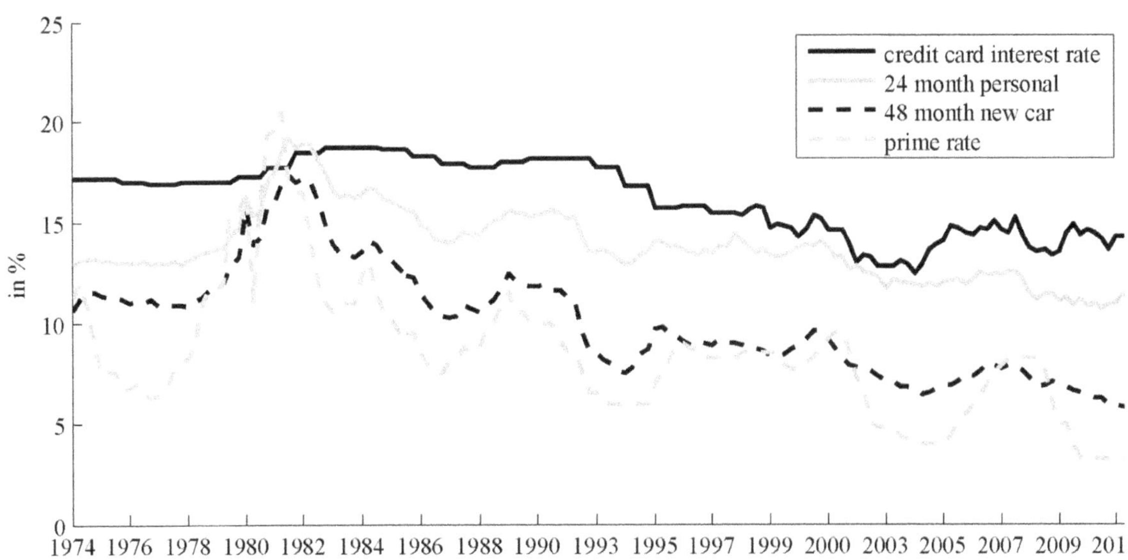

Later, Hvide (2002, Footnote 1, p. 15) interpreted the "unintended borrowers" as "being overconfident about their future ability to avoid overdrawn accounts." Empirical evidence for such overconfident behaviour was found by Yang et al. (2007). With a unique data set that included the actual repayment behaviour as well as customers intended repayment behaviour, they could show that unrealistic optimism makes customer less sensitive to low interest rates and more sensitive to high annual fees.[1] Credit card customers commonly have more than one credit card, often from different banking networks, resulting in a multihoming condition. Agarwal et al. (2005, 2009), and Zinman (2007) showed that customers in such a situation still borrow at a high interest rate. The phenomena of borrowing on high interest rates is even more widespread due to the credit card puzzle: where customers borrow on their credit cards, even when they have enough cash. Telyukova and Wright (2008) showed that the credit card debt puzzle can be explained by the fact that people hold cash instead of using it to pay off their credit card debt so they are able to cover unexpected expenses that cannot be paid by credit card.

A typical credit card market contains several parties (see Figure 2): the consumer, the consumer's bank, the merchant, the merchant's bank and a card network company. Consumers buy from merchants through their bank credit cards and pay the amount back to their banks; the card network companies – such as Visa or MasterCard – function as an intermediary between the merchant's and consumer's banks to authorize credit card payments. Merchants receive the payment, reduced by interchage, from their bank. The intercharge fee is split between the credit card issuer and the participating banks. Credit card markets are two-sided, i.e. the credit card company acts as a platform between merchant and customer.

Various papers including Rochet and Tirole (2002, 2003), Rochet and Wright (2010), Evans et al. (2011) and Wright (2004) have analysed the effects of two-sided markets, focusing on the optimal combination of consumer and merchant fees (see Verdier (2010) for an overview). The intercharge fee is also a money transfer between the cash-paying customers and those using credit cards, since merchants generally do not charge separate prices to credit card customers (Schuh et al., 2010). After acquiring the card, setting the conditions (credit limit, interest rates and repayment cycle) and paying charges such as membership fees and annual fees, a credit card can be used in the same way as cash (Brito and Hartley, 1995). Some credit card issuers offer a cash-back program which means that customers receive a bonus for every dollar spent on their credit card. In many cases the annual fee can be waived for new customers.

Most credit cards have a grace period, typically one month that allows consumers to avoid interest charges by paying the outstanding balance in full at the end of this period, and a minimum amount that needs to be repaid during this period. If users repay less than the minimum amount – not paying at all is also an option – they are said to become delinquent customers and, additional to the interest charges, late fees are imposed. Consumers who stay delinquent for longer than a certain number of billing cycles are called defaulters. If consumers borrow more than the credit limit set by the bank, an over-limit fee is charged.

To our knowledge, no work has been done in the area of agent-based modelling regarding the question of overconfidence in credit card markets. Other agent-based models with credit cards markets exist: In a number of papers, Alexandrova-Kabadjova et al. (2011) developed an agent-based model for the credit card market (Artificial Payment Card Market) focussing on the interaction between consumers, merchants and credit card issuers/acquirers.

Figure 2. Overview of the Credit Card Market.

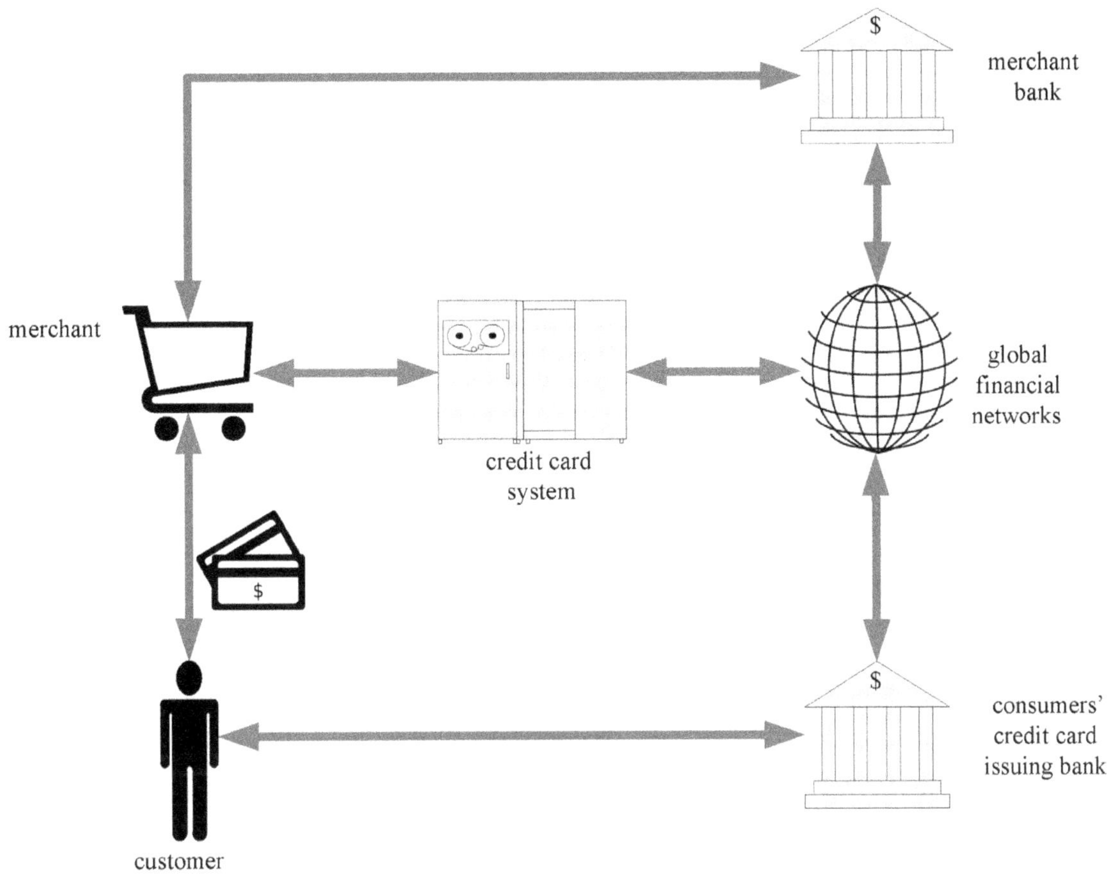

MODEL

With the model presented here the following hypotheses are tested: (a) Do information barriers allow credit card issuers to charge higher interest rates. (b) If Ausubel (1991)'s adverse selection theory holds, how does the mix in the population influence the pricing behaviour of credit card issuers? (c) Does overconfidence about one's own financial means cause "unintended borrowers" to revolve more often. (d) Would a credit card market with no overconfidence have lower interest rates? (e) How much does "keeping up with the Joneses", when consumers' propensity to buy is more or less influenced by their peers, lead to overconsumption and credit card abuse?

The model is populated by $i = 1,....,n$ consumers and $j = 1,...,m$ credit card issuers. Credit card issuers offer one type of credit card. Consumers have a subscription to one of these credit card issuers and they have cash as another payment instrument[2]. Cash subsumes all forms of non-credit payment-instruments and is used as a benchmark. Consumers prefer to buy products by using one of the two available payment instruments. In the following, credit card issuers and consumers are described in more detail.

Credit Card Issuers

Credit card issuers try to increase their profit π_{jt} by competing for customers, which is done by setting the conditions of the credit card. These conditions include interest charges p_{jt} and annual fees q_{jt}, where annual fees are charged 12 months after the subscription started. Also part of the conditions is enticements e_{jt} for new subscribers and/or a bonus b_{jt} for every unit borrowed on the credit card. The credit card issuers require a minimum payment, either a certain amount or a fixed percentage of the balance, whatever is higher. Unlike in many other subscription markets, there are two types of penalties: over-limit fees o and late fees l. These penalties are a major income source of credit card issuers and amplify the consumer default risk (Massoud et al., 2011).[3] Consumers exceeding their credit limit are chosen randomly in each period t. Besides the profit cut caused by bonuses and enticements, credit card issuers face costs for offering a subscription. We distinguish between interest expenses V_{jt} and operational charges C_{jt}. Loan losses L_{jt} through the inability of customers to repay their debt reduce profit even further.[4] The subsequent profit is

$$\pi_{jt} = X_{jt}p_{jt} + n_{jt}q_{jt} - X_{jt}(b_{jt} + V_{jt}) - \bar{n}_{jt}e_{jt} - C_{jt} - L_{jt} + o_{jt} + l_{jt}$$

where n_{jt} is the number of customers of issuer j in t, $\bar{n}_{jt}$ is the number of new customers of issuer j in t and X_{jt} is the overall usage of issuer j's customers.

Credit card issuers can be ranked, based on their profit, and two groups can be selected: "successful" credit card issuers (the top ρ_T percentage), and "not successful" credit card issuers (the bottom ρ_L percentage or those who made a loss, whatever is larger). Companies that belong to either of these two groups, change conditions to increase their profit, or, in the case of the "not successful" group, to make a profit at all. The "not successful" companies randomly copy one condition from the most successful company. It is assumed that credit card issuers do not know all the market forces, so they do not know in advance if a lower price will attract more customers, or if a higher price allows them to exploit their current customers. To reject this, the "successful" credit card issuers randomly change one condition. The better a company's ranking, the more selective it can be with new customers.

With a certain probability, credit card issuers deny a subscription to revolvers.

Consumer

In each time step t, consumers have the choice to buy one of the available k products. These products have different prices P_{kt} and a different lifespans λ_{kt}. Consumers' decision-making about consumption, particularly if there is a financial choice involved, is complex and has been the subject of many theories and approaches. Kamleitner and Kirchler (2007) presented a framework of this process, which is simplified to suit our model. Modelling the complete household budgeting would go beyond the scope of this work. It is assumed that the products available are not necessaries like food, housing, health care and expenses relating to maintaining employment, such as day care, clothing and transportation; i.e. it is assumed that those expenses have already been covered. Kantona (1975) called this "discretionary expenditure", which is characterized by the following three features: (i) There is no compelling need to make this expenditure at a given time, (ii) they are not governed by a habit, and (iii) the decision to buy them is not made at the spur of the moment. These groups could be, for example, consumer electronics, travelling or fashion.

The major influence of the purchasing decision is the propensity $D_{it}^{(k)} \in [0,1]$ to buy product k, hereafter called "desire". For example, $D_{it}^{(k)} = 0.7$ gives a probability of 70% that agent i will buy the product k in t if he or she can afford it. With increasing desire consumers can replace a product before its lifespan runs out, and since they are discretionary they do not need to be replaced straight away after the lifespan expired. The total desire $D_{it}^{(k)} \in [0,1]$ that agent i has for the product is the sum of the individual's desire $d_{it}^{(k)}$ and the social effect $f_{it}^{(k)}$ arising from the influence of the agent's friends (Janssen & Jager, 2003). To model this: Each agent i is connected with f other agents who can be seen as his friends.[5] The influence of the desire for product k goes as follows: the desire for the product increases when more friends bought product k in the last period. The individual desire $d_{it}^{(k)}$ on the other hand is heterogeneous and decreases by a random factor as the time since the purchase of a certain product increases. A very low desire leads to an abandonment of the purchase while a higher desire leads to an intention to buy.

Along with the decision to buy, consumers consider the affordability of the product. Consumers have two ways to pay for the product: cash or credit card. Cash subsumes various forms of non-credit payment instruments available, such as debit cards and paper money. The availability of credit facilities means that a consumer can purchase products on credit; the consumer can still afford to purchase a product despite his or her low income in the current period. When buying a product, a combination of both payment instruments is not allowed. The choice of payment instrument depends on the situational circumstances; there are situations when one payment instrument is easier than the other (Kamleitner & Kirchler, 2007). The consumer's willingness to use the less-convenient payment method depends on the desirability for the product; if $D_{it}^{(k)}$ does not exceed a certain threshold δ_i, the agent only checks his or her ability to use the more convenient payment instrument.

Checking one's cash balance is simple, with the cash available consisting of the current discretionary income Y_{it} and any discretionary income not used in the previous periods. The consumers' monthly discretionary income Y_{it} varies over time.[6] In general, discretionary income is expected to be constant overtime, Y_i^* and to follow a similar distribution to the total income. McDonald (1984) showed that income follows a log-normal distribution. Therefore, we set the income

$$Y_i^* = \xi e^z,$$

where ξ is a constant and $z \sim N(0;1)$. As unforeseeable events can influence this amount (e.g. the washing machine irreparably breaks down and must be replaced, or a bonus at work), we introduce an error term U_{it} representing unobserved characteristics of discretionary income.

$$Y_{it} = \max(0; Y_i^*(1 + U_{it})),$$

where the error term, $U_{it} \sim N(0,1)$.

If a consumer chooses to use a credit card and the card is not at its limit, he or she estimates his or her future income to see if he or she can repay the credit card bill in full before interest charges apply (convenience user) or pay the desired percentage of the balance in the next period (unintended borrower).[7] Repayment preferences are set at beginning and do not change over time.

Consumers do not know their future income, but they must estimate it so they can decide if it is possible to repay the credit card instalments in their preferred manner. While actual future discretionary income is unknown to the consumers, they do have certain exceptions about the future income $\tilde{Y}_{it}$ based on the average of the previous τ time periods. Following Lichtenstein et al. (1982), Russo and Schoemaker (1992), and Klayman et al. (1999), overconfidence is defined $\omega_i \in [0,1]$ as the overestimation of the precision of income estimates. ω_i is the confidence interval surrounding the agent's estimation. So an overconfident agent underestimates the standard deviation making his income estimation more peaked around the mean.

An overly optimistic income expectation leads to agents not being able to repay the full balance before interest charges apply, meaning they become revolvers. If the required minimum cannot be repaid, agents become delinquent for this period. Agents that have been delinquent T^{Del} consecutive periods default, meaning that they cannot use their credit card for T^{Def} periods; after this length of time, it is assumed that they have recovered and they restart with zero funds.[8]

After using their credit card, consumers calculate their costs:

$$c_{it} = x_{it}(p_{jt} - b_{jt}) + q_{jt},$$

where x_{it} is the consumer i's outstanding credit card balance. Consumers hesitate to look around for another contract, and so in this model there are two possible ways to motivate consumers to look for a new contract: they consider their costs c_{it} too high compared to the average costs in the population (i.e. c_{it} exceeds a threshold γ), or they receive a stimulus with a probability ς_{it} .

According to the black box model of consumer behaviour from Sandhusen (2000) (see Figure 3), a stimulus can have different origins, such as an advertising campaign, or just a friend who recently changed subscription and told others about it. When consumers receive a stimulus, they evaluate the alternatives by calculating the costs for each different credit card issuer κ known to them. Unaware of κ 's conditions and their usage in $t+1$, consumers use the values from t:

$$\hat{c}_{it} = x_{it}(p_{\kappa t} - b_{\kappa t}) + q_{\kappa t} - e_{\kappa t}.$$

Figure 3. Black Box Model.

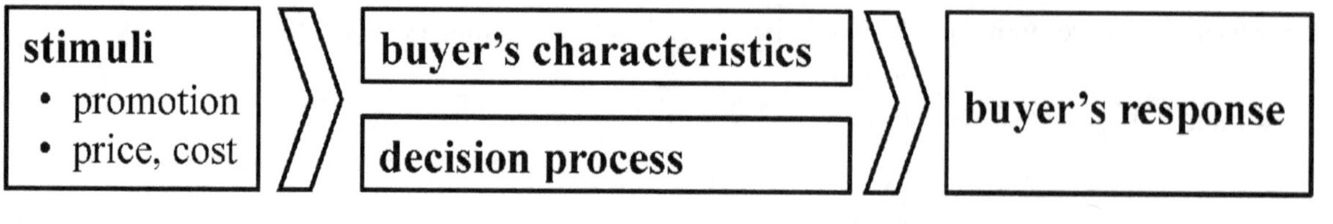

It is assumed that consumers are short-sighted and only look at the next period. The number of credit card issuers known to consumer i is denoted by v_{it}. At this point, the switching costs S_{it} come into the equation, since consumers only switch contracts if the expected savings are lower than the expected switching costs. For example, if one saves only $1 on a new subscription but has to invest time, postage, etc., worth $30, one would hardly do so. So only if

$$c_{it} - \hat{c}_{it} > S_{it}$$

will the consumer switch credit card issuers. If there is more than one credit card issuer that fulfils this condition, consumers choose the one with the lowest costs. After a contract switch, S increases to the $\max(S_t)$ for η time periods.

COMPUTATIONAL EXPERIMENTS

Settings

$T = 500$ time steps are analysed, each time step is equal to the normal monthly billing cycle of a credit card. The model needs around 200 periods to stabilize, because the initial credit card debt in $t = 1$ was too low, therefore, the actual analysis time was set to $t = 201$ to $t = 400$. $m = 20$ credit card issuers compete for $n = 500$ customers. Based on the Consumer Action Credit Card Survey (Consumer Action, 2009), a periodical survey that examines the features of several credit cards from several financial institutions in the U.S., in $t = 1$, the initial annual fees are set to, $q_{j1} \sim U\left[18,150\right]$, charged by 20% of issuers, and the interest charges are set to $p_{jt} \sim N(0.1283, 0.035^2)$,where $p_{jt} \geq 0.0425$ and $p_{jt} \leq 0.23$. In the imitation process, it is not possible for p_{jt} to fall below 0.08. Over-limit and late fees are between $10 and $40.One percent of consumers is randomly chosen to exceed the credit card limit by a random percentage. The minimum payment required is set between 2%and 5% of the outstanding debt (minimum $20) per period. Enticements $e_{jt} \sim U\left[0, e_{j1}\right]$ for new subscribers and bonuses $b_{jt} \sim U\left[0, 0.01\right]$ for every dollar spent are offered by 20% of issuers. For the sake of simplicity, the interest expenses $V = 0.02$ are identical for all issuers and do not change over time, and the operational charges C are set to zero. During the imitation process the market leader changes one condition in each time step, i.e. $\rho_T = 0.05$, and four companies copy one condition of the market leader, $\rho_L = 0.20$. Empirical data could not be found for all parameters. The crucial parameters – income, credit card limit and product prices – were therefore calibrated against the percentage of default, which averaged around 6% between1991 and 2011 (maximum 11.52%) (Fitch-Ratings, 2011). Additionally, we require that 20% of customers with the most credit card debt have 90% of credit card debt (Foster et al., 2010). Based on this calibration we set the price of the three product groups as $P_{1t} \sim \left[1500, 7000\right]$, $P_{2t} \sim \left[4000, 5000\right]$ and with durabilities of $\lambda_{1t} \sim \left[1, 6\right]$, $\lambda_{2t} \sim \left[6, 10\right]$, $\lambda_{3t} \sim \left[1, 3\right]$.The constant ξ is set to 830, i.e. around 16% of agents have a discretionary income of 0 in each time step. Customers use the previous $\tau = 7$ time periods to calculate their usage. The initial credit card debt is set for each customer between zero and the credit card limit. Consumers' desire is $D_{it}^{(k)} \in [0,1]$, where the default proportion is: social effect $f_{it}^{(k)} \in [0,0.2]$ and individual desire $d_{it}^{(k)} \in [0,0.8]$. The desire δ_i at which a consumer is willing to change to the less convenient method to pay varies: $\delta_i \in [0,1]$. In 50% of the times the credit card is the easier method to use. The parameters set in the "small world" network are arbitrarily set to $\zeta = 0.1$ and $f = 4$.[9]Defaulting consumers are replaced after 2 periods.

If not varied to test how different switching costs influence the behaviour of customers, the switching costs are set to $S \in [0,10]$ and the time period after a contract switch customer have high cost is $\eta = 6$. In each time step 50% of customers receive a stimulus. The threshold to change credit card issuer is set to $\gamma = 0.9$ for "unintended borrowers" and $\gamma = 0.75$ for revolvers. Every customer knows about half of the credit card issuers $(\nu = 0.5)$. The probability that the market leader accepts a revolver is 5%, whereas the company with the highest losses takes all of them, and all other companies follow a linear relationship between these two extremes. For comparison reasons we only look at the two extreme cases, so we define agents with $\omega_i > 0.9$ as non-overconfident and agents with $\omega_i < 0.1$ as overconfident. This limitation to only two groups is in line with other studies about overconfidence (see, for example, Rouchier and Tanimura, 2012). In the starting period each customer has a randomly assigned credit card. Credit cards offer a grace period of one time step, during this time no interest charges apply; a large fraction of credit card users repay their debt during this period.

Figure 4. displays a sharp increase in turnover, equalling the total money spent on consumption in t and the amount of credit taken in the first periods, followed by a decrease. This comes from the initial settings of the credit card debt. Although not starting with zero credit card debts, the set credit card debt in $t = 1$ is still low, allowing consumers to use their credit card extensively. In the light of this starting time, the actual analysis time was chosen to be periods 201-400.

Figure 4. Turnover and credit taken averaged over 500 runs and 500 customers.

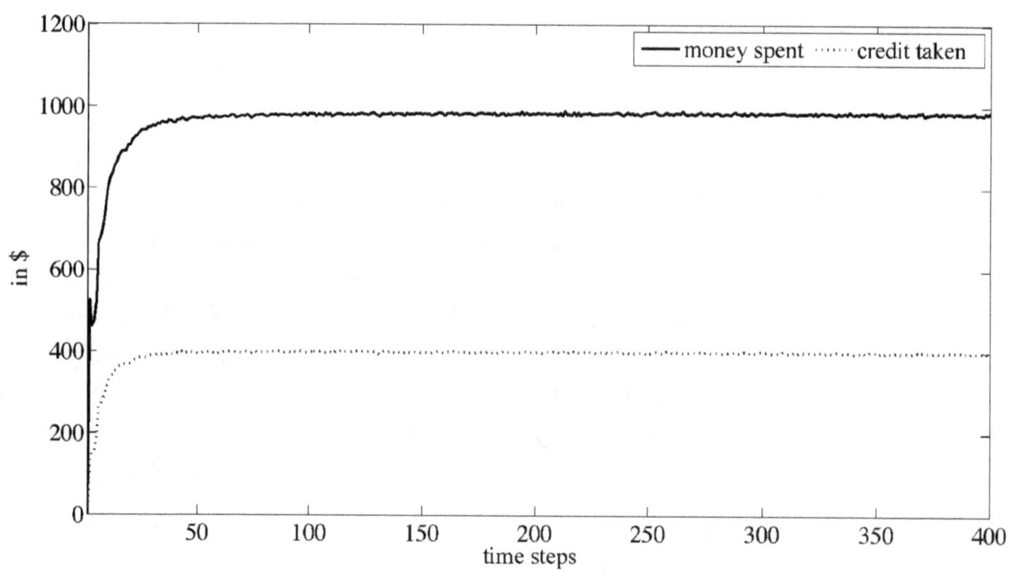

RESULTS

In the first experiment the effects of varying the number of issuers known, v , is analysed for different level of switching costs and a population with the same number of revolvers and unintended borrowers. Figure 5shows the average interest rate over 500 runs for different ν . As Ausubel (1991) suggested, very little market knowledge leads to high interest rates. This is in line with the results from the general model, where market in-transparency leads to higher costs for customers.

In the second experiment the percentage of revolvers in the population is varied. If Ausubel (1991) is right with his adverse selection hypothesis, in an environment with 90% convenient customers, issuers do not have to fear major loan losses from bad customers and should, therefore, compete for customers by lowering interest rates. Figure 6 shows that the interest rate is higher in a population with mainly revolvers. Unaware of customer type, the percentage of credit card issuers offering an enticement to customers is not affected by the percentage of revolvers.

There are more bonuses and enticements offered when there are fewer revolvers in the population (Figure 7) and that less issuers charge an annual fee (Figure 8). Figure 9 displays (a) that issuers' profit is decreasing over time and (b) that in a population with only unintended borrowers' profits higher. This supports Ausubel's findings.

The decreasing profit results from decreasing interest rates, which are caused by the high turbulence, compared to the other markets.

To test if overconfident consumers revolve more often, a population containing only convenience users, where half of them are very overconfident $(\omega_i > 0.9)$ and the other half is not overconfident $(\omega_i < 0.1)$ is analysed. In regards to spending money and credit card usage there is no significant difference between the two customer groups (Figure 10).

Figure 5. Effect of the number of credit card issuers known by the consumer, v , on the interest rate for different switching costs at $t = 300$. The interest rate is the average interest rate over all issuers in $t = 300$.

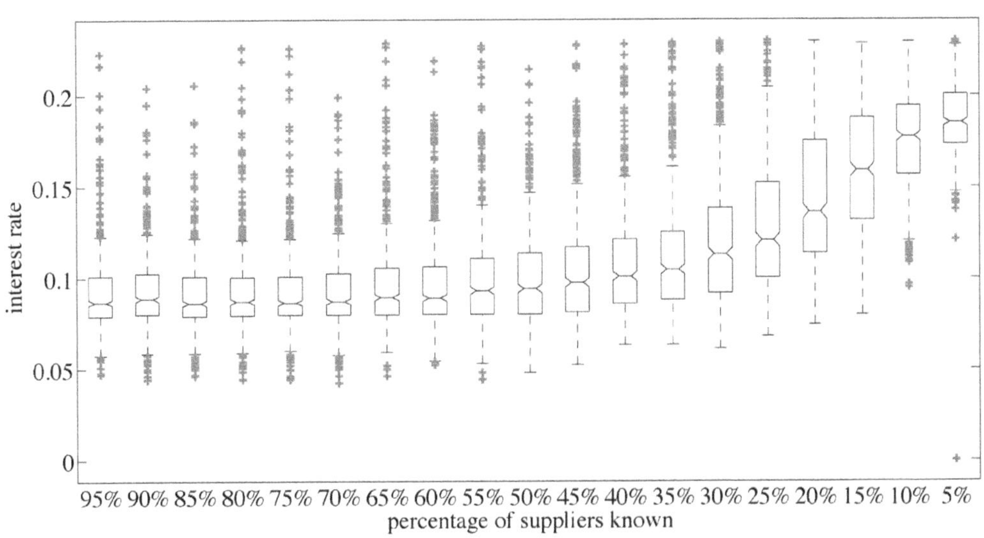

Figure 6. Effect of the percentage of revolvers in the population on the interest rate at different points in time.

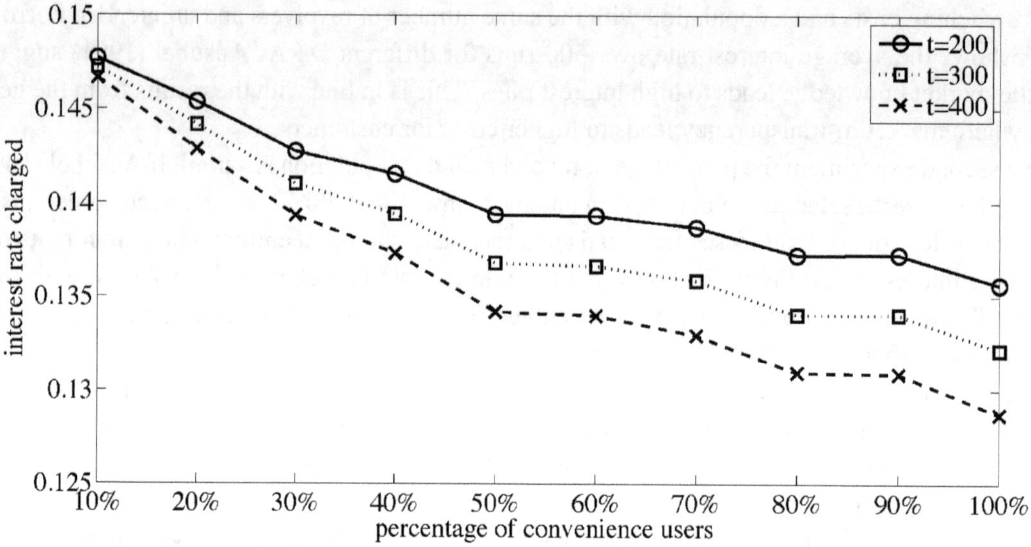

Figure 7. Effect of the percentage of revolvers in the population on the bonus.

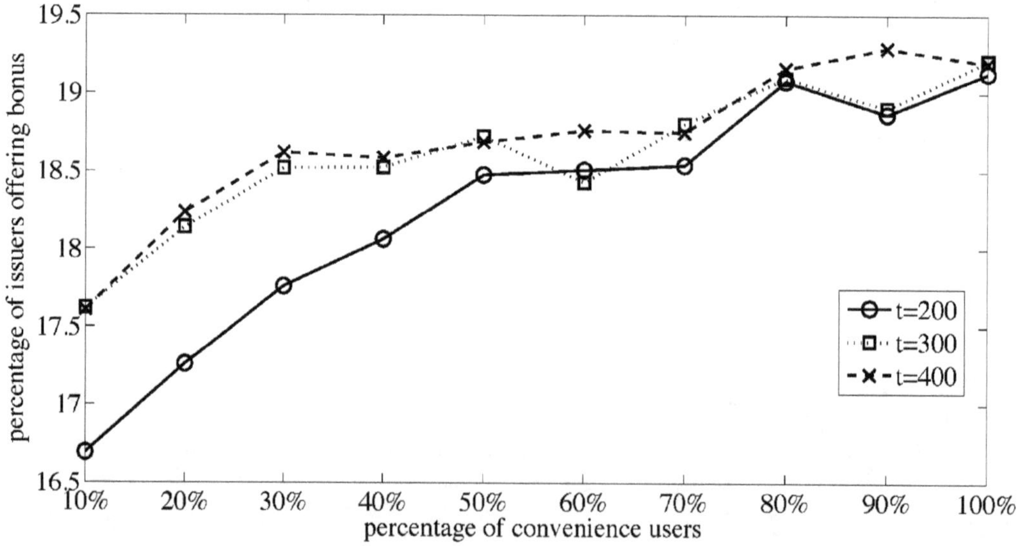

But as Ausubel (1991) suggested, overconfident users have a significantly higher probability to revolve (Figure 11). According to Ausubel (1991) revolvers are one reason for high interest rates. Therefore, the following analysis is done for a population with 50% revolvers and 50% convenience users. A population with only overconfident consumers ($\omega_i > 0.9$) is compared to one with only non-overconfident consumers ($\omega_i < 0.1$).

Figure 8. Effect of the percentage of revolvers in the population on the annual fee.

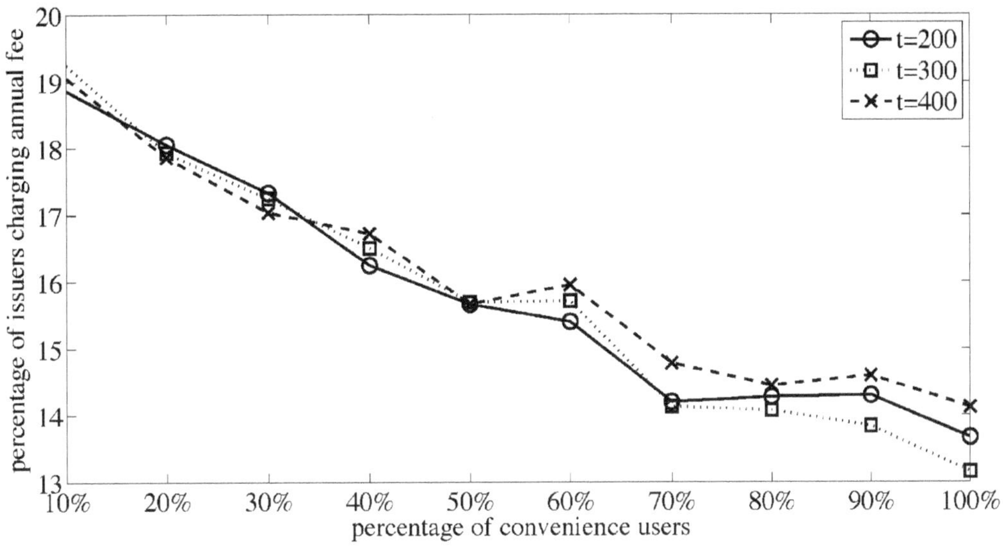

Figure 9. Effect of the percentage of revolvers in the population on the profit.

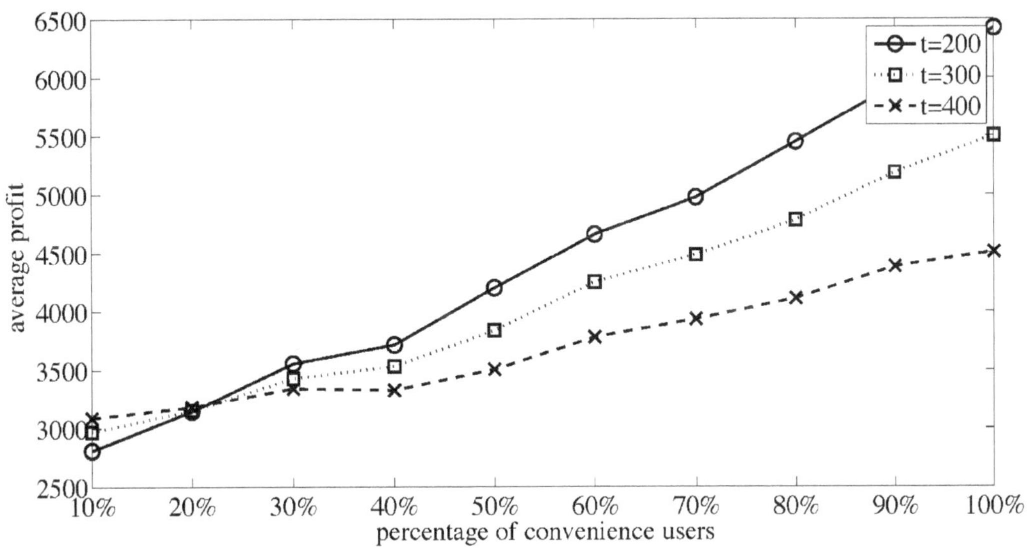

Table 1 shows the average interest rate and the average span (difference between the highest and the lowest interest rate per run) for various points in time. Throughout time, the interest rate charged is higher for a population with only overconfident consumers. Table 1also shows that the turbulence (the number of contract switches) is higher when there are only overconfident consumers. Overconfidence leads issuers to charge higher interest rates which results in more competition. A t-test showed that the differences are significant at all 5 points in time at a significance level of 0.01. Hence, not only low

Figure 10. Comparison of the amount of money spent (M) *and credit taken* (x) *for overconfident* $(\omega > 0.9)$ *and non-overconfident* $(\omega_i < 0.1)$ *consumers at* $t = 300$.

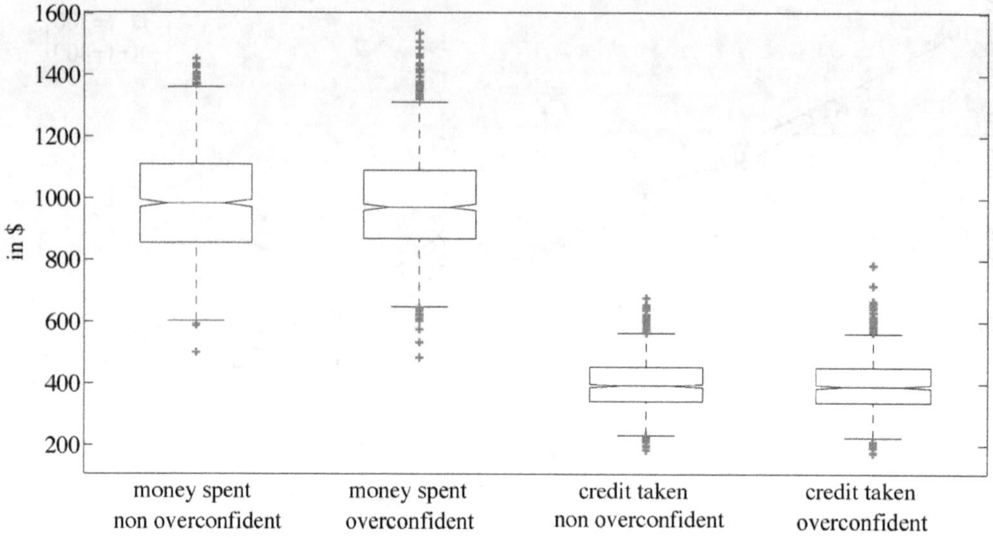

Figure 11. Probability to revolve over time.

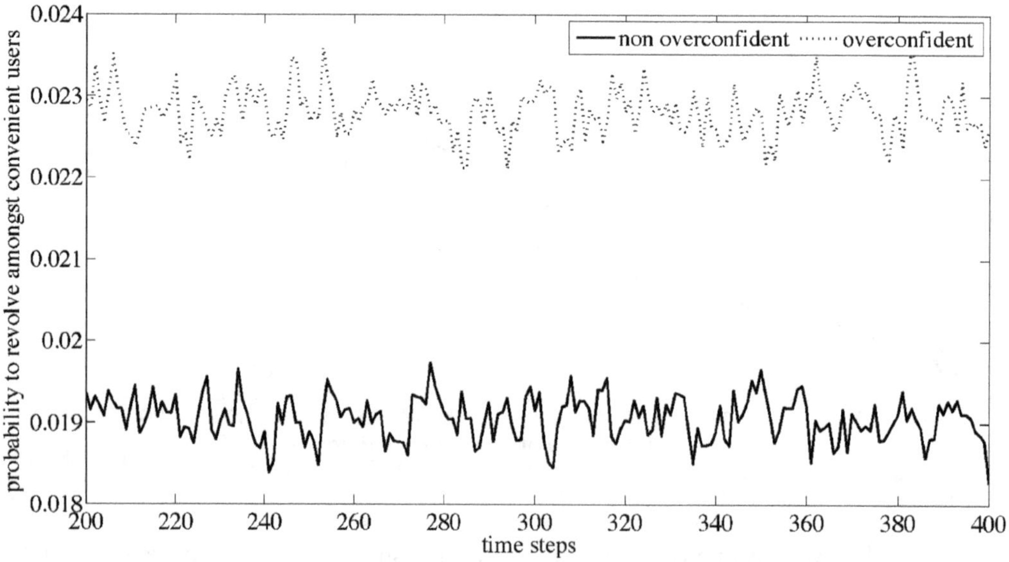

market transparency leads to higher interest rates in the credit card market, but interest rates are also here higher in a population with more revolvers and overconfidence. This supports Ausubel (1991)'s findings, particularly the author's adverse selection hypothesis: overconfidence leads to more revolving credit card debt and a higher proportion of revolvers in the population leads to higher interest rates.

Table 1. Comparison of Interest Rate Development

	Overconfident			Non-Overconfident		
Time	**Average p**	**Span**	**Turbulence**	**Average p**	**Span**	**Turbulence**
200	13.65	0.1	0.45	13.53	0.1	0.41
250	13.52	0.1	0.43	13.38	0.09	0.41
300	13.37	0.09	0.44	13.23	0.1	0.41
350	13.21	0.1	0.43	13.07	0.1	0.41
400	13.05	0.09	0.44	12.92	0.1	0.41

Another explanation for high credit card debt is known under the term "Keeping up with the Joneses" and refers to that comparison with one's neighbours or peer group can lead to overconsumption and excessive use of credit.

Given the model assumptions detailed here, it is not possible to explain the common problem of high revolving credit card debt. High revolving credit card debt can result from lacking self-control (Della Vigna & Malmendier, 2004; Shefrin & Nicols, 2014), from using credit cards as an insurance against income and consumption fluctuation (Brito & Hartley, 1995), or from the increase in consumption caused by "keeping up with the Joneses".

Consumer debt does not depend on a consumer's income but instead on the "social meaning" that the purchase of products has (Christen & Morgan, 2005).This is a form of peer pressure, which has been said to cause overconsumption and more credit card usage (Burton, 2008). Figure 12 displays higher consumption in a population with strong individual desire, whereas peer pressure leads to more credit card usage in our model (two-sample t-test with 0.01 significance level). θ does not influence the turbulence, but this solely emerges from the model mechanisms. Since the main purpose of the model was to test the effect of overconfidence, the purchasing decision is driven by desire, which was modelled – to capture realism – as a combination of peer pressure and individual desire. With the number of friends being small and identical for all customers, peer pressure increases quickly as more friends purchase a certain product, while the individual desire increases by an increment in each period the customer did not buy.

CONCLUSION AND FUTURE RESEARCH

This paper presented an agent-based model where consumers make decisions about consumption and payment method used. Their decisions are based on their propensity to buy, effected by both their friends' consumption behaviour and by their expectations about future income, which may be distorted due to overconfidence. Furthermore, credit card issuers can compete for customers by changing their conditions. The model allows the analysis of how consumer overconfidence can influence consumer behaviour and the credit card market. Despite several strong simplifications by the model, it can be seen as a method to analyse behaviour of credit card users with and without overconfidence. Allowing customers to have more than one credit card or introducing debit cards in the models could be potential extensions.

Figure 12. Average amount of money spent, credit taken and turbulence, right box always very high individual desire $\theta > 0.9$ and the left box low individual desire $\theta < 0.1$ at $t = 300$.

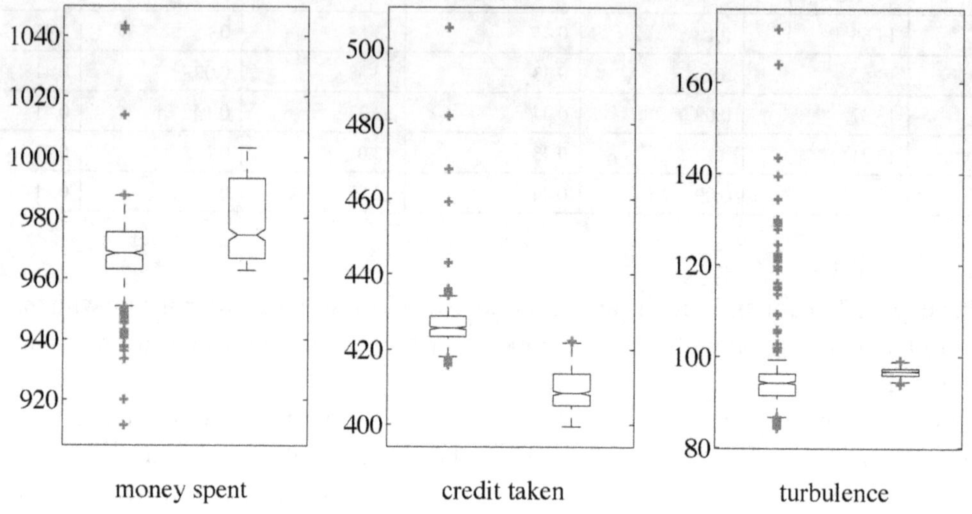

Figure 13. Average profit over time, when no intercharge fee (ICF) and various levels of ICF charged.

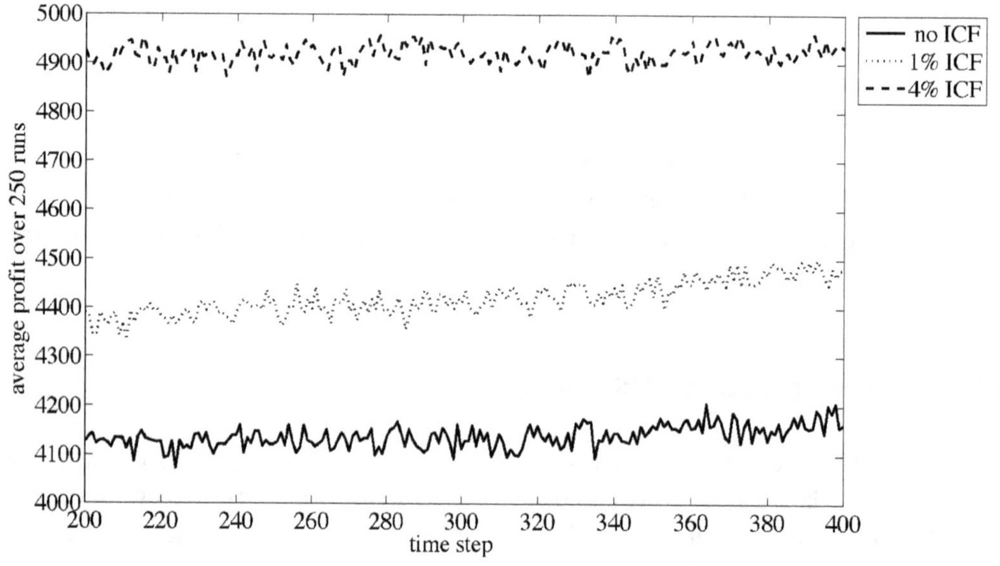

REFERENCES

Agarwal, S., Chakravorti, S., & Lunn, A. (2010). *Why do banks reward their customers to use their credit cards?* Working Paper No. 2010-19, Federal Reserve Bank of Chicago.

Agarwal, S., Chomsisengphet, S., Liu, C., & Souleles, N. S. (2006, November). Do Consumers Choose the Right Credit Contracts? Retrieved from http://ssrn.com/abstract=843826

Agarwal, S., Paige, M. S., & Tobacman, J. (2009). Payday Loans and Credit Cards: New Liquidity and Credit Scoring Puzzles? *The American Economic Review*, *99*(2), 412–417. doi:10.1257/aer.99.2.412

Alexandrova-Kabadjova, B. (2009). Impact of interchange fees on a nonsaturated multi-agent payment card market. *Intelligent Systems in Accounting Finance & Management 01/2009*; *16*(1-2):33-48.

Alexandrova-Kabadjova, B., Tsang, E., & Krause, A. (2011). Market structure and information in payment card markets. *International Journal of Automation and Computing*, *8*(3), 364–370. doi:10.1007/s11633-011-0593-1

Ausubel, L. M. (1991). The failure of competition in the credit card market. *The American Economic Review*, *81*(1), 50–81.

Brito, D. L., & Hartley, P. R. (1995). Consumer rationality and credit cards. *Journal of Political Economy*, *103*(2), 400–433. doi:10.1086/261988

Burton, D. (2008). *Credit and consumer society*. Routledge London.

Calem, P. S., & Mester, L. J. (1995). Consumer behavior and the stickiness of credit-card interest rates. *The American Economic Review*, *85*(5), 1327–1336.

Census, U. S. (2011). *Statistical abstract of the United States. Indiana*. Washington: Government Printing Office.

Christen, M., & Morgan, R. M. (2005). Keeping up with the Joneses: Analyzing the effect of income inequality on consumer borrowing. *Quantitative Marketing and Economics*, *3*(2), 145–173. doi:10.1007/s11129-005-0351-1

Consumer Action. Credit card survey. Online: (2009). Retrieved from http://www.consumer-action.org/news/articles/2009 credit card survey

Consumer Action. Credit card survey. Online. (2010/2011). Retrieved from http://www.consumer-action.org/news/articles/2010–2011creditcardsurvey.

Credit card – rising interchange fees have increased costs for merchants, but options for reducing fees pose challenges. (2009). United States Government Accountability Office – Report to Congressional Addressees

Della Vigna, S., & Malmendier, U. (2004). Contract design and self-control: Theory and evidence. *The Quarterly Journal of Economics*, *CXIX*(2), 353–402. doi:10.1162/0033553041382111

Evans, D. S., Schmalensee, R., Noel, M. D., Chang, H. H., & Garcia-Swartz, D. D. (2011). *Platform Economics: Essays on Multi-Sided Businesses*. Retrieved from http://ssrn.com/abstract=1974020

U.S. credit card abs performance may be nearing plateau [Press release] Fitch-Ratings. (2011, October 11). Retrieved from http://www.fitchratings.com/creditdesk/pressreleases/detail.cfm?prid=730344

Foster, K., Meijer, E., Schuh, S., & Zabek, M. A. (2010). *The 2008 survey of consumer payment choice*. Federal Reserve Bank of Boston.

Hvide, H. K. (2002). Pragmatic beliefs and overconfidence. *Journal of Economic Behavior & Organization, 48*(1), 15–28. doi:10.1016/S0167-2681(01)00221-9

Janssen, M. A., & Jager, W. (2003). Simulating market dynamics: Interactions between consumer psychology and social networks. *Artificial Life, 9*(4), 343–356. doi:10.1162/106454603322694807 PMID:14761255

Kamleitner, B., & Kirchler, E. (2007). Consumer credit use: A process model and literature review. *Revue Européenne de Psychologie Appliquee. European Review of Applied Psychology, 57*(4), 267–283. doi:10.1016/j.erap.2006.09.003

Kantona, G. (1975). *Psychological economics*. Elsevier Science Ltd.

Klayman, J., Soll, J. B., González-Vallejo, C., & Barlas, S. (1999). Overconfidence: It depends on how, what, and whom you ask. *Organizational Behavior and Human Decision Processes, 79*(3), 216–247. doi:10.1006/obhd.1999.2847 PMID:10471362

Lichtenstein, S., Fischhoff, B., & Phillips, L. D. (1982). Calibration of probabilities: The state of the art to 1980 (pp.306-334). In Kahneman D., Slovic P., Tversky A. (Eds.), *Judgment under uncertainty: Heuristics and biases*.

Massoud, N., Saunders, A., & Scholnick, B. (2011). The cost of being late? The case of credit card penalty fees. *Journal of Financial Stability, 7*(2), 49–59. doi:10.1016/j.jfs.2009.12.001

McDonald, J. B. (1984). Some generalized functions for the size distribution of income. *Econometrica, 52*(3), 647–665. doi:10.2307/1913469

Rochet, J.-C., & Tirole, J. (2002). Cooperation among competitors: Some economics of payment card associations. *The Rand Journal of Economics, 33*(4), 549–570. doi:10.2307/3087474

Rochet, J.-C., & Tirole, J. (2003). Platform Competition in Two-Sided Markets. *Journal of the European Economic Association, 1*(4), 990–1029. doi:10.1162/154247603322493212

Rochet, J.-C., & Tirole, J. (2011). Must-take cards: Merchant discounts and avoided costs. *Journal of the European Economic Association, 9*(3), 462–495. doi:10.1111/j.1542-4774.2011.01020.x

Rochet, J.-C., & Wright, J. (2010). Credit card interchange fees. *Journal of Banking & Finance, 34*(8), 1788–1797. doi:10.1016/j.jbankfin.2010.02.026

Rouchier, J., & Tanimura, E. (2012). When overconfident agents slow down collective learning. *Simulation, 88*(1), 33–49. doi:10.1177/0037549711428948

Russo, J. E., & Schoemaker, P. J. (1992). Managing overconfidence. *Sloan Management Review, 33*(2), 7–17. PMID:10120627

Sandhusen, R. L. (2000). *Marketing*. Barron's Educational Series (3rd ed.).

Schuh, S. D., Shy, O., & Stavins, J. (2010). *Who gains and who loses from credit card payments? Theory and calibrations*. FRB of Boston Public Policy Discussion Paper 10-3.

Shefrin, H., & Nicols, C. M. (2014). Credit card behavior, financial styles, and heuristics. *Journal of Business Research*, *67*(8), 1679–1687. doi:10.1016/j.jbusres.2014.02.014

Shefrin, H., & Thaler, R. H. (1988). The behavioral life-cycle hypothesis. *Economic Inquiry*, *26*(4), 609–643. doi:10.1111/j.1465-7295.1988.tb01520.x

Stango, V. (2003). Strategic responses to regulatory threat in the credit card market. *The Journal of Law & Economics*, *46*(2), 427–452. doi:10.1086/377291

Stango, V., & Zinman, J. (2009). What do consumers really pay on their checking and credit card accounts? Explicit, implicit, and avoidable costs. *The American Economic Review*, *99*(2), 424–429. doi:10.1257/aer.99.2.424

Taylor, A., & Higham, D. J. (2009). CONTEST: A controllable test matrix toolbox for MATLAB. [TOMS]. *ACM Transactions on Mathematical Software*, *35*(4), 26. doi:10.1145/1462173.1462175

Telyukova, I. A., & Wright, R. (2008). A model of money and credit, with application to the credit card debt puzzle. *The Review of Economic Studies*, *75*(2), 629–647. doi:10.1111/j.1467-937X.2008.00487.x

Thaler, R. H. (1999). Mental accounting matters. *Journal of Behavioral Decision Making*, *12*(3), 183–206. doi:10.1002/(SICI)1099-0771(199909)12:3<183::AID-BDM318>3.0.CO;2-F

Verdier, M. (2011). Interchange fees in payment card systems: A survey of the literature. *Journal of Economic Surveys*, *25*(2), 273–297. doi:10.1111/j.1467-6419.2009.00607.x

Watts, D. J. (2003). *Small Worlds: The dynamics of networks between order and randomness*. Princeton University Press.

Wright, J. (2004). Determinants of optimal interchange fees in payment systems. *The Journal of Industrial Economics*, *52*(1), 1–26. doi:10.1111/j.0022-1821.2004.00214.x

Yang, S., Markoczy, L., & Qi, M. (2007). Unrealistic optimism in consumer credit card adoption. *Journal of Economic Psychology*, *28*(2), 170–185. doi:10.1016/j.joep.2006.05.006

Zinman, J. (2007). *Household borrowing high and lending low under no-arbitrage*. Darthmore College Working Papers.

KEY TERMS AND DEFINITIONS

Accidental Borrowing: Unplanned borrowing exceeding one's credit card limit.

Agent-Based Model: Computational models for simulating the actions and interactions of autonomous agents.

Behavioural Bias: Deviations from rational thinking or good judgment.

Credit Card: Card issued by a card network company allowing the holder to borrow funds.

Overconfidence: Overestimations of one's abilities.

Overconsumption: Consumption exceeding one's personal means.

Subscription Market: Market with repeated purchases and contracts that tie customers to a certain supplier.

Endnotes

1 In addition to Ausubel's findings, other explanations have arisen from behavioural economics for poor credit card choice: limited attention to prices, mental accounting, and anchoring.

2 Cash and credit card represent the type of payment instrument; multihoming is therefore not needed in this model.

3 Penalties are a demonstrated substitute for interest rate charges, and are charged more often by credit card issuers with a higher market share (Massoud et al. (2011)). One possible extension of the model presented here is to allow penalties to change, based on the market share of the credit card issuer or on the interest rate, but this is not important within the context of overconfidence.

4 Intercharge fees charged to merchants would increase the profit even further. Alexandrova-Kabadjova (2009) showed the impact of intercharge fees on the credit card market.

5 The "small world" concept introduced by Watts (2003) is used here, but a random or a static network leads to similar results. The network is modelled by using the Matlab code provided by Taylor and Higham (2008).

6 Discretionary income is defined here as funds available after obtaining necessaries. Another way to see discretionary income is in the context of mental accounting: Customers divide their current income into separate, non-transferable portions like rent, groceries, holidays (Thaler (1999)) or into current spendable income, current assets and future in come (Shefrin and Thaler (1988)).

7 Revolvers assume that their discretionary income will not drop after, they assume that if they are able to pay this amount in, they will also be able to pay in later periods.

8 Consumers do not try to reduce the probability to default by controlling or reducing their credit card debt by controlling their spending.

9 Further research could be done by varying and to see how quickly products spread through the market.

Chapter 9
Implementation Aspects of Indicators Related to Payments Timing

Alexandros Kaliontzoglou
Bank of Greece, Greece

Alexander Pascal Müller
Deutsche Bundesbank, Germany

ABSTRACT

Timing analysis in an RTGS payment system offers input to operators, overseers and supervisors about the behavior of the system or individual participants. Timing related indicators can be used as a monitoring tool to identify liquidity circulation problems. Study of the behavior of participants may help identify changes due to business practices shifts, reactions to unexpected events or even to various types of stress. Furthermore, the indicators can be used in simulation studies, where the impact to timing of different levels of induced stress to a system or changes of its institutional features may be measured and compared. This chapter explores the experiences and challenges while setting up and evaluating two payments timing indicators for the European RTGS TARGET2. The indicators are the "value weighted average settlement time" as well as a form of payments "delay" indicator. The goal is to present specific aspects of a methodological framework for implementing such indicators, for possible replication based on granular transaction level data of other RTGS payment systems.

INTRODUCTION[1]

Real-Time Gross Settlement Systems effecting the final settlement of individual payments continuously during their business hours are predominant in settling high value and time critical payments (Kokkola, 2010, p. 48ff.). The various times of payment processing within an RTGS (i.e. submission time, settlement time, earliest/latest debit times) represent useful pieces of information for payment system operators as well as oversight and supervision authorities, because they may have a significant impact

DOI: 10.4018/978-1-4666-8745-5.ch009

on the liquidity flows for the system as a whole. They also have the potential of being correlated to various business practices of participants or to reflect financial stress faced by single participants or groups sharing a common characteristic (i.e. country level, corporate groups).

This chapter presents two indicators related to payments timing, the "value weighted average payment settlement time" and a form of a payments "delay" indicator. The indicators have been selected based on the existing literature and they are under evaluation with respect to their quality and usefulness as part of the research activities in the context of the Eurosystem large value RTGS TARGET2 (Kokkola, 2010, p. 178) . The two indicators capture the most important time-related aspects of payments: the time when they are settled and the time they spend in the system before being settled. These aspects are important when analyzing the liquidity management behavior of the entity under monitoring (i.e. system, single participant or group of participants).

Setting up and implementing indicators that are based upon granular transaction level data to produce a composite output requires the adoption of a relevant methodological framework answering to several questions:

- Which types of payments should be taken into account by the indicators?
- What payment attributes (shared commonly in RTGS systems) should be addressed when implementing the indicators?
- What levels of aggregation are useful for monitoring (at platform/group/participant levels)?
- Which types of transaction flows are available based on the aggregation level?
- What graphical representations offer a concise visualization of the indicator output?
- What types of output characteristics can be considered as significant signals?

The answers to these questions depend on the type of monitoring agent (infrastructure operator or oversight authority) and the objectives of the use of the indicators. Such objectives are the following:

- Analysis of system performance and participant behavior for the purposes of financial stability and prudential supervision. This objective requires explorative in-depth analysis of specific periods, events or groups of participants.
- Setup of continuous monitoring, where a predefined indicator is continuously calculated as close to real time as possible. This involves the definition of thresholds of signaling indicators and the development of monitoring tools.
- Evaluation and comparison of the output data of different scenarios in simulation results.

The technical specificities of the payment system involved might have an impact on the methodological principles, but overall these types of indicators are applicable to any RTGS system. This paper aims to answer the above questions for the set of indicators selected based on the experience of the implementation for TARGET2, to showcase how similar indicators based on granular transaction level data may be designed and implemented.

BACKGROUND

Relevant work has been presented in Massarenti, Petriconi, and Lindner (2012), where, among others, the paper analyses the daily average of interbank payments volume and value within the day for four years of TARGET2 operations and the corresponding cumulative volumes and values. The daily average value settled indicator is calculated as a function of settlement time, providing a measurement of when the most value is settled within the day. The paper also defines and analyses the patterns of one type of payment delay indicator. The indicator is calculated as the difference between the introduction time of an interbank payment and its settlement time, measured in seconds. It is presented in the paper in the form of a daily average value (simple and value weighted) as a function of time. The delay indicator takes into account the introduction time, earliest debit time and opening time of the system. One consequence of the above approaches to indicators is that, in order to show the evolution of patterns over a long period of time (i.e. several days, months or years), one would have to juxtapose different data series representing the time periods, thus making the comparison complex. On the other hand, this approach makes it possible to identify typical intraday patterns by showing the average settled value during the day over a given time period. The indicator pattern analysis capabilities are discussed only at the TARGET2 system level, without investigating the potential of time related indicators for the behavioral analysis of specific participants or groups of participants. Similar studies focusing on the timing of payments within the day have also been performed in other RTGS systems such as CHAPS in Becher, Galbiati and Tudela (2008) and Fedwire in McAndrews and Rajan (2000).

The value weighted average settlement time of payments indicator has been proposed in Heijmans and Heuver (2011) for interbank payments, excluding interbank loans and client transactions. The paper explores the value of the indicator for monitoring the behavior of specific participants in the Dutch TARGET2 component as a candidate for early warnings in case of liquidity stress. The recording of a moving average is proposed for filtering the noise produced by day-to-day variations. It is also suggested that this indicator may be further complemented as part of the full analysis with daily timing indicators similar to the ones used in Massarenti et al. (2012), which would nevertheless mostly be able to focus into specific days, rather than the whole matching studied period. It is important to note that the paper proposes a rich list also of other financial stability indicators derived from payment data that may be consulted in order to formulate a more complete picture of the behavioral patterns of the entity studied.

The same indicator has also been proposed in the original consultative version of (Bank of International Settlements, 2012, p. 8), as part of a proposed set of intraday liquidity management monitoring indicators that could be requested by banking supervisors, so that they may monitor a bank's intraday liquidity risk management. The indicator is presented as a way for supervisors to identify changes to the timing of a bank's intraday outgoing payments over time. Following up on the public consultation of the consultative document, the indicator has been removed from the final version of the document (Bank of International Settlements, 2013). The public comments state various reasons against including such an indicator in the framework, some of which were related to the confusion regarding the indicator specification (such as the concept of time it uses in a multi-jurisdiction environment and the payment flows included), the potential inability of a single participant to acquire the actual settlement time of each payment, overlap of the indicator's results with other indicators of the framework and a perceived risk that the indicator promotes late submission of payments.

The timing of payments settlement has also been investigated as a form of measure for free riding of participants in TARGET2 in Diehl (2013, pp. 12-17). The goal is essentially the identification of participants that are deliberately withholding incoming liquidity for certain reasons, at the expense of the smooth liquidity circulation in the system. Among others, two time based indicators are proposed that make use of a form of average settlement time as part of their calculation, a so called "time-based measure" and an "early payment indicator". From an implementation perspective, the indicators are based on dividing the total time of active payment submission to slices, covering the active hours for TARGET2 and then bundling up the payments within a minute together in the same time band. The indicators are constructed by combining different indexes for incoming and outgoing payments that would characterize a participant as a free rider. The paper introduces a concrete approach for setting up indicators that identify a particular behavioral pattern.

A form of a settlement delay indicator has been discussed in Koponen and Soramäki (1998, p. 59) which has been defined as the value of queued payments at a specific point in time divided by the total value of outgoing payments at that point in time. The ratio takes a value between zero and one, representing the two extremes when all the payments are settled immediately and when all outgoing value is queued correspondingly. It is used to evaluate the results of several simulations of different payment system setups. The indicator produces a value per minute based on the information contained within the queueing mechanism of the payment system, not individual transactions. The indicator is value-weighted, therefore linking the delays with the payment value, but does not take into account the actual time that the payment remained in the queue (all queued payments are treated equally with respect to their share in the delay).The delay indicator proposed in Schulz (2011, p. 20), represents the average queue duration for queued payments, calculated as the total queueing time for each queued payment divided by the total number of queued payments. In this case the actual time spent in the queue is taken into account, but high value payments do not proportionately affect the delay. This indicator is used in the context of a simulated RTGS system with calibrated data. Both concepts could also be applied to real world systems if similar data as it was provided by the simulation software is available from the system queuing mechanism.

The notion of monitoring different types of indicators as early warnings for stress or problems has been expanding in the literature throughout the last years, especially following the financial crisis that started in 2008. The combination of various types of indicators can be seen as a consultative instrument for financial stability authorities. One source of information and data for such indicators is payment system data. As referenced above in Heijmans and Heuver (2011) and Bank of International Settlements (2013), there are several types of indicators related to intraday liquidity sources, use of collateral pledged for credit lines, reserve requirements, payment flows and money markets volumes and rates forming a whole "indicator ecosystem" that may provide signals about the health of the system as a whole and its individual participants. This idea has also been explored in Laine, Numellin and Snellman (2011) where an oversight indicator in the form of a grid, based on liquidity usage in TARGET2 in combination with interest rates on overnight loans, is proposed for financial stability analysis purposes. In Tölö, Jokivuolle and Virén (2014) the authors further drill down into micro-level data related to single participants overnight money market transactions identified from payment system data, in comparison with their credit default swap prices (CDS) in order to investigate how such short-term information can act as early warning for stress and a measure for a bank's creditworthiness in the context of banking supervision.

The literature highlights the importance of the time related attributes of payments as part of the everyday business practices of participants in the payment system. The main idea behind the present work was to use the already proposed in the literature value weighted average settlement time indicator as a starting point for studying the patterns of payments in TARGET2 at all aggregation levels and then complement the pattern analysis with additional indicators that enable analysts to formulate a more complete picture of the liquidity management profile of the entities studied. Essentially, the first timing indicator was used as a basis to setup a consistent implementation framework upon which other, potentially more complex indicators (such as the delay indicator) may be built, in terms of queries, scripts and parameterization required. At the same time, this work provides insight on challenges faced and solutions that had to be adopted while building the framework, as a result of trying to match the theoretical model representing the indicators to the actual underlying raw payment data.

DEFINITION OF INDICATORS

Value Weighted Average Payments Settlement Time

The ***"value weighted average settlement time indicator"*** produces a measure of the actual timing of the payments settlement. The indicator calculated for the payments of a single day is defined as follows:

$$\frac{\sum_{i=1}^{n}\left(paymentsValue_i * settlementTime_i\right)}{\sum_{i=1}^{n} paymentsValue_i}$$

where:

- $\boldsymbol{paymentsValue_i}$ is the value of payment i
- $\boldsymbol{settlementTime_i}$ is the settlement time of payment i
- $\boldsymbol{n}$ is the total number of payments in day i

The output of the indicator is time scaled and shows the average time of settlement. The output produced is a **daily value**. Theoretically, the indicator could also be calculated for longer periods. Still, the daily frequency is most adequate for the majority of purposes.

The indicator can be relevant for the analysis of system performance, participant behavior and financial stability. From a system performance point of view, operators and overseers should favor a settlement time as early as possible. The indicator can provide the capability to evaluate the need for changes to the system design, rules or incentives for participants targeting introduction behavior if the average settlement time is considered to be too late and the effect of such changes if they are implemented. One example of a possible change to be evaluated is the introduction of throughput guidelines, which incentivize or oblige an early submission of payments. In simulation studies the indicator can be used as evaluation criterion, since given identical input data, earlier average settlement time is equivalent to faster payment processing. The effect of changes to system design affecting payment processing can then be evaluated before it is actually implemented. Still, for a general evaluation of settlement efficiency in a simulation study, the delay indicator is considered more appropriate because it encompasses more information, as discussed below. From a participant behavior point of view, the indicator can lead to valuable insights when it is calculated for several single participants and clusters of participants sharing the same patterns are formed. From a financial stability point of view, sudden and large changes in the indicator might be used as an early warning indicator both for single participant as well as for the system as a whole.

It should be noted that unsettled payments are not taken into account by the indicator because the focus is on the time when payments are actually settled. This reduces the comparability of indicator values with different amount of unsettled payments. Nevertheless, as shown in the next section, the delay indicator takes them fully into account so that their effect can also be measured. Therefore there is a strong complementarity between the two indicators, which enhances the potential value of their combined output as part of the analysis of time related patterns.

Payments Delay

The payments delay indicator is defined as:

$$\frac{\sum_{i=1}^{n} value_i \left(t_{2,i} - t_{1,i}\right)}{\sum_{i=1}^{n} value_i \left(t_{3,i} - t_{1,i}\right)} \in [0...1]$$

where:

- $t_{1,i}$ is the time when payment i is available to be settled[2]
- $t_{2,i}$ is the actual settlement time of the payment i (which should be equal to $t_{3,i}$ if the payment remains unsettled)
- $t_{3,i}$ is the end of day for the type of payment i, i.e. the latest possible settlement time
- ***value$_i$*** is the value of payment i
- ***n*** is the total number of payments in day i

The delay indicator expresses the time payments stay in the queue (if any) against the theoretical total time they could have stayed in the queue before they would become unsettled, weighted by the value of the payments. A value of zero means no delay and happens when the introduction time is the same as the settlement time ($t_{1,i} = t_{2,i}$), while a value of 1 indicates the maximum delay and happens when the payment is either settled or becomes unsettled at the end of day ($t_{2,i} = t_{3,i}$). The end of day settlement time ($t_{3,i}$) depends on the sub-category of the payment if the system has specific cut-off times for different sub-categories. The output produced is a **daily** value ranging between 0 (all payments have been directly settled) and 1 (all payments have been queued until the end of the day or remained unsettled).

The indicator is more focused on potential problems in the payment processing since it measures undesired delays. It takes into account both settled and unsettled payments and therefore provides a complete picture of the studied entity's performance. It builds upon and extends existing relevant indicators referenced in the literature in the background section firstly by taking into account both the total time payments are queued and their value and secondly by including in the calculation the attributes of every single payment. The latter characteristic enables analysts to study the contribution to the delays at the lowest possible aggregation level. Furthermore, in contrast to indicators that mostly depend on the difference between $t_{1,i}$ and $t_{2,i}$ (which is expressed in seconds), the proposed delay indicator, as constructed, takes into account also attributes that depend on the latest possible settlement time for a payment and is a dimensionless value ranging between 0 and 1 that can be better utilized as comparison tool.

Due to its structure, the indicator is sensitive to introduction time and signals an improvement of settlement execution when only average introduction time is increasing. The combination of $t_{3,i}$ with $t_{1,i}$ (forming the denominator of the indicator formula fraction) makes the indicator sensitive to how close to its latest possible settlement time the payment becomes available. For example, a payment introduced late within the day would have greater negative impact[3] on the indicator than a payment introduced earlier within the day, if the two payments have the same value and the same time difference between their introduction and settlement time. This essentially means that payments closer to the end of day trade phase (a time period with heavy demand for payment settlement) are considered to contribute towards signaling greater delays. This behavior is consistent with the perceived positive effect of early introduction of payments in a payment system and also highlights again the strong complementarity between the two indicators.

Similarly to the previous indicator, the delay indicator may contribute to different types of analysis. The application at system level can be used as tool for financial stability purposes, especially when studying various actual or probable adverse events that may affect the smooth operation of the payment system and potentially introduce additional delays to payments. Therefore the indicator is particularly useful for the comparison of output of different scenarios in simulation analysis, with each scenario involving the introduction of different types and levels of stress. In that case the indicator should be applied on simulated rather than primary system data. The indicator can also be used for simulated data to assess the system performance with changes in the system design.

When applied at lower aggregation levels, the indicator is suitable for the continuous monitoring of the delay profile over time of single participants or groups of participants and when combined with other types of information it may also contribute towards identifying potential early warnings for stress, or other problematic situations.

It should be noted that two reasons for delays can be distinguished in theory: The first are the characteristics of a participant, in particular the level of its available liquidity. The second are the characteristics of the RTGS itself, in particular its technical performance and institutional features like hybrid liquidity saving elements. In practice, the indicator is not able to differentiate between these two reasons. However, since the technical setup and institutional features of a system remain constant over time, when the indicator is used for continuous monitoring a change could be interpreted as being caused by a change in participant behavior or conditions. Since TARGET2 demonstrates a high level of technical performance, changes in the indicator output shouldn't be expected to stem from technical difficulties. Furthermore, for the comparison of simulation results, the comparison of indicator output can be focused on comparing scenarios with changed system setup and participant behavior or conditions on the one hand and scenarios with constant system setup and changed participant behavior or conditions on the other hand, which allows to attribute the change in the delay to one of the two reasons.

The delay indicator is only capturing the difference between the time when a payment becomes available for settlement in the system and the settlement itself. It cannot capture the delay between the time when the payment manager knows that the payment is due and its actual submission time into the system. Such internal delays could lead to an overestimation of the settlement speed when e.g. the submission to the system only takes place when enough liquidity is available on the participant's account. Nevertheless, the combined output of payment timing and delay indicator would signal an increase in the average payment time when the submission to the system is delayed by the participant due to liquidity constraints. In addition, behavioral changes which are of particular interest from the perspective of continuous monitoring can be identified anyway. In this context, it is also worth analyzing the potential incentives for participants for early or late submission of the respective system, like e.g. rules requiring early submission, pricing schemes with intraday differentiation or the availability and cost of intraday credit. Based on this evaluation of the incentives for a specific submission behavior, the interpretation of the indicator output should be adapted to the respective system.

The use of intraday credit by the participants could be considered as an additional complementing indicator for systems with free intraday credit. The availability of intraday credit is significantly reducing the number of queued payments and thereby reducing delays. An increase in the use of intraday credits could therefore be interpreted as a pre-step to increasing delays. Heijmans and Heuver (2011) suggest a graphical implementation of such an indicator.

For both indicators, it is important to note that this continuous monitoring should be based on a "per participant (or per group) per payment system" fashion, without combining data from different payments systems, as the differences in the time definition itself in different jurisdictions worldwide and the operational schedule of each payment system would be very hard to be combined in a coherent framework. This also means that the comparison of indicator output across different payment systems should be performed with caution. The comparison might not produce meaningful results especially in the case of the "value weighted average settlement time" indicator, due to the possible different operational times between different systems. The delay indicator is less affected by this because it is based in time differences rather than specific times, as long as the specific start and end of day trade phase times of each system are correctly defined when the indicator is configured. Further discussion on the aggregation levels for applying the indicators follows in the section "Implementation methodology".

IMPLEMENTATION METHODOLOGY

This section presents the methodology adopted for setting, configuring, running and analyzing the two indicators and analyses common steps taken and specificities encountered. The methodology is mainly based on answering the questions stated in the introduction section. Furthermore, within the relevant context, the section also elaborates on the challenges faced.

It is important to note that the implementation methodology at certain points is affected by the overall technical context of the system upon which this work has been based, namely TARGET2. Nevertheless, a lot of TARGET2 features are common among RTGS systems and therefore quite similar approaches could be applied to different systems for similar indicators calculated by processing granular transaction data. For example, at a minimum the indicators require the introduction and settlement times of a payment and the start and end of day trade phase times, which should be attributes present and available in most RTGS. Features such as latest or earliest debit time may be optionally used only when available (further information on how the indicators handle time related attributes is provided later in the chapter). In contrast, especially as far as timing of payments is concerned, a lot of the methodological decisions do not directly apply to netting systems where the timing of the payments is heavily dependent on the settlement during cycles that happen at specified intervals during the day.

From a technology perspective, the indicators were implemented as SQL scripts running on a database with availability on granular transaction level data from TARGET2. The scripts were implemented to have as input variables specific sets of parameters that essentially filter the data for processing. Apart from the basic filter of the period under investigation (year and months), the rest of the options are addressed in the sections that follow, because they have a direct link to the answers of the fundamental questions presented in the introduction section of this paper.

The requirement for access to granular transaction data mandates rather strict limitations to the possible entities that may be able to replicate a similar approach for analysis or monitoring purposes. The acquisition of certain data elements, such as the exact payment settlement time, may be challenging to achieve for member institutions of a payment system. As a result, the implementation of similar indicators is feasible mostly for regulatory authorities that have either direct access to the transaction level data themselves (i.e. they are the system's overseer or operator in their own capacity), or can access them through the payment system operator.

Payment Types

The selection of payment types (and possibly sub-types, based on how they are classified within the payment system) that should be included in the dataset to be processed for the calculation of any indicator, is one of the most crucial steps to be taken as it heavily affects the quality of the final output. Careful analysis needs to take place in order to include within the dataset payments which are meaningful in the context of the specific indicator. As a general rule, for time related indicators it is worth separating all time-fixed payments and to calculate indicators only for those payments where a minimum of discretion exists for a bank's payment manager. This task is not straightforward in many cases, since the payment categories are not always designed primarily for analytical purposes, but for the technical processing of the settlement.

As discussed in Massarenti et al. (2012, p. 5), some categories of time-fixed payments are easy to identify, such as the ancillary system payments. Specifically in TARGET2, this type of payments also has a higher priority than standard interbank payments and is therefore treated differently in terms of queuing. Furthermore, exceptionally high value important payments where one participant is the central bank, may skew the indicator and should therefore be removed as well. Finally, payments where there is no change of ownership of the money transferred should also be excluded from the dataset, because their timing is not important from a behavioral pattern point of view.

In the context of TARGET2, ECB (2014, p. 18) presents the categories of payments supported by the system along with shares in volume and value for 2013, as shown in Table 1.

In the present work, a similar approach was adopted to the above with a set of caveats. The basis of the datasets drew from the pool of Category 1 payments, but the technical implementation was configured as to be able to produce combined data where Customer Payments could be excluded or included as demanded, so that the effect of Customer Payments to timing could also be studied. As it was expected, for larger participants, Customer Payments had almost negligible effect to the "value weighted average settlement type", due to their much lower value in comparison to Interbank Payments. There were only a few cases of smaller sized participants where this type of payments could influence the indicator, especially in periods where very few Interbank Payments took place. For these participants, the inclusion of Customer Payments in the dataset could be essential for the full picture of the patterns analysis.

The removal of payments that represent money market loans, similar to the DNB approach referenced above, could be another enhancement of indicator filtering capabilities. This could be achieved through the combination of the payment data with data from a Furfine implementation that is also available for research purposes and has been utilized in Arciero, Heijmans, Heuver, Massarenti, Picillo and Vacirca

Table 1. TARGET2 payment categories and share in total volume/value for 2013

Category	Description	Volume (%)	Value (%)
1	Payments to third parties (customer and interbank payments)	77	33
2	Operations with the central bank (i.e. monetary operations, cash transactions)	7	14
3	Ancillary system payments (payments related to ancillary systems such as other payment systems or securities clearing and settlement systems)	13	29
4	Liquidity transfers (between payment systems or between different accounts of the same participant)	3	23

In Massarenti et al. (2012, p. 5), the analysis is restricted to Category 1 payments, which are further distinguished in sub-category 1.1 Customer Payments and 1.2 Interbank Payments, as Category 1 payments are considered more prone to staying in the queue due to insufficient liquidity. In Heijmans and Heuver (2011), Customer Payments are excluded from calculations due to them usually not being delayed, as clients are assumed to have sufficient liquidity on their accounts. Furthermore, a subset of Interbank Payments representing interbank loans is also excluded, on the basis that they "differ in nature from "real" payments" (p. 16). In particular, due to trade practices or standards, the discretionary space for the timing of the payment could be limited.

(2013). This functionality has not been implemented yet nevertheless, due to its technical complexity and potential impact on the current implementation performance.

The analysis of indicator output also revealed certain strange patterns, which lead to a further filtering of the payments. Interbank Payments may include sub-categories of payments that cannot be actually influenced by the participant submitting the payment. One such sub-category are the TARGET2 "mandated payments" (ECB, 2013, p. XXII), which, although "interbank", may be used as part of ancillary system settlement, cash operations and in a specific case also with monetary policy operations. Further analysis showed there were cases where their value was high, their appearance was regular and they happened at steady times, therefore they affected significantly the average time produced by the indicator, but not the actual patterns of the relevant participants. In those cases these transactions were filtered out of the dataset.

Another point to be considered when filtering payment types is potential inconsistencies between the time windows available for settlement. In the case of TARGET2 this is in particular the case due to distinction between a day-trade phase and night time settlement (ECB, 2013, p. 328ff.) This has been solved by focusing on the Category 1 payments which are only settled in the day-trade phase.

These examples from TARGET2 show that the implementation process requires an in depth analysis of the available data. It turned out to be beneficial to consider different filters for payments to be included and to investigate whether the differences in the outcome were as expected. One lesson learnt here was not to directly rely on the indicator result but to perform cross-checks to test for the plausibility of the results before finally deciding on the filters to be used. Still, not one single filter for payment types proved to be second to none.

One aspect which has not been addressed in the current work is the fact that Liquidity Transfers (Category 4 transactions) may also contain certain interbank transactions that are taking place as part of correspondent banking. These payments may have high values, and therefore could be potentially affecting significantly both value weighted timing indicators (especially for participants or groups that are very active in correspondent banking), but work is still needed in order to securely identify these transactions within the dataset.

Payment Attributes

Time and Date Attributes for Payments

Usually payments data are quite complex in the sense that they may encompass a lot of diverse pieces of information. This is especially true for time related information, for which a payment may be accompanied by several time-related attributes: introduction time to the system, settlement time, latest debit time and earliest debit time (for example see definition of execution time for TARGET2 payments at ECB (2013, p. 60)). Furthermore, the operational model of a payment system may define various different times for day trade phases and cut-offs (i.e. for TARGET2 the schedule is defined in ECB, (2013, p. 327)). For date related data, the most important distinction is between the date that a payment is introduced to the system, the date during which the payment should be introduced for settlement and the date when the payment actually gets settled or discarded, which may as well be different, depending again on the operational model of the system (i.e. especially in the case of TARGET2 for which the operational day spans over two calendar days) and the relevant supported functionality.

These attributes are very important for the selection of the data variables to be processed for the implementation of time-based indicators. As shown in the section "Definition of Indicators", the value weighted average settlement time indicator only uses the actual settlement time and the corresponding settlement date.

The delay indicator is a far more complex construct, requiring the processing of several different time and date attributes. For example, the variable $t_{1,i}$ defined as "the time when payment i is available to be settled" should be the latest time amongst three values: the actual introduction time, the earliest debit time (EDT) and the opening time of the system, as also noted in Massarenti et al (2012). It is important that these times are processed in correlation with the date that the payments were scheduled for settlement in the system and not the date they were actually introduced. The capability of a payment manager to submit payments for settlement a certain number of days in advance is called a "warehouse functionality" of the payment system (i.e. for TARGET2 this functionality is defined in ECB (2013, p. 62)). For example in TARGET2, a warehoused payment is processed at the beginning of the business day it is scheduled for settlement and this has to be taken into account when calculating the delay indicator. For non-warehoused payments, $t_{1,i}$ is set as the EDT if it exists or the introduction time. Under normal circumstances, the introduction time should always be earlier than EDT, but the possibility of introduction time being later could also be taken into account when implementing the indicator, to cover all cases.

The value of $t_{2,i}$ should be the value of the actual settlement time if the payment was settled. For unsettled payments $t_{2,i}$ should be set as the maximum time a payment may stay in the system before becoming discarded, i.e. $t_{2,i}=t_{3,i}$.

$t_{3,i}$ expresses the theoretical maximum time a payment may stay in the system before becoming discarded. There are two identified cases, depending on whether a latest debit time (LDT) has been set or not. If the LDT has been defined, this should be used as it expresses the maximum time the payment would have stayed in a queue in the system. If there is no LDT, the value is set as the cut-off time defined in the system's operational schedule for the corresponding type of payments. In the case of TARGET2, they are defined as "end of day trade phase 1" (currently 17.00) for payment type 1.1 (Customer payments) and "end of day trade phase 2" (currently 18.00) for all other payments, as documented in ECB (2013, p. 327). In the implementation we faced the issue that customer payment that are introduced after their cut-off time but before the cut-off for other payments are technically still entering the system but then remain unsettled. These transactions had to be filtered out since they led to a negative value when calculating $t_{3,i}$ - $t_{1,i}$.

Final Payment Status

A payment usually can have one of three final states at the end of day trade phase: settled, unsettled or cancelled. As already mentioned, in our implementation framework, the value weighted average settlement time takes only settled payments into account and the delay indicator takes settled and unsettled payments into account. Cancelled payments (i.e. for TARGET2 this functionality is defined in ECB (2013, p. 511)) are always filtered out from processing, mostly on the grounds that they express the intent of the payment manager to revoke them (and therefore they should never have been introduced to the system). The possibility that their cancellation was due to them taking too long could be a reason against filtering out these payments. Nevertheless their inclusion would have the adverse effect of making the indicator treat them as unsettled. Especially in the case of high value payments, their inclusion has been observed to significantly distort the indicator output in certain cases.

Exclusion of Noise in Data

There are further cases of noise in data which should be eliminated. The datasets provided as input for the calculation of the indicators may contain various test data. For example there might be cases of non-operation days that are included in the datasets which contain a few low value tests payments. Calculating the indicator for these days might significantly distort the output (i.e. a few only low value early payments would produce a very early average settlement time for that day) and they should therefore be filtered out. The implementation therefore should also provide the possibility to filter out specific dates from the datasets.

Aggregation Levels

Timing indicators may be useful as a monitoring tool for various purposes. A payment system operator and / or overseer are interested in the timing behavior of the system as a whole in order to ensure the smooth flow of liquidity, and therefore system operation. The whole of the system is therefore one of the aggregation levels that should be supported in the design of an implementation framework. One level of aggregation lower, regulatory authorities (overseers and supervisors) could also see potential in the pattern analysis of certain groups of participants that share a common characteristic. The two most significant levels of aggregation of this kind are at country level and at corporate group level. But also other groups of single participants sharing common characteristics are possible like e.g. small vs. large banks, or groups of banks having different business models. Finally, mostly supervisory authorities are interested in data that can be drilled down to the single participant level, for the monitoring of behavioral changes related to the timing of payments as part of the overall management of intraday liquidity. Still, also for single financial institutions a consolidation of several accounts can be necessary if a single entity from economic and legal aspects is not acting as single entity from a technical point of view and e.g. using subaccounts.

The implementation for the indicators includes a set of parameters that define the aggregation level and the participants that will be taken into account for the filtering of payments. More specifically, a parameter allows the script user to define the type of the participant to be either a single participant or a country or a group of participants and then setting an identifier that enables searching through the transaction data for payments that match that particular identifier pattern. For single participants and groups, the identifier is a BIC (or group of BICs), while for countries the identifier is the two digit country name (i.e. GR for Greece) in the account which is based on the National Central Bank (NCB) through which a participant is connected to TARGET2. The script combines the two information items to define the required level of aggregation.

In the cases of a full system or country level, during the analysis of the indicator output, there appeared a need to also be able to exclude certain BICs from the dataset, in order to verify whether the corresponding participants had a severe impact on the indicator output and to visualize how the indicator pattern would have been, had that participant not sent or received any payments. Therefore the implementation was also enriched with the capabilities of excluding BICs from the dataset and also creating different identifiers for the filtered datasets to facilitate comparison between indicator output data that has been generated about the same entity for the same period and aggregation level with modified included participant payments.

Transaction Flows

Several distinctions can be made between the transaction flows to be studied. The first and most important distinction is the distinction between incoming and outgoing payments. This distinction depends on the aggregation level. For the system level, only a single flow exists and the indicators are calculated for all payments within the input dataset. For lower aggregation levels, the indicators should be calculated separately for incoming and outgoing flows, which correspond to the payments received by or sent from the unit studied (group, country, participant).

Another distinction could be made between cross-border and domestic payments. Such an analysis is of particular interest in a multi-country system like TARGET2. One could also distinguish between intra-group and extra-group payments, i.e. payments to or from participants belonging to the same or a distinct corporate group. Again, also the creation of other groups is possibly meaningful.

Further work that is still ongoing is the inclusion of input variables related to the actual "ordering institution" and "beneficiary institution" of payments (this information is conveyed in the swift messages used for the payments, as shown in ECB (2013)). The inclusion of such parameters to the implementation would enable the analysis of differences in the behavior of a single participant for the timing of its "own" payments and payments sent for others.

The combination of these different distinctions is quickly leading to a high number of time series of indicator output so that it should be carefully analyzed which combinations are of particular relevance.

Output Data Graphical Representation

After having calculated the indicator values, it has to be decided which statistical variables offer a concise representation of the indicator output. Of course, the set of available options is already influenced by the decision made about aggregation level and transactions flows. In the implementation of the indicators for TARGET2 we opted for an approach representing the indicator value for each level of aggregation in a separate graph, i.e. one graph for each participant, the whole system or other aggregations to be studied. Other representations with more input data quickly led to overburdened figures.

The indicator is calculated as a time series of daily indicator values. Plotting the indicator values directly as a line turned out to be confusing due to the volatility of the daily values. We therefore implemented the calculation of a moving average to smoothen out the daily spikes and enable better visualization of trend changes. In order to still take into account the volatility, we added a confidence interval as a shaded area which is calculated as the 90% confidence interval of the values of the values for the period for which the moving average has been calculated. This representation is particularly useful for a continuous monitoring or the analysis of long horizons of real world data. It should be noted that the potential inclusion of any of the indicators in an everyday monitoring framework for early warnings, would imply the recording and visualization of the indicator value at intervals as close to real-time as possible. For example, depending on data availability, the delay indicator could be even produced as a "health check" monitor refreshed within the hour and provided to the system operator via their monitoring tools. Compared to other data sources for monitoring financial stability, payment data is promptly available. However, getting closer to almost real-time availability of the indicators discussed here can pose technical challenges concerning data extraction and automated and fast calculation of the indicators. In an early warning framework, one would also need to focus more on signals. The line graphs with moving averages would need to be augmented with thresholds to identify outliers of daily values.

One alternative representation to the single value output of the delay indicator could be considered, by disaggregating and combining time attributes from both the "value weighted average settlement time" and the "delay" indicator. This can be achieved by separately calculating the two parts of the numerator value:

$$\frac{\sum_{i=1}^{n}\left(value_i * t_{1,i}\right)}{\sum_{i=1}^{n} value_i}$$

and

$$\frac{\sum_{i=1}^{n}\left(value_i * t_{2,i}\right)}{\sum_{i=1}^{n} value_i}$$

where:

- $t_{1,i}$ is the time when payment i is available to be settled
- $t_{2,i}$ is the actual settlement time of the payment i (which is equal to the latest possible settlement time if the payment remains unsettled)

The normalization of the indicator between 1 and 0 is then discarded, and two values representing a value weighted average time are calculated. These two values can be plotted as two lines representing average introduction and settlement time with the area between the two lines representing the delay. This representation has the advantage to already include the complementary information from the average settlement time indicator and to signal both changes in introduction behavior and in settlement delay. It has the disadvantage that different transaction flows, in particular incoming and outgoing payments, are more difficult to be represented in one single graph.

To analyze simulation output, line graphs are less useful since typically the number of available daily values is smaller. In this case, the representation of bar charts for each day and values for different scenarios turned out to be a good solution. Another solution is to calculate an overall average for the whole period simulated in order to compare only one value per scenario. Here, a box-plot approach could be used to still take into account the volatility between single days being simulated. It also turned out to be beneficial to represent differences between the indicator values between different scenarios being simulated. Both relative and absolute differences could be of interest depending on the concrete type of analysis.

The graphical representation of the indicator output could be augmented by including other indicators not related to the timing of payments. We used in particular the net flow of payments of a single participant (i.e. the difference between the value of incoming and outgoing payments) in the monitoring graphs. Other indicators of financial stress could also be used in order to identify correlation with the timing related indicators.

INDICATOR OUTPUT EVALUATION

Value Weighted Average Settlement Time

The following figure depicts the output of the value weighted settlement time at the system level for TARGET2 Category 1 payments for the three years period 2011-2013.

The results are remarkably stable, indicating that the average settlement time in the system does not fluctuate over time, remaining close to midday between 12:19 and 12:34. These results agree with the cumulative intraday distribution of value presented in Massarenti et al. (2012, p. 20), where it is shown that 60% of the total daily value is settled before noon, without much deviation from the years 2008 to 2011. Given the fact that there are no throughput guidelines for TARGET2, this is a positive characteristic for the liquidity circulation profile in TARGET2.

At lower aggregation levels the situation may be quite different than the system level in terms of pattern volatility. Due to confidentiality reasons, no actual output data lower than system aggregation levels can be presented in this chapter. Nevertheless, some general observations will be discussed here.

When drilling into lower aggregation levels the behavioral pattern changes requiring particular attention take one of the following forms:

- Entity is starting to pay significantly earlier or later than before.
- The entity's counterparties start sending payments to the entity significantly earlier or later than before.

Figure 1. Value weighted average settlement time in TARGET2 for 2011-2013

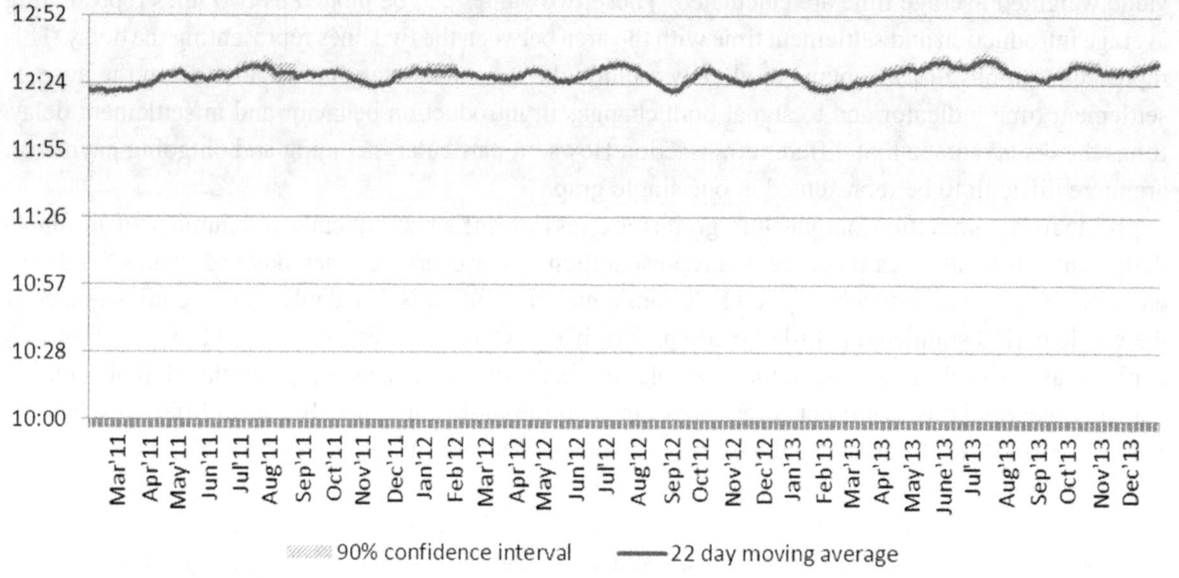

The above can be seen changing in a parallel fashion (i.e. they both start paying earlier or both paying later) or a cross-over exists with both patterns reversing at the same time.

At country level, the indicators fluctuate significantly, something which heavily depends on the market size and composition. From the experience collected so far through the data analysis, it was evident that in countries with more concentrated markets, as it was expected, the indicators are prone to be heavily influenced by a small number of critical participants, which altogether affect the country profile. In some cases, it helps to utilize features that enable analysis to isolate or altogether remove the effects of single entities to be able to get a more unbiased view of the relevant market segments. The output analysis also shows that in smaller markets, concentrated bursts of high value payments or even single payments of considerably high value may also influence the indicators' output.

Similar results were collected further down at single participant or group level, where in some cases a shift of a participants' timing pattern could be correlated with certain events happening in the respective markets or the participants themselves, which could justify a change in the business practices of the participant or have induced a certain degree of liquidity stress. These effects were sometimes pronounced in indicator output, following some of the more serious events that happened during the recent financial crisis. Furthermore, it was interesting to note the parallel changes in the settlement time of payment flows happening between participants belonging to the same group or having a parent company-subsidiary relationship, especially in a cross-border context, where the patterns may be influencing both the country-to-country and the participant-to-participant graphs, depending on the magnitude.

Payments Delay

The following figure depicts the output of the delay indicator at the system level for TARGET2 Category 1 payments for the three years period 2011-2013.

Figure 2. Payments delay in TARGET2 for the years 2011-2013

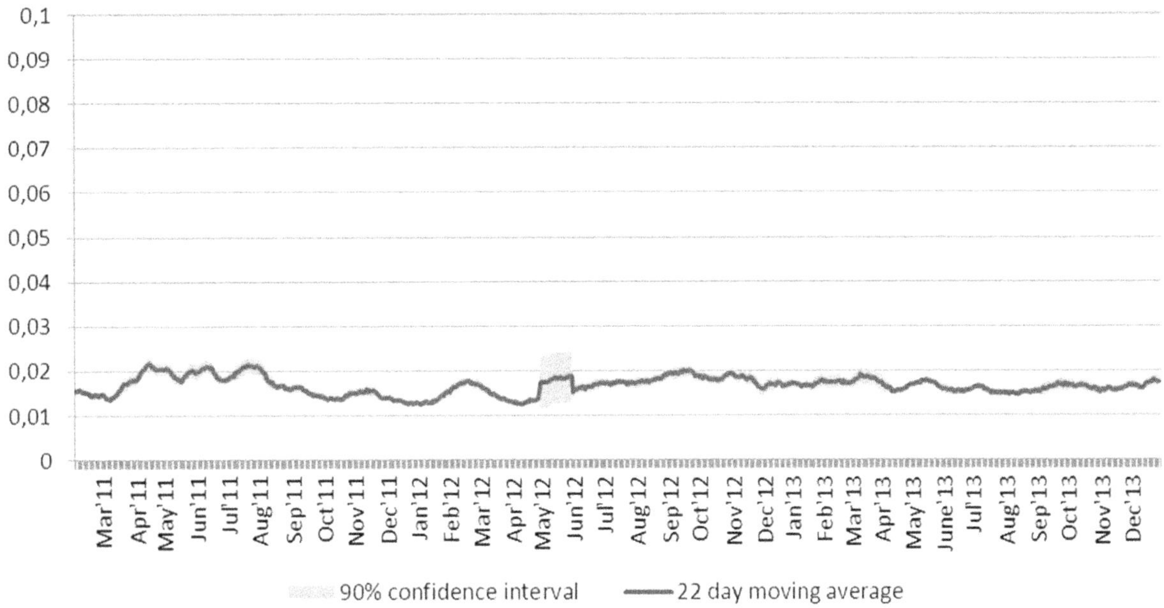

Similarly to the value weighted settlement time indicator, the delays are relatively stable as well and kept at a significantly low level (between 0,012 and 0,022), which could be seen as evidence of a smooth operation of the system at a macro level. The 90% confidence interval is quite stable as well, except for May 2012, when a single outlier due to an unsettled large value payment distorts the overall 22 day trend. This again shows that, these indicators are quite sensitive to significant pattern changes, which may warrant further investigation as to probable causes.

At lower aggregation levels, from the delay indicator perspective, the pattern changes requiring particular attention are the following:

- Entity is starting to experience significant delays while sending payments.
- The entity's counterparties are starting to experience significant delays while sending payments to the entity.

The analysis of delay data at country and participant level shows that, in contrast to the value weighted average settlement time, the patterns are closer to the system level picture. The delays in the system are kept at low level, even very close to zero for certain participants. Nevertheless, based on the sample of participants for which indicator data were collected, there are also a few cases where the delay may have reached as high as 0,81 for individual days, which should be considered a significant deviation to the system average. Although few, these cases can be correlated with a relatively high degree of certainty to specific events with a negative impact that happened throughout the financial crisis, suggesting that the delay indicator stress event identification and prediction potential might be higher than other time related indicators.

Another pattern which has been observed within the sample of participants studied, is that when a participant experiences outgoing delays, the affected participants (for which the delay is incoming), do not seem to propagate any kind of delay in their own outgoing payments, i.e. no contagion effects are apparent.

Output Evaluation Challenges and Potential Uses

The most important keyword in the abovementioned pattern changes of the previous sections is "significant", where the analyst needs to define thresholds for the magnitude of each change, in order to identify patterns of interest. Candidate key parameters for the pattern analysis are the following:

- The definition of thresholds for the significance of the change, which could take the form of a change percentage or flat time difference value within a specific time frame, i.e. a greater than 1h 30m increase or decrease of the value weighted average settlement time within a period of 30 days.
- The definition of lower and upper bound thresholds for the indicator value itself, i.e. a delay of more than 0.1.

The definition of the above parameters may be based on past behavioral patterns shown by the indicators in correlation with events or facts or other indicators known about the entity under investigation. Once the parameters have been defined, the indicators could be integrated in an early warning framework, where several indicators are combined to give feedback about changes in business practices, events that impacted the participant or disrupted payment operations, out of the ordinary behaviors or even liquidity stress, which would be the most interesting case in terms of early warning potential. Nevertheless, based on the experience so far by the study of the indicators output during the recent economic crisis, when payments would have been more probable to be impacted by liquidity stress, one may conclude that the definition of the above mentioned parameters is a very challenging task.

One example is the interpretation of a specific timing pattern where a participant starts to pay its highest value payments significantly earlier than before (i.e. several hours earlier than usual). Would that mean that it has just simply changed its business practices and its liquidity position is so strong that it can "afford" this behavior, or would it mean that it is trying to convince the markets that it faces no liquidity problems? The event context during the change might help with favoring towards one or the other cases (i.e. a severe degradation of the participant's credit rating or a known period of severe loss of deposits), but one cannot be totally certain unless they bring the issue to actual payment manager of the participant. There are cases where a sequence of changes may lead towards better situation profiling, such as when a participant starts to pay significantly earlier for a period and afterwards becomes a late payer when they can no longer afford doing so. Even then though, indicator output cannot be conclusive, unless other monitored indicators or variables (such us for example deposits monitoring) lead towards the same observations. An analyst should pursue the thorough combination of different types of indicators, possibly stemming from a different economic area to payment systems altogether (i.e. bond spreads), in order to setup an as complete as possible picture of the entity under study. This combination can also lead to the definition of composite indicators that combine different data, possibly with adjustable weights, that should be better suited for early warning frameworks.

Currently, there is work in progress for the implemented indicators quality, predictive capabilities and reliability to be assessed against a testing framework for early warning indicators based on signaling analysis. The goals of this work will be to assess the indicators' signal strength and how early warnings can be detected. It has to be critically assessed whether the indicators are not only an interesting piece of the puzzle in analyzing stress-periods ex-post. Their value would increase if stable causal interpretations of changes in the indicator values could be identified.

Simulation Analysis

The output evaluation discussed so far is of particular interest from a perspective of financial stability and participant behavior. On the other hand, the use of the indicators turned out to be very useful from a perspective of system performance, which is of high interest for the operator of the system in particular. The calculation of the indicators at system level has shown very stable patterns, indicating a very good performance of the actual system. While the cross-system comparability is rather limited, given the many technical challenges in implementing the indicator for a particular system, the indicators are in addition particularly valuable to evaluate the output of simulation studies of one single system. In this context, the main benefit of the indicators (especially the delay indicator) is that they allow the direct assessment of the system performance given a particular set of input data with one single value, but at the same time they take into account more detailed aspects than simpler indicators like e.g. the number of unsettled or queued payments.

In the Eurosystem, the indicators have been used to evaluate the usefulness of institutional features of TARGET2 by comparing indicator values in setups with and without these features. These have been further combined in scenarios which also include different levels of induced stress.

Figure 3 is an example of the delay indicator being used in simulation output analysis. It is presented in Diehl and Müller (2014), a study aimed at quantifying the impact of the institutional feature of bilateral limits in TARGET2. Several stress scenarios have been simulated in that study by applying changes to the original data from TARGET2. The figure shows the comparison of the effect of limits between scenario 3 and scenario 4 of the study. For scenario 3, artificial late payers have been created by delaying the introduction time of transactions of a group of participants and virtual limits have been set against these participants. For scenario 4 in addition to the changes made for scenario 3, a 90% haircut to the availably intraday credits for all participants has been applied in order to simulate the effect of limits with tighter liquidity conditions, i.e. a higher level of stress, ceteris paribus. In order to assess the effect of limits, the stress scenarios have been simulated once with the virtual limits being effectively set and once without the virtual limits being set. The figure shows the additional delay that is caused by limits in each stress scenario. It is calculated as the difference of the values of the delay indicator in the setup of the respective stress scenario without and with limits in percent of the value of the delay indicator in the setup with limits:

$$\frac{\text{delay indicator (stress scenario}_i\text{,without limits)- delay indicator (stress scenario}_i\text{,with limits)}}{\text{delay indicator (stress scenario}_i\text{,with limits)}}$$

It can be interpreted as the share of delay in the setup with limits that is caused by the limits. The interpretation of the figure is that the additional delay due to limits is much smaller in the scenario 4 with a higher level of stress compared to the scenario 3. The delay indicator has been used in this study

Figure 3. Comparison of delayed payments between different stress scenarios. Simulated period: Days in January 2013.

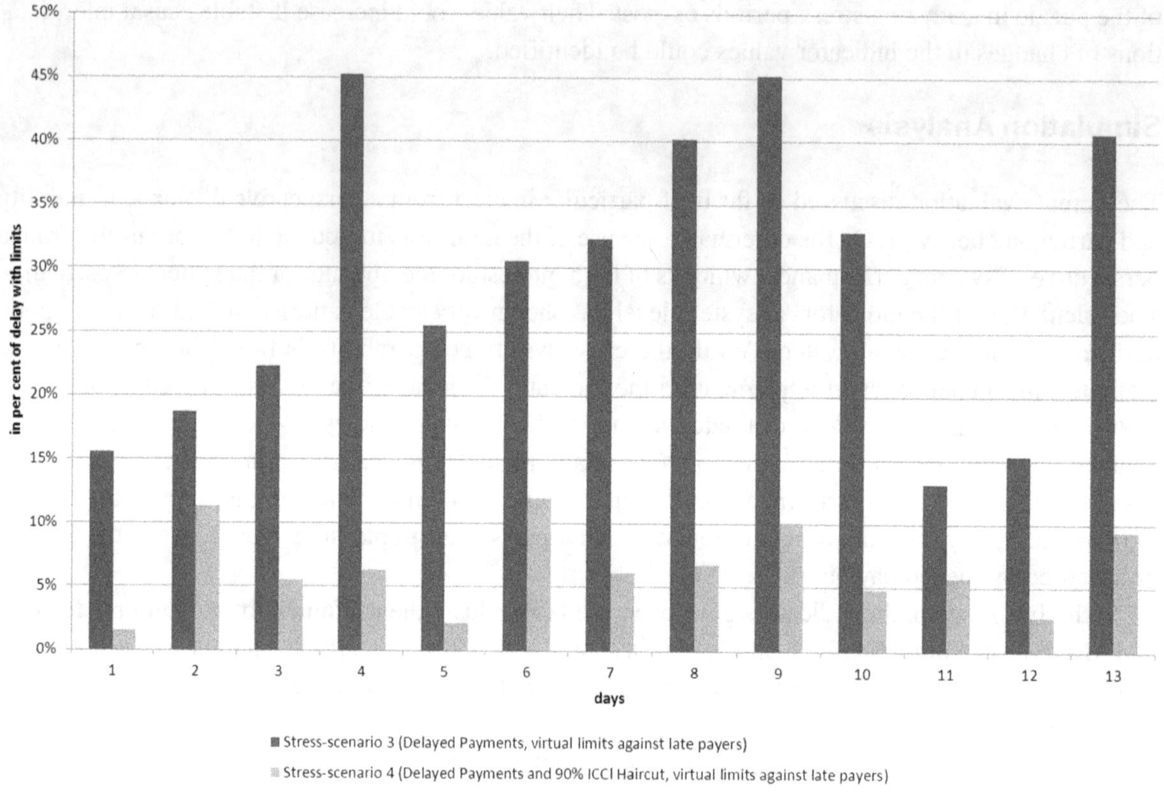

to evaluate the system performance after changing system parameters: the setting (or not) of limits and the imposing (or not) of stress conditions. Its distinctive advantage in this context is that different aspects of system performance, in particular the number and value of queued and unsettled payments and the length of delays, are condensed to one figure which can be easily numerically compared and interpreted as "the lower the better". In the example presented here, the conclusion was drawn that the positive effects of limits on system performance are higher in scenarios with a higher level of stress.

CONCLUSION

The experience of implementing the two timing indicators within the context of TARGET2 has validated the need for an extensive and elaborate design of processes when one tries to derive useful composite output from very rich granular transaction data. In order to set up an indicator framework one should analyze all relevant characteristics of payments, common in most RTGS systems, such as payment types, payment attributes, aggregation levels, transaction flows and statistical variables. The indicators should then be implemented in a way that facilitates the maximum configurability and parameterization that address the pursued analysis goals, including identified special cases.

After the indicators have been implemented, usually the first phase of processing indicator output from real world data includes the identification of possible correlations between the past behavior of the entities under study with external events (i.e. changes in the general business environment of the market, organizational changes, negative assessments or ratings) or other indicators known about it (i.e. other financial variables) and the formulation of corresponding observations, estimations and stylized facts. Nevertheless, if the ultimate goal for the implemented indicators is to be used for regular monitoring or even as part of a framework for early warnings, it is considered important that the specific implementation should be further tested in a systematic way with respect to the indicator's signal strength and predictive capabilities so that proper thresholds are defined for the characterization of situations. Furthermore, it is extremely important that any potential early warning about the degradation of an entity's payments timing profile is followed up by a cross-referencing procedure with other variables known about that particular entity, within the respective monitoring framework.

For the analysis of output in simulation studies, the indicators are actively used in the Eurosystem and turned out to offer a concise representation of the overall system level performance. They are therefore a valuable evaluation criterion for policy recommendations based on the simulation results.

REFERENCES

Arciero, L., Heijmans, R., Heuver, R., Massarenti, M., Picillo, C., & Vacirca, F. (2013). How to Measure the Unsecured Money Market? The Eurosystem's Implementation and Validation Using TARGET2 Data, De Nederlandsche Bank Working Paper No. 369.

Monitoring indicators for intraday liquidity management [Consultative document]. (2012). Basel Committee on Banking Supervision, Bank for International Settlements.

Monitoring tools for intraday liquidity management. (2013). Basel Committee on Banking Supervision, Bank for International Settlements.

Becher, C., Galbiati, M., & Tudela, M. (2008). The timing and funding of CHAPS sterling payments. *Economic Policy Review*, *14*(2), 113–133.

Diehl, M. (2013). Measuring free riding in large-value payment systems: the case of TARGET2. *Journal of Financial Market infrastructures*, 1/3, 1-23.

Diehl, M., & Müller, A. (2014). Analysis of the use and impact of limits. *Journal of Financial Market Infrastructures*, *3*(1), 33–60.

TARGET2 Single Shared Platform: User Detailed Functional Specifications. (2013). European Central Bank.

TARGET Annual Report 2013. (2014). European Central Bank.

Heijmans, R., & Heuver, R. (2011). Is this bank ill? The diagnosis of doctor TARGET2. De Nederlandsche Bank Working Paper No. 316.

Kokkola, T. (Ed.). (2010). *The Payment System*. European Central Bank Publications.

Koponen, R. & Soramäki, K. (1998). *Intraday liquidity needs in a modern interbank payment system - a simulation approach*. Bank of Finland Publications.

Laine, T., Nummelin, T., & Snellman, H. (2011). *Combining liquidity usage and interest rates on overnight loans: an oversight indicator*. Bank of Finland Publications.

Massarenti, M., Petriconi, S., Lindner, J. (2012). Intraday patterns and Timing of T2 Interbank payments. *Journal of Financial Market Infrastructures*, 1/2, 3-23.

McAndrews, J., & Rajan, S. (2000). The timing and funding of Fedwire funds transfers. *Economic Policy Review*, *6*(2), 17–32.

Schulz, C. (2011, February). *Liquidity requirements and payment delays. Participant type dependent preferences*. European Central Bank Working Paper Series No 1291.

Tölö, E., Jokivuolle, E., & Virén, M. (2014). *Do private signals of a bank's creditworthiness predict the bank's CDS price? Evidence from the Eurosystem's overnight loan rates*. Bank of Finland Research Discussion Paper No. 9.

ENDNOTES

1 The authors of this paper are members of one of the user groups with access to TARGET2 data in accordance with Article 1(2) of Decision ECB/2012/9 of 29 July 2012 on access to and use of certain TARGET2 data. The Bank of Greece, the Deutsche Bundesbank and the PSSC have checked the paper against the rules for guaranteeing the confidentiality of transaction-level data imposed by the PSSC pursuant to Article 1(4) of the above mentioned issue. The views expressed in the paper are solely those of the authors and do not necessarily present the views of the Eurosystem. The authors would like to especially thank Mr. Matti Hellqvist for the help, comments and original ideas provided to this work.

2 This time takes into account also special features of the payment system, such as warehoused payments, where the time when the payment is introduced is different from the time the payment is available for settlement. These are explained in more detail later in the chapter in the "Payment Attributes" section.

3 In this context, negative impact means signaling a higher delay, i.e. leading to a higher value of the indicator.

Chapter 10
Intraday Liquidity Flows within the Financial Market Infrastructures in Mexico

Biliana Alexandrova-Kabadjova
Banco de Mexico, Mexico

Ronald Heijmans
De Nederlandsche Bank, The Netherlands

Liliana Garcia-Ochoa
Banco de Mexico, Mexico

Antoaneta Serguieva
University College London, UK

ABSTRACT

In this chapter, the authors present a methodology to study the flow of funds in large-value payment systems (LVPSs). The algorithm presented differentiates the flow of payments into two categories: 1) external funds, i.e. funds transferred from other financial market infrastructures (FMIs) or provided by the central bank, and 2) the reuse of incoming payments within the same FMI. Using individual transaction data, the algorithm evaluates to what extent incoming payments are used to cover obligations. The method also studies the flow of intraday liquidity under the framework of its provision within Mexican FMIs. The aim is to evaluate the impact of intraday liquidity provision, and understand how liquidity is transmitted to participants in the Mexican Large Value Payment System, or SPEI®.

INTRODUCTION[1]

The worldwide economic crisis has revealed that liquidity problems in (large) banks can occur suddenly, and with serious consequences for (global) financial stability. The most recent and widely referenced example is the collapse of Lehman Brothers. The interest in intraday liquidity management has grown since then, from both academics and financial authorities such as central banks. Studying intraday liquidity flows, provides valuable insight into: (i) the provision of liquidity and efficient use levels, (ii) potential liquidity risks in settling payment obligations, and (iii) the degree of interdependence between financial market infrastructures (FMIs) in terms of liquidity, in particular between large value payment and securities settlement systems (LVPSs and SSSs). The insight for central banks can be towards establishing rules and guidelines that improve the robustness of these FMIs, reduce risks between interdependent FMIs, and enhance the frameworks that implement liquidity provision into FMIs.

DOI: 10.4018/978-1-4666-8745-5.ch010

To smooth the settlement of transactions in FMIs, central banks provide (intraday) liquidity to participants in their LVPSs. This liquidity, together with liquidity from financial institutions' payment obligations, flows through different FMIs. Further, the liquidity is redistributed among participants either as transfers or secured/unsecured lending/borrowing among them. Therefore, the adequate level (from both an aggregate and individual perspective) and price of the liquidity provided by the central bank are required conditions to achieve efficiency. To that end, central banks must have solid knowledge of two aspects of the financial system. The first is the emerging network among participants. This reveals the structure of the interdependency among financial institutions. Given that some of these institutions are direct participants in more than one FMI, the overall network of funds transfers among FMIs must be taken into account. The second aspect is the behavior of the participants related to intraday liquidity management, i.e., decisions made during the day with respect to the number/value of payment obligations. We have identified three factors affecting decisions on how many payment orders should be sent for settlement by a participant throughout the day.[2] Those factors are: (i) the amount of central bank money the participant has access to, (ii) the amount of funds the institution can obtain in terms of borrowing from other participants, if required, and (iii) the volume of payments received due to existing obligations either to the participant or its clients at a particular time in the day.

In this chapter, the authors define a methodology to study the flow of funds observed in LVPSs related to the management of external funds of the participants – i.e., funds transferred from other FMIs or provided by a central bank – and the reuse of incoming payments by the participants. An algorithm is developed, using individual transaction data, to distinguish to what extent incoming payments are used to cover obligations. This approach is applied to study the flow of intraday liquidity under the framework of its provision in the Mexican FMIs. Three systems are involved in this process: (i) SPEI® (an equivalent to a real-time gross settlement (RTGS) system), (ii) SIAC - a system that provides liquidity to credit institutions, and (iii) DALÍ (the Mexican SSS). SPEI® and SIAC are administrated by the central bank, whereas DALÍ is administrated by the private institution S.D. INDEVAL.[3]

Furthermore, this chapter evaluates the impact of the intraday liquidity provision mechanism in order to understand how liquidity is transmitted to all participants in SPEI®, i.e., among those with access to central bank money and those that do not have a SIAC account. Currently, there are ninety-eight direct participants in SPEI® identified under four categories: (i) private multiple-purpose banks (commercial banks or CBs), (ii) public development banks (DBs), [4] (iii) brokerages (Bs), and (iv) other nonbank financial institutions (NBFIs). The liquidity provision to the FMIs is performed through two channels. The first channel is performed through overdrafts guaranteed by monetary regulation deposits and granted as direct deposits at Banco de México (BdM). The second uses intraday repos on sovereign debt. Overdrafts are allowed to credit institutions (CBs and DBs) that have current accounts in SIAC, and their limits are determined according to the amount of monetary regulation deposit each participant has. Intraday repos are executed in DALÍ by credit institutions[5] and brokerages.[6] There is a limit to the total value of repo operations a financial institution can perform, depending on capital. There are fifty direct participants in SIAC. Forty-four of them are private banks, whereas six are public banks.

The authors use all individual transactions in SPEI® for the year 2013 to calculate to what extent incoming payments cover participants' obligations, which are referred to as recycled. In the case of SPEI®, incoming payments could be either obligations received from other parties or borrowing from other participants. It is assumed that the rest of the payments are covered with funds coming from other FMIs. Further, given the same time period, we calculate on an aggregate level, the overdraft registered in

SIAC, and the Banco de México intraday repos performed in DALÍ. We compare on a daily basis and per hour, the calculated funded payments vs. the real amount of overdrafts and repos provided to the system.

The outline of this chapter is as follows. In the next (or second) section, an overview of the literature is provided as background. The main body of the chapter comprises three liquidity-related issues. First, the mechanism of liquidity provision is presented (in the third section). Second, we discuss how we distinguish among the use of external funds vs. incoming payments (in section four). Third, the interactions between FMIs are analyzed in section five. The chapter ends with final remarks and recommendations for future research, discussed in section six.

BACKGROUND

The main focus of this chapter is liquidity flows and intraday patterns in (the Mexican) LVPS. This section provides overviews of the literature on these flows and patterns. In addition, we provide insight on other research topics related to FMI (data) analysis. Most countries in the industrialised world have implemented real-time gross settlement (RTGS) systems (Bech and Hobijn, 2007). Therefore, most analysis on large value payment systems focus on RTGS systems rather than netting. The interest in liquidity flows in payment systems has increased in the last decade, especially since the collapse of Lehman Brothers.

An early investigation is provided by Humphrey (1986). He assessed the potential disruptive effects of systemic risk in a net settlement system using data on transactions from a randomly selected business day on CHIPS.[7] He simulated a large participant's failure by unwinding all the day's transactions to and from that participant. To check robustness, Humphrey also replicated the exercise with data from another business day. The main results show that: 1) on both days, approximately 37% of CHIPS institutions default as a consequence of a major direct participant's default and 2) on the two different days, different institutions are affected. Angelini, Maresca and Russo (1996) presented an empirical assessment of the potential size of the domino effect, i.e., that one bank's failure to pay leads to other banks' payment failures, in the Italian netting system. A bank's settlement failure is simulated and the impact on the rest of the system measured. Their main findings are that (i) the average number of systemic crises recorded in their simulations is small and (ii) the systemic crises are also small, both in terms of the number of institutions involved (less than 1%) and of losses (less than 3% of the total average daily debtor balances). The simulation performed by Humphrey in the U.S. system had a much larger systemic risk impact. According to Angelini et al. (1996), the difference is mainly due to the much smaller volume of funds flowing through the Italian system and due to structural differences.

Leinonen and Soramäki (2005) studied the optimisation of liquidity usage and settlement speed. One of their main findings is that if liquidity costs are low enough relative to delay costs, participants will pay as soon as the obligation arises. Within a narrow range of relative costs of liquidity and delay, participants will switch from maximum delay to immediate settlement. Hellqvist and Koskinen (2005) present a methodology for stress testing securities clearing and settlement systems with simulations based on actual system data. Their method can be used for assessing the consequences of operational failures of clearing parties within the systems. It can also be used to quantify the possibility of spillover effects resulting from operational failures in securities clearing and settlement systems. One of their findings is that stress testing the settlement system for Finnish money market instruments shows that the system does not seem to pose a significant systemic risk to the Finnish financial markets. Even in a severe disturbance affecting one participant, the liquidity effect on the other participants was for the most part minor when taking into consideration the participants' liquidity reserves.

Hellqvist and Snellman (2007) present a simulation model of the Finnish securities settlement system for equities. Results of the simulations show that operational failure of individual clearing participants should last more than one settlement day to cause a significant impact in the settlement system under study. No contagion from failures in the securities settlement system was observed on the large value payment system. The main settlement algorithm mitigated the impact of the scenarios in the settlement system efficiently.

Armantier, Arnold and McAndrews (2008) seek to quantify how the changing environment in which Fedwire (the biggest large value payment system of the United States) operates has affected the timing of payment value transferred within the system.[8] They observe several trends in payment timing from 1998 to 2006. After 2000, the peak in payment activity shifts to later in the day. Indeed, post-2000, greater concentration of payments occurs after 17:00. At the same time, however, several factors have been associated with increased payment activity early in the day, such as 1) the creation of the Continuous Linked Settlement (CLS) Bank, an institution that settles U.S. dollar payments early in the morning, 2) changes to the Clearing House Interbank Payments System's (CHIPS) settlement practices, and 3) expanded Fedwire operating hours. Despite these developments, they find that the distribution of payment activity across the day still peaks more in the late afternoon.

Becher, Galbiati and Tudela (2008) investigate the factors influencing the timing and funding of payments in the CHAPS Sterling system, drawing where appropriate on comparisons with payment activity in Fedwire. Their results show that the settlement of time-critical payments in CHAPS supplies liquidity early in the day. Liquidity can be recycled to fund less urgent payments. Moreover, CHAPS throughput guidelines provide a centralized coordination mechanism that essentially limits any tendency toward payment delay.[9] Furthermore, the relatively small direct membership of CHAPS facilitates coordination, enabling members to maintain a constant flux of payments during the day.

As in RTGS systems, liquidity demand is relatively high due to the fact that each transaction is settled individually, and it is desired that banks do not delay (unnecessary) payments. If participants in the system do delay payments, this will have a direct effect on the liquidity position of their counterparties. If a participant choses to pay after it has received its incoming payments, it is called a free-rider. Diehl (2013) addresses the question of how free-riding in LVPSs should be properly measured. He developed several measures for identifying free-riding. Free-riding can be measured at an individual bank level. His analysis shows that a combination of at least two measures is recommended for capturing the effects of free-riding. His results are based on nine important banks in the German part of TARGET (the European RTGS system). The evaluated measures show stable payment behaviour of most participants over time. However, his results also show some remarkable regime shifts, which provide interesting insights on a single participant.

Massarenti et al. (2012) studied the intraday patterns and timing of all TARGET2 interbank payments.[10] They provide insight on the intraday patterns of TARGET2 payments and (the evolution of) settlement delay. One of their results is that the first hour and a half and the last hour are the most crucial times during the system's operating hours in terms of the numbers of payments processed (opening hours) and value of payments (closing hour). Their analysis provides only a system-wide view and can be used by operators and overseers of central banks. Other transaction-level data analyses are simulations aiming to investigate operational outages in the payment system or investigate liquidity shocks.

Heijmans and Heuver (2014) study the different liquidity elements which can be identified from LVPS transaction data. They develop a method for how LVPS transaction data can be used to identify liquidity stress in the market as a whole and at an individual bank level. The stress indicators look at liquidity obtained from the central bank (monetary loans), unsecured interbank loans (value and interest rate), the use of collateral, and the payments on behalf of their own business and that of their clients.

In the case of Mexico, two simulation studies have been conducted by Alexandrova-Kabadjova and Solís-Robleda (2012, 2013) to analyze the settlement rules of SPEI® and the liquidity management of commercial banks that are direct participants. Based on transaction data, the authors study the behaviour of the selected financial institutions related to the reuse of incoming payments. They found that despite the growing volume of low value payments processed in real time through SPEI®, settlement is performed efficiently. Furthermore, the authors argue that observed patterns in the commercial banks' intraday behavior, particularly in the hours in which the highest volumes of low value payments are sent, could be a sign of coordination among participants. However, a study accounting for all direct participants in SPEI® has not been done.

Another method used over the last decade to study FMI transaction data is network topology. The ideas of network theory can be applied to the field of economics, for example, to study systemic risk. There is a vast literature analyzing the interactions of various financial markets such as equity and bond markets (Pericoli and Sbracia, 2003). Inaoka et al. (2004) and Soramäki et al. (2006) have started to describe large value financial payment systems (in Japan and the U.S., respectively) from a network perspective. Bech and Garratt (2012) analyze the effects of a wide-scale disruption on the functioning of the interbank payment system. Pröpper et al. (2013) investigate the influence of the chosen timeframe on the properties of the payment network. In addition, they look at the central role of highly connected nodes. Other recent studies introduce a framework for investigating financial market infrastructures, including payment systems, and incorporating them at the meso-level within multiplex or multilayer networks of the financial system, see Serguieva (2013) and Bravo-Benitez et al. (2015).

Martinez-Jaramillo et al. (2014) provide an empirical study of the Mexican banking system's network and its implications for systemic risk. To measure and monitor the systemic risk in the Mexican payment system, they present topological metrics for the interbank exposures and the payment system network. One of their main findings is that the structures of the payments and exposures networks are different in terms of connectivity. The topology of the exposures network changed after the collapse of Lehman Brothers, whereas the structure of the payments network does not change.

All these papers have in common that they look at (transaction-level) data of one payment system (or an FMI), and an RTGS system. However, they do not look at the interactions between these systems. This chapter also looks at the interactions between the most important FMIs.

THE MECHANISM OF LIQUIDITY PROVISION

The participants with access to intraday liquidity provided by BdM, i.e., credit institutions (like multi-purposed commercial banks and public development banks), have current accounts in SIAC.[11] SIAC is the system that grants collateralized overdrafts (CPSS, 2011). In addition, credit institutions and brokerages can also obtain intraday liquidity from BdM through government debt repos, which are carried out within the SSS, DALÍ. Figure 1 schematically presents the different sectors of direct participants and the infrastructures involved in liquidity provision. Through these liquidity channels, the central bank gives

Figure 1. Liquidity Provision
BdM – Banco de México
DALÍ – the Mexican Security Settlement System
SIAC – the system holding current accounts for the banks allowing direct access to liquidity provided by BdM
B – Brokerages
CB – Private Multiple–Purpose Banks (Commercial Banks)
DB – Public Development Banks

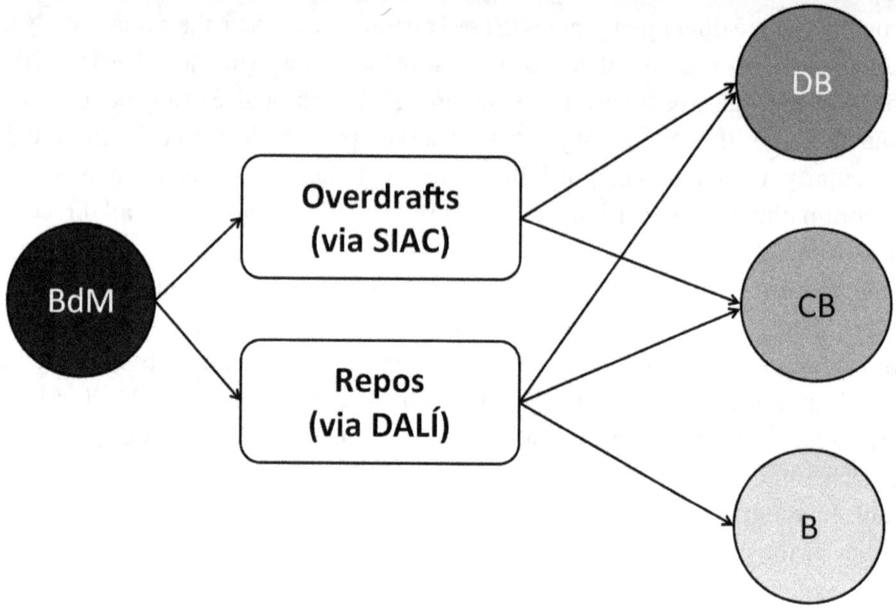

shape to a vivid and complex interaction structure, which has recently been the subject of several studies (Martinez-Jaramillo et al., 2014; Bravo-Benitez et al., 2014; Alexandrova-Kabadjova et al., 2014).

SPEI® is a payment system that is an RTGS equivalent (CPSS, 1997). It is operated by BdM, and direct participants are allowed to perform payment obligations and fund transfers. It operates under an equivalent to RTGS scheme, as a bilateral and multilateral net settlement process is executed at the latest every 3 seconds after receiving a new instruction. In addition, low and large value payments between banks and third parties are processed simultaneously in SPEI®. This creates rich liquidity flow among participants, so that institutions that have direct access to SPEI® receive funds that allow them to cover their payment obligations. Figure 2 presents the weighted links that connect SPEI® with the following FMIs - SIAC, CLS and DALÍ. SIAC and DALÍ have been introduced earlier in the chapter, while CLS is the Continuous Linked Settlement system that processes foreign exchange settlements under a Payment vs. Payment (PvP) scheme. The figure classifies the direct SPEI® participants by sector. This introduces the meso-level related to the LVPS and its interactions with the rest of the components. We observe from the figure that the most weighted connections are commercial banks and DALÍ. Notice that direct participants in SIAC are allowed only to make fund transfers to SPEI®, which in turn could be used as the connecting point to DALÍ.

Figure 2 presents on an aggregated level the existing network between SPEI®, DALÍ, CLS and the rest of the direct participants in SPEI®, in which the weights of the links constitute the volume of

Figure 2. Volume of Transactions in SPEI® Processed in 2013, in MXN Billions:
per Sector – Commercial Banks (CBs), Development Banks (DBs), Brokerages (Bs), Non-Bank Financial Institutions (NBFIs), and the direct participant BdM, as well as FMIs – SIAC, DALÍ, CLS.

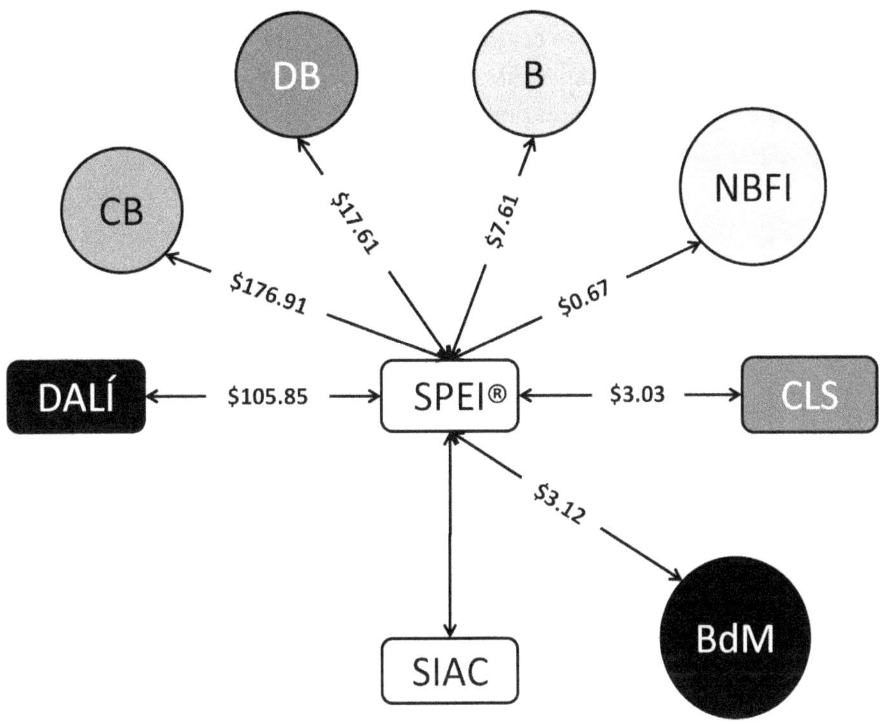

transactions settled in SPEI®. Certainly from the perspective of operations volume settled in DALÍ, the weighted links are different. Also, the direct participants in DALÍ do not overlap completely with the direct participants of SPEI®. This chapter focusses on the volume of transactions settled in SPEI® in order to evaluate the flow of liquidity between the LVPS and the SSS. In the next section, we propose a methodology to evaluate the use of external funds vs. incoming payments in the settlement of payment obligations in SPEI®. For future research, creating the weighted links of the DALÍ transactions will allow completion of the network structure between the FMIs we are analyzing.

USE OF EXTERNAL FUNDS VS. INCOMING PAYMENTS IN SPEI®

In the previous section, the rules of intraday liquidity provision were discussed. In the present section, direct participants' behavior, determined by the sector they belong to, is explained in terms of decisions related to the management of external funds and incoming payments.

Given that SPEI® operates under an equivalent to RTGS scheme, it imposes higher pressure on the level of liquidity required in comparison to a Deferred Net Settlement (DNS) scheme. Nevertheless, payments are settled under continuing bilateral and multilateral netting. For that reason, it is important to measure how much this liquidity-saving mechanism reduces pressure on the amount of external funds used. Given the high number of retail payments that settle during a day, we further assume participants use incoming payments to cover other obligations - this process also reduces the demand for external funds.

Commercial banks and development banks are credit institutions and have access to central bank money in SIAC, as well as accounts in SPEI® and DALÍ. Brokerages have accounts in SIAC, SPEI® and DALÍ, but do not have direct access to central bank money. NBFIs have accounts only in SPEI® and DALÍ. The algorithm we apply to the transaction data for calculating the level of recycled and externally funded payments in SPEI® made by institutions is presented as follows:

Let I be the set of participants in SPEI® and T the set of cycles in one day. We define P_{it}^{rec} as the sum of the amount of payments received by each $i \in I$ in each cycle $t \in T$, whereas P_{it}^{sent} is the sum of the amount of payments sent by each participant $i \in I$ in each cycle $t \in T$. Let S_{it} be the positive balance of each participant $i \in I$ in each cycle $t \in T$, given that $S_{i0} = 0$ for all i. Further, we define F_{it} as the amount of own funds for each $i \in I$ in each $t \in T$ calculated according to the transactional data, given that $F_{i0} = 0$ for all i.

For each cycle:

$$A_{it} = P_{it}^{rec} - P_{it}^{sent} \tag{1}$$

$$F_{it} = F_{it-1} - \left(S_{it-1} + A_{it}\right), S_{it} = 0, if\left(S_{it-1} + A_{it}\right) < 0 \tag{2}$$

$$S_{it} = \left(S_{it-1} + A_{it}\right), if\left(S_{it-1} + A_{it}\right) \geq 0 \tag{3}$$

The initial value of the variables S_{it} and F_{it} are given as 0, since the liquidity provision in SPEI® is on a daily basis and does not transfer from one day to another. S_{it} is an auxiliary variable, whereas F_{it} is a cumulative variable, i.e., S_{it} allows us to keep track of the incoming funds that are used to cover other obligations such that if these funds are not available, the value of S_{it} is zero at any time during the day. The value of F_{it} on the other hand, represents the overall need for external funds, e.g., F_{iD} gives the sum of external funding that institution i really needed during that day, as D denotes the last settlement period t in the set T of settlement cycles for the day. From the historical data, we have been able to identify for each real cycle the transactions that have been settled together, such that each cycle t corresponds to a settlement cycle executed by SPEI® with the exact transactions corresponding to that cycle. Then $\sum_{i \in CreditInsituttions} \left(F_{iD}\right)$ will produce the daily levels of external funds throughout the year 2013 for the dark grey area, whereas $\sum_{i \in CreditInstitutions} \sum_{t \in T} \left(P_{it}^{sent}\right) - \sum_{i \in CreditInstitutions} \left(F_{iD}\right)$ will produce the light grey area in Figure 4, corresponding to the transactions covered with incoming payments by credit institutions. This area is labelled in Figure 4 as “Incoming payments CI.”

The institutions with direct access to liquidity provided by BdM through SIAC evaluate in advance the levels they need to settle obligations throughout the day in SPEI®, DALÍ, and CLS. Based on these pre-evaluated amounts, they then transfer funds from their accounts in SIAC to their accounts in SPEI®, and use the accounts in SPEI® and DALÍ to settle their obligations throughout the day.

Figure 3 presents detailed information on a daily basis for 2013 on the use of external funds vs. incoming payments in SPEI® by type of participant. The need for external funding for CIs, NBFIs, BdM, CLS, and DALÍ are presented within the texture gray and darkest gray areas, whereas the proportion of incoming payments used to cover outstanding obligations are presented within the light texture grey and bright grey areas. The proportion of the use of incoming payments is calculated as the total payments made by direct participants in SPEI® and connected FMI on each day minus the amount determined by the algorithm as the external funding needed on that day. Overall, the percentages corresponding to external funds vs. incoming payments represents $36\% - 64\%$. The black dotted line in the figure corresponds to the overdrafts taken form SIAC by the credit institutions. In Table 1, the corresponding proportions used of incoming payments vs. external funds are presented per type of participant and per FMI.

In Figure 3 we observe that overdrafts in SIAC cover most external funds flowing through the FMI and direct participants, in particular during the second half of the year. Further, in Table 1 we notice that BdM does not wait for incoming payments, which is to be expected. It is important to stress that the use of incoming payments in the case of CIs and NBFIs does not necessarily imply payment free of charge. Money market transactions take place in SPEI® in such a way that those operations are among

Figure 3. Use of External Funds vs. Incoming Payments in SPEI® in MXN Billions
by Type of Participant

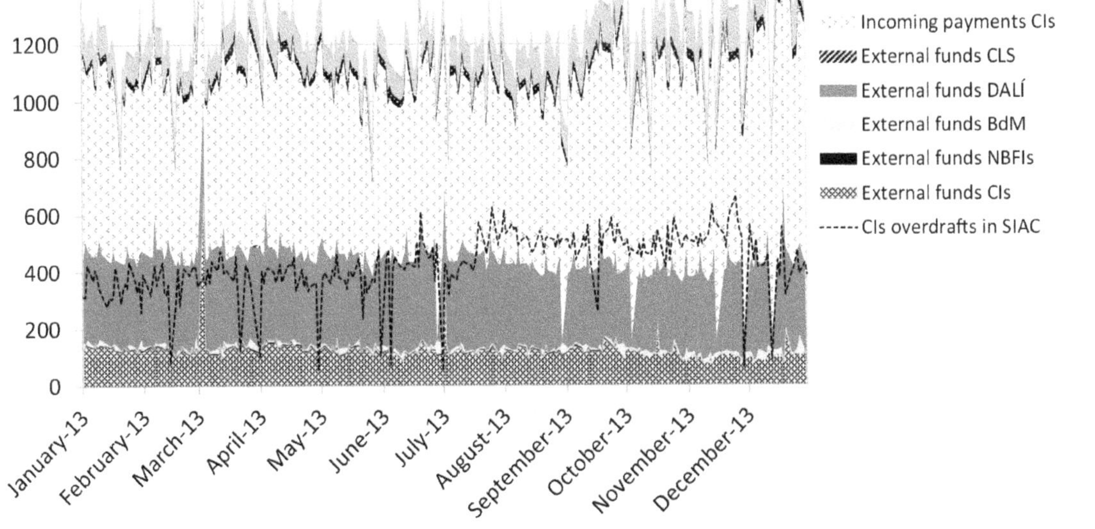

Figure 4. Intraday Use of External Funds vs. Incoming Payments in SPEI® in MXN Billions by Type of Participant

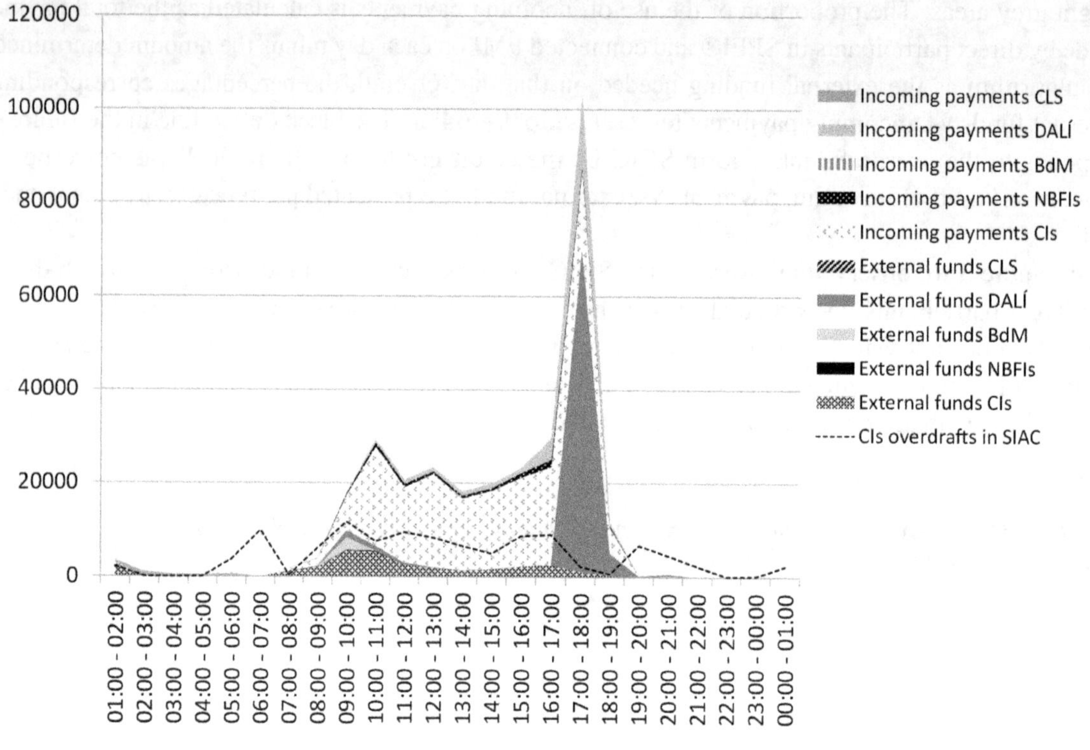

Table 1. Average percentage of incoming payments vs. external funds per sector

	Incoming payments	External funds
CIs	85%	15%
NBFIs	91%	9%
BdM	1%	99%
CLS	99%	1%
DALÍ	26%	74%

the incoming payment amounts used to cover outstanding obligations, identified by the algorithm. In the case of CLS and DALÍ, the observed behavior is related to the rules established in those FMIs and should not be interpreted as strategic behavior on the part of the institutions that are participants in CLS and DALÍ. In the next section, we take a close look to the interactions among FMIs that emerge.

INTRADAY INTERACTIONS AMONG FINANCIAL MARKET INFRASTRUCTURES UNDER THE LIQUIDITY PROVISION RULES

In the previous sections, two of the aspects of policy provision were discussed, 1) the mechanism of providing liquidity, and 2) the methodological approach that allows us to distinguish how participants cover their payment obligations using external funds and incoming payments. In this section we present our findings related to the interdependency among FMIs. The interaction among infrastructures arises from different factors, including the fact that the sets of direct participants in different FMIs significantly overlap. In the present study, we focus exclusively on the nature of flows that are coming into and are going out of SPEI®.

The analysis of FMIs allows for more comprehensive data investigation due to the availability of intraday transactions between financial institutions, while financial stability analysis is usually based on exposures between institutions on a daily basis. Those represent to some extent the redistribution of liquidity among participants. In this chapter we find out how liquidity is introduced into the system before the redistribution (unsecured and secured lending-borrowing among participants) takes place. Following our methodology, we are able to observe how funds coming from SIAC flow among different FMIs, in particular between DALÍ and SPEI®. In this respect, arriving at the meso-level of the financial system, the flow of interdependencies among FMIs brings the investigation to the level of big-data analytics and allow for a synergetic focus on operational efficiency and stability. The intraday analysis highlights effects that are not observed and therefore ignored when the investigation is limited to daily data.

Figure 4 presents the intraday profile of different types of SPEI® participants. It reveals information about the links between SPEI® and other infrastructures such as DALÍ and CLS, for the year 2013. The black dotted line in the figure corresponds to the amounts taken form SIAC by the credit institutions and the same textures and scale of grey colors of the previous figure are used to represent the different type of participants. The calculation per hour is performed as follows – the total amount taken in the hour between 1:00 and 2:00 for the 250 business days in that year, then the total amount taken in the hour between 2:00 and 3:00, etc until 24:00. A working day in SPEI® and SIAC starts at 19:00 on the previous calendar day and ends at 17:30 on the current calendar day. Balances in SIAC and SPEI® are opened at 0 at the beginning of the operational day. The figure reveals that the credit institutions start transferring funds from their accounts in SIAC to SPEI® at the opening hour of 19:00 onwards, anticipating their payment obligations for the forthcoming day, and later continue transferring throughout the day to top up their SPEI® accounts. In contrast, almost all payment transactions take place between 6:00 and 18:00.

Though the majority of payments are positioned in the centre of the graph in the intraday schedule, there is also a volume of transactions that takes place mostly between 24:00 and 2:00. These are related to settlements in the CLS and their coordination with the European market. Therefore, they present links of SPEI® with another market infrastructure – the CLS foreign exchange settlements. The CLS coordinates the transfer of currencies, and related payments appear as transactions between SPEI® participants. CLS operates in Mexico between 24:00 and 5:00, which corresponds to 7:00 – 12:00 Central European Time. Incoming payments from CLS are observed in the figure only between 1:00 and 5:00.

A link with DALÍ, another market infrastructure, is presented by the thick dark grey area and the light grey area on top in Figure 4. The account of DALÍ in SPEI® acts as a bridge between SPEI® and DALÍ. CIs and brokerages in SPEI® transfer amounts to their accounts in DALÍ through the account of DALÍ in SPEI®. They also transfer amounts to their accounts in SPEI® through the account of DALÍ in SPEI®. Thus, the account of DALÍ in SPEI® receives or sends payments throughout the day from/

to other participants in SPEI®. We apply our algorithm to evaluate obligations of DALÍ in SPEI® met through incoming payments in SPEI®, and this is presented on the top of areas by the light grey area in the figure in the hours between 8:00 and 19:00. The dark grey area represents non-recycled financing payments from DALÍ's account to other SPEI® participants. The data analysis and the figure reveal that a significantly larger proportion of DALÍ's payments are non-recycled or are externally financed. The external financing in the case of DALÍ has a different meaning from the external financing for credit institutions, identified by the algorithm used to cover payment obligations in SPEI®. In the case of SPEI®, the external financing for credit institutions comes from SIAC, with the main purpose to provide liquidity for these institutions throughout the day in SPEI®. The external financing for DALÍ comes from credit institutions (primary commercial banks) that are participants in DALÍ transferring amounts to their DALÍ account in SPEI®, with the purpose of transferring balances. The balances themselves are results from the activity within DALÍ as a separate system, and within that security settlement system transactions can also be analysed as recycled and externally financed. The focus here is on SPEI® as the RTGS equivalent payment system and one of the market infrastructures in Mexico. We will consider in a follow-up study the detailed analysis of the mechanism within DALÍ. The balance transfers to DALÍ's account in SPEI® are mainly used to close the borrowing from SIAC down to 0 for the day. As observed from the data, the payments from DALÍ's account in SPEI® take place towards the end of day – mainly between 16:00 and 18:00. Thus, the analysis of transaction data facilitates discovering different behaviours of SPEI® participants.

Figure 4 includes information about the intraday profile in the year 2013 of NBFIs and CIs. NBFIs, except brokerages, cannot get external to SPEI® financing for their obligations in SPEI®. Brokerages can obtain intraday liquidity from the BdM through government debt repos via DALÍ, by fulfilling specific requirements of the law. That mechanism also involves an additional link or interdependence with DALÍ, as another market infrastructure. The detailed intraday information, analysed and presented in Figure 4, captures the externally financed obligations in SPEI® of brokerages, as the very thin black area above the texture area of external funds used by CIs. The internally financed or recycled payments of these institutions are captured by the black with white dots area between the incoming payments used by CIs and the incoming payments from DALÍ at the top of the figure. The analysis further shows that unsecured lending is taking place in SPEI® from CIs to NBFIs, which implies that the area represented as "Incoming payments NBFI" also includes those transactions, which are costly for NBFIs.

The texture grey area at the bottom of Figure 4 corresponds to externally financed obligations of CIs – CBs and DBs. The thickest light texture grey area represents their internally financed obligations. Notice that here the internally and externally financed transactions overlap throughout the day, and the system is used very efficiently by credit institutions as their internally financed obligations exceed those externally financed once by a significant margin. The highest volume of externally financed obligations takes place during the morning hours. The main mechanism of external financing for CBs and DBs is through SIAC. However, they can sell securities holdings in DALÍ to finance obligations in SPEI®, as well. Therefore, this further involves intraday interactions between financial market infrastructures. Overall, credit institutions receive sufficient external financing through SIAC, and thus need no further financing through DALÍ. However, this scenario may not be in place for an individual credit institution, as different banks are granted access to different levels of liquidity through SIAC. Some banks may not have access to sufficient SIAC funding, and would use the mechanism through DALÍ or through unsecured interbank lending that takes place in SPEI®. The analysis here is at the level by type of institution. However, the database is by individual institution and we will investigate in a follow-up study at the finer granularity. Our algorithms and analysis currently classify the borrowing/lending payments as incoming payments. A consecutive focus will be on detection of transactions redistributing liquidity.

Figure 5 shows use of external funds vs. incoming payments on a weekly base. Following the same colour and texture code as in Figure 3 and Figure 4, we would like to comment on two observations. First, throughout the week there is no significant difference in the volume of external funds used in SPEI and the external funds coming from DALÍ. Furthermore, SIAC overdrafts are stable during the week and are usually sufficient to cover the external funds. Second, on Thursdays, external funds coming from DALÍ increase in comparison with the other weekdays. Nevertheless, overdrafts in SIAC do not increase accordingly on Thursdays. This could imply that regular unsecured loan repayment is taking place in SPEI on Thursdays.

Finally, analysing Figure 4 and Figure 5, we can conclude that liquidity flows among FMIs allow us to explain participants' behaviour better, allowing for analysis of the dynamics in interactions for different time patterns, namely intraday and weekly. Overall, the indications are that operations in 2013 were stable, as the observed behaviour is mostly steady and repetitive.

Figure 5. On Average Weekly Use of External Funds vs. Incoming Payments in SPEI® in MXN Billions by Type of Participant

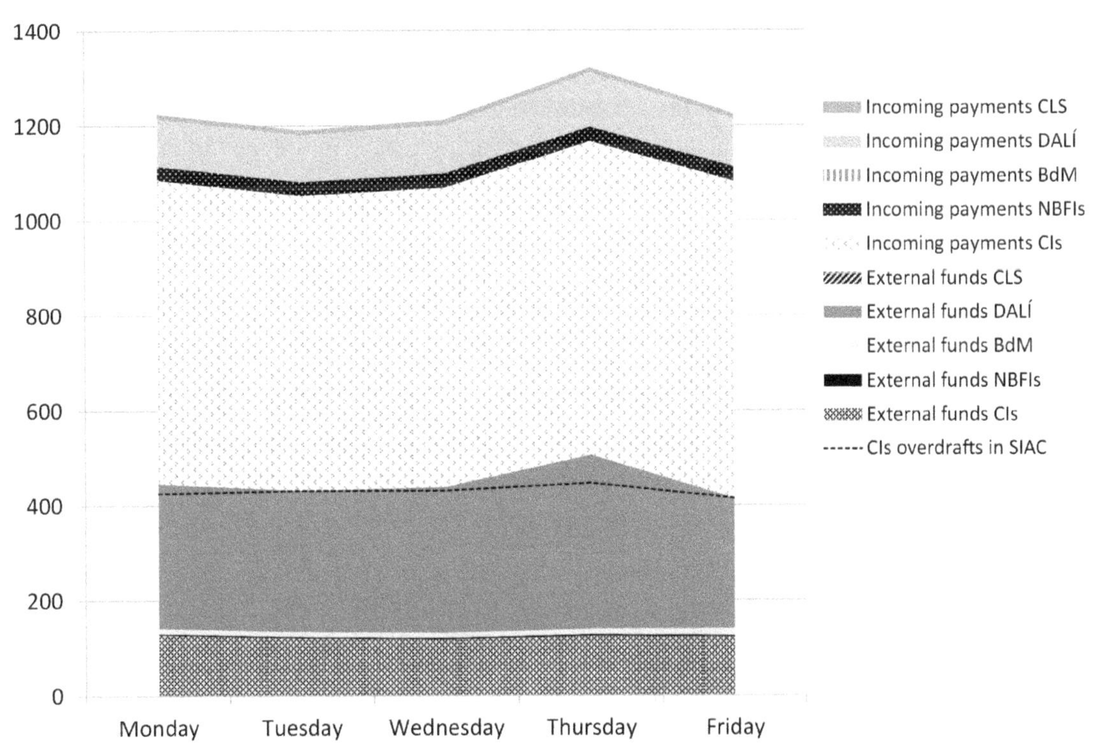

CONCLUSION AND FUTURE RESEARCH DIRECTIONS

In this section, a summary of the overall chapter is provided, along with a discussion of future research directions, and concluding remarks.

Liquidity issues have been one of the strongest lines of research for studies related to payment systems in more than a decade. This focus reveals the significant role of liquidity for the sound functioning not only of the payment system, but for financial market infrastructures overall. The analysis in the present study contributes to this research focus. The proposed methodology for analyzing the flow of funds observed in LVPS and the presented algorithm allow separation of payments in two categories. The first is related to the funds transferred from other FMIs, or provided by a central bank, whereas the second category comprises the incoming payments from other participants used to cover obligations. Further, the analytical approach has been applied to distinguish to what extent incoming payments are used to cover payment obligations. The framework of liquidity provision in the Mexican FMIs is used to evaluate the performance of the developed algorithm, with a particular focus on the connection between the RTGS equivalent and the securities settlement systems, and to an extent on the connection with CLS.

The present study learns about participants' behavior related to the use of incoming payments. Other important factors remain to be investigated. It is necessary to introduce into the algorithm and process information on who initiates an operation – is it a participant's client or the participant itself? This should be followed by an evaluation to what extent payments initiated by a third party increase demand on liquidity or help to reduce pressure through recycling. In addition, we should gain more insight into the mechanism of redistribution of funds among participants by including in the analytical framework the unsecured/secured lending transactions. For instance, if the payment is initiated by the participant, is it a lending/borrowing operation, or does it follow under different categories? These kinds of identifiers will be incorporated into the methodological approach we have introduced in this chapter, allowing us to further contribute to the understanding of intraday liquidity operations of the different sectors participating in FMIs.

REFERENCES

Alexandrova-Kabadjova, B., Serguieva, A., & Garcia-Ochoa, L. (2014, July). Formation of Tectonic Wave Networks: Dynamics of the Mexican Payment System Structure. *Proceedings of the 2014 International Conference on Behavioral, Economic and Socio-Cultural Computing* (pp. 1–7). IEEE Press. doi:10.1109/BESC.2014.7059524

Alexandrova-Kabadjova, B., Serguieva, A., Heijmans, R., & Garcia-Ochoa, L. (2015). Direct participants' behaviour through the lens of transactional analysis: the case of SPEI. In H. Takayasu, N. Ito, I. Noda & M. Takayasu (Eds.) *Proceedings of the International Conference on Social Modeling and Simulation, plus Econophysics Colloquium 2014*. Springer Proceedings in Complexity, Springer, forthcoming.

Alexandrova-Kabadjova, B., & Solís-Robleda, F. (2012). The Mexican experience in how the settlement of large payments is performed in the presence of high volume of small payments. In M. Hellqvist & T. Laine (Eds.), *Diagnostics for the financial markets - computational studies of payment system* (pp. 431–460). Finland: Bank of Finland. doi:10.2139/ssrn.2191794

Alexandrova-Kabadjova, B., & Solís-Robleda, F. (2013). Managing Intraday Liquidity: The Mexican Experience. In B. Alexandrova-Kabadjova, S. Martinez-Jaramillo, A. Garcia-Almanza, & E. Tsang (Eds.), *Simulation in Computational Finance and Economics: Tools and Emerging Applications* (pp. 143–160). Hershey, PA: Business Science Reference; doi:10.4018/978-1-4666-2011-7.ch008

Angelini, P., Maresca, G., & Russo, D. (1996). Systemic risk in the netting system. *Journal of Banking & Finance, 20*(5), 853–868. doi:10.1016/0378-4266(95)00029-1

Armantier, O., Arnold, J. & McAndrews, J. (2008, September). Changes in the timing distribution of Fedwire funds transfers. *FRBNY Economic Policy Review*.

Bech, M., & Garratt, R. (2012, August). Illiquidity in the Interbank Payment System Following Wide-Scale Disruptions. *Journal of Money, Credit and Banking, 5*(5), 903–929. doi:10.1111/j.1538-4616.2012.00515.x

Bech, M., & Hobijn, B. (2007). Technology diffusion within central banking: The case of the real-time gross settlement. *International Journal of Central Banking, 3*, 147–182.

Becher, C., Galbiati, M. & Tudela, M. (2008). The timing and funding of CHAPS Sterling payments. *FRBNY Economic Policy Review*, September.

Bravo-Benitez, B., Alexandrova-Kabadjova, B., & Martinez-Jaramillo, S. (2015). (forthcoming). Centrality measurement of the Mexican large value payments system from the perspective of multiplex network. *Journal of Comparative Economics*. doi:10.1007/s10614-014-9477-0

Real-time gross settlement systems. (1997, March). Committee on Payment and Settlement Systems. Basel, Switzerland: Bank for International Settlements.

Payment, clearing and settlement systems in the CPSS countries, Volume 1. Committee on Payment and Settlement Systems. (2011, September). Basel, Switzerland: Bank for International Settlements.

Diehl, M. (2013). Measuring free riding in large-value payment systems: The case of TARGET2. *The Journal of Financial Market Infrastructures, 1*(3), 31–53.

Heijmans, R., & Heuver, R. (2012). Preparing Simulations in Large Value Payment Systems using Historical Data. In B. Alexandrova-Kabadjova, S. Martinez-Jaramillo, A. Garcia-Almanza, & E. Tsang (Eds.), *Simulation in Computational Finance and Economics: Tools and Emerging Applications* (pp. 46–68). Hershey, PA: Business Science Reference; doi:10.4018/978-1-4666-2011-7.ch003

Heijmans, R., & Heuver, R. (2014). Is this bank ill? The diagnosis of doctor TARGET2. *Journal of Financial Market Infrastructures, 2*(3), 3–36.

Hellqvist, M., & Koskinen, J. (2005). Stress testing securities clearing and settlement systems using simulations. In H. Leinonen (Ed.), *Liquidity, risks and speed in payment and settlement systems - a simulation approach, No E31* (pp. 321–350).

Hellqvist, M., & Snellman, H. (2007). Simulation of operational failures in equities settlement. In H. Leinonen (Ed.), *Simulation studies of liquidity needs, risks and efficiency in payment networks: Proceedings from the Bank of Finland Payment and Settlement System Seminars 2005-2006* (pp. 283-320).

Humphrey, D. (1986). Payments finality and risk settlement failure. In A. Saunders and L White (Eds.), Technology and the regulation of financial markets: Securities, futures and banking (pp. 97-120). Lexington, MA: Lexington Books.

Inaoka, H., Ninomiya, T., Taniguchi, K., Shimizu, T., & Takayasu, H. (2004). Fractal Network derived from banking transaction: An analysis of network structures formed by financial institutions. *Bank of Japan Working Paper Series*, 04-E-04.

Leinonen, H., & Soramäki, K. (2005). Optimising liquidity usage and settlement speed in payment systems. In H. Leinonen (Ed.), *Liquidity, risks and speed in payment and settlement systems - a simulation approach* (pp. 115-148). *Proceedings from the Bank of Finland Payment and Settlement System Seminars 2005*.

Martinez-Jaramillo, S., Alexandrova-Kabadjova, B., Bravo-Benitez, B., & Solorzano-Margain, J. P. (2014, March). An empirical study of the Mexican banking systems network and its implications for systemic risk. *Journal of Economic Dynamics & Control*, *40*, 242–265. Retrieved from http://www.sciencedirect.com/science/article/pii/S0165188914000189 doi:10.1016/j.jedc.2014.01.009

Pericoli, M., & Sbracia, M. (2003). A Primer on Financial Contagion. *Journal of Economic Surveys. Wiley Blackwell*, *17*(4), 571–608.

Pröpper, M., Van Lelyveld, I., & Heijmans, R. (2013). Network Dynamics of TOP Payments Measuring free riding in large-value payment systems: The case of TARGET2. *The Journal of Financial Market Infrastructures*, *1*(3), 3–29.

Serguieva, A. (2013, May). Systemic risk identification, modelling, analysis, and monitoring: An integrated approach, *Working Paper arXiv: general finance / computational engineering, finance and science*, 1310.6486, 1–19. Retrieved from http://arxiv.org/ftp/arxiv/papers/1310/1310.6486.pdf

Soramäki, K., Bech, M. L., Arnold, J., Glass, R. J. & Beyeler, W. E. (2006, March). The topology of interbank payment flows. *Federal Reserve Bank of New York Staff Reports*, 243.

KEY TERMS AND DEFINITIONS

Central Bank Money: The money that Central bank gives as a loan to commercial banks in order to make payment orders through interbank payment systems.

DALÍ: Is the security settlement system, which operates under the "delivery versus payment" (DVP) scheme. It also performs the functions of Central Security Depository.

Direct Participants: The institutions with direct access to the facilities of LVPS.

Intraday Liquidity: The funds used by participants through the day to cover payment obligations.

Large Value Payment System (LVPS): It is a Financial Market Infrastructure that provides the functionality for exchange of transactions with high monetary value among direct participants. It is governed by laws, rules and standards that establish the framework of interaction among institutions given a specific set of instruments, procedures, and technical means.

SIAC: Is the system that provides liquidity into the financial market infrastructure in Mexico and it is operated by the central bank. The credit institutions' and brokerages' current accounts are held in this system. SIAC also manages the accounts of government entities that, by law, must be in account with Banco de México.

SPEI®: Is a real time payment system, owned and operated by Banco de México. It performs electronic transfers among participants and third party (clients), as it settles large- and small-value payments. Pay-ins and pay-outs for CLS are also settled through SPEI.

ENDNOTES

1 The authors would like to acknowledge Lorenza Martínez, Miguel Díaz, Francisco Solís, Javier Pérez, Ramón De la Rosa, Rafael Jiménez, Aldo Marini, Avigayl González, the Financial Computing and Analytics Research Group at University College London, and the Financial Mathematics Group at King's College London for their support for this work. Further, the authors would like to thank the anonymous reviewers for their comments and valuable insights, to Dorothy Walton for proofreading the manuscript and to Juan Rocha, Armando Bravo, Liliana Ortiz, Rafael Villar and Reyna Pérez for their support with the data. The views express in this chapter are those of the authors and do not necessarily reflect those of Banco de México or De Nederlandsche Bank.

2 By law, customer (or third-party) payments in Mexico should be processed and settled immediately after reception of an order, whereas participant-initiated payments are ruled by contractual obligation, and we assume that some flexibility could occur regarding the decision on time of settlement.

3 S.D. INDEVAL, Institución para el Depósito de Valores, S.A. de C.V.

4 The legal framework of the commercial and development banks is established by the Credit Institutions Act.

5 Numeral M.73 of Circular 2019/95 establishes the rules regarding multipurpose commercial banks, whereas numeral BD.51 of Circular 1/2006 refers to public development banks.

6 Numeral CB.2 of Circular 115/2002 establishes the rules on brokerage houses.

7 CHIPS is the netting system of the United States.

8 The timing of payments is relevant for the (re)distribution of liquidity, especially real time gross settlement systems. These systems require relatively large amounts of liquidity. The sooner a participant pays, the sooner the receiving parties can reuse this liquidity to fulfil payment obligations.

9 The CHAPS Clearing Company imposes a set of throughput guidelines whereby participants are expected to make 50% of their payments by value by 12.00 p.m. and 75% by 2.30 p.m., as an average over a calendar month.

10 TARGET2 is the most important large value payment system of the Eurosystem.

11 Brokerages also have current accounts but not access to overdrafts.

Section 3
Economics of Single Types of Financial Market Infrastructures

Chapter 11
Payment System Analysis:
The Central Bank Perspective

Alexander Pascal Müller
Deutsche Bundesbank, Germany

ABSTRACT

Together with the growing importance of stable and efficient payment systems, payment systems analysis has gained importance in the recent years. Central banks play the most prominent role in this field since they have unique responsibilities but also unique opportunities. This chapter will systematize the different aspects of payment system analysis and show their respective importance from a central bank perspective. This will be done both from a theoretical but also from a practical point of view by giving examples of actual work in this field. Three types of Payment system analysis will be distinguished: Payment system analysis in the broad sense of the term, the analysis of particular payment systems and the use of payment system data.

INTRODUCTION[1]

Together with the growing importance of stable and efficient payment systems, payment system analysis has gained in importance in recent years. Central banks play the most prominent role in this field as they have unique responsibilities and at the same time unique opportunities. This chapter will systematize different aspects of payment system analysis and show their respective importance from a central bank perspective, both from a theoretical and a practical point of view. The most important current and recent research questions will be discussed and results of payment system analysis as performed in different central banks will be presented.

Payment system analysis is not *per se* a goal of central banks. Its basic aim should be to support and found the making of political and business decisions in the various business areas of a central bank, mainly by the central bank itself but also by other market participants. The discussion of the practical examples of payment system analysis will show that the term "analysis" has a very broad meaning here. Nevertheless, the common factor for all the cited examples is that information about or derived from payment systems is used for a systematical investigation of a research question related to the political and operative tasks of the central bank.

DOI: 10.4018/978-1-4666-8745-5.ch011

Payment system analysis from a central bank perspective can be linked to the various tasks fulfilled by a central bank. The most prominent tasks of a central bank are monetary policy, payments and financial stability.[2] The importance of payment system analysis is most straightforward in the second case. Payment system analysis in this field is linked to the tasks of central banks associated with ensuring the smooth operation of the payment system in broad terms but also with cash management. Central banks potentially play three main roles in this field: First, some are directly active in operating payment infrastructures and also in cash handling. Second, most of them shape the overall payment system landscape through their "catalyst role", facilitating agreements and rules between different market participants. Third, most central banks act as a payment system overseer and influence the regulatory framework of the payment system. However, it transpires that ensuring the functioning of the payment system is also closely tied to the objectives of financial stability and monetary policy. This means that payment system analysis can also contribute to these central bank tasks. There is a historical link between clearing and settlement and central banking due to the fact that some central banks were founded as central clearing institutions. Monetary policy, financial stability and payments are all based on the provision of central bank money as the ultimate settlement asset. Monetary policy is operationally dependent on payment infrastructures and these infrastructures are part of the financial system whose stability has to be safeguarded. Therefore, analysis of these infrastructures is indirectly connected with monetary policy and financial stability and data from these infrastructures can be put to direct use for these purposes.

The structure of the chapter is geared to the three different types of payment system analysis, defined as: Payment system analysis in the broad sense of the term, analysis of specific payment systems and use of payment system data. With regard to the first definition, the term "the payment system" relates to the entire set of instruments, banking procedures and interbank funds transfer systems employed to facilitate the circulation of money in an economy; this toolbox is then the object of analysis. In the second definition, "payment systems" is synonymous with interbank funds transfer systems, i.e. the definition is more technical and these technical systems are the object of analysis. In the third definition, data derived from payment systems is used for other, secondary purposes which go beyond the functioning of the systems.

The final section describes the particular central bank perspective, showing that the distinctiveness of the central bank perspective in payment system analysis is based on four elements:

- First, the uniqueness of the tasks performed by central banks, in particular their monopoly in terms of providing central bank money and the possibility of acting as lender of last resort.
- Second, their strong operational role in payments based on their specific risk profile concerning business and liquidity risk.
- Third, the fact that central banks act in the public interest.
- Fourth, the multitude and variety of the tasks of a central bank.

PAYMENT SYSTEM ANALYSIS IN THE BROAD SENSE OF THE TERM

In the case of payment system analysis in the broad sense of the term, "the payment system" relates to the entire set of instruments, banking procedures and interbank funds transfer systems employed to facilitate the circulation of money in an economy. In this context, the ultimate goal of payment system analysis is to provide knowledge about the optimal structure of the payment system as a whole. The most commonly used criteria are "efficient" and "safe" processing of the various types of payments. These criteria reflect the most important aspects of a payment system: Reducing transaction and liquidity costs of an economy and increasing public trust in the monetary system.

Research Questions

Analytical work in this area is focused on payment instruments. Three main fields of activity can be distinguished:

- Choice of payment instruments.
- Innovation of new or improved instruments.
- Security of instruments.

The first main field of analytical work conducted by central banks consists of studies on the choice of payment instruments. The basic research question here is: "Which payment instruments are used and for what reasons?" Recent examples include publications by the Federal Reserve System (2014), the Reserve Bank of Australia (Ossolinski et al., 2014) and the Deutsche Bundesbank (2012). By conducting such studies, central banks learn about the preferences of market participants with regards to payment instruments. At the same time, these studies help to identify inefficient payment habits, efficiency being defined differently to users' revealed preferences. The research question would then be normative: "Which payment instruments should be used and for what reasons?" In this context, studies focus on the cost of payments instruments such as the work presented by Schmiedel et al. (2012) or the relationship between efficiency of retail payments and the real economy as presented by Hasan et al. (2013). Central banks could base their efforts to promote specific payment instruments on such studies. Other central banks, like the Deutsche Bundesbank, adopt a neutral approach with the user preferences as the sole criterion.

The second important field of analytical work is innovative payment instruments. An overview of innovations in retail payments is provided by the Committee on Payment and Settlement Systems (2012). In recent years, virtual currency schemes, in particular, have become a topical issue. Analytical work in this field currently concentrates mainly on descriptive studies of the technical features of such instruments and their increasing importance. However, it is a necessary first step to present the different schemes in a structured manner as done by the European Central Bank (2012). Other papers focus on the identification and discussion of the distinctive features of virtual currencies. Ali et al. (2014a) discuss the distributed ledger as being a significant innovation that could transform the financial system. For central bank analysts, the impact of virtual currencies on the role and tasks of central banks is another notable research field, as discussed in Ali et al. (2014b).

The third important field of analytical work is the security of instruments, which is mainly tackled by central banks in their role in payment systems oversight. Since the security of an instrument is a difficult factor for users to judge, an assessment by the central bank in its capacity as a public authority can avoid market failures. However, a stronger scientific foundation of the recommendations given by central banks in this area could be developed.

Importance for the Different Roles of a Central Bank in Payment Systems

Analysis of the payment system in the broad sense of the term contributes in particular to the catalyst role of a central bank. A well-structured overall understanding of the entire payment system enhances its policy decisions. Since moral suasion and the mere force of a given argument are often of key importance in this field, a thorough analysis following scientific standards and empirical foundations will also increase the influence of the central bank on the payment system landscape. At the same time, the central bank frequently serves as a neutral arbitrary, not least in the field of payment instruments where providers of different instruments compete against one another with their rival business models and the central bank is able to provide neutral scientific studies.

Analysis of the payment system landscape in general also contributes to the oversight role of a central bank, e.g. by delivering singular axiomatic studies to derive oversight or regulatory principles. The most important document in this context are the Principles for Financial Market Infrastructures (PFMI). Those principles are based on knowledge acquired through analytical work.

ANALYSIS OF SPECIFIC PAYMENT SYSTEMS

Having discussed the three main fields of payment system analysis in a broad sense, we will now turn our attention to the analysis of specific payment systems. A payment system in the broad sense of the term is composed of a multitude of technical infrastructures, which themselves are also called payment systems. "Payment system" in this context refers to interbank funds transfer systems, meaning technical mechanisms designed by an operator to clear and or settle monetary obligations. The focus here is on cashless payments.

Research Questions

Four main fields of research can be distinguished.

- Institutional analysis of assigning the task of operator to different types of actors, in particular central banks or private operators.
- Analysis of system design and functional development.
- Analysis of participant behavior and system structure.
- Optimization of business models.

Institutional Analysis

The most fundamental question to be answered for a particular payment system is who should be the operator of that system, and specifically whether this role should fall to the central bank or a private entity. A broad consensus has emerged in the literature that central banks do and should play an important operational role. This consensus is also supported by historical and descriptive studies of the operational role of central banks. One fundamental argument is that only central banks can provide central bank money which plays a central role as ultimate settlement asset (see Committee for Payment and Settlement Systems (2003), Manning et al. (Ed.), 2009, p. 15ff.). Another reason for their strong operational role is their uniquely low risk concerning liquidity and business risk.

Despite this consensus in principle, the role of central banks in payment systems is still debatable as a matter of degree and not of substance. Norman et al. (2011) argue that the historical link between clearing and settlement and central banking was not imperative. Johnson and Steigerwald (2008) discuss trade-offs in defining the role of a central bank in the payment system. Oliver and Weiner (2010) focus on the role of central banks as the operator responsible for the subcategory of retail payments. A prevalent position is that central banks should play a stronger operational role for systemically important large value payment systems (LVPS) than for retail payment systems (RPS), with RPS settling a larger number but less time-critical and lower value payments.

System Design and Functional Development

Going beyond the question of principle of whether the central bank should be an operator at all, the analysis is focused on technical aspects of payment systems. This large field of analytical work can be summarized under the keywords system design and functional development. New systems can be built based on the insights gained here and existing systems can be optimized. One can distinguish between ex-ante analysis which evaluates the effects of a system design prior to its implementation and ex-post analysis which evaluates existing features. The spectrum of possible analytical questions ranges from fundamental questions of system design such as net versus gross settlement to detailed analysis of individual features such as single settlement algorithms.

One fundamental question of system design which has been intensively debated is net versus gross settlement, deferred net settlement systems (DNS) versus real-time gross settlement systems (RTGS). Examples are Kahn and Roberds (1998, 2001). Manning et al. (Ed.) (2009, pp. 51), provide a good overview of the arguments and the publications in this field. The main trade-off faced is between liquidity demands and risk: DNS bear the risk of accruing interbank credit exposures prior to settlement while RTGS tend to have higher liquidity demands. Manning el al. (Ed.) (2009, pp. 67), identify public intervention as the main driver of the growing importance of RTGS, mainly caused by the increased volume and value of payments which lead to an increase in the importance of credit risk exposures in DNS. While the scope of the theoretical argument has now largely been exhausted, the global trend towards having RTGS still provides opportunities to analyze the consequences of implementing such systems in practice. The study conducted by Tsuchiya (2013) on the effects of switching from DNS to RTGS in Japan is just one example. Parallel to this, the emergence of hybrid systems including liquidity saving elements in RTGS has generated a new field suitable for analysis.

In general, more detailed research questions focus on singular features of a particular payment system like the liquidity saving elements in a hybrid system. Three studies deserve mention as examples here, beginning with an evaluation of the introduction of a Liquidity Saving Mechanism in CHAPS, the United Kingdom's large value payment system. Here, the effects of several system designs were evaluated ex-ante in a simulation study presented by McLafferty and Denbee (2012). Based on these results, a specific design was implemented in the real system, after which the effects were evaluated once again. The findings, presented in Davey & Gray (2014), show that the real world effect lags behind the predicted effect in the simulation studies but remains positive in overall terms. The second case concerns a detailed analysis of a singular feature of a payment system included in a study by Diehl & Müller (2014), who analyze the use and the impact of limits as a specific liquidity saving feature in TARGET2, the RTGS for the Eurozone, in a simulation. The third study was presented by Clarke and Hancock (2014) and focuses on the impact of various liquidity saving features of Australia's RTGS system RITS using simulation techniques. These three examples of empirical studies of liquidity saving features are complemented by studies carried out by Martin and McAndrews (2008) and Galbiati and Soramäki (2010), who evaluate liquidity saving mechanisms in a theoretical model.

Participant Behavior and System Structure

For central banks it is not only necessary to understand the details of the functioning of a system for system design and functional development, but also the behavior of the participants and risks in the system. In a first step, the goal of analysis is to derive stylized facts of participant behavior, to find typical payment patterns and to categorize participants and structures. Complexity reduction techniques are applied here. In a second step, an analysis can be carried out to detect and quantify types of behavior and structures with potentially harmful systemic effects. This analysis can then be linked to system design and functional development by providing a better understanding of the implications of behavioral patterns for the functioning of the system. Taking this further, in a third step, it would be possible to identify conditions for the occurrence of such behavior or structures. Again, this analysis can be linked to system design and functional development with a view to developing technical solutions and instruments to prevent such behavior or structures.

The most prominent example of behavior with potentially harmful systemic effects is the deliberate delaying of outgoing payments. Such behavior is referred to as "free-riding" on account of the fact that participants "free-ride" on incoming liquidity from other participants instead of using their own liquidity. To cite an example, Diehl (2013) presents methods for quantifying free-riding in TARGET2. Measuring this phenomenon is useful for an operator because, in extreme cases, such behavior could induce a gridlock throughout the system if all the participants were to wait for incoming payments before sending out their own payments. Delaying payments additionally entails the risk that, in the event of operational problems, less time is available before the end of the business day to resolve such problems and yet still settle those payments. All in all, the payment submission behavior of participants is an important topic for analysis, as outlined in Armantier et al. (2008), Bech (2008) and Becher et al. (2008a).

The most prominent example of system structures investigated is the level of tiering of a payment system. A tiered system is a system where a number of direct participants provide various indirect participants with access to the system in order to settle their transactions. Studies on this topic analyze the extent to which indirect participation in the system as opposed to direct participation affects the functioning of and risk contained in the system. As an example, Finan et al. (2013) discuss tiering in CHAPS. Analyzing tiered structures is relevant for an operator inasmuch as such a structure can lead to increased risk. The direct participant is required to settle payments on behalf of other parties while the indirect participants have to rely on their access points. Both aspects result in reciprocal dependencies which materialize in credit, liquidity and operational risk. In return, participants in such a system benefit from economies of scale by bundling tasks at the direct participant interface.

Stress testing of payment systems, which links aspects of the analysis of system design and functional development with the analysis of participant behavior and system structure, is an important field of analysis for central banks, both as overseers and as operators. The resilience of the system against various types of stress can be tested in stress testing exercises. Commonly used scenarios include operational failures, liquidity or solvency problems of single participants or a degradation of systemic variables such as overall liquidity conditions. A crucial methodological challenge in this context is to distinguish between causes and remedies falling within the area of responsibility of the participants and those falling under the remit of the system operator.

Business Optimization

Of somewhat less practical importance for analytical work of central banks as operators is the optimization of the business models in order to maximize profit. As a general rule, central banks act in the public interest and profit maximization is not one of their primary objectives. Nevertheless, in their role as operators, they are still keen to run efficient and cost-saving systems. Analyzing the general efficiency of a system is helpful in achieving this goal. In addition, there is often a desire to recover costs and this could be supported by analytical work.

Methods

The methods used to analyze single payment systems are manifold. The most basic method applied for analyses of singular systems are descriptive studies. Summers (Ed.) (2012) provides case studies and lessons from experience for several payment systems. Such descriptive studies provide a solid base for practitioners to base their decisions on experiences made by others. With regard to further analytical work, they can be used as a platform for more systematic comparative studies, albeit subject to limits due to the wide variety of systems in place. For example, Bech et al. (2008) provide a study of the development of payment systems worldwide and identify global trends.

Complexity-reducing statistical techniques are particularly important for descriptive analysis. Network analysis has recently gained in importance in this context as it allows the complex structure of a payments network to be reduced to single indicators. In addition, graphical network analysis can be a useful tool for highlighting, quantifying and assessing characteristics and changes in the characteristics of a payment network. Significant progress has been made here since the pictures presented in Soramäki et al. (2006) and Becher et al. (2008b).

Formal theoretical models have been used for the evaluation of payment systems. Bech (2008) applies a game theoretical approach to model intraday liquidity management. Martin and McAndrews (2008) evaluate liquidity saving mechanisms using a general model. However, although models can become very sophisticated, they are unable to cover all the features of the system. In particular, the sequential nature of the settlement process poses a challenge for models because the treatment of single transactions among a huge volume of payments needing to be settled can change the overall outcome.

For the above reason, simulation studies have turned out to be a powerful tool for empirical studies on system design and functional development. Diehl (2012) provides an epistemological assessment of simulation studies. Despite their weaknesses, simulations can be considered an adequate method for a large set of research questions. This is particularly true from a practical perspective, compared with theoretically superior methods which have only very limited applicability. The most obvious example is real world experiments, which are superior in theory but not feasible in practice. The main weakness of simulations is a strong ceteris paribus assumption, not allowing for behavioral responses on the part of the participants in the payment system. Agent-based modeling is a method that can be used to overcome this shortcoming, as discussed in Arciero and Picillo (2012).

To sum up, formal theoretical models are the standard for evaluating the basic principles of a typical feature. Empirical studies focusing on the general characteristics of a common feature of payment systems, comparing systems and going beyond fundamental questions such as DNS versus RTGS, are a less frequent alternative. This circumstance is attributable to the varied nature of the detailed functions of the various payment systems across the globe. Work on system design and functional development for singular features in fact typically examines different alternatives relating to system design for a single system and simulation studies focus on a specific real world system, investigating the details of its complex settlement algorithms.

The studies by Becher et al. (2008a) and Diehl and Müller (2014) are a good example of this complementing plurality of methods. While the former provides a formal theoretical model of the effects of a bilateral net sender limit, the latter provides an empirical study of the use and impacts of limits in TARGET2.

Object of Analysis

The empirical payment system analysis discussed in this section consists mostly of analysis focusing on LVPS. On the one hand, from a practical point of view, data access is more complicated for RPS, particularly if the central bank is not the operator itself. As said above, the operational role of central banks is less strong for retail payments which are mostly settled in networks comprising several interconnected individual RPS including internal systems of banks and banking groups. At the same time, due to the huge number of low value transactions processed in RPS, working with this data would require disproportionate computational resources. On the other hand, the systemic impact of an individual RPS is small compared to LVPS. Taking the higher practical difficulties and the lower impact together leads to a cost-benefit analysis that favors focusing on an empirical analysis of individual payment systems on LVPS. Turning to retail payments, the analysis places a stronger emphasis on instruments, as discussed in the section on payment system analysis in the broad sense of the term.

Importance for the Different Roles of a Central Bank in Payment Systems

Analyses of specific payment systems are of crucial importance for central banks acting as operators if the central bank happens to be the operator of the payment system being analyzed. On the one hand, the incentive for such analysis stems directly from its operational role as it is in the operator's own interest to understand and improve the system. On the other hand, the knowledge gathered from its experience of the daily business as an operator facilitates this analysis.

Analyses of specific payment systems are also important for central banks when they act as overseers. The objects and methods of analysis used for oversight purposes are often similar to those employed by operator institutions. In general, the assessment of payment systems for oversight purposes is enhanced by analysis focused on the operative aspects of a system. Analysis from an oversight perspective concentrates on the risk inherent in the individual payment system, while analysis from an operational perspective may have a broader focus, albeit with risk reduction almost always included as an object of analysis. Analysis from an oversight perspective can also be undertaken for systems operated by other institutions, thereby enlarging the set of potential objects of analysis.

In the case of a central bank acting as an overseer, this may also entail analytical work regarding the operational role. In particular, the PFMI require specific analytical work to be conducted by the operator of a financial market infrastructure. Stress testing with deteriorated liquidity conditions is required by the PFMI under principle 7 on liquidity risk. Moreover, identification of critical participants is a precondition for the requirements stipulated in principle 13 concerning operational risks. In this context, simulations of the consequences of operational failures on the part of single participants represent an advanced method for identifying such critical participants. Tiered participation arrangements must be monitored in accordance with principle 19.

USE OF PAYMENT SYSTEM DATA

Having dealt with the analysis of specific payment systems, we will now highlight the subject of analysis using payment system data for other purposes. The objectives of payment system analysis for central banks are not restricted to the tasks of a central bank directly linked to the payment system in its broader meaning and payment systems in the narrower sense of this term. Payment system data can also be used in other business areas for which a central bank may be responsible.

Financial Stability

One key field of use for payment system data analysis is financial stability. In the first instance, there are close links between the oversight of payment systems or other market infrastructures and financial stability. It goes without saying that any improvement of systems operated by the central bank itself simultaneously has a positive direct impact on financial stability. But the potential of payment system analysis goes far beyond these originary fields.

Using data from payment systems it is possible to derive a multitude of indicators so as to monitor risks for the financial system as whole but also single participants. Examples are the analysis of net flows between sectors or participants. A basic indicator could be to identify participants with large net outflows which could signal liquidity or even solvency problems, or map the evolution of payment timing. Kaliontzoglou and Müller's chapter in this book provides a detailed discussion of the implementation aspects of indicators related to payment timing.

In terms of monitoring, the task of payment systems analysis is to identify meaningful indicators with predictive power. Payment system analysis therefore needs to be combined with other financial stability-related analysis and payments data supplemented with additional data from other sources. Furthermore, implementing such indicators is a technically demanding task that requires a good understanding of the institutional features of the payment system from which the data is derived. Heijmans and Heuver (2014) present an overview of financial stability indicators based on payment system data for the Netherlands which could also be applied in other contexts. However, devising meaningful indicators of liquidity or solvency using payment system data remains a challenge.

Monetary Policy

Payment system analysis can also aid monetary policy, which in most cases is the foremost task of central banks. Monetary policy operations and money market transactions, which constitute the first element of the transmission mechanism of monetary policy, are settled via payment systems. Monetary policy and payment systems are therefore closely intertwined as described in Schmitz (2006) and Keister et al. (2008). Payment system analysis can assist operational monetary policy in optimizing liquidity provision to and liquidity use by the banking sector.

This first part of the monetary transmission mechanism consisting of monetary policy operations and money market transactions can be tracked in close detail using payment systems data. This is of special importance because in many cases no other data sources offering such granularity are available. Nevertheless, in most instances not even payment system data enable direct identification of money market transactions. Several central banks have therefore tried to identify money market transactions in payment data by applying the "Furfine-algorithm", based on the work of Furfine (1999).

The basic logic of this method is rather simple: The payout and payback of a money market loan are identified in the transactions of the payment system. They are matched based on the assumption that a money market loan leads to a round value payment from the creditor to the debtor and a payment of the same value plus the interest rate from the debtor to the creditor after maturity. The algorithm can apply further conditions and refinements to the matching process. It has to be calibrated in a way that optimizes the occurrence of false positive and false negative matches. This calibration poses a challenge inasmuch as data for a validation are not available in most cases – exactly this lack of data sources was the rationale behind developing the algorithm. Still, partial validation is possible either with aggregated money market data, e.g. by replicating an available average interest rate with the identified transactions, or by using granular data partially covering the entire market, e.g. from one trading platform.

Some authors, for example Armantier and Copeland (2012), have published critical assessments of the quality of the data generated by algorithms using this methodology, based on data for the fed funds market. Kovner and Skeie (2013) use another evaluation method and conclude that the results are a meaningful measure of overnight fed funds activity, but reiterate various caveats. Other central banks have implemented such algorithms leading to promising results of partial validations. Arciero et al. (2013) present an implementation for the Eurosystem based on TARGET2 data validated with aggregate indicators and granular data from trading platforms. Akram and Christophersen (2013) present an implementation for Norway validated with data on money market activity reported by a panel of banks to the central bank. Rempel (2014) proposes another estimation of the vulnerability of the algorithm to false identifications and methodological improvements. At this juncture, one can conclude that a successful implementation of such an algorithm poses great methodological challenges but should not be rejected outright . The reliability of the results will certainly depend on the technical characteristics of the payment system as well as the structure of the market to be analyzed.

National Accounting

Outside the broad area covered by monetary policy, payment system data can also be used for economic analysis related to national accounting. Several attempts have been made to use such data in connection with GDP "nowcasting" or forecasting. GDP data is usually published with a time lag. Using payment system data could help to deliver more timely indications commonly referred to as nowcasting. Again, the basic logic is rather simple: It hinges on the assumption that every economic activity culminates in a payment sooner or later. It follows that the total volume and value of payments made and economic activity should be highly correlated. Nevertheless, the practical implementation again poses significant challenges. Gill et al. (2012) present a basic discussion of the use of electronic indicators of economic activity. The SWIFT indicator described in SWIFT (2012) is a prime example of an attempt at GDP nowcasting. Galbraith and Tkacz (2013) find mixed evidence for the benefits of using payments data for GDP nowcasting.

Payment system data can also help us to understand cross-country capital flows. This type of analysis has been of particular importance in the Eurozone where TARGET2 balances (see Cour-Thimann, 2013) are a subject of much discussion. These balances reflect the net cross-border flows of funds of participants in one country with TARGET2 participants in all the other countries. They are therefore a valuable source of information for making an in-depth analysis of an integral aspect of total cross-border capital flows in the Eurozone. Similar analysis is also possible on a global scale, based on information delivered by cross-border payment flows. However, if the scale of such an analysis is extended beyond the scope of one country or one system, data availability steadily worsens. While such data could generally be supplied by global infrastructure providers such as SWIFT, problems of confidentiality and access rights still persist.

Combining Data Sources

Analysis of payment system data for purposes other than the payment system itself can be enriched by combining it with data sources for other FMIs, especially in the financial stability context. While payment systems data relate to the settlement of financial transactions, these could be matched with data from trade repositories covering the trading leg. Data on the unsecured money market identified in the payment system should be combined with data on secured money market transactions. CCPs could be used as further data sources. From this perspective, payment system data are just one of a range of data sources from FMIs that can be used to get deeper insights into the functioning of financial markets. In this regard, central banks can also cooperate with other supervisory authorities.

THE CENTRAL BANK PERSPECTIVE

The particularity of the central bank perspective in payment system analysis rests upon the combination of unique opportunities and unique responsibilities. Its distinctiveness is based on four elements:

- First, the uniqueness of the tasks performed by central banks, in particular their monopoly in terms of providing central bank money and the possibility of acting as lender of last resort.
- Second, their strong operational role in payments based on their specific risk profile concerning business and liquidity risk.
- Third, the fact that central banks act in the public interest.
- Fourth, the multitude and variety of the tasks of a central bank.

Unique Research Questions

The first element, the uniqueness of central bank tasks, leads to a specific responsibility in the form of specific research questions arising in payment system analysis. Central banks have a monopoly when it comes to providing central bank money and they can always act as lender of last resort. For this reason, only central banks are in a position to operate payment systems that effect settlement in central bank money, to conduct monetary policy and to enhance financial stability. Central banks have an inherent interest in conducting analysis in all these fields, and payment system analysis can contribute to all of them.

Privileged Data Access

The first three elements generate unique opportunities in the form of offering privileged access to data. Despite the importance of cash, primarily for customer payments, a very large proportion in terms of volume and even more in terms of the value of the payment obligations is settled using payment systems. All these transactions are to some extent registered in databases which can then be accessed for payment system analysis. Owing to the unique richness of this available data, payment systems analysis is predominantly empirical in nature. Central banks have privileged access to such data for two reasons.

The first reason is that, as operators, central banks have direct access to full datasets detailing transactions handled by their own systems. In this regard, the first two elements, i.e. central banks' monopoly in terms of providing central bank money and their specific risk profile, form the foundation for this data access as they are the reason why central banks perform a strong operational role with regard to particularly important payment systems. The second reason for their privileged access to data is that central banks are commonly endowed with the power to collect data from other actors. The third element, i.e. their mandate to act in the public interest, is the bedrock of this power. In the context of payment systems, the aforementioned powers arise from the central bank's role as an overseer and, in some cases, also as a macroprudential supervisor of financial market infrastructures. Being able to combine its own data with data collected from third parties puts the central bank in a privileged position to conduct analysis based on this data pool. The same applies when combining payment systems data with data on other financial market segments.

It goes without saying that these privileges come with increased responsibilities: The issue of confidential treatment of data is highly important for central banks, as the information relates to customers, i.e. the users of the payment system, when data is collected by the central bank as the operator or the information is provided by third parties on a confidential basis. Central banks are under a strong responsibility here to protect the interests of both their customers and data-providing third parties. A strict and credible separation between oversight and operations is also required in order to ensure a level playing field between systems operated by central banks and systems operated by other actors.

Owing to the high sensitivity of the used data, the results of payment system analysis are for the most part not published and only used internally. Hence, the examples cited in this chapter represent a mere fraction of actual payment system analysis. That being said, one could argue that by having such exclusive access to data on payment systems central banks in fact have a moral obligation to analyze this data and to publish the aggregated results. An ample publication of results would go some way towards levelling out their privileged access to data. In-depth public knowledge of the factors determining the performance of a given payment system and the influence of participants' behavior on that system can also serve the public interest: It can enhance the efficiency and stability of the payment system by providing guidance to participants on how they might adjust their behavior. When publishing the results of any analysis, it is important to strike a balance between protecting confidentiality and achieving benefits, both for the central bank itself and for the general public.

This trade-off undoubtedly varies depending on the topic and depth of the analysis and the individual target audience. The results of payment system analysis are in the first instance intended for an audience of experts. But on a more general level, central banks may find that it is in their interest for the public to enhance its knowledge of the payment system. Kokkola (2010) is an example of a basic introduction to the payment system. Moreover, results obtained from analytical work, be this at a simplified or an abstract level, could serve as useful input in publications targeted at a broad audience, without compromising confidentiality. All in all, it is fair to say that central banks would not only benefit from fostering such an environment but that they also have an obligation to increase knowledge about the functioning of payment systems by publishing the results of their analysis provided confidentiality is respected.

Interdependent Research Questions

The particularity of the central bank perspective in payment system analysis also rests upon the simultaneous assumption of different tasks and the assumption of different roles, i.e. the fourth element. Here, discussion of examples of payment system analysis related to the different tasks expected of a central bank shows that the different roles executed by a central bank are interdependent. A strong operational role in payment systems, for example, will provide the data and the technical knowledge necessary for the analysis of payment system data. The task of maintaining financial stability leads to an interest in this data for the specific purpose of generating early warning indicators. Studies on payment timing are performed using payment data for financial stability indicators. At the same time, studies on payment timing are also important for analysis directly related to the functioning of the system and therefore the central bank's operational role in payment systems. As discussed in detail by Kaliontzoglou and Müller in their chapter of this book, a payment timing indicator can be useful both as a financial stability indicator and as a system performance indicator in simulation studies. This example highlights the economies of scope which exist between the different strands of payment system analysis.

To sum up, the uniqueness and sheer variety of central bank tasks together with the very particular status which central banks enjoy allow these institutions privileged access to data, thus enabling them to combine these different aspects and play the role in payment systems analysis, at the same time obliging them to act in a responsible way.

REFERENCES

Akram, Q. F., & Christophersen, C. (2013) *Inferring interbank loans and interest rates from interbank payments - an evaluation.* Norges Bank Working Paper 26.

Ali, R., Barrdear, J., Clews, R., & Southgate, J. (2014a). Innovations in payment technologies and the emergence of digital currencies. *Bank of England Quarterly Bulletin, Q3*, 262–275.

Ali, R., Barrdear, J., Clews, R., & Southgate, J. (2014b). The economics of digital currencies. *Bank of England Quarterly Bulletin, Q3*, 276–286.

Arciero, L., Heijmans, R., Heuver, R., Massarenti, M., Picillo, C., & Vacirca, F. (2013). *How to measure the unsecured money market? The Eurosystem's implementation and validation using TARGET2 data.* DNB Working Paper No. 369.

Arciero, L., & Picillo, C. (2013). Liquidity Management in the Large Value Payment Systems: Need for an Agent-Based Model's Complex Approach. In B. Alexandrova-Kabadjova, S. Martinez-Jaramillo, A. Garcia-Almanza, & E. Tsang. (Eds.), Simulation in Computational Finance and Economics: Tools and Emerging Applications (pp. 84–102). Hershey: IGI Global. doi:10.4018/978-1-4666-2011-7.ch005

Armantier, O., Arnold, J. & McAndrews, J. (2008). *Changes in the Timing and Distribution of Fedwire Funds Transfers.* Federal Reserve Bank of New York Economic Policy Review, 14(2) Special Issue: The Economics of Payments, 83-112.

Armantier, O., & Copeland, A. (2012). *Assessing the quality of Furfine-Based algorithms.* Federal Reserve Bank of New York Staff Report No. 575.

Bech, M. (2008). *Intraday Liquidity Management: A Tale of Games that Banks Play.* Federal Reserve Bank of New York Economic Policy Review 14(2) Special Issue: The Economics of Payments, 7-23.

Bech, M., Preisig, C. & Soramäki, K. (2008). *Global Trends in Large-Value Payments.* Federal Reserve Bank of New York Economic Policy Review 14(2) Special Issue: The Economics of Payments, 59–81.

Becher, C., Galbiati, M. & Tudela, M. (2008). *The Timing and Funding of CHAPS Sterling Payments.* Federal Reserve Bank of New York Economic Policy Review 14(2) Special Issue: The Economics of Payments, 113-133.

Becher, C., Millard, S., & Soramäki, K. (2008). *The network topology of CHAPS Sterling*. Bank of England Working Paper 355.

Clarke, A., & Hancock, J. (2014). Payment system design and participant operational disruptions. *Journal of Financial Market Infrastructures*, *2*(2), 53–76.

The role of central bank money in payment systems. (2003). Committee on Payment and Settlement Systems.

Innovations in retail payments. (2012). Committee on Payment and Settlement Systems.

Cour-Thimann, P. (2013). *Target Balances and the Crisis in the Euro Area. CESifo Forum* (Vol. 14). Special Issue.

Davey, N., & Gray, D. (2014). How has the Liquidity-saving Mechanism reduced banks' intraday liquidity costs in CHAPS? *Bank of England Quarterly Bulletin*, *Q2*, 180–189.

Deutsche Bundesbank (2012). *Payment behaviour in Germany in 2011: An empirical study of the utilisation of cash and cashless payment instruments.*

Diehl, M. (2012). The Use of Simulations as an Analytical Tool for Payment Systems. In B. Alexandrova-Kabadjova, S. Martinez-Jaramillo, A. Garcia-Almanza, & E. Tsang. (Eds.), Simulation in Computational Finance and Economics: Tools and Emerging Applications (pp. 29–45). Hershey: IGI Global.

Diehl, M. (2013). Measuring free-riding in large-value payment-systems: The case of TARGET2. *Journal of Financial Market Infrastructures*, *1*(3), 1–23.

Diehl, M., & Müller, A. (2014). Analysis of the use and impact of limits. *Journal of Financial Market Infrastructures*, *3*(1), 33–60.

Virtual currency schemes. (2012). European Central Bank.

The 2013 Federal Reserve Payments Study. (2014). Federal Reserve System.

Finan, K., Lasaosa, A., & Sunderland, J. (2013). Tiering in CHAPS. *Bank of England Quarterly Bulletin, Q4*, 371–378.

Furfine, C. (1999). *The microstructure of the federal funds market.* Financial Markets. *Institutions and Instruments*, *8*(5), 24–44. doi:10.1111/1468-0416.00031

Galbiati, M., & Soramäki, K. (2010). *Liquidity-saving Mechanisms and Bank Behaviour.* Bank of England Working Paper 400.

Galbraith, J. & Tkacz, G. (2013). *Nowcasting GDP: Electronic Payments, Data Vintages and the Timing of Data Releases.* CIRANO Scientific Series, 2013, s-25.

Gill, T., Perera, D., & Sunner, D. (2012). *Electronic Indicators of Economic Activity.* Reserve Bank of Australia Bulletin. *June Quarter*, *2012*, 1–12.

Hasan, I., De Renzis, T., & Schmiedel, H. (2013). *Retail Payments and the Real Economy.* ECB Working Paper Series No. 1572.

Heijmans, R., & Heuver, R. (2014). Is this bank ill? The diagnosis of doctor TARGET2. *Journal of Financial Market Infrastructures*, *2*(3), 3–36.

Johnson, C., & Steigerwald, R. (2008). The Central Bank's Role in the Payment System: Legal and Policy Aspects (pp. 445–470). Proceedings of Seminar on Current Developments in Monetary and Financial Law. Washington, D.C.: International Monetary Fund.

Kahn, C., & Roberds, W. (1998). Payment System Settlement and Bank Incentives. *Review of Financial Studies*, *11*(4), 845–870. doi:10.1093/rfs/11.4.845

Kahn, C., & Roberds, W. (2001). Real-Time Gross Settlement and the Costs of Immediacy. *Journal of Monetary Economics*, *47*(2), 299–319. doi:10.1016/S0304-3932(01)00047-2

Keister, T., Martin, Antoine, M. & McAndrews, J. (2008). Divorcing Money from Monetary Policy. *Federal Reserve Bank of New York Economic Policy Review*, 14(2) Special Issue: The Economics of Payments, 41-56.

Kokkola, T. (Ed.). (2010). *The Payment System*. Frankfurt: European Central Bank.

Kovner, A., & Skeie, D. (2013). *Evaluating the Quality of Fed Funds Lending Estimates Produced from Fedwire Payments Data*. Federal Reserve Bank of New York Staff Report No. 629.

Manning, M., Nier, E., & Schanz, J. (Eds.). (2009). *The economics of large-value payments and settlement: Theory and policy issues for central banks*. Oxford: University Press.

Martin, A. & McAndrews, J. (2008). *An Economic Analysis of Liquidity-saving Mechanisms. Federal Reserve Bank of New York Economic Policy Review*, 14(2) Special Issue: The Economics of Payments, 25–39.

McLafferty, J., & Denbee, E. (2012). Liquidity Saving in CHAPS: A Simulation Study. In *Simulation in Computational Finance and Economics: Tools and Emerging Applications* (pp. 120–142). Hershey: IGI Global.

Norman, B., Shaw, R., & Speight, G. (2011). *The history of interbank settlement arrangements: exploring central banks' role in the payment system*. Bank of England Working Paper 412.

Oliver, R., & Weiner, S. E. (2010). The Role of Central Banks in Retail Payments: The Central Bank as Operator. In *The Changing Retail Payments Landscape: What Role For Central Banks?* (pp. 199–216). Kansas City: The Federal Reserve Bank of Kansas City.

Ossolinski, C., Lam, T., & Emery, D. (2014). *The Changing Way We Pay: Trends in Consumer Payments*. Reserve Bank of Australia Research Discussion Paper, RDP2014-5.

Rempel, M. (2014). *Improving Overnight Loan Identification in Payments Systems*. Bank of Canada Working Paper 2014-25.

Schmiedel, H., Kostova, G., & Ruttenberg, W. (2012). *The social and private costs of retail payment instruments. A European perspective*. ECB Occasional Paper Series, No. 137.

Schmitz, S. (2006, November). How payment systems affect monetary policy. Central Banking, 17, N 2.

Soramäki, K., Bech, M., Arnold, J., Glass, R., & Beyeler, W. (2006). *The Topology of Interbank Payment Flows*. Federal Reserve Bank of New York Staff Report No. 243.

Summers, B. (Ed.). (2012). *Payment Systems: Design, Governance and Oversight*. London: Central Banking Publications.

The SWIFT Index [Technical description]. (2012). SWIFT.

Tsuchiya, S. (2013). The effects of settlement methods on liquidity needs in Japan: An empirical study based on funds-transfer data from BOJ-NET. *Journal of Financial Market Infrastructures*, *1*(4), 109–131.

ENDNOTES

1 This paper represents the judgments and views of the author and does not necessarily reflect the opinion of the Deutsche Bundesbank.

2 Financial stability is used here in the broadest sense of the term, encompassing various possible institutional arrangements with potential responsibilities of central banks comprising various tasks related to regulation, macroprudential and microprudential supervision and resolution regimes for banks and other actors in the financial system.

Chapter 12
Liquidity Saving Mechanisms in Payment Systems and Settlement Liquidity:
The Experience of Japan's Next-Generation RTGS Project

Masashi Nakajima
Reitaku University, Japan

ABSTRACT

Payment systems are one of the key Financial Market Infrastructures (FMIs) and have showed remarkable progress over the past two decades. The first half of this chapter focuses on the evolutionary process of payment systems, starting with the Deferred Net Settlement (DNS) system and progressing to the Real-Time Gross Settlement (RTGS) system. Subsequently, much more sophisticated payment systems have been put in place, which include the "Hybrid System," and the "RTGS system with Liquidity Saving Mechanism (LSM)." In the latter half of this chapter, experience from the "Next-Generation Real-Time Gross Settlement" (RTGS-XG) project of BOJ-NET is discussed. BOJ-NET is the large-value payment system operated by Bank of Japan (BOJ). BOJ-NET added an LSM in 2008 and became an RTGS system with LSM. The impact of the LSM's introduction is analyzed, which includes the liquidity-saving effect, the average waiting time in the queue, the turnover ratio, and the volume of idle liquidity.

INTRODUCTION

Over the past two decades, payment systems have evolved drastically. In particular, Large-Value Payment Systems (LVPSs) have achieved breakthrough innovations in settlement mechanism design. LVPSs generally process very large-value, inter-bank payments and play a key role in the financial system.

Considering the theoretical background of this development, it is recognized that the purpose of the evolution was to improve payment systems' two evaluation criteria, safety and efficiency. More importantly, the ultimate aim was to overcome the trade-off between the two.

DOI: 10.4018/978-1-4666-8745-5.ch012

In the early days, there were only two types of payment systems. One was the Deferred Net Settlement (DNS) system, and the other was the Real-Time Gross Settlement (RTGS) system. There was a serious trade-off relationship between the two systems, or more concretely, between safety and efficiency in payment systems.

Looking more closely, the DNS system has the advantage in efficiency but is inferior in terms of safety. This is because the DNS system requires only a small amount of liquidity for settlement because of its use of 'netting'. In netting, participants' net positions are settled at the end of the day. The DNS system, however, is vulnerable to settlement risk because of the time gap between when the payment is sent to the system and when the net position is finally settled at the end of the day. This means that 'settlement finality' cannot be achieved until the end of the day. In addition to the late finality, the DNS system is exposed to 'systemic risk' in that the failure of one participant may cause significant liquidity or credit problems and might threaten the stability of financial market as a whole.

On the other hand, the RTGS system is superior in terms of safety, but is not as efficient in the usage of liquidity. The merit is achieved because each payment is settled individually on a real-time basis and immediately becomes final in the RTGS system. The downside, however, is that it requires a higher level of liquidity for settlement. Liquidity here refers to the account balance of each participant (typically a bank) at the central bank.

EVOLUTIONAL PROCESS OF PAYMENT SYSTEMS

Global Evolution of Payment Systems: Beyond the Trade-off between Safety and Efficiency

Historically, almost all LVPSs started their operation as DNS systems. In due course, settlement mechanisms were changed and they became RTGS systems, with the main purpose of the improvement being to reduce settlement risk. Since LVPSs settle huge amounts of funds, it was most important for the system operators, usually the central banks, to reduce settlement risk and avoid systemic risk.

Although the RTGS system is robust with respect to settlement risk, it has the drawback of requiring a large amount of liquidity for settlement. In the case of a DNS system, the liquidity required at the end of the day is the net position between the outgoing and incoming payments, usually just a small portion of the total outgoing payment amount. In the RTGS system, by contrast, the full liquidity value is required for each outgoing payment in order to make a settlement. Therefore, the liquidity burden is rather heavy in the RTGS system.

In order to ease this liquidity burden, the Liquidity Saving Mechanism (LSM) was newly invented. In an LSM, the outgoing and incoming payments are matched and settled simultaneously, either bilaterally or multilaterally. That is, the LSM allows participants to send payments on the receipt of payments from others, which activates the netting effect and enables settlements with a small amount of liquidity. The settlement engine continues to search and match payments during the day, which facilitates near real-time settlement, and intraday finality.

In this way, the RTGS system with LSM is currently the cutting-edge payment system in the world, achieving a good balance between safety and efficiency (see Table 1). These payment system developments are described in the following part of this section.

Table 1. Safety and Efficiency in Payment Systems

	Safety **(robust to settlement risk)**	*Efficiency* **(require less liquidity for settlement)**
DNS system	× (vulnerable to settlement risk and systemic risk)	○ (settlement with less liquidity)
RTGS system	○ (real-time finality)	× (require a lot of liquidity)
RTGS system with LSM	○ (intraday finality)	○ (settlement with less liquidity)

Note: ○ means superiority and × indicates inferiority.

From DNS System to RTGS System

The worldwide shift from DNS to RTGS system started in the late 1990s as central banks became increasingly concerned that DNS systems were vulnerable to settlement risk. The payment systems that central banks operate have huge settlement values including interbank payments and fund settlements for government bonds. Consequently, their first priority was to reduce settlement risk. By this means, central banks directed their efforts at converting their systems to RTGS (Nakajima, 2012).

The Committee on Payment and Settlement Systems (CPSS) of the Bank for International Settlements (BIS) published the "RTGS Report" in 1997. The report played an important role in spreading awareness of settlement risk, and the importance of an RTGS system to eliminate the risk inherent in DNS system. It studied the generic features and the issues associated with RTGS systems including intraday liquidity. It also discussed the policy implications for central banks, and advocated the wider usage of RTGS systems for the purpose of risk reduction.

The adoption of the RTGS system started in major industrialized countries in the late 1990s and spread gradually to the Asia-Pacific region, Latin America, the Middle East, and Africa.

According to the World Bank's survey, 116 out of 139 countries (or 83%) used RTGS systems as of the end of 2010 (World Bank, 2011). The survey showed that 34% of the RTGS systems were implemented in 1999 or earlier, 50% in 2000-2006, and 16% in 2007-2010 (see Figure 1).

According to another survey by the Federal Reserve Bank of New York, 15 RTGS systems were introduced in 2002, making it the peak year for respective introductions (Bech & Hobijn, 2007). RTGS system has become a standard approach for large-value payment system in each country.

Introduction of Hybrid Systems

Another new direction was the innovative introduction of Hybrid systems, which were also a shift away from DNS systems.

Characteristics of Hybrid Systems

Traditional DNS systems made the net settlement only once at the end of the day. Typically, a method of "Full Netting" was executed with all participants incorporated into the calculation of the net positions. The major difference to DNS system is that a Hybrid system makes net settlements at frequent intervals, and the transfer of funds becomes final at the time of these settlements during the day. A "Partial Netting" mechanism is often employed in Hybrid system, whereby a limited number of participants, typically two or three, is incorporated into the netting process.

Figure 1. Implementation Year of RTGS Systems

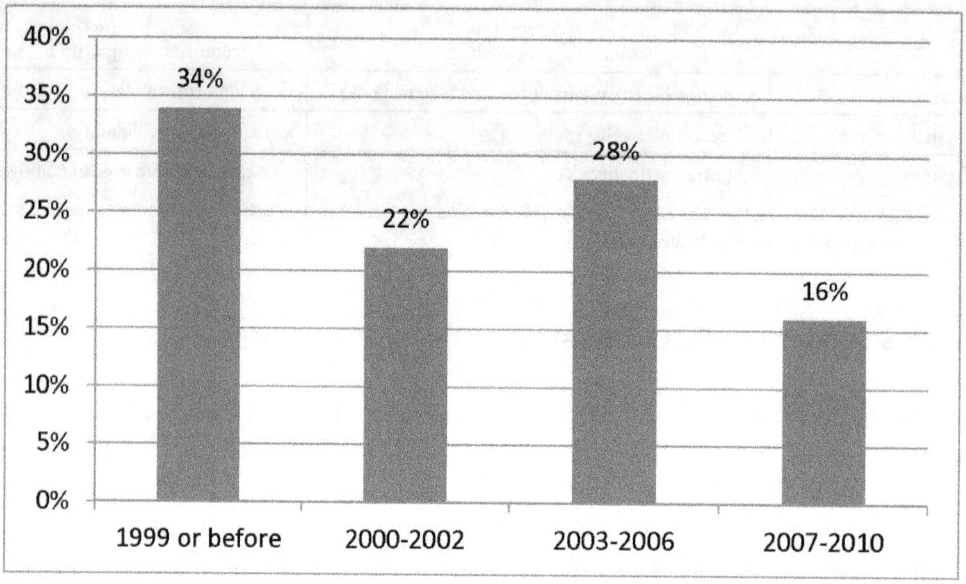

Note :Total number of countries using RTGS system was 116 at the end of 2010.

Source: World Bank (2011)

By means of these frequent netting mechanisms, Hybrid systems realized earlier settlement finality. On top of it, Hybrid system can execute the settlement with minimal liquidity. The net difference amount of the outgoing and incoming payments is enough to proceed the settlement, because the Hybrid system settlement is a type of net settlement.

In this way, Hybrid systems succeeded in combining 'liquidity saving features,' the DNS system's merit, and 'immediate finality,' the RTGS system's advantage. A payment system that successfully combines the merits of DNS and RTGS systems is referred to as "Hybrid system" (Nakajima, 2011).

Deployment of Hybrid Systems

The world's first Hybrid system was "EAF2" in Germany. In March 1996, it became a Hybrid system by making bilateral and multilateral net settlements at regular intervals. This was a revolutionary change from the DNS system's single net settlement at the end of the day. In April 1999, Paris Net Settlement (PNS) in France adopted the similar new features of continuous net settlement and became the world's second Hybrid system. Following EAF2 and PNS, Clearing House Interbank Payments System (CHIPS) in the US became the world's third Hybrid system by adopting the innovative "CHIPS Finality" scheme in February 2001 (Nakajima, 2011).

In 2007, "TARGET2" was introduced as a payment system that covered the entire euro area and was operated on a single technical platform. At this point, EAF2 and PNS were abolished and absorbed into TARGET2. Therefore, CHIPS is the only existing Hybrid system at this time.

Even belonging to the same category, there are some differences in the processing methods of Hybrid systems. In EAF2 and PNS, the bilateral and the multilateral nettings were executed as completely separate processes. On the contrary, CHIPS executes these two nettings as a simultaneous parallel process (see Table 2).

RTGS System with Liquidity Saving Mechanism

Learning from the mechanism of the Hybrid system, a completely new idea was sparked. That was to combine the Hybrid function with the RTGS function in a payment system. It was a giant step forward and a real breakthrough idea to solve the long-lasting trade-off problem.

Characteristics of RTGS System with LSM

This kind of system that combines RTGS and LS functionality is referred to as "RTGS system with LSM." The LSM is a mechanism of frequent nettings (or offsetting) that was invented in Hybrid systems. To be more precise, LSM allows banks to release queued payments on the receipt of offsetting payments. As a result, banks can make settlements with less liquidity.

An RTGS system with LSM is a combination of the pure RTGS system and the Hybrid system. In this sense, the Hybrid system could be positioned as the transitional payment system between DNS system and RTGS system with LSM.

RTGS system can eliminate both the settlement risk and systemic risk. However, the elimination of risk is achieved at the cost of an increased need for intraday liquidity. And the liquidity is costly for banks at all times either in the form of an explicit fee or implicit opportunity cost for collateral. Thus, LSM can compensate the drawback of RTGS system by saving the liquidity needs.

Two Settlement Modes of RTGS System with LSM

RTGS system with LSM has two settlement modes: RTGS mode, and Liquidity Saving mode (LS mode). In the RTGS mode, payments are processed in real-time and become final instantly. In the LS mode, payments are placed in each participant's queue. The algorithm then searches for a combination of payments that can be settled according to the liquidity conditions of the relevant participants. Once such a combination is found, the algorithm picks up the intended payments from the queue and settles them.

"Offsetting," often used in LS mode, is a simultaneous processing of several payments on a gross basis. Although the offsetting takes place in gross settlement form, outgoing payments can be paired with incoming payments enabling settlement to be made with minimal liquidity, i.e. the net difference between the two.

Table 2. Differences in Processing Methods of Hybrid Systems

Hybrid System	*Bilateral Netting*	*Multilateral Netting*
EAF2 (Germany)	Every 20 minutes before noon	Two nettings in the afternoon
PNS (France)	Continuous nettings during the day	At an appropriate time when the unsettled payments have accumulated.
CHIPS (US)	Balanced release engine selects the processing type from three options; Individual release, Bilateral release, and Multilateral release.	

In general, a participant can use the settlement account's full liquidity in RTGS mode, and only the assigned liquidity for LS mode. With this assignment of liquidity, the RTGS mode can make settlements without delay, and the LS mode can achieve settlements with smaller liquidity usage. The LS mode makes settlement to the maximum that offsetting will allow, i.e. within the liquidity limits of the paying participant. Usually, the LS mode utilizes a combination of both bilateral and multilateral offsetting.

Participants of the RTGS system with LSM can decide which mode to use depending on the nature of the payments. More concretely, participants can use RTGS mode for urgent and time-critical payments, while LS mode can be employed for payments that are not time sensitive.

Since RTGS system with LSM combines two settlement modes, it is sometimes referred to as "Integrated system." The RTGS mode realizes a high level of safety with early finality, while the LS mode facilitates a high level of efficiency using less liquidity. As a result, this system successfully resolves the traditional trade-off problem between safety and efficiency in payment systems. Therefore, RTGS system with LSM can currently be described as the most advanced payment system in the world.

Introduction of RTGS System with LSM

RTGS systems with LSM have already been introduced in several countries (see Table 3).

In February 1999, the Bank of Canada introduced the Large Value Transfer System (LVTS), which was the world's first RTGS system with LSM. It had two modes: Tranche 1, which was the RTGS mode and, Tranche 2, which was the LS mode (Arjani & McVanel, 2006). In November 2001, the Deutsche Bundesbank introduced "RTGS^{plus}," which was another prime example of RTGS system with LSM. It also had two modes: 'EX payment,' which was the RTGS mode, and 'Limit payment,' which was the LS mode (Deutsche Bundesbank, 2000). These functionalities of RTGS^{plus} were succeeded by TARGET2, the second generation of TARGET, operated by the Eurosystem. In sum, TARGET2 belongs to the family of RTGS systems with LSM.

There are also examples of RTGS system with LSM in Asia: "MEPS+" in Singapore, "BOJ-NET" in Japan, and "BOK-Wire+" in Korea.

The most recently-introduced RTGS system with LSM was "CHAPS" in the UK. CHAPS introduced LSM functionality in April 2013, whereby the LSM briefly suspends processing the RTGS mode and

Table 3. RTGS Systems with Liquidity Saving Mechanism in selected countries

Country	*RTGS System with LSM*	*Timing of introduction*
Canada	LVTS	February 1999
Germany	RTGS^{plus}	November 2001
Italy	new BIREL	April 2004
Singapore	MEPS +	December 2006
EU	TARGET2	November 2007
Japan	BOJ-NET(RTGS-XG)	October 2008
Korea	BOK-Wire+	April 2009
UK	CHAPS	April 2013
Switzerland	SIC	planned

switches to a "matching cycle" every two minutes (Denbee & McLafferty, 2013). During the matching cycle, which lasts around 20 seconds, the offsetting algorithm runs to match and settle batches of non-urgent payments. The system alternates between bilateral and multilateral offsetting. Some offsetting is made to the queue sorted by value from the smallest to the largest payment, and other offsetting takes place according to submission time with the oldest payments processed first. Any payments not settled by a matching cycle remain in the queue and the system will attempt to match and settle them in the next cycle, two minutes later (Dent & Dison, 2012).

The trend of RTGS system with LSM expansion appears to be continuing. For instance, Swiss National Bank is currently discussing the possibility of enhancing the functionality of "Swiss Interbank Clearing" (SIC) by introducing LSM. The bank ran simulations to analyze which of the alternative algorithms is most effective in reducing settlement delay and liquidity usage (Oleschak & Nellen, 2013).

As a result of the expansion of RTGS system with LSM, the traditional RTGS system without LSM has come to be referred somewhat sarcastically as a "pure RTGS system" or a "conventional RTGS system."

Offsetting as a Gridlock-preventing Feature

Some payment systems adopt the offsetting mechanism only for the limited purpose. This kind of usage of offsetting should be discussed separately from the usage of the mechanism as one of main settlement modes in the RTGS system with LSM. In such a payment system, the offsetting mechanism is used purely to prevent the gridlock in the system. More specifically, the functionality is run only when a certain volume of payments remain unsettled for a certain period. This means the usage of the mechanism is only at a fixed time interval or for the special cases.

The usages of the offsetting mechanism for gridlock-prevention can be seen in several payment systems, including "CHATS" in Hong Kong, "SIC" in Switzerland, and "RITS" in Australia (see Table 4).

In the case of CHATS, the multilateral offsetting, which was introduced in January 2006, runs at 30-minute intervals. The same kind of gridlock-prevention functionality is called "Circles Processing Mechanism" in SIC, and "Auto-offset Facility" in RITS.

These payment systems can be classified as "pure RTGS systems," in which payments are settled in RTGS mode according to the simple first-in first-out (FIFO) rule. In these systems, the offsetting mechanism runs only occasionally in order to clear the outstanding payment queues at a certain time or when necessary. Therefore, the two usages of offsetting should be differentiated: one is the use of offsetting only for gridlock prevention, while the other is the adoption of offsetting as a separate settlement mode alongside the RTGS mode.

Table 4. RTGS Systems with Gridlock-preventing feature

Country/Area	*Payment system*	*Gridlock-preventing feature*
Hong Kong	CHATS	RTGS Liquidity Optimizer
Switzerland	SIC	Circles Processing Mechanism
Australia	RITS	Auto-offset Facility
New Zealand	ESAS	Auto-offset Functionality (bilateral offsetting) Freeze Frame (multilateral offsetting)

EXPERIENCE FROM THE BOJ-NET NEXT-GENERATION RTGS PROJECT

This section takes a close look at the BOJ-NET Next-Generation RTGS (RTGS-XG) project. BOJ-NET is a large-value payment system operated by Bank of Japan (BOJ). It is mainly used for interbank payments for money market and government bond transactions. It also settles the net positions of private-sector netting systems, that is, the Foreign Exchange Yen Clearing System (FXYCS), and Zengin Data Telecommunication System (Zengin System).

The RTGS-XG was a project to enhance the functionality of BOJ-NET. As a result, Japan's payment landscape changed drastically, and through this project, BOJ-NET became one of the RTGS systems with LSM, as described above.

Outline of the RTGS-XG Project

In October 2008, BOJ-NET added an LSM and became a RTGS system with LSM from a previously pure RTGS system. The project comprised three components: (i) to establish a centralized queuing function, (ii) to introduce Liquidity-Saving Features (LSF), and (iii) to develop a special account for these LSF (see Figure 2).

Queuing Function

With respect to the payment systems in major countries, it is quite common that each has a centralized queuing function. BOJ-NET, however, did not have a queuing function before the RTGS-XG project.

The queuing function established by the RTGS-XG entails a payment being placed in the waiting queue when there is insufficient liquidity for settlement in the payer's account. The queuing function

Figure 2. Three Components of RTGS-XG Project

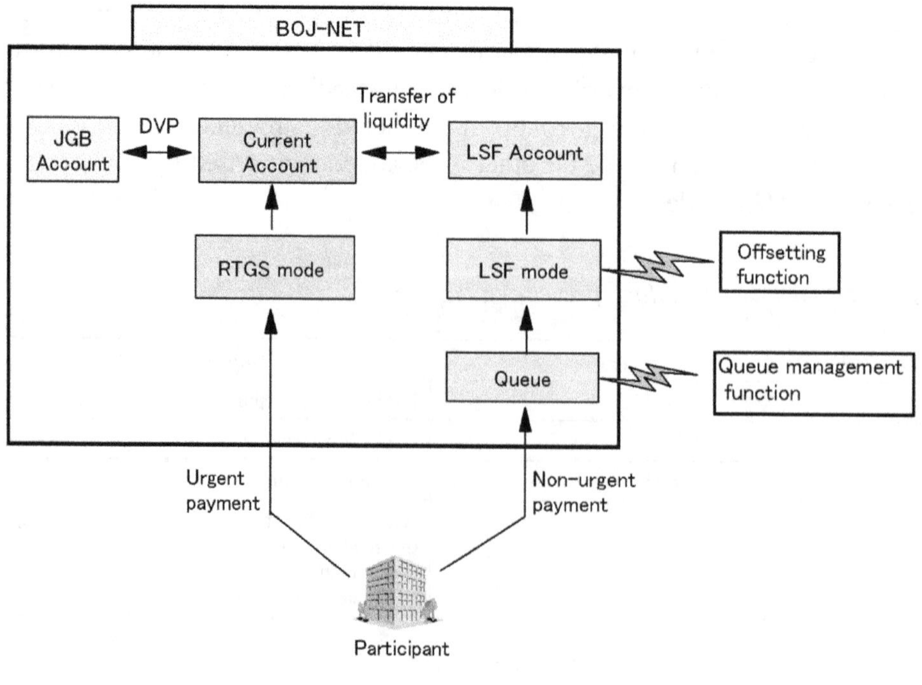

provides good incentives for participants to submit payments early in the day because the greater the number of payments in the queue, the greater the probability of settling payments from other participants.

Participants of BOJ-NET are able to monitor their settlement situation in real time, including the balance in the account, the settlement status of each payment, and the waiting payments in the queue. Each participant is also able to actively control the payments in the queue with the "queue management function," which includes assigning payment priority, and reordering and cancelling payments.

With regard to the "payment priority," each participant is able to assign a priority to each payment, being "high" or "normal." The queue is managed separately between the high priority and the normal priority payments. Needless to say, the high priority payments are given preference for settlement. Thus, if any high priority payments remain in the respective queue, the normal priority payments are not processed.

Liquidity-Saving Features (LSF)

In the RTGS-XG project, LSF was introduced, which is identical to the LSM in other RTGS systems with LSM, which provide the 'offsetting mechanism.' Offsetting is the simultaneous processing of outgoing and incoming payments on a gross basis. If there is a payment of 30 from Bank A to Bank B, and there is a payment of 100 from Bank B to Bank A, these two payments are processed simultaneously, if the net outflow has sufficient cover. The result of this processing is that Bank A's account increases by 70, and Bank B's account decreases by 70 (see Figure 3). This kind of offsetting is referred to as "bilateral offsetting." It is noteworthy that the outcome of the bilateral offsetting is exactly the same as the netting of the two payments.

The RTGS-XG has two offsetting mechanisms: "bilateral offsetting" and "multilateral offsetting." The bilateral offsetting algorithm runs continuously throughout the day and is the primary function for settlements. On the other hand, the multilateral offsetting algorithm runs only at a fixed time (four times a day), and is regarded as a complementary function to bilateral offsetting.

Figure 3. Two offsetting mechanisms in Liquidity-Saving Features (LSF)

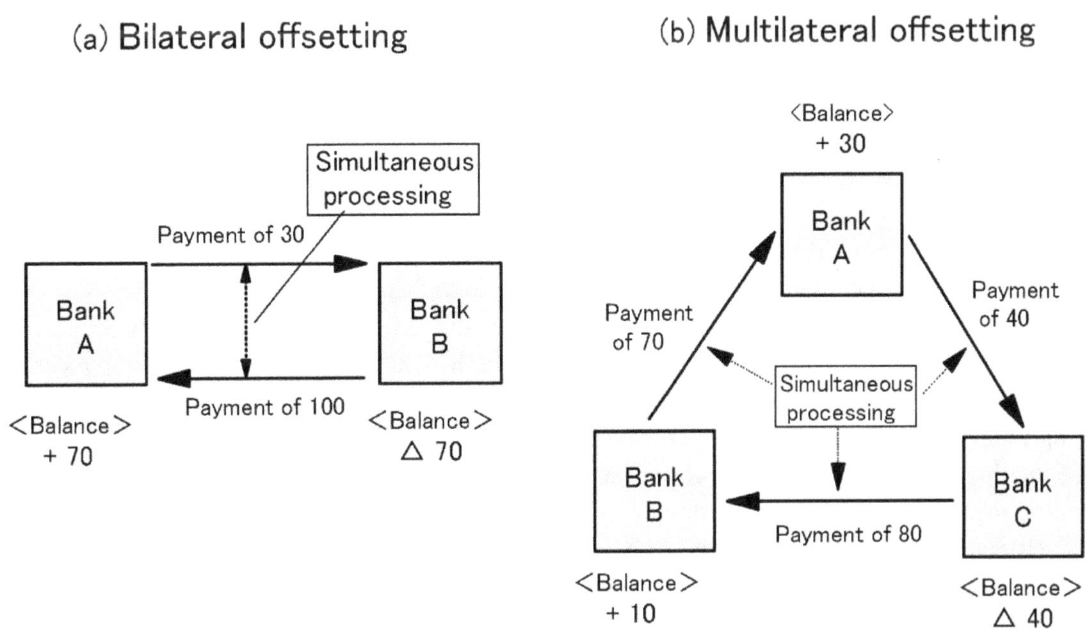

Dedicated Account for LSF

The RTGS-XG has two kinds of accounts: one for the LSF settlement and the other for the RTGS settlement. Participants using the LSF mode are required to hold a dedicated account for LSF settlements ("LSF account"). Moreover, LSF settlement is only available for payments between LSF accounts. Meanwhile, the "RTGS account" is used for settlements in RTGS mode, and is also used for reserve requirements. No settlement takes place between a participant's LSF account and other participants' RTGS accounts.

First thing in the morning, each participant is required to transfer the funds necessary for the day's LSF settlements from the RTGS account to the LSF account. The transfer of additional funds to the LSF account is possible at any time during the day, if more liquidity is necessary for the LSF settlement. In this manner, LSF mode adopts a prefund mechanism, where the necessary fund for settlement should be put in LSF account in advance of settlement. Owing to this prefund nature, LSF mode is free from settlement risk and systemic risk.

At the end of the day, the balance in the LSF account is automatically transferred back to the RTGS account, leaving the balance of each LSF account at zero. In this way, participants need to manage two liquidity positions, the LSF account, and the RTGS account. The liquidity management burden, however, is not particularly onerous because the participants are able to transfer liquidity freely between the two accounts throughout the day.

Most interbank and customer transactions are eligible for settlement via the LSF account; however, some transactions should be settled only in the RTGS account. These include the transactions with BOJ and the government, the settlement obligation arising from the clearing systems (including Zengin system and Bill and Cheque Clearing Systems), and the cash legs of securities transactions.

Three Settlement Patterns in LSF account

There are three settlement patterns in the LSF account (see Figure 4). As presented above, the LSF function consists of a centralized queuing function and offsetting mechanisms.

First, when the new payment is entered into the system, the offsetting mechanism searches for a potential set of payments that can be offset. If such a pair is found, the two opposite payments are picked up from the queue and settled simultaneously. This kind of settlement is called "bilateral offsetting," as mentioned before. The required condition for bilateral offsetting is that the difference between the incoming and outgoing payment does not exceed the payer's LSF account balance. That is, the payer's LSF balance should cover the net debit amount.

Second, if the offsetting mechanism cannot find a counter payment that can be matched with the new payment, the latter is settled via gross settlement in real time, assuming there are sufficient funds in the payer's LSF account. This kind of settlement is referred to as "single gross settlement."

Third, if the new payment cannot be settled with the above two settlement methods because of an insufficient balance on the payer's account, it is placed in the waiting queue. The offsetting mechanism then attempts "multilateral offsetting" at four fixed times (10:30, 13:30, 14:30, 15:30) each day to find a group of offsetting payments from all the queued payments.

Of the three settlement patterns, bilateral and multilateral offsetting are the settlements that use the offsetting mechanism. Both these settlement methods have liquidity-saving effects. Meanwhile, single gross settlement is the gross settlement of a single payment at real time, which is exactly the same as the RTGS function and has no effect of liquidity-saving.

Figure 4. Flowchart of Three Settlement Patterns in LSF account

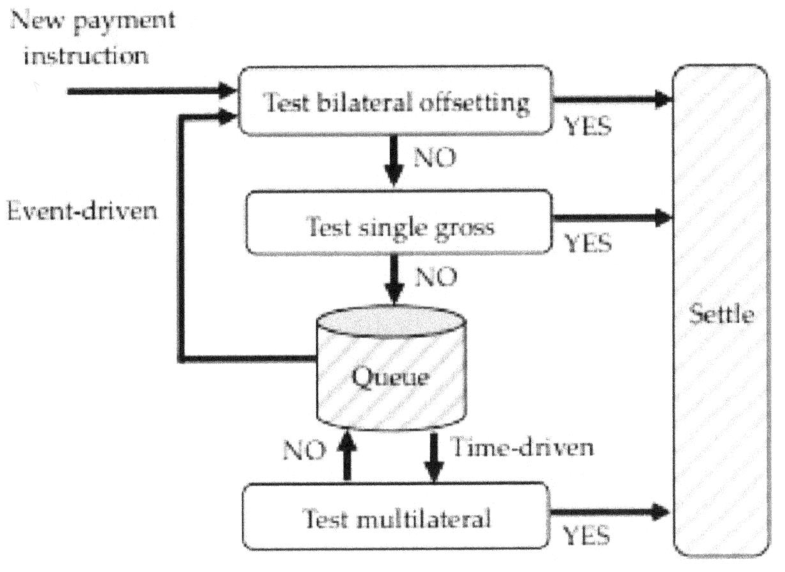

Source: Tsuchiya[2013]

Intraday Overdraft of BOJ

BOJ provides intraday liquidity to BOJ-NET participants in the form of an intraday overdraft. The usage thereof is free of charge but eligible collateral is necessary to borrow temporary funds from BOJ. The intraday overdraft is, however, only provided to the RTGS account and there is no intraday credit facility for LSF accounts.

Thus, a participant needing to obtain intraday liquidity from BOJ must first increase the RTGS account's liquidity and then transfer it to the LSF account.

Reconstruction of Payment Systems in Japan

Consolidation of Large-Value Payments

The RTGS-XG project also included the reconstruction of several payment systems in Japan, which brought significant changes to the Japanese payment landscape. Before the project, large-value payments in Japan were dealt with by three different payment systems. First, BOJ-NET was the main settlement channel for large-value payments mainly for money market and securities transactions. The second was FXYCS, which predominantly handled foreign exchange related payments. The last was Zengin System, which handled customer payments. In terms of the FXYCS and Zengin Systems, the final settlements of participants' net positions were made at BOJ-NET at the end of the day. Until then, unsettled positions accumulated, and the settlement risk resided among the participants during the daytime on every business day.

Since the project's implementation, all large-value payments are consolidated into BOJ-NET and settlements are made near real-time with intraday finality (see Figure 5). This means that the RTGS-XG project achieved a substantial reduction of settlement risk in the Japanese payment market.

Consolidation in Two Stages

The consolidation of large-value payments was made in two stages. Phase 1 was in October 2008 when FXYCS payments were consolidated into BOJ-NET. Phase 2 took place in November 2011 when large-value retail payments were consolidated into BOJ-NET from Zengin System (see Figure 6). With respect to the consolidated large-value payments, the settlement methods were changed from the end-of-the-day DNS to the LSF settlement in near real-time in BOJ-NET.

Consolidation of FXYCS Flows (Phase 1)

In October 2008, FXYCS payments were changed, and forwarded to BOJ-NET. At the same time, the DNS mode of FXYCS was abolished. In other words, the payments sent from the FXYCS participants are forwarded to and settled in BOJ-NET by either LSF or RTGS mode (see Figure 7). FXYCS's RTGS mode, which was mainly used for the pay-ins/pay-outs to/from the CLS Bank, continues to be used. The main flows of FXYCS were changed to go through FXYCS and be forwarded to BOJ-NET, where the payments are processed with the LSF mode.

FXYCS's framework, which includes the system rules, the participation rules, and the cost sharing arrangement, was maintained. In particular, the direct and indirect participant framework was important because BOJ-NET does not have an indirect participation scheme.

Figure 5. Consolidation of Large-Value Payment Flows

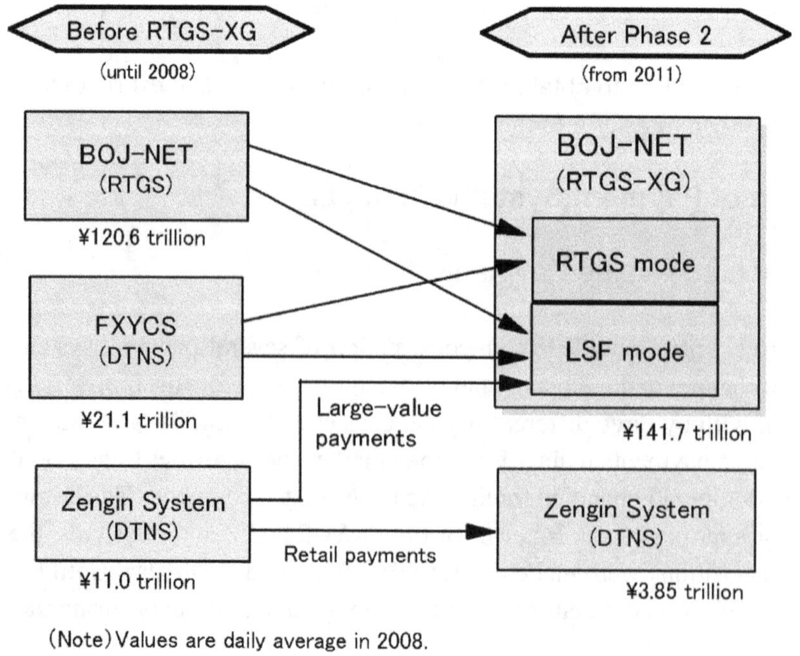

Figure 6. Change of Division of Roles among Japanese Payment Systems

	Before RTGS-XG	After Phase 1	After Phase 2
Money market payments	RTGS	RTGS with LSF	RTGS with LSF
FXYCS payments	DNS	RTGS with LSF	RTGS with LSF
large-value retail payments	DNS	DNS	RTGS with LSF

Source: Tsuchiya[2013]

Figure 7. Consolidation of Payment Flow from FXYCS

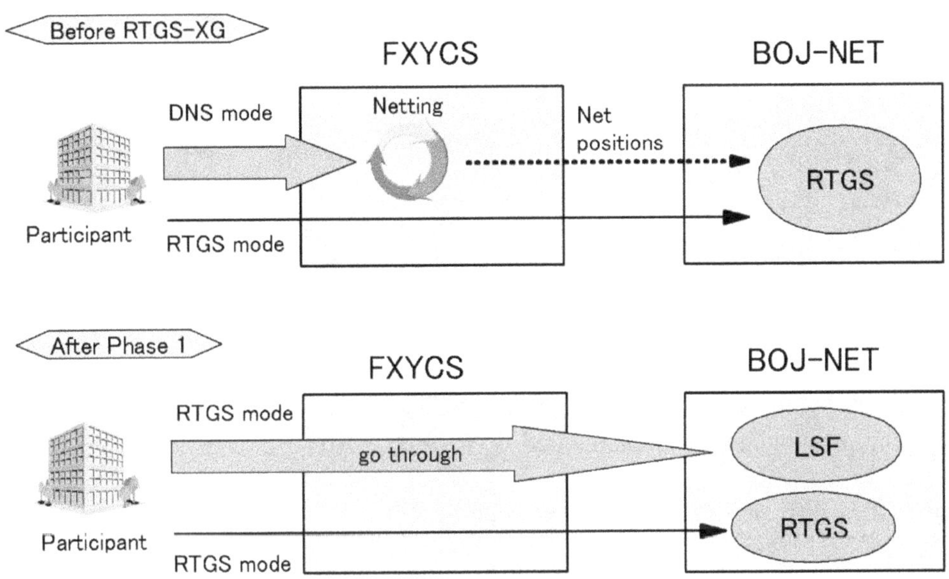

With the new scheme, most of the payments simply pass through FXYCS and the settlements take place within BOJ-NET. In sum, the role of FXYCS was significantly reduced by the aggregation of the payment flow to the enhanced BOJ-NET.

Consolidation of Large-Value Zengin Payments (Phase 2)

In terms of the Zengin System, a new "Interface Mechanism" was developed, which picks up large-value payments (\100 million and up) from the Zengin payment flow and sends them to BOJ-NET. The forwarded large-value Zengin payments are processed with LSF mode at BOJ-NET.

The remaining small-value payments are processed in the Zengin System with the netting process as before (see Figure 8). By this consolidation, Zengin System became a pure retail payment system without processing large-value payments.

Figure 8. Consolidation of Large-Value Zengin Payments

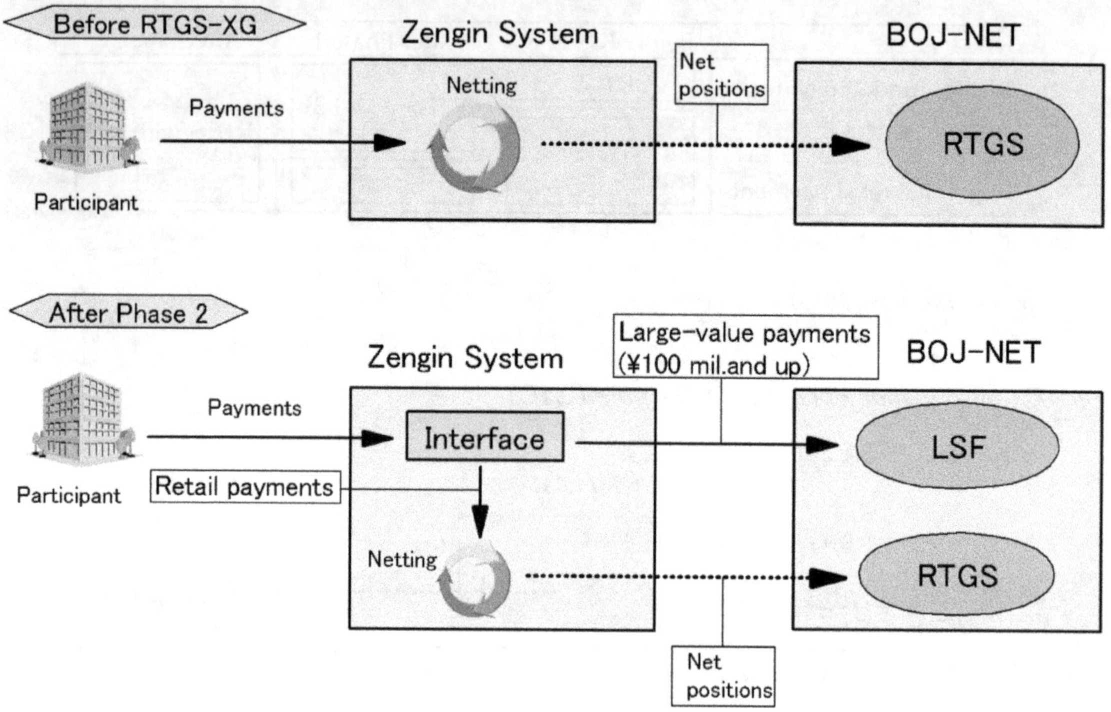

When the Interface Mechanism sends large-value payments to BOJ-NET, only interbank payment information is sent, while customer information remains in the Zengin System. This aggregation of large-value Zengin payments was implemented in November 2011.

Settlement Situation of BOJ-NET after RTGS-XG

After Phase 1, all FXYCS payments were transferred and settled in BOJ-NET. After Phase 2, only a small portion (0.2% to be exact) of the Zengin payments in volume terms were shifted to BOJ-NET's LSF mode. In value terms, however, the large-value Zengin payments comprise three-quarters (76% more precisely) of Zengin payments, which are given the near real-time finality in new BOJ-NET. Therefore, the consolidation of large-value Zengin payments into BOJ-NET is not insignificant from a risk reduction perspective.

As the result of the Phase 1 and Phase 2 consolidations, FXYCS payments accounted for 8%, and the large-value Zengin payments 10% of BOJ-NET's daily average value in 2013 (see Table 5). This means the consolidations increased BOJ-NET's settlement value by about 20%. As for the shifted payments, the settlement method was changed from net settlement at the end of the day to near real-time settlement with intraday finality, leading to a huge reduction in settlement risk.

The LSF mode handles three types of transactions: money market payments, FXYCS payments, and large-value Zengin payments, and handles more than 50% of the total BOJ-NET settlement value. On the other hand, government bond payments account for most of the settlements in RTGS mode, where Delivery versus Payment (DVP) is achieved between the RTGS account and the government bond account.

Table 5. Breakdown of Payments in BOJ-NET- Daily average value, 2013

	Settlement mode	Value (in \ trillion)	Share (%)
Money market payments	LSF	40.8	(35.0)
FXYCS payments		8.7	(7.5)
Large-value Zengin payments		11.9	(10.2)
Government bond payments	RTGS	44.6	(38.3)
Others		10.5	(9.0)
Total	--	116.5	(100.0)

Source: "Payment and Settlement Statistics," BOJ

Impact on Liquidity by RTGS-XG Project

In the new environment after RTGS-XG project, the participants of BOJ-NET faced new challenges in liquidity management. They need to manage the two separate liquidities in both LSF account and RTGS account.

It is a well-known fact that there is a trade-off between liquidity and delay risk. If the liquidity in LSF account is not enough, LSF settlement does not proceed smoothly and settlement delay comes into being. On the other hand, if the liquidity in LSF account is more than enough, the efficiency in liquidity usage comes down, which undermines the liquidity-saving effects of newly-introduced LSF mode.

Before RTGS-XG, the participants did not need to worry about splitting the liquidity into two accounts, since only a single account was admitted for each participant. Therefore, RTGS-XG brought a complete new challenge for the participants, which was the first-time experience for them.

Liquidity-Saving Effects of RTGS-XG

According to the BOJ's estimate, the liquidity required for settlement, calculated as the total of each participant's daily peak debit position, was \14 trillion before Phase 1. After Phase 1, the requisite liquidity, calculated as the total of each participant's daily peak LSF account balance value, was reduced to \12 trillion (BOJ, 2010). The difference between the two figures, i.e., \2 trillion or 15% of the total required liquidity, was regarded as the outcome of the liquidity-saving effects. After Phase 2, the effect showed a small decrease and fell below \ 2 trillion.

By way of comparison, the Bank of England (BOE) indicates the liquidity-saving effect from the introduction of the LSM to CHAPS to be around 20% compared to a basic RTGS system (Davey & Gray, 2014). Moreover, when the Bank of Korea's BOK-Wire+ was launched in 2009, the liquidity-saving effect within a month of its launch was approximately 20%, of previous liquidity requirements in the BOK-Wire RTGS system (Norman, 2010).

The reason BOJ-NET's liquidity-saving effect was smaller than that of CHAPS can be partially attributed to the number of direct participants. BOJ-NET has around 500 direct participants and CHAPS has only about 20. It is a well-known fact that the smaller the participants become, the larger the number of payments available to offset. Therefore, a concentrated membership brings about a higher liquidity-saving effect.

Another reason was the difference of settlement mechanisms between the two systems. The Liquidity-Saving Feature (LSF) of CHAPS is more sophisticated than that of BOJ-NET. And more important factor should be the market conditions when RTGS-XG was introduced; more concretely, under the super-easy monetary policy of BOJ (to be discussed in detail).

Average Settlement Time Moved Forward

Phase 2 also moved forward BOJ-NET's average settlement time, which is calculated as the weighted average of the settlement time of each payment by value. According to the BOJ's estimate, the average settlement time shifted from around 12:00 p.m. to approximately 11:00 a.m. after Phase 2. This means the average settlement time was brought forward about one hour.

Moving the average settlement time forward was for a fact mainly the result of shifting the large-value Zengin payments from the end-of-day settlement with netting to the intraday settlement with offsetting. This time-shift provides more evidence of the reduction of settlement risk in the overall Japanese payment market.

Utilization Ratio of Offsetting Mechanisms

The settlement data after Phase 2 shows that bilateral and multilateral offsetting account only for approximately 20% of total settlements in the LSF account. This means the remaining 80% are conducted by means of single gross settlement which is identical to RTGS function and has no netting effect.

This figure shows that participants tend to place ample liquidity in their LSF accounts early in the day, and that there is sufficient (or more than enough) liquidity to settle the large portion of payments on a gross basis without the necessity of offsetting mechanisms

Average Waiting Time

The ample liquidity in LSF account is also confirmed by the "average waiting time", which is the average length of time a payment is on hold in the waiting queue.

The average waiting time after Phase 2 is 59 seconds for large-value Zengin payments, 3 minutes and 12 seconds for money market payments, and 4 minutes and 59 seconds for FXYCS payments (BOJ, 2013). The waiting times are substantially shorter than with CHAPS, where payments are in the queue for approximately seven and a half minutes on average (Davey & Gray, 2014). Bank of Japan seems to be content to these time lengths, by stating that "the settlements are accomplished within a short time" (BOJ, 2013).

Liquidity Placed in the LSF Account for Settlement and Idle Liquidity

Aggregate amount of liquidity placed in the LSF account for settlement by all participants was \ 15 trillion before Phase 2. This amount increased to \ 23 trillion after Phase 2, an increase of more than 50%. The additional \ 8 trillion of liquidity was almost equal to the value of large-value Zengin payments (\ 8.3 trillion), which were added to the LSF settlement at Phase 2.

The total balance all participants held at BOJ, which was made of required reserves and excess reserves, was about \ 27 trillion after Phase 2. This meant that the participants injected to the LSF account around 85% of all the liquidity they had. Before Phase 2, the ratio was just around 55%.

Participants tend to place their surplus liquidity into the LSF account, meaning that they hold far more than the minimum necessary for LSF settlements. Consequently, some "idle liquidity" came into existence, which was the liquidity not used for settlements in LSF account. According to the BOJ's estimate, the idle liquidity was about \ 3 trillion (about 20% of the liquidity injected) before Phase 2. This jumped to about \ 8 trillion (about 35% of the liquidity injected into LSF accounts) after Phase 2 (Tsuchiya, 2013).

Judging from these data, participants must have increased their liquidity input into LSF account by the amount equal to the increase in the settlement value of the day. Contrary to their expectations, however, the required liquidity did not increased as expected and the idle liquidity was boosted significantly. This indicated that Phase 2 enabled to make settlements with far less liquidity than before. In fact, Phase 2 led to an increase in the settlement efficiency. It appears that participants could not recognize or adjust fully to the new circumstance of higher efficiency. The enhanced settlement efficiency was brought about because more payments were being processed using the offsetting mechanism.

This showed that it was possible that participants were not aware of the increased settlement efficiency. Consequently, participants increased LSF account liquidity mechanically to conform with the increase in settlement value resulting from the consolidation of large-value Zengin payments. Another possibility is that participants sought to hold idle liquidity as a precaution. In other words, participants wanted to maintain a liquidity cushion in case there were unexpected payment needs immediately after the major role-sharing change between the payment systems.

The implication of the fact is that there could be some room to reduce the liquidity put into the LSF accounts. This adjustment would occur when participants fully notice and become accustomed to the higher level of settlement efficiency in LSF mode.

LSF Account Turnover Ratio

The turnover ratio can be regarded as a useful measure of liquidity efficiency in a payment system. It is the ratio of the total value of payments made in the system to the total value of liquidity that is used for settlement. When the ratio is high, liquidity is being circulated at great speed from one account to another in the system, and a large volume of payments are being settled with a fairly small amount of liquidity. Such a payment system can pride itself on excellent liquidity efficiency. When the ratio is low, on the other hand, it suggests the velocity of liquidity circulation in the system is not very high. In this type of payment system, a larger amount of liquidity is necessary for the settlement of a certain volume of payments.

Unfortunately, the turnover ratio of BOJ-NET's LSF account is not particularly high at 4 times before Phase 2. The ratio showed a sharp decline to 2 times after Phase 2, reflecting the surplus liquidity put in the LSF accounts (see Figure 9).

The turnover ratio of CHIPS in the US is around 500-600 times and the ratios of Fedwire and CHATS are about 12 times. Compared with these ratios, the BOJ-NET LSF accounts' 2 times is comparatively low and indicates that there is still room for improvement.

It is noteworthy that the turnover ratio in BOJ-NET differs depending on the category of financial institutions. While securities companies have the lowest ratio of 1 time, the ratio of major commercial

Figure 9. Turnover Ratio and Idle Liquidity in LSF Account

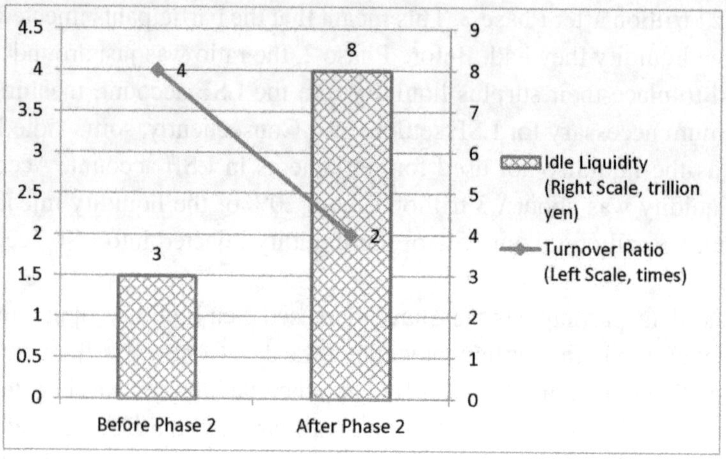

Source: BOJ

banks stands at 3 times, which is higher than the average. On the other hand, trust banks have the highest ratio of 9 times. Trust banks, which are large providers of funds to the money market, tend to receive the large amount of refund early in the morning. Therefore, they can make smooth settlements with the refund and large amount of liquidity input to the LSF account is not necessary. This indicates that not only the input liquidity amount but the financial trades they made are also the determining factor of turnover ratio.

The low turnover ratio can partly be attributed to the new BOJ-NET algorithm, which uses only the bilateral offsetting as a main function. However, the weighty reason is that participants are placing excessive liquidity into their LSF accounts. This is indicated by the evidence of the huge amount of idle liquidity not being used for settlement. In fact, the turnover ratio declined from 4 times to 2 times after Phase 2, which was coincided with the increase of idle liquidity from \ 3 trillion to \ 8 trillion around the same time. This suggests the main issue lies on the liquidity management of the participants.

Comparison of Algorithm with CHAPS

Part of the reason for the low turnover ratio could be attributed to the settlement mechanism of new BOJ-NET. In order to bring out the characteristics of BOJ-NET, it might be useful to compare the algorithm of BOJ-NET with that of other system. And CHAPS would be a good target for comparison, because it is the most recent RTGS system with LSM and has a state-of-art functionality (see Table 6).

The first difference is the relationship between RTGS mode and LSM mode. In BOJ-NET, these two modes are operated in a completely separate way as two independent mechanisms throughout the day. In CHAPS, two modes are operated in a single stream of processing, where RTGS mode is switched to LSM mode (matching cycle) every two minutes.

Second difference is the number of accounts the participants hold. In BOJ-NET, the participants should hold two accounts at BOJ, namely, RTGS account and LSF account. In CHAPS, each participant has a single account at BOE. Every settlement of CHAPS is made in these accounts.

Table 6. Comparisons between BOJ-NET (RTGS-XG) and CHAPS

Evaluation Criteria	*BOJ-NET (RTGS-XG)*	*CHAPS*
Relationship between RTGS mode and LSM mode	Completely separated in two independent mechanisms	Operated in a single stream of processing. Switched from RTGS mode to LSM mode (matching cycle) every two minutes
Number of accounts for participants	Two accounts: RTGS account and LSF account	One account
Usage of two offsetting mechanisms	Bilateral offsetting is utilized continuously throughout the day. Multilateral offsetting runs only four times a day.	Either bilateral or multilateral offsetting is utilized in each matching cycle (every two minutes).
Queue sorting order	Basically, first-in, first-out (FIFO) basis. Participants can change the order of queued payments.	Sorting order is different for each offsetting. 1) From the smallest to the largest payment, 2) From the oldest to the newest payment, 3) From the largest to the smallest payment
Split of liquidity	Liquidity is divided into two accounts.	Liquidity is concentrated in a single account.
Management of liquidity	Participants should manage two liquidities.	Participants manage only one liquidity in a single account.
Turnover Ratio	2 times	12 times

Third point is the usage of two offsetting mechanisms. In BOJ-NET, bilateral offsetting is utilized continuously during the day and multilateral offsetting runs only four times a day. In sum, bilateral offsetting serves as the main functionality for settlement and multilateral offsetting is for the supplementary only in BOJ-NET. In CHAPS, either bilateral or multilateral offsetting is utilized in each matching cycle which takes place every two minutes. This means that CHAPS allocates an important responsibility to multilateral offsetting as well as bilateral offsetting. The limited usage of multilateral offsetting in BOJ-NET appears to have some impact on the low turnover ratio.

Forth difference is queue sorting order. In BOJ-NET, queued payments are always sorted simply on first-in, first-out (FIFO) basis, though participants can change the order of payments later. In CHAPS, sorting is different for each offsetting. In some offsetting, sorting is made from the smallest to the largest payment, and in other offsetting, sorting order is from the oldest to the newest payment. It is a quite new concept to change the queue sorting order each time, which could lead to an increased efficiency and higher turnover ratio.

Fifth issue is the management of liquidity. In BOJ-NET, liquidity is divided into two accounts, i.e., RTGS account and LSF account. Therefore, participants should manage two liquidities. On the other hand, liquidity is concentrated in a single account in CHAPS. It is only necessary to manage a single liquidity for the CHAPS participants.

It is undeniable that these differences in system design contribute to some extent to the wide gap of turnover ratio between the two systems: 2 times for BOJ-NET and 12 times for CHAPS.

Reason for Ample Liquidity Placed in LSF Account

As mentioned above, settlements are made smoothly at BOJ-NET in the post-Phase 2 period. There is no doubt that the major reason for the situation is the abundant liquidity being injected into the LSF account by the participants.

The reasoning is supported by the following facts: i) the average waiting time of payment is very short, ii) 80% of settlements are conducted via single gross settlement without offsetting mechanisms, iii) the level of idle liquidity is very high, and iv) the turnover ratio is rather low.

Then, why do participants put such an abundant liquidity to LSF account? Several reasons can be named as follows.

Low Liquidity Cost

First, the LSF was introduced when the BOJ's monetary policy was extremely loose, and accompanied by an exceptionally low interest rate. The interbank overnight call loan rate has been below 0.1% and shows a zero-interest-rate environment. This means the liquidity cost for the bank was almost zero. In addition, BOJ provided ample liquidity to the market, resulting in huge "excess reserves," that is, bank

Figure 10. Money Market Rate and Excess Reserves

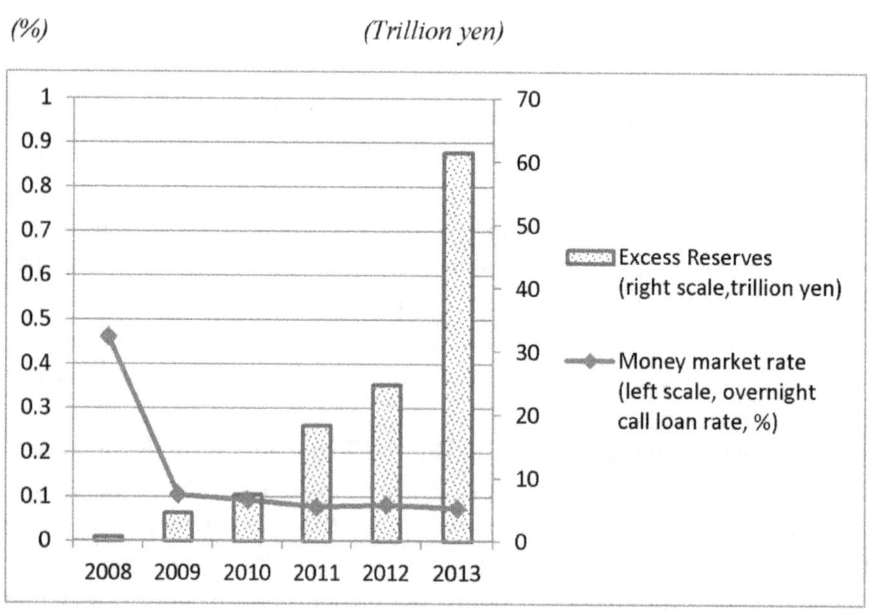

Source: BOJ

reserves exceeding those required (see Figure 10). In sum, the ultra-easy monetary policy enabled participants to hold abundant liquidity at an extremely low cost.

Usually, liquidity is costly for banks and they want to minimize its use. However, who cares about economizing on liquidity usage when the cost for the liquidity is negligibly minimal? Therefore, one can argue that the prevailing monetary policy is the primary reason for participants injecting plentiful liquidity into the LSF account.

Market Practices

Second, market practices also seemed to have an impact on the large volume of liquidity in the LSF account. At the same time as RTGS-XG project, Japan's payment industry stipulated the industry guidelines for payment timing according to payment type (see Table 7).

For money market transactions (i.e., federal funds transactions), borrowers are required to make repayment as soon as possible after 9:00 a.m. and no later than 10:00 a.m. on the repayment date. This is referred to as the "repayment-first rule."

Market participants made another rule called the "throughput guidelines" for FXYCS payments. These guidelines require that participants send and settle 65% of the daily volume, and 55% of the daily value of FXYCS payments by 11:00 a.m.

With respect to large-value Zengin payments, the industry instituted the "one-hour rule." This requires each bank to maintain an adequate balance on its LSF account so that interbank settlement is completed in a short time, and the transmission from the sender's bank branch to the receiver's bank branch can be completed in less than one hour.

If a bank breaks one of these rules, its reputation in the Japanese market would be damaged. As credibility is most important in the banking industry, banks put great effort into ensuring compliance with aforementioned industry guidelines. This can be regarded as another reason why banks inject ample liquidity into their LSF accounts.

Third, the precautionary motive also plays a certain role in maintaining a sizeable LSF account balance. With respect to large-value Zengin payments, banks tend to make earlier settlements to offer satisfying service to the sending and receiving remittance customer. It is, however, quite difficult to ascertain the

Table 7. Market guidelines for each type of payment

Type of payment	*Rule*	*Details*
Money market payments	Repayment-first rule	Money market borrowers are required to repay the borrowed funds as soon as possible after 9:00 a.m., and no later than 10:00 a.m. on the repayment date.
FXYCS payments	Throughput guidelines	Banks are required to send and settle 65% of the daily volume, and 55% of the daily value by 11:00 a.m.
Large-value Zengin payments	One-hour rule	Banks are required to maintain an adequate balance on their LSF accounts so that the interbank settlement is completed, and the payment message reaches the receiver's branch in less than one hour.

Precautionary Motive

precise amount required for same-day customer payments. And there is some uncertainty about total customer payment flows of the day. Thus, banks try to maintain a certain liquidity cushion for precautionary demand. There is a trade-off between liquidity savings and payment delay. Since liquidity costs are extraordinarily low, banks give priority to minimize the delay for their customers.

Due to the combination of these three factors, banks have tended to have more-than-adequate liquidity in their LSF accounts, with some liquidity not used for settlements. In other words, there is some room for the participants to reduce their LSF account liquidity.

CONCLUSION

Merits of RTGS-XG

The RTGS-XG of BOJ-NET had several merits.

Delivering Intraday-Finality

First, the RTGS-XG delivered "intraday-finality" to all large-value payments in Japan. Before the RTGS-XG project, the large-value payments that were settled in the FXYCS and Zengin systems could achieve settlement finality only at the end of the day. By adding the LSF and consolidating all large-value payments into BOJ-NET, all such payments can see settlement finality with near real-time during the day.

Reducing Liquidity Cost

Second, the RTGS-XG succeeded in reducing participants' liquidity costs. By utilizing the LSF mechanism, a participant can offset outgoing payments with incoming payments from other banks, and make settlements with less liquidity, i.e. the net difference between the payments.

Achieving Compliance with Global Standard

Third, the RTGS-XG brought compliance with the global standard. The Core Principles for Systemically Important Payment Systems ("The Core Principles") has been the global standard for payment systems since 2001. The Core Principles require "intraday finality" as a best practice for all large-value payment systems in countries with large volumes of high-value payments and sophisticated financial markets. This condition is, beyond doubt, applicable to the Japanese market.

With the RTGS-XG project, all large-value payments are consolidated into BOJ-NET and settled with intraday finality. This means that the introduction of RTGS-XG and the reorganization of payment systems in Japan brought conformity with The Core Principles. It was another RTGS-XG achievement to meet the global standard successfully.

Impact of New Functionality and Settlement Behavior of Banks

The RTGS-XG was intended to improve both the safety and efficiency of settlements. Both objectives are close to being accomplished with one exception. Turnover efficiency, or the efficiency of RTGS-XG liquidity, is not high enough because participants place more liquidity into their LSF accounts than the minimum required. Japanese banks tend to do so because the liquidity is easily obtainable with an exceptionally low cost. They hold the liquidity for precautionary reasons in addition to the liquidity required for transactions. This behavior has resulted in a lowering of settlement efficiency in the RTGS-XG.

Thus, it can be concluded that the impact of introducing new functionality in a payment system should not be discussed in isolation. On the contrary, the feedback effect of the participants' settlement behavior and liquidity management must also be taken into account. Finally, we can draw the conclusion that the new functionality's liquidity level or the magnitude of the liquidity-saving effect can be determined by the cross-interaction between the settlement mechanism and the participants' liquidity management behavior.

Toward Further Improvement of Liquidity Saving

It is not always true that the required liquidity for a payment system is constant. In the case of BOJ-NET, the LSF accounts' liquidity level has the potential to be decreased with respect to precautionary demand. The reason is twofold.

Normalization of Monetary Policy

First, BOJ's monetary policy is likely to be normalized in years to come, resulting in a higher market interest rate, and a decrease in the supply of banks' excess reserves. This would also entail a significant increase in liquidity costs for banks. In that case, they would be more likely to try to reduce the liquidity holding in the LSF accounts.

Acquiring Settlement Pattern

Second, as time progresses, participants are likely to become accustomed to the daily and monthly settlement pattern in the LSF accounts. Once the necessary liquidity level is fully recognized, the banks are likely to control the volume of liquidity injected more carefully. Such careful control would reduce the liquidity held for a precautionary motive and increase the liquidity saving.

Toward Improvements in Turnover Ratio

If these two conditions are met, the turnover ratio of LSF accounts would rise substantially. It would contribute significantly to achieving the desired objective of the RTGS-XG project, which is to make a number of settlements with intra-day finality and with less liquidity. The interim target would be the turnover ratios of Fedwire and CHATS, which are about 12 times. Then, the final objective would be that of CHIPS (500-600 times).

FUTURE RESEARCH DIRECTIONS

The payment system evolution is not over yet. As the most recent RTGS system with LSM, CHAPS has showed another more sophisticated option for realizing the liquidity saving mechanism. Therefore, an avenue for further study could be to analyze the liquidity-saving effect of each LSM type, and in particular using a simulation model populated with actual payment-system settlement data.

REFERENCES

Arjani, N. & McVanel, D. (2006, March). *A Premier on Canada's Large Value Transfer System.*

Real-Time Gross Settlement Systems Report. (1997, March). Bank for International Settlements.

Payment and Settlement Systems Report 2009. (2010). Bank of Japan.

Payment and Settlement Systems Report 2012-2013. (2013). Bank of Japan.

Bech, M., & Hobijn, B. (2007, September). Technology Diffusion within Central Banking: The Case of Real-Time Gross Settlement. *International Journal of Central Banking, 3, 3.*

BOJ-NET Funds Transfers after the Implementation of Phase 1 of the Next Generation RTGS Project. (2009, July). *Bank of Japan Review.*

Davey, N., & Gray, D. (2014). How Has the Liquidity Saving Mechanism Reduced Banks' Intraday Liquidity Costs in CHAPS? *Bank of England Quarterly Bulletin, 2014*, Q2.

Denbee, E., & McLafferty, J. (2013). Liquidity Saving in CHAPS: A Simulation Study. In B. Alexandrova-Kabadjova et al. (Eds.), *Simulation in Computational Finance and Economics: Tools and Emerging Applications* (pp. 120–142). IGI Global.

Dent, A., & Dison, W. (2012). The Bank of England's Real-Time Gross Settlement Infrastructure. *Bank of England Quarterly Bulletin, 2013*, Q3.

Martin, A., & McAndrew, J. (2008, September). An Economic Analysis of Liquidity-Saving Mechanisms: *FRBNY. Economic Policy Review.*

Nakajima, M. (2008). Global Trends of Payment Systems and the Next-Generation RTGS Project in Japan. In T. Kubota (Ed.), Cyberlaw for Global E-Business: Finance, Payment, and Dispute Resolution (pp. 109–127). Hershey, PA: IGI Global. doi:10.4018/978-1-59904-828-4.ch006

Nakajima, M. (2011). Payment System Technologies and Functions: Innovations and Development. Hershey, PA: IGI Global. doi:10.4018/978-1-61520-645-2

Nakajima, M. (2012, February-March). *The Evolution of Payment Systems: The European Financial Review* (pp. 8–9).

Nakajima, M., & Shukuwa, J. (2013). *All about Payment Systems* (3rd ed.) [in Japanese]. Tokyo, Japan: Toyo Keizai Inc.

Norman, B. (2010, *May*). Liquidity Saving in Real-Time Gross Settlement Systems — An Overview. *Bank of England Financial Stability Paper No.7.*

Oleschak, R., & Nellen, T. (2013, *October*). Does SIC need a heart pacemaker? *Swiss National Bank Working Papers.*

Payment Systems Worldwide: A Snapshot. (2011World Bank - Financial Infrastructure Series.

RTGS^{plus}: the Bundesbank's New System for Individual Payments. (2000, June). *Deutsche Bundesbank Monthly Report.*

Tsuchiya, S. (2013). The Effects of Settlement Methods on Liquidity Needs: Empirical Study based on Funds Transfer Data: *Bank of Japan Working Paper Series, No.13-E-2*

KEY TERMS AND DEFINITIONS

DNS (Deferred Net Settlement) System: A payment system that effects the settlement of obligations between or among system participants on a net basis at some later time. Typically, net settlement is made at the end of the day.

Idle Liquidity: Liquidity (account balance) that was not used for settlement.

LSM (Liquidity Saving Mechanism): A mechanism in a payment system by which outgoing and incoming payments are matched and settled simultaneously, either bilaterally or multilaterally. This mechanism allows participants to send payments on the receipt of payments from others, which brings forth the netting effect.

Offsetting: A simultaneous processing of several payments on a gross basis. This is often used in an LSM. Typically, bilateral offsetting and multilateral offsetting are used in combination.

RTGS (Real-Time Gross Settlement) System: A payment system that effects the real-time settlement of obligations between participants individually on a real-time basis with gross value (without netting).

RTGS System with LSM: A payment system which has both the RTGS and LSM functions for the settlement of payments.

RTGS-XG (Next-Generation Real-Time Gross Settlement) Project: A project to enhance the functionality of BOJ-NET. The project had two main objectives. One was to introduce the Liquidity-Saving Feature to BOJ-NET. The second was to consolidate all large-value payments to BOJ-NET. This was implemented by BOJ between 2008 and 2011.

Turnover Ratio: A ratio of the total value of payments made in a payment system to the total value of liquidity that is used for settlement.

Chapter 13
CCPs: A Challenge for Practical Oversight

Anna Pliquett
Deutsche Bundesbank, Germany

ABSTRACT

As a first step a short summary of the historical development of CCPs is provided, followed by an outline of the concept and core functions CCPs. Then an illustration of the main risk management safeguards of CCPs is provided. This includes an excursus regarding the hier-archical structure of clearing and regarding procyclical considerations with respect to CCPs. The outline of CCP counterparty risk management is complemented by a brief overview of other risks, including liquidity risk, legal risk, and operational risk. The consideration of the risk profile of CCPs is concluded with some insight into the main factors determining the oversight of CCPs' governance. The full picture of CCPs from an oversight perspective is given by placing the CCPs in the clearing process and the outlining the resulting challenges for regulatory oversight. The chapter concludes with a description of the manifold layers of today's oversight of CCPs.

INTRODUCTION

For a long time, central counterparties (CCPs) have been an essential element of the financial market infrastructure and the post-trade processing of financial market transactions[1]. With their growing role in the financial markets CCPs became subject of regulatory debates of increasing intensity. In particular after the financial crisis of 2007, with heightened efforts to guarantee systemic financial stability, CCPs, arguably ensuring operational efficiency and counterparty discipline, have become a focal point of the reform of financial market infrastructure.

International standards now require the use of CCPs also in traditionally bilaterally cleared OTC derivatives markets. Expectations toward CCPs are rather high. Earlier CCPs were praised as an example of private market innovation and self-regulation that can be effective for achieving public policy goals of safety, soundness and broader financial stability (Kroszner, 1999, p. 30; Moskow, 2006, p. 37). Now

DOI: 10.4018/978-1-4666-8745-5.ch013

international standards foresee an extensive range of minimum requirements to ensure their safety[2]. In some cases CCPs are even expected to support the management of systemic risk (Bank of England, 2013, p. 2).

In spite of the high expectations, current regulatory developments are ambiguous about the role of CCPs. They do favor CCPs as a solution for major weaknesses in the financial system and worry about their failure constituting a "financial Armageddon" (Green, Jenning-Mares, & Smith, 2013, p. 1). Because all transactions are concentrated in one institution, CCPs can be seen as source of systemic vulnerabilities representing the biggest too-big-to-fail institutions the financial system has ever contained.

Admittedly, CCPs have had a track record of low failure rate in comparison to other financial institutions like banks, financial service providers or insurance companies[3]. Nevertheless, the smooth functioning and financial soundness of CCPs are essential for financial stability and cannot be taken for granted (Bernanke, 2011, p. 1). CCPs have their own vulnerabilities and the importance of these for the entire financial system has only increased with the recently strengthened role of CCPs in the financial architecture.

Given their central role in the financial architecture, it is vital that regulatory oversight of CCPs rests on a clear understanding of the functioning of these institutions, the various mechanisms how they are connected to the financial system, the sources of fragility and the factors influencing a CCP's ability to withstand market disruptions. With this in mind, the primary purpose of this paper is to illustrate the workings of CCPs and the main and recently evolving challenges for their practical oversight[4]. It is intended to show that a mechanical approach to CCP oversight needs to be avoided. While relevant quantitative indicators for regulatory oversight purposes can be identified, the varying nature of CCPs and their vulnerabilities makes it necessary to adopt a CCP-specific and holistic oversight approach. In order to conduct effective regulatory oversight of a CCP an in-depth knowledge of the individual CCP, a clear operationalization of the individual regulatory mandate and the pragmatic application of the relevant requirements are necessary. This naturally contradicts a uniform, granular approach on an international scale.

This chapter is organized as follows:

The three particular phases of historical evolution of clearing of financial instruments (Moser, 1998, p. 8) - alternating between counterparty discipline and operational efficiency – which led to the prevalence of so called true CCPs are explained. This allows for a succinct demonstration of the basic functions and the main principles of virtually all CCPs today (Kroszner, 2006, p. 38).Then an illustration of the main risk management safeguards of CCPs is provided. The full picture of CCPs from an oversight perspective is given by placing the CCPs in the clearing process and outlining the resulting challenges for regulatory oversight. The chapter concludes with a description of the manifold layers of today's regulatory oversight of CCPs.

WHAT DOES THE HISTORICAL EVOLUTION OF CCPS REVEAL ABOUT THEIR FUNCTIONING?

The First Steps: Counterparty Discipline by Restricted Membership and Margining

Originally, only few selected counterparties were allowed trading on an exchange. Membership of an exchange served to provide some certification of the trustworthiness of counterparties. Since membership in an exchange was valuable, its possible loss provided some incentives for the fulfillment of obligations even in case of adverse developments (Bliss & Papathanassiou, 2006, p. 11). The first step of innovation aimed at more discipline in the marketplace: the counterparties' right to call for margin (posting of collateral) was established[5]. In case a counterparty with accumulating losses on its position would abstain from fulfilling its obligations, the other counterparty could reimburse oneself by seizing the collateral posted as margin. Hence, the introduction of a margining regime - as long as the accumulated losses did not exceed the value of margin collateral posted - reduced the incentives for non-performance and effectively shielded performing counterparties from its effects. The right to call margin was further enforced by the establishment of the norm - also recognized by the courts - that failure to post margin would be considered a default on the counterparties' contracts. This feature continues to be the most important disciplinary measure of modern CCPs as well.

In addition, exchange rules introduced measures requiring from counterparties a periodic demonstration of continued capacity to pay. It was recognized that the possibility of accumulating substantial losses by counterparties increases with the time remaining in the term of a financial transaction. A failing counterpart would have incentives to gamble for resurrection, thereby further increasing the size of the possible losses (Moser, 1998, p. 9). However, when positions are regularly re-evaluated and losses collected from the counterparties, loss accumulation for individual counterparties could be curtailed and the build-up of potential losses could be limited. This way the magnitude of the final settlement payments (Rutz, 1989, p. 357) and the uncollateralized portion of the price change realized at the next re-evaluation would be reduced. In addition, this regular collection and redistribution of losses and gains not only required the counterparties to demonstrate their financial ability to perform, but also contributed to an early detection of non-performance. In case of derivatives, this regular re-evaluation would take the form of daily settlement based on the end-of-day prices. This would set the market value and currently payable amounts between counterparties to zero, while the contracts remained outstanding (Moser, 1998, p. 6). This daily re-evaluation could occur by re-novating contracts each day on the basis of the new settlement price (settled-to-market) with losses collected in cash and passed through to counterparts incurring profits (futures-style margining, variation margin). In case of securities transactions or other derivatives, transactions might remain open at trade price but losses arising from the marking-to-market would be collected as margin collateral. Profits would be at the most credited toward the margin requirement of the counterparty incurring the profit but not paid out in cash (premium-style margining) (EACH, 2001, p. 3). This backward looking component of margining covering current exposure is still in place in today's CCPs in both forms.

The historically restricted feature of participation in the trading on an exchange remained an important characteristic of modern CCPs as well (Bliss & Papathanassiou, 2006, p. 13). Requirements relating to participating counterparts' (i.e. clearing members[6]) financial health (solvency), to their ability to meet margin calls on a short notice (liquidity) and their operational reliability are necessary for a CCP to be able to manage its risks effectively (Rehlon & Nixon, 2013, p. 6). CCPs typically retain a legal relationship only with their clearing members usually on a principal to principal basis (Wendt, 2006, p. 3, CCP12, 2009, p. 1). The guarantees provided by CCPs extend therefore only to clearing members and encompass only the positions of those members[7]. Market participants can decide not to shoulder the considerable technological and operational investments necessary for participating directly in the processes of the CCP or they might not satisfy the membership criteria of a CCP. Such market participants can still centrally clear as clients attached to a clearing member.

Client clearing is not new in the world of exchange-traded products, where it is often referred to as indirect clearing or in the terminology of exchange-traded derivatives as non-member clearing. Non-members are trading participants of an exchange which are not clearing members at the CCP at the same time. Such trading participants need to connect to trading participants acting also clearing members of the CCP serving the exchange. For this purpose, non-member trading participants have to give up their trades to their chosen clearing member.

Clearing members are then entrusted with administering the funds and transactions of such clients on the clients' behalf and expected to guarantee the performance of their client's trades toward the CCP and assume responsibilities for handling a non-performance of clients[8]. This pyramid structure offers numerous advantages of efficiency for risk monitoring and mitigation (Bernanke, 1990, p. 142) and accordingly, clearing members with significant client business play an important function for a CCP. To protect themselves and the CCP against client defaults, members are generally required to set a minimum level of margin for their clients according to rules set down by the CCP. One of two methods is usually used to determine the proportion of margin passed on to the CCP. Under net margining, clearing members are permitted to net together the long and short positions of different clients and post margin on aggregate net positions. Under gross margining, members are required to deposit margin with the CCP sufficient to cover the gross positions of their clients. In either case, the members must collect the same minimum amount of margin from their clients. The main difference lies in the proportion of client margin that they are required to pass through to the CCP.

From the CCP's perspective, gross margining has the advantage that if a clearing member defaults as a result of a client default, then the entire client margin that the member has passed through to the CCP is available to protect the CCP against loss. Gross margining systems, however, reduce the earnings of clearing members on client margin funds, and it is sometimes argued that this makes clearing members more vulnerable to bankruptcy, and more likely to raise clearing fees. In practice, net margining systems predominate. At the end, clearing members transform diverse credit risks from a wide array of clients to the lower credit risk of the member (usually a bank) towards the CCP and shield the CCP from client defaults. The robustness of the overall central clearing function depends, therefore, also on the financial health and the ability of clearing members to provide efficient client clearing.

All told, some of the core CCP functions and thus the central clearing function[9] is carried out not only at the level of the CCP, but also at further levels of the clearing chain by clearing members and their clients potentially acting as clearing providers to further clients, as well. As a result, the clearing chain is complex and characterized by many levels of intermediation (Bliss & Papathanassiou, 2006, p. 29). CCPs are integrated in the network of market participants in a hierarchical arrangement of a multi-tiered structure, which involves possibly several intermediaries up to the end investor.

Due to introduction of the clearing obligation for OTC derivatives, however, this traditional client-clearing member-CCP relationship is currently undergoing significant changes. Additionally driven by the regulatory objective of greater protection of customer assets, the use of individual segregation solutions for clients at CCP level is increasing. The evolving design of the central clearing pyramid has a significant impact on the processes and risk profile of a CCP and its linkage with other parts of the financial system. Important factors in this regard are the level of client margining (Knott & Mills, 2002, p. 163), the types and number of accounts maintained by a CCP and its clearing members, and the level of aggregation and segregation of positions, margin requirements and collateral[10]. The structure of client clearing has also a great influence on the design of the process for handling non-performance, especially concerning the liquidation or transfer of clients' accounts (portability).

The Second Step: Efficiency by Netting

The second innovative step aimed at reducing the high costs of protection from nonperformance losses (margining): the exchange or rather its clearinghouse undertook the calculation of counterparties' net obligations to post margins and to settle contracts. The aggregation of the related transactions of counterparties (by identifying offsetting commitments and replacement of the obligations of the original transactions with net obligations) reduced the size of open positions, the amount of necessary collateral and thus the cost of maintaining open positions.

It has to be conceded, that depending on the historical development of a marketplace, in some cases the task of netting is at present taken up by securities settlement systems instead of CCPs (London School of Economics, 2005, p. 5, Hasenpusch, 2009, Ch. 2.1.3.2). Such settlement netting[11] concerns the netting of delivery instructions for the transfer of cash, securities or another underlying. It contributes significantly to the efficiency and cost reduction of the settlement process as it results in a single position for a specific security to be delivered or received, and a single cash payment to be made for each participating counterpart (Ripatti, 2004, p. 11). Settlement netting leaves the offsetting positions non-extinguished, so that the original individual obligations are neither satisfied nor discharged (Hasenpusch, 2009, Ch. 2.1.2.2.1.2.). The division of tasks between market infrastructures and the de facto involvement of a CCP in securities settlement is an important determinant for the CCPs payment and delivery obligations.

In the case of derivatives, the historical development of fungible and thus easily substitutable contracts by the derivatives exchange allowed for the possibility to settle contracts not only by delivery, but also by payment of differences in value. The provision of such offsets or setoffs is considered as one of the main functions of CCPs. In case of some financial instruments, it is crucial for the existence and functioning of highly liquid markets (Edwards, 1983, p. 386), as it enables market participants to freely enter and leave the market (Bliss & Papathanassiou, 2006, p. 4). The rules of most derivatives CCPs typically provide for the automatic netting and cancellation of offsetting transactions, thereby reducing all outstanding residuals to a single debit/credit between the CCP and each participant (Bliss & Steigerwald, 2006, p. 26). New obligations of alike transactions were incorporated into the running total (either reducing or increasing it).

There is a legal risk that in the event of a counterpart's bankruptcy the multilateral netting arrangement between the clearinghouse and its members would not be upheld under the national law. In order to mitigate this risk, many jurisdictions have afforded CCPs a special legislative protection to ensure that their netting is valid (BIS, 1997, p. 19). Also current legislations take into account the importance of the domestic and supra-national insolvency protection of CCPs (EACH, 2001, p. 10). Since the legal concepts and terminology for netting vary across jurisdictions, the enforceability of all netting provisions has to be supported by legal opinions (EACH, 2001, p. 10).

For a modern CCP the level and legal enforceability of netting is an important factor for the actual financial risk faced by it (Rehlon & Nixon, 2013, p. 4). Netting benefits have an impact on clearing members, too. In particular they determine the liquidity needs arising from their contractual obligations and the size of possible liquidity demands on them in stressed market conditions. Furthermore, the reduction of individual contract obligations is affecting market participants' books and balance sheets. To the extent, that national legislation limits the trading volume of a given participant to a certain percentage of its balance sheet or capital, the extent of position taking and leverage for such participants could depend on the amount of netting provided by the CCP (Ripatti, 2004, p. 19).

The Third Final Step: A True CCP with Novation, Centralization of Margining and Loss Mutualisation

The third evolutional step increased both, discipline and efficiency in the marketplace, and transformed the clearinghouse into a central counterparty (CCP): the clearinghouse was interposed to each side of the cleared transactions between counterparties buying and selling, thereby taking the buy side of every transaction to sell and the sell side to every transaction to buy. The clearinghouse acting in an agency role was replaced by a central, synthetic trading counterparty acting in a substituted principal role (Bliss & Steigerwald, 2006, p. 24; Knott & Mills, 2002, p. 162).

This legal process involving the substitution of the original counterparty by a new contractual counterparty is called contract novation. In case of CCPs novation serves as a legal device to facilitate a higher order of netting at the CCP. The moment of novation is determined by the rules of the CCP and the market it serves. In historical times regular novation by the CCP could take a week or longer and still even a few years ago in some markets end-of-day CCP-novation was the norm. Today's automated markets with straight-through processing (e. g. securities or derivatives exchanges) often employ the approach known as open offer. Based on a prior agreement between the CCP and its members, the CCP makes an unconditional offer to enter into pairs of contracts on the terms agreed upon by the members. The clearing members never formally enter into a contract and thus novation is in effect simultaneous. If transactions are conducted off-exchange (e. g. block trades) or the CCP clears OTC products (e. g. repos or OTC-derivatives) novation means the distinct discharge of the contract between the original counterparties as well as its replacement by two new legal relationships. Even in such cases, novation might be a matter of less than 10 seconds (CFTC guidance, issued 26/09/2013).

As a result of each novation – regardless of the applicable approach - CCPs run a matched and market-neutral book: in their normal course of business they enter two offsetting positions and are not exposed to a change in the market value of their trades. In this regard they are fundamentally different from other, risk taking financial institutions. However, in case of a non-performance by a member (member default) the CCP's book becomes unmatched and subject to market risk[12]. Hence, central counterparty novation centralized counterparty risk in the clearinghouses (Bliss & Steigerwald, 2006, p. 25) and left them with a series of contingent exposures to their members. This development made it necessary to centralize at the CCP the risk monitoring and management, the mechanisms for until the bilateral margining, collateral posting, payments and deliveries and the handling of non-performance of members, as well.

Calculation methods concerning the margin requirements developed from the setting of fixed margins for each type of contract to complex analyses of the member's entire portfolio with a CCP. CCPs preserved a great level of discretion concerning the methodology used to calculate potential future exposures, so that methodologies today vary greatly among CCPs. Differences result on the one hand from the specific risks inherent to the product types constituting the positions managed and processed by a CCP. On the other hand differences arise also from a CCP's assumed ability to replace the positions upon the default of a member. This is in turn is determined by the time required for the process of replacing a defaulting members transactions, and the liquidity and size of the market. Since the exact loss potential for a CCP depends also on the specific terms of the contract with its members, the margin methodology has to reflect also transaction terms and specifications correctly or at least conservatively.

In addition, the actual extent of the protection level provided by the margining regime to a CCP is greatly affected by the type, price stability and liquidity of the assets accepted as margin collateral. In case of non-cash assets or cash in foreign currency an unchanged position can become under-margined (member perspective) or under-protected (CCP perspective) solely due to changes in the value of such collateral. In the situation of non-performance the realized proceeds from the liquidation of the seized collateral would be lower than assumed. The relevant collateral value assigned to securities collateral has therefore to take into account not only as current market values as possible, but also the potential for the market value of the security posted as margin collateral to decline (haircuts).

Similar to the underlying principle of the variation margining regime, the principle of regularity and timeliness is of paramount importance also for the margining process for potential future exposures of a modern CCP. Intraday, possibly real-time margining can anticipate an excessive build-up of variation margin payments during the day and reduce the magnitude of variation margin payments on the next morning. It also enables the CCP to quickly respond to an increased or concentrated member position or to limit margin erosion due to falling collateral values. The design of the intraday margining (thresholds and frequency) should be in line with the risk appetite of the CCP, since it has a significant influence on its risk exposure. The intraday margining process places high demands not only on the processes of the CCP, but also on the clearing members with additional costs due to liquidity need, collateral management and back office processing (Wendt, 2006, p. 2).

In summary, modern CCPs need to monitor member positions virtually continuously in order to evaluate risks accurately. This allows CCPs to be able to enforce margin calls under all market conditions and at a speed appropriate for the asset class (Deutsche Börse Group, 2014, p. 19). This way CCPs can adjust their margin requirement in response to additional trading activity of the members. Main determinants of an effective margining process, therefore, are

- the frequency of re-evaluation of member positions and margin requirements using the most realistic and reliable market prices,
- the effective control of members margin collateral against the exposure calculated,
- the speed of adjustments and coordination with the members resulting either in a reduction of the risk exposure or in the collection of increased margin requirements,
- the processing of new collateral, and
- the accuracy and frequency of evaluating collateral value and of prudent collateral haircuts.

Risk exposures for a CCP are much larger and more difficult to manage in the derivatives market than in the securities market (spot), as derivative transactions give rise to longer exposures and need more market sensitive risk management procedures (Bliss & Papathanassiou, 2006, p. 2). The repo market comes somewhere between the two, with durations that are shorter than on the derivatives market but longer than on the spot market (Riksbank, 2002, p. 48). As for a CCP clearing OTC-derivatives, these contracts are often more complex and reliable prices are less clearly observable, so that they require the use of more complex pricing models, which may increase model risk for the CCP. Also, any default procedures implemented by the CCP for OTC contracts must accommodate the relative illiquidity of the instruments being cleared (ECB, 2010, p. 108).

Due to the imposition of a central counterparty in all transactions the handling of non-performance was changed radically, as well. Non-performance or default is synonymous with a counterpart's permanent inability to meet future, deferred payments resulting from its set of transactions. With the CCP in the middle, the non-performance of a counterpart should not have any effect on the CCP's obligations to other performing counterparts, i. e. to deliver cash or securities or fulfill obligations resulting from a derivative position (Wendt, 2006, p. 4). In such situations the CCP's originally matched position would become unbalanced and the CCP would seek to return to a matched book of contracts. To this end, the CCP would have to enter into replacement transactions to secure the necessary security or money and to reestablish or replace the original trade to close its now one-sided derivative position (Bliss & Steigerwald, 2006, p. 25). Losses could incur to the CCP, when, in the meantime, prices and market values change, and the replacement transaction becomes more expensive than the original one. These losses, however, could be covered by the margin collateral posted to the CCP by the non-performing counterparty (Riksbank, 2002, p. 50).

As the clearinghouse providing the CCP service was backed by the members of the exchange as shareholders, a loss mutualisation regime was introduced. In case losses were realized in excess of the posted margin of the defaulters, they were distributed based on previously agreed rules for loss allocation among the clearing members e. g. by buying additional shares in the equity of the clearinghouse. From this point a waterfall of financial resources to be used in the event of clearing member default crystallized. It underwent only minor changes with the development of modern CCPs and remains at the center of their risk management.

The CCP service of the clearinghouse and its loss mutualisation regime reduced the likelihood and the size of potential non-performance losses to be borne by surviving counterparties. It also made the effects of non-performance more predictable and containable thus preventing or mitigating contagion. Until then, such non-performance affected the circle of direct counterparties in an unimpeded way, often resulting in a further default cascade.

As most authors on this subject have emphasized, the main defining characteristics of a CCP are and continue to be netting, novation, and risk management, including loss mutualisation. These core CCP services have to be supported by other activities of the CCP, bringing to markets the benefit of discipline and efficiency (Aigrain, 2013, p. 154): the means for rapid resolution of disputes between counterparties, objectively obtained and independent contract and collateral valuations, the capability of the CCP timely to determine the due payments of all participants and the capability to manage risk exposures, only to name a few.

HOW MANY SAFEGUARDS DO CCPS HAVE?

Understandably, the primary focus of regulatory oversight lies on the financial risk profile of CCPs and their ability to handle non-performance. Conceding that the actual risks incurring a CCP depend on the product types, the specific terms of its contracts with members as well as the scope of services offered, three typical safeguards for controlling counterparty risk (with variations in their specific constitution) were established by CCPs to backstop the guarantee provided by them (Bernanke, 2011, p. 5). Past failures of CCPs have shown that an adequate implementation of the three safeguards is a prerequisite to avoid them. CCP failures were caused mostly due to failure to increase margin requirements in response to greater market volatility, due to lack of position limits and failure to identify and react to a concentration of market risk and exposure at one or few clearing members and due to failure of clearing members to implement adequate margining with respect to their clients. The counterparty risk management measures of CCPs have to be supplemented by measures for liquidity risk management, which is equally important for the robustness of the CCPs.

First Safeguard: Minimize Probability of Default

First, there are safeguards designed to minimize the probability of failure of the members by CCPs restricting access to their services to high quality counterparties. From a regulatory oversight perspective, the degree of restriction on direct access to a CCP and the development of membership is a relevant factor. Membership requirements have an impact on the CCPs ability to muster the necessary resources to handle member defaults. A broad and heterogeneous membership might increase volume but add complexity to the governance and the default management processes of a CCP. Then again, a small concentrated membership might be less cumbersome in this respect but increase concentration risk for the CCP, by pushing counterparty risk towards the members. Thus, there is an inherent tension between the prudential and competitive implications of membership requirements and a trade-off between openness and risk mitigation. The same holds for the implementation of qualitative and quantitative metrics as access criteria, where a trade-off exists between flexibility on the one side and clarity and objectivity on the other side. Thus, benchmarks for regulatory oversight purposes are inherently market specific and regulator dependent (Lazarow, 2011, p. 7).

Second Safeguard: Minimize Loss Given Default

Second, there are safeguards designed to minimize the loss to the CCP if a member should fail, so that the probability of losses resulting from replacement cost risk on the member's cleared positions (sums then owed by a defaulting member to the CCP) exceeding the amount of margin held is very small (in most cases less than 1 percent).

From regulatory oversight perspective, it is not only important that a CCP establishes adequate, statistically robust methodologies and implements back-testing of their performance to ensure that the methodologies measure risk correctly. It is just as important, that a CCP implements adequate procedures and invests into data collection, storage and analysis technologies. For a comprehensive review, regulatory oversight would have to consider also, whether the money settlement and custodial arrangements of the CCP and its members and the trade management processes allow the frequency and speed to reevaluate positions and post collateral required by the (intraday) margining process of the CCP.

The definition of an event constituting member default is subject to an agreement between the CCP and its clearing membership and is fixed in the rulebook of the CCP. This can include non-payment of cash obligations, non-delivery of securities, failure to satisfy margin requirements or the commencement of an insolvency procedure against the member. For the CCP non-payment and non-delivery would be most critical, since the CCP would be stuck in a one-sided way with the corresponding cash payments and delivery obligations to other clearing members. In case a member fails to meet additional margin requirements, the CCP would still be able to meet its obligations, but it would be exposed to unmitigated counterparty risk. The opening of insolvency proceedings is a clear and objective criterion, but might come late in the process and introduce legal restrictions concerning the actions of the CCP during the default management process.

The longer a defaulting member's positions remain open, the larger is the likelihood of potential negative changes in their market value. Thus, it is a key issue for the CCP to speedily close out the defaulting clearing member's positions. This expediency and the possible market impact of a close-out depend on the size of the defaulting member's positions and the liquidity of the markets in which they were held (BIS, 1997, p. 25). Also, the processes necessary to hedge or to transfer the defaulter's positions can require significant human and technical resources.

In this processes CCPs usually draw on the operational and financial assistance of their members. Clearing members are expected to participate in the hedging of the defaulter portfolio by providing trained staff to conclude the necessary transactions and by pricing and bidding for the portfolio of the defaulting member. CCPs are required to regularly test their default management processes; the lessons learned from such fire drills can afford relevant insights also for the regulatory oversight. That said, real financial markets are complex and tightly coupled, and thus prone to act in novel and unpredictable ways. Politics and policy will be also influencing even during crises and are difficult to predict (Pirrong. 2011, p. 25).

The default management process is a key element of a CCP's defenses. However, it is easier to describe than to prove as fit for purpose and overseers need to probe very deeply to ensure that they are adequate (Aigrain, 2013, p. 155). Furthermore, the default management process is dynamic and uncertain. As mentioned above, due to their role resulting from novation CCPs may engage in several actions altering the fundamentals of a transaction that may differ from CCP to CCP. CCPs can also buy or borrow securities for the account of the clearing member to ensure compliance with the settlement obligations of the clearing member. Furthermore, in case of deliveries of securities, CCPs may ask the buyer to accept partial delivery and charge him with the costs if he does not accept. CCPs can even change the delivery obligation of a derivative contract from physical delivery to cash payment in case it is unable to deliver a security pursuant to market conditions. Also, CCPs can restrict the novation of new transactions of the defaulter only to those which would reduce the member's risk position.

Given the complexity associated with the default management process, it is difficult to accurately predict the amount of financial resources that a CCP would need in order to properly manage such an event, especially in times of stress. On the one hand CCPs strive to reduce the uncertainty around a default event and implement clearly defined and transparent rules and procedures including rules concerning measures for hedges and the participation of non-defaulting members in the closing out of the defaulted member's portfolio. On the other hand, CCPs retain certain discretion as regards the timelines to meet their cash and securities obligations following a default. Altogether, the design of the default management process should provide the necessary flexibility to protect the CCP and the non-defaulting members.

Third Safeguard: Loss Mutualisation

Third, there are safeguards designed to cover losses that exceed the value of the defaulting member's resources controlled by the CCP (Ripatti, 2004, p. 23). To this end, the risk mutualisation regime of the CCP spreads those losses over the other members, reducing their impact on any one member (Bliss & Papathanassiou, 2006, p. 3).The final aim is to remove the possibility of contagious disruption to the activities of non-defaulting members. The design and enforcement of the above mentioned default procedures has to ensure that shortfalls are immediately detected and damage is kept to a minimum.

For the calculation of back-up default resources, CCPs develop stress testing methodologies to assess the potential impact of tail risks and risks which may not be captured by the margin model and verify the adequacy of their financial resources. Stress scenarios have to include infrequently incurring tail events such as extreme, but plausible market conditions, historical and hypothetical market scenarios. Stress testing necessitates numerous default assumptions (number and timing of defaults, handling of clients, interdependencies of the defaulting member), as well. Logically, stress scenarios and stress testing methodologies are inherently arbitrary. CCPs possess in this regard even greater discretion than regarding the other modeling techniques applied by them for margining but they are confronted with similarly high standards from a regulatory oversight perspective concerning the processes and governance as for the case of margining.

In contrast to banks, financial resources to be provided to CCPs are directly related to the outcome of stress testing (EACH, 2011, p. 3). Current international standards require CCPs to cover the two largest member default exposures. The financial resources of a CCP should then amount at least to the exposure of those members who the stress testing results identify as producing the first and second largest losses in excess of their margin requirement in the event of their default. The informative value of this quantitative indicator for the oversight or even outsiders is however limited. This is due to the subjectivity of the measure, its inherent limitations and the fact that both the members in question and the size of the exposure are likely to change over time, even daily. A more relevant impact of the requirement of stress testing lies in the improved information basis and awareness at the CCP, which results from the necessary daily processes for monitoring member portfolios and calculating their sensitivity to stressed market factors.

From a process view, CCPs conventionally rely on a "waterfall" of resources to absorb defaults (Pirrong. 2011, p. 21). The default waterfall of a modern CCP consists of the financial resources provided by the defaulting member (margin collateral and default fund contribution), by the CCP (so called "skin in the game"), by non-defaulting members (remaining default fund and replenishments) and other back-up arrangements (e. g. parental guarantees).

In principle, the various elements of the default waterfall can be ordered and segmented in a variety of ways. The order and magnitude in which the different financial resources available to the CCP are drawn down are key in creating appropriate incentives for all parties concerned, namely clearing members and CCP (Rehlon & Nixon, 2013, p. 5). The interposition of a layer consisting of the CCPs own resources in the default waterfall means exposing CCP capital to losses from member defaults. It is considered as one of the strongest incentives for a CCP to control risk, monitor members and choose margin levels prudently (Pirrong, 2011, p. 21). It is argued, that there might be considerable asymmetry between possible fee revenue increases by lowering standards and the potential losses in case of a member default (Deutsche Börse Group, 2014, p. 18).

CCPs can set risk management policies along the continuum of options between pure defaulter pays model and non-defaulter-pay frameworks, too. Defaulter pays models increase margin and the targeted confidence level of margining. This way the defaulter's assets controlled by the CCP are always sufficient to cover potential losses resulting from the default reducing the size and relevance of a default fund. In contrast, a non-defaulter-pay model reduces the weight of margins and aims to cover losses through a larger default fund (Haene & Sturm, 2009, p. 7). The weighting of margins and default fund and the entire default waterfall requires a delicate balance between moral hazard, the CCP's value proposition and the attractiveness of membership, members' incentives for participating in the default management process and monitoring the CCP's risk management. Consequently, it is crucial that CCPs strike a balance concerning the relationship between initial margining and default fund that is right for them (IMF, 2010, p. 18). From a regulatory oversight perspective, the default waterfall should be assessed holistically (Lazarow, 2011, p. 9), since all components of the risk management framework have an impact on its adequacy.

Most Important Safeguard: Liquidity Risk Management

Counterparty risk management of a CCP cannot be discussed without considering liquidity risk. The default of a member exposes the CCP not only to losses in the amount of the replacement value of the member's portfolio, thereby possibly posing a risk to its solvency. Having access to sufficient cash and securities to meet payment and delivery obligations on time is another challenge (Chande, Labelle, & Tuer, 2010, p. 48). Payment obligations of a CCP can have a wide variety: pass-throughs of profits on outstanding contracts and of option payments, reimbursements of cash collateral posted as margin or payments for deliveries (BIS, 1997, p. 17).

As long as the CCP does not replace the contracts impacted by the member default, it must fulfill the above payment obligations on the other side of the contracts to non-defaulting members from its own resources. In fact, it is critical that the CCP performs its obligations without delay so that questions about its solvency do not arise. From a liquidity risk perspective, CCPs have also to take into account the effects of potential payment or delivery delays, which would follow from a temporary inability of a member to fulfill its obligations caused by events not related to its financial strength (operational failures). The resulting liquidity pressure on the CCP in such cases might be significantly higher, since depending on its collateral arrangements (pledge with security interest or title transfer) the CCP might have no recourse to the margin collateral posted by the member in delay (pre-conditions for default not fulfilled).

Liquidity risk is a particularly interconnected risk category as it involves several trade-offs with other components of the CCPs activity and risk management framework. Trade-offs surrounding liquidity risk and the availability of liquid resources exist in connection with the netting levels as the daily cash movements of CCPs can be substantial, with the collateral framework of a CCP, with its investment policy and with its settlement processes, as well as with its default management procedures.

Margin collateral is the most important source of liquidity for CCPs. The acceptance of high-quality liquid collateral, adequate monitoring of haircuts and implementation of concentration limits allows the CCPs to liquidate or pledge collateral while minimizing losses and market impact and has thus a great influence on the CCPs ability to generate liquidity. In fact, the distribution of margin between cash and non-cash collateral provided by members and the incentives implemented towards the provision of cash collateral is just as important. The balance between cash and non-cash collateral is a trade-off between higher protection (overcollateralization in case of non-cash collateral) and higher liquidity. The CCP may be exposed to liquidity risk even if margin collateral is posted in cash. This is because most CCPs seek to minimize the opportunity costs for their members and pay interest to the clearing members resulting from short term investments of cash margins. The risk that a CCP cannot liquidate its investments to obtain cash is one of the most important liquidity risk CCPs are exposed to (Wendt, 2006, p. 5).

CCPs also arrange liquidity lines with financial institutions. However, commercial bank credit lines depend on the ability and the willingness of the bank to provide liquidity and depending on the market situation might not be considered as absolute assurances. CCPs could in theory or in practice obtain emergency liquidity support from their central banks. Central bankers, however, are cautious to explicitly commit to the provision of an emergency credit line, since this could disincentivize the CCP to implement appropriate risk management tools.

From a regulatory oversight perspective, it can be useful to differentiate between 'business as usual' liquidity risk management of a CCP and liquidity risk management in case of a member default or delay or other non-default related stress scenarios depending on the CCPs involvement in the settlement process. Some of the basic elements of stress testing of liquidity risk are the same as for stress testing the financial resources of a CCP. However, the inventory of potential events which may have an impact on the liquidity risk of a CCP will be idiosyncratic. The assessment of the quantitative impact of liquidity stress events for some cash flows would be straight forward but substantial (cash settled products), for others would have to be modeled and depend on various assumptions and model parameters (derivatives). In addition, the stress testing of liquidity risk will have to make assumptions on the CCP's access to liquidity sources (EACH, 2011, p. 12).

ARE CCPS MORE THAN INSTITUTIONS DESIGNED TO MANAGE COUNTERPARTY RISK?

For a comprehensive understanding of the risk profile of a CCP, practical oversight has to take into account that a CCP is an integral part of the clearing process, which is the first step in the overall post-trading process implemented in the capital markets. CCPs link trading and settlement by providing several administrative processes that are necessary for the reconciliation and resolution of obligations between counterparties[13]. According to this process-view (in sharp contrast to the risk-view), a clearinghouse is an organization that establishes and records obligations arising from trading on a marketplace and ensures that those obligations are processed according to the relevant rules (CCP12, 2009, p. 1).

The main measures for counterparty and liquidity risk management for the event of member default were described earlier. They are embedded into the business as usual processes of the CCP. These comprise

- netting,
- processing of transactions after execution until the successful fulfillment of the legal obligations either at expiration, settlement day or any day on which legal obligation is fulfilled,
- management of transactions between execution and fulfillment (corporate actions, position transfers, give-ups and take-ups)[14],
- sending instructions to settlement institutions (CSDs, custodians and payment banks) with regard to the legal fulfillment of obligations resulting from transactions, and with regard meeting margin requirements,
- practical measures ensuring that the member delivering has the securities to deliver the day before delivery, as well as
- issuing of reports regarding transactions, modifications and exposure components of their members (EACH: Functional Definition of a Central Counterparty Clearing House).

By sending settlement instructions to the respective settlement institutions the CCP creates a link to payment systems and the securities settlement system (custodians and central securities depositories). CCPs standardize and automate trade capture and post trade processing and implement straight-through-processing to back office systems of their members. Thus, they make trade processing more efficient and provide a golden record of each trade, its status, and payments relating to it, as well as information about the full portfolio of positions (CCP12, 2010, p. 1). As part of this process, CCPs provide operational cash management to their members: they verify the transactions and records credits and debits, account for any subsequent trades of the contract and oversee the ultimate delivery and liquidation of the contract, process cash instructions from netting, premium payments, realized profit and loss cash instructions, fines and fees, unrealized profits and losses, income events and margin calls.

For the oversight perspective, this process-view highlights several important points.

First, problems on the clearing side at the CCP could spill over to the settlement side (Ripatti, 2004, p. 23). CCPs are not only institutions designed to insure counterparty risk (Koeppl & Monnet, 2010, p. 2). By centralizing information, recordkeeping, payments and risks associated with credit and liquidity, CCPs concentrate activities which would otherwise be performed by many institutions. Clearing and settlement procedures vary significantly from one country to another. The specifics of a particular CCP are significantly influenced by local realities stemming from historical developments, legal and cultural precedents, but also by the characteristics of the cleared products, by the nature of its market participants and its organic development as well as its business strategy. In addition, the design of the settlement procedures determines the risk profile of the CCP as regards liquidity, settlement and custody risk. Hence, an in-depth knowledge of the relevant settlement processes is a prerequisite for the effective regulatory oversight of a CCP.

Second, a prominent part of the institutional structure of the clearing and settlement systems is their interconnectedness with the banking system (Bernanke, 1990, p. 138). Banks are operationally part of the clearing process not only as clearing members but as payment or settlement banks, liquidity providers and investment counterparts for CCPs. Banks can be also a major source of credit for all parties in the clearing chain by providing credit lines to clearing members or clients for posting variation margin or for the purchase of securities on credit. In a business as usual context, the smooth operation of the financial market clearing and settlement system is based on the presumption that the banking system is sound and can satisfy demands for withdrawal of funds at all times (Bernanke, 1990, p. 139).

In addition, CCPs are not only closely linked with the banking system, but perform a banking function by facilitating the transfer of funds between contracting counterparties and their agents (Edwards, 1983, p. 370; Bernanke, 1990, p. 140). The specific payment instruments which the CCPs use to transfer funds to discharge the payment leg of the obligation can vary. They depend on the participants to the transaction and the value of the associated payment. From a central bank point of view, CCPs are considered as part of the overall payment mechanisms of a country[15] and there clearly exists a connection between the safety of the payment systems and the clearing system. CCPs are recognized as having the similar inherent risks as those associated with systemically important payment mechanisms[16].

Funds transfer resulting from settlement and margin calls happens in a payment system monitored by the CCP. It involves numerous intermediate steps not only the transfer of assets, but possibly the extension of credit. A disturbance of the clearing process would result in the disturbance of the payment process. This could happen when steps in the transaction sequence are blocked or delayed due to concerns about the financial condition (solvency or liquidity) of the participants in the clearing chain (clearing members or CCP). The crash in October 1987 and the resulting demand for liquidity brought the payment systems in the US close to a brink, revealed weaknesses in the design of payment flows between the CCPs, their members and the liquidity providers of both (Bernanke, 2011, p. 8) and highlighted the important role that payment systems play in connecting clearing systems with each other, with the banking system and with the rest of the economy (Rutz, 1989, p. 393).

Third, CCPs have a number of working relationships resulting in interfaces with other institutions: markets (exchanges, trading platforms and flow providers), payment systems (by central banks and by commercial banks, CLS), securities settlement systems (CSDs and custodians), critical service providers (IT-providers and SWIFT) and other market participants (investment counterparties and third-party custodians). Most of these institutions fall under the new umbrella term of financial market infrastructures (abbreviated as FMIs)[17]. The concept of a financial market infrastructure is defined as a set consisting of five elements. One element is on the payments side: the systemically important payment system. The other four are on the securities/derivatives side, and in post-trade order they are the trade repository, the central counterparty, the securities settlement system and the central securities depository. These five types of FMI collectively perform the crucial role of clearing and settlement of financial transactions economy-wide. They constitute the systemically important part of the financial infrastructure.

The above mentioned links of a CCP with other FMIs are the necessary consequence of either the structure of the industry (a vertically integrated post-trade securities chain) or the adherence to one of the internationally accepted oversight principles for financial market infrastructures[18]. An FMI like a CCP may in itself already be fairly complicated, but when these mutual links are also taken into account, one can truly say that the whole ensemble is complex (Berndsen, 2012, p. 1).

Furthermore, interdependencies among CCPs and other financial market infrastructures exist even in the absence of explicit operational links and are growing as the landscape of central clearing becomes dominated by fewer and larger CCPs supporting more integrated markets and consolidated, global firms. The same globally active banks participate in many of the major CCPs and the CCPs often rely on similar sets of banks for payment services, funding, settlement and liquidity (Bernanke, 2011, p. 12).

Fourth, regulatory oversight has to consider both, the operational and financial component of clearing (Rutz, 1989, p. 347), since even if the CCP's risk management procedures are in theory sound; their effectiveness is still dependent on the competent implementation of those procedures (Hills, Rule, & Parkinson, 1999, p. 131). Technological innovation is constantly evolving to improve the speed of processing, the certainty, reliability, safety, convenience, universality and due to economies of scale the cost basis of the clearing process (Guadamillas & Keppler, 2002, p. 3). At the same time, this leads to an increased operational and technological risk. The breakdown of hardware, software or communications systems of a CCP could not only impair the CCPs own ability to calculate and monitor its risk exposure, but also hamper the smooth functioning of the markets they serve and the risk management capabilities of their members. Due to the connectedness of clearing operations, operational risk can be contagious as well. The 1987 stock market crash provided a market wide test for securities and derivatives CCPs, as well as their interlinkages with other systems and with their members. Surging volumes of trades and extraordinary price volatility laid open operational inconsistencies and caused severe operational stress at CCPs and clearing members (Bernanke, 2011, p. 7).

For this reasons, most CCPs impose operational requirements concerning payment, collateral and delivery arrangements, systems with adequate operational support and back-up as well as trained staff toward their members, payment banks and CSDs or custodians (EACH, 2001, p. 2). These requirements should be applied also to operations outsourced to third parties. Hence, from regulatory oversight perspective, CCPs not only concentrate counterparty credit risk, but also operational risk associated with their own failure or with the failure of interlinked infrastructures.

Fifth, it is widely acknowledged that CCPs can contribute to the stability of the financial system. By facilitating an efficient, transparent and orderly management of defaults, CCPs can reduce price volatility and the incidence of extreme price moves that can occur when a large member defaults (Pirrong, 2011, p. 11). As mentioned above, CCPs can eliminate but at least mitigate the potential for default cascades. However, it is well known that many, micro-prudentially sensible policies can be macro-prudentially dangerous (Pirrong, 2011, p. 12).

The fact that CCPs can adjust margins in response to changes in market conditions limits their vulnerability (Pirrong, 2011, p. 22). But CCPs financial demands on their members can affect market dynamics and may be destabilizing. Depending on the margining methodology of a CCP, it is possible that a CCP during periods of market exuberance succumbs to market pressure and relaxes its margin requirements, so that when conditions deteriorate, it has to tighten them sharply. According to the size and interconnectedness of the CCP, this could amplify swings in market conditions. In case of margin calls, market participants that must meet margin calls may respond by selling assets or reducing positions. This reaction can depress prices, lead to a downward revision of asset values that requires a further margin call and so on (Biais, Heider, & Hoerova, 2013, p. 165). The margin dynamic can lead to exaggerated, systemically destabilizing price movements (Pirrong, 2011, p.12).

Furthermore, during periods of great price swings, CCP members might be confronted with large (variation) margin calls and scramble to secure liquid assets in a very short period of time (hours) to meet their obligations toward the CCP. Spikes in demand for liquidity can impose acute funding risks in the financial system and also lead to inefficient asset sales. The strain on the funding system and market liquidity can affect even market participants not directly connected to the CCP (Pirrong, 2011, p. 12).

Such procyclicality or systemic disturbance is to be avoided from a system risk regulatory perspective. Destabilizing, excessive margining is, however, not in the interest of the CCPs, either. Historically, CCPs imposed limits curtailing calls for excessive amounts of margin which could have forced a counterparty into default (Moser, 1998, p. 24). Resulting from their (quasi-)cooperative structure concerning loss allocation, CCPs have great incentives to ensure that the loss absorbency of their clearing members is adequate and stable. Clearing members should be able to anticipate and meet extraordinary demands for liquidity, which might become necessary in case of dramatic changes in prices of the cleared products. Both are critical for the functioning of the loss mutualisation regime of a CCP. Accordingly, the discipline imposed by the CCPs on their members serve primarily to protect the integrity of the CCP, but should have the secondary effect of inducing members to be better able to meet margin requirements as well as bear losses in excess of margin deposits (Edwards, 1983, p. 376).

That said, CCPs were originally not designed as macro-prudential institutions with responsibility to improve the safety and soundness of the broader financial system. The potential procyclical effects of the CCPs' margin requirements are therefore currently in the focus of the regulatory oversight.

ARE THERE ANY CHALLENGES REMAINING FOR THE PRACTICAL OVERSIGHT OF CCPS?

Although the distance from households to CCPs is large, it is now generally accepted, that the public depends on the safety, soundness and efficiency of CCPs. CCPs are nodal entities as their routing of payments and deliveries creates a choke point and concentrate substantial financial and operational risk. Failure at these nodes or loss of confidence in the CCPs has then, by definition, systemic implications. CCP failure would create an enormous uncertainty in the financial markets (about the status of initiated transactions and about the financial positions of the participants of the CCP). Furthermore, a major disturbance in the processing of payments and could lead to possible liquidity shortages of affected participants (Ripatti, 2004, p. 24). From this logically follows, that it is not sufficient for the clearing, settlement and payment systems to avoid collapse. Their strength must be such that market participants will have enough confidence in the robustness and integrity of the systems to avoid taking actions which could bring them down. Especially, for CCPs to fulfill their economic functions, everyone must believe they are completely safe (Tucker, 2014, p. 6) As the CCPs moved into the center of attention, calls for more granular regulation and a more uniform, consistent regulatory oversight of CCPs became frequent.

It is important to keep in mind, however, that each CCP is actually a unique set of rules, processes and operational arrangements. They are established for the management, mitigation and allocation of the risks arising from a unique set of transactions between unique groups of market participants. One of the important lessons from the history of clearing is that CCPs emerged gradually and slowly as a result of experience and experimentation (Kroszner, 2006, p. 38). The evolution of clearing mechanisms to reconcile and resolve obligations between counterparties (Moser, 1998, p. 4) has been shaped by the counterparties desire to control their risk of losses from non-performance on financial transactions

(Moser, 1998, p. 7; Hasenpusch, 2009, Ch. 2.1.2.2.1). Adjustments and innovations to central clearing arrangements like CCPs continue to be necessary according to developments of financial markets and its participants. Therefore it is important that CCPs still retain some scope and discretion to influence how risk is managed.

Furthermore, there remains a prevalent need for an in-depth knowledge of an individual CCP's rules, regulations, and procedures. Significant regional differences persist from the diverging ways marketplaces came to introduce CCP clearing, from the differing historical development of CCPs, from the variable division of tasks among the entities processing financial market transactions, from the institutional and legal setup of CCPs and from the specifics of the relevant legal frameworks. Regulatory oversight will continue to concentrate in large part on the structural attributes of CCP aiming to ensure that the CCP's structure, rules and regulations, procedures are designed and applied in ways that genuinely reduce the risks. Under the umbrella of common main characteristics of CCPs reflected in the relevant international standards the practical oversight of CCPs and its priorities remain significantly determined by the specific characteristics of the central clearing and central counterparty function of a jurisdiction.

Moreover, the assigned scope and objective of regulatory oversight is still evolving and greatly differs according to the mandate of a regulator. An institutional view employed mostly by prudential supervisory regimes focus on the robustness of the entity providing central counterparty clearing[19]. The instrumental perspective of securities markets supervision is based on the instruments used for transferring value (financial instruments including stocks, bonds, derivatives), while the oversight of conduct risks concerns customer protection. The oversight function of central banks[20] in most cases encompasses a functional view and monitors the robustness and effectiveness of the central clearing system as part of the financial transactions value chain. Consequently, central bank oversight aims to contain systemic risk, or, more precisely, infrastructural systemic risk. This is the part of systemic risk where FMIs - if they do not meet the principles - could transmit shocks from one part of the financial sector to another or cause a shock through an internal failure.

A further dimension to the regulatory oversight of CCPs was added with the establishment of the macro prudential policy framework. Under the heading of macro prudential supervision, policy makers and supervisors aim to preserve financial stability by preventing the build-up of systemic risk and containing shocks to the financial sector and the real economy as a whole. This perspective strives to encompass the chain of effects between the CCP and other parts of the financial system resulting from the interconnectedness of individual financial institutions and markets, as well as their common exposure to economic risk factors. From a systemic risk point of view, CCPs might be exposed to contagion risk among their membership, so called knock-on systemic risk (Bliss & Papathanassiou, 2006, p. 5), a risk that the default of a member will cause other members to fail to meet their obligations when due or even default (Ripatti, 2004, p. 12). The default of a large member can also lead to informational asymmetries that could cause trading to freeze up or necessitate a large number of counterparties simultaneously replacing defaulted contracts resulting in liquidity strains and possible market breakdown. Furthermore, a major economic shock could simultaneously affect a large number of members (Bliss & Papathanassiou, 2006, p. 6). To make matters more complicated, this variety of regulatory oversight objectives and mandates is realized in a different institutional set-up and legal framework in each jurisdiction leading to great differences in the oversight approaches and its tools.

In summary, a particular challenge for the regulatory oversight of CCP lies, therefore, in its evolving nature and the fact that CCP-oversight is most successful if its effectiveness is never tested. Further challenges for regulatory oversight emerge from the need to find a balance between individuality and consistence. Regulatory oversight also strives to accomplish a common view in spite of the fundamental regional differences in its set-up and targeted objects. The final objective seems to be that CCPs are rigged up to a much broader definition of market stress, than the one they were originally designed for.

REFERENCES

Aigrain, J. (2013, April). CCPs as instruments of stability and risk mitigation. *Banque de France Financial Stability Review*, 17.

Clearing arrangements for exchange-traded derivatives. (1997, March). CPSS Publications, 23. Bank for International Settlements.

The Bank of England's approach to the supervision of financial market infrastructures (2013, April). Bank of England.

Bernanke, B. S. (1990). Clearing and settlement during the Crash. *Review of Financial Studies*, *3*(1), 133–151. doi:10.1093/rfs/3.1.133

Bernanke, B. S. (2011). Clearinghouses, Financial Stability, and Financial Reform. Proceedings of the 2011 Financial Markets Conference. Stone Mountain, Georgia.

Berndsen, R. (2012). Letter from the editor in chief, Journal of Financial Market Infrastructures.

Biais, Bruno, Florian Heider, Marie Hoerova (2013, April). Incentive compatible centralized clearing. *Banque de France Financial Stability Review*, 17.

Bliss, R. R., & Papathanassiou, C. (2006). Derivatives clearing, central counterparties, and novation: The economic implications [Working paper]. Wake Forest University.

Bliss, R.R., & Steigerwald, R.S. (2006). Derivatives Clearing and Settlement: A Comparison of Central Counterparties and Alternative Structures. *Economic Perspectives*, 4Q/2006

Chande, N., Labelle, N., & Tuer, E. (2010, December). Central Counterparties and Systemic Risk. *Bank of Canada, Financial System Review.*

Staff Guidance on Swaps Straight-Through Processing. (2013, September 26). U.S. Commodity and Futures Commission.

Edwards, F. R. (1983). The Clearing Association in Futures Markets: Guarantor and Regulator. *Journal of Futures Markets*, *3*(4), 1983. doi:10.1002/fut.3990030404

Standards of Risk Management Controls used by Central Counterparty Clearing Houses. (2001, November). European Association of CCP Clearing Houses.

Best Practices for CCP Stress Testing. (2011, November). European Association of CCP Clearing Houses.

The Payment System. (2010European Central Bank.

Green, P. J., Jennings-Mares, J. C., & Smith, D. (2013), Avoiding Armageddon: Resolution Regimes for Central Clearing Counterparties, Morrison Foerster, Derivatives: Financial Products Report, Vol. 14 No. 8

Guadamillas, M., & Keppler, R. (2002). Securities Clearance and Settlement Systems – A Guide to Best Practices

Haene, P., & Sturm, A. (2009). Optimal Central Counterparty Risk Management. *Swiss National Bank*, Working Paper No. 2009-7

Hanley, W. J., McCann, K., & Moser, J. T. (1995), Public benefits and Public Concerns: An Economic Analysis of Regulatory Standards for Clearing Facilities. *Federal Reserve Bank of Chicago,* Working Paper WP-95-12

Hasenpusch, T. P. (2009). *Clearing Services for Global Markets*. Cambridge, United Kingdom: Cambridge University Press. doi:10.1017/CBO9780511635557

Hills, B., Rule, D., Parkinson, S., & Young, C. (1999). *Central Counterparty Clearing Houses and Financial Stability, Financial Stability Review June 1999*. Bank of England.

How central counterparties strengthen the safety and integrity of financial markets. (2014). *Deutsche Börse Group.* Deutsche Börse Group and Eurex Clearing.

Making Over-the-Counter Derivatives Safer: The Role of Central Counterparties. (2010, April). Global Financial Stability Report, International Monetary Fund (IMF).

Knott, R., & Mills, A. (2002, December). Modeling Risk in Central Counterparty Clearing Houses: A Review. Bank of England.

Koeppl, T.V. (2011). Time for Stability in Derivatives Markets, Commentary, C.D. Howe Institute, No. 329

Koeppl, T.V., & Monnet, C. (2010), The Emergence and Future of Central Counterparties, Working Paper 1241. Queen's University.

Kroszner, R. (1999, November). Can the Financial Markets Privately Regulate Risk? The Development of Derivatives Clearing Houses and Recent Over-the-Counter Innovations. *Journal of Money, Credit and Banking.*

Kroszner, R. (2006, April 3). Central Counterparty Clearing: History, Innovation, and Regulation. Proceedings of the Joint Conference on Issues Related to Central Counterparty Clearing. Frankfurt, Germany.

Lazarow, A. (2011), Lessons from International Central Counterparties: Benchmarking and Analysis. Bank of Canada Discussion Paper 2011-4

Securities trading, clearing, central counterparties and settlement in EU 25 – an overview of current arrangements. (2005, June). London School of Economics.

Moser, J. T. (1998). Contracting innovations and the evolution of clearing and settlement methods at futures exchanges. Federal Reserve Bank of Chicago working paper, No. WP-1998-26.

Moskow, M. H. (2006, April 4). Public policy and central counterparty clearing. Proceedings of Issues Related to Central Counterparty Clearing. Frankfurt, Germany.

Pirrong, C. (2011, May). The Economics of Central Clearing: Theory and Practice. ISDA Discussion Paper.

Rehlon, A., & Nixon, D. (2013). Central counterparties: What are they, why do they matter and how does the Bank supervise them? Bank of England. *Quarterly Bulletin, 2013*, Q2.

Riksbank. (2002). Central counterparty clearing for the securities market. Financial Stability Report 2.

Ripatti, K. (2004). Central counterparty clearing: constructing a framework for evaluation of risks and benefits. *Bank of Finland discussion papers.*

Rutz, R. D. (1989). Clearance, Payment, and Settlement Systems in the Futures, Options, and Stock Markets. *Board of Trade Clearing Corporation, Chicago, IL.*

The Global Association of Central Counterparties). (2009), The Value of Proposition of Central Counterparty Clearing Houses, Working Paper

Tucker, P. (2014, April 11). Are clearinghouses the new central banks? Proceedings of the Over-the-counter Symposium. Chicago, Il.

Wendt, F. (2006). Intraday Margining of Central Counterparties: EU Practice and Theoretical Evaluation of Benefits and Costs. *De Nederlandsche Bank Working Paper No. 107.*

KEY TERMS AND DEFINITIONS

Clearing: The process of transmitting, reconciling, and, in some cases, confirming transactions prior to settlement, potentially including the netting of transactions and the establishment of final positions for settlement. For the clearing of futures and options, this term also refers to the daily balancing of profits and losses and the daily calculation of collateral requirements.

Central Counterparty: An entity that interposes itself between counterparties to contracts traded in one or more financial markets, becoming the buyer to every seller and the seller to every buyer and thereby ensuring the performance of open contracts.

Central Securities Depository: An entity that provides securities accounts, central safekeeping services, and asset services, which may include the administration of corporate actions and redemptions, and plays an important role in helping to ensure the integrity of securities issues (that is, ensure that securities are not accidentally or fraudulently created or destroyed or their details changed).

Securities Settlement System: An entity that enables securities to be transferred and settled by book entry according to a set of predetermined multilateral rules. Such systems allow transfers of securities either free of payment or against payment.

Margin: Collateral that is collected to cover potential changes in the value of each participant's position (that is, potential future exposure) over the appropriate close-out period in the event the participant defaults.

Current Exposure: The loss that an FMI (or in some cases, its participants) would face immediately if a participant were to default. Current exposure is technically defined as the larger of zero or the market value (or replacement cost) of a transaction or portfolio of transactions within a netting set with a counterparty that would be lost upon the default of the counterparty.

Potential Future Exposure: Any potential credit exposure that an FMI could face at a future point in time. Potential future exposure is technically defined as the maximum exposure estimated to occur at a future point in time at a high level of statistical confidence. Potential future exposure arises from potential fluctuations in the market value of a participant's open positions between the time they are incurred or reset to the current market price, and the time they are liquidated or effectively hedged.

Haircut: A risk control measure applied to underlying assets whereby the value of those underlying assets is calculated as the market value of the assets reduced by a certain percentage (the "haircut"). Haircuts are applied by a collateral taker in order to protect itself from losses resulting from declines in the market value of a security in the event that it needs to liquidate that collateral.

Liquidity Risk: The risk that a counterparty, whether a participant or other entity, will have insufficient funds to meet its financial obligations as and when expected, although it may be able to do so in the future.

Payment System: A set of instruments, procedures, and rules for the transfer of funds between or among participants; the system includes the participants and the entity operating the arrangement.

Replacement Cost Risk: The risk of loss resulting from the replacement of the original contract at current market prices that may be changing rapidly during periods of stress.

Procyclicality: The changes in risk-management requirements or practices that are positively correlated with business or credit cycle fluctuations and that may cause or exacerbate financial instability.

Segregation: A method of protecting customer collateral and contractual positions by holding or accounting for them separately from those of the direct participant (such as a carrying firm or broker).

ENDNOTES

1 Post-trade services refer to the activities after a trade has been concluded.

2 Principles for financial market infrastructures, Committee on Payment and Settlement Systems (CPSS) and the International Organization of Securities Commissions (IOSCO), 2012

3 The resilience of the CCPs – in particular, their ability to manage their liquidity and ensure the integrity of transactions under stressed conditions – was tested by financial shocks and crises. Even though most CCPs of the time survived all of these episodes, they can provide a relevant insight for regulatory oversight purposes into potential vulnerabilities (Bernanke, 2011, p. 145). The three occurrences of CCP failures have often been analyzed in literature: of the CCP of the sugar exchange in Paris in 1974, of the Malaysian CCP of the futures exchange for palm oil in Kuala Lumpur in 1983 and of the Hong Kong Futures Exchange in 1987.

4 This chapter uses the term oversight to refer to prudential supervision, oversight carried out by central banks and securities market supervision.

5 The posting of margin in advance makes a deliberate default unattractive when price ranges are in the normal range (Wendt, 2006, p. 6).

6 For convenience, the terms "member" or "clearing member" is used to describe participants in central clearing arrangements, whether or not they are organized as mutual organizations. According to EACH (2001, p. 1) not all CCPs use the description "clearing member" to describe firms from whom they collect margin and through whom all the clearing transactions are channeled. Some CCPs use the term "clearing participant" rather than "clearing member" to avoid any impression that such participants are members of a mutually owned company or association.

7 According to EACH (2001, p. 1), some CCPs, although having a clearing member structure, extend their financial guarantee to clients of those clearing members who are brokers. This end-client model operates in Greece, Portugal, Scandinavia, Spain, and on an optional basis in France.

8 This service was sometimes compared to the correspondent services offered by banks (Moser, 1998, p. 4).

9 Clearing is defined as the processing of transactions after the execution of buy and sell orders in preparation for the transfer of ownership of the product and the fulfillment of obligations, as well as the performance of additional services, such as the netting of obligations to ensure fewer processes and cash flows, and in particular the evaluation and management of all relevant sources of risk in order to reduce the probability of failure to meet obligations.

10 Traditionally, most CCPs maintained for their clearing members an account for their own positions and collateral (proprietary or house account), and a group of other accounts for their customers' positions and collateral. With the introduction of individual segregation this account structure will change fundamentally.

11 Settlement netting is also known as clearance on a net basis (London School of Economics, 2005, p. 6).

12 In contrast, in payments and securities settlement systems credit extension is a system design choice (Bliss and Papathanassiou, 2006, p. 2).

13 The final phase of a trade life cycle is settlement, when the legal obligation is fulfilled. In case of securities, this happens with the exchange of ownership of the securities for cash and vice versa. In case of derivatives, this occurs when the duration of the contract expires or when an offsetting contract is entered into.

14 In securities markets, the services necessary to maintain the life cycle of a trade and to enable settlement are provided by the central securities depository of a country.

15 A payment system is defined as the collection of institutions, instruments, rules and procedures, standards and technical means used to exchange financial value between two parties discharging an obligation. In case of clearing and settlement systems the exchange of value consists both the exchange of securities or other underlyings and the exchange of cash.

16 In contrast to the clearing of financial transactions, in case of payment clearing the clearer does not become a legal party to a transaction, does not act as a guarantor and is not involved in facilitating settlement by delivery (Kroszner, 1999, p. 14).

17 Financial market infrastructure refers to terms that were previously often used in a loose way, such as "the payment system", "clearing and settlement" or "post-trade infrastructures".

18 Examples are the link between the SIPS and the SSS (delivery versus payment) and the link between CCPs and SIPS (requirement to settle in central bank money where practicable and available).

19 Prudential supervision of CCPs can be part of the banking supervision in case the CCP has a banking license.

20 Central banks have an interest in ensuring the smooth functioning of securities clearing and settlement systems because of the potential impact a major disruption may have on two of their key responsibilities: the smooth implementation of monetary policy and the smooth functioning of payment systems and overall stability (Ripatti, 2004, p. 35).

Chapter 14
Ownership, Incentives and Regulation of CCP Risks

Louise Carter
Reserve Bank of Australia, Australia

Jennifer Hancock
Reserve Bank of Australia, Australia

Mark Manning
Reserve Bank of Australia, Australia

ABSTRACT

This chapter develops a framework to analyse the factors influencing central counterparties' (CCPs') risk controls and the role of regulation. The framework illustrates the importance of sound regulation of CCPs and helps to explain why different CCPs may make different risk management choices. Key factors include ownership, governance and the profile and preferences of participants. International standards for the design and operation of CCPs and other financial market infrastructures (FMIs) are reflected in the Principles for Financial Market Infrastructures (PFMIs). Modelling key elements of these standards, the chapter demonstrates the importance of a flexible regulatory framework that achieves the desired level of stability while allowing the mix of risk controls applied by each CCP to vary according to its particular incentives and operating environment. The chapter goes on to discuss the emerging trends towards competition and interoperability between CCPs and cross-border provision of clearing services, and consider the implications for CCPs' risk management choices.

1. INTRODUCTION

The financial strains of 2008 underscore the important role played by CCPs in the financial system. Indeed, in September 2008, the successful unwinding of Lehman Brothers positions across several CCPs worldwide illustrated the potential benefit of centralised risk management and a centralised default-management process (Gregory, 2014; Norman 2011). Furthermore, while liquidity and trading activity in many over-the-counter (OTC) markets was constrained during this period by tight counterparty limits,

DOI: 10.4018/978-1-4666-8745-5.ch014

markets served by CCPs experienced less disruption. This would seem to reflect market participants' confidence in the capacity of CCPs to adequately manage risks associated with trading in financial markets. In light of this experience, the G20 has committed to regulatory reform to provide for central clearing of all standardised OTC derivatives (G20, 2009).

While greater use of CCPs may address some important issues, the market structure of clearing and the robustness of CCP risk management will determine the extent to which increased central clearing contributes to greater financial stability. The question has been raised, for instance, as to whether CCPs should be permitted to have a profit orientation and whether they should instead be regarded purely as utilities (Tucker, 2013). While a number of studies have demonstrated the benefits of central clearing for netting efficiency – at least when clearing of a single or related products is not fragmented across multiple CCPs (Jackson and Manning, 2007; Duffie and Zhu, 2011; Heath, Kelly and Manning, 2013; Duffie et al., 2014) – the potential concentration of risk in CCPs is also widely recognised (Renault, 2010; Tucker, 2013; Anderson and Joeveer, 2014; Powell 2014). More generally, on the policy drive towards central clearing, Pirrong (2011) argues 'although [the rules] may reduce some risks, they will simply relocate others, while creating some new ones'.

Our principal focus in this chapter is on the risk management choices made by CCPs and how these decisions can be influenced by regulation and other features of the operating environment. We develop a model to examine the coverage and reliability of CCPs' financial resources. Our model builds on the optimal margining approach of a user-owned CCP developed by Baer *et al* (2004). A similar approach has been used by Haene and Sturm (2009) to examine the optimal balance of margin and pooled financial resources for a user-owned CCP that faces regulatory requirements on the coverage of its financial resources.

Considering first an operating environment with no regulation, we find that, other things being equal, a for-profit CCP that relies on its own capital to fund any shortfall above a defaulted participant's initial margin will seek to minimise the potential call on its own resources by increasing margin requirements to the maximum level consistent with its clearing participants' continued willingness to trade. If, on the other hand, any shortfall is funded by *ex post* loss allocation to participants, this contingent obligation will be taken into account in participants' trading decisions. Margin requirements are then likely to be correspondingly lower. If a CCP is user owned, it will similarly take into account the opportunity cost to participants of posting initial margin and meeting any shortfalls, and hence will generally prefer to set margin requirements at a lower level, relying more on *ex post* loss allocation to participants.

We also demonstrate that an unregulated CCP relying only on *ex post* funding to meet a shortfall has a strategic option to wind down rather than meet its obligations. Furthermore, if a CCP anticipates public support in the event that it faces a shortfall, its privately optimal strategy may be to set margin requirements lower than it otherwise would. This could impose significant social costs, underscoring the important role for regulation in influencing the coverage and reliability of a CCP's financial resources.

We therefore model the implications of regulation, focusing principally on two core elements of the internationally-agreed *Principles for Financial Market Infrastructures* which were published by the Committee on Payment and Settlement Systems (CPSS) – now the Committee on Payments and Market Infrastructures (CPMI) – and the International Organization of Securities Commissions (IOSCO) in 2012 (PFMIs; CPSS-IOSCO, 2012): pre-funded financial resources, sufficient to cover losses arising in the event of the default of the largest participant in extreme but plausible market conditions; and recovery plans that comprehensively address any unfunded losses, underpinned by a special resolution regime for CCPs. Appropriate enforcement of these regulatory settings eliminates the wind-down option and the moral hazard associated with anticipated government support.

We further demonstrate that, notwithstanding regulation, CCPs will still make different choices on their relative reliance on initial margin versus a pre-funded default fund. These choices will reflect their particular ownership and governance structures and the preferences of their participants. As long as the minimum regulatory standards are rigorously enforced, regulation should accommodate legitimate differences in risk management settings. It is important, however, that there is transparency of CCPs' risk management arrangements and that participants fully understand – and can manage – both their *ex ante* and potential future obligations.

The importance of regulation is amplified by a number of trends emerging in the financial market infrastructure, including competition between CCPs and cross-border provision of CCP services.[1] These are likely to shape CCPs' risk management choices and potentially also create challenges for CCP regulators.

The rest of the chapter is structured as follows. Section 2 offers some background on CCP risk controls and the high-level determinants of risk control choices. Section 3 formalises some of these ideas in a model of CCPs' risk control choices, with and without regulation. This section demonstrates how certain requirements in the PFMIs may be captured in the model and how these can alter outcomes. Section 4 goes on to discuss how competition between CCPs and cross-border provision of clearing are changing the market structure of CCP clearing. This section describes how these trends have shaped clearing of different products (cash equities, exchange traded derivatives and OTC derivatives). It then goes on to consider, with reference to the model, some challenges that these trends pose for regulators seeking to meet their public policy objectives. Section 5 concludes.

2. CCPs: RISK CONTROL CHOICES

CCPs initially emerged to support anonymous derivatives trading on commodities exchanges (Moser, 1998; Norman, 2011). Since the parties to a derivatives contract agree to fulfil obligations sometime in the future, counterparty credit risk is an important consideration. Should one of the parties default before fulfilling its contractual obligations, the remaining party must 'replace' the trade in the market, potentially at an adverse price. It is this 'replacement cost' risk that a CCP is designed to manage.

The CCP interposes itself between the original contracting parties to a trade, becoming the buyer to the seller and the seller to the buyer (through a process known as novation), and employs a range of risk-management tools to offer contracting parties the assurance that it will be able to fulfil its contractual obligations. In this way, market participants need only monitor the CCP rather than every potential trading participant in a particular market. Since in providing this assurance the CCP concentrates counterparty risk management, it is crucial that its risk controls are sound.

In this section, we describe the risk-management tools typically applied by CCPs before going on in Section 3 to develop a model framework to illustrate the determinants of the choice between alternative risk controls.

2.1 The Three Layers of CCP Risk Controls

Hills *et al* (1999) describe the range of risk–management strategies used by a CCP, illustrating how they may be applied to both reduce the probability of a clearing participant default and to manage the scale of any loss given default. The authors categorise such techniques according to the specific type of risk they aim to alleviate.

In a similar vein, we identify three layers of risk controls typically applied by a CCP:

- The first layer of risk controls is *ex ante controls on exposures*, which limit the trades that the CCP is willing to accept. In order for a loss to crystallise, a clearing participant default must be accompanied by an adverse move in market prices, such that the CCP incurs a loss closing out the defaulted participant's positions.[2] The CCP therefore seeks to restrict the types of participants and the products it is prepared to deal with, as well as, where feasible, the size of positions. Setting minimum requirements for the financial standing of participants directly affects the probability of a default event.
- The second layer of risk controls, *defaulter-pays protections*, seeks to manage the risk associated with exposures once they have been novated to the CCP. These protections generally take the form of margin (or other collateral) requirements. Knott and Mills (2002) survey the alternative statistical approaches to margin setting and a range of studies – including Figlewski (1984), Day and Lewis (2004) and Gemmill (1994) – explore margin coverage in practice. Margin is typically imposed to cover both current and potential future exposures:
    - *Current exposure.* This is the exposure that relates to observed changes in market prices. To cover this exposure, *variation* margin is generally collected at least daily from participants with mark-to-market losses and paid out to the participants with mark-to-market gains. In this way, participants realise gains and losses on an ongoing basis and the CCP's exposure in respect of all open positions is re-set to zero at the start of each day.
    - *Potential future exposure.* This is the CCP's exposure to potential future price moves that may arise, in the event a participant defaults, between the last variation margin settlement and the time the defaulted participant's positions can be closed out. The CCP collects *initial* margin as collateral to cover such prospective future price moves..
    - Finally, a CCP often also collects *additional* margin from participants that have particularly large or concentrated positions, or in response to adverse information on a participant's financial position.
- A third layer of protection is provided by *prefunded pooled financial resources* or *ex post loss allocation.* In the event of a default in more extreme market conditions, initial and additional margin posted by the defaulted participant may not be sufficient to fully cover any losses arising. Hence, a CCP will also establish arrangements for dealing with any shortfall. Such arrangements typically comprise pooled financial resources (sometimes referred to as a default fund or clearing guarantee fund), made up of pre-funded contributions by the CCP and clearing participants, sometimes supplemented with the power to call for additional contributions from participants *ex post.*

One way of gauging the robustness of a CCP's risk framework is to consider the 'quality' of its risk controls in terms of a set of inter-related attributes:

- *Coverage.* Taking into account both initial margin collected directly from participants and the size of pre-funded pooled financial resources, stress tests may be used to establish whether the CCP's available financial resources would provide adequate coverage in the event of the default of one or more of the CCP's largest clearing participants in all but the most extreme circumstances. One aspect of this is to consider non-cash collateral eligibility criteria and cash collateral reinvestment criteria. In particular, the level of coverage achieved will in part be determined by how well collateral assets hold their value in stressed market circumstances.[3]

- *Reliability*. For a given level of coverage, reliability describes the certainty with which the CCP could enforce its claim on, and realise, its financial resources to meet its obligations in the event of a participant default. Fully pre-funded financial resources are likely to be highly reliable, since they are already held by the CCP. The reliability of promissory resources, such as *ex post* contributions by surviving participants, may be less assured.
- *Liquidity* determines the *speed* with which the CCP can access its financial resources.
- *Incentives*. The composition of financial resources may also have implications for incentives faced by both participants and the CCP itself. For instance, Koeppl and Monnet (2008) demonstrate that the collection of margin addresses the problem of limited enforcement in financial contracts. By placing the *ex post* burden on the defaulting party, these arrangements give participants an incentive to perform on their obligations. In the case of additional resources such as prefunded pooled financial resources or *ex post* loss allocation, however, the cost of a default is borne proportionally by the providers of those resources. It is important, therefore, that the providers of such resources also have adequate control over the risk-management framework such that they can assess the likelihood of a call on their contributed resources.
- *Replenishability*. Finally, financial resources should be replenishable. Following a default event, continued confidence in the CCP will depend on whether it can demonstrate its capacity to withstand the default of another participant. In this regard, some financial resources may be more readily replenishable than others and there may be a case for a CCP to have a variety of funding channels open to it.

The spirit of these attributes is reflected in the PFMIs, which set 24 best-practice standards for providers of centralised payment, clearing, settlement and trade-reporting infrastructures. Of these standards, 22 are relevant to CCPs, establishing a range of requirements designed to promote the safe and efficient provision of CCP services. The PFMIs set requirements in a range of areas, including not only the management of financial risks, but also matters such as legal and governance arrangements, operational risk management, access and participation and disclosure.

Perhaps the most notable *coverage* requirement is that a CCP hold sufficient financial resources to cover the joint default of the participant and its affiliates in any extreme but plausible scenario that would cause the largest aggregate credit exposure. This is the so-called 'cover one' requirement. A CCP with a more complex risk profile – perhaps due to the products that it clears – or that is systemically important in multiple jurisdictions would be subject to the higher requirement that it hold sufficient financial resources to cover the default of the *two* participants (plus affiliates) that generate the largest aggregate exposure ('cover two'). Similar coverage requirements apply in relation to a CCP's coverage of liquidity exposure.

The PFMIs also specify collateral eligibility criteria that support the coverage criterion, as well as *reliability* and *liquidity*, by requiring that the coverage requirement be met with *pre-funded* margin and pooled financial resources. Cash collateral must be invested in assets with low market, credit and liquidity risk. Any non-cash collateral posted by participants to meet their margin obligations or contributions to pooled resources similarly should be of low market, credit and liquidity risk, and also subject to conservative haircuts. Where a CCP has access to central bank liquidity, it may be able to assist its management of liquidity risk by holding collateral in assets that are eligible in the central bank's operations.

Furthermore, to ensure appropriate *incentives*, a minimum proportion of these resources should be 'defaulter pays'. The PFMIs specify that margin requirements should be set conservatively, to cover at least 99 per cent of potential future price moves over an appropriate closeout period. Accordingly, in the vast majority of cases the obligations of a defaulted participant would be expected to be covered by margin alone, without drawing on the CCP's additional financial resources.

Finally, the PFMIs also require that a CCP prepare recovery and wind-down plans to give transparency as to how it would respond in a distress situation that threatened its viability. A recovery plan should include rules and procedures to allocate uncovered credit losses and address liquidity shortfalls in the event of a participant default, and also mechanisms to deal effectively with non-default losses (such as losses on reinvestment of cash margin). Recovery plans should also address the *replenishment* of pre-funded pooled financial resources utilised by the CCP in meeting its obligations following a default; the CCP must also maintain plans to raise new capital.

2.2 Non-Regulatory Determinants of CCP Risk Controls

While the PFMIs are expected to be implemented in every jurisdiction, they are written at a sufficient level of generality to allow equivalent outcomes to be achieved in different ways. For instance, some risk management tools are at least partly, allowing CCPs to achieve equivalent reliability and coverage with a different mix of tools. The literature on CCPs offers some guidance as to the source of the differences in risk frameworks observed in practice. Empirically, it is difficult to isolate the influence of each source, but it is nevertheless possible to establish some basic principles which can be considered further using the model in Section 3.

2.2.1 Ownership and Profit Orientation

Over time, the ownership structure and profit motives of CCPs have diversified away from the traditional user-owned structure described by Kroszner (1999, 2006). While many retain the traditional mutual structure, others are now owned by the exchange (or exchanges) they serve, other financial institutions or arms-length private shareholders (CPSS, 2010). Some also face direct competition in the markets they support (see Section 4). Evolution from the traditional user-owned structure has often been associated with the demutualisation of the exchanges with which many CCPs are vertically integrated. This change in ownership structure and profit orientation has naturally altered some CCPs' objectives, incentives and capabilities, with implications for their private risk-management choices. Some of the potential implications of alternative ownership and profit structures are discussed below.

Since, in the traditional user-owned model, the pooled financial resources of the CCP are funded primarily via either pre-funded or promissory contributions from the participant-owners of the CCP, each clearing participant will be at least partly responsible for the losses of any other clearing participant, should such losses exceed initial margin. In theory, this should give participants in a user-owned CCP an incentive to establish risk controls that minimise the potential call on their resources. Indeed, this is one of the critical principles identified by Kroszner (2006): 'a CCP's governance arrangements must provide those with 'skin in the game' with substantial influence over the CCP's risk controls'.

Nevertheless, since any such loss is shared across all participants, while each participant faces the full opportunity cost of up-front margin payments, a user-owned CCP may place greater emphasis on pooled financial resources than defaulter-pays protections.[4] Indeed, Haene and Sturm (2009) find that it is always optimal for a cost-minimising, user-owned CCP to establish a default fund. This result reflects the fact that once margins are set above a certain level, the risk that a non-defaulting participant's default fund contributions will be used to cover the defaulting participant's losses is small. Accordingly, the mutualised protection of the default fund offers a lower cost alternative to margins. If the marginal cost of collateral s higher than the probability of default, the default fund will be the only risk control applied.

In contrast to a user-owned CCP, the interests of an externally owned for-profit CCP may not be fully aligned with those of its participants, either individually or in aggregate. In particular, a for-profit CCP may have an incentive to increase clearing fee revenues by encouraging a higher volume of trade, perhaps by lowering margins or allowing greater opportunities for netting and margin offsets. The strength of this revenue-seeking incentive is likely to depend on how, in the event of a default, the for-profit CCP would fund any shortfall above margin to meet its obligations.

- In a for-profit model in which the CCP's own capital comprises the majority of its non-margin financial resources, the CCP may seek to minimise the potential for a call on its own capital by placing greater emphasis on margin than either pre-funded pooled financial resources or ex post loss allocation. This emphasis may be stronger if a for-profit CCP is capital constrained and would find it difficult to replenish its pooled resources following a drawdown.
- On the other hand, where a for-profit CCP would fund a shortfall through participant contributions, its incentives are likely to be very different. Objectively, there are significant benefits to relying on participant contributions. As a more dispersed and diversified source of funding, they may be more reliable. They may also be more readily replenishable than a CCP's own capital. However, an externally-owned, for-profit CCP that relied *solely* on such contributions would have no skin in the game, and absent other disciplinary mechanisms its revenue incentives may dominate its private risk-management choices. Since the CCP would bear none of the financial costs of a default, it may have a reduced incentive to monitor its participants and to prevent defaults.

These incentives may be tempered by participants' willingness to continue to trade. In some cases, there may also be a direct vehicle for participants to influence the CCP's risk-management choices – for example, a user risk committee or other user-governance committee. Such mechanisms would restore the important discipline provided by those responsible for funding the CCP's financial resources. Otherwise, it is important that the regulator understands the private preferences of a for-profit CCP that does not commit a material amount of its own capital, and carefully monitors its risk-management choices.

2.2.2 Product and Market Characteristics

Product and market characteristics are also likely to have a significant bearing on a CCP's choice of risk controls. There are several potential factors:

- *Trading spillovers*. A number of empirical studies of this question have demonstrated that increased margin requirements reduce the volume of futures contracts novated to CCPs (e.g., Telser (1981), Hartzmark (1986) and Hardouvelis and Kim (1995)).
- *Margin calculations*. Some products are more amenable to standard margin calculations than others. Where products are subject to pricing discontinuities, standard defaulter-pays margining techniques may not be easily applied. For instance, margining single-name credit-default swaps is

complicated by the potential for a reference-entity default event to trigger a cliff-edge price fall. Under such circumstances, greater reliance may be placed on non-margin financial resources, potentially requiring strict participation requirements to minimise the potential for a call on these resources.

- *Default management.* If market liquidity is such that a CCP would face difficulties in closing out a defaulter's positions, it will potentially seek higher margin protection and restrict participation to highly credit-worthy participants. In such circumstances, a CCP may also establish bespoke *ex ante* arrangements with its participants (or others in the market) to assist in closing out positions should a default occur, as typically applied by some CCPs serving OTC derivatives markets.
- *Structure of market participation.* A wholesale market comprised primarily of large institutional participants is likely to exhibit greater homogeneity in credit quality than a retail-oriented market with a large number of small brokers. As noted by Hills *et al* (1999) and Jackson and Manning (2007), heterogeneity limits a CCP's capacity to apply both a uniform margin rate across participants and pooled financial resources (particularly in the case of a user-owned CCP). In this case, participants of higher financial standing would tend to subsidise those of lesser standing. Relatively high threshold participation requirements and tiered participation may therefore be more likely to be observed in heterogeneous markets.

3. A MODEL OF CCPS' RISK CONTROLS

In this section we present a model of CCP risk controls. Our principal focus is on how different preferences and funding structures may affect the size and composition of a CCP's financial resources and how regulatory action may shape private incentives. The analysis takes into account how risk-management choices affect participation in the CCP, and by implication the level of trading activity.

The model builds on Baer *et al* (2004) and applies a constrained optimisation framework to three highly stylised CCPs:

- A mutualised, *user-owned* CCP that sets margin requirements to maximise the expected collective pay-off of its participants and would fund any shortfall in the event of a default using either pre-funded participant contributions or *ex post* loss allocation to participants.
- A *for-profit CCP with equity funding* that sets margin requirements to maximise expected profits and would fund any shortfall in the event of a default using its own capital (either pre-funded/allocated or raised *ex post*).
- A *for-profit CCP with participant funding* that sets margin requirements to maximise expected profits and would fund any shortfall in the event of a default using either pre-funded participant contributions or *ex post* loss allocation to participants.

These are highly stylised models and in practice CCPs often do not fit neatly into these categories. Nevertheless the National Securities Clearing Corporation (a subsidiary of the Depository Trust and Clearing Corporation) is an example of a user-owned CCP and ASX Clear is a for-profit CCP that would fund any shortfall using its own capital. The for-profit model with participant funding is relatively common, particularly where a CCP is vertically integrated with a demutualised exchange. Chicago Mercantile Exchange (CME) is an example of a for-profit CCP with pre-funded resources that are predominantly funded by participants. In general, however, even where a for-profit CCP relies on pre-funded participant contributions or *ex post* loss allocation to participants, it will typically have at least some skin in the game. See the Appendix for a list of CCPs and their ownership structure.

In the model we start with an *unregulated* CCP, before going on to consider the implications of *regulation*. Consider a simple environment, with *n* traders and a CCP that interposes itself between buyers and sellers in a liquid market for a single financial product; the 'rest of the economy' is ignored. We consider an infinite stream of trading days, each comprising five sub-periods:

- At *t0*, the CCP sets the mix of risk controls to apply to all trades executed during the coming day. An unregulated CCP chooses the level at which to set initial margin, *m*, taking into account expected *ex post* funding requirements to meet any shortfall arising in the event of a participant default. A regulated CCP sets initial margin taking into account a minimum requirement for total *pre-funded* financial resources, which may be achieved through either margins or a pre-funded default fund. A regulated CCP must also address any losses beyond its prefunded financial resources. The CCP receives all initial margin and, where relevant, pre-funded financial resources, in cash, and invests these in risk-free, liquid instruments, ensuring that they can be liquidated on a timely basis, with little or no loss of value, to meet obligations arising in the event of a participant default.
- At *t1*, trading participants make their trading decisions. If the value of a trade net of all related costs imposed by the CCP (fees, margin requirements, pre-funded contributions to the default fund or *ex post* loss allocation) is positive, participants will trade a fixed value, *T*; if it is negative, they will trade zero.[5] There are no pre-funded non-margin financial resources in the unregulated case. This participation constraint therefore acts as an effective upper limit on the level of margin requirements. While trading participants are assumed to be homogenous in respect of their financial standing, *n/2* traders value the financial product at *v* over the prevailing price for the financial product, *p*, while *n/2* traders value it at *v* under the prevailing price. We assume that $v \geq E(|\Delta P|)$.
- At *t2*, nature draws from a symmetric distribution of price changes for the financial product, $F(\Delta p)$.
- At *t3*, one trader may default with probability, δ. For simplicity, only a single participant can default in expectation.[6]
- At *t4*, if a trader has defaulted at *t3*, the CCP closes out the risk associated with the defaulter's positions, drawing on the margin posted by the defaulter and, in the case of a regulated CCP, other pre-funded financial resources in the default fund. If these resources are not sufficient, an unregulated CCP may choose to wind down rather than fund any shortfall by absorbing or allocating losses. This will depend on the continuation value of the CCP – that is, the discounted stream of expected future profits. We also consider the case in which the CCP assesses the likelihood of government support to meet a shortfall. Finally we turn to how regulation conditions the CCP's *ex post* options by requiring a recovery plan that comprehensively and reliably addresses any shortfall.

3.1 Unregulated CCP

In this section, we first apply the framework outlined above to the case of an unregulated CCP that operates in an environment with no government sector and no possibility of government support in the event of a clearing participant default. In Section 3.1.5, we consider how the expectation of public support may alter the CCP's risk-management choices.

3.1.1 User-Owned CCP

The user-owned CCP is assumed to be owned in equal shares by its users. It aims to set margin requirements so as to maximise the expected collective pay-off, *V*, discounted over an infinite future horizon at rate *d*:

$$\max_{m} E\left(V\right) = \frac{T}{1-d}\left[n\left(v-cm\right) - \delta(1+R)\int_{m}^{\infty}(\Delta p - m)f(\Delta p)d(\Delta p)\right] \quad (1)$$

Subject to $v \geq cm + \frac{\delta\left(1+R\right)}{\left(n-1\right)}\int_{m}^{\infty}(\Delta p - m)f(\Delta p)d(\Delta p)$

where *v* is the net gain from trade on each of the *n* participants' open positions, *T*; *c* is the opportunity cost to participants associated with posting margins, *m*. We assume that the CCP invests margin received at the risk-free rate of return and therefore *c* is the difference between the risk-free return and the expected rate of return the participant could earn if it invested the funds in risky assets. Without loss of generality, fixed operating costs are assumed to be equal to zero.

The expected pay-off is decreasing in the expected shortfall in the event of a participant default, shown as the second term in square brackets in Equation (1). As noted, in the unregulated case, there are no pre-funded non-margin financial resources: any shortfall is met via *ex post* contributions from participants.[7]

The participation constraint states that trading will only take place if the net gain from a unit of trade exceeds the per-unit expected cost of trading. This comprises the opportunity cost of posting margins and the expected cost of funding a shortfall *ex post*. Since each participant owns an equal share of the CCP, each survivor is ultimately called upon to contribute an equal share of the cost of any shortfall in the event of a default. These funds are raised at single-period cost, *R*. Since $v \geq E(\Delta p)$, the participation constraint holds at $m=0$.

Throughout this section we focus on the case in which the expected default shortfall is less than the 'continuation value' of the CCP (i.e., the discounted sum of expected utility should the CCP continue into perpetuity) and therefore the CCP (or equivalently its participants) would fund the default via an agreed loss allocation mechanism.[8]

However, even though *in expectation* the CCP expects to continue operating following a default, should the *observed* shortfall in financial resources in the event of a default exceed the CCP's continuation value it will wind down rather than fund the shortfall. This strategic option arises because the unregulated CCP relies on *ex post* funding. In this sense, any inability to enforce *ex post* funding reduces the reliability of the CCP's risk-management framework.

3.1.2 For-Profit CCP with Equity Funding

The for-profit CCP with equity funding aims to maximise its expected profit, with revenue earned from ad-valorem fees, *g*, on each participant's open positions.[9] The CCP optimises the objective function in Equation (2), subject to the participation constraint.[10] [11]

$$\max_{m} E\left(\pi\right) = \frac{T}{1-d}\left[ng - \delta\left(1+R\right)\int_{m}^{\infty}(\Delta p - m)f(\Delta p)d(\Delta p)\right] \quad (2)$$

Subject to $v \geq cm + g$

It is assumed that the CCP operates in a contestable market and therefore is a price-taker of clearing fees.

In the participation constraint, participants take into account both clearing fees and the opportunity cost of posting margin in their decision to trade. In the this case, it is assumed that the CCP relies entirely on its own funds. It will therefore meet any shortfall by raising capital *ex post* at the single-period cost, *R*. In practice, *R* may differ between the user-owned and for-profit CCPs.

As before, we restrict attention to the case in which the CCP has a positive net expected continuation value in the event of a participant default. However, should a default occur, the CCP again has the strategic option to wind down rather than fund the shortfall if the observed default shortfall cost exceeds its continuation value.

3.1.3 For-Profit CCP with Participant Funding

The for-profit CCP with participant funding again aims to maximise its expected profit, with revenue earned from ad-valorem fees. Since in this case, any shortfall is ultimately funded by participants, the CCP does not incur any cost in the event of a default. Instead, costs associated with default are borne entirely by the participants. Therefore, the CCP's profit-seeking incentives are not constrained by costs associated with raising funds to cover defaults. The CCP optimises a margin-independent objective function, with the cost of funding defaults reflected only in the participation constraint.

$$\max_{m} E\left(\pi\right) = \frac{T}{1-d}ng \quad (3)$$

Subject to $v \geq cm + g + \dfrac{\delta\left(1+R\right)}{\left(n-1\right)}\int_{m}^{\infty}(\Delta p - m)f(\Delta p)d(\Delta p)$

As before, we restrict attention to the case in which the CCP has a positive net expected continuation value in the event of a participant default.

3.1.4 Risk Management Choices of the Unregulated CCPs

The optimal margin choices of the three types of unregulated CCP are presented in Table 1. These again focus on the case in which the CCPs expect to continue rather than wind down in the event of a default that exhausts the defaulted participant's margins.

If unconstrained, the for-profit CCP with equity funding will seek full margin coverage, with no reliance on *ex post* funding sources. The unconstrained user-owned CCP, on the other hand, will set margin requirements at below full coverage, relying on *ex post* contributions from surviving participants to meet any shortfall arising in the event of a participant default. This reflects the fact that the user-owned CCP

Table 1. Margin Choices of the Unregulated CCPs[1]

	Constrained (participation constraint binds)	**Unconstrained (participation constraint does not bind)**
User owned CCP	$m = \frac{1}{c}\left[v - \frac{\delta(1+R)}{n-1}\int_m^{\infty}(\Delta p - m)f(\Delta p)d(\Delta p)\right]$	$m = F^{-1}\left(1 - \frac{nc}{\delta(1+R)}\right)$
For profit CCP with equity funding	$m = \frac{v-g}{c}$	$m = F^{-1}(1)$
For profit with participant funding	$m = \frac{1}{c}\left[v - g - \frac{\delta(1+R)}{n-1}\int_m^{\infty}(\Delta p - m)f(\Delta p)d(\Delta p)\right]$	Profit independent of margin choice

[1]Note that reduced form analytical solutions cannot be found for the constrained margin choices in the cases of the user-owned CCP and the for-profit CCP with participant-funded pooled financial resources.

faces both costs and benefits from increasing margin requirements: while higher margin requirements reduce the expected shortfall cost in the event of a default, they also increase the opportunity cost to participants. When the default probability is low and opportunity costs are high, the user-owned CCP will rely more on *ex post* contributions relative to defaulter-pays (margin) protections. The for-profit CCP with equity funding, on the other hand, only takes into account participants' opportunity cost of posting margin if the participation constraint binds; otherwise it seeks only to minimise expected shortfall costs by setting margin requirements at a high level.

The for-profit CCP with equity funding will, however, be bound by its participation constraint, since the level of margin requirements that secures full coverage when prices can move over an infinite range will exceed the finite maximum level at which traders will be prepared to participate in the CCP. For the user-owned CCP, the participation constraint lies close to the margin level at which expected pay-offs approach zero. It is therefore unlikely that this constraint will bind.[12]

Perhaps the most interesting case, therefore, is that in which the participation constraint binds only for the for-profit CCP. In this case, the for-profit CCP with equity funding will set higher margin requirements than the user-owned CCP as long as:

$$\frac{v-g}{c} > F^{-1}\left(1 - \frac{nc}{\delta(1+R)}\right) \tag{4}$$

Whether this holds depends on the parameter values: the greater the difference between the participants' net gain from trade, v, and clearing fees, g, and the lower the probability of default, the more likely it is that the for-profit CCP will set higher margin requirements. The intuition is that if gains from trade are sufficiently high, participants in the for-profit CCP will, for a given c, be willing to accept higher margin requirements, since there will still be a net benefit from trading. And the lower the probability of default, the lower the expected cost of any shortfall to the user-owned CCP. Accordingly, the user-owned CCP will optimally place greater reliance on *ex post* funding relative to defaulter-pays protections.

In the case of the for-profit CCP with participant funding, profit is independent of margin choice when the participation constraint doesn't bind. The outcome is therefore indeterminate. When the participation constraint binds, however, the expression for the optimal margin choice is similar to that in the case of the constrained user-owned CCP. The constraint is, however, more likely to bind, since participants will also take into account clearing fees, g. As n increases, the expected shortfall term tends towards zero and the optimal margin choice tends towards $\frac{v-g}{c}$, as in the case of the constrained for-profit CCP with equity funding.

3.1.5 Expected Government Support

We now consider the implications of expected government support. In the model, the government seeks to ensure continuity of CCP services. This recognises that CCPs are key components of the financial system, delivering services critical to the smooth functioning of financial markets. Indeed, some have argued recently that CCPs have become the ultimate 'too-important-to-fail' institutions (Tucker, 2013; Coeuré, 2014).

In the event of a participant default that left a CCP facing a shortfall, it could be difficult for the government to credibly commit to not supporting the CCP. The government's continuation value is similar to that of the user-owned CCP, reflecting the net gains from trade, but we also add a 'spillover' cost to capture the potential knock-on effect of a CCP failure on the rest of the economy. The cost to the government of meeting a shortfall reflects the cost of fiscal distortion associated with raising taxes from the rest of the economy.

Introducing the expectation of public support significantly alters the problem facing an unregulated CCP. If the optimal level of margin requirements is set such that, in expectation, the government's continuation value for the CCP will exceed the size of the shortfall to be funded, the CCP can reasonably anticipate that it will receive public support. That is, the CCP realises that the government cannot commit to allowing it to fail. The CCP's (or equivalently its users') private expected shortfall cost is therefore zero.[13]

If the government cannot commit to allowing it to fail, it is reasonable to assume that a user-owned CCP will set m at the lowest level at which it would receive public support in the event of a shortfall: either at $m=0$, or, where the government would provide support only over some range of positive margin requirements, at the lower bound of this range. This is intuitive: if a CCP expects public support, it no longer has to cover the cost of a default (through either margin or *ex post* funding), and therefore has no incentive to set margin requirements in excess of the minimum level required to ensure such support. The higher the spillover cost and the lower the cost of fiscal distortion, the more likely it is that the government will provide support over the entire range of margin requirements on which the CCP will receive a positive expected pay-off.

It is always in the interests of an otherwise constrained for-profit CCP, including one with participant-funded pooled financial resources, to set margin requirements such that it would receive public support. Accordingly, its expected profits will be independent of margin. However, if the government can only be expected to provide support over a range of positive margin, there is a possibility the constraint will bind; this is more likely the higher the clearing fee, g, relative to the participants' per-unit gain from trade, v.

Comparing these outcomes with the unconstrained choices in Table 1, the expectation of public support is likely to lead to a lower optimal margin choice for both user-owned and for-profit CCPs.

3.2 Regulated CCP

Since public support is costly, and yet the government may find it difficult to commit to not providing support *ex post*, the government will introduce regulation to enforce 'self-insurance' by the CCP. In particular, the government will set minimum standards for the quality of the CCP's risk control framework. To illustrate the implications of regulation within the model, we introduce:

- *Pre-funded financial resources.* An *ex ante* requirement to hold sufficient pre-funded financial resources, either in the form of margins or pooled financial resources, to meet any shortfall arising up to an 'extreme but plausible' price change, $|\Delta P^*|$. This may be regarded as equivalent to the cover one requirement in the PFMIs.[14] The price change to be covered would in practice be calibrated with reference to stress-test outcomes. By enforcing a default management framework that draws on a regulated minimum quantum of pre-funded resources in a defined order in the event of a participant default (the so-called 'default waterfall'), the regulator aims to improve reliability and eliminate the wind down option available to an unregulated CCP that relies only on *ex post* funding.
- *Recovery plans.* A participant default in conjunction with a price change in excess of $|\Delta P^*|$ would, however, lead to an unfunded shortfall in the CCP. The PFMIs specify that CCPs' recovery plans should include mechanisms to address any such unfunded losses and also to replenish any drawdown of pre-funded non-margin financial resources. Such mechanisms might include *ex post* loss-allocation agreements with participants, such as committed supplementary calls on participants to 'top-up' pooled pre-funded resources or haircutting of participants' variation margin gains (CPSS-IOSCO, 2014; Gibson, 2013; ISDA, 2013). A special resolution regime for CCPs, such as is encouraged by international policymakers (Financial Stability Board (FSB), 2014a) and is being introduced in a number of jurisdictions (Council of Financial Regulators, 2012; UK Government, 2014), will sit behind the regulatory framework as a backstop to recovery plans. In combination with a special resolution regime for CCPs, recovery plans to allocate unfunded losses aim to enhance the reliability of *ex post* funding sources and eliminate the moral hazard associated with expectations of government support. In the model, therefore, each regulated CCP's objective function explicitly takes into account the cost and impact of loss allocation and replenishment requirements. We assume that unfunded losses are allocated to participants in the case of both the user-owned CCP and the for-profit CCP with participant funding; and to shareholders in the case of the for-profit CCP with equity funding.

3.2.1 User-Owned CCP

The positioning of the CCP's optimal margin choice relative to $|\Delta P^*|$ determines both the objective function and the solution to the optimisation. The regulated user-owned CCP sets margin requirements according to Equation (5).

If $\left|\Delta P^*\right| > m$:

$$\max_m E\left(V\right) = \frac{T}{1-d}\left[\begin{array}{l} n\left(v - cm\right) - \delta(1+2R)\int\limits_m^{|\Delta P^*|}(\Delta p - m)f(\Delta p)d(\Delta p) \\ -\delta(1+R)\int\limits_{|\Delta P^*|}^{\infty}(\Delta p - m)f(\Delta p)d(\Delta p) - \delta R(\left|\Delta P^*\right| - m)\int\limits_{|\Delta P^*|}^{\infty}f(\Delta p)d(\Delta p) - c(\left|\Delta P^*\right| - m) \end{array}\right] \quad (5)$$

Subject to

$$v \geq cm + \frac{\delta(1+2R)}{(n-1)}\int\limits_m^{|\Delta P^*|}(\Delta p - m)f(\Delta p)d(\Delta p) + \frac{\delta(1+R)}{(n-1)}\int\limits_{|\Delta P^*|}^{\infty}(\Delta p - m)f(\Delta p)d(\Delta p) + \frac{\delta R}{(n-1)}(\left|\Delta P^*\right| - m)\int\limits_{|\Delta P^*|}^{\infty}f(\Delta p)d(\Delta p) + \frac{c(\left|\Delta P^*\right| - m)}{n}$$

If $m \geq \left|\Delta P^*\right|$, Equation (1) applies.

The final term in the square brackets of Equation (5) captures the cost to the CCP of the pre-funded default resource requirement. This is sized to capture the excess in the cover one requirement over margin collected from the defaulted participant. The funds are contributed by the participant owners of the CCP, at a per-period opportunity cost of *c*.

The second, third and fourth terms in the square brackets capture three distinct sources of the expected default cost to the CCP, when $\left|\Delta P^*\right| > m$:

- If a participant default coincides with a price change of $\left|\Delta P^*\right| > \Delta p > m$, the CCP must fund the entire cost of the shortfall over margin by drawing on its pool of pre-funded resources. The risk-free return on these funds is also forgone in that period and hence a single-period cost of *R* is incurred. Any funds drawn must be immediately replenished so that the CCP is protected against a subsequent default. This replenishment incurs a single-period cost of R. These expected costs, per unit of trade, are captured by the term,

$$\delta(1+2R)\int\limits_m^{|\Delta P^*|}(\Delta p - m)f(\Delta p)d(\Delta p).$$

Given the length of this expression, in the remainder of this section, we define this term as 'Covered Shortfall' = CS.

- In the event of a price change in excess of $\left|\Delta P^*\right|$, the CCP must again draw on its pool of pre-funded resources to cover the loss up to $\left|\Delta P^*\right|$ and then cover the unfunded component via *ex post* loss allocation to participants. As in the model with only *ex post* funding of a shortfall, each surviving participant is ultimately called upon to contribute an equal share of the cost of any shortfall in the event of a default. The risk-free return on the pre-funded component is again forgone, with a single-period cost of *R* incurred in raising the unfunded component. These expected costs, per unit of trade, are captured by the term:

$$\delta(1+R)\int_{|\Delta P*|}^{\infty}(\Delta p-m)f(\Delta p)d(\Delta p).$$

Again, given the length of this expression, in the remainder of this section, we define this term as 'Uncovered Shortfall' = US.

- Also in the event of a price change in excess of $|\Delta P*|$, the CCP must again replenish any funds drawn, up to $|\Delta P*|$. This replenishment also incurs a single-period cost of R. This expected cost, per unit of trade, is captured by the term:

$$\delta R(|\Delta P*|-m)\int_{|\Delta P*|}^{\infty}f(\Delta p)d(\Delta p).$$

The expected costs of pre-funding, replenishment and loss allocation are also reflected in the participation constraint. The *n* and (*n-1*) terms reflect the mutualisation among participants.[15]

3.2.2 For-Profit CCP with Equity Funding

The objective function of the for-profit CCP with equity funding also depends on the positioning of the CCP's optimal margin choice relative to $|\Delta P*|$.

If $|\Delta P*|>m$:

$$\max_{m} E\left(V\right)=\frac{T}{1-d}\left[ng-CS-US-\delta R(|\Delta P*|-m)\int_{|\Delta P*|}^{\infty}f(\Delta p)d(\Delta p)-c(|\Delta P*|-m)\right] \tag{6}$$

Subject to $v\geq cm+g$

If $m\geq|\Delta P*|$, Equation (2) applies.

In this case, the CCP funds pre-funded non-margin resources using its own equity, at a unit opportunity cost of c. The CCP also bears the full cost of meeting any shortfall ex post and replenishing pre-funded resources. These are reflected in the terms of Equation (6) that are equivalent to those described for the user-owned CCP. Since participants bear none of the cost of pre-funded or ex post default resources, the participation constraint remains as in Equation (2).

3.2.3 For-profit CCP with participant funding

Finally, the objective function of the for-profit CCP with participant funding is given by Equation (7).

If $\left|\Delta P^*\right| > m$:

$$\max_{m} E\left(\pi\right) = \frac{Tng}{1-d} \tag{7}$$

Subject to

$$v \geq cm + g + \frac{1}{(n-1)}\left(CS + US + \delta R(\left|\Delta P^*\right| - m)\int_{\left|\Delta P^*\right|}^{\infty} f(\Delta p)d(\Delta p)\right) + \frac{c(\left|\Delta P^*\right| - m)}{n}$$

If $m \geq \left|\Delta P^*\right|$, Equation (3) applies.

As in Equation (3), since the CCP bears none of the cost of meeting a shortfall in the event of a participant default, its expected profit is independent of margin. These costs are, however, reflected in the participation constraint. This constraint is similar to that for the regulated user-owned CCP, but with the addition of the clearing fee, g.

3.2.4 Risk-Management Choices of the Regulated CCPs

Solving the problems described by Equations (5) – (7), Table 2 details the optimal margin choices of the regulated CCPs. As noted, the CCPs' optimal choices depend on the position of *m* relative to $\left|\Delta P^*\right|$. Accordingly, the table presents margin choices separately for $m \geq \left|\Delta P^*\right|$ and $m < \left|\Delta P^*\right|$, as well as separately for the cases in which the participation constraints binds and those in which it doesn't bind.

It is clear that, if unconstrained, the for-profit CCP with equity funding will again have an incentive to set margin requirements as high as possible. The optimal level is full coverage. Indeed, there is no valid solution to this CCP's problem for the unconstrained case with $\left|\Delta P^*\right| > m$. As before, we focus on the practical case that the for-profit CCP with equity funding is bound by the participation constraint. In this case, the optimal choice is as in the unregulated case. This is intuitive since participants face neither the cost of pre-funded nor *ex post* funded default resources and therefore the constraint is unchanged. In practice, however, it is likely that the market-clearing level of fees, *g*, would be higher than when CCPs were unregulated. This would reflect the opportunity cost to CCPs of pre-funding non-margin financial resources, and the expected cost of meeting any shortfall in those resources.

In the case of the user-owned CCP, where it is unconstrained and $m \geq \left|\Delta P^*\right|$, the optimal margin choice is as in the unregulated case. This recognises that all losses in the event of default would be met through margin and *ex post* funding, as before. In the more likely case that $m < \left|\Delta P^*\right|$, however, regulation leads to a higher optimal margin choice:

Table 2. Margin Choices of the Regulated CCPs[1]

		Constrained (participation constraint binds)	***Unconstrained (participation constraint does not bind)***
User owned CCP	$m \geq \lvert \Delta P^* \rvert$	$m = \frac{1}{c}\left[v - \frac{\delta(1+R)}{(n-1)}\int_{m}^{\infty}(\Delta p - m)f(\Delta p)d(\Delta p)\right]$	$m = F^{-1}\left(1 - \frac{nc}{\delta(1+R)}\right)$
	$m < \lvert \Delta P^* \rvert$	$m = \frac{1}{c\left[\left(1-\frac{1}{n}\right) - \frac{\delta R}{(n-1)}\int_{\lvert \Delta P^* \rvert}^{\infty} f(\Delta p)d(\Delta p)\right]}\left[v - \frac{(CS+US)}{(n-1)} - \lvert \Delta P^* \rvert\left(\frac{1}{n} + \frac{\delta R}{(n-1)}\int_{\lvert \Delta P^* \rvert}^{\infty} f(\Delta p)d(\Delta p)\right)\right]$	$m = F^{-1}\left(1 - \frac{(n-1)c}{\delta(1+2R)}\right)$
For profit CCP with equity funding	$m \geq. \lvert \Delta P^* \rvert$	$m = \frac{v-g}{c}$	$m = F^{-1}(1)$
	$m < \lvert \Delta P^* \rvert$	$m = \frac{v-g}{c}$	$m = F^{-1}\left(1 + \frac{c}{\delta(1+2R)}\right) > F^{-1}(1)$; therefore, n/a.
For profit CCP with participant funding	$m \geq \lvert \Delta P^* \rvert$	$m = \frac{1}{c}\left[v - g - \frac{\delta(1+R)}{(n-1)}\int_{m}^{\infty}(\Delta p - m)f(\Delta p)d(\Delta p)\right]$	Profit independent of margin choice
	$m < \lvert \Delta P^* \rvert$	$m = \frac{1}{c\left[\left(1-\frac{1}{n}\right) - \frac{\delta R}{(n-1)}\int_{\lvert \Delta P^* \rvert}^{\infty} f(\Delta p)d(\Delta p)\right]}\left[v - g - \frac{(CS+US)}{(n-1)} - \lvert \Delta P^* \rvert\left(\frac{1}{n} + \frac{\delta R}{(n-1)}\int_{\lvert \Delta P^* \rvert}^{\infty} f(\Delta p)d(\Delta p)\right)\right]$	Profit independent of margin choice

[1]Note that reduced form analytical solutions cannot be found for the constrained margin choices in the cases of the user-owned CCP and the for-profit CCP with participant funding.

$$m(regulated) = F^{-1}\left(1 - \frac{(n-1)c}{\delta(1+2R)}\right) > m(unregulated) = F^{-1}\left(1 - \frac{nc}{\delta(1+R)}\right).$$

If constrained, the margin choices of the user-owned CCP and the for-profit CCP with participant funding are again as in the unregulated case where $m \geq \lvert \Delta P^* \rvert$. Whether margin is higher or lower than in the unregulated case if $m < \lvert \Delta P^* \rvert$ depends on parameter values. While the solutions are long expressions, they capture the trade-off between *ex ante* opportunity costs – of posting margin and pre-funded financial resources – and the expected *ex post* cost of loss allocation and replenishment. Intuitively, margins will be increasing in the value of trading and the probability of default, and decreasing in the opportunity cost, *c*, and the number of participants.

3.3 Discussion

The analysis shows that by eliminating the wind-down option and addressing the moral hazard associated with expectations of government support, regulation generally increases the level of margin requirements a CCP will optimally set.

The for-profit CCP with equity funding prefers to rely on margins, subject to its participants' continued willingness to trade. The user-owned CCP, by contrast, prefers to keep margin requirements somewhat lower. Nevertheless, since there is an opportunity cost to holding pre-funded non-margin financial resources that does not exist when all non-margin financial resources are committed only *ex post*, the user-owned CCP will generally optimally set margin requirements higher than when unregulated. Similarly, when constrained, the for-profit CCP with participant funding takes into account participants' preferences and aims to find the appropriate balance between margins and non-margin financial resources so as to meet regulatory requirements while ensuring continued trade.

The analysis reveals that, notwithstanding equivalent regulatory requirements, the ownership and funding structure of a CCP will, subject to minimum margin requirements, determine its risk management choices – in this case, the balance between margins and non-margin financial resources. As long as regulatory requirements are met, observed differences in margin levels may be seen as the outcome of the CCPs' optimisation, reflecting their own and their participants' preferences. A given level of stability and resilience can be achieved with a variety of different risk frameworks. It is important, therefore, that the regulatory framework is sufficiently flexible to accommodate such differences.

Nevertheless, for all parties to make optimal choices it is important that there is transparency of CCPs' risk management arrangements, including for instance how precisely pre-funded financial resource requirements are calibrated to meet $|\Delta P^*|$. There should also be transparency in the balance between margin and non-margin financial resources, and full disclosure of a CCP's recovery plans that set out how it would respond in a distress situation that threatened its viability. Transparency is necessary to ensure that participants fully understand – and can manage – both their *ex ante* and potential future obligations.

Some relevant aspects have not been modelled. In the case of the for-profit CCP with predominantly participant funding, for instance, the absence of the incentive and discipline provided by a material level of 'skin in the game' for the CCP could have implications for financial stability. Strong regulatory oversight and enforcement will be particularly important in such circumstances, as will governance arrangements, such as a user risk committee.

4. DEVELOPMENTS IN THE POST-TRADE MARKET STRUCTURE

A number of emerging trends in the trading and post-trade market structure seem likely to have significant implications both for CCPs' risk management choices and for regulators' enforcement of international standards (RBA, 2014). This section discusses some of these developments and, with reference to the model in Section 3, considers their potential implications.

The relevant developments include:

- *Competition between CCPs.* Over the past decade there has been an expansion in the number and types of trading venues. This trend reflects the increasing sophistication and declining cost of technology and the continued globalisation of finance. Developments in the trading market structure and the emergence of strategies such as algorithmic and high-frequency trading have also increased traders' focus on the cost of clearing. This has led to competition and interoperable links between CCPs in some markets.

- *Cross-border provision of clearing*. Where competition in both trading and clearing has emerged, it has often come from market operators and CCPs seeking to expand their scale and geographical scope in other markets. Participant demands have also been a relevant driver. Cross-border provision of services has been facilitated by a range of public policy initiatives aimed at promoting greater harmonisation of financial regulation across markets.

These trends are shaping the market structure in a number of market segments.

4.1 Developments Across Product Markets

4.1.1 Cash Equities

Over time, advances in technology have significantly altered the market structure of trading in cash equity markets, with competition between venues becoming more prevalent. For instance, as of November 2014 securities listed on the New York Stock Exchange are traded on 13 lit venues, with around a third of turnover in the S&P 500 index executed off-market or on 'dark' venues.[16] At the same point in time, seven lit venues compete for trading in securities listed on the London Stock Exchange, with around half of the turnover in the FTSE 100 index taking place outside of the lit venues (Fidessa Fragmentation Index, n.d.).

Even though there is now competition between trading venues, in most markets there remains a monopoly provider of post-trade services for cash equities. However, this has changed in Europe and could change in other markets.

In 2007, the Markets in Financial Instruments Directive (MiFID) removed legislative barriers to competition between European trading venues. This led quickly to newly created trading facilities contesting the markets of a number of established exchanges. While these new trading venues competed with each other in most of the major equities markets throughout Europe, initially they each directed trades to a particular CCP. As they tended to use different CCPs to the incumbent exchanges, this introduced some competition at the clearing level.

Over time, interoperable links have been established between some CCPs. These allow CCPs to directly compete for trades executed on a particular trading venue. With interoperability, participants can avoid the loss of netting that occurs when positions are fragmented across multiple CCPs, although this comes at the cost of new exposures between the interoperating CCPs themselves which must be managed (see Section 4.2.2). It is estimated that around half of all share trading in Europe occurs on trading venues that offer participants a choice of CCP (Stafford, 2013a). EuroCCP, LCH.Clearnet Ltd and SIX x-clear have a three-way interoperability link to compete for trades executed on BATS Chi-X Europe, Turquoise and UBS MTF (BATS, n.d.). LCH.Clearnet Ltd and SIX x-clear also compete for equity trades executed on the London Stock Exchange and the SIX Swiss Exchange (Stafford, 2014). In mid 2014, the London Stock Exchange announced that it would also allow trades to be cleared through EuroCCP (Stafford, 2014). As a result of the increased competition and market integration across Europe, a report prepared for the European Commission found that on average clearing fees across Europe decreased by 73 per cent between 2006 and 2009 (Oxera, 2011).

However, the competitive pressure on clearing of European cash-equities led to the merger in 2013 of two of Europe's largest CCPs, EuroCCP and the European Multilateral Clearing Facility (EMCF), now collectively known as EuroCCP. Prior to the merger, EuroCCP operated at a loss, with its parent – the

Depository Trust & Clearing Corporation – reportedly injecting more than €100 million into EuroCCP over its four years of operation. While EMCF was initially profitable, its market share declined and it made a loss just prior to the merger (Stafford, 2013b).

4.1.2 Exchange Traded Derivatives

Trading and clearing of exchange traded derivatives tends to be structured in vertical silos, with few examples to date of inter-CCP links other than a small number of cross-margining arrangements between CCPs that clear different contracts referencing the same (or related) underlyings. There have been some instances of successful challenges by competing derivatives trading venues, which have typically also involved a shift in liquidity between vertically integrated CCPs. While overall evidence is mixed, the successes include the following:

- The most frequently cited example of a successful challenge is the entry of Deutsche Terminbörse (DTB, now Eurex group) into the market for German government debt (Bund) futures in 1990. These futures were previously traded exclusively on the London International Financial Futures Exchange (Liffe, now part of Intercontinental Exchange, ICE). After quickly gaining a market share of around 20 per cent, DTB's share remained steady for several years until regulatory changes that permitted remote access to DTB's electronic platform encouraged a further migration of activity. At this time Liffe offered only floor trading. As of early 1998, the two exchanges had equal market shares, but thereafter trading shifted rapidly; by September of that year, DTB had captured the entire market (Cantillon and Yin, 2007 and 2011; Pirrong, 2005).
- ICE began listing natural gas futures contracts in 2002, in competition with the incumbent New York Mercantile Exchange (NYMEX, now part of the CME group). While the NYMEX main contract is physically delivered, the ICE contract is cash settled. In response to competition, NYMEX has started offering a cash settled contract. Both exchanges continue to compete, with NYMEX maintaining around two-thirds of this market as of September 2014 (CME, n.d.; ICE, n.d.).
- The Order Machine (TOM), part-owned by NASDAQ, has operated a derivatives trading platform in the Netherlands since 2011. The venue lists single-name and equity-index options contracts on Dutch underlyings, in competition with ICE. As of November 2014, TOM had captured a market share of over 30 per cent across the contracts it lists (TOM, n.d).
- In 2013, NLX – owned by NASDAQ OMX – began to offer interest rate contracts similar to the short term rate contracts traded on Liffe (now ICE) and long term rate contracts on Eurex. NLX is competing on lower fees and greater margin offsets via its CCP (LCH.C Ltd). By the end May 2014, NLX's most successful contract had gained a share of around 15 per cent of the market (Eurex, n.d., ICE, n.d.; NASDAQ, n.d).

By contrast, three exchanges – Eurex, ELX and Euronext – each failed in attempts to capture liquidity in short term US dollar-denominated interest rate futures contracts between 2003 and 2009, with CME successfully defending its monopoly position (Cameron, 2012).

4.1.3 OTC Derivatives

While migration of standardised OTC derivatives transactions to central clearing had begun prior to 2009, since the global financial crisis, domestic and overseas regulatory reforms have encouraged greater use of CCPs in the OTC derivatives market (Gregory, 2014; Murphy, 2013). This has been most evident in the OTC interest rate derivatives market, for which the value of centrally cleared trades increased five-fold from June 2007, to account for substantially more than half of the total notional value outstanding globally by the end of 2013.

Unlike cash equities and exchange traded derivatives, which rely on central clearing to facilitate anonymous trading on an exchange, counterparty exposures related to derivatives traded bilaterally in OTC markets have traditionally been risk managed on a bilateral basis. While collecting initial margin is a core aspect of CCP risk management, this has not normally been the case for non-centrally cleared OTC derivatives. Consequently, during the global financial crisis, when counterparty defaults became more likely – and in the case of Lehman Brothers actually occurred – OTC derivatives users often did not have sufficient collateral to offset actual or potential losses. This may have accelerated the transmission of stress between trading counterparties.

Following the crisis there has been a concerted public policy push to reduce counterparty risk in the OTC derivatives market, in part by increasing central clearing of OTC derivatives. Over half of FSB member jurisdictions anticipate having a central clearing framework in effect by end 2016 (FSB, 2015). Consistent with the Basel III capital standards, most jurisdictions impose higher capital requirements for non-centrally cleared OTC derivatives exposures. This acts as an incentive to move to central clearing. This incentive will be further strengthened by the introduction of initial margin requirements for non-centrally cleared OTC derivatives exposures, which is scheduled for September 2016 (BCBS-IOSCO, 2015).

Participants in OTC derivatives markets tend to organise their trading activity and post-trade processes on a multicurrency basis. Consequently, the most prominent CCPs that clear OTC derivatives are also organised on a multicurrency basis with a highly international participant base. As a result, the move to central clearing of OTC derivatives has highlighted the challenges in regulating cross-border provision of clearing services. Increasingly OTC derivatives CCPs are subject to regulation in multiple jurisdictions. For example, LCH.Clearnet Limited is primarily supervised by the Bank of England and subject to EU regulation, but is also subject to some form of regulation in Australia, Canada, China, Japan, Switzerland and the US (FSB, 2015.

4.2 Implications for CCP's Risk Management Choices and Regulation

We now consider the implications of the emerging trends towards competition and interoperability between CCPs and cross-border provision of clearing services for CCP's risk management choices, with reference to the model set out in Section 3.

4.2.1 Competition

The benefits and risks of competition in central clearing are well known (CPSS, 2010; Zhu, 2011). While competition may lead to lower clearing fees, broaden market participants' access to central clearing and encourage innovation, theoretically it could also encourage CCPs to compromise risk controls to lower costs in a 'race to the bottom'. The different margin outcomes arising in our model are not a product of a race to the bottom. They are due to different optimisation problems faced by a regulated CCP affecting the mix of margins and pre-funded pooled financial resources to meet any shortfall arising from an extreme but plausible price change ($|\Delta P^*|$). Nevertheless, a race to the bottom could arise if regulators did not adequately enforce the requirement that all CCPs had sufficient pre-funded default resources.

Where CCPs compete, open positions could potentially be split across CCPs. Further, if the trading decision was modelled as a continuous function of margin (i.e. $T(m)$), overall open trading positions could be lower, since fragmentation of exposures would be likely to lead to fewer offsetting positions and therefore higher margin requirements. Since CCP clearing is a scale business, a reduction in open positions would, all other things being equal, make a for-profit CCP less profitable or, in the case of a user-owned CCP, reduce the expected collective pay-off. As noted, prior to the recent re-consolidation in Europe, there was some evidence that competition was making CCP clearing of cash equities less profitable.

Competition could have a variety of implications for the market structure and the depth of liquidity across trading venues and CCPs. On the one hand, the market could become segmented, splitting the number of traders across the competing CCPs. For a user-owned CCP or a for-profit CCP with participant funded default resources, this would other things being equal increase the likelihood that the participation constraint was binding, since shortfalls would be mutualised across a smaller number of participants. On the other hand, opening up markets to competition could attract traders that were previously unable to gain access, potentially increasing both T and n for a given CCP. With other parameters held constant, the optimal margin level, m, for that CCP would decline. And if competition arose from a cross-border trading venue and CCP, other trading, netting and mutualisation opportunities could emerge (see Section 4.2.3, below).

Competition could also occur between for-profit and user-owned CCPs. Competing CCPs may face different costs of raising funds, with implications for the outcomes of their respective optimisation problems. Similarly, while the model assumes that for-profit CCPs are price-takers in respect of clearing fees, in reality competing CCPs may charge different clearing fees reflecting the scale of their respective businesses and other idiosyncratic market factors. As has been observed in European cash equity markets, competitive pressures may lead CCPs to lower such clearing fees. With identical products and no barriers to choosing between CCPs, competition within a market could prove unsustainable in the medium run as participants shift to the CCP that maximises their net gain from trade. This could be self-fulfilling as scale, netting benefits and mutualisation opportunities further lower costs. This is consistent with the experience to date in competition for exchange traded derivatives.

If competition was unsustainable in the medium term, markets would have to accommodate entry and exit of CCPs. This may be undesirable, given the high costs to market participants of transitioning between CCPs. Connecting to a new CCP entails significant legal, technology and operational costs. It is also a time-consuming process, which for some participants can take several months. Should a CCP subsequently exit, forcing participants to transfer to a new CCP, these connection costs would be borne again, with possible market disruption during the transition. More research is encouraged to better understand the dynamics of competition in these markets, including the implications for risk management choices, to ensure an appropriate regulatory response.

4.2.2 Interoperability

Sustained competition has been observed in the clearing of European cash equities, where interoperability mitigates the unnetting associated with fragmented clearing venues, and allows participants to avoid duplicating CCP membership fees, default fund contributions and other participation requirements. Interoperability should allow for overall open positions across competing CCPs to remain unchanged, even where they are a continuous function of margin; although these could still be spread across the competing CCPs.

Interoperable links between CCPs also create a direct counterparty exposure between those CCPs that must be managed. However, work by Cox, Garvin and Kelly (2013) suggests that under a wide variety of plausible assumptions the inter-CCP netting benefit outweighs the cost arising from inter-CCP exposures. Since derivatives exposures typically have a much longer duration than securities exposures, the risk from inter-CCP links could be higher in derivatives markets than in securities markets. Consequently, regulatory approval of interoperability arrangements in EU derivatives markets has been postponed pending further review.

More generally, competition and links inherently add complexity to the post-trade landscape. Following the introduction of the first inter-CCP links in Europe, regulators developed a number of risk-management conditions for new link arrangements in securities markets. These conditions have since formed the basis for an FMI links principle in the PFMIs, as well as guidelines for assessing interoperability arrangements issued by the European Securities and Markets Authority in June 2013 (ESMA, 2013).

4.2.3 Cross-Border Provision of Clearing Services

Even in European cash equity markets, where sustained competition has been observed, there is some evidence of re-consolidation. Consolidation and cross-border provision of clearing services may be modelled as an increase in the number of traders that clear via a given CCP. By creating opportunities for wider mutualisation, this would relax the participation constraint of user-owned CCPs or for-profit CCPs that rely on participant funding, other things being equal lowering the optimal margin level. In a continuous trading model, open positions would rise in response to the fall in margin.

Cross-border provision of clearing services brings a CCP within the scope of regulation in multiple jurisdictions. To ensure harmonisation of regulatory requirements, such as $|\Delta P^*|$, and more generally address the need for a resilient and efficient global framework for central clearing, in January 2012 the FSB articulated 'four safeguards':

- Fair and open access by market participants to CCPs, based on transparent and objective criteria.
- Cooperative oversight arrangements between relevant authorities, both domestically and internationally and on either a bilateral or multilateral basis, that result in robust and consistently applied regulation and oversight of global CCPs.
- Resolution and recovery regimes that ensure the core functions of CCPs are maintained during times of crises and that consider the interests of all jurisdictions where the CCP is systemically important.
- Appropriate liquidity arrangements for CCPs in the currencies they clear.

The PFMIs touch on all of these issues, and CPMI and IOSCO have recently published further guidance on FMI recovery planning (CPMI-IOSCO, 2014). At the same time, the FSB has finalised an annex to the *Key Attributes of Effective Resolution Regimes for Financial Institutions* (2011) setting out the legal and institutional arrangements a jurisdiction should put in place to deal with a distressed systemically important non-banks, including CCPs (FSB, 2014a).

In support of the requirement that CCPs have appropriate liquidity arrangements in the currencies they clear, central banks have committed to ensuring that there are no technical obstacles to providing liquidity assistance to a CCP that is fundamentally sound but faces a shortage of liquidity at very short notice (FSB, 2012).

5. CONCLUSION

The objective of this chapter has been to explore the determinants of a CCP's risk-management choices and gauge the role of regulation in influencing private decisions.

Applying an optimising framework that builds on Baer et al (2004), we have demonstrated that, other things being equal, ownership and funding structures potentially have an important bearing on a CCP's risk management choices. We also show that expectations of public support may lead private decisions to deviate from the socially optimal choice. Robust regulation is therefore required to ensure appropriate incentives to manage risks.

This highlights the importance of enforcing international best-practice standards for CCP risk management, as reflected in the PFMIs. These establish minimum standards for the key parameters of CCPs' risk controls, including the quality of their default resources. Adapting the model to incorporate a minimum level of coverage of pre-funded financial resources and appropriate recovery plans, as required under the PFMIs, we demonstrate that the scope for strategic risk management choices and moral hazard is removed. Nevertheless, within the parameters of the regulatory framework, CCPs will optimally reach different risk control decisions, reflecting their private incentives. Transparency and sound governance arrangements are essential to ensure that CCP participants fully understand the risks they bear as participants of CCPs.

We have also discussed some emerging trends in the trading and post-trade market structure which are likely also to have a bearing on CCPs' risk management choices. We leave for future research explicit modelling of these developments as well as other more detailed requirements under the PFMIs.

REFERENCES

Anderson, R., & Joeveer, K. (2014). The Economics of Collateral, *Financial Markets Group Discussion Paper* No 732

Baer, H., France, V., & Moser, J. (2004). Opportunity Cost and Prudentiality: An Analysis of Collateral Decisions in Bilateral and Multilateral Settings. *Research in Finance*, *21*, 201–227.

BATS. (n.d.). Clearing Interoperability. Retrieved from http://www.batsglobalmarkets.com/europe/equities/clearing/products/interoperability/

BCBS-IOSCO (Basel Committee on Banking Supervision and the Board of the International Organization of Securities Commissions) (2013). *Margin Requirements for Non-centrally Cleared Derivatives - Final Document*, September

Cameron, M. (2012). The Power Behind the Throne. *CME and the Fight for Futures Supremacy Risk Magazine*, *24*(10), 21–26.

Cantillon, E., & Yin, P. (1998). How and When Do Markets Tip? Lessons from the Battle of the Bund, *European Central Bank Working Paper* No 2007–766.

Cantillon, E., & Yin, P. (2011). Competition Between Exchanges: A Research Agenda. *International Journal of Industrial Organization*, *29*(1), 329–336.

CCP12. (n.d.). CCP12 Membership. Retrieved from https://ccp12site-main.pbworks.com/w/page/55831310/CCP12%20Membership

Coeuré, B. (2014). *'The Unknowns of Central Clearing', Speech.* European Central Bank.

Council of Financial Regulators (2012). Review of Financial Market Infrastructure Regulation: Letter to the Deputy Prime Minister and Treasurer, February.

Cox, N., Garvin, N., & Kelly, G. (2013). Central Counterparty Links and Clearing System Exposures, *RBA Research Discussion Paper* No 2013-12.

CME. (n.d.). CMEG Exchange Volume Report – Monthly. Retrieved from http://www.cmegroup.com/wrappedpages/web_monthly_report/Web_Volume_Report_CMEG.pdf

CPSS (Committee on Payment and Settlement Systems) (2010). *Market Structure Developments in the Clearing Industry: Implications for Financial Stability*, November.

CPSS-IOSCO (CPSS - Technical Committee of the International Organization of Securities Commissions) (2012). *Principles for Financial Market Infrastructures*,April.

CPMI-IOSCO (Committee on Payments and Market Infrastructures – IOSCO) (2014). *Recovery of Financial Market Infrastructures: Final Report*, October.

Day, T., & Lewis, C. (2004). Margin Adequacy and Standards: An Analysis of the Crude Oil Futures Market. *The Journal of Business*, *77*(1), 101–135.

Duffie, D., & Zhu, H. (2011). Does a Central Clearing Counterparty Reduce Counterparty Risk? *The Review of Asset Pricing Studies*, *1*(1), 74–95.

Duffie, D., Scheicher, M., & Vuillemey, G. (2014). Central Clearing and Collateral Demand, *NBER Working Paper* No 19890.

Eurex (n.d.). Monthly Statistics. Retrieved from http://www.eurexchange.com/exchange-en/market-data/statistics/monthly-statistics

Fidessa Fragmentation Index. (n.d.) Retrieved from http://fragmentation.fidessa.com/

Figlewski, S. (1984). Margins and Market Integrity: Margin Setting for Stock Index Futures and Options. *Journal of Futures Markets*, *4*, 385–416.

Financial Stability Board (FSB) (2011). *Key Attributes for Effective Resolution Regimes for Financial Institutions*, October.

FSB (2012). *OTC Derivatives Market Reforms Third Progress Report on Implementation*, June.

FSB (2014a). *Key Attributes of Effective Resolution Regimes to Financial Institutions*, October.

FSB (2014b). *OTC Derivatives Market Reforms Eighth Progress Report on Implementation*, November.

G20 (Group of Twenty) (2009). Leaders' Statement, Pittsburgh Summit, 24–25 September

Gemmill, G. (1994). Margins and the Safety of Clearing Houses. *Journal of Banking & Finance*, *18*, 979–996.

Gibson, M. (2013). 'Recovery and Resolution of Central Counterparties', *RBA Bulletin*, December, 39–48.

Gregory, J. (2014). Central Counterparties: Mandatory Clearing and Bilateral Margin Requirements for OTC Derivatives, Croydon, Great Britan: Wiley.

Haene, P., & Sturm, A. (2009). Optimal CCP Risk Management, *Swiss National Bank Working Papers* No. 2009-7.

Hardouvelis, G., & Kim, D. (1995). Margin Requirements, Price Fluctuations and Market Participation in Metal Futures. *Journal of Money, Credit and Banking*, *27*(3), 659–671.

Hartzmark, M. (1986). The Effects of Changing Margin Levels on Futures Market Activity, the Composition of Traders in the Market and Price Performance. *The Journal of Business*, *59*(2), 147–180.

Heath, A., Kelly, G., & Manning, M. (2013). OTC Derivatives Reform: Netting and Networks, *Liquidity and Funding Markets, Proceedings of a Conference*, Reserve Bank of Australia, Sydney, pp 33–73

Hills, B., Rule, D., Parkinson, S., & Young, C. (1999). CCP Clearing Houses and Financial Stability. *Bank of England Financial Stability Review*, *6*, 122–134.

ICE. (n.d.). Historical Daily Volume. Retrieved from https://www.theice.com/marketdata/reports/26

ISDA (International Swaps and Derivatives Association) (2013). CCP Loss Allocation at the End of the Waterfall August.

Jackson, J., & Manning, M. (2007). Comparing the Pre-settlement Risk Implications of Alternative Clearing Arrangements, *Bank of England Working Paper* No. 321.

Knott, R., & Mills, A. (2002). Modelling Risk in CCP Clearing Houses: A Review. *Bank of England Financial Stability Review*, *13*, 162–174.

Koeppl, T., & Monnet, C. (2008). CCPs, *Centre for Financial Studies Working Paper* No. 42.

Kroszner, R. (1999). Can the Financial Markets Privately Regulate Risk? The Development of Derivatives Clearinghouses and Recent Over-the-Counter Innovations. *Journal of Money, Credit and Banking*, *31*(3), 596–618.

Kroszner, R. (2006). Central Counterparty Clearing: History, Innovation, and Regulation, Speech, Board of Governors of the Federal Reserve System, April

Moser, J. (1998). Contracting Innovations and the Evolution of Clearing and Settlement Methods at Futures Exchanges, *Federal Reserve Bank of Chicago Working Paper Series*, No. 1998-26

Murphy, D. (2013). *OTC Derivatives: Bilateral Trading and Central Clearing*. Hampshire, UK: Palgrave Macmillan.

NASDAQ. (n.d.). Historical Market Data. Retrieved from http://www.nasdaqomx.com/transactions/markets/nlx/marketdata/historic-market-data

Norman, P. (2011). *The Risk Controllers. Central Counterparty Clearing in Globalised Financial Markets*. UK: John Wiley and Sons.

Oxera (2011). Monitoring Prices, Costs and Volumes of Trading and Post-trading Services, Report prepared for the European Commission DG Internal Market and Services, May.

Pirrong, C. (2005). Bund for Glory, or, It's a Long Way to Tip a Market, University of Houston Department of Finance, 8 March.

Pirrong, C. (2011). The Economics of Central Clearing: Theory and Practice, *ISDA Discussion Paper Series*, No. 1, May

Pirrong, C. (2013). Financial Exchanges. *Competition and Vertical Integration in Financial Exchanges Competition Policy International*, *7*(2), 90–102.

Powell, J (2014). A Financial System Perspective on Central Clearing of Derivatives, Speech, Board of Governors of the Federal Reserve System, November.

RBA (2014). *Submission to the Financial System Inquiry*, March.

Renault, F. (2010). Concentration Risk and the Optimal Number of Central Counterparties for a Single Asset, *Banque de France Financial Stability Review*, No. 14, July, 169–176

Santos, T., & Schienkman, J. (2001). Competition Among Exchanges. *The Quarterly Journal of Economics*, *116*(3), 1027–1061.

Stafford, P. (2014). LSE to Allow Customers to Clear Trades on EuroCCP, *Financial Times*, 21 May.

Stafford, P. (2013a). UK Gives Green Light to EuroCCP-EMCF Deal, *Financial Times*, 21 October.

Stafford, P. (2013b). EuroCCP cuts settlement feeds for UK and Irish Stocks, *Financial Times*, 12 August.

Telser, L. (1981). Margins and Futures Contracts. *Journal of Futures Markets*, *1*(2), 225–253.

TOM (The Order Machine) (n.d). Statistics. Retrieved from http://tommtf.eu/statistics/

Tucker, P. (2013). Central Counterparties in Evolving Capital Markets: Safety, Recovery and Resolution *Banque de France Financial Stability Review*, No. 17, April, 179–184

UK Government (2014). *Consultation Outcome – Secondary Legislation for Non-Bank Resolution Regimes*, June

Zhu, S. (2011). Is There a "Race to the Bottom" in Central Counterparties Competition? De Nederlandsche Bank Occasional Studies Vol 9 No 6.

KEY TERMS AND DEFINITIONS

Additional Margin: A form of defaulter-pays protection that is often collected from participants with particularly large or concentrated positions against a CCP, or in response to adverse information on a participant's financial position.

Central Counterparty (CCP): An FMI that interposes itself between the original contracting parties to a trade, becoming the buyer to the seller and the seller to the buyer.

Financial Market Infrastructure (FMI): An organisation that is used by its members to facilitate clearing, settling, or recording payments, securities, derivatives, or other financial transactions.

Initial Margin: A form of defaulter-pays protection that is collected in respect of all positions novated to the CCP to cover prospective future price moves (potential future exposure) before the risk associated with a defaulter's positions can be closed out.

Interoperability: An arrangement that links different CCPs, allowing participants of one CCP to seamlessly deal with participants of another CCP.

Novation: A process through which the original obligation between a buyer and a seller is discharged through the substitution of the CCP as seller to the buyer and buyer to the seller, creating two new contracts.

Principles for Financial Market Infrastructures (PFMIs): The internationally agreed standards for Financial Market Infrastructures developed by CPMI and IOSCO.

Pooled Financial Resources: Sometimes referred to as a default fund or clearing guarantee fund, these are financial resources contributed by a CCP and its participants that are pooled, and therefore can be used to cover the default of any participant.

Recovery Plan: A CCP's plan to address any unfunded losses and replenish any drawdown of pre-funded pooled resources.

Variation Margin: Funds that are collected from participants with mark-to-market losses and paid out to the participants with mark-to-market gains. As a result, participants realise gains and losses on an ongoing basis and the CCP's exposure in respect of all open positions is re-set to zero at the start of each day.

ENDNOTES

1 These trends are discussed in (RBA, 2014).

2 Should a participant default, the CCP must continue to honour the defaulted participant's obligations to its original counterparty. The CCP must, therefore, replace the defaulted participant's trades so as to rebalance its portfolio and 'close out' the financial risk associated with this ongoing obligation.

3 Collateral assets should also be free from wrong-way risk; that is, the risk that the value of collateral posted by a clearing participant is adversely correlated with the credit quality of that participant.

4 A user-owned CCP might also be expected to set high participation requirements so as to maintain a broadly homogeneous and high-quality participation base.

5 In a richer setting, trade may be modelled as a continuous function of margins:. $T = T(m), \quad \frac{\partial T}{\partial m} < 0$

6 For simplicity, and without loss of generality, we assume that the defaulted participant will be replaced by a new entrant, maintaining the total number of participants at n in each period.

7 Since replacement cost risk to the CCP only crystallises if the default of a long participant coincides with a price decline, or if the default of a short participant coincides with a price increase, we need model only one side of the distribution of price changes.

8 The condition for continuation is:

$$\frac{1}{1-d}\left[n(v-cm)-d\delta(1+R)\int_{m}^{\infty}(\Delta p-m)f(\Delta p)d(\Delta p)\right]\geq(1+R)\int_{m}^{\infty}(\Delta p-m)f(\Delta p)d(\Delta p)$$

We assume that each participant has an equal share in the ownership of the CCP and therefore the CCP expects to share losses equally in funding the shortfall, allowing the CCP to continue into the next period.

9 The absence of an equivalent term in Equation (1) reflects the assumption that any fees charged by a user-owned CCP would be returned to its participant owners in the form of dividends. They can therefore be ignored for the purposes of the optimisation.

10 For simplicity, we assume that the CCP passes the full return it earns on margin funds back to its participants. In practice, any spread earned on margin funds held can be a source of revenue for a CCP. Including this in the objective function would provide an additional incentive for the for-profit CCP to set higher margins.

11 The model could equally be expressed in terms of volume-based clearing fees, which are commonly applied by CCPs, without altering the qualitative outcome of the model.

12 As *n* increases, the maximum margin level that participants will bear approaches the margin level at which expected pay-offs equal zero. The participation constraint therefore becomes almost equivalent to a non-negative pay-off constraint for the CCP.

13 In practice, it might reasonably be expected that a government would require some change in governance or ownership of a CCP for which it provided support, thus imposing some cost on the CCP's owners.

14 See Principle 4, Key Consideration 4 of the PFMIs (p37). This Key Consideration also specifies that 'a CCP that is involved in activities with a more-complex risk profile or that is systemically important in multiple jurisdictions should maintain additional financial resources to cover a wide range of potential stress scenarios that should include, but not be limited to, the default of the two participants and their affiliates that would potentially cause the largest aggregate credit exposure for the CCP in extreme but plausible market conditions'. The model could easily be adapted to accommodate such a 'cover two' requirement, by allowing for multiple defaults within a single period. The qualitative results would, however, be similar. We note that the PFMIs also specify a minimum level of pre-funded coverage in the form of margin (Principle 6, Key Consideration 3), but for simplicity do not explicitly model this here.

15 The term $\frac{c(|\Delta P^{*}|-m)}{n}$ reflects an individual participant's share of the opportunity cost of pre-funding per unit of trade. This cost is incurred for the entire period, since in the event of default, these funds would be replenished.

16 Dark trading is that which takes place without pre-trade transparency; that is, orders are not known to the rest of the market before they are matched and executed.

APPENDIX

Table 3 contains a list of the product scope and ownership structure for CCPs that are members of CCP12, which is a global industry association for CCP. 'ETD' refers to exchange traded derivatives, while 'OTCD' refers to over-the-counter derivatives.

Table 3. Ownership of CCPs that are Members of CCP12

Organisation	Home Country	Products Cleared	Ownership Structure
Mercado de Valores de Buenos Aires S.A. (Merval)	Argentina	Equities	For-profit
ASX Limited (ASX)	Australia	Equities, ETD, OTCD	For-profit
BM&F Bovespa (BM&F)	Brazil	Debt securities, Equities, ETD, OTCD, Repos	For-profit
TMX Group (TMX)	Canada	Debt securities, Equities, ETD	For-profit
Contraparte Central S.A. (CCLV)	Chile	Equities, ETD	For-profit
Shanghai Clearing House (SHCH)	China	OTCD	N/A
Cámara de Riesgo Central de Contraparte de Colombia S.A (CRCC)	Colombia	ETD	For-profit
Dubai Commodities Clearing Corporation (DCCC)	Dubai	ETD	N/A
Eurex Group (Eurex)	Germany	Debt securities, Equities, ETD, OTCD, Repos	For-profit
Hong Kong Exchanges & Clearing Ltd (HKEx)	Hong Kong	Equities, ETD, OTCD	For-profit
Indian Clearing Corporation Ltd. (ICCL)	India	Debt securities, Equities, ETD	N/A
National Securities Clearing Corporation Limited (NSCCL)	India	Debt securities, Equities, ETD	For-profit
The Clearing Corporation of India Ltd (CCIL)	India	Debt securities, OTCD	User-owned
Tel Aviv Stock Exchange (TASE)	Israel	Equities, ETDs	User-owned
Cassa di Compensazione e Garanzia S.p.A. (CC&G)	Italy	Debt securities, Equities, ETD, Repos	For-profit
Japan Securities Clearing Corporation / Tokio Stock Exchange, Inc. (JSCC/TSE)	Japan	Debt securities, Equities, ETD, OTCD	User-owned
Grupo BMV (BMV)	Mexico	Debt securities, Equities	N/A
National Clearing Company of Pakistan Limited (NCCPL)	Pakistan	Equities	For-profit
KDPW_CCP (KDPW)	Poland	Debt securities, Equities, ETD, OTCD, Repos	User-owned
National Clearing Centre (NCC)	Russia	Equities, ETD, OTCD	For-profit
Singapore Exchange Ltd (SGX)	Singapore	Debt securities, Equities, ETD, OTCD	For-profit
Johannesburg Stock Exchange (SAFCOM)	South Africa	Debt securities, Equities, ETD	For-profit
Korea Exchange (KRX)	South Korea	Debt securities, Equities, ETD, OTCD	For-profit
SIX X-clear Ltd. (SIX)	Switzerland	Debt securities, Equities	User-owned
Gre Tai Securities Market (GTSM)	Taiwan	Debt securities, Equities, ETD	User-owned

continued on following page

Table 3. Continued

Organisation	Home Country	Products Cleared	Ownership Structure
Taiwan Futures Exchange (Taifex)	Taiwan	ETD	User-owned
Taiwan Stock Exchange (TWSE)	Taiwan	Debt securities, Equities	N/A
Thailand Clearing House Co. Ltd. (TCH)	Thailand	Debt securities, Equities, ETD	For-profit
Intercontinental Exchange (ICE)	UK	ETD, OTCD	For-profit
LCH.Clearnet Group Ltd (LCH)	UK	Debt securities, Equities, ETD, OTCD, Repos	For-profit
Chicago Mercantile Exchange Group (CME)	USA	ETD, OTCD	For-profit
The Options Clearing Corporation (OCC)	USA	ETD, OTCD	Owned by partner exchanges
NASDAQ OMX Clearing AB (NASDAQ)	USA/ Sweden	ETD, OTCD, Repo	For-profit
Depository Trust & Clearing Corporation (DTCC)	USA/ UK	Debt securities, Equities, Repo	User-owned
Sources: BIS, CCP12 (n.d.), CCP websites, FSB (2014b)			

Chapter 15
Mind the Gap:
Undercollateralization in the Global and Canadian OTCD Markets

Jorge Cruz Lopez
Bank of Canada, Canada

ABSTRACT

We provide estimates of the collateral gap in the global and Canadian OTCD markets. Using the latest available data as of December 31 2011, it is estimated that current exposures after netting are \$3.9T globally and \$71B in Canada. The estimated amount of available collateral after correcting for re-hypothecation in each market is \$767B and \$48B, respectively. Thence, the current gap in variation margins stands at \$3.1T globally and at \$23B in Canada. The initial margin that would be required to centrally clear OTCD is estimated at \$4T globally and \$104B in Canada. The rate of collateralization has increased globally, but specially in Canada. In 2001, 92% of global and 72% of Canadian current exposures were undercollateralized; currently, the figures are 80% for global and 30% for Canadian current exposures. The high level of collateralization and the lack of re-hypothecation could make the Canadian market more resilient to systemic shocks. Further, it is likely that the upcoming regulatory reforms will have a more subtle impact on Canadian banks than on banks elsewhere.

INTRODUCTION

The global Over-the-Counter derivatives (OTCD) market has experienced very rapid growth in recent years; particularly during the first six years of the last decade (see Figure 1). A significant part of this growth was the product of financial deregulation during the late 1990s and early 2000s, which allowed investors to trade customized bilateral contracts that required little or no collateral to guarantee their performance[1]. Exchange traded derivatives (ETD), on the other hand, experienced a more moderate growth due to their more strict and standardized terms, which required firms to fully collateralize their exposures; thus, making them relatively more costly to trade.

DOI: 10.4018/978-1-4666-8745-5.ch015

Figure 1. Notional values of the OTCD and ETD Markets (in USD trillions)

Note: OTCD and ETD amounts are represented in the left and right axis, respectively. Global values were obtained from the Bank for International Settlements (2012a). Canadian figures correspond to the six largest banks (RBC, TD, BMO, CIBC, BNS and NBC). Canadian values from 2007 to 2011 were obtained from the Office of the Superintendent of Financial Institutions (OSFI, 2012). Values from 2001 to 2006 were obtained assuming that the share of these six banks represents on average 2.10% and 2.7% of the global OTCD and ETD market, respectively. This assumption is consistent with the data reported by CMIC (2011) and the average share of the Canadian markets since 2007.

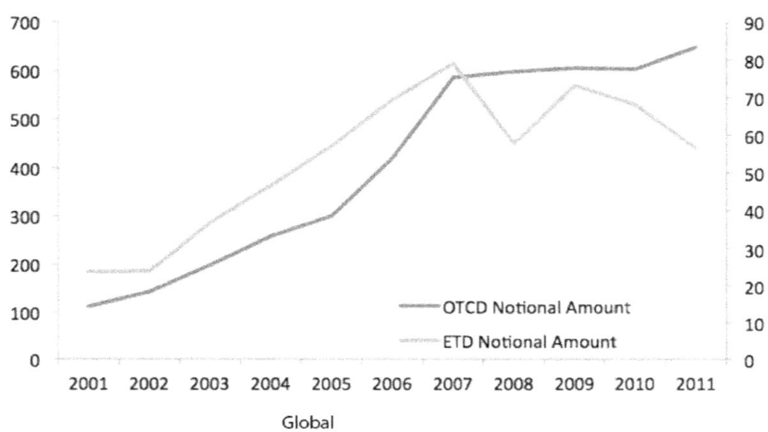

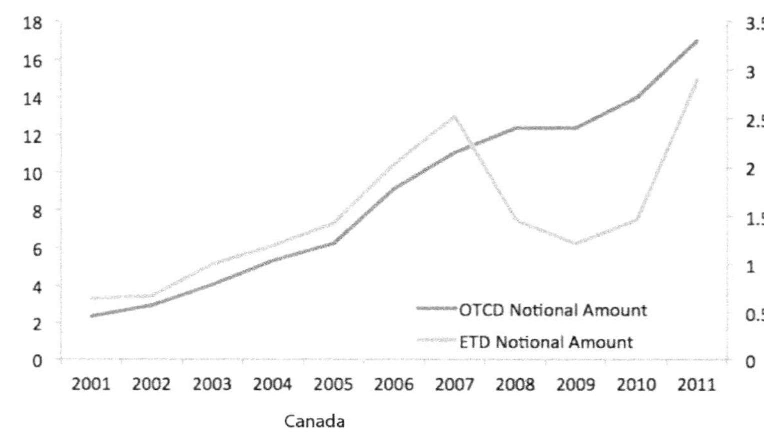

Today, OTCD contracts exceed, in notional terms, exchange traded ones by a factor of ten globally and by a factor of five in Canada. Nevertheless, during the crisis of 2008, it became apparent that the global OTCD market did not have the transparency and stability of its exchange traded counterpart. The lack of standardization and traceability in this market prevented efficient netting, which complicated the efforts of regulators to restructure the positions of financially distressed institutions. More importantly, the absence of a consistent collateral policy left many contracts undercollateralized and several counterparties exposed to large credit losses.

The undercollateralization of the OTCD market, also known as the collateral gap, remains one of the main risks faced by the financial system. It is also at the center of the regulatory changes proposed by the members of the G20 in 2009, which aim at restructuring derivatives markets by migrating OTC derivatives to central counterparties (CCPs).

The objective of this chapter is to provide estimates of the collateral gap globally and in Canada. The collateral gap is usually defined as the amount of additional assets needed to collateralize current exposures (i.e., positive replacement values after netting) in the OTCD market. Current exposures correspond to the dollar amount that investors would lose in their OTCD positions if their counterparties suddenly defaulted. Defined this way, the collateral gap focuses on current collateral needs by measuring the additional amount of collateral needed to protect against immediate losses.

In recent years, however, due to the regulatory reforms calling for the central clearing of OTCD contracts, the collateral gap is sometimes defined as the amount of assets needed to collateralize potential future exposures. These exposures correspond to the maximum dollar amount that investors could lose in their OTCD positions during a pre-specified period of time (usually the next five to ten days), assuming a set of scenarios or distributions. Defined this way, the collateral gap focuses on future collateral needs by measuring the additional amount of collateral needed to protect against potential future loses.

In the context of central clearing, the first definition resembles the additional variation margin that would be required by a CCP to settle all outstanding claims across investors after marking-to-market all positions. In the same context, the second definition corresponds to the amount of initial margin that would be needed if outstanding OTCD positions were initiated in (or migrated to) a CCP. In order to distinguish between both definitions, this chapter makes an explicit distinction between the current gap in variation margins and the amount of initial margin that would be needed to centrally clear OTC derivatives, denoted the CCP effect.

The methodology used to produce the estimates presented in this chapter draws from the approaches used by Singh (2010), Cecchetti, Gyntelberg and Hollanders (2009) and Rowady (2010) but revises their assumptions. The results show that as of December 31, 2011 current exposures after permissible netting are $3.9 trillion globally and $71 billion in Canada. The amount of available collateral after correcting for re-hypothecation is $767 billion and $48 billion, respectively. Thus, the current gap in variation margins stands at $3.1 trillion globally and $23 billion in Canada. The CCP effect is estimated at $4 trillion globally and $104 billion in Canada. Therefore, it is likely that current regulatory reforms will have a significant impact on the overall collateral gap if the level of available collateral does not increase in the market.

The remainder of this chapter is organized as follows. Section 2 describes the data used in the analysis. Section 3 presents the estimates of the collateral gap in the global and Canadian OTCD markets, and Section 4 concludes and provides policy implications.

NOTIONAL VALUES, COLLATERAL IN CIRCULATION AND GROSS CREDIT EXPOSURES

Three data series are used to produce the collateral gap estimates presented in this chapter. The first data set consists of global notional values and gross credit exposures published by the Bank for International Settlements (BIS, 2012a and BIS, 2012b, respectively). The second data set consists of global collateral in circulation amounts published by the International Swaps and Derivatives Association (ISDA, 2012). The third set of data corresponds to Canadian notional values and gross credit exposures published by the Office of the Superintendent of Financial Institutions (OSFI, 2012). In order to assess the time variation of the collateral gap, annual data from December 2001 to December 2011 is used in the analysis[2].

Canadian data was only obtained for the six largest banks (RBC, TD, BMO, CIBC, BNS and NBC). The assumption made here is that these banks cover the entire market. This is a reasonable assumption given that these institutions account for 95% of local OTCD transactions in notional terms (CMIC, 2011). Canadian gross credit exposures from 2007 to 2011 were obtained directly from OSFI (2012). However, OSFI does not report data prior to 2007. Thus, from 2001 to 2006 Canadian gross credit exposures are implied from global values by assuming that Canada represents 2.10% of the international OTCD market. This figure corresponds to the average Canadian share of the global market in notional terms from 2007 to 2011 and is consistent with the data reported by CMIC (2011). Canadian collateral in circulation for the full sample period is implied from global amounts using the same assumption.

The notional amount in a derivatives contract is the nominal or face amount that is used to calculate the payments made to the counterparties. This amount usually does not change hands and is only used as a reference value[3]. Gross credit exposure is defined as the sum of positive market values (or replacement costs) across market participants after bilateral netting. It measures the current exposure between counterparties[4]. Collateral in circulation is defined as the total amount of collateral collected and received by market participants when conducting OTCD transactions. It is important to note that because collateral in circulation adds collateral received and collateral pledged, it double counts the amount of available collateral in the OTCD market. Furthermore, notice that this measure does not account for all of the eligible collateral assets in the balance sheets of financial institutions; instead, it only accounts for the amount of collateral used to guarantee OTCD transactions. While it is true that financial institutions could re-channel some of their assets to increase the level of collateral in circulation, the objective in this chapter is to measure the collateral gap (i.e., the amount of additional assets that would be needed to fully collateralize OTCD transactions), and not the potential collateral shortage in the entire financial system. Figure 1 plots the evolution of notional amounts globally and in Canada. Figure 2 plots the evolution of global gross credit exposures and collateral in circulation.

Figure 2 clearly shows a significant increase in gross credit exposures starting in 2007 and peaking in 2008 globally and in 2009 in Canada. This increase in exposures can be attributed to the excess market volatility and increased default occurrences that characterized the onset of the financial crisis. After 2008, exposures remained high relative to earlier years, but they became more stable. The relative stability of credit exposures in recent years may be partially explained by the increased consolidation of financial firms, the more efficient netting of outstanding claims, and the slow growth of the global OTCD market since the beginning of the financial crisis (see Figure 1).

Not surprisingly, the collateral in circulation in the global OTCD market follows the pattern of gross credit exposures. More collateral was required by counterparties at the end of 2007 and during 2008 to

Figure 2. Gross Credit Exposures and Collateral in Circulation (in USD billions)

Note: Global gross credit exposures were obtained from the BIS Statistical Release of OTC Derivatives Statistics at end-December 2011 (BIS, 2012b). Global collateral in circulation amounts were obtained from ISDA Margin Survey 2012 (ISDA, 2012). Canadian values correspond to the six largest banks (RBC, TD, BMO, CIBC, BNS and NBC). Canadian gross credit exposures from 2007 to 2011 were obtained from the Office of the Superintendent of Financial Institutions (OSFI, 2012). Canadian gross credit exposures from 2001 to 2006 and collateral in circulation amounts for the full sample period were obtained by assuming that the share of these six banks represents on average 2.10% of the global OTCD market. This figure corresponds to the average Canadian share of the global market in notional terms from 2007 to 2011 and is consistent with the data reported by CMIC (2011).

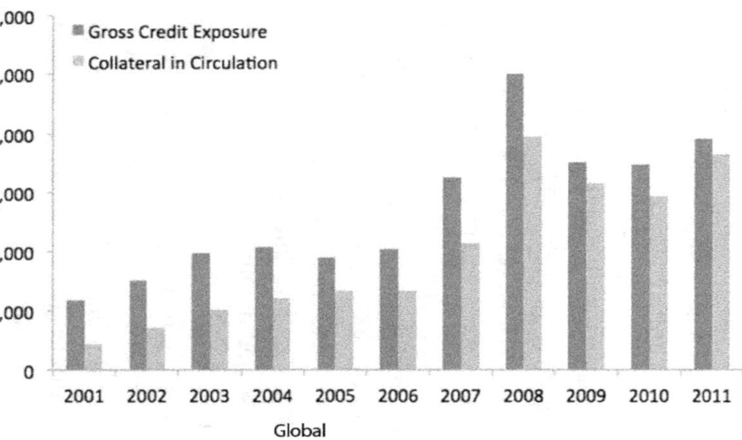

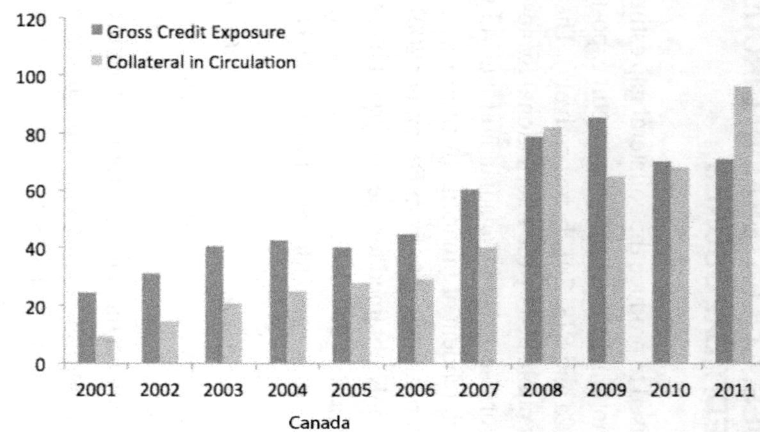

cope with the adverse credit environment of the crisis. Since then, the amount of collateral in circulation has been increasing relative to gross credit exposures. A significant amount of global collateral in circulation, however, is the product of re-hypothecation. This means that a dollar of collateral can be re-used (or re-hypothecated) by financial institutions to cover more than one dollar of gross exposure. Before 2008, Singh (2011) documents that about 67% of collateral available to the major global dealers was the product of re-hypothecation. After 2008, re-hypothecation accounted for 58% of their collateral. In addition, ISDA (2012) shows that most of the large and medium dealers re-hypothecate collateral; primarily cash (91% gets re-hypothecated) and marketable securities (44% gets re-hypothecated). In contrast, re-hypothecation in the Canadian market is almost nonexistent; therefore, a dollar of collateral covers a dollar of gross exposure. This practice may explain to a large extent the resiliency of the Canadian OTCD market during the financial crisis and its relatively stable growth in recent years (see Figure 1). An interesting feature of Figure 2 is that for 2011, collateral in circulation exceeds gross credit exposures in the Canadian market. While the level of collateralization relative to gross exposures has significantly increased in recent years, this does not mean that all gross exposures are fully collateralized in Canadian. As mentioned before, collateral in circulation double counts the amount of available collateral in the market. Therefore, as explained in the next section, there is still a significant gap in the variation margin of Canadian institutions.

THE COLLATERAL GAP

Figure 3 presents the estimates of the collateral gap in the global and Canadian OTCD markets. The procedure used to compute these estimates draws from the methodologies advocated by Singh (2010), Cecchetti, Gyntelberg and Hollanders (2009) and Rowady (2010) but revises their assumptions. For simplicity, the remainder of this chapter refers to each one of these approaches as the IMF, BIS and TABB methods, respectively, because of the affiliation of their corresponding authors.

Unlike the BIS and TABB methods that only focus on one side of the collateral gap, the approach adopted here explores both its current and potential future state after central clearing is enforced in the OTCD market. In addition, the assumptions made regarding the amount of available collateral and current credit exposures in the market are in line with what the existing data actually measures. Table 1 summarizes the assumptions behind the estimates presented in Figure 3 and those of alternative methodologies. Box 1 explains these assumptions in detail and Figure 4 presents the estimates obtained by using alternative specifications.

Panel A of Figure 3 shows the current gap in variation margins and Panel B shows the initial margin that would be required to centrally clear OTC derivatives (i.e., the *CCP effect*). The solid bars on the first panel correspond to the values on the left axis and show that as of December 31, 2011 the amount of current exposures after netting (i.e., the sum of the variation margin gap and available collateral) in the global market is $3.9 trillion. The amount of available collateral after correcting for double counting and re-hypothecation is $767 billion. Therefore, the global gap in variation margin stands at $3.1 trillion. In Canada, there are $71 billion of net current exposures outstanding. After accounting for the $48 billion of available collateral in the market, the Canadian gap in variation margin stands at $23 billion.

The solid lines in the graphs of Panel A plot on the right axis the ratio of the gap in variation margin to net current exposures. This is a measure of the proportion of current exposures that remain undercollateralized in the market. In 2001, 92% of global and 72% of Canadian current exposures were undercol-

Figure 3. The Collateral Gap in the Global and Canadian OTCD Markets (in USD billions).

Note: The solid bars in Panel A (upper part of this figure) plot on the left axis the current gap in variation margins and the level of available collateral. The solid lines in the graphs plot on the right axis the ratio of the gap in variation margin to net current exposures. The graphs in Panel B (lower part of this figure) show the CCP Effect; that is, initial margin that would be required to centrally clear OTC derivatives. Available collateral corresponds to half of the collateral in circulation reported by ISDA (2012) after correcting for re-hypothecation. Following Singh (2011), it is assumed that 67% and 58% of collateral in circulation is the product of re-hypothecation from 2001 to 2007, and from 2008 to 2011, respectively. Variation margin needs are defined as the amount of assets required to collateralize gross credit exposure amounts published by the BIS (2012b). The CCP Effect is estimated by taking the ratio of initial margin plus default fund contribution to notional in the ETD market (0.61%) and applying it to the notional value of the entire OTCD market.

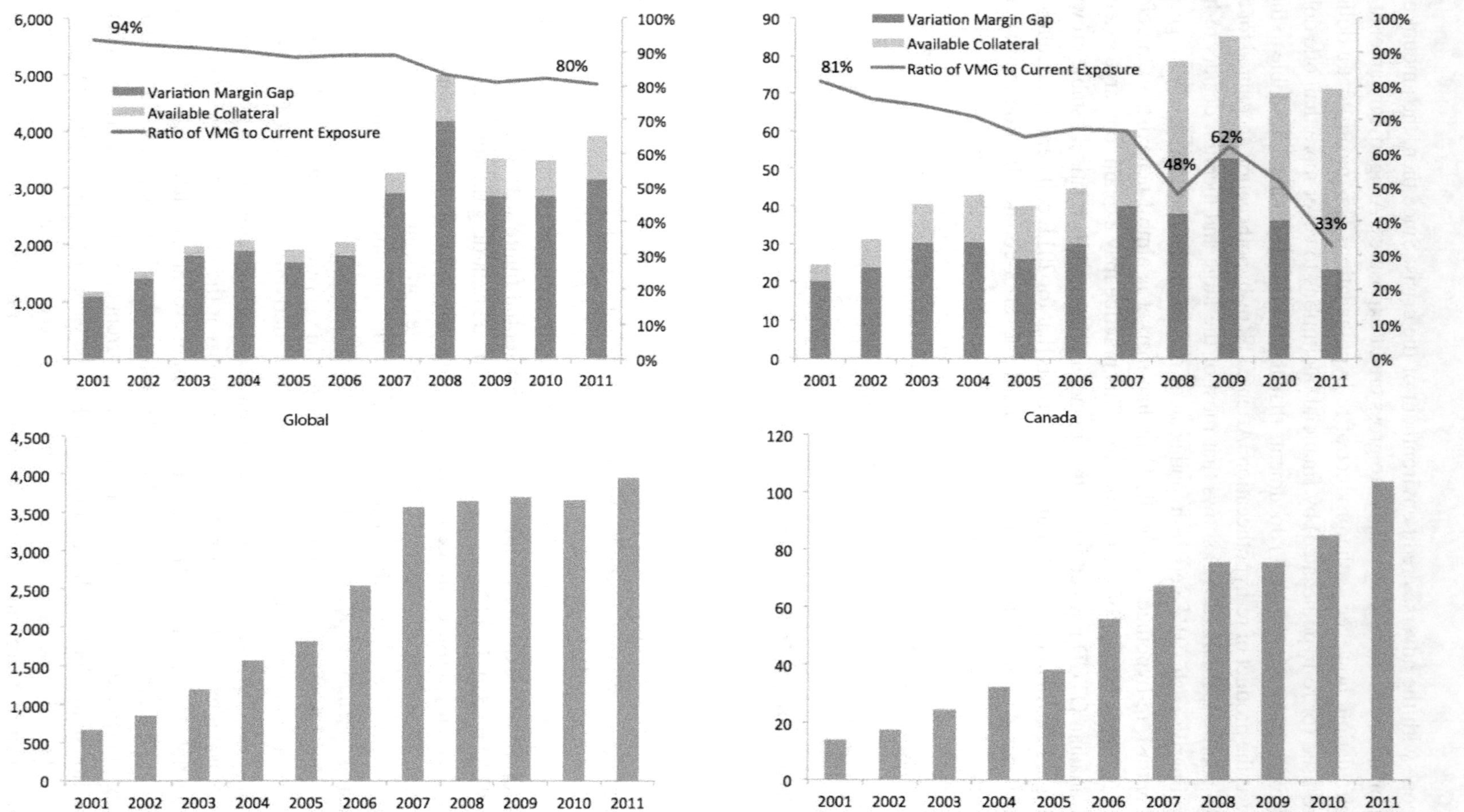

Table 1. Assumptions Made by Different Methods to Estimate the Collateral Gap

	Proposed Method	IMF	BIS	TABB
Designed to measure	- Variation margin gap - CCP-effect	- Variation margin gap - CCP-effect	- Variation margin gap	- CCP-effect
Need to estimate	- Available collateral - Net current exposures - Net potential future exposures	- Available collateral - Net current exposures - Net potential future exposures	- Available collateral - Net current exposures	- Available collateral - Net potential future exposures
Data inputs	- Collateral in circulation - Gross credit exposures - Notional amounts	- Collateral in circulation - Gross credit exposures - Notional amounts	- Collateral in circulation - Gross credit exposures	- Collateral in circulation - Notional amounts
Available Collateral	- Half of the collateral in circulation reported by ISDA. - Correction for re-hypothecation.	- Half of the collateral in circulation reported by ISDA. - Correction for re-hypothecation.	- Total collateral in circulation reported by ISDA. - No correction for re-hypothecation.	- Half of the collateral in circulation reported by ISDA. - No correction for re-hypothecation.
Current Exposure	- Total gross credit exposures reported by BIS.	- Half of the gross credit exposures reported by BIS.	- Total gross credit exposures reported by BIS.	
Potential Future Exposure	- Take the ratio of initial margin plus default fund contribution to notional in the ETD market (0.61%). Apply this ratio to the entire notional of the OTCD market.	- Take the ratio of initial margin plus default fund contribution to notional in the ETD market (0.33%). Apply this ratio to 2/3 of the notional of the OTCD market.		- Take the ratio of initial margin plus default fund contribution to notional in the ETD market (0.61%). Apply this ratio to the entire notional of the OTCD market.
Additional assumptions	- The ETD market and the OTCD market have similar risk characteristics.	- The ETD market and the OTCD market have similar risk characteristics.		- The ETD market and the OTCD market have similar risk characteristics.

Note: The table summarizes the assumptions followed by the method used to estimate the collateral gap in this chapter, and those used by the IMF (Singh, 2010), the BIS (Cecchetti, Gyntelberg and Hollanders, 2009) and the TABB Group (Rowady, 2010). Box 1 describes each one of these assumptions in detail.

lateralized. Currently, 80% of global and 30% of Canadian current exposures remain undercollateralized. As can be seen from the figure, the ratio has steadily decreased over time, particularly after the financial crisis, both globally and in Canada. However, the trend confirms the fact that Canadian financial institutions tend to behave relatively more conservatively, especially in recent years.

It is particularly interesting to see from the figure that even though Canada accounts for only 2.5% of the global OTCD market in notional terms, it holds approximately 6% of the globally available collateral. This high concentration of collateral in Canada can be explained to a great extent by the lack of re-hypothecation in the market. Re-hypothecation is a common practice in major financial centres like the US and the UK. The common use of re-hypothecation in these markets allows investors to re-use collateral assets to guarantee the performance of several transactions; thus, increasing the amount of collateral in circulation. Ultimately, however, if a large portion of credit risk materializes, as it did during the financial crisis, re-hypothecated assets are generally insufficient to cover all of the transactions that they guarantee.

The absence of re-hypothecation and the low and decreasing level of the gap in variation margins relative to current exposures imply that Canada may be more resilient to systemic shocks derived from OTCD transactions.

Figure 4. Alternative Estimates of the Collateral Gap (in USD billions)

Note: Panel A (upper part of this figure) shows estimates of the current gap in variation margins using the proposed methodology in this chapter, and that followed by the IMF (Singh, 2010) and the BIS (Cecchetti, Gyntelberg and Hollanders, 2009) methods. Panel B (lower part of this figure)shows the estimates of the initial margin required to centrally clear OTC derivatives using the metodology followed in this chapter, which corresponds to theTABB method (Rowady, 2010), and the IMF method (Singh, 2010) assuming that the entire OTCD market is centrally cleared.

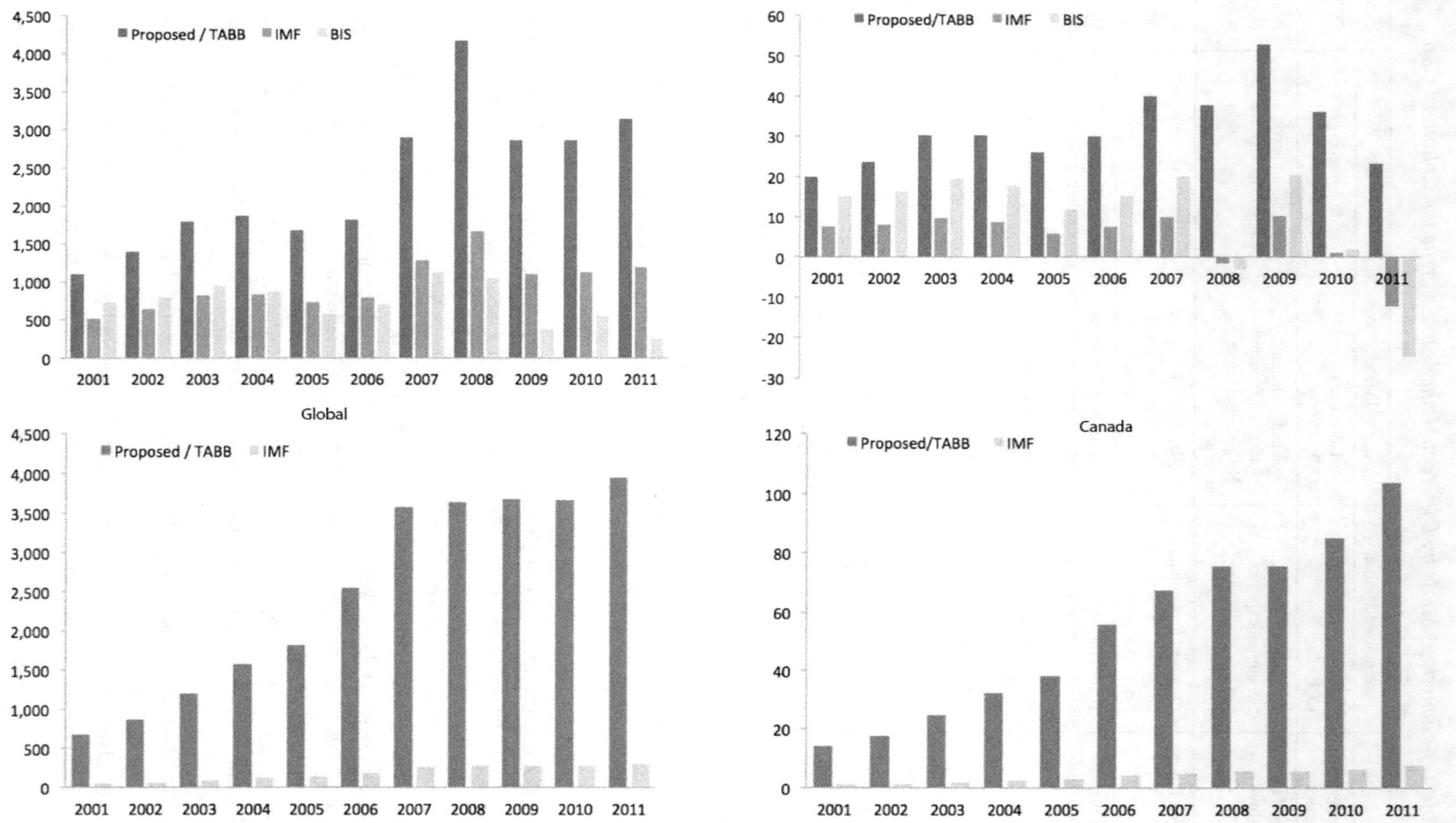

Moreover, it could be argued that the upcoming regulatory reforms aimed at closing the collateral gap may have a more subtle impact on Canadian banks than on other banks around the world.

Panel B of Figure 3 shows the estimated impact of centrally clearing the entire OTCD market. As of December 31, 2011, the amount of collateral assets needed to migrate all OTC derivatives to CCPs is estimated at $4 trillion globally and $104 billion in Canada. These results are in line with the 2.5% share of the global OTCD market that Canada represents in notional terms. However, they assume that the risk structure of the OTCD and ETD markets are comparable and that the margining systems used by CCPs will remain unchanged after they are mandated to clear new products. Cruz Lopez, Harris and Pérignon (2011) and Cruz Lopez, Harris, Hurlin and Pérignon (2012) show that current margining systems at CCPs do not incorporate risk homogeneity across investors and across underlying assets. Therefore, adding new products to the clearing mix of existing CCPs or creating new specialized CCPs that rely on current margining systems, could lead to an increase in the probability of joint defaults across clearing members. Hence, CCPs may adjust, and potentially increase, their collateral requirements to cope with the additional risk of clearing new contracts.

The impact of central clearing reforms on individual financial institutions is unclear given the data used in this chapter. While the demand for collateral might increase as the result of current regulatory

Box 1. Assumptions and comparison to alternative methods

In the estimates presented in Figure 3, available collateral corresponds to half of the collateral in circulation reported by ISDA (2012) after correcting for re-hypothecation. Half of the amount of collateral in circulation is taken because ISDA figures count collateral twice, once as received and once as delivered. In addition, this single counted collateral amount needs to be corrected for re-hypothecation, which allows a dollar of collateral to be re-used to secure more than one dollar of credit exposure. Correcting for re-hypothecation allows us to find the amount of collateral actually available in the OTCD market; that is, the amount of collateral that can be used to cover credit exposures *one-to-one*. This is particularly important in our context because we are interested in assessing the amount of additional assets needed to *fully collateralize* or *settle* credit exposures.

Using the findings of Singh (2011), it is assumed that 67% and 58% of global collateral in circulation is the product of re-hypothecation from 2001 to 2007, and from 2008 to 2011, respectively. However, re-hypothecation is assumed to be absent in the Canadian market. The BIS and TABB methods significantly overstate the amount of available collateral in the OTCD market because both of them fail to correct for re-hypothecation. Furthermore, the BIS method uses the full amount of collateral in circulation reported by ISDA and does not adjust for double counting.

Variation margin needs are defined as the amount of assets required to collateralize current exposures. They are measured by the total gross credit exposure amounts published by the BIS in its Statistical Release of OTC derivatives (BIS, 2012b). The full amounts are taken because by definition gross credit exposures only measure the sum of positive replacement costs after netting. The IMF method of Singh (2010) assumes that gross credit exposures include both positive and negative replacement costs (i.e., derivatives payables and receivables) and halves their value to estimate net current exposures. Singh (2010) seems to make this assumption based on the adjustment approach used by the BIS to extrapolate their results to the entire market. This adjustment uses the negative replacement values of reporting firms to imply the credit exposures of non-reporting firms. However, gross credit exposures do not add positive and negative replacement values by construction, and are unlikely to double count current exposures in the economy[5].

The amount needed to collateralize potential future exposures corresponds to the initial margin that would be required by a CCP to clear the OTCD market. In order to estimate this value, the ratio of initial margin to notional is estimated in the ETD market at 0.61%. This ratio is then applied to the entire notional amount of the OTCD market. The ratio of 0.61% is the same as that estimated by the TABB method for global amounts, so the estimates proposed here for the CCP effect, correspond to those advocated by the TABB method. This specification is selected because when the ratio of 0.61% is used for the Canadian market, the results approach the average potential future exposures of the six largest banks during the sample period. The critical assumption here is that the ETD market and the OTCD market have similar risk characteristics. If this is the case, the ratio of initial margin to notional is equivalent in both markets. Singh (2010) adopts a similar approach to estimate the impact of central clearing. However, he estimates the initial margin to notional ratio for specific types of OTC products and CCPs to avoid the assumption that risks are similar between OTC and centrally cleared markets. He obtains an average ratio of 0.05%, which yields very low initial margin requirements relative to potential future exposures, at least for the six largest Canadian banks. For example, for 2011 this method implies that the initial margin required to centrally clear all of the OTC derivatives of these six banks is $8 billion, whereas their potential future exposures for that year is $92 billion. Finally, Singh (2010) assumes that only two thirds of the OTCD market will be centrally cleared. This assumption is removed from the results presented in Figure 4, to make the results comparable across methods. Therefore, all of the estimates correspond to the effect of clearing the entire OTCD market.

reforms, their impact on the collateral balances of individual institutions is an open question that needs to be investigated. In addition, measuring potential collateral shortages in the system requires a dedicated analysis that incorporates evidence on the OTCD portfolio composition and the level of eligible assets of individual financial institutions. Cruz Lopez (2012) offers a preliminary analysis of these issues using data on the six largest Canadian banks.

CONCLUSION AND POLICY IMPLICATIONS

This chapter presented estimates of the collateral gap in the global and Canadian OTCD markets. The collateral gap, or the level of undercollateralization, in variation margins currently stands at $3.1 trillion globally and $23 billion in Canada. This means that 80% of global and 30% of Canadian current exposures remain undercollateralized. This proportion has steadily decreased since 2001, particularly after the financial crisis, from 92% and 72% for the global and Canadian markets, respectively. The trend in the gap of variation margins confirms the fact that Canadian financial institutions have historically behaved relatively more conservative, particularly in recent years.

It is estimated that an additional $4 trillion and $104 billion of collateral will be required to centrally clear the entire global and Canadian OTCD markets, respectively. These amounts assume that all OTC products and asset classes will be centrally cleared and, therefore, do not account for potential exclusions currently being considered by policy makers. In addition, while it is expected that the demand for collateral assets will increase as the result of regulatory reforms, their impact on the collateral balances of individual institutions needs to be investigated. Further research should consider measuring potential shortages of collateral by incorporating granular data on the OTCD portfolios and eligible assets held by these institutions.

Finally, and important finding in this chapter is that Canada has a strong position relative to the rest of the world. The results show that despite accounting for only 2.5% of the global OTCD market in notional terms, Canadian institutions hold approximately 6% of the collateral assets available globally. This high concentration of collateral in local financial institutions, coupled with the absence of re-hypothecation, allow the Canadian economy to be more resilient to systemic shocks derived from OTCD transactions. Furthermore, this implies that the regulatory reforms aimed at closing the collateral gap will tend to have a more subtle impact on Canadian banks than on other banks around the world.

NOTE

Disclaimer: The views expressed in this chapter are those of the author and not those of the Bank of Canada.

REFERENCES

Avdjiev, S., Schrimpf, A., & Vause, N. (2011, September 2011). Highlights of the BIS International Statistics. *BIS Quarterly Review*.

Derivatives Statistics. (2012a). Bank for International Settlements. Retrieved from: www.bis.org/statistics/derstats.htm

Annual Statistical Release. (2012b, *December 2011*). Bank for International Settlements.

Cecchetti, S.G., Gyntelberg, J., and Hollanders, M. (2009, September 2009). Central Counterparties for Over-the-Counter Derivatives. *BIS Quarterly Review*.

Cruz Lopez, J. A., Harris, J. H., & Pérignon, C. (2011). Clearing House, Margin Requirements, and Systemic Risk. *Review of Futures Markets*, *19*, 39–54.

Cruz Lopez, J. A., Harris, J. H., Pérignon, C., & Hurlin, C. (2012). *CoMargin: A System to Enhance Financial Stability*. Working Paper, Bank of Canada, HEC Paris, University of Orleans and Syracuse University.

Cruz Lopez, J. A., Mendes, R., & Vikstedt, H. (2013). The Market for Collateral: The Potential Impact of Financial Regulation. Financial System Review, Bank of Canada, June 2013.

Data Analysis CMIC Canadian OTC Derivatives Landscape [Strategy Paper]. (2011). Canadian Market Infrastructure Committee.

International Swaps and Derivatives Association, Incorporation (2012). *ISDA Margin Survey 2012*. Annual Statistical Release.

Financial Data – Banks. (2012). Office of the Superintendent of Financial Institutions Canada. Retrieved from: http://www.osfi-bsif.gc.ca/osfi/index_e.aspx?ArticleID=554

Rowady, E. Jr. (2010). *The Global Risk Transfer Market: Developments in OTC and Exchange-Traded Derivatives. Presentation*. TABB Group.

Singh, M. (2010). *Collateral, Netting and Systemic Risk in the OTC Derivatives Market*. Working Paper, International Monetary Fund.

Singh, M. (2011). *Velocity of Pledged Collateral: Analysis and Implications*. Working Paper, International Monetary Fund.

KEY TERMS AND DEFINITIONS

Central Counterparty: Organization that facilitates trading in derivatives and equities markets.

Collateral: Asset offered by a borrower to a lender to secure a loan.

Derivative: A financial instrument whose price depends on another underlying asset.

Over the Counter Derivatives: Derivatives traded outside formal exchanges like the Chicago Mercantile Exchange.

Re-Hypothecation: The re-use of collateral posted by borrowers for the own purposes of a lender.

ENDNOTES

1 All dollar figures in this paper are quoted in USD.
Due to the bilateral and customized nature of OTC derivatives, it is often difficult to net or close outstanding contracts with current counterparties. Therefore, some of the growth in the OTCD market can also be attributed to transactions designed to offset outstanding positions.

2 Higher data frequency would be ideal, however, collateral in circulation amounts reported by ISDA are only available on an annual basis.

3 Exceptions to this rule are Foreign Exchange Swaps. These contracts quote two notional amounts, each one in different currencies, that the counterparties are required to exchange on the expiration date.

4 Gross credit exposure as defined by the BIS (2011) is also known as gross positive replacement cost, current exposure after netting or net current exposure, where net denotes that exposures are measured after bilateral netting.

5 For a more detailed explanation of the computation of gross credit exposures see Avdjiev, Schrimpf and Vause (2011).

Chapter 16
The Changing Role of CSDs in the Post-Trade Industry in Europe
Impact of the CSD-Regulation and T2S

Ariena van Wageningen
De Nederlandsche Bank, The Netherlands

ABSTRACT

In this chapter Central Securities Depositories (CSDs) are analyzed, in playing an essential role in the European post-trade market. The background is presented, describing their services both on domestic level, and in a cross border context in Europe. CSDs have introduced (self) regulation and this chapter outlines the efforts they are making to remove existing barriers in a still fragmented European post-trade market, in order to achieve more efficiency. Particular attention is given to the changes and challenges the CSDs face with respect to the Central Security Depository Regulation (CSDR) and Target2-Securities (T2S), which is an initiative of the Eurosystem and is expected to go live as of June 2015. T2S will connect CSDs within the European area, performing as a cross border securities settlement engine.

1. INTRODUCTION: THE FUNCTIONING OF CSDs AND THE IMPACT OF CSD REGULATION AND THE IMPLEMENTATION OF T2S

The smooth functioning of the post-trade industry, including settlement, is essential for Europe's economy, and the working of capital and financial markets. CSDs (including the SSS function, see box 1) play a crucial role in securities settlement industry and they need to comply to rules and regulations aiming at the smooth, safe and efficient functioning of the post-trade market.

Cross border securities settlement in the EU is still complex and complicated. Market parties have put an effort and made progress in breaking down to so called private sector "Giovannini barriers". These barriers were identified in 2001 by a group chaired by Alberto Giovannini as the sources of fragmentation.

DOI: 10.4018/978-1-4666-8745-5.ch016

Furthermore, they came up with the European Code of Conduct for clearing and settlement in 2006 to which they committed themselves, to comply to rules with a view to improve transparency and access.

In 2012, CPSS and IOSCO replaced and harmonized three existing sets of international standards set out for systemically important payment systems, securities settlements systems, and central counterparties, with the Principles for Financial Market Infrastructures. These Principles provide for minimum requirements and more detailed guidance to cover new risk-management areas and new types of FMIs.

Furthermore, further harmonization through the whole cross border settlement chain for different kind of products and services was needed to further improve efficiency. The industry needed a further push by means of the CSD-Regulation (CSDR) and the initiative of the Eurosystem, Target2-Securities (T2S).

The European Commission was of the opinion that CSDs, playing a crucial role in the securities market, would need their own rules by means of the CSDR. The objective of the CSDR is to improve safe and efficient cross border securities settlement, by enhancing legal and operational conditions for settlement, and laying down uniform requirements. The CSDR should follow the Principles for financial market infrastructures developed by CPSS-IOSCO. The Commission and European Securities and Markets Authority (ESMA) should ensure consistency with existing standards and their future developments when drawing up or proposing to revise the regulatory technical standards and implementing technical standards as well as the guidelines and recommendations referred to in the CSDR, in close cooperation with the ESCB.

Furthermore, the Eurosystem has an interest in safe and efficient settlement of these securities, especially on a cross border basis. Therefore, around 2006 the Eurosystem central banks and the ECB took the lead in developing a platform, Target2-Securities (T2S), which should make cross border securities settlement more easy.

2. CSDs SERVICES TODAY, INCLUDING SSS FUNCTIONS

CDS perform custody services (registration and safekeeping) and activities related to issuing, including bringing new issues to the market, asset servicing, asset protection, asset safekeeping for several securities instruments, corporate actions, fund business. Furthermore, they carry out the settlement of securities in exchange for cash and the processing of securities transactions in financial markets.

Box 1. The definitions of both a SSS and a CSD which has slightly been changed during the last decade

Central Securities Depositories (CSDs)
A CSD plays a crucial role in the securities settlement industry, safekeeping securities and processing these by book entry. In 2001 CPSS IOSCO recommended that securities should be immobilized and transferred by book entry in CSDs to the greatest extent possible and CPSS IOSCO provides guidance with a set of principles for CSDs. According to CPPS IOSCO CSDs have unique risks associated with their function and design. A CSD should therefore have appropriate rules and procedures in place to help ensure the integrity of securities issues, minimize and manage the risks associated with safekeeping and transfer of securities. According to the Principles for financial market infrastructures, a CSD should maintain securities in an immobilized or dematerialized form for their transfer by book entry as mentioned in the Today, in market practice, a CSD often perform SSS functions, incorporating confirmation, clearing and settlement functions.

Securities Settlement Systems (SSSs)
In 2001 an SSS was defined as an institution which performs the full set of arrangements for confirmation, clearance and settlement of securities trades and safekeeping of securities across a securities market An SSS can furthermore be described as a system permitting the transfer of securities either Free of Payment (FoP) or Delivery versus Payment (DvP). The most recent definition of CPSS/IOSCO of an SSS is more narrow: an SSS enables securities to be transferred and settled by book entry according to a set of predetermined multilateral rules In many countries CSDs also operate an SSS but this is not included in the more narrow definition of a CSD. There are several entities which combine the functions of both an SSS and a CSD (BIS, PFMIs, CPSS IOSCO 2012).

Not only CSDs provide these services. A variety of entities, mostly banks, are also active in this field as a custodian, having developed economies of scale and servicing the foreign and cross border securities settlement business.

CSDs were established by markets some decades ago, with the main and common goal to eliminate the physical movements of securities which were traded on the financial markets by dematerializing securities (so they only exist in electronic form) and immobilizing the securities (eliminating physical movement) enabling the transfer of title by book entry form. Central banks and national authorities supported this, having an interest in the smooth functioning of the securities markets. Because of this, CSDs did get and still have a specific status, laid down in national rules and CSDs are regulated by supervisors and overseers.

Custody can be described as the safekeeping (holding) and administration of securities and financial instruments for third parties. The safekeeping business changed during the years because the physical safekeeping became less important due to immobilization and dematerialization, and it became more and more a reconciliation process and an information exchange business. CSDs offer custody services outside their markets by appointing a multi-direct or single market custodian bank as sub-custodian, and by opening other accounts in CSDs (links), holding securities issued elsewhere on behalf of their clients.

Asset services are related to the holding of assets. A CSD needs to ensure the investor receives the securities to which he is entitled to, by processing the rights and obligations associated with the securities. The services include: collection of dividends and interests, corporate actions, payment of tax, voting rights and shareholders' meetings by proxy. There are different kind of legal, operational and regulatory requirements determining how participants can hold securities at a CSD, based on national legal systems, which has consequences on asset protection, servicing and operational procedures and costs. CSDs offer a variety of account holding structures for the investor-side of CSD activities, recording ownership of outstanding securities, which basically can be divided in two main ones: direct and indirect account structures, mixed structures are common, combining features of both. A direct holding structure means that CSD holds accounts for final owners of securities (for single end investors, registered in a single entity), in an indirect holding system omnibus accounts (multiple beneficiary) are held that belong to multiple end-investors. In addition, the term segregated securities accounts exist, to distinguish from an omnibus account, separating particular activities, assets or categories of clients, or intermediaries. In order to create a safe environment for post-trade transactions CSDs offer straight-through processing of securities.

The other type of securities accounts are the issuer accounts which are relevant for the issuance of securities and the notary function, for the initial bookkeeping and registration of these securities in a specific account of the issuer. Issuer services are provided by CSDs as a "first entry point" for newly issued securities. Issuers use CSDs to deposit new securities, whether fully dematerialized, immobilized or still in physical form. By holding these securities on accounts on behalf of their clients, CSDs make it possible to process the securities in book-entry form, without the need to physically moving paper based certificates. The services however, vary significantly among CSDs from country to country, providing full or partial services related to corporate actions, shareholders' information, tax services, reporting, etc.

Furthermore, CSDs provide liquidity and collateral management services, managing operational costs, and customers risks, developing tools and algorithms to perform collateral management services. These are mostly the larger, more sophisticated CSDs, which are able to combine such systems and a large pool of assets which can be mobilized against exposures.

Finally, CSDs which operate an SSS offer settlement services, the actual delivery of the securities and the corresponding payment in a Delivery versus Payment (DvP) procedure, or Free of Payment (FoP) delivery of securities. The main models for interaction between securities and payment systems are the interfaced model (communicating and interacting through an interface) and the integrated model (securities and cash accounts are maintained on a single technical platform, in commercial bank or central bank money). CSDs settle transactions in global and international securities and domestic securities traded across borders through links, so securities can be transferred between CSDs through book-entry processes, on a FoP or DvP basis (securities are usually first delivered FoP).

3. CSDs CRITICAL ROLE IN THE POST-TRADE CHAIN AND CROSS BORDER SECURITIES SETTLEMENT

There are many parties involved in a cross border transaction, compared to the USA *(see figure 1)*, including CSDs, one or more local custodians, agents, banks and central banks, offering different services in several countries, varying from one provider to another.

The post-trade market in Europe is still fragmented due to obstacles that are still in place which result from divergent national and domestic rules, with different regulations, operational and technical standards and procedures.

There are differences in governance structure, and different categories of ownership. Basically these can be divided in a state- exchange- or user-owned or hybrid model, and there is a distinction between profit or not for profit activities. Furthermore, market parties have to deal with various standards, operational procedures and market specific practices. In order to process a cross-border securities settlement transaction, market parties need to access different national systems, which need to be linked properly to work efficiently. This complexity leads to additional costs for a cross-border transaction compared to a domestic transaction. The cost of securities settlement increases with the number of providers and individual components in a cross-border environment. Moreover, CSDs are mostly national monopolies, with their rules and governance based on national legislation, so there is little room for competition among European providers, this also leads to inefficiency and high costs and prices for cross-border transactions.

CSDs perform both domestic and cross border settlement services. Settlement processing plays a vital role in the post-trade chain. To achieve that the securities market works, close cooperation between market parties and intermediaries is needed, based on harmonized market and contractual arrangements, standards, procedures and processes. These need to be supported by a sound legal basis, including laws, rules and regulations.

For a more efficient handling of cross border securities further integration in the EU market is needed. To measure how much integration has been achieved so far, and to assess the status of the infrastructure, it is useful to look at the following conditions, as mentioned by Schmiedel and Schönenberger: 1) market parties should face the same set of rules, i.e. same technical requirements, prices, legal framework and business practices 2) equal access for all users to the same services and financial instruments on the same conditions, regardless the location of the user or the provider and 3) Equal treatment within a system and across systems, eliminating national differences in settlement procedures. They concluded that true integration has not progressed very fast, although market providers acknowledge the importance of pan-European systems.

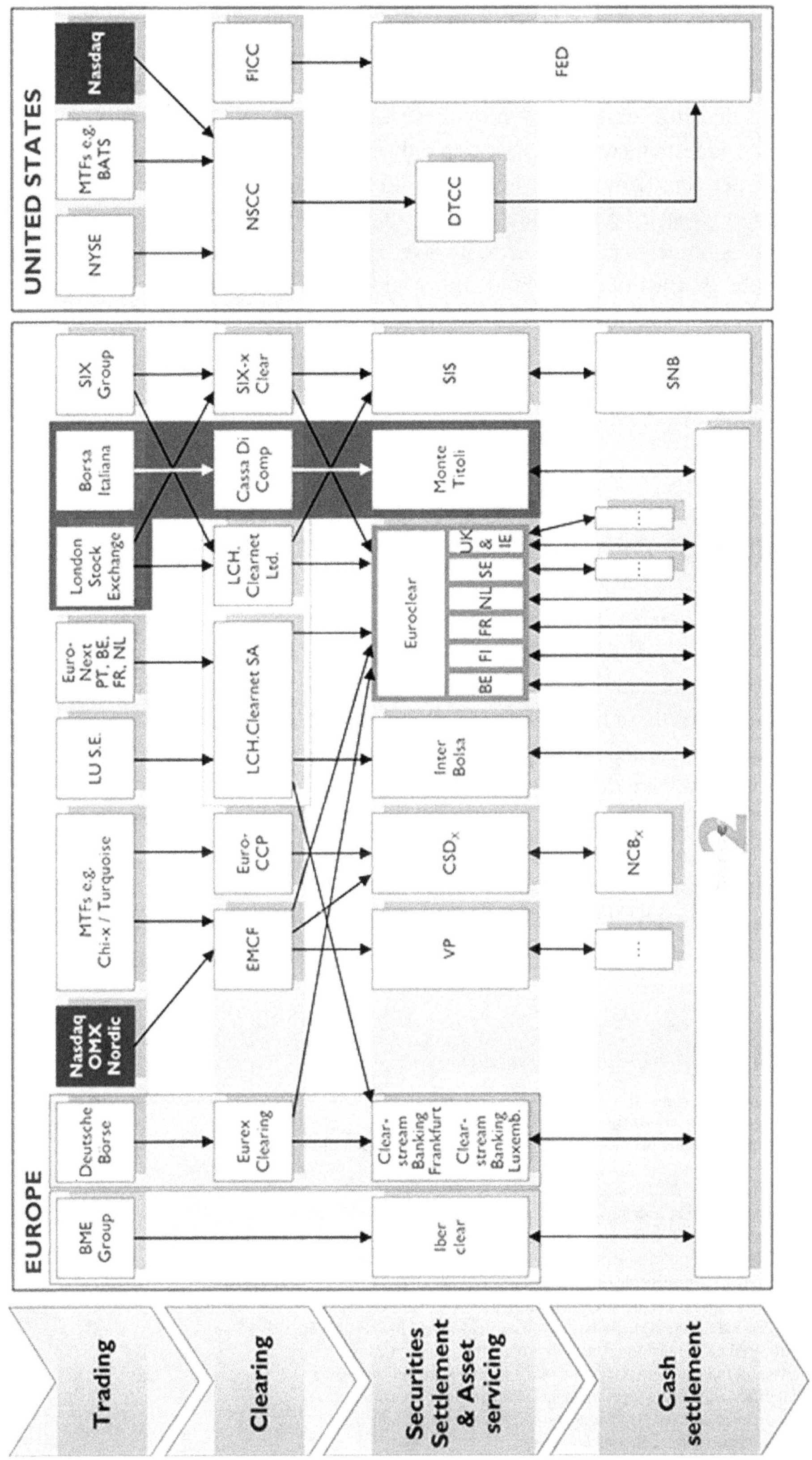

Figure 1. The European vs. the U.S. FMI Landscape (Source: ECB)

The inefficiencies in a cross-border context that are still in place seem to be reflected in the costs and prices of cross-border settlement. The costs and prices of post-trading services are monitored by Oxera, under the authority of DG Internal Market and Services. The Oxera Study of 2011 indicates that prices and costs of using infrastructure providers (cost per transaction) in general are coming down. For CSDs, clearing and settlement costs have generally declined. The average reduction across all financial centres was 25 per cent (from €0.48 in 2006 to €0.36 in 2009) for equities and 35 per cent for fixed income securities (from €0.53 in 2006 to €0.34 in 2009), but post-trading services still can be more expensive if cross-border transactions are involved. Overall costs of CSD services have fallen, but the costs of domestic transactions have come down more than those for cross-border ones. Cross-border transactions are still substantially more costly (4.1 times as much as domestic transactions in 2006, 2.6 in 2009), although the difference between domestic and cross-border transactions for CSD clearing and settlement services has fallen by 36 per cent, and for account provisioning and asset servicing by 12 per cent between 2006 and 2009.

4. PROGRESS IN IMPROVING THE EFFICIENCY, INTEGRATION, SAFETY AND SOUNDNESS OF THE POST-TRADE INFRASTRUCTURE.

Integration of the European post trade industry should lower the cross border settlement costs to the level of domestic ones, while breaking down the so-called Giovannini barriers (box 2) should improve European Union clearing and settlement arrangements. The objective of the Giovannini Group was to identify the sources of these inefficiencies and to assess the arrangements which were in place at that time. These barriers were and are still hindering the creation of a true integrated securities- and financial market in Europe. They are divided in the following categories 1) technical or market-practice barriers (mentioned in bold) 2) legal barriers and 3) barriers related to tax procedures. Removing these barriers would lead to a true integrated European securities market, supporting the functioning of the financial markets, which are important for economic growth.

In 2006, the market infrastructures presented and committed themselves to a voluntary Code of Conduct, to prevent further regulation, with the aim to 1) increase price transparency 2) to improve an open

Box 2. Removing the private sector barriers

1. National differences in information technology and interfaces
2. National clearing or settlement restrictions that require the use of multiple systems
3. National differences in rules governing corporate actions, beneficial ownership and custody
4. Absence of intra-day settlement finality
5. Practical impediments to remote access to national clearing and settlement systems
6. National differences in settlement periods
7. National differences in operating hours/settlement deadlines
8. National differences in securities issuance practice
9. National restrictions on the location of securities
10. National restrictions on the activity of primary dealers and market-makers
11. Domestic withholding tax procedures disadvantaging foreign intermediaries
12. Tax collection functionality integrated into a local settlement system
13. National differences in the legal treatment of interests in securities
14. National differences in the legal treatment of bilateral financial clearing
15. Uneven application of conflict-of-law rules

and transparent access and interoperability 3) service unbundling and accounting separation. In 2008, the European Commission stated that this had injected "momentum in the market" and that indeed the "industry is so far living up to its commitments".

In November 2009 the Council concluded on the basis of the Commission Report on "The Code of Conduct on clearing and settlement: three years of experience" that competition has indeed increased and that progress has been made in terms of increased efficiency and reduced prices costs for investors. However, comparing prices remain difficult, for CSDs have differences in business models, commercial and technical/operational barriers remain, because the market standards, practices still are different.

Nowadays, there are still some of the private sector Giovannini barriers which are hindering the creation of a true integrated securities- and financial market in Europe. The industry has introduced several standards and harmonised procedures to which they have committed themselves and the post-trade industry has made substantial progress in eliminating the Giovannini private sector barriers, especially regarding barrier 1 (diversity of IT platforms) and 6 (differences in settlement periods). Barrier 8, national differences in securities instruments, has been taken care of and eliminated. Securities instruments are now identified by one standardised identifier: ISIN. A standardized SWIFT protocol for communication in the EU, defining message formats between systems and their members, has been implemented by March 2011. Market parties are now making use of ISO 15022, in the near future they will make use of 20022 (the successor to ISO 15022) standard for Financial Services Messaging, containing descriptions of messages and business processes. This will be used through the entire value chain which will reduce back-office costs. The industry has furthermore taken action to streamline the differences in settlement periods by harmonizing and shortening the settlement cycle to T+2. However, vital differences still remain with respect to corporate action processing (barrier 3), operating hours and settlement deadlines, and settlement finality (barrier 4 and 7).

Although the post-trade industry did make progress, it needed a further push. CSDs were confronted with further regulation, the CSDR, and with T2S.

5. IMPACT OF THE CSD REGULATION AND T2S ON THE ROLE OF CSDs

5.1 CSD Regulation

With the CSDR, he European Commission aims at addressing the lack of safety and efficiency of securities settlement in a cross border situation. CSD transactions are generally processed safely and efficient within their own countries, but when handling cross border securities transactions, the risks, possible 'fails' and costs could increase.There are a number of safety issues resulting from the length of a settlement cycle (an extended settlement cycle creates a longer period of counterparty risk exposure), and paper based securities which increases the settlement cycle and the risks of settlement fails. The barriers which are still in place (limitation of securities issuers access to CSDs, differing national licensing regimes), results in a still complex fragmented market which has a negative impact on cross border efficiency.

Therefore, the objective of the CSDR is to improve safe and efficient cross border securities settlement, by enhancing legal and operational conditions for settlement, and laying down uniform requirements. The European Parliament adopted the CSDR in July 2014. Following the approval by the Council of the European Union the CSDR entered into force 17 September 2014. According to the CSDR CSDs provide at least two of the three core services: the notary service, meaning initial recording of securities in a book-entry system, central maintenance services by providing and maintaining securities accounts at the top tier level, and settlement services by operating a securities settlement system (SSS).

The rules of the CSDR include: an obligation to represent all transferable securities in book-entry form and to record these in the CSD, the securities should be in immobilized or dematerialized form. Furthermore the Regulation means a compulsory move to a settlement cycle of two business days after trade date (T+2), for all transactions in transferable securities traded on organized trading venues. Additionally, a harmonized settlement discipline regime will be in place: penalty mechanisms and buy-in procedures for market participants that fail to deliver their securities four days after the agreed settlement date will have to buy them in the market and deliver them to their counterparties. The creation of a settlement discipline regime across Europe is intended to improve market discipline. Links among CSDs are important to facilitate cross-border securities settlement. To enhance the smooth functioning of these links, the authorization and supervision of these links are defined more precisely.

Furthermore, CSDs may provide non-banking type of services, which do not imply credit or liquidity risks. These may include securities lending, collateral management services, matching, processing of corporate actions. Finally, CSDs may provide banking type of services directly related to their core or ancillary services. These may include providing cash accounts, and accepting deposits, cash- and securities lending and borrowing, under certain conditions and standards which are in place for the performance of these bank-related ancillary services.

5.2 The Impact of the CSDR on CSDs

The CSDR will have an impact on the post trade market and the role of CSDs with respect to efficiency, safety and transparency, and the CSDR will promote competition and choice.

Safety

With the introduction of the CSDR there will be consistency with the CPSS IOSCO principles and existing standards. The CPSS IOSCO principles on risk management are made binding, and there are rules in place on banking type of ancillary services on the management of credit and liquidity risks. CSDs are subject to an additional capital surcharge that reflect these risks (article 54). There will be stricter rules on settlement discipline (buy in regime, and penalties for late settlement) and T+2 which will shorten the exposure to settlement risk, favoring the use of central bank money (where available). Market parties involved are now discussing how this regime can be implemented, giving input for technical standards ESMA is required to draft under the CSDR.

Efficiency

National differences in settlement periods in the EU have led to different procedures in front- and back offices, resulting in possible extra costs, mismatches of funding or disfunctioning of liquidity provision. A common settlement period facilitates the identification of the intended settlement date for all parties involved and supports settlement discipline measures. The T+2 requirement for the EU equity market will make cross border processing more easy. Stakeholders committed themselves to migrate to T+2 on European level, taking action already around the adoption of the CSDR: markets announced to move to T+2 on 6 October 2014.

Transparency

There will be a published price list and unbundled pricing of CSD services, making the price transparency provision of the Code of Conduct of Clearing and Settlement of 2006 binding. Also, the governance structure of a CSD will change, there will be an obligation to have independent directors in the board and a stronger role of users will be in place, with an obligation to have an independent user committee (article 27,28). Furthermore, the reporting on settlement fails at EU level will enhance the visibility on settlement efficiency across markets.

Promoting Competition and Choice

CSDs will be subject to a common set of rules across the EU and benefit from uniform licensing and a EU wide passport. This will remove the existing barriers of access across Europe. Although authorized by national regulators, central securities depositories will now be governed by the same prudential requirements across the EU. The new rules also confirm the principle of non-discrimination for market participants and issuers of securities to access CSDs in any EU country (free choice of issuers). Issuer CSDs remain at the "top tier level" guaranteeing the integrity if the issue, custodians wanting to enter the business would need a CSD license, and need to fulfill the same requirements. It is expected that CSDs as national monopolies cease to exist, and the focus will be on a cross border rather than on the national scope of services. Some CSDs may perform banking type of services, competing with custodian banks, and/or perform functions similar to a CCP.

Legal Certainty and Transparency in the Securities Holding Chain

The legal certainty issue on "who owns what" is not being handled in the CSDR. The CSDR does not specify the responsibilities of all the parties involved in the securities holding chain This needs to be laid down in the Securities Law Legislation (SLL) which is - unfortunately - still in the pipeline. The SSL should define the following:

- A framework aiming at legal certainty and transparency with respect to determination of the jurisdiction whose law is applicable to the rights of holders of securities throughout the sequential links in a cross-border holding chain; and
- Minimum requirements with respect to investor protection throughout the sequential links in a cross-border holding chain.
- In addition, the SLL should facilitate the passing on of information and instructions with regard to corporate actions, shareholder meetings and voting through the sequential links in a cross-border holding chain.

5.3. The Initiative of the Eurosystem: T2S

One of the Eurosystem's basic tasks is "to promote the smooth operation of payment systems" (Article 3.1 of the Statute of the European System of Central Banks and of the European Central Bank). In promoting safety, the Eurosystem aims to ensure systemic stability in payment, clearing and settlement systems. Complementing its objective of ensuring systemic stability, the Eurosystem aims to promote the efficiency of payment, clearing and settlement systems. In relation to this the Eurosystems NCBs play a fundamental role as operator of TARGET2, in providing fast and safe settlement in central bank money.

The safe and efficient functioning of market infrastructures is an important element of a sound currency and is essential for the maintenance of financial stability. The Eurosystem has therefore "a keen interest in the prudent design and management of market infrastructures operating in its currency". Within this context, the Eurosystem decided to develop T2S, based on and within the legal perimeter of TARGET2 (see box 3). Box 3 TARGET, TARGET2 and TARGET2-Securities

TARGET, which went live in 1999, was a decentralized system linking the distinctive central banks systems for settlement of euro payments in Central Bank Money and cross border delivery of collateral in Eurosystem monetary policy operations and intraday credit operations This first generation TARGET system was replaced by the second generation TARGET2. The decentralized platform structure was replaced by a Single Shared platform. TARGET2 is the backbone for all payment and settlement arrangements in euro, and the core system for liquidity management, and the system is used for settlement operations of a large number of ancillary systems such as securities clearing and settlement systems.

The Eurosystem decided that T2S is developed and operated on the TARGET platform. The intention is to exploit synergies and provide and efficient solution to CSDs and their users. (General Principles T2S URD 5.2). It will not only provide an efficient securities settlement platform, but will also offer both liquidity and collateral management services through dedicated cash accounts which will lead to liquidity savings and a single collateral pool for T2S markets.

T2S is centralizing and harmonizing cross border securities settlement. T2S will settle transactions for the entire euro area in euro and for some non-eurozone countries and non-euro currencies to the 24 CSDs which outsource their securities settlement business, and connect to T2S. T2S will offer a common interface, message standards and a common settlement window. *See figure 2,3.*

T2S aims to facilitate post-trading integration by offering core, neutral and borderless pan-European cash- and securities settlement in Central Bank Money. CDSs participation in T2S is not compulsory, they themselves have to decide whether or not to join T2S. CSDs which outsource their securities settlement business to T2S can provide their customers with harmonized and commoditized delivery-versus payment (DvP) services in an integrated technical environment with cross border capabilities. 24 CSDs made their decision, and will connect to T2S, consolidating settlement volumes on one single platform, bringing economies of scale and improved settlement efficiency, with the aim of lowering the settlement fee in Europe.

T2S, which is owned by the Eurosystem, is expected to go-live as of June 2015, and that CSDs will migrate in four waves, until February 2017. Both securities and cash will by then be integrated on one single IT platform (the integrated model). The Eurosystem is committed to recovering the full development and running costs of T2S through the fees charged to the CSDs which outsource their securities settlement activities to the Eurosystem. The CSDR makes it more easy to outsource to the Eurosystem as a public entity "where that outsourcing is governed by a dedicated legal, regulatory and operational framework which has been jointly agreed and formalized by the public entity and the relevant CSD"(article 20.5). The Framework Agreement, the core legal document governs the rights and obligations of the Eurosystem NCBs en the CSDs in relation to the development and operation of T2S.

The DvP price for T2S has been set at 15 cent per instruction, which is much lower than the price today. The price will be fixed for the period from June 2015, to December 2018, under certain conditions: non-euro currencies add at least 20% to the euro settlement volume; the securities settlement volume in the EU is not more than 10% lower than the volumes projected by the T2S Programme Office, which in turn are based on market advice.

Figure 2. (Source: ECB)

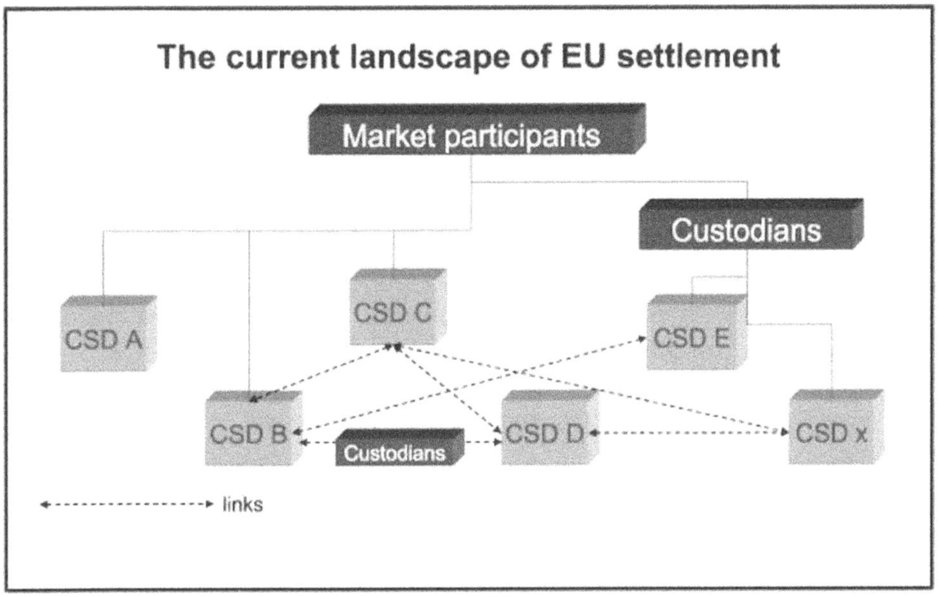

Figure 3. (Source: ECB)

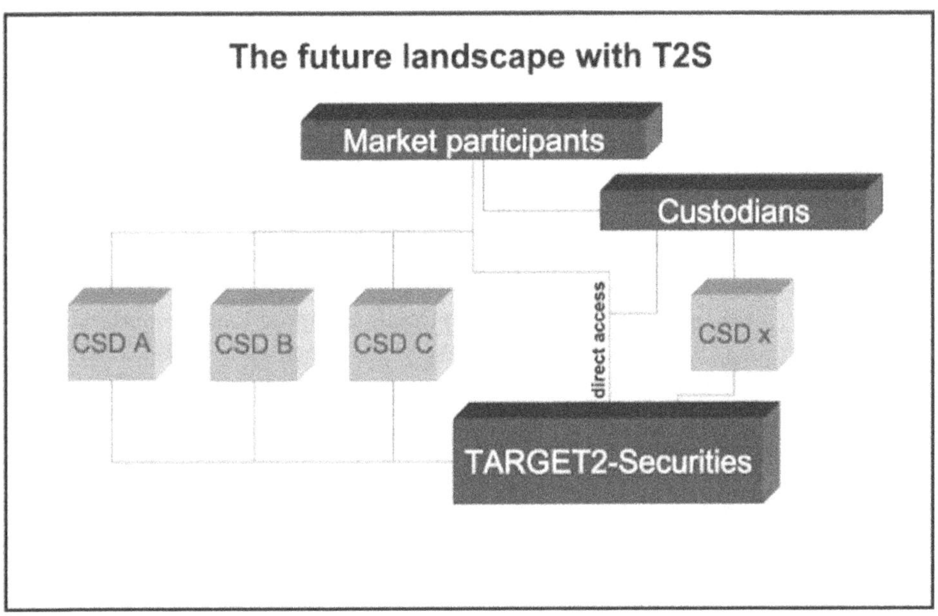

T2S shall process all types of securities which CSD's are settling today: debt instruments, equities, investment funds, warrants. These need to comply with certain criteria: the securities need to an ISIN code, held in book-entry form with a CSD, and fungible from a settlement procedure perspective (amounts/fractions of securities are interchangeable).

T2S will not only provide an efficient securities settlement platform, it offers both liquidity and collateral management services through the dedicated cash accounts which leads to liquidity savings, and a single collateral pool for all T2S markets.

Also it has an impact on the users (the banks).T2S supports the possibility to establish a direct technical connection to the T2S platform upon agreement with the respective CSD. Users can choose whether they will operate as a Directly Connected Participant (DCP) or as a Indirectly Connected Participant (via the CSD). A DCP can directly connect to T2S through a technical interface, either on the cash or securities side, or both, under certain conditions: A DCP needs to adapt to the communication channels of T2S, needs to be certified by the Eurosystem, and authorized by the CSD or NCB. A DCP may use the following services: queries, reporting, sending settlement and/or cash instructions. This supports a DCPs collateral and liquidity management.

Finally, market parties have committed themselves to further contributing to harmonisation within and outside of the context of T2S. The T2S Harmonisation Group was set up as a substructure of the T2S Advisory Group and has identified relevant harmonisation issues and established standards for the T2S community. In its Fourth progress report it was concluded that the implementation process of these operational, technical and legal standards is progressing well, with T2S markets either having already achieved compliance or having made clear plans to do so before migration. A set of standards for corporate actions was defined (based on the corporate actions market standards). The results of annual gap-analysis surveys still show a lack of progress, so it is expected that not all T2S markets will achieve full compliance by the time of migration on this standard. Furthermore, a harmonised rule for settlement finality, the moment of entry of a transfer order into the system, is still in the progress of being defined. The aim is to agree on a common T2S rule and to ensure compliance by all market parties.

CSDs are now preparing for connecting to and the implementation of T2S. It requires investments of CSDs to adapt to T2S. They need to reshape their businesses to T2S and their existing legacy systems, to update their IT systems, have to connect to T2S, map their account structure with the T2S account structure, and change their technical and operational settlement procedures and legal arrangements. To what degree they would or could adapt to T2S is a decision they have to make, depending on their investment costs and how and to what extent these can be recovered and/or passed on to their customers. Mercier and Sauer have investigated the degree of optimal reshaping and the optimal prices to model the choice of CSDs.

5.4. Impact of T2S on CSDs

T2S as an operator and settlement engine will contribute to removing some of the industry related Giovannini barriers, and contribute to safety, efficiency and transparency. At the same time, CSDs could be moving up the value chain, creating new business.T2S could however also lead to concentration risks, which need to be mitigated.

Safety

T2S will offer cross border securities settlement services against cash in central bank money. As mentioned in the Principles for FMIs and the CSDR CSDs should settle the cash using central bank money through accounts opened with a central bank of issue of the relevant currency where practical and available. Furthermore, the aim is to harmonize settlement finality standards which will foster further financial stability and legal certainty.

Efficiency

T2S will use the ISO 20022 standard from the start,T2S will offer a common interface, message formats and shall have a calendar of opening days, with a harmonized settlement window, for opening and closing times. Once T2S is in operation, there will be one IT platform, allowing to connect any securities account at any participating CSD with any cash account, and operating hours and deadlines will be the same for all market parties involved. The processing of corporate actions will not be carried out on the T2S platform, but there will be a set of T2S standards to harmonize CSDs interaction with T2S regarding the settlement of corporate actions.

Transparency

T2S settlement rules and procedures shall be common to all participating CSDs, which will have equal access conditions, and be subject to a harmonized contractual arrangements and a common fee structure will be in place. All the operational and legal arrangements are laid down in (legal) documents, as well as the governance and pricing structure and principles. These are all accessible for all the stakeholders involved through the website of the ECB.

Promoting Competition and Choice

T2S will play a role a as a catalyst by creating new business. Market parties are already finding new business solutions for their clients within the context of T2S. There are plans for integrating ICSD and CSD services (through connectivity) and T2S makes liquidity pooling more easy, providing a single pool of assets, both domestic and international, so CSDs will be able to give their customers the opportunity to consolidate all their assets. Furthermore, there is a need to manage collateral cross border more efficiently. CSDs offer these services for international business, but this is still fragmented along national lines. T2S will enhance collateral management services of their participants, facilitating interoperability between CSDs and offering DCPs direct connectivity, decreasing the costs of collateral and liquidity management. Issuers will benefit from T2S as they will have an easy access to cross-border investors, allowing for pan-European distribution. This will broaden their investor reach and reduce funding costs.

T2S will change the securities settlement business in the near future for both CSDs, SSSs, their services and their customers by centralizing securities settlement transactions. Through T2S, CSDs are able to establish cross border links and they could offer asset servicing for the entire Euro area. Access through one single CSD, offering different ways to connect toT2S, as well as asset servicing close to home markets while at the same time connecting to one European wide platform will be possible. The (fixed) fee will reduce pure settlement costs, and it is expected that this would increase cross border volumes. It is expected that T2S will lead to further competition between CSDs and custodians, further cooperation, and/or mergers and acquisitions between CSDs, and it may lead to closing down (domestic) business. Access to multiple markets through one CSD could be an opportunity for some CSDs, being able to offer value added services with sufficient economies of scale in the EU market, but it could be complicated for small CSDs, and it would be difficult to survive if they do not have any possibility to offer these services.

T2S will change the landscape of the post-trade infrastructures. Custodians are becoming CSDs (BNY Mellon), and there are newly established CSDs (LSE Luxembourg, Lux CSD). T2S could be the start of a "shake out" of CSDs, the larger European custodian banks taking the lead in competing with CSDs, while at the same time CSDs with a banking license under the CSDR might compete with the custodians offering banking type of services.

Centralization of Activities

Through the centralization of these activities, T2S offers CSDs a common settlement infrastructure, a safe and efficient European platform for both domestic and cross border securities settlement. T2S enhances the efficiency of securities settlement across Europe based on harmonized rules and conditions, and standard procedures, while at the same time T2S promotes safety by keeping central banks cash account management within the central banks, its scope therefore exclusively limited to central bank money. Consequently, T2S allows CSDs to manage their risks more effectively and efficiently, and, in some instances, eliminate certain risks.

On the other hand, by performing centralized activities, T2S concentrates risks and creates interdependencies between and among CSDs and financial institutions. Participants are dependent on each other, with regard to collateral and liquidity that is needed, and there could be disruptions and delays in the settlement, caused by the system and or the participants, and in the technical/operational environment (software, hardware, connectivity). Furthermore, when operating one single IT platform, if the system fails/falls out, this could ultimately result in systemic risk. T2S identified these risks, and (business continuity) measures and procedures are in place and laid down in legal documentation, operational rules and procedures.

Role and Definition of T2S

The Framework Agreement states it very clear in the preamble: "T2S is a settlement solution and is not a CSD or a Securities Settlement System". Parties involved agreed to that. The agreement also mentions that CSDs will use T2S Services for securities settlement and that the contracting CSD will outsource certain IT activities necessary for the Eurosystem to operate T2S. To that extent T2S is an IT platform, following a strictly technical approach, with a database functionally compiling and electronically storing accounts related data, in a common location. The respective securities accounts remain legally attributed to the CSDs, which themselves are designated as a system under the Settlement Finality Directive (SFD). T2S is explicitly not a system within the meaning of the SFD.

Furthermore, as earlier mentioned in the CPSS/IOSCO definition of an SSS, it enables securities to be transferred and settled by book entry according to a set of predetermined multilateral rules. These multilateral rules are defined in the legal documentation of T2S (a set of common rules). T2S has common participants, the CSDs, which themselves are FMIs, which offer services to their clients, the banks. T2S interconnects as such institutions and markets, which are linked to and dependent upon one another through T2S.

It might be argued that T2S could be seen as a Financial market infrastructure. The CPSS/IOSCO defines an FMI "as a multilateral system among participating institutions, including the operator of the system, used for the purposes of clearing, settling or recording payments, securities, derivatives or other financial transactions". According to the CPSS/IOSCO an FMI can differ significantly, it may be owned and operated by a central bank (group of central banks) and regulated differently. Furthermore, in a footnote it is mentioned that the term FMI 'in market parlance' may be used to a functional entity to carry out centralized, multilateral settlement (page 7).

Oversight on T2S

The Eurosystem will perform oversight on T2S. The Eurosystem performs its oversight tasks on the basis of standards and recommendations it has developed by itself or in cooperation with other central banks and authorities.

As mentioned in the Framework Agreement the Eurosystem "is responsible for carrying out efficient oversight of their market in infrastructure". At the same time, the contracting CSD is responsible to the Relevant Competent Authorities with regard to the compliance with the Legal and Regulatory Requirements.The Eurosystem already assesses TARGET2. It is expected that the Eurosystem will also perform oversight on T2S as well, making use of the Principles for FMIs, taking also into account the rules laid down in the CSDR, in close cooperation with ESMA and other competent authorities which are responsible for oversight on CSDs.

6. CONCLUSION

The functioning of CSDs has changed during the last decade with the aim of removing the still remaining barriers and fragmentation in Europe, due to differences in rules, regulations, and operational procedures which are in place on domestic level. The post-trade industry in Europe has introduced the Code of Conduct, and several standards and harmonized procedures to which they have committed themselves in order to break down the Giovannini industry barriers. So far, the market parties involved have achieved more efficiency, which resulted in lower costs and prices of both domestic and cross-border transactions. However, both the CSD-Regulation as well as T2S as operator seem to be needed to further improve efficiency, safety and transparency in the post-trade environment and enhance market integration. In addition, they both will have impact on the cross-border securities settlement business models in the near future, for CSDs and their clients. T2S, which has to prove itself as of the go-live, is defined as an IT platform, and performs as such as a securities settlement engine for cross border transactions for CSDs and its participants (the users) in central bank money in euro in the Eurozone.

REFERENCES

AFME Post trade settlement committee taskforce on CSD account structure (2012) *CSD Account structure: issues and proposals*, 3-4. Retrieved from http://www.afme.eu/Documents/Discussion-papers.aspx

The Work of the Clearing and Settlement Advisory and Monitoring Experts' Group, Brussels. (2008). CESAME. Retrieved from http://ec.europa.eu/internal_market/financial-markets/docs/cesame/cesame_report_en.pdf

Chan, F., Fontan, F., Rosati, S., & Russo, D. (2007). The securities custody industry (pp. 6-10). Occasional paper series ECB. Frankfurt, 16.

CSD Regulation of the European Parliament and of the Council on improving securities settlement in the European Union and on central securities depositories (CSDs) (2014). European Union. Retrieved from http://ec.europa.eu/internal_market/financial-markets/central_securities_depositories/index_en.htm

European Code of Conduct for clearing and settlement. (2006). EACH, ECSDA, FESE. Retrieved from http://ec.europa.eu/internal_market/financial-markets/docs/code/code_en.pdf

CSD Issuer Services. (2013) ECSDA - European Central Securities Depositories Association. Retrieved from http://www.ecsda.eu/uploads/tx_doclibrary/2013_10_ECSDA_IS_Report.pdf

Improving the efficiency, integration and safety and soundness of cross border post-trading arrangements in Europe, Brussels, 3rd progress report. (2008). European Commission. Retrieved from http://ec.europa.eu/internal_market/financial-markets/docs/clearing/ecofin/20080311_ecofin_en.pdf

The Code of Conduct on clearing and settlement: three years of experience, Financial Services Policy and Financial Markets, Brussels. ECOFIN. (2009). European Commission. Retrieved from http://ec.europa.eu/internal_market/financial-markets/docs/code/2009-11-06-code-report-ecofin_en.pdf

Forth T2S Harmonisation Progress Report. (2014). T2S Advisory Group. Retrieved from http://www.ecb.europa.eu/paym/t2s/pdf/fourth_t2s_harmonisation_progress_report.pdf??ca8dad7f68af5c5edd9087cdc73d400a

Cross-Border Clearing and Settlement Arrangements in the European Union. (2002). Giovannini Group. Retrieved from http://ec.europa.eu/internal_market/financialmarkets/docs/clearing/first_giovannini_report_en.pdf

Second Report on EU Clearing and Settlement. (2003). Giovannini Group. Retrieved from http://ec.europa.eu/internal_market/financial-markets/docs/clearing/second_giovannini_report_en.pdf

Kokkola (2010) *The Payment System: payments, securities and derivatives, and the role of the Eurosystem*, 66 - 68, 84 - 85, 173 – 179. Frankfurt.

Mercier and Sauer. (2013). Optimal central securities depository reshaping toward TARGET2-Securities. *Journal of Financial Market Infrastructures*, *2*(2), 3–51.

Nicaud (2012) *Payment systems, design, governance and oversight, edited by Bruce J. Summers*, Central banking Publications, London

Oxera (2011) *Monitoring prices, costs and volumes of trading and post-trading services, report prepared for the European Commission DG internal market and services*, Oxford and Brussels. Available: http://ec.europa.eu/internal_market/financial-markets/docs/clearing/2011_oxera_study_en.pdf

Principles for financial market infrastructures. (2012BIS. Basel, Switzerland. *CPPS-IOSCO*, *5-9*, 13.

Recommendations for securities settlement systems. (2001BIS. Basel, Switzerland: CPSS-IOSCO.

Schmiedel and Schönenberger. (2005) Integration of securities market infrastructures in the Euro Area. Occasional paper series ECB, Frankfurt, 20-21

T2S Framework Agreement (2012) Retrieved from http://www.ecb.europa.eu/paym/t2s/pdf/csd_FA/T2S_Framework_Agreement_Schedules.pdf??136c1c40cce184cf0474fcea50179129

T2S User Requirement Document 5.3 (2014) Retrieved from http://www.ecb.europa.eu/paym/t2s/pdf/urd_v5-03.pdf??c11cd4527ac7dc75c315924e60cc3277

T2S website: http://www.ecb.europa.eu/paym/t2s/html/index.en.html

KEY TERMS AND DEFINITIONS

Central Securities Depository: An institution holding securities, enabling securities transactions to be processed by book-entry, providing settlement services.

Custody: The safekeeping (holding) and administration of securities and financial instruments for third parties.

Post-Trade Industry: The companies which provide clearing and settlement processing services for their clients after trading of securities has taken place.

Safekeeping: The storage of securities in a protected area, for instance a Central Securities Depository.

Securities Settlement Industry: The securities settlement processing services, see post-trade industry.

Settlement: The completion of a transaction which discharges obligations of securities transfers between one or more parties.

Chapter 17
Central Securities Depositories and Securities Clearing and Settlement:
Business Practice and Public Policy Concerns

Alistair Milne
Loughborough University, UK

ABSTRACT

This chapter describes the emergence of national and international central securities depositories (CSDs) and the systems of tiered account-based security ownership they support. It examines clearing and settlement risks, including principal risk now largely removed by DVP, and liquidity risk reduced but far from fully removed by multilateral netting. Liquidity demand and the complexity of some underlying transactions results in a surprisingly high volume of postponed settlements (trade fails). Systems of clearing and settlement were resilient during the crisis of 2008, but the remarkable complexity of these networks suggests two policy concerns that need further examination. Problems in clearing and settlement could still magnify or transmit systemic financial risk in a future crisis, if firms do not again obtain public sector support; and the sheer complexity of clearing and settlement arrangements may both create operational risks and heighten barriers to entry, hence reducing competition and raising costs to investors.

1. INTRODUCTION

The execution of every financial market transaction is followed by a series of further processes, ensuring the resulting obligations are carried out as agreed and helping counterparties manage the risks of contractual failure. These processes are referred to collectively as 'clearing and settlement.'

This chapter explains what clearing and settlement is and the institutional arrangements that support it including the role of central securities depositories and custodian banks. It also discusses the challenges of

DOI: 10.4018/978-1-4666-8745-5.ch017

promoting competition and efficiency and in clearing and settlement (and related services) and avoiding the transmission and amplification of systemic financial risk through clearing and settlement systems.

Before clearing and settlement can even begin there must be agreement on what has taken place in the trade. This requires matching of the two sides of the trade and confirmation of trade details such as price and quantity. In past times, before automated computer trading was commonplace, the processes of matching and confirmation required considerable manual reconciliation. Today, as trade execution is itself becoming increasingly automated, so is the subsequent matching and confirmation of trade details.

After matching and confirmation all financial trades must then be cleared and finally settled. Clearing refers to everything prior to settlement, establishing who owes what to whom and when. But the same word is often used as shorthand for 'central counterparty clearing', when the obligations to make payments or deliver securities arising from a financial trade are transferred to a central counterparty (or CCP); which thus becomes the buyer to every seller and the seller to every buyer. Not every financial transaction is 'cleared' through a CCP, but every financial transaction must be 'cleared' before it is settled. [1] After clearing comes settlement i.e. the agreed exchange of money and ownership.

It is not necessary to have a degree in automotive engineering in order to drive a car or to be a qualified plumber in order to run a bath. So why should these post-trade processes matter to anyone who is not a technical specialist? They are in fact a central concern to many others: to traders and investment managers, because of the substantial associated costs and risks associated with processing of financial trades; to final investors and also competition authorities, because clearing and settlement arrangements are a potential barrier to competition and hence source of unnecessary trading costs; and to central bankers and 'macroprudential' regulators because problems in clearing and settlement can potentially lead to system wide disruption of financial markets.

This chapter not only describes the process of clearing and settlement, it also draws attention to particular aspects of clearing and settlement where policy makers may need to pay particularly close attention. Clearing and settlement operations have evolved over time to become remarkably complex. This complexity creates business challenges, especially for management of liquidity, which could potentially have systemic consequences for the wider financial system. This complexity may also increase the barriers to entry that can discourage competition in trade settlement and securities services.

The chapter is organised as follows. Section 2 describes how ownership (or title) is recorded and transferred in today's financial markets, focussing on the hierarchical or tiered accounts in which securities are held. These are contrasted with earlier paper based systems of recording ownership that were widely used before the days of computers.

Section 3 then outlines the main issues of risk and cost involved in securities clearing and settlement. It examines four closely related issues: (a) 'principal risk' i.e. the risk that the purchased security is not delivered or the money promised is not paid and how this is overcome through 'Delivery v. Payment' or DVP; (b) the remaining replacement and operational risks that are further controlled through central counterparty clearing; (c) the close link between securities settlement, custodian accounts and the provision of liquidity for securities market transactions; and (d) the puzzle of surprisingly high levels of reported trade fails (i.e. postponements of final settlement).

Section 4 discusses two of the major challenges for industry and policy makers that arise in the context of securities clearing and settlement. The first is the maintenance of systemic financial stability and the possibility that a financial crisis might be amplified by problems emanating from securities clearing and settlement. The second are the appropriate steps to promote competition and reduce costs to final investors both in asset servicing and in financial market transactions. Section 5 summarises and concludes.

2. OWNERSHIP OF SECURITIES: A BRIEF HISTORY FROM BEARER BONDS TO BYTES

Paper Vs Account Based Ownership

In order to understanding today's systems of securities ownership, it is helpful to review how these emerged from the earlier paper-based arrangements used for recording and transferring the ownership of publically traded securities, before the advent of computerisation.[2]

For many years, until the late 1960s, most public traded securities were held as 'bearer bonds'. The name itself is misleading: a bearer bond could just as well represent a share of a corporate equity as well as a fixed income security. So what is a bearer bond? It is a negotiable instrument, meaning that ownership is transferred through the exchange of the physical paper instrument in return for payment

A comparison that some readers may be familiar with is the endorsement of the negotiable cheque.[3] The owner of a certificate representing the ownership of a security, whether dividend paying or fixed income, endorsed their certificate of ownership so passing ownership rights to whoever held the certificate in their physical possession. The reason for doing this was to reduce the costs of trading, at the expense of relatively higher costs of securing the endorsed certificates in strong rooms. Fixed income securities were often also originally issued in bearer form, typically with detachable paper 'coupons' which were physically presented in order to claim interest payments.

As well as bearer bonds, there were two other alternative historically important arrangements for the paper based recording of title to a tradable security. In the London stock market, the leading global venue for the trading both of equity and bonds, change in ownership in many domestic (UK) securities used a different approach, the so called 'deed of transfer'. Ownership was established solely by the record of ownership in a central register as signified by a certificate. The deed of transfer was a further legal document which, signed by the seller and accompanied by the share certificate, allowed the buyer to apply to the company registrar (the keeper of the list of owners of the security) for the cancellation of the original certificate and the issue of a new certificate in their name.

A third approach to change in ownership, known as 'inscription', was found also in London, for example at the Bank of England for most British government bonds, and also in Vienna at the Wiener Giro- und Cassen-Verein established by the Vienna stock exchange in 1872 and in Germany in similar institutions the Kassenverein. For such inscribed securities there were no certificates at all, instead ownership was recorded only through book entry (the inscription) in a central registrar. The seller simply signed their approval for the transfer of ownership on the registrar. This offered another relatively low cost means of transferring ownership, provided that the seller could be physically present to complete the transfer.

Beginning in the late 1960s, as trading volumes rose, these paper based system of trading and settlement became unacceptably costly and inefficient. There was then a shift away from paper based arrangements, towards electronic recording and transfer of securities ownership and the development of the now standard arrangements for account based holding of securities.

These new arrangements have two key distinguishing features:

- The ultimate record of all issued securities is kept in a 'centralised securities depository' or CSD.
- Ownership of securities is recorded by holdings in securities accounts that can be traced back to the CSD.

In some respect the CSD is similar to the long established inscription arrangements found in late 19th century London, Austria and Germany. Certificates, either in registered or bearer form are no longer necessary. Change in ownership is recorded purely through book-entry. There is however one major difference: securities accounts need not be held directly with the CSD. Market participants much more commonly hold these accounts indirectly with custodian banks or other financial institutions in order to benefit from other services (such as income and tax management, processing of corporate actions such as share buy backs or acquisitions or the execution of transactions). These intermediaries in turn maintain matching securities account that can be traced back down (possibly through further accounts) to the ultimate record of issue at the CSD.

This resulting 'multi-tiered' ownership of shares and other securities typically required accompanying development of legal conventions and the passage of relevant legislation. Ownership rights are exercised through a hierarchy of account holdings. Figure 1 illustrates such a hierarchy incorporating the additional layer of intermediation required for a cross-border ownership.

A necessary support for these arrangements is that law recognises holdings of securities at each level as fungible i.e. not a direct claim on a specific security but a general claim on all the securities of that particular kind held at the next lower level in the hierarchy. For example here the final investor has a claim on a share of the securities held by a custodian, not a claim on an identifiable share certificate held at the central securities depository.

This legal principle of 'fungibility' facilitates trading in a number of ways. For example it makes it possible for custodians and for CSDs to lend securities to trading participants for delivery in settlement; this is a key aspect of managing security flows. It also makes it feasible to establish links between Central Securities Depositories in order to effect cross border delivery. This link is simply another level of the ownership hierarchy.

Account based ownership underpins the substantial and international custodian banking industry.[4] Originally, in the old days of paper based title, the core function of a custodian bank was safekeeping of certificates (hence the name 'custodian'). Today the business has moved on, exemplified by the global custodian banks – notably JP Morgan, State Street, The Bank of New York Mellon and also CitiGroup and BNP Paribas – who are the principal providers of security accounts for both domestic and international investors.[5] Their business model is charging fees to investors for providing a combination of transaction

Figure 1. The hierarchy of cross-border security ownership

Final Investor (typically an institution such as a pension fund)

Account with Global Custodian

Account with Local Sub-Custodian

Account with Central Securities Depository (CSD)

services (supporting the clearing and settlement of securities trades, securities lending) and asset services (collection of dividend and coupon income, tax payments, and exercise of shareholder rights such as proxy voting and take up of rights issues). These activities are all IT based and heavily capital intensive.

The Creation of National and International CSDs

This shift from paper to account based holding of securities occurred first in the United States.[6] This was a response to the Wall Street paper work crisis of the 1960s (when the back offices of Wall Street firms were overwhelmed by rapidly increasing trading volumes, leading to transfer of title often lagging several weeks behind the original trade execution). The first response in 1968 was the immobilisation of certificates within the Central Certificate Service of the New York Stock exchange. Following the report of the ad-hoc US Banking and Securities Industry Committee, this service was spun out as the Depository Trust Corporation or DTC, creating a national US central securities depository in 1972 serving all the various US exchanges. A final step in the creation of the modern US securities clearing and settlement landscape came in 1999, various clearing houses for the different regional and New York exchanges were merged to form the NSCC (the national securities clearing corporation) and this was in turn merged with the DTC within a single industry owned holding company, the Depository Trust Clearing Corporation or DTCC. By this means the US acquired a single national infrastructure for all securities clearing and settlement (some bonds, e.g. municipals, continue to be held in depositories outside of the DTCC, but links with DTCC ensure that these are still accessible via this single infrastructure).

Similar difficulties with the settlement of securities held in paper form led the establishment of the two European based international central securities depositories, or ICSDs, Euroclear and Cedel, both created to provide settlement services for the international bond market that developed in Europe in the 1960s.[7] Euroclear was founded in 1968 as an international bond settlement system by the Brussels office of Morgan Guaranty. Cedel was founded in 1971 as an alternative bond settlement system to compete with Euroclear. Cedel was subsequently acquired by DeutscheBorse and renamed as Clearstream International.

Since the late 1960s national CSDs have been established in all major financial centres, typically with either central bank or exchange sponsorship. One of the last to follow this route was London with launch of CREST (now a subsidiary of Euroclear) as the UK CSD in 1996. London could delay because it had a remarkably efficient system of paper based clearing and settlement, based on a two week trading-account period (bonds and shares were traded for settlement at the end of every fortnight); but this system was really only suited to a the kind of membership based exchange in which every participant was well known to other participants and hence, because counterparty default risks were comparatively low, there was no urgency to complete settlement.

Originating as it did from paper based processing it remained however relatively costly, compared to the more advanced systems of electronic settlement based on security accounts, and also inappropriate to the more anonymous and competitive trading environment that emerged in London after the 1986 'big-bang' removed barriers to entry. Shifting to modern T+3 CSD settlement by then standard in other financial centres proved to be difficult, but was eventually achieved by 1996.[8]

Recently, in October 2014, London together with the rest of Europe shifted to T+2 settlement for equity trades. The major markets in the US and Asia are now discussing a similar shift for the settlement of equity trades from T+3 to T+2 (see for example (DTCC, 2014a, 2014b)).[9]

A legal detail is that in some cases (e.g. France, Denmark, Norway, Italy) the CSD is dematerialised i.e. certificates have no legal status and securities are represented purely as entries on a computer database. Where local law allows it, dematerialization is a useful tidying up of the arrangements for holding of securities; but this makes relatively little practical difference. Even if securities are deposited in physical certificated form (this is the case for example in the US where the large retail investor base has led to the retention of physical share certificates alongside CSD accounts with DTC, instead of full dematerialisation), the investors, custodians and others can still exchange claims on these securities against each other purely electronically.

Today CSDs, both national and international, and custodian banks work together and at the same time compete with each other. It is a natural step for a national CSD, working alongside the system for national large value payments, to use its processing systems to offer post trade settlement services i.e. managing the settlement cycle through the various stages of clearing i.e. indicating to each party of the trade their obligations whether delivery of security or in order for the trade to be settled and the point in time at which that obligation must be met; positioning i.e. obtaining confirmation from participants that they are ready to meet these obligations; guaranteeing services ; and finally completing i.e. initiating the appropriate payment and delivery instructions so that delivery with finality is achieved. But conceptually these CSD settlement and depository services are distinct functions and indeed, with appropriate links, a CSD can provide a settlement service for a security that is in fact held with another depository.

An example of such value added services is that Euroclear and Clearstream each maintain link with a network of custodian banks, national depositories and central banks and offer settlement services around the world. They also maintain a link with each other (known as 'the bridge'). This bridge allows DVP where the two sides of the trade choose to settle through the two different systems. Other bilateral links have been developed between various national CSDs to facilitate cross border trading. Examples include links between CREST and the Swiss depository SIGA and between the Italian CSD Monte-Titoli and the Scandinavian CSDs.

3. SETTLING THE TRADE: MANAGING COSTS AND RISKS

This section examines the costs and risks involved in securities clearing and settlement. It begins by offering an analogy with the 'closing' of a house purchase, and then discusses the various risks and operational efficiencies involved in these processes.

Almost all security ownership is nowadays represented by the holding balances in security accounts, as described in Section 2. Settlement must be possible against the accounts of the various national central securities depositories (CSDs) or international central securities depositories (ICSDs, i.e. Euroclear Bank in Brussels and Clearstream International in Luxembourg) which are the ultimate record of securities issued.

Settlement can also take place on security accounts held with other institutions, for example custodian banks such as JP Morgan, State Street or The Bank of New York Mellon. This is relatively easy if both buyer and seller hold securities accounts with the same custodian, in this case settlement is simply an internal transfer of securities from one client account to another and no transfer of securities is required at the CSD. If the buyer and seller hold securities at different custodian banks, then a matching transfer of securities must take place on the books of the CSD to ensure that the total security accounts in each custodian match against a corresponding 'omnibus' account at the CSD.

Table 1 presents the analogy between the closing of a house purchase and the clearing and settlement of an equity transaction. As any house purchaser or equity trader will know, these practical processes, taking place from the initial agreement to trade until its eventual completion, are costly and all too often can go wrong.

As Table 1 illustrates, in each case there are two sides to the trade, a buyer and a seller, who are brought together by a broker. A difference is that in the standard purchase or sale of a security in a public market there is no need ever to know the identity of the counterparty.[10]

In the case of both a house and a security purchase there is a record of ownership. Records of house ownership can still be paper based (practice varies considerably between countries, and even within for example different US states). As described in Section 2 most securities holdings are now account based, typically with custodian banks. Again in each case the transfer of ownership requires a payment of an agreed sum of money in exchange for title. With large sums of money involved there are obvious risks involved, notably default or counterparty risk (does the seller really have title to this property? Will the buyer pay as agreed at the time of settlement?) and operational risk (are all the legal requirements for completing the transaction in order? Will the final steps be taken at their scheduled time?).

Details of settlement do vary from one financial transaction to another. In house purchases the money must be transferred to a third party (in some countries an 'escrow' account, in others an agent such a lawyer working on behalf of the seller) before the keys to a property are released. Once the keys are transferred then the money is passed on to the seller.

Settlement of a securities purchase similarly requires a transfer of ownership in exchange for a monetary payment. Settlement of foreign exchange and derivative transactions is a little different, undertaken entirely through the exchange of monetary payments. But the underlying risks – whether in housing, securities or in other financial transactions – are similar. This discussion will focus on four aspects of risk and cost: principal risk (and DVP), replacement risk (and netting), liquidity risk and securities borrowing, and finally the puzzle of high rates of settlement postponement.

a) Principal Risk and DVP

In securities transactions most default risk is nowadays avoided by ensuring that settlement is 'DVP' or delivery against payment. This is very similar to the requirement for 'cash on delivery' sometimes

Table 1. Clearing and Settlement – a Comparison

	House Purchase	Equity or Bond Purchase
Intermediary	Realtor	Broker
Record of ownership	The relevant municipal or county record of deeds	An account held with securities depository or custodian
Transfer of ownership	Closing (also called settlement) with exchange of money for title	Settlement through exchange of money and securities
Preparation for transfer	Title search	Confirmation, matching and netting
Risk and cost reduction	Use of an escrow account for closing Title insurance	Simultaneous delivery against payment (DVP) Transfer of obligations to a clearing house or central counterparty.

used for the purchase of physical goods. Settlement, the exchange of securities for money, goes ahead only once both the securities are ready for delivery i.e. ready and waiting in the seller's security account for transfer to the buyer's securities account *and* money is ready in the buyer's bank account ready for transfer to the seller's bank account. Once this is confirmed then both transfers are authorised. DVP avoids the possibility of paying money for securities that are not delivered or delivering securities that are not paid (so called 'principal risk').

While DVP eliminates principal risk, it was far from trivial technical challenge to fully implement in the major markets as they moved from paper-based to electronic settlement. It was only following an influential report (G30 Working Group, 1988) emphasising the large exposures to principal risk in global securities markets, that the major financial centres adopted DVP. This required close co-operation with central banks because full DVP required the simultaneous adoption of so called 'Real Time Gross Settlement' (RTGS) in order that high value payments in central bank money could be initiated and completed simultaneously with the transfer of securities, hence eliminating principal risk.

This G30 report, developed under the chairmanship of John Reed, addressed a variety of problems of inconsistency in settlement arrangements between countries, including incompatible systems and procedures, different settlement arrangements and variation in the length of settlement cycle, all of which were a cause for concern, both because they hindered cross-border trade and as a source of systemic risk. The G30 recommendations were for: trade confirmation and affirmation on a compatible basis for both domestic and international markets by T+1; settlement on a rolling basis by T+3, "Delivery versus payment" or DVP in all settlements preferably via electronic or book entry payments with 'same day funds'; use of a central securities depository; encouragement of securities lending; and use of netting mechanisms where appropriate; and finally standard numbering systems. All there were to be in place by 1992 and remain best practice in all established financial markets today.

The G30 report set out what are now considered to the basic standards for post-trade execution at the domestic level. Taken together with various reports of the Basel committee on payments and settlements it encouraged continued improvement in the speed and operation of payment and settlement cycles. A significant structural shift has been from batched settlement (e.g. the settlement at the end of a two week account period such as used to be used in the London Stock Exchange) to rolling settlement, with settlement a fixed period after the date of trade (e.g. t+3 implying final settlement 3 days after the trading date) and trades that fail to settle on this day deferred to the following day.

Implementation of DVP varies somewhat from one jurisdiction to another. A subsequent central bank report on the practicalities of implementing the G20 proposals, (CPSS, 1992), distinguished three models actually being applied to the achievement of DVP. Model 1 which fully eliminates principal risk, is real time exchange of securities and payments on a gross basis. This model – adopted in the major financial centres such as London, New York and Tokyo, however requires complementary development of RTGS capability in large value payment systems and can place substantial liquidity demands on market participants at times of stress. Model 2 involves gross exchange of securities, followed relatively closely, typically overnight, by a subsequent net payment in cash. This model does not fully eliminated principal risk and requires further safeguards to ensure that the subsequent net cash payments are forthcoming. Another possibility is what the CPSS refer to as model 3, in which cash and securities are exchange simultaneously on a net basis. This also eliminates fully principal risk, but can lead to difficulties in the event of participant default with large subsequent knock on impact on other market participants through high levels of trade failure. As can be seen each approach to DVP has its own advantages and disadvantages.

Cross border settlement, increasingly common as financial markets have become more globalised, requires additional processes for handling transfer, both of money and of ownership, between jurisdictions; this can involve, for example, the settlement of monetary obligations in commercial bank rather than central bank money; and additional tiered arrangements for recording ownership by foreign investors. Thus for example ICSD settlement for Eurobonds by Euroclear and Clearstream is in commercial rather than central bank money, reflecting customer requirement for multi-currency settlement which makes settlement in central bank money impractical. Participants maintain cash accounts for finance settlement with the commercial banking arms of the ICSDs. Settlement is DVP and multi-currency in these accounts, but principal risk is not quite so effectively removed, since there is a residual albeit small risk of failure of these banks and the money deposited in them.

b) Operational Costs, Replacement Risk and Multilateral Netting

DVP in central bank money can eliminate principal risk, but does not remove the remaining residual risk of trade failures. If either money or securities are not ready for delivery then DVP cannot take place and there will be a delay in settlement. Dealing with such problems adds to operational costs and can potentially cause liquidity problems for one or both counterparties. In the event that settlement is not just delayed but does not take place at all, e.g. because of counterparty bankruptcy, then there are the additional costs and potential losses of having to replace the failed trade with a newly executed trade.

These replacement risks are just one of the operational costs and risks associated confronted by modern day systems of security settlement. Another key challenge is business continuity. Systems need to be robust in the event of a major disturbance such as a terrorist attack or other catastrophic event. There is a desire on the part of market participants to exploit technology and economies of scale in order to reduce both processing costs and operational risks. Thus in Europe, over the past two decades, there has been a considerable effort to develop pan-European arrangement for the clearing and settlement of securities trades (for example Target-2 securities, discussed below) to take full advantage of the cost reductions from economies of scale). The discussion here focuses though on replacement risk and the reduction in this operational risk through multilateral netting.

It is useful to distinguish different reasons for a delay in settlement. One, only touched on here, is operational integrity of the systems themselves. All market participants, both intermediaries and final investors, suffer enormous costs of the clearing and settlement systems themselves break down. There is therefore close monitoring of the operational integrity of these systems by both industry and regulators. Great care is taken with operational tasks such as software upgrades, to ensure that there is no break in service. Much of the costs of operating clearing and settlement infrastructure are operational.

Even when the systems themselves are robust, there is always still the possibility that a counterparty may fail to deliver either cash or collateral as promised. This has two consequences: in extremis, if the counterparty is bankrupt and will never deliver, then the consequence is a replacement risk, the trade must be replaced and market prices may have moved substantially and create a large cost for so doing. In most cases the counterparty is still trading and can be expected, eventually, to deliver; but this creates a liquidity problem, the securities broker must obtain the cash or collateral to deliver to clients.

These risks may be quite small for each individual trade, but in active securities markets with large trade volumes they are far from trivial. The front-line tool for reducing this replacement and liquidity risk is ‘multilateral netting’ through a central counterparty. A central counterparty (also referred to as a clearing house or central counterparty clearing house) is an institution that is interposed between buyers and sellers on a financial market, acting as the buyer to every seller and the seller to every buyer. Figure 2 illustrates:

There is a potentially dramatic reduction in the number of trades to be settled. On a bilateral basis market participants have $(nn-1)/2$ bilateral positions. This is reduced to only n with a central counterparty. With 1,000 participants in the market, potential number of positions needing to be settled could be reduced from 499,500 to only 1000! The central counterparty must of course be extremely safe – if the central counterparty were to fail, then all participants in the market would be seriously affected.

Central counterparty clearing has been used for the best part of a century in derivative exchanges.[11] Examples include Chicago Mercantile Exchange Clearing for the main US derivatives exchanges and London Clearing House which developed as the central counterparty for the London derivatives exchange LIFFE and the London commodities exchanges (although a few years ago it lost the LIFFE contract).

As operational risks and costs have increased in securities markets, along with trading volumes, stock exchanges in all the major financial centres have adopted central counterparty clearing for their securities markets as well as exchange traded derivatives. This has several benefits in terms of reduced risk and cost.[12]

- It provides the maximum amount of multilateral netting. As illustrated in Figure 1, the introduction of a central counterparty results in automatic and full netting of all positions. In the case of the US securities markets this reduces the volume of trades that need to be settled by 98% (Morris & Goldstein, 2010) and as technology promotes even larger numbers of smaller trades this percentage netting efficiency is growing even higher.
- In the context of an order driven market, such a stock exchange or automated execution facility, they allow 'anonymity of trading' to be preserved – (something that happens automatically in a quote driven market because a market maker stands between buyers and sellers deal).
- They facilitate standardisation of post-trade processing, including both initial confirmation and matching, and then the subsequent clearing, and final settlement. Every trade is handled by the central counterparty and the systems of all other market participants must work effectively with the CCP.

Figure 2. Pre-settlement netting: Bilateral versus central counterparty

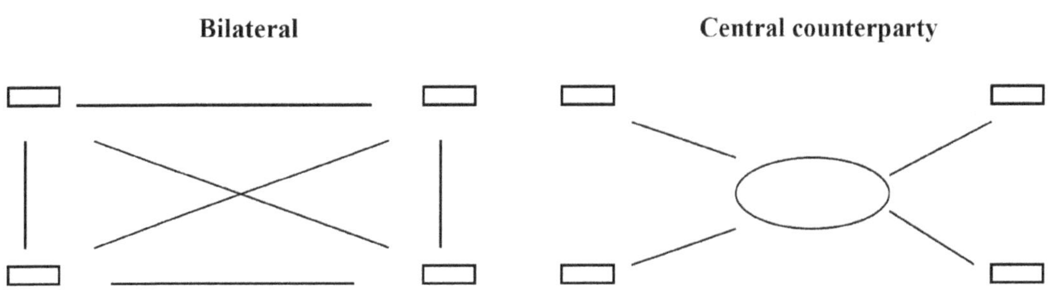

- Finally central counterparties facilitate so called "Continuous Net Settlement". When a trade settlement fails, because either the buyer fails to provide cash, or the seller fails to provide the security, then the position can be marked to market, and carried over and netted with all of the following day's trades for settlement one day later.

Also, as discussed in Section 4, a CCP can if it is accompanied by open access reduce entry barriers and hence support greater competition both trade execution and the provision of post trade services.

c) Liquidity Risk and Securities Borrowing

A third and closely related risk in securities settlement is liquidity risk, the risk that either cash or securities may not be available to settle remaining (unnetted) trades. This subsection provides a brief discussion of the role of custodian banks and CSDs in providing the necessary liquidity in securities accounts for completion of trades. The challenge is a long standing one in securities markets: it may not be necessary to be in possession of securities ready for delivery at the time an order to sell a security is submitted; this is only necessary at the time of settlement.[13]

As a result there is a market for securities borrowing and lending, through which market participants can temporarily borrow securities from the accounts of other market participants and deliver them for settlement.[14] Historically, this was achieved in London markets through a fee known as 'contango', paid by a purchaser of securities for borrowing money against the loan of the security and thus being able to delay full payment and in effect financing a long position on margin.[15]

Occasionally, when there was abnormal demand for securities for settlement, these fees reversed in sign and a payment, then referred to as 'backwardation', was made by the lender of money to the owner of securities for the privilege of having possession of the security for settlement (an unusual situation arising only when there is substantial unsatisfied demand for that particular security in the cash market, arising for example if many securities have been sold forward in futures or forward contracts and there a sharp change in market sentiment leading to substantial closing of these positions and a hence a shortage of securities.)

This has now evolved into securities lending, one of the main services provided by custodian banks to their broker and investor clients. They can for a fee arrange for a loan of securities to take place on their books between one client's account and another, matched by a loan from a cash account held by the security borrower to a cash account of the security lender. Investors are normally happy for their securities to be loaned out because this earns them a small additional income. The cash lenders are willing to receive a lower remuneration than they would from simply keeping the cash on deposit in order to have securities for settlement.

This securities lending is closely related to, and economically a close substitute for, the practice of "repo" or sale and repurchase agreements between investment banks and their clients. In both cases a security is used as collateral for borrowing of cash. The differences between the two arrangements are institutional: repo is used primarily for financing long positions in bonds and other fixed income securities; while securities lending is primarily used for obtaining equities for the settlement of short trading positions.

The tiered ownership described in Section 2 has resulted in another substantial difference between settlement arrangements used today and those used the paper based systems of the 1960s and earlier. In those days securities settlement meant exchange between the final buyers and final sellers of securities, money exchanged for either a physical certificate or for a change of entry in an inscribed security holdings record book. Today securities settlement means exchange of money for securities in held *in securities accounts with the brokers responsible for executing client orders*. This difference matters because the first responsibility for managing the liquidity and settlement risks in securities trading falls on the brokers rather than on their clients. They can of course ask clients to accept the costs, for example by requiring them to pre-fund trades, but the response of the clearing and settlement system to liquidity shocks is different and – an issue for further research – may be a source of systemic risk.

Figure 3 illustrates how, in order to trade, buyers and sellers hold securities in securities accounts held with the brokers who execute their instructions to trade. This may require transferring securities from an investment account held with a custodian bank. The securities broker in turn holds securities accounts with a custodian or CSD and cash accounts with central bank. After the trade is executed the trade is settled, from the customers perspective, by movement of securities into (or out of) these accounts with a matching and opposite cash payment out of held with custodian

This figure highlights these ways in which modern settlement arrangements that differ from those in the old days of paper based settlement. As already discussed, final buyers and sellers now hold both securities accounts and cash accounts with the brokers who execute security purchases and sales on their behalf. This is different from past practice when investors would have held only cash accounts with brokers (such a thing as a 'security account' did not then exist) and physically delivered security certificates for settlement (or physically presented themselves for a change of inscribed book entry.)

Also, as discussed, delays in settlement and resulting liquidity risk, are nowadays an immediate concern for the broker, the intermediaries, but do not impinge directly on their final customers. If settlement is at T+2 then the broker dealer will credit the buyers account with that security on T+2. If as happens occasionally the security is not delivered into the brokers own custodian account, then they will have to themselves borrow the security in order to meet their client obligations. This is very different from arrangements under the old paper based system of clearing and settlement when clients not brokers were responsible for managing liquidity risks using contango (margin) or backwardation (security borrowing) according to whether they were short of cash or short of securities.

Figure 3. The hierarchy of ownership in a trading environment

Buyer (asset manager, cash only institution such as an insurance fund or a leveraged institution such as hedge fund)		Seller (asset manager, cash only institution such as an insurance fund or a leveraged institution such as hedge fund)	
Investment accounts	Trading accounts	Trading accounts	Investment accounts
Cash and security accounts with Commercial Bank/Custodian Cash and security accounts with Central Bank/CSD	Cash and security Accounts with Security Broker Cash and security accounts with Central Bank/CSD	Cash and security accounts with Security Broker Cash and security accounts with Central Bank/CSD	Cash and security accounts with Commercial Bank/Custodian Cash and security accounts with Central Bank/CSD

The consequence is that under modern systems it is the security brokers who carry all these liquidity risks. They must therefore always be ready to borrow securities either in the securities lending market (used primarily for equities) or the repo market (used primarily for bonds). Thus brokers rely on both repo and securities lending as a source of liquidity. Repo lending is the main instrument for exchange of liquidity in the short term money markets. Securities lending is the corresponding instrument for provision of liquidity to those broker dealers in order to support their customers in taking short positions in equity markets.

d) When is Settlement a Settlement? The Puzzle of Trade Fails

The move over past decades from paper based and manual processes in clearing and settlement has accompanied a switch from manual (face to face and telephone based) trade execution to automated computer based or computer assisted orders for trade execution. These developments have long promised to lead to full automation of trading processes, from initial order through trade execution to final settlement, something described as 'straight through processing' or STP.

In theory in today's financial markets where the large proportion of trades are initiated on a computer, either automatically or through a mouse-click, the post-trade process should be highly automated with only minimum manual intervention. However in practice, while there has indeed been considerable degree of automation of post trade services, an essential requirement to cope with the greatly increased trading volumes in modern computerised and screen based markets, it has also for a number of reasons proved difficult to achieve complete STP. Instead a surprisingly high proportion of trades fail. This is due to the challenges facing security brokers in managing both their cash and securities liquidity.

There has been progress. In the 1990s and earlier, when a large proportion of orders to trade and execution was manual, for example through voice instructions, then substantial resources had to be devoted to the initial matching and confirmation of trades. Securities markets have in the past two decades largely shifted to computerised trading, either through manual orders entered on a computer screen or through computerised algorithmic trading. These change have substantially reduced those trade fails arising because the original trade agreement itself was flawed because inconsistency of instructions on the two sides of the trade.

It is though still quite common for settlement to be delayed by one or more days (rather confusingly these are still referred to as 'trade fails' even though the trade has not failed, rather instead settlement has been delayed). For this reason fully straight through processing has proved to be elusive, especially in either cross-border trades and in trades involving a number of underlying a participants, for example both exchange traded and actively managed fund. As a result trade fails, i.e. settlement delays, are still comparatively high in some types of trades and some trade fails can still require relatively expensive manual intervention before they are finally cleared and settled.

The analysis of (Bradley, Fawls, Litan, & Sommers, 2011) (of the Kauffmann Foundation and the Basis Point Group) drawing on DTCC data has drawn attention issue of trade fails. (The Economist, 2011), in an article based on their work, highlights the high levels of trade fails, especially at times of systemic financial stress, for example at the time of the failures of Lehman Brothers and Bear Stearns (see Figure 4), and in particular instruments. In 2010-2011 US trade failures were especially high in Exchange Traded Funds, accounting for around $7bn per day of the $10bn per day of failed equity trades in 2010. Trade failures in US Treasuries and Mortgage Backed Securities were even higher.

Figure 4. US Daily Trade Fails

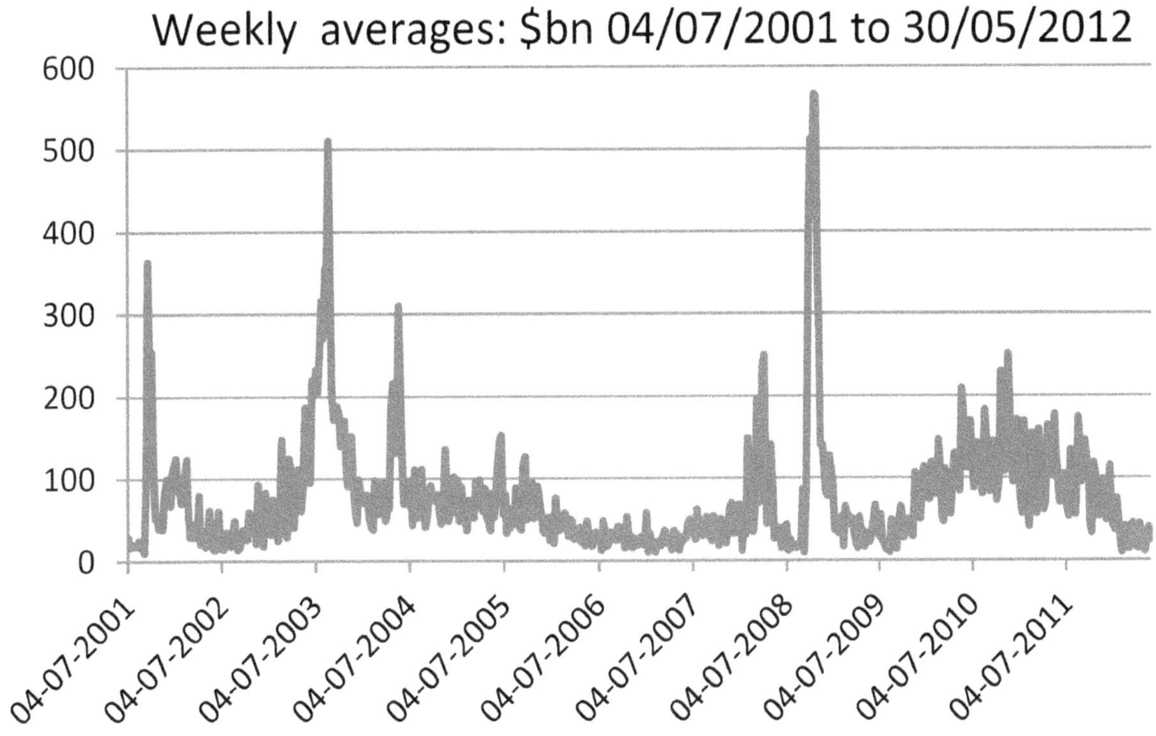

Note: The data in this figure was provided by the Basis Point Group consultancy. The data has been put together from statistical releases on the US Federal Reserve Bank of New York website for US treasury, Federal agency, other mortgage-backed and corporate securities trade fails reported by the US Primary Dealers (see http://www.newyorkfed.org/markets/statrel.html, http://www.newyorkfed.org/markets/gsds/search.html and http://www.newyorkfed.org/markets/pridealers_current.html).

Do these levels of trade failure matter, given that final customers are not directly affected? Clearly it involves cost and risk to securities brokers but provided these risks are understood and managed then these not need be a cause of further concern. (Amery, 2011) reports a range of views on the ETF trade failures, some market participants regarding them as a benign consequence of the different tools used by brokers to manage collateral and liquidity (as already explained customers positions are determined by the trade not settlement, with the broker responsible for making up any losses arising from settlement failure); others including (Bradley et al., 2011) view them as potentially large source of systemic risk with the possibility of a cascade of trade failures leading to systemic financial problems.

(ECSDA, 2012) reports some statistics for trade failures in European markets. For example they report (Annex 1) March 2012 figures for the UK and Ireland – which have some of the lowest trade failure rates across Europe – indicating that 3.82% of the total volume of securities trades for which Euroclear UK and Ireland (the CSD) receives settlement instructions remain unmatched at T+2, the day before intended settlement; with 1.27% of trades by value failing to settle on the intended settlement day of T+3 and only a further 0.27% of trades settling one day late on T+4.

There are several underlying reasons for these sometimes surprisingly high levels of observed trade fails (see discussion in (ECB, 2011; Fleming & Garbade, 2005)):

- Failure of the cash leg of settlement is hardly ever a cause of trade fails, but problems arise relatively often with the security leg of settlement either because it can be difficult to secure the specific security required for settlement or because the securities dealer prefers not to use up their cash liquidity in securities borrowing. Failure volumes approaching 5% of average daily total equity market trading in 2011 have been reported in the US ((Mollenkamp, Podkul, & Toonkel, 2012)). Even higher US trade failure rates occur in Treasury and government agency bond markets.
- Market participants may consciously choose postponement of settlement as an alternative to securities borrowing because the penalty for a postponement are relatively low. Changes in regulatory penalties for settlement delay in the US have reduced rates of trade fails, but they have not disappeared entirely ((SEC, 2011))
- Settlement postponement in US treasury securities trades have been high during periods when there were relatively low quantities of securities available for lending (see (Fleming & Garbade, 2007)
- Settlement postponement is also associated with relatively complex deals, such as cross border participation or multiple participants in a fund transactions, the accounts of each of which must be credited with cash or securities.
- Settlement postponement can rise during periods of market stress when liquidity is scarce.

4. POLICY CONCERNS: THE CHALLENGE OF COMPLEXITY

This section discusses briefly two policy issues that arise in relation to securities clearing and settlement. The first is systemic risk, the second implications of post-trade clearing and settlement arrangements for competition and the cost and quality of services to final investors holding and transacting in securities. It will be argued here that there is at least some 'prima facie' evidence that the complex modern arrangements for holding securities and transferring ownership both reduce competition in securities services and heighten systemic risk. Policy makers need to pay close attention.

Systemic Risk in Securities Clearing and Settlement

Central banks across the world are closely involved in securities clearing and settlement and are especially concerned with the possibility that problems in clearing and settlement processes might amplify or transmit systemic financial problems. These concerns are regularly addressed at global level by the Committee on Payment and Market Infrastructures hosted at the Bank for International Settlements (formerly known as the Committee on Payment and Settlement Systems, see (CPMI, 2014)).

During the global financial crisis of 2007-2009 securities clearing and settlement systems proved to be remarkably robust, and did not amplify or transmit systemic risk (Borio, 2010). This is in sharp contrast with the 1987 Stock Market crash in the US where clearing and settlement systems came under great strain, with several problems including the failure of the Fedwire large value payments system, contributing substantially to the resulting panic (see (Bernanke, 1990) for summary discussion and more detailed references).

There were though, as we have seen above, heightened rates of trade fails in 2008 at those times of greatest systemic financial stress when firms were scrambling for liquidity. (Bradley et al., 2011) argue that these trade fails, while not overwhelming the wider financial system on these occasions, still have the potential to result in such large "cascades" of trade fails that this could lead to widespread transmission of systemic financial problems.

Problems also arose in the global crisis of 2008 in closely related market arrangements, notably in repo markets. Because of loss of confidence in their quality as collateral, the ability to repo sub-prime MBS and other structured credit securities disappeared. 'Haircuts' widened i.e. the amount that could borrowed against securities using repo fell.[16]

There were particular problems in US tri-party repo markets (see (Copeland, Duffie, Martin, & McLaughlin, 2012). Tri-Party repo is an arrangement, more common in the US than in other markets, where a security that is pledged in repo is placed with a third party custodian bank. A key problem during the crisis was that the convention in the US for custodian banks involved in this business, chiefly JP Morgan and The Bank of New York, was to return securities pledged in overnight repo to their owners at the beginning of the next working day, leaving the matching loan as an uncollateralized daylight exposure.[17] This substantially increased counterparty risk because the lender of money was exposed to the substantial counterparty risk of loan not being repaid later in the day.

Another obvious substantial and uncontrolled counterparty risks that emerged during the crisis, rather less closely related to clearing and settlement, was in over the counter credit default swap markets, against AIG and monoline insurers (these events are of course well documented, see for example (Milne, 2009)). This risk is the principal rationale for the newly introduced requirements for trade reporting and clearing and OTC derivative markets, but was not directly related to securities clearing and settlement.

The fact that clearing and settlement problems did not play a major role in the global financial crisis of 2008, does not imply that the role of securities clearing and settlement in a future systemic financial crisis can be entirely ignored. While clearing and settlement systems did not themselves amplify problems in the crisis, almost all participants in these systems were protected by emergency liquidity provision from central banks (and in many cases by explicit or implicit uncollateralised support from governments e.g. the widespread guarantees by the UK and other governments on many bank liabilities or the direct support by the US government to Citigroup and, through TARP lending, to many other US financial institutions). It is difficult to know what the counterfactual would have been: how would clearing and settlement systems have stood up had there not been extensive public sector support for financial institutions across the world?

The intention of regulators, going forward, is that such widespread support will not be repeated in any future crisis. In this case could liquidity or other problems then emerge in securities clearing and settlement? Or could exposures in clearing and settlement prove to be an obstacle to the orderly resolution of securities brokers, as envisaged in the US Dodd-Frank act or the Single Resolution Mechanism in European Banking Union?

Addressing these questions in any detail goes beyond the main scope of this chapter, providing a description of clearing and settlement processes and the associated default and liquidity risks. What can be concluded from the material offered here is that modern clearing and settlement arrangements are extremely complex, involving intricate and to a substantial extent largely undocumented networks of account holdings together with explicit (and sometimes implicit) credit and liquidity exposures. This complexity is itself a potential source of systemic problems. The behavioural incentives on market participants, especially in relation to the hoarding of securities or cash liquidity at times of financial stress are unclear and poorly understood. There are indications (for example from the data on "trade fails" i.e. postponed settlement, during the height of the global crisis), that systemic problems can still arise in modern systems of clearing and settlement during periods of market stress.

One aspect of this is the widespread practice amongst securities brokers of using assets, both cash and securities collateral, deposited with them by clients as tools for their own liquidity management. The best known example is rehypothecation i.e. when a dealer uses securities placed by clients in their securities accounts as collateral for cash borrowing by the dealer. Unwinding these positions, as was for example required following the failure of Lehman Brothers in 2008, can be difficult. The legal details matte, (see discussion in (Murphy, 2013)). The consequences of rehypothecation depends upon whether the transfer of cash and collateral is a transfer of title (with the security actually changing ownership) or whether ownership is unaffected by the pledging of collateral. At least in theory, if title is not pledged, the security should not be trapped in a bankruptcy of an intermediary in the rehypothecation chain. In practice the operating systems of the institutions involved may not be sophisticated enough to distinguish pledged securities to which they do not have title from other securities to which they do have title, so clients are exposed to loss in bankruptcy when they believe they are legally protected.

It may reasonably be asked whether there are not simpler mechanisms for the post-trade exchange of securities title and cash between final investors might not be worked out, imposing less operational and liquidity demands on broker dealers and hence reducing systemic risk in clearing and settlement. This is a major open issue for further research.

Complexity and Competition and Efficiency in Securities Transaction Services.

The remainder of this section discusses of the relationship between clearing and settlement infrastructure and competition and efficiency in the full range of securities transaction services, from initial trade execution through to final settlement.[18] It first describes the debates on regulation of clearing and settlement in the European Union and then draws some more general policy lessons.

This topic of competition and efficiency in securities clearing and settlement has been the subject of considerable attention in the European Union where it has been argued that fragmentation of clearing and settlement infrastructure along national lines has increased costs and reduced competition, as a result reducing both market liquidity and substantially increasing transaction costs.

A number of studies, for example (Lannoo & Levin, 2002; NERA Consulting, 2004) have compared costs in US and EU securities clearing and settlement arguing that the presence of the DTCC as a single US infrastructure has supported both greater efficiency of settlement (exploiting fully economies of scale) and by allowing trades to be settled in a single system support greater liquidity in trading venues. Cross-border trades within the European Union have been especially costly.

Because of this European policy makers have adopted the development of pan-European securities arrangements for clearing and settlement as a key objective, in the development of single markets in financial services across Europe.[19] The policy debate in Europe on clearing and settlement was substantially taken forward by the two reports of the Giovannini group (Giovannini Group, 2002, 2003) which identified fifteen separate barriers to integrated pan-European clearing and settlement, including market practice, law and regulation and technical interoperability. However even after some years progress in overcoming these barriers was limited, an outcome which (Giovannini, 2010) ascribes principally to weaknesses in the political process and the resulting failure to introduce a European directive to force a common legal framework on all participants in European clearing and settlement.

Progress has however been made in some of the more technical obstacles to pan-European clearing, with the creation of a pan-European securities settlement infrastructure: Target2 Securities or T2S. This has been commissioned and overseen by the European Central Bank (see (ECB, 2014) for the technical details of the project and (Lannoo & Valiante, 2009) for a critical review of this initiative). T2S when it comes on stream (this is now scheduled for 2015) will provide a platform supporting securities accounts that is closely linked to the Target2 platform for Euro large value payments, thus facilitating DVP settlement. All European CSDs will be able to link their own securities accounts into Target2, so a financial institution e.g. a custodian bank, by opening securities accounts with one CSD will be able to offer settlement services in any European security. According to the ECB this will overcome six of the fifteen Giovannini barriers to pan-European clearing and settlement – some fifteen years after the Giovannini group first considered how to create a common clearing and settlement framework.

This slow and hesitant progress towards integrated arrangements for European securities clearing and settlement, illustrates many more general issues of competition and efficiency which arise in securities clearing and settlement.[20] These include the following:

- Clearing and settlement infrastructures are technical monopolies. Operating clearing and settlement on a 'for profit' basis is problematic because participants to the two sides of a trade typically have no choice about where ultimate settlement takes place, this is determined by the CSD that holds the ultimate securities accounts.
- One common response, this is the situation of the DTCC in the United States and Euro-Clear in Europe, is for the infrastructure to be user-owned and operated on an 'at cost' basis. The users though, in the case of DTCC are the major securities brokers, not final investors, so it may be argued that DTCC still operates to serve producer interests. This arrangement does however encourage competition between trading platforms.
- An alternative arrangement, which applies for example to Deutsche Börse Clearstream, the German clearing and settlement infrastructure which also owns the ICSD Clearstream International, is for the infrastructure to be owned by an exchange. This 'silo' arrangement has certain advantages, for example making it technically easier to have 'straight through processing' from trade execution to final settlement. The problem here is that the exchange, especially if is a 'for profit' as most exchange now are, may be tempted to use the market power created by its monopoly on clearing and settlement to charge higher fees above cost.
- Clearing and settlement arrangements have a major impact on competition for associated services such as securities lending and transaction reporting. In particular existing infrastructures, even when they are not for profit, have a vested interest in the growth of their own clearing and settlement solutions and the opportunities for new business that this creates. According to (Giovannini, 2010) a number of market participants were disappointed by the failure to develop a common legal framework that would encourage competition in securities settlement, believing that it gave too much competitive advantage to the largest provider Euroclear. Euroclear was in turn disappointed by the decision to create T2-S because it undermined the value of the investment it had already undertaken in its own pan-European settlement solution.
- As in other 'network' industries, greater technical inter-operability and the removal of access barriers can reduce the market power of the owners of clearing and settlement infrastructures. Achieving greater interoperability requires standardisation at both the technical level e.g. communications and messaging and at the business process level. But the necessary co-operation on

standardisation can be difficult to achieve, especially if this involves substantial new investments.[21] Access regulation may be required to allow other suppliers to compete on 'downstream' services such as securities lending and transaction reporting.

The analysis provided in this chapter suggests a possible concern about competition and efficiency in securities clearing and settlement. As already emphasised, the interaction between securities brokers and custodian banks, on the one hand, and clearing and settlement infrastructures including CSDs on the other, is remarkably complicated, both in terms of the operational challenges of managing account flows and also the resulting responsibilities for managing cash and securities liquidity.

A consequence may be that it is very difficult for a new entrant to challenge the role of incumbent securities brokers. Arguably the sheer complexity of securities ownership and securities clearing and settlement entrenches the market power of securities brokers, at the expense of higher charges to final investors. While this goes beyond the scope of the present chapter, it is another issue where further research is again merited.

5. CONCLUSION

The purpose of this chapter has been to describe the legal and economic arrangements behind the ownership of securities and transfer of securities title. It aims to be both backward-looking, providing a brief history of how arrangements for ownership and sale have evolved over time; and forward-looking, discussing some of the current challenges in clearing and settlement, both from both a business and policy perspective.

While this chapter contains a lot of technical detail (clearing and settlement is an activity where technical details matter) a few issues can be highlighted. Section 2 has explained the tiered account based securities ownership arrangements that emerged in the late 1960s and early 1970s as securities processing was computerised. These arrangements are very different from the old paper based arrangements that preceded them. They allow the underlying securities, all ultimately located in a central securities depository, to be represented by a hierarchy of securities accounts offered by other financial intermediaries, with each account representing securities in an account at a lower level.

While these arrangements have supported the dramatic increases in the volume of trading on today's financial markets, they have also fundamentally shifted the responsibilities for management of cash and liquidity in securities trading. Whereas under older arrangements these were the responsibilities of final investors, now it is the intermediaries, the securities brokers, who have the ultimate responsibility for delivering cash and securities to settle trades.

Over the past quarter of a century 'principal risk' – i.e. the risk of delivering a security and not getting paid, or paying and not getting title – has been largely eliminated through 'delivery versus payment' of DVP. It is now standard practice in all markets to have payment and delivery made either simultaneously or at least for payment to follow very soon after delivery. There are still however substantial liquidity risks in securities markets, and in the underlying processes of clearing and settlement. These liquidity risks are one major reason why postponement of settlement between brokers (so called 'trade fails' although this is a bit of a misnomer since the original trade is typically valid) remain so surprisingly high.

In some respects modern clearing and settlement systems are impressive technical achievements. They have successfully provided business continuity even under extreme stress (for example the 9-11 attacks in New York). The operational costs of trading have been closely controlled, even while trading volumes have massively increased over past decades. Clearing and settlement systems also proved to be resilient during the 2008 crisis, in sharp contrast to their degradation during the 1987 stock market crash. This was due to the adoption of DVP but also because of the widespread guarantees and public sector support to market participants.

Despite these achievements, authorities will need to continue closely monitoring the possibility of systemic problems in securities and settlement systems. The sheer complexity of modern securities ownership arrangements, and the challenge to securities brokers of managing liquidity, result in a very complex network of credit and cash obligations. So it remains an open question as to whether breakdown of clearing and settlement might transmit systemic problems in a future financial crisis. Another potential problems is that arrangements ("recovery and resolution plans" also known as "living wills") for resolution of large financial firms might prove infeasible because clearing and settlement exposures cannot be dealt with in an orderly fashion.

Clearing and settlement systems are also a potential competition concern. The need to clear and settle through a shared system creates market power and if this market power is exploited final investors in securities may pay substantially more than underlying costs, both for clearing and settlement services and for the trade execution that relies on subsequent clearing and settlement. Institutional arrangements, such as user ownership and/ or interoperability and pen access can and do limit this market power. But a concern remains that the sheer complexity of clearing and settlement systems still acts as a barrier to entry in securities brokerage.

REFERENCES

Clearance and Settlement Systems in the World's Security Markets. (1988). G30 Working Group. Retrieved from http://www.group30.org/rpt_43.shtml

America's dodgy financial plumbing: Too big a fail count. (2011). *The Economist*. Retrieved from http://www.economist.com/node/18774844?frsc=dgla

Amery, P. (2011). Delayed ETF Settlements—What's The Problem? www.etf.com. Retrieved October 07, 2014, from http://www.etf.com/sections/features/9403-delayed-etf-settlementswhats-the-problem.html?fullart=1&start=2

Armstrong, F. E. (1934). *The Book of the Stock Exchange* (2nd ed.). Pitman.

Bernanke, B. S. (1990). Clearing and Settlement during the Crash. *Review of Financial Studies*, *3*(1), 133–151. doi:10.1093/rfs/3.1.133

Beutel, F. K. (1940). The Development of State Statutes on Negotiable Paper Prior to the Negotiable Instruments Law. *Columbia Law Review*, *40*(5), 836–865. doi:10.2307/1117594

Borio, C. (2010). Ten propositions about liquidity crises. *CESifo Economic Studies*, *56*(1), 70–95. doi:10.1093/cesifo/ifp031

Bradley, H., Fawls, R. A., Litan, R. E., & Sommers, F. (2011). *Canaries in the Coal Mine: How the Rise in Settlement "Fails" Creates Systemic Risk for Financial Firms and Investors*. SSRN Electronic Journal; doi:10.2139/ssrn.1773633

The role of margin requirements and haircuts in procyclicality. (2010). CGFS. Retrieved from http://www.bis.org/publ/cgfs36.pdf

Chan, D., Fontan, F., Rosati, S., & Russo, D. (2007). The securities custody industry. *ECB Occasional Paper*, (68).

Cont, R., & Kokholm, T. (2014). Central Clearing of OTC Derivatives: Bilateral vs multilateral netting. *Statistics & Risk Modeling*, *31*(1), 3–22. doi:10.1515/strm-2013-1161

Copeland, A., Duffie, D., Martin, A., & McLaughlin, S. (2012). Key mechanics of the US tri-party repo market. *Economic Policy Review*, 17–28.

CPMI. (2014). Committee on Payments and Market Infrastructures (CPMI). Retrieved from http://www.bis.org/cpmi/

CPSS. (1992). *Delivery versus payment in securities settlement systems*. Retrieved from http://www.bis.org/cpmi/publ/d06.htm

Currie, W. (2007). Computerising the Stock Exchange: A comparison of two information systems. *New Technology, Work and Employment*, *12*(2), 75–83. doi:10.1111/1468-005X.00025

DTCC Partners with the Industry to Implement T+2 in the U.S. (2014a). *DTCC*. Retrieved from http://www.dtcc.com/news/2014/april/22/shortening-settlement-cycle.aspx

DTCC Recommends Shortening the U.S. Trade Settlement Cycle. (2014b). *DTCC*. Retrieved from http://www.dtcc.com/~/media/Files/Downloads/WhitePapers/T2-Shortened-Cycle-WP.pdf

Duffie, D., Scheicher, M., & Vuillemey, G. (2015). Central Clearing and Collateral Demand. *Journal of Financial Economics*, *116*(2), 237–256. doi:10.1016/j.jfineco.2014.12.006

Settlement Fails Report on Securities Settlement Systems (SSS) Measures To Ensure Timely Settlement (p. 9). (2011). ECB. Retrieved from https://www.ecb.europa.eu/pub/pdf/other/settlementfails042011en.pdf

Target-2 Securities. (2014). ECB. Retrieved from http://www.ecb.europa.eu/paym/t2s/html/index.en.html

2012 Statistical Exercise on Matching and Settlement Efficiency. (2012). ECSDA. Retrieved from http://ecsda.eu/wp-content/uploads/2014/07/2012_09_18_ECSDA_Statistical_Exercise.pdf

Short selling. (2012). ESMA. Retrieved from http://www.esma.europa.eu/page/Short-selling

Faulkner, M. C. (2008). An introduction to securities lending. Handbook of Finance.

Fleming, M. J., & Garbade, K. (2005). Explaining settlement fails. *Current Issues in Economics and Finance, 11*(9).

Fleming, M. J., & Garbade, K. D. (2007). Dealer behavior in the specials market for US Treasury securities. *Journal of Financial Intermediation*, *16*(2), 204–228. doi:10.1016/j.jfi.2006.12.003

Giovannini, A. (2010). Why the European Securities Market is Not Fully Integrated. In *Europe and the Euro* (pp. 255–283). University of Chicago Press. doi:10.7208/chicago/9780226012858.003.0008

Cross-border clearing and settlement arrangements in the European Union. (2002). Giovannini Group. Retrieved from http://ec.europa.eu/internal_market/financial-markets/docs/clearing/first_giovannini_report_en.pdf

ICMA. Frequently Asked Questions on repo. (2014). Retrieved from http://www.icmagroup.org/Regulatory-Policy-and-Market-Practice/short-term-markets/Repo-Markets/frequently-asked-questions-on-repo/

Lannoo, K., & Levin, M. (2002, January). The Securities Settlement Industry in the EU: Structure, Costs and the Way Forward. *CEPS Reports in Finance and Banking No., 26*, 1.

Lannoo, K., & Valiante, D. (2009). Integrating Europe's Back Office: 10 Years of Turning in Circles. Retrieved from http://papers.ssrn.com/abstract=1416108

Michie, R. (2006). *The global securities market: a history*. Oxford University Press. doi:10.1093/acprof:oso/9780199280612.001.0001

Milne, A. (2005). *Standard setting and competition in securities settlement (No. 23-2005)*. Helsinki: Bank of Finland.

Milne, A. (2007a). Competition and the rationalization of European securities clearing and settlement. In D. G. Mayes & G. E. Wood (Eds.), The Structure of Financial Regulation (p. 370–). Taylor & Francis (Routledge). doi:10.4324/9780203962312.ch12

Milne, A. (2007b). The industrial organization of post-trade clearing and settlement. *Journal of Banking & Finance, 31*(10), 2945–2961. doi:10.1016/j.jbankfin.2007.03.002

Milne, A. (2009). The Fall of the House of Credit (p. 380). Cambridge, UK: Cambridge University Press. Retrieved from http://www.cambridge.org/gb/knowledge/isbn/item2428039/?site_locale=en_GB doi:10.1017/CBO9780511596643

Milne, A. (2012). OTC central counterparty clearing: Myths and reality. *Journal of Risk Management in Financial Institutions, 5*(3), 335–346.

Mollenkamp, C., Podkul, C., & Toonkel, J. (2012, January). Persistent trade failure problem gets partial fix. *Reuters*. Retrieved from http://www.ft.com/cms/s/0/97ff6658-d87b-11e0-8f0a-00144feabdc0.html#axzz3EifgnBQU

Morris, V. B., & Goldstein, S. Z. (2010). *The Life Cycle of a Security*. Lighbulb Press. Retrieved from http://www.dtcc.com/~/media/Files/Downloads/Settlement-Asset-Services/Underwriting/LCoaS.pdf

Murphy, D. (2013). *OTC Derivatives: Bilateral Trading and Central Clearing: An Introduction to Regulatory Policy, Market Impact and Systemic Risk*. Palgrave Macmillan. doi:10.1057/9781137293862

Norman, P. (2007). *Plumbers and Visionaries: Securities Settlement and Europe's Financial Market* (Vol. 437). John Wiley & Sons.

Pirrong, C. (2012). Clearing and Collateral Mandates: A New Liquidity Trap? *Journal of Applied Corporate Finance, 24*(1), 67–73. doi:10.1111/j.1745-6622.2012.00366.x

SEC. (2011). *Impact of Recent SHO Rule Changes on Fails to Deliver* (p. 18). Retrieved from http://www.sec.gov/spotlight/shortsales/failsmemo042511.pdf

Second report on EU clearing and settlement arrangements. Directorate-General for Economic and Financial Affairs. (2003Giovannini Group. European Commission.

The Direct Costs of Clearing and Settlement: An EU-US Comparison. (2004). NERA Economic Consulting. London: Coproation of London. Retrieved from http://www.cityoflondon.gov.uk/business/economic-research-and-information/research-publications/Documents/2007-2000/direct-costs-of-clearing-and-settlement-executive-summary.pdf

Clearing and Settlement. (2014). The European Commission. Retrieved from http://ec.europa.eu/internal_market/financial-markets/clearing/index_en.htm

KEY TERMS AND DEFINITIONS

Brokerage: A financial institution that facilitates the buying and selling of financial securities between a buyer and a seller.

DVP: Delivery versus Payment scheme.

Liquidity Risk: the risk arriving from the lack of possibility that an investment cannot be bought or sold quickly enough to prevent or minimize a loss.

Netting: The legal framework, under which one or more series of related transactions among parties are canceled and a new obligation to make only the net payments is created.

Principal Risk: In securities transactions is the risk that the security is not delivered after the payment is made or the risk that a payment is not received after a security was delivered.

Repurchase Agreement (repo): It is a short term financing transaction securities in which securities are sold with the promise of buying (repurchasing) them back.

Securities Lending: Securities lending involves a temporary transfer of the ownership of a security to a borrower who is required to put up collateral. These type of securities transactions are commonly used in short selling trading strategies.

Short Selling: A trading strategy which involves borrowing a security in order to sell it immediately with the expectation of buying it at a lower price in the future.

ENDNOTES

1. Further confusion arises from inconsistencies in usage; for example the Euroclear group is a leading European provider of settlement and related banking services, but it is not a CCP that centrally clears trades.
2. Standard histories of securities markets, for example (Michie, 2006), contain little or no information on clearing and settlement arrangements. Much of the description here is gleaned from (Armstrong, 1934).

3 The widespread use of bearer bonds relies on the concept of a "negotiable instrument", deeply rooted in US law and commercial practice but with much more limited British practice. (Beutel, 1940) provides an historical account.

4 See (Chan, Fontan, Rosati, & Russo, 2007) for a fuller account of the work of custodian banks.

5 These named banks were the leading providers of custodian services in 2006, see (Chan et al., 2007) Table 2.

6 These developments are described in (Norman, 2007).

7 See (Norman, 2007) for an account of this history and some of the colourful characters involved.

8 The initial effort was the Taurus project, which turned out to be a complete failure, with costs spiralling out of control and the complex outsourced software never being delivered in a useable form. Eventually in March 1993, after expenditure of £70mn, the project was cancelled. A small team from the Bank of England, with experience of the Bank's involvement in high value payment systems, was brought in and they successfully delivered a fully functional CSD and electronic settlement system, CREST, which went live in 1996, at a cost of only £30mn. (Currie, 2007) provides a fuller comparison of the Taurus and Crest projects.

9 T+2 means final transfer of title to a security by the morning of the second working day following the execution of a trade. Government bonds are already often settled T+2 and money market transactions same day.

10 Typically today a securities trade is executed by computer (automatically or through manual execution via a computer screen) and often – if obligations are transferred to a central counterparty -- the other side of the transaction remains anonymous even during subsequent clearing and settlement.

11 (Milne, 2012) provides a short account, with further references, of the history of exchange trade derivatives clearing and the challenges of providing similar services in OTC markets.

12 The discussion of central counterparties (CCPs) in this chapter focuses on their role in securities markets and in particular their role in reducing operational and liquidity risks. There is in addition (and see also Cruz, Manning et alia as well as Pliquett in this volume) a large literature on the somewhat different role of central counterparties in derivatives markets (where counterparty risk is so much more important), and in particular on the controversies over the requirement agreed at the 2009 G-20 Heads of Government Pittsburgh Declaration for many OTC derivative transactions to be guaranteed by CCPs. This recent research has focused on the implications of OTC derivative clearing for collateral demand, counterparty and systemic risk, for example (Cont & Kokholm, 2014; Duffie, Scheicher, & Vuillemey, 2015). Some, e.g. (Pirrong, 2012), argue that CCP clearing in OTC markets can exacerbate rather than reduce systemic risk.

13 Recent regulations, e.g. the European Union ban on so called 'naked' short selling (introduced by Regulation (EU) No 236/2012 on short selling and certain aspects of credit default swaps, see (ESMA, 2012)) means that nowadays it is often necessary to borrow the security first before selling. Naked short selling means executing an order to sell a security without the seller already holding that security in a securities account. It is still possible to take a short position without doing this, first borrowing the security and then executing an order to sell. A puzzle (see below) is why the ban on naked short selling has not eliminated 'trade fails'.

14 (Faulkner, 2008) provides a fuller account of the operation of securities lending. A succinct discussion of both securities lending and repo is provided by (ICMA, 2014).

15 As described by (Armstrong, 1934) under the traditional fortnightly system of accounts settlement these deals were arranged by stock brokers in the London markets on behalf of clients and recorded in their so called "Contango book". Before World War I substantial net long positions in securities were held using contango.

16 See (CGFS, 2010), Table 1, many of these repo markets disappeared altogether.

17 The underlying problem is operational design. Similar tri-party repo facilities in Europe, for example those provided by Euroclear use intraday DVPO settlement to avoid such daylight exposures.

18 No attempt is made here to discuss the related question of whether modern tiered security title arrangements limit competition in portfolio services such as asset management and custodian banking.

19 Key documents relating to these debates can be found at (The European Commission, 2014).

20 For further discussion of the industrial economics of securities clearing and settlement see (Milne, 2007b) and the various contributions to the same special issue of that journal.

21 For further discussion of standardisation in clearing and settlement see (Milne, 2005, 2007a).

Chapter 18
Undressing the Global Derivatives Market:
Trade Repositories: Past, Present and Future

Marco Massarenti
European Central Bank, Germany

ABSTRACT

Trade repositories are market infrastructures collecting and maintaining the records of over-the-counter (OTC) derivatives transactions for a large number of asset classes. They have been under the spotlight since the G20 meeting in Pittsburgh and have recently gained very high importance in the field. Reporting obligations have started or will be coming into force in the near future worldwide. The purpose of this chapter is to describe the history and landscape of trade repositories, to outline advantages of having these market infrastructures in place and to briefly review the literature available based on data stemming from trade repositories.

INTRODUCTION

Trade repositories are the youngest financial market infrastructures, yet they have gained very high importance in relatively short time. From their introduction to the wide audience in 2009, trade repositories have been established in every major economy in the world and their data scrupulously safeguarded is now being chased by regulators, supervisors and researchers alike. But what is really a trade repository and what can be done with the data it contains?

The purpose of this chapter is threefold: first, it describes the history of trade repositories and their landscape for the main financial jurisdictions worldwide (Europe, United States and the main economies in the Asia Pacific region), also highlighting the pros and cons of the established frameworks. Second, it outlines some of the advantages of increased transparency in the OTC derivatives markets for counterparties, regulators and academics.[1] Finally, it reviews the literature available based on trade repository data, usually focusing on Credit Default Swap (CDS) contracts recorded in the Depository Trust and Clearing Corporation (DTCC) as early as 2006.

DOI: 10.4018/978-1-4666-8745-5.ch018

THE HISTORY

A trade repository is a market infrastructure collecting and maintaining the records of over-the-counter (OTC) derivatives transactions for a large number of asset classes, comprising (i) credit, (ii) interest rate, (iii) equity, (iv) foreign exchange, (v) commodity, (vi) and other derivatives. A trade repository is thus a large-scale database of OTC transactions that should overcome the inherent opacity of OTC derivatives markets thus increasing market transparency. Trade repositories will help public authorities and market participants in monitoring market developments more closely and analysing specific issues in depth, such as build-up and distribution of exposures in any market segment.

The first market infrastructure similar to a trade repository, the Trade Information Warehouse (TIW), was launched in November 2006 by DTCC in collaboration with market participants. From its original aim of centralizing the maintenance and automated processing of OTC derivatives contracts, TIW expanded its functionalities in November 2007 by adding a central settlement engine for calculating, netting and issuing payments between counterparties becoming, by default, the storage facility for every automatically confirmed trade. That means it also served as an electronic central registry for CDS traded by the largest majority of global derivatives dealers in more than thirty countries.

DTCC and TIW came under the spotlight in the aftermath of the bankruptcy of Lehman Brothers:[2] market rumours suggested that $400 billion on CDS naming Lehman Brothers would have changed hands and investors' fear reached a peak when markets closed on Friday 10 October 2008 (Bodson, 2013). However, TIW data reported about $72 billion in CDS written on Lehman Brothers and registered in the trade repository. In just over a month, the payment obligations arising from these trades were calculated, netted on a bilateral basis for a total amount of approximately $21 billion and sent to CLS for final settlement on a multi-lateral net basis with other foreign exchange trades for a final amount just over $5 billion, a reduction of more than 90% from the initial bilateral exposure. The data held in TIW helped calming the global financial markets and facilitated the netting process. Soon after, in November 2008, DTCC began disclosing weekly data on outstanding gross and net notional values for the top 1000 underlying CDS single-name entities and all indices. It represented the first public release of CDS data and enhanced market transparency on this particular asset class. The concept of the Trade Repository was thus born!

However, it was only in late 2009 that trade repositories became worldwide known to market participants, central bankers, regulators and financial journalists alike. In the 24-25 September 2009 summit in Pittsburgh, the G20 leaders agreed that all standardized OTC derivatives should be cleared through central counterparties (CCPs) and reported to trade repositories. The Trade Repository machine was thus started. The goal of the regulators was to enhance market transparency, helping public authorities and market participants to monitor more closely market developments. Several consultation rounds between the Committee of European Securities Regulators (CESR), the Bank for International Settlements (BIS), central banks and market participants worldwide followed. Ultimately, the Financial Stability Board (FSB) and its OTC Derivatives Working Group (ODWG) were mandated to monitor progress and compliance with the commitments set in the Pittsburgh meeting.[3] Meanwhile, new trade repositories for equity derivatives, interest rates swaps, commodity swaps and foreign exchange swaps were gradually introduced across the world.

Europe

Trade repositories in Europe are overseen by the European Securities and Market Authority (ESMA) under the European Market Infrastructure Regulation (EMIR). The first European trade repositories to receive the ESMA label were DTCC (UK), KDPW (Poland), Regis-TR (Luxembourg) and Una-Vista (UK) in November 2013, followed shortly after by ICE Trade Vault (UK) and CME Trade Repository (UK). All registered trade repositories cover all derivatives asset classes irrespective of whether trades have taken place on or off exchange, except for ICE Trade Vault, not recording foreign-exchange and other derivatives. The reporting obligation began in February 2014, including reporting of all trades executed after 16 August 2012 (back-loading). The reporting requirements apply to a very large number of entities involved in derivatives trading, including corporates, broker-dealers, asset managers and hedge funds.

Despite having a good level of competition, interoperability of trade repositories remains a big challenge to overcome. As the main purpose of recording OTC transactions was to enhance market transparency and thus better identify systemic risk, having separate reporting databases does the job only partly. Data from all trade repositories needs to be aggregated by asset class in a standardized and manageable form. Different fields, data formats and IT infrastructures may pose significant challenges in aggregating data coming from several providers. A single data warehouse for all euro trades coming from all European trade repositories would be the best solution in terms of usability, efficiency and transparency.

One further peculiarity of the European framework is the threshold-less dual-side reporting requirement. That means, both sides of a traded OTC contract should be reported to a trade repository. This requirement increases significantly the number of reporting entities and, when not properly understood, may also pose the risk of double- and under-reporting.

United States

In the United States, the Commodity Futures Trading Commission (CTFC) oversees swap data repositories (SDR) under the Dodd-Frank Wall Street Reform and Consumer Protection Act (Dodd-Frank Act). Contrary to EMIR, the reporting mandate in US is single sided, that means that only one side of an OTC trading needs to be reported. Up to July 2014 seven SDRs have applied to the CTFC. Three of them have withdrawn their application while for the remaining four their final registration is pending after having been granted a provisional registration. BSDR (a Bloomberg subsidiary) and DTCC report all types of OTC derivatives; CME instead does not report equity while ICE Trade Vault records only credit and other derivatives.

Aiming at increasing market transparency, CTFC began publishing weekly reports on aggregated swaps market data on November 14, 2012. Soon after, on January 1, 2013, market participants started reporting new transactions and historical data to SDRs. This data was then collected from the SDRs by the CTFC, processed and incorporated in the weekly Swaps Reports. These reports represented the first release of swap data to the general public complementing publications by other institutions (e.g. Bank for International Settlements (BIS)) based on different data sources. Currently, the weekly reports comprise detailed information on interest rate swaps (IRSs), including cross-currency swaps, and CDS. The reports provide weekly data on the gross notional outstanding amount, the value and number of transactions. For IRSs, data is broken down by cleared status, currency, tenor and participant type while for CDSs break downs include cleared status, participant type and grade status.[4] For the moment, data on fx, equity and other commodity swaps only include the gross notional amount outstanding.

Despite the high level of information published weekly by the CTFC, transaction-level data are kept in the individual SDRs and are not made public, even upon anonymization to maintain the confidentiality of the data. At the same time, a global US trade repository is not yet foreseen.

Asia-Pacific

The Asia Pacific landscape is completely different from the European and the U.S. ones. Given the high number of jurisdictions and the strong difficulties in establishing pan-Asian regulations, the majority of countries moved forward in implementing the G20 recommendations on mandatory reporting of derivatives trades on an individual basis. The only attempt to establish a common trade repository in the region is represented by an initiative of the Association of South East Asian Nations (ASEAN), comprising Brunei, Cambodia, Indonesia, Laos, Malaysia, Myanmar, Philippines, Singapore, Thailand and Vietnam. The ASEAN trade repository (ATR) should be established by 2015 and be made accessible to the public through the internet. Nevertheless, some members of ASEAN have also proceeded with the setting up of national trade repositories.

Mandatory reporting of derivatives trades in the Asia Pacific region began in 2013. Japan commenced operation in April with a dual system. Participants can report to the Global Trade Repository - Japan, a private data warehouse operated by DTCC, or can report directly and for free to the JFSA (Financial Services Agency of Japan). However, as this requires the establishment of IT solutions, only some large Japanese or high volume traders opted for this channel.

Australia split the reporting go-live in three waves: first in October 2013 for all swap dealers registered in the US with the CTFC; then in April 2014 credit and interest rate derivatives for financial institutions with total gross notional outstanding larger than AU$50 billion and in October 2014 for other OTC; finally, for all other financial institutions reporting will be mandatory for credit and interest rate derivatives as of October 2014 and for other OTC as of April 2014. Currently in Australia there is only one registered trade repository, GTR – Australia.

In Singapore the reporting mandate started in February 2014, following a wave-scheme similar to the one in Australia: in February the 17 largest banks, in April all other Singapore licensed banks, in July finance companies, trustees, fund managers and insurers and finally in October other major derivative holders. The reporting obligations cover credit and interest rate derivatives first, with fx, equity and commodity reported in the second phase starting in October 2014. As in Japan and Australia, the only authorized trade repository, supervised by the Monetary Authority of Singapore (MAS), is GTR – Singapore.

The Hong-Kong's Monetary Authority (HKMA) stands out for its different approach: rather than authorize and supervise trade repositories, it has created its own market infrastructure, the Hong-Kong Trade Repository (HKTR), which went live in July 2013. Entities can report directly to the HKMA or via an intermediary, such as DTCC.

Other Asian countries have also established trade repositories or are moving forward implementing reporting obligations: in India a number of derivatives trade need to be reported to the Clearing Corporation of India; in South Korea trades in all asset classes need to be reported to the Bank of Korea, the Financial Supervisory Service or the Korea Exchange as all serve as trade repositories; in China mandatory central clearing begun in January 2014 for credit, FX and interest rate derivatives and it is expected that will be followed by a reporting mandate, despite the known resistance of the Chinese government to release data as many financial institutions in China are state-owned.

DTCC's GTR currently represents the only pan-Asian trade repository, covering Japan, Australia, Singapore and Hong-Kong (as reporting agent). Such solution allows market participants trading in several markets to benefit from a single contractual obligation as well as setting up a common IT infrastructure. As the same time, regulators could potentially access a single trade repository covering different markets, enabling them to better analyse the Asian market as a whole, identify sources of systemic risk and prepare countermeasures against contagion effects.

LOOKING AHEAD

When the G20 leaders at the September 2009 summit in Pittsburgh agreed that all standardized OTC derivatives should be cleared through CCPs and reported to trade repositories, their goal was to enhance market transparency in the very opaque derivatives market, given the OTC nature of most of the trades. With the beginning of mandatory reporting, aggregate information on (global) derivatives market is timely made available to the public. Regulators and market participants will both benefit from increased transparency.

Market participants will have access to reliable information on prices and volumes, thus reducing information asymmetry and fostering competition. Counterparties will be able to better manage their exposure risks and improve their risk management practices. In addition, provided that public authorities entrust trade repositories with a public function, they could also become official registries with a notary function, reducing legal risk. Ultimately, greater pre-trade information improves market stability, in particular during periods of turmoil, and may even lead to higher trading volumes and liquidity.

Regulators, including central banks, banking and market supervisors, should be able to conduct effective macro- and micro-prudential supervision, detect market abuse, identify sources of systemic risk and establish early warning mechanisms. In particular, having access to detailed transaction-level data, would allow public authorities to monitor risk taking by individual counterparties as well as concentrations of exposures to individual market participants or to specific asset classes, preventing similar cases as the one of AIG (Duffie *et al.*, 2010): unfortunately, the TIW data in 2008 could not provide an early warning regarding the large CDS exposure of AIG, leading to the bailout of the insurance group by the US government.

Academics and practitioners will also benefit from increased data access, even in anonymized form. The market microstructure of all derivatives assets classes could be analyzed in depth, leading to a better understanding of the price formation and discovery processes, transaction costs, participants' behaviors and trading strategies. Transaction-level data allows studying intraday trading movements (news response) and patterns (seasonality). Eventually, the possibility to combine data on OTC derivatives traded in different markets worldwide would allow having a global picture of trading dynamics around the clock.

As reported by Bodson (2013), a single centralized trade repository will bring several advantages in terms of reporting accuracy and control, timeliness, data management and analysis and set common best practice. Ultimately, this global trade repository may be viewed as a public good, in that it could be provided to the all relevant stakeholder by public or private entities on a non-profit basis. However, the current setup presents several deficiencies. Different data and IT standards, different reporting requirements and sometimes even multiple trade repositories in the same jurisdiction make trade reporting complicated for market participants and sub-optimal for regulators and supervisors. In addition, there is a number of privacy related obstacles that may prevent a regulator to access certain counterparty information. More importantly, due to the current legal setup, regulators in the EU do not have access to data in US and vice versa. A stronger cooperation among regulators worldwide, a greater degree of standardization in data and IT standards and higher harmonization in the reporting requirements could only help both parties: market participants will incur in lower costs for IT, staff, legal departments and perhaps vis-à-vis trade repositories; regulators will be able to access a single data warehouse with standardized data format and information.

For all these reasons, the FSB in February 2014 launched a public consultation[5] on how to optimally aggregate OTC derivatives data stored in trade repositories in a number of jurisdictions, proposing three options: (i) physically centralised; (ii) logically centralised; (iii) collection of raw data from individual trade repositories. Having a physically or logically centralised global trade repository for all OTC derivative trades executed in every major currency was identified as the best option. However, reaching this milestone will require time and large efforts by all parties involved. Despite highlighting some technical issues (e.g. the necessary use of common identifiers such as the Legal Entity Identifier), the report expressed serious concerns about the legal barriers currently in place. Ultimately, the global industry's wish of having a global trade repository needs to find the optimal balance with the governments' desire to establish domestic repositories and to limit data access to regulators from different jurisdictions.

LITERATURE REVIEW

With reporting obligations being implemented or coming into force in the near future, and data access being granted to regulators, central bankers and supervisors, the literature on trade repository is expected to grow rapidly. Nevertheless, a sizeable literature making use of trade repository data already exists, although focusing mostly on CDS data. The purpose of this section is to review the most relevant works available in the literature and to give some examples on how trade repositories data have been used for research and policy purposes. It is not meant to be an in-depth literature review on the derivatives market.

Market Microstructure

As it is often the case with new financial market dataset, one of the first topics to be studied with trade repository data was market microstructure. Chen *et al.* (2011) use three months of global CDS transaction data on trading frequency, trade sizes, currencies and market participants to describe the market composition, the trading dynamics and the level of standardisation in the CDS market. They reach a number of conclusions: (i) trading activity for the majority of single-name CDS is rather low (less than once a day), except for event-driven periods of high clustering. Only a few single-name CDS (mostly sovereigns) are traded actively and in bigger volumes; (ii) a high proportion of CDS transactions is standardised and clearing-eligible; (iii) market makers have an important liquidity-providing role in the CDS market; (iv) large trades with customers are not hedged immediately with offsetting trades for the same reference entity, corroborating anecdotal evidence that dealers, when hedging, do so over a longer time horizon.

Oehmke and Zawadowski (2012) use disaggregated data on individual single-name CDS to document that (i) CDSs are used for both hedging and speculating (taking views on the default probabilities of the underlying reference entities); (ii) the CDS market functions as an *"alternative trading venue"* for both hedging and speculating in the underlying bond: sometimes investors seem preferring the CDS market to directly trading the underlying instrument, in particular when the market for the particular bond is illiquid or fragmented; (iii) CDS markets may help to compress spreads for bond issuers, thus improving firms' access to wholesale financing.

Systemic Risk and Contagion

Another topic analysed in depth was systemic risk and contagion. One of the first papers to assess the systemic risk in the global derivatives market is Markose (2012).[6] The study is based on 2009:Q4 FDIC reporting and individually collected firm level data covering gross notional, gross positive/negative fair value and the netted derivatives assets and liabilities for 202 financial firms, including 20 SIFIs and 18 broker dealers. Figure 1 presents the number of participants in each of the derivatives asset classes (equity, commodity, fx, credit and interest rate). The large majority of the institutions (126) trade in one market only, 23 in two products, 8 in three, 10 in four and finally 8 in all five asset classes. The author describes the network as fragile, given the high concentration of exposures among a few central nodes and suggests designing a set of taxes for the global derivatives Systemically Important Financial Institutions with the aim to minimize the costs imposed to other financial institutions and the tax payers.

Figure 1. Participants in derivatives markets based on gross notional data for fx (48), interest rate swaps (189), equities (25), commodities and others (22), and CDS (23). Source: Markose (2012).

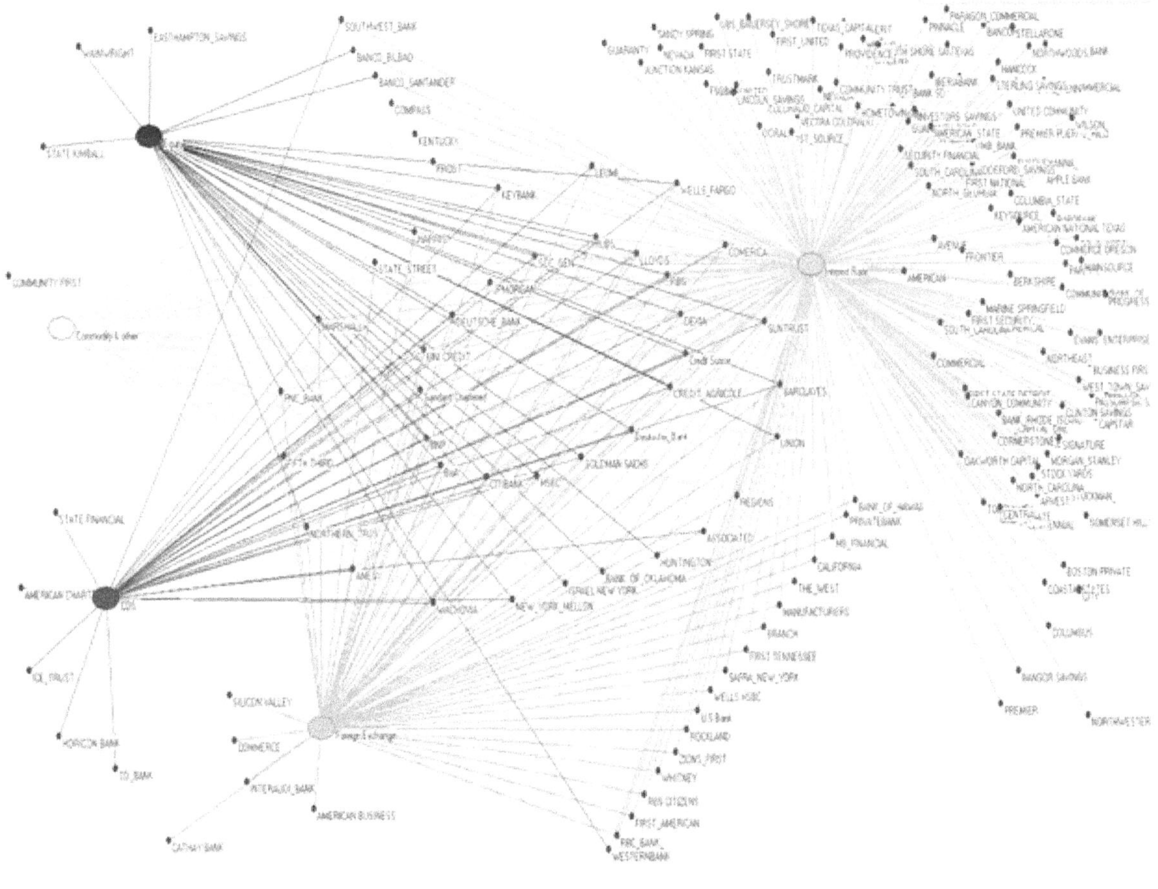

Brunnermeier *et al.* (2013) study the potential systemic and contagion risk deriving from a major credit event caused by the default of a key CDS market player or CDS reference entity. They use DTCC data on weekly bilateral CDS exposures between all European and non-European counterparties for each European reference entity from November 2006 until January 2012. They find that the CDS market is highly concentrated at the counterparty level with the top-ten traders accounting more than 70% of gross protection bought or sold. They also report that on average major traders sell protection while smaller traders buy CDS, similarly to the mechanics of several interbank markets. Looking at the network structure, there are around 800 market participants having more than 3,500 bilateral links, making the EU CDS network a large and complex one. The network of bilateral CDS exposures is quite concentrated, centred around the fifteen global derivatives players (G15, defined as *"super-spreaders"*) and presents the typical core-periphery structure (Figure 2).

Figure 2. The CDS network structure. The 15 largest CDS players are represented as coloured nodes in the centre (black nodes are net sellers, grey nodes are net buyers) while their large net exposures are represented by dark grey lines. For each coloured node, the 10 largest bilateral net selling exposures are shown, together with their underlying gross (the node size) and the net (the link) exposures. Source: Brunnermeier et al. (2013).

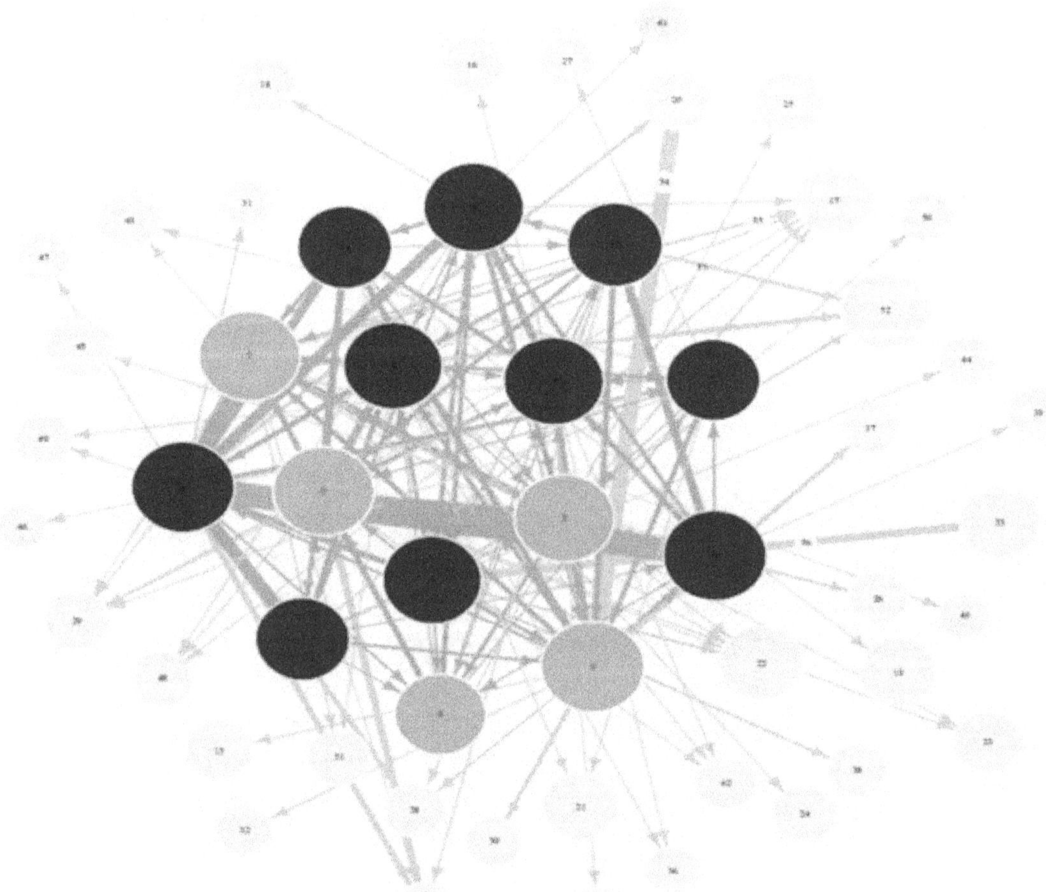

On contagion, a sovereign credit event in the CDS market may be absorbed quite smoothly, as it was the case after the Greek credit event. The contagion is more likely to spread from direct sovereign bond exposures, typically large by domestic banks, rather than sovereign CDS exposures, affecting more foreign banks. Nevertheless, the degree and magnitude of contagion risk strongly depends on the players involved. For example, the *"super-spreader"* institutions are more vulnerable to contagion risk than other players given their strong exposure to counterparty risk and their high interconnectedness in the CDS market. Finally, risk-bearing capacity of the financial system, behavioural effects, confidence channels and regulators' response will all play a key role in a major credit event.

The follow-up paper by Clerc *et al.* (2014) focuses on the network topology of CDS exposures on European reference entities based again on weekly anonymised DTCC data, recording the notional value of CDS positions outstanding each Friday from 4 January 2008 until 27 January 2012. They consider four different network representations, corresponding to different levels of CDS aggregation: financials, non-financials, sovereigns and the whole CDS market. In general, the authors describe the CDS market as a *"scale-free"* network, where most dealers are exposed to a few others but exposures are highly concentrated following a power-law distribution. Market participants are either directly linked to each other or indirectly via two or three counterparties only and those with many links tend to be connected to players with few and vice-versa. The study reveals that the network structure remains overall stable from 2008 until 2012, although a higher degree of concentration of exposures is somewhat observed. As in Brunnermeier *et al.* (2013), the network of CDS exposures would be resilient in most cases: (i) first, the likelihood of one of the *"super-spreader"* being hit by a random shock is very low; (ii) second, should one of the most interconnected players indeed being negatively affected, the network may function normally given its other highly interconnected hubs. The authors explain that contagion effects may arise when random shocks affect two or more of the major players. Thus, from a financial stability perspective, targeted interventions to the more connected players in the CDS market are more likely to be successful in preventing contagion effects. The authors conclude highlighting that (i) access to supervisory data is of extreme importance for regular monitoring of the CDS market and (ii) that regular monitoring should also apply to the shadow banking, comprising institutions such as asset managers and hedge funds, both playing an increasing role in this market segment.

Another example is Peltonen *et al.* (2013), who analyse the CDS market in a similar fashion as in the previous two cited papers, although introducing a new dimension in their study. First, the authors describe the network structure of the aggregated CDS market, showing topological similarities with interbank networks and the *"scale-free"* nature. Second, they provide econometric analysis on the relationship between the characteristics of a reference entity (debt characteristics, riskiness and location) and the properties of the corresponding CDS market (size, activity and concentration of the CDS network). The results show that CDS market size and activity are significantly impacted by characteristics of the underlying bond exposure and the risk characteristics of the CDS.

NOTE

Disclaimer: The views in this article are those of the author only and should not be represented as the views of the European Central Bank (ECB).

REFERENCES

Bodson, M. (2013). *New Infrastructures for a sounder financial system.* Banque de France, Financial Stability Review, 17

Brunnermeier, M., Clerc, L., El Omari, Y., Gabrieli, S., Kern, S., Memmel, C., et al. (2013). *Assessing contagion risk from the CDS market.* ESRB Occasional Paper, 4

Kathryn, C., Fleming, M., Jackson, J., Li, A., & Sarkar, A. (2011). *An Analysis of CDS Transactions: Implications for Public Reporting*. Federal Reserve Bank of New York Staff Reports, 517

Clerc, L., Gabrieli, S., Kern, S., & El Omari, Y. (2014). *Monitoring the European CDS market through networks: implications for contagion risks*, Banque de France Working Paper, no. 417.

Duffie, D., Li, A., & Lubke, T. (2010). *Policy Perspectives on OTC Derivatives Market Infrastructure.* Federal Reserve Bank of New York Staff Reports, 424

Markose, S. (2012). *Systemic Risk from Global Financial Derivatives: A Network Analysis of Contagion and Its Mitigation with Super-Spreader Tax.* IMF Working Paper, 12/282

Oehmke, M., & Zawadowski, A. (2012). *The Anatomy of the CDS Market* [Working Paper].

Peltonen, T. A., Scheicher, M., & Vuillemey, G. (2013). *The network structure of the CDS market and its determinants.* ECB Working Paper, 1583

ENDNOTES

1 The Financial Stability Board (FSB) proposed that repos and securities lending should also be reported to trade repositories. At the time of drafting this article, the law making process was still on-going.

2 In 2008 TIW successfully managed 11 credit events, including Lehman Brothers Holding Inc., Fannie Mae, Freddie Mac and Washington Mutual. Approximately $285 billion (in aggregate gross notional value) of CDS contracts were netted down to $12 billion in actual payments, executed via CLS Bank.

3 Other international groups that worked on standardising trade repositories reporting, setting minimum requirements and monitoring in general the progress in implementing the G20 recommendations comprise the Committee on Payments and Settlement Systems (CPSS), the International Organisation of Securities Commissions (IOSCO) and the OTC Derivatives Regulators' Forum (ODRF).

4 For more information see http://www.cftc.gov/MarketReports/SwapsReports/index.htm

5 In September 2014 the FSB released the final report after having reviewed the comments received in the public consultation.

6 The paper does not use trade repository data per se. However, it presents a perfect example of what could be done with data stemming from a global data warehouse.

Compilation of References

Cross-Border Clearing and Settlement Arrangements in the European Union. (2002). Giovannini Group. Retrieved from http://ec.europa.eu/internal_market/financialmarkets/docs/clearing/first_giovannini_report_en.pdf

Cruz Lopez, J., Mendes, R., & Vikstedt, H. (2013). The Market for Collateral: The Potential Impact of Financial Regulation. *Bank of Canada, Financial System Review.*

House Report 112-471 - Part 1 - Swap Data Repository and Clearinghouse Indemnification Correction Act of 2012. (2012). The Library of Congress. Retrieved from http://thomas.loc.gov/cgi-bin/cpquery/?&dbname=cp112&sid=cp112jN8jw&refer=&r_n=hr471p1.112&item=&&&sel=TOC_3197&

Second Report on EU Clearing and Settlement. (2003). Giovannini Group. Retrieved from http://ec.europa.eu/internal_market/financial-markets/docs/clearing/second_giovannini_report_en.pdf

TARGET Annual Report 2013. (2014). European Central Bank.

2012 Statistical Exercise on Matching and Settlement Efficiency. (2012). ECSDA. Retrieved from http://ecsda.eu/wp-content/uploads/2014/07/2012_09_18_ECSDA_Statistical_Exercise.pdf

7. U.S.C. §7a-1 (2011).

A glossary of terms used in payments and settlement systems. CPSS. Bank for International Settlements.

About the International Organization of Securities Commissions. (n. d.). *The International Organization of Securities Commissions.* Retrieved from http://www.iosco.org/about/

Adams, R. M., Bauer, P. W., & Sickles, R. C. (2002). Scope and Scale Economies in Federal Reserve Payment Processing. *Federal Reserve Bank of Cleveland Research Department Working Paper,* 02-13.

AFME Post trade settlement committee taskforce on CSD account structure (2012) *CSD Account structure: issues and proposals*, 3-4. Retrieved from http://www.afme.eu/Documents/Discussion-papers.aspx

Agarwal, S., Chakravorti, S., & Lunn, A. (2010). *Why do banks reward their customers to use their credit cards?* Working Paper No. 2010-19, Federal Reserve Bank of Chicago.

Agarwal, S., Chomsisengphet, S., Liu, C., & Souleles, N. S. (2006, November). Do Consumers Choose the Right Credit Contracts? Retrieved from http://ssrn.com/abstract=843826

Agarwal, S., Paige, M. S., & Tobacman, J. (2009). Payday Loans and Credit Cards: New Liquidity and Credit Scoring Puzzles? *The American Economic Review*, *99*(2), 412–417. doi:10.1257/aer.99.2.412

Aigrain, J. (2013, April). CCPs as instruments of stability and risk mitigation. *Banque de France Financial Stability Review*, 17.

Akram, Q. F., & Christophersen, C. (2013) *Inferring interbank loans and interest rates from interbank payments - an evaluation.* Norges Bank Working Paper 26.

Albert, R., & Barabási, A.-L. (2002). Statistical mechanics of complex networks. *Reviews of Modern Physics, 74*(1), 47–97. doi:10.1103/RevModPhys.74.47

Alexandrova-Kabadjova, B. (2009). Impact of interchange fees on a nonsaturated multi-agent payment card market. *Intelligent Systems in Accounting Finance & Management 01/2009*; *16*(1-2):33-48.

Alexandrova-Kabadjova, B., Serguieva, A., Heijmans, R., & Garcia-Ochoa, L. (2015). Direct participants' behaviour through the lens of transactional analysis: the case of SPEI. In H. Takayasu, N. Ito, I. Noda & M. Takayasu (Eds.) *Proceedings of the International Conference on Social Modeling and Simulation, plus Econophysics Colloquium 2014.* Springer Proceedings in Complexity, Springer, forthcoming.

Alexandrova-Kabadjova, B., Serguieva, A., & Garcia-Ochoa, L. (2014, July). Formation of Tectonic Wave Networks: Dynamics of the Mexican Payment System Structure.*Proceedings of the 2014 International Conference on Behavioral, Economic and Socio-Cultural Computing* (pp. 1–7). IEEE Press. doi:10.1109/BESC.2014.7059524

Alexandrova-Kabadjova, B., & Solís-Robleda, F. (2012). The Mexican experience in how the settlement of large payments is performed in the presence of high volume of small payments. In M. Hellqvist & T. Laine (Eds.), *Diagnostics for the financial markets - computational studies of payment system* (pp. 431–460). Finland: Bank of Finland. doi:10.2139/ssrn.2191794

Alexandrova-Kabadjova, B., & Solís-Robleda, F. (2013). Managing Intraday Liquidity: The Mexican Experience. In B. Alexandrova-Kabadjova, S. Martinez-Jaramillo, A. Garcia-Almanza, & E. Tsang (Eds.), *Simulation in Computational Finance and Economics: Tools and Emerging Applications* (pp. 143–160). Hershey, PA: Business Science Reference; doi:10.4018/978-1-4666-2011-7.ch008

Alexandrova-Kabadjova, B., Tsang, E., & Krause, A. (2011). Market structure and information in payment card markets. *International Journal of Automation and Computing, 8*(3), 364–370. doi:10.1007/s11633-011-0593-1

Ali, R., Barrdear, J., Clews, R., & Southgate, J. (2014a). Innovations in payment technologies and the emergence of digital currencies. *Bank of England Quarterly Bulletin, Q3*, 262–275.

Ali, R., Barrdear, J., Clews, R., & Southgate, J. (2014b). The economics of digital currencies. *Bank of England Quarterly Bulletin, Q3*, 276–286.

Allen, F., & Carletti, E. (2013). What Is Systemic Risk? *Journal of Money, Credit and Banking, 45*(1).

America's dodgy financial plumbing: Too big a fail count. (2011). *The Economist.* Retrieved from http://www.economist.com/node/18774844?frsc=dg|a

Amery, P. (2011). Delayed ETF Settlements—What's The Problem? www.etf.com. Retrieved October 07, 2014, from http://www.etf.com/sections/features/9403-delayed-etf-settlementswhats-the-problem.html?fullart=1&start=2

Andersen, K., & Madsen, I. (2009). A Quantitative Assessment of Interantional Best Practice for Business Continuity Arrangements in Payment Systems. In H. Leinonen, (Ed.), *Simulation analysis and stress testing of payment networks* (pp. 17–58). Proceedings from the Bank of Finland Payment and Settlement System Seminars 2007-2008.

Anderson, R., & Joeveer, K. (2014). The Economics of Collateral, *Financial Markets Group Discussion Paper* No 732

Anderson, S., Dion, J.P., & Perez-Saiz, H. (2013, May). To link or not to link? Netting and exposures between central counterparties. *Journal of Financial Market Infrastructures,* 1(4), 3-29.

Angelini, P., Maresca, G., & Russo, D. (1996). Systemic risk in the netting system. *Journal of Banking & Finance*, *20*(5), 853–868. doi:10.1016/0378-4266(95)00029-1

Annual Statistical Release. (2012b, *December 2011*). Bank for International Settlements.

Application of "Security-Based Swap Dealer" and "Major Security-Based Swap Participant" Definitions to Cross-Border Security-Based Swap Activities . (2014, June 25). U.S. Securities and Exchange Commission. Retrieved from http://www.sec.gov/rules/final/2014/34-72472.pdf

Arciero, L. (2010). Evaluating the impact of shocks to the supply of overnight unsecured money market funds on the TARGET2-Banca d'Italia functioning: a simulation study (pp. 169–192). In M. Hellqvist & T. Laine (Ed.), Diagnostics for the financial markets–computational studies of payment system. Helsinki: Scientific Monographs.

Arciero, L., & Picillo, C. (2013). Liquidity Management in the Large Value Payment Systems: Need for an Agent-Based Model's Complex Approach. In B. Alexandrova-Kabadjova, S. Martinez-Jaramillo, A. Garcia-Almanza, & E. Tsang. (Eds.), Simulation in Computational Finance and Economics: Tools and Emerging Applications (pp. 84–102). Hershey: IGI Global. doi:10.4018/978-1-4666-2011-7.ch005

Arciero, L., Heijmans, R., Heuver, R., Massarenti, M., Picillo, C., & Vacirca, F. (2013). *How to measure the unsecured money market? The Eurosystem's implementation and validation using TARGET2 data.* DNB Working Paper No. 369.

Arciero, L., Heijmans, R., Heuver, R., Massarenti, M., Picillo, C., & Vacirca, F. (2013). How to Measure the Unsecured Money Market? The Eurosystem's Implementation and Validation Using TARGET2 Data, De Nederlandsche Bank Working Paper No. 369.

Arculus, R., Hancock, J., & Moran, G. (2010). The impact of payment system design on tiering incentives (pp. 379–410). In M. Hellqvist & T. Laine (Ed.), Diagnostics for the financial markets–computational studies of payment system. Helsinki: Scientific Monographs.

Arjani, N. & McVanel, D. (2006, March). *A Premier on Canada's Large Value Transfer System.*

Arjani, N. M. (2007). Examining the tradeoff between settlement delay and intraday liquidity in Canada's LVTS: a simulation approach (pp. 87–122). In H. Leinonen (Ed.), Simulation studies of liquidity needs, risks and efficiency in payment networks. Helsinki: Scientific Monographs.

Arjani, N. M. (2007). Examining the tradeoff between settlement delay and intraday liquidity in Canada's LVTS: a simulation approach. In H. Leinonen (Ed.), *Simulation studies of liquidity needs, risks and efficiency in payment networks* (pp. 87–121). Bank of Finland Publications.

Armantier, O., & Copeland, A. (2012). *Assessing the quality of Furfine-Based algorithms.* Federal Reserve Bank of New York Staff Report No. 575.

Armantier, O., Arnold, J. & McAndrews, J. (2008). *Changes in the Timing and Distribution of Fedwire Funds Transfers.* Federal Reserve Bank of New York Economic Policy Review, 14(2) Special Issue: The Economics of Payments, 83-112.

Armantier, O., Arnold, J. & McAndrews, J. (2008, September). Changes in the timing distribution of Fedwire funds transfers. *FRBNY Economic Policy Review.*

Armstrong, F. E. (1934). *The Book of the Stock Exchange* (2nd ed.). Pitman.

Ausubel, L. M. (1991). The failure of competition in the credit card market. *The American Economic Review*, *81*(1), 50–81.

Authorities' access to trade repository data. (2013, April). *Committee on Payment and Settlement Systems and the Board of the International Organization of Securities Commission.* Retrieved from http://www.bis.org/publ/cpss108.pdf

Avdjiev, S., Schrimpf, A., & Vause, N. (2011, September 2011). Highlights of the BIS International Statistics. *BIS Quarterly Review*.

Baer, H., France, V., & Moser, J. (2004). Opportunity Cost and Prudentiality: An Analysis of Collateral Decisions in Bilateral and Multilateral Settings. *Research in Finance*, *21*, 201–227.

Baker, S. (2012). Clearing houses: failure not an option. *Financial News*. Retrieved from http://www.efinancialnews.com/story/2012-04-16/clearing-houses-failure-not-an-option?ea9c8a2de0ee111045601ab04d673622

Barabási, A.-L. (2003). *Linked*. New York: Plume.

Barabási, A.-L., & Albert, R. (1999). Emergence of scaling in random networks. *Science*, *286*(5439), 509–512. doi:10.1126/science.286.5439.509 PMID:10521342

Barank, J. (2013). *Financial Market utilities and Key Financial Market Infrastructure Elements*. Nova Science Publishers.

Bargigli, L., di Iasio, G., Infante, L., Lillo, F., & Pierobon, F. (2013). *The multiplex structure of interbank networks* (Working Paper Series – Economics No.26/2013). DISEI.

BATS. (n.d.). Clearing Interoperability. Retrieved from http://www.batsglobalmarkets.com/europe/equities/clearing/products/interoperability/

Baxter, G. J., Dorogovtsev, A., Glotsec, V., & Mendes, J. F. F. (2014). Avalanches in multiplex and interdependent networks. In G. D'Agostino & A. Scala (Eds.), *Networks of networks: the last frontier of complexity* (pp. 37–52). Cham, Switzerland: Springer. doi:10.1007/978-3-319-03518-5_2

BCBS-IOSCO (Basel Committee on Banking Supervision and the Board of the International Organization of Securities Commissions) (2013). *Margin Requirements for Non-centrally Cleared Derivatives - Final Document*, September

Bech, M. (2008). *Intraday Liquidity Management: A Tale of Games that Banks Play*. Federal Reserve Bank of New York Economic Policy Review 14(2) Special Issue: The Economics of Payments, 7-23.

Bech, M., & Atalay, E. (2008). *The topology of the Federal Funds Market* (Federal Reserve Bank of New York Staff Report No.354). New York: Federal Reserve Bank of New York.

Bech, M., & Hobijn, B. (2007, September). Technology Diffusion within Central Banking: The Case of Real-Time Gross Settlement. *International Journal of Central Banking, 3, 3.*

Bech, M., & Soramäki, K. (2005a). Gridlock Resoluation and Bank Failures in Interbank Payment Systems (pages 151–178). In H. Leinonen (Ed.), Liquidity, risks and speed in payment and settlement systems: a simulation approach. Helsinki: Suomen Pankki.

Bech, M., & Soramäki, K. (2005b). Systemic Risk in a Netting System Revisited (pp. 277–298). In H. Leinonen (Ed.), Liquidity, risks and speed in payment and settlement systems: a simulation approach. Helsinki: Suomen Pankki.

Bech, M., Preisig, C. & Soramäki, K. (2008). *Global Trends in Large-Value Payments*. Federal Reserve Bank of New York Economic Policy Review 14(2) Special Issue: The Economics of Payments, 59–81.

Becher, C., Galbiati, M. & Tudela, M. (2008). *The Timing and Funding of CHAPS Sterling Payments*. Federal Reserve Bank of New York Economic Policy Review 14(2) Special Issue: The Economics of Payments, 113-133.

Becher, C., Galbiati, M. & Tudela, M. (2008). The timing and funding of CHAPS Sterling payments. *FRBNY Economic Policy Review*, September.

Becher, C., Millard, S., & Soramäki, K. (2008). *The network topology of CHAPS Sterling*. Bank of England Working Paper 355.

Becher, C., Galbiati, M., & Tudela, M. (2008). The timing and funding of CHAPS sterling payments. *Economic Policy Review*, *14*(2), 113–133.

Bech, M., & Garratt, R. (2012, August). Illiquidity in the Interbank Payment System Following Wide-Scale Disruptions. *Journal of Money, Credit and Banking*, *5*(5), 903–929. doi:10.1111/j.1538-4616.2012.00515.x

Bech, M., & Hobijn, B. (2007). Technology Diffusion within Central Banking: The Case of Real-Time Gross Settlement. *International Journal of Central Banking*, *3*, 147–182.

Bech, M., & Hobijn, B. (2007). Technology diffusion within central banking: The case of the real-time gross settlement. *International Journal of Central Banking*, *3*, 147–182.

Becker, L. (2014, May 23). EU regulators concerned by CFTC's foreign CCP rules. *Risk Magazine*. Retrieved from http://www.risk.net/risk-magazine/news/2346603/eu-regulators-concerned-by-cftcs-foreign-ccp-rules

Becker, L., & Madigan, P. (2014, June 16). EC to snub US in first wave of CCP equivalence decisions. *Risk Magazine*. Retrieved from http://www.risk.net/risk-magazine/news/2350239/ec-to-snub-us-in-first-wave-of-ccp-equivalence-decisions

Bedford, P., Millard, S., & Yang, J. (2005). Analysing the Impact of Operational Incidents in Large-Value Payment Systems: A Simulation Approach (pp. 247-274). In H. Leinonen (Ed.), Liquidity, Risks and Speed in Payment and Settlement Systems–A Simulation Approach. Helsinki: Suomen Pankki.

Bedford, P., Millard, S., & Yang, J. (2005). Analysing the impact of operational incidents in large-value payment systems: a simulation approach. In H. Leinonen (Ed.), *Liquidity, risks and speed in payment and settlement systems – a simulation approach* (pp. 247–274). Bank of Finland Publications.

Benos, E., Garratt, R., & Zimmerman, P. (2012). Bank behaviour and risks in CHAPS following the collapse of Lehman Brothers. *Bank of England Working Paper, 451*.

Bernanke, B. (2011, April). *Clearinghouses, financial stability, and financial reform*. Remarks at the 2011 Financial Markets Conference, Federal Reserve Bank of Atlanta, Stone Mountain, Georgia.

Bernanke, B. S. (2011). Clearinghouses, Financial Stability, and Financial Reform. Proceedings of the 2011 Financial Markets Conference. Stone Mountain, Georgia.

Bernanke, B. S. (1990). Clearing and settlement during the Crash. *Review of Financial Studies*, *3*(1), 133–151. doi:10.1093/rfs/3.1.133

Berndsen, R. (2010, March). Toward a Uniform Functional Model of Payment and Securities Settlement Systems. *De Nederlandsche Bank Working Paper*, No. 243.

Berndsen, R. (2011, February 25). *What is happening at Scrooge Digiduck's Warehouse?* Inaugural address at Tilburg University.

Berndsen, R. (2012). Letter from the editor in chief, Journal of Financial Market Infrastructures.

Berndsen, R. (2012). Letter from the editor. *The Journal of Financial Market Infrastructures*, 1(2), Winter 2012/2013.

Best Practices for CCP Stress Testing. (2011, November). European Association of CCP Clearing Houses.

Beutel, F. K. (1940). The Development of State Statutes on Negotiable Paper Prior to the Negotiable Instruments Law. *Columbia Law Review*, *40*(5), 836–865. doi:10.2307/1117594

Biais, Bruno, Florian Heider, Marie Hoerova (2013, April). Incentive compatible centralized clearing. *Banque de France Financial Stability Review*, 17.

Bjelland, J., Canright, G., & Engo-Mønsen, K. (2008). Web link analysis: Estimating document's importance from its context. *Telektronikk*, *1*, 95–113.

Bliss, R. R., & Papathanassiou, C. (2006). Derivatives clearing, central counterparties, and novation: The economic implications [Working paper]. Wake Forest University.

Bliss, R.R., & Steigerwald, R.S. (2006). Derivatives Clearing and Settlement: A Comparison of Central Counterparties and Alternative Structures. *Economic Perspectives*, 4Q/2006

Bodson, M. (2013). *New Infrastructures for a sounder financial system.* Banque de France, Financial Stability Review, 17

Bodson, M. C. (2013). New Infrastructures for a sounder financial system (trade repositories). *Banque de France. Financial Stability Review*, *17*, 91–99.

BoF. (2013). BoF PSS2 v3.2.1 User Manual. BoF.

BOJ-NET Funds Transfers after the Implementation of Phase 1 of the Next Generation RTGS Project. (2009, July). *Bank of Japan Review.*

Bolt, W., & Humphrey, D. (2005, July). Public Good Issues in TARGET: Natural Monopoly, Scale Economies, Network Effects and Cost Allocation. *ECB Working Paper Series*, 505.

Bonacich, P. (1972). Factoring and weighting approaches to status scores and clique identification. *The Journal of Mathematical Sociology*, *2*(1), 113–120. doi:10.1080/0022250X.1972.9989806

Boots, B. N. (1984). Evaluating principal eigenvalues as measures of network structure. *Geographical Analysis*, *3*, 270–275.

Borio, C. (2010). Ten propositions about liquidity crises. *CESifo Economic Studies*, *56*(1), 70–95. doi:10.1093/cesifo/ifp031

Boss, M., Elsinger, H., Summer, M., & Thurner, S. (2004). The network topology of the interbank market. *Quantitative Finance*, *4*(6), 677–684. doi:10.1080/14697680400020325

Bradley, H., Fawls, R. A., Litan, R. E., & Sommers, F. (2011). *Canaries in the Coal Mine: How the Rise in Settlement "Fails" Creates Systemic Risk for Financial Firms and Investors.* SSRN Electronic Journal; doi:10.2139/ssrn.1773633

Bravo-Benitez, B., Alexandrova-Kabadjova, B., & Martinez-Jaramillo, S. (2015). (forthcoming). Centrality measurement of the Mexican large value payments system from the perspective of multiplex network. *Journal of Comparative Economics*. doi:10.1007/s10614-014-9477-0

Brito, D. L., & Hartley, P. R. (1995). Consumer rationality and credit cards. *Journal of Political Economy*, *103*(2), 400–433. doi:10.1086/261988

Brummer, C. (2010). Post-American Securities Regulation. *California Law Review*, *98*(2), 327–384.

Brunnermeier, M., Clerc, L., El Omari, Y., Gabrieli, S., Kern, S., Memmel, C., et al. (2013). *Assessing contagion risk from the CDS market.* ESRB Occasional Paper, 4

Buhr, W. (2003). *What is Infrastructure*? University Siegen Discussion Paper, No. 107-03.

Buldyrev, S. V., Parshani, R., Paul, G., Stanley, H. E., & Havlin, S. (2010). Catastrophic cascade of failures in interdependent networks. *Nature*, *15*(464), 1025–1028. doi:10.1038/nature08932 PMID:20393559

Burton, D. (2008). *Credit and consumer society.* Routledge London.

Bush, S., & Hamilton, J. (2014, April 26). Banks' Overseas Swaps Moves Drawing CFTC Attention. *Bloomberg*. Retrieved from http://www.bloomberg.com/news/2014-04-25/banks-overseas-swaps-moves-said-to-draw-cftc-attention.html

Calem, P. S., & Mester, L. J. (1995). Consumer behavior and the stickiness of credit-card interest rates. *The American Economic Review*, *85*(5), 1327–1336.

Cameron, M. (2012). The Power Behind the Throne. *CME and the Fight for Futures Supremacy Risk Magazine*, *24*(10), 21–26.

Cantillon, E., & Yin, P. (1998). How and When Do Markets Tip? Lessons from the Battle of the Bund, *European Central Bank Working Paper* No 2007–766.

Cantillon, E., & Yin, P. (2011). Competition Between Exchanges: A Research Agenda. *International Journal of Industrial Organization*, *29*(1), 329–336.

Capel, J. (2011, March). Banks' international liquidity management in the future: What role can financial market infrastructures play? *Journal of Payments Strategy & Systems*, *5*(1), 1.

Capital requirements for bank exposures to central counterparties - final standard. (2014, April). *Bank for International Settlements*. Retrieved from http://www.bis.org/publ/bcbs282.htm

Capital requirements for bank exposures to central counterparties . (2012, July). Bank for International Settlements. Retrieved from http://www.bis.org/publ/bcbs227.pdf

Cardillo, A., Gómez-Gardeñes, J., Zanin, M., Romance, M., Papo, D., del Pozo, F., & Boccaletti, S. (2013). Emergence of network features from multiplexity. *Scientific Reports*, *3*(1344), 1–6. PMID:23446838

Carr, G. (2013, May 20). Emir futures margin rules create 'regulatory arbitrage'. *Energy Risk*. Retrieved from http://www.risk.net/energy-risk/news/2269032/emir-futures-margin-rules-create-regulatory-arbitrage

CCP12. (n.d.). CCP12 Membership. Retrieved from https://ccp12site-main.pbworks.com/w/page/55831310/CCP12%20 Membership

Cecchetti, S.G., Gyntelberg, J., and Hollanders, M. (2009, September 2009). Central Counterparties for Over-the-Counter Derivatives. *BIS Quarterly Review*.

Census, U. S. (2011). *Statistical abstract of the United States. Indiana*. Washington: Government Printing Office.

Chan, D., Fontan, F., Rosati, S., & Russo, D. (2007). The securities custody industry. *ECB Occasional Paper*, (68).

Chan, F., Fontan, F., Rosati, S., & Russo, D. (2007). The securities custody industry (pp. 6-10). Occasional paper series ECB. Frankfurt, 16.

Chande, N., Dion, J.P., McVanel, D., & Slive, J. (2012, December). The Canadian Approach to Central Clearing for Over-the-Counter Derivatives. *Bank of Canada Financial System Review*, 43-49.

Chande, N., Labelle, N., & Tuer, E. (2010, December). Central Counterparties and Systemic Risk. *Bank of Canada, Financial System Review*.

Christen, M., & Morgan, R. M. (2005). Keeping up with the Joneses: Analyzing the effect of income inequality on consumer borrowing. *Quantitative Marketing and Economics*, *3*(2), 145–173. doi:10.1007/s11129-005-0351-1

Cirasino, M., Garcia, J. A., & Tumpel-Gugerell, G. (2014). Materialising the expected benefits from financial infrastructure integration: The "Guidelines for the Successful Regional Integration of Financial Infrastructures. *Journal of Payments Strategy & Systems*, *8*(2), 119–128.

Clarke, A., & Hancock, J. (2010). Participant operational disruptions: the impact of system design (pp. 193–218). In M. Hellqvist & T. Laine (Ed.), Diagnostics for the financial markets–computational studies of payment system. Helsinki: Scientific Monographs.

Clarke, A., & Hancock, J. (2014). Payment system design and participant operational disruptions. *Journal of Financial Market Infrastructures*, *2*(2), 53–76.

Clauset, A., Shalizi, C. R., & Newman, M. E. J. (2009). Power-law distributions in empirical data. *SIAM Review*, *51*(4), 661–703. doi:10.1137/070710111

Clearance and Settlement Systems in the World's Security Markets. (1988). G30 Working Group. Retrieved from http://www.group30.org/rpt_43.shtml

Clearing and Settlement. (2014). The European Commission. Retrieved from http://ec.europa.eu/internal_market/financial-markets/clearing/index_en.htm

Clearing arrangements for exchange-traded derivatives. (1997, March). CPSS Publications, 23. Bank for International Settlements.

Clerc, L., Gabrieli, S., Kern, S., & El Omari, Y. (2014). *Monitoring the European CDS market through networks: implications for contagion risks*, Banque de France Working Paper, no. 417.

CME. (n.d.). CMEG Exchange Volume Report – Monthly. Retrieved from http://www.cmegroup.com/wrappedpages/web_monthly_report/Web_Volume_Report_CMEG.pdf

Coeuré, B. (2014, January 23). Risks in CCPs. Proceedings of "Mapping and Monitoring the Financial System: Liquidity, Funding, and Plumbing". Financial Research & Financial Stability Oversight Council. http://www.ecb.europa.eu/press/key/date/2014/html/sp140331.en.html

Coeuré, B. (2014). *'The Unknowns of Central Clearing', Speech*. European Central Bank.

Cohen, R., & Havlin, S. (2003). Scale-Free Networks Are Ultrasmall. *Physical Review Letters*, *5*, 1–4. PMID:12633404

Committee on Payment and Market Infrastructures and the Board of the International Organization of Securities Commission [CPSS IOSCO]. (2014, October). *Recovery of financial market infrastructures*. Retrieved from http://www.bis.org/cpmi/publ/d121.pdf

Committee on Payment and Settlement Systems – CPSS. (2008). The interdependencies of payment and settlement systems. Basel: Bank for International Settlements (BIS).

Communiqué. (2014, February 22-23). Finance Ministers and Central Bank Governors. Presented at the Meeting of Finance Ministers and Central Bank Governors, Sydney. Retrieved from https://www.g20.org/sites/default/files/g20_resources/library/Communique%20Meeting%20of%20G20%20Finance%20Ministers%20and%20Central%20Bank%20Governors%20Sydney%2022-23%20February%202014_0.pdf

Conrad, K., & Seitz, H. (1994). The economic benefits of public infrastructure. *Applied Economics*, *26*(4), 303–311. doi:10.1080/00036849400000077

Consultative Document - Capitalisation of bank exposures to central counterparties, 4. (2010, December). Bank for International Settlements. Retrieved from http://www.bis.org/publ/bcbs190.pdf

Consumer Action. Credit card survey. Online. (2010/2011). Retrieved from http://www.consumer-action.org/news/articles/2010–2011creditcardsurvey.

Consumer Action. Credit card survey. Online: (2009). Retrieved from http://www.consumer-action.org/news/articles/2009 credit card survey

Cont, R., & Minca, A. (2014). Credit default swaps and systemic risk. *Available at SSRN 2487947*.

Cont, R., & Kokholm, T. (2014). Central Clearing of OTC Derivatives: Bilateral vs multilateral netting. *Statistics & Risk Modeling*, *31*(1), 3–22. doi:10.1515/strm-2013-1161

Copeland, A., Duffie, D., Martin, A., & McLaughlin, S. (2012). Key mechanics of the US tri-party repo market. *Economic Policy Review*, 17–28.

Corcoran, A. M. (2013). International Standards for Central Counterparties and Replumbing the Financial System: Retrofitting Listed Derivatives Infrastructure for the Global OTC Derivatives Market. *Futures and Derivatives Law Report*, *33*(4), 1–29.

Core Principles for Effective Banking Supervision. (2012, September). *Basel Committee on Banking Supervision*. Retrieved from http://www.bis.org/publ/bcbs230.pdf

Core principles for systemically important payment systems. (2001, January). *Bank for International Settlements*. Retrieved from http://www.bis.org/publ/cpss43.pdf

Council directive 2008/114/EC. (2008). *Official Journal of the European Union*. Retrieved from http://eur-lex.europa.eu/LexUriServ/LexUriServ.do?uri=CELEX:32008L0114:EN:NOT

Council of Financial Regulators (2012). Review of Financial Market Infrastructure Regulation: Letter to the Deputy Prime Minister and Treasurer, February.

Cour-Thimann, P. (2013). *Target Balances and the Crisis in the Euro Area. CESifo Forum* (Vol. 14). Special Issue.

Cox, N., Garvin, N., & Kelly, G. (2013). Central Counterparty Links and Clearing System Exposures, *RBA Research Discussion Paper* No 2013-12.

CPMI. (2014). Committee on Payments and Market Infrastructures (CPMI). Retrieved from http://www.bis.org/cpmi/

CPMI-IOSCO (Committee on Payments and Market Infrastructures – IOSCO) (2014). *Recovery of Financial Market Infrastructures: Final Report*, October.

CPSS (2012b, April). *Principles for financial market infrastructures*, BIS.

CPSS (2013). *Statistics on payment, clearing and settlement systems in the CPSS countries – Figures for 2011*, BIS, January 2013.

CPSS (Committee on Payment and Settlement Systems) (2010). *Market Structure Developments in the Clearing Industry: Implications for Financial Stability*, November.

CPSS. (1992). *Delivery versus payment in securities settlement systems*. Retrieved from http://www.bis.org/cpmi/publ/d06.htm

CPSS. (2011, September). Payments, clearing and settlement systems in the CPSS countries, 1, BIS.

CPSS. (2012). *Principles for Financial Market Infrastructures: Disclosure Framework and Assessment Methodology*. Bank for International Settlements.

CPSS. (2012a November). Payments, clearing and settlement systems in the CPSS countries, 2, BIS.

CPSS: History, organisation, cooperation. (n.d.). Bank for International Settlements. Retrieved from http://www.bis.org/cpss/cpssinfo01.htm

CPSS-IOSCO (CPSS - Technical Committee of the International Organization of Securities Commissions) (2012). *Principles for Financial Market Infrastructures,*April.

Craig, B., & von Peter, G. (2014). Interbank tiering and money center banks. *Journal of Financial Intermediation, 23*(3), 322–347. doi:10.1016/j.jfi.2014.02.003

Credit card – rising interchange fees have increased costs for merchants, but options for reducing fees pose challenges. (2009). United States Government Accountability Office – Report to Congressional Addressees

Cross-border clearing and settlement arrangements in the European Union. (2002). Giovannini Group. Retrieved from http://ec.europa.eu/internal_market/financial-markets/docs/clearing/first_giovannini_report_en.pdf

Cruz Lopez, J. A., Harris, J. H., Pérignon, C., & Hurlin, C. (2012). *CoMargin: A System to Enhance Financial Stability.* Working Paper, Bank of Canada, HEC Paris, University of Orleans and Syracuse University.

Cruz Lopez, J. A., Mendes, R., & Vikstedt, H. (2013). The Market for Collateral: The Potential Impact of Financial Regulation. Financial System Review, Bank of Canada, June 2013.

Cruz Lopez, J. A., Harris, J. H., & Pérignon, C. (2011). Clearing House, Margin Requirements, and Systemic Risk. *Review of Futures Markets, 19*, 39–54.

CSD Factbook. (2013). ECSDA. Brussels, Belgium.

CSD Issuer Services. (2013) ECSDA - European Central Securities Depositories Association. Retrieved from http://www.ecsda.eu/uploads/tx_doclibrary/2013_10_ECSDA_IS_Report.pdf

CSD Regulation of the European Parliament and of the Council on improving securities settlement in the European Union and on central securities depositories (CSDs) (2014). European Union. Retrieved from http://ec.europa.eu/internal_market/financial-markets/central_securities_depositories/index_en.htm

Culler, D., Pal Singh, J., & Gupta, A. (1997). *Parallel computer architecture: A hardware / software approach.* Morgan Kaufmann Publishers.

Currie, W. (2007). Computerising the Stock Exchange: A comparison of two information systems. *New Technology, Work and Employment, 12*(2), 75–83. doi:10.1111/1468-005X.00025

D'Souza, R. M., Brummitt, C. D., & Leicht, E. A. (2014). Modeling interdependent networks as random graphs: connectivity and systemic risk. In G. D'Agostino & A. Scala (Eds.), *Networks of networks: the last frontier of complexity* (pp. 73–94). Cham, Switzerland: Springer. doi:10.1007/978-3-319-03518-5_4

Data Analysis CMIC Canadian OTC Derivatives Landscape [Strategy Paper]. (2011). Canadian Market Infrastructure Committee.

Davey, N., & Gray, D. (2014). How Has the Liquidity Saving Mechanism Reduced Banks' Intraday Liquidity Costs in CHAPS? *Bank of England Quarterly Bulletin, 2014*, Q2.

Davey, N., & Gray, D. (2014). How has the Liquidity-saving Mechanism reduced banks' intraday liquidity costs in CHAPS? *Bank of England Quarterly Bulletin, Q2*, 180–189.

Day, T., & Lewis, C. (2004). Margin Adequacy and Standards: An Analysis of the Crude Oil Futures Market. *The Journal of Business, 77*(1), 101–135.

DB Research (2014, September). Fintech – Die digitale (R)evolution im Finanzsektor. *Deutsche Bank Research*, 23.

Della Vigna, S., & Malmendier, U. (2004). Contract design and self-control: Theory and evidence. *The Quarterly Journal of Economics*, *CXIX*(2), 353–402. doi:10.1162/0033553041382111

Denbee, E., Garratt, R., & Zimmerman, P. (2010). Methods for evaluating liquidity provision in real-time gross settlement payment systems (pp. 53–76). In M. Hellqvist & T. Laine (Ed.), Diagnostics for the financial markets–computational studies of payment system. Helsinki: Scientific Monographs.

Dent, A., & Dison, W. (2012). The Bank of England's Real-Time Gross Settlement Infrastructure. *Bank of England Quarterly Bulletin*, *2013*, Q3.

Denzel, M. A. (2014). Die Errichtung der Hamburger Bank 1619. In Lindenlaub et alii, 38-50.

Derivatives Statistics. (2012a). Bank for International Settlements. Retrieved from: www.bis.org/statistics/derstats.htm

Deutsche Börse Group. Eurex Clearing (Eds.) (2014). How central counterparties strengthen the safety and integrity of financial markets.

Deutsche Bundesbank (2012). *Payment behaviour in Germany in 2011: An empirical study of the utilisation of cash and cashless payment instruments.*

Devriese, J., & Mitchell, J. (2006). Liquidity risk in securities settlement. *Journal of Banking & Finance*, *30*(6), 1807–1834. doi:10.1016/j.jbankfin.2005.09.008

Diehl, M. (2012). The Use of Simulations as an Analytical Tool for Payment Systems. In B. Alexandrova-Kabadjova, et al. (Eds): *Simulation in Computational Finance and Economics: Tools and Emerging Applications*, 29-45. Retrieved from http://www.igi-global.com/book/simulation-computational-finance-economics/64901

Diehl, M. (2012). The Use of Simulations as an Analytical Tool for Payment Systems. In B. Alexandrova-Kabadjova, S. Martinez-Jaramillo, A. Garcia-Almanza, & E. Tsang. (Eds.), Simulation in Computational Finance and Economics: Tools and Emerging Applications (pp. 29–45). Hershey: IGI Global.

Diehl, M. (2013). Measuring free riding in large-value payment systems: the case of TARGET2. *Journal of Financial Market infrastructures*, 1/3, 1-23.

Diehl, M. (2013). Measuring free riding in large-value payment systems: The case of TARGET2. *The Journal of Financial Market Infrastructures*, *1*(3), 31–53.

Diehl, M. (2013). Measuring free-riding in large-value payment-systems: The case of TARGET2. *Journal of Financial Market Infrastructures*, *1*(3), 1–23.

Diehl, M. (2013). The Use of Simulations as an Analytical Tool for Payment Systems. In B. Alexandrova-Kabadjova, S. Martinez-Jaramillo, A. Garcia-Almanza, & E. Tsang (Eds.), *Simulation in Computational Finance and Economics: Tools and Emerging Applications* (pp. 29–45). Hershey, PA: Business Science Reference; doi:10.4018/978-1-4666-2011-7.ch002

Diehl, M. (in press). FMI: The backbone of financial systems. *Analyzing the Economics of Financial Market Infrastructures*.

Diehl, M., & Müller, A. (2014). Analysis of the use and impact of limits. *Journal of Financial Market Infrastructures*, *3*(1), 33–60.

Dirninger, C. (2014). Der bargeldlose Zahlungsverkehr der Sparkassen 1908. In: Lindenlaub et al., 216-228.

Dodd -Frank Indemnification Briefing Paper . (n.d.) The Depository Trust & Clearing Corporation. Retrieved from http://164.109.172.95/legal/government_relations/downloads/briefing/Indemnification.pdf

Dodd-Frank Wall Street Reform and Consumer Protection Act of 2010, H. R. 4173, 111th Congress (2010).

DTCC Partners with the Industry to Implement T+2 in the U.S. (2014a). *DTCC*. Retrieved from http://www.dtcc.com/news/2014/april/22/shortening-settlement-cycle.aspx

DTCC Recommends Shortening the U.S. Trade Settlement Cycle. (2014b). *DTCC*. Retrieved from http://www.dtcc.com/~/media/Files/Downloads/WhitePapers/T2-Shortened-Cycle-WP.pdf

Dubrau, F. (2014). CSD regulation: A major change for the post-trade arena. *Journal of securities operations & custody*, 6(3), 212-219.

Duffie, D., Li, A., & Lubke, T. (2010). *Policy Perspectives on OTC Derivatives Market Infrastructure*. Federal Reserve Bank of New York Staff Reports, 424

Duffie, D., Scheicher, M., & Vuillemey, G. (2014). Central Clearing and Collateral Demand, *NBER Working Paper* No 19890.

Duffie, D. (2014). Financial Market Infrastructure: Too Important to Fail. In M. Bailey & J. Taylor (Eds.), *The U.S. Financial System – Five Years After the Crisis. Hoover Institution and Brookings Institute, 2014*.

Duffie, D., Scheicher, M., & Vuillemey, G. (2015). Central clearing and collateral demand. *Journal of Financial Economics*, *116*(2), 237–256. doi:10.1016/j.jfineco.2014.12.006

Duffie, D., & Zhu, H. (2011). Does a Central Clearing Counterparty Reduce Counterparty Risk? *The Review of Asset Pricing Studies*, *1*(1), 74–95.

Edwards, F. R. (1983). The Clearing Association in Futures Markets: Guarantor and Regulator. *Journal of Futures Markets*, *3*(4), 1983. doi:10.1002/fut.3990030404

Erdos, P., & Rényi, A. (1960). On random graphs. *Publicationes Mathematicae*, *6*, 17–61.

Estrada, D. & Morales, P. (2008, March). *La estructura del mercado interbancario y del riesgo de contagio en Colombia* (Reporte de Estabilidad Financiera). Bogotá, Colombia: Banco de la República.

Eurex (n.d.). Monthly Statistics. Retrieved from http://www.eurexchange.com/exchange-en/market-data/statistics/monthly-statistics

European Code of Conduct for clearing and settlement. (2006). EACH, ECSDA, FESE. Retrieved from http://ec.europa.eu/internal_market/financial-markets/docs/code/code_en.pdf

Evans, D. S., Schmalensee, R., Noel, M. D., Chang, H. H., & Garcia-Swartz, D. D. (2011). *Platform Economics: Essays on Multi-Sided Businesses*. Retrieved from http://ssrn.com/abstract=1974020

Faulkner, M. C. (2008). An introduction to securities lending. Handbook of Finance.

Feasibility Study on Approaches to Aggregate OTC Derivatives Data. (2014b). Financial Stability Board.

Fidessa Fragmentation Index. (n.d.) Retrieved from http://fragmentation.fidessa.com/

Figlewski, S. (1984). Margins and Market Integrity: Margin Setting for Stock Index Futures and Options. *Journal of Futures Markets*, *4*, 385–416.

Financial Data – Banks. (2012). Office of the Superintendent of Financial Institutions Canada. Retrieved from: http://www.osfi-bsif.gc.ca/osfi/index_e.aspx?ArticleID=554

Financial Stability Board (FSB) (2011). *Key Attributes for Effective Resolution Regimes for Financial Institutions*, October.

Finan, K., Lasaosa, A., & Sunderland, J. (2013). Tiering in CHAPS. *Bank of England Quarterly Bulletin, Q4*, 371–378.

Fleming, M. J., & Garbade, K. (2005). Explaining settlement fails. *Current Issues in Economics and Finance, 11*(9).

Fleming, M. J., & Garbade, K. (2002). When the back office moved to the front burner: Settlement fails in the Treasury market after September 11. *Economic Policy Review*, *8*(2).

Fleming, M. J., & Garbade, K. D. (2007). Dealer behavior in the specials market for US Treasury securities. *Journal of Financial Intermediation*, *16*(2), 204–228. doi:10.1016/j.jfi.2006.12.003

Forth T2S Harmonisation Progress Report. (2014). T2S Advisory Group. Retrieved from http://www.ecb.europa.eu/paym/t2s/pdf/fourth_t2s_harmonisation_progress_report.pdf??ca8dad7f68af5c5edd9087cdc73d400a

Foster, K., Meijer, E., Schuh, S., & Zabek, M. A. (2010). *The 2008 survey of consumer payment choice*. Federal Reserve Bank of Boston.

Frankfurter Kassenverein (1963). *Der Frankfurter Kassenverein.* Überblick über seine Geschichte und Funktionen.

Fricke, D., & Lux, T. (2014). Core-periphery structure in the overnight money market: Evidence from the e-MID trading platform. *Computational Economics*. doi:10.1007/s10614-014-9427-x

FSB (2012). *OTC Derivatives Market Reforms Third Progress Report on Implementation*, June.

FSB (2014a). *Key Attributes of Effective Resolution Regimes to Financial Institutions*, October.

FSB (2014b). *OTC Derivatives Market Reforms Eighth Progress Report on Implementation*, November.

Fujimoto, R. M. (2000). *Parallel and distributed simulation systems*. John Wiley & Sons, Inc Publications.

Fundtech (2013). Immediate Payments – Innovation is Knocking [White Paper]. *Fundtech*.

Furfine, C. (1999). *The microstructure of the federal funds market.* Financial Markets. *Institutions and Instruments*, *8*(5), 24–44. doi:10.1111/1468-0416.00031

G20 (Group of Twenty) (2009). Leaders' Statement, Pittsburgh Summit, 24–25 September

G20 Leaders Statement: The Pittsburgh Summit. (2009). Proceedings of *G20 Information Centre*. Retrieved from http://www.g8.utoronto.ca/g20/2009/2009communique0925.html

Galbiati, M., & Soramäki, K. (2010). *Liquidity-saving Mechanisms and Bank Behaviour.* Bank of England Working Paper 400.

Galbiati, M., & Soramäki, K. (2013). Liquidity Saving Mechanisms and Bank Behavior in Payment Systems. In B. Alexandrova-Kabadjova, S. Martinez-Jaramillo, A. Garcia-Almanza, & E. Tsang (Eds.), *Simulation in Computational Finance and Economics: Tools and Emerging Applications* (pp. 103–119). Hershey, PA: Business Science Reference; doi:10.4018/978-1-4666-2011-7.ch006

Galbraith, J. & Tkacz, G. (2013). *Nowcasting GDP: Electronic Payments, Data Vintages and the Timing of Data Releases.* CIRANO Scientific Series, 2013, s-25.

Gao, J., Buldyrev, S. V., Stanley, H. E., & Havlin, S. (2012). Networks formed from interdependent networks. *Nature Physics*, *8*(1), 40–48. doi:10.1038/nphys2180 PMID:23005189

Garratt, R., & Zimmerman, P. (2013). Does a CCP Reduce Counterparty Risk in a Scale-Free Network? [Unpublished manuscript].

Gemmill, G. (1994). Margins and the Safety of Clearing Houses. *Journal of Banking & Finance, 18*, 979–996.

Gensler, G. (2011, March 22). *Remarks, OTC Derivatives Reform, European Parliament, Economic and Monetary Affairs Committee, Brussels, Belgium* [Speech transcript]. Retrieved from http://www.cftc.gov/PressRoom/SpeechesTestimony/opagensler-75

Gibson, M. (2013). 'Recovery and Resolution of Central Counterparties', *RBA Bulletin*, December, 39–48.

Gill, T., Perera, D., & Sunner, D. (2012). *Electronic Indicators of Economic Activity*. Reserve Bank of Australia Bulletin. *June Quarter*, *2012*, 1–12.

Giovannini, A. (2010). Why the European Securities Market is Not Fully Integrated. In *Europe and the Euro* (pp. 255–283). University of Chicago Press. doi:10.7208/chicago/9780226012858.003.0008

Gómez-Gardeñes, J., Reinares, I., Arenas, A., & Floría, L. M. (2012). Evolution of cooperation in multiplex networks. *Scientific Reports*, *2*(620), 1–6. doi:10.1038/srep00620 PMID:22943006

Good practice principles on supervisory colleges. (2010, October). *Basel Committee on Banking Supervision*. Retrieved from http://www.bis.org/publ/bcbs177.pdf

Gorton, G., & Metrick, A. (2012). Securitized banking and the run on repo. *Journal of Financial Economics*, *104*(3), 425–451. doi:10.1016/j.jfineco.2011.03.016

Gould, P. R. (1967). On the geographical interpretation of eigenvalues. *Transactions of the Institute of British Geographers*, *42*(42), 53–86. doi:10.2307/621372

Goyal, S., & Vigier, A. (2010). Robust networks. Retrieved from http://www.econ.cam.ac.uk/faculty/goyal/wp10/robustnet-works55.pdf

Green, P. J., Jennings-Mares, J. C., & Smith, D. (2013), Avoiding Armageddon: Resolution Regimes for Central Clearing Counterparties, Morrison Foerster, Derivatives: Financial Products Report, Vol. 14 No. 8

Gregory, J. (2014). Central Counterparties: Mandatory Clearing and Bilateral Margin Requirements for OTC Derivatives, Croydon, Great Britan: Wiley.

Griffith, S. J. (2014). Substituted Compliance and Systemic Risk: How to Make a Global Market in Derivatives Regulation. *Minnesota Law Review*, *98*, 1291–1371.

Guadamillas, M., & Keppler, R. (2002). Securities Clearance and Settlement Systems – A Guide to Best Practices

Gulan, A., Haavio, M., & Kilponen, J. (in press). From Finnish great depression to great recession. *Bank of Finland Publications.*

Güntzer, M. M., Jungnickel, D., & Leclerc, M. (1998). Efficient algorithms for the clearing of interbank payments. *European Journal of Operational Research*, *106*(1), 212–219. doi:10.1016/S0377-2217(97)00265-8

Gutheil-Knopp-Kirchwald, G. (2012). Infrastruktur – ein Begriff im Wandel der Zeiten. Lecture at the IFIP-Jahrestagung "Öffentliche Infrastruktur im Wandel", Vienna, June 15, 2012.

Haene, P., & Sturm, A. (2009). Optimal CCP Risk Management, *Swiss National Bank Working Papers* No. 2009-7.

Haene, P., & Sturm, A. (2009). Optimal Central Counterparty Risk Management. *Swiss National Bank*, Working Paper No. 2009-7

Haldane, A.G. (2009, April). *Rethinking the financial network*. Speech delivered at the Financial Student Association, Amsterdam, Netherlands.

Hanley, W. J., McCann, K., & Moser, J. T. (1995), Public benefits and Public Concerns: An Economic Analysis of Regulatory Standards for Clearing Facilities. *Federal Reserve Bank of Chicago,* Working Paper WP-95-12

Hardouvelis, G., & Kim, D. (1995). Margin Requirements, Price Fluctuations and Market Participation in Metal Futures. *Journal of Money, Credit and Banking*, *27*(3), 659–671.

Hartzmark, M. (1986). The Effects of Changing Margin Levels on Futures Market Activity, the Composition of Traders in the Market and Price Performance. *The Journal of Business*, *59*(2), 147–180.

Hasan, I., De Renzis, T., & Schmiedel, H. (2013). *Retail Payments and the Real Economy.* ECB Working Paper Series No. 1572.

Hasenpusch, T. P. (2009). *Clearing Services for Global Markets.* Cambridge, United Kingdom: Cambridge University Press. doi:10.1017/CBO9780511635557

Heath, A., Kelly, G., & Manning, M. (2013). OTC Derivatives Reform: Netting and Networks, *Liquidity and Funding Markets, Proceedings of a Conference*, Reserve Bank of Australia, Sydney, pp 33–73

Heijmans, R. (2009). Simulation in the Dutch Interbank Payment System: A Sensitivity Analysis. *DNB Working Paper.*

Heijmans, R., & Heuver, R. (2011). Is this bank ill? The diagnosis of doctor TARGET2. De Nederlandsche Bank Working Paper No. 316.

Heijmans, R., & Heuver, R. (2013). Preparing Simulations in Large Value Payment Systems using Historical Data. In B. Alexandrova-Kabadjova, S. Martinez-Jaramillo, A. Garcia-Almanza, & E. Tsang (Eds.), *Simulation in Computational Finance and Economics: Tools and Emerging Applications* (pp. 46–68). Hershey, PA: Business Science Reference; doi:10.4018/978-1-4666-2011-7.ch003

Heijmans, R., & Heuver, R. (2014). Is this bank ill? The diagnosis of doctor TARGET2. *Journal of Financial Market Infrastructures*, *2*(3), 3–36.

Hellqvist, M. (2009). Participants' internal intraday limits in large value payment systems, chapter 09, pp. 255–276. In Hellqvist (2009).

Hellqvist, M., & Koskinen, J. (2005). Stress testing securities clearing and settlement systems using simulations (pp. 324–350). In H. Leinonen (Ed.), Liquidity, risks and speed in payment and settlement systems: a simulation approach. Helsinki: Suomen Pankki.

Hellqvist, M., & Snellman, H. (2007). Simulation of operational failures in equities settlement (pp. 283–320). In H. Leinonen (Ed.), Simulation studies of liquidity needs, risks and efficiency in payment networks. Helsinki: Scientific Monographs.

Hellqvist, M., & Snellman, H. (2007). Simulation of operational failures in equities settlement. In H. Leinonen (Ed.), *Simulation studies of liquidity needs, risks and efficiency in payment networks: Proceedings from the Bank of Finland Payment and Settlement System Seminars 2005-2006* (pp. 283-320).

Hellqvist, M. (2012). *Diagnostics for the financial market - computational studies of payment systems.Proceedings from the Bank of Finland Payment and Settlement System Seminars 2009*-2011. Bank of Finland.

Hellqvist, M., & Koskinen, J. (2005). Stress testing securities clearing and settlement systems using simulations. In H. Leinonen (Ed.), *Liquidity, risks and speed in payment and settlement systems - a simulation approach, No E31* (pp. 321–350).

Heuver, R. (in press). Compressing the number of transactions in order to increase performance of simulations. *Bank of Finland Publications.*

Hills, B., Rule, D., Parkinson, S., & Young, C. (1999). CCP Clearing Houses and Financial Stability. *Bank of England Financial Stability Review*, *6*, 122–134.

Hills, B., Rule, D., Parkinson, S., & Young, C. (1999). *Central Counterparty Clearing Houses and Financial Stability, Financial Stability Review June 1999*. Bank of England.

How central counterparties strengthen the safety and integrity of financial markets. (2014). *Deutsche Börse Group*. Deutsche Börse Group and Eurex Clearing.

How Regulation Will Reshape FX and Rates Markets: Part 3. [Special Report]. (2014, July 24). *Deutsche Bank Markets Research*.

Humphrey, D. (1986). Payments finality and risk settlement failure. In A. Saunders and L White (Eds.), Technology and the regulation of financial markets: Securities, futures and banking (pp. 97-120). Lexington, MA: Lexington Books.

Hvide, H. K. (2002). Pragmatic beliefs and overconfidence. *Journal of Economic Behavior & Organization*, *48*(1), 15–28. doi:10.1016/S0167-2681(01)00221-9

ICE. (n.d.). Historical Daily Volume. Retrieved from https://www.theice.com/marketdata/reports/26

ICMA. Frequently Asked Questions on repo. (2014). Retrieved from http://www.icmagroup.org/Regulatory-Policy-and-Market-Practice/short-term-markets/Repo-Markets/frequently-asked-questions-on-repo/

IFC. (2013). *Progress in Responsible Financial Inclusion*. Washington: International Finance Corporation.

Imakubo, K., & McAndrews, J. J. (2007). Funding levels for the new accounts in the BOJ-NET (pp. 123–148). In H. Leinonen (Ed.), Simulation studies of liquidity needs, risks and efficiency in payment networks. Helsinki: Scientific Monographs.

Imakubo, K., & McAndrews, J. J. (2007). Funding levels for the new accounts in BOJ-NET. In H. Leinonen (Ed.), *Simulation studies of liquidity needs, risks and efficiency in payment networks* (pp. 123–148). Bank of Finland Publications.

Implementation monitoring of PFMIs: first update to the Level 1 report. (2014, May). *Committee on Payment and Settlement Systems and the Board of the International Organization of Securities Commission*. Retrieved from http://www.bis.org/cpmi/publ/d117.pdf

Implementing OTC Derivatives Market Reforms. (2010, October 25). *Financial Stability Board*. Retrieved from http://www.financialstabilityboard.org/publications/r_101025.pdf

Improving the efficiency, integration and safety and soundness of cross border post-trading arrangements in Europe, Brussels, 3rd progress report. (2008). European Commission. Retrieved from http://ec.europa.eu/internal_market/financial-markets/docs/clearing/ecofin/20080311_ecofin_en.pdf

in 't Veld, D., & van Lelyveld, I. (2014). Finding the Core: Network Structure in Interbank Markets. *Journal of Banking & Finance*, *49*, 27–40. doi:10.1016/j.jbankfin.2014.08.006

Inaoka, H., Ninomiya, T., Taniguchi, K., Shimizu, T., & Takayasu, H. (2004). Fractal Network derived from banking transaction: An analysis of network structures formed by financial institutions. *Bank of Japan Working Paper Series*, 04-E-04.

Inaoka, H., Ninomiya, T., Tanigushi, K., Shimizu, T., & Takayasu, H. (2004). *Fractal network derived from banking transaction* (Bank of Japan Working Paper Series No. 04-E04). Tokyo: Bank of Japan.

Innes, A.M. (1913, May). What is Money? *The Banking Law Journal.*

Innes, A. M. (1914, Dec./Jan.). *The Credit Theory of Money. The Banking Law Journal,* 31, 151–168.

Innovations in retail payments. (2012). Committee on Payment and Settlement Systems.

International Swaps and Derivatives Association, Incorporation (2012). *ISDA Margin Survey 2012.* Annual Statistical Release.

Interpretive Guidance and Policy Statement Regarding Compliance with Certain Swap Regulations. 78 Fed. Reg. 144 (2013, July 26) (to be codified 17 CFR pt. 1).

Iori, G. (2004). An analysis of systemic risk in alternative securities settlement architectures, *European Central Bank, Working paper, 404.*

Iori, G., & Deissenberg, C. (2008). An Analysis of Settlement Risk Contagion in Alternative Securities Settlement Architectures. In *Computational Methods in Financial Engineering* (pp. 299–315). Springer Berlin Heidelberg.

ISDA (International Swaps and Derivatives Association) (2013). CCP Loss Allocation at the End of the Waterfall August.

Ivanov, P. Ch., & Bartsch, R. P. (2014). Network physiology: mapping interactions between networks of physiologic networks. In G. D'Agostino & A. Scala (Eds.), *Networks of networks: the last frontier of complexity* (pp. 203–222). Cham, Switzerland: Springer. doi:10.1007/978-3-319-03518-5_10

Jackson, J., & Manning, M. (2007). Comparing the Pre-settlement Risk Implications of Alternative Clearing Arrangements, *Bank of England Working Paper* No. 321.

Janssen, M. A., & Jager, W. (2003). Simulating market dynamics: Interactions between consumer psychology and social networks. *Artificial Life*, *9*(4), 343–356. doi:10.1162/106454603322694807 PMID:14761255

Johnson, C., & Steigerwald, R. (2008). The Central Bank's Role in the Payment System: Legal and Policy Aspects (pp. 445–470). Proceedings of Seminar on Current Developments in Monetary and Financial Law. Washington, D.C.: International Monetary Fund.

Johnson, K., McAndrews, J., & Soramäki, K. (2005). Economising liquidity with deferred settlement mechanisms (pp. 179–216). In H. Leinonen (Ed.), Liquidity, risks and speed in payment and settlement systems: a simulation approach. Helsinki: Suomen Pankki.

Jones, H. (2013, November 5). Global watchdog says new body with teeth needed to police markets. *Reuters.* Retrieved from http://uk.reuters.com/article/2013/11/05/g20-regulation-idUKL5N0IQ2G820131105

Kahn, C., & Roberds, W. (1998). Payment System Settlement and Bank Incentives. *Review of Financial Studies*, *11*(4), 845–870. doi:10.1093/rfs/11.4.845

Kahn, C., & Roberds, W. (2001). Real-Time Gross Settlement and the Costs of Immediacy. *Journal of Monetary Economics*, *47*(2), 299–319. doi:10.1016/S0304-3932(01)00047-2

Kamleitner, B., & Kirchler, E. (2007). Consumer credit use: A process model and literature review. *Revue Européenne de Psychologie Appliquee. European Review of Applied Psychology*, *57*(4), 267–283. doi:10.1016/j.erap.2006.09.003

Kane, E. J. (2009). Discussion of "An Industrial Organization Approach to the Too Big to Fail Problem" by Jean-Charles Rochet. In *Prepared for Federal Reserve Bank of Boston 54th Economic Conference in Chatham, MA (October).*

Kantona, G. (1975). *Psychological economics.* Elsevier Science Ltd.

Kathryn, C., Fleming, M., Jackson, J., Li, A., & Sarkar, A. (2011). *An Analysis of CDS Transactions: Implications for Public Reporting*. Federal Reserve Bank of New York Staff Reports, 517

Keister, T., Martin, Antoine, M. & McAndrews, J. (2008). Divorcing Money from Monetary Policy. *Federal Reserve Bank of New York Economic Policy Review*, 14(2) Special Issue: The Economics of Payments, 41-56.

Kenett, D. Y., Gao, J., Huang, X., Shao, S., Vodenska, I., & Buldyrev, S. V. et al. (2014). Network of interdependent networks: overview of theory and applications. In G. D'Agostino & A. Scala (Eds.), *Networks of networks: the last frontier of complexity* (pp. 3–36). Cham, Switzerland: Springer. doi:10.1007/978-3-319-03518-5_1

Key Attributes of Effective Resolution Regimes for Financial Institutions. (2011, October) *Financial Stability Board.* Retrieved from http://www.financialstabilityboard.org/wp-content/uploads/r_111104cc.pdf?page_moved=1

Key Attributes of Effective Resolution Regimes for Financial Institutions. (2014, October 15) *Financial Stability Board.* Retrieved from http://www.financialstabilityboard.org/wp-content/uploads/r_141015.pdf

Key Attributes of Effective Resolution Regimes for Financial Institutions. (2014a). Financial Stability Board.

Klayman, J., Soll, J. B., González-Vallejo, C., & Barlas, S. (1999). Overconfidence: It depends on how, what, and whom you ask. *Organizational Behavior and Human Decision Processes*, *79*(3), 216–247. doi:10.1006/obhd.1999.2847 PMID:10471362

Kleinberg, J. M. (1998, January). Authoritative sources in a hyperlinked environment.*Proceedings of the 9th ACM-SIAM Symposium on Discrete Algorithms*, 668-677.

Knott, R., & Mills, A. (2002, December). Modeling Risk in Central Counterparty Clearing Houses: A Review. Bank of England.

Knott, R., & Mills, A. (2002). Modelling Risk in CCP Clearing Houses: A Review. *Bank of England Financial Stability Review*, *13*, 162–174.

Koeppl, T., & Monnet, C. (2008). CCPs, *Centre for Financial Studies Working Paper* No. 42.

Koeppl, T.V. (2011). Time for Stability in Derivatives Markets, Commentary, C.D. Howe Institute, No. 329

Koeppl, T.V., & Monnet, C. (2010), The Emergence and Future of Central Counterparties, Working Paper 1241. Queen's University.

Kokkola (2010) *The Payment System: payments, securities and derivatives, and the role of the Eurosystem*, 66 - 68, 84 - 85, 173 – 179. Frankfurt.

Kokkola, T. (Ed.). (2010). *The Payment System*. European Central Bank Publications.

Kolaczyc, E. D. (2009). *Statistical analysis of network data*. New York: Springer. doi:10.1007/978-0-387-88146-1

Koponen, R. & Soramäki, K. (1998). *Intraday liquidity needs in a modern interbank payment system - a simulation approach.* Bank of Finland Publications.

Koponen, R., & Soramäki, K. (1998). *Intraday liquidity needs in a modern interbank payment system – a simulation approach.* Bank of Finland Publications. Retrieved from http://www.suomenpankki.fi/fi/julkaisut/tutkimukset/erillis-julkaisut/ Pages/E14.aspx

Koponen, R., & Soramäki, K. (2005). Intraday Liquidity Needs in a Modern Interbank Payment System: A Simulation Approach. (pp. 74–117). In H. Leinonen (Ed.), Liquidity, risks and speed in payment and settlement systems: a simulation approach. Helsinki: Suomen Pankki.

Korsgraad, S. (2012, Fall). Auto-collateralization as a liquidity-saving mechanism. *Journal of Financial Market Infrastructures*, 1(1), 2-27.

Kovner, A., & Skeie, D. (2013). *Evaluating the Quality of Fed Funds Lending Estimates Produced from Fedwire Payments Data*. Federal Reserve Bank of New York Staff Report No. 629.

Kovner, A., Vickery, J., & Zhou, L. (2014). Do Big Banks Have Lower Operating Costs? Federal Reserve Bank of New York Economic Policy Review, 20(2).

Kroszner, R. (2006). Central Counterparty Clearing: History, Innovation, and Regulation, Speech, Board of Governors of the Federal Reserve System, April

Kroszner, R. (2006, April 3). Central Counterparty Clearing: History, Innovation, and Regulation. Proceedings of the Joint Conference on Issues Related to Central Counterparty Clearing. Frankfurt, Germany.

Kroszner, R. S. (2006, April 3). *Central Counterparty Clearing: History, Innovation, and Regulation*. Proceedings of of Chicago joint conference on issues related to central counterparty clearing, Frankfurt, Germany.

Kroszner, R. (1999). Can the Financial Markets Privately Regulate Risk? The Development of Derivatives Clearinghouses and Recent Over-the-Counter Innovations. *Journal of Money, Credit and Banking*, *31*(3), 596–618.

Kroszner, R. (1999, November). Can the Financial Markets Privately Regulate Risk? The Development of Derivatives Clearing Houses and Recent Over-the-Counter Innovations. *Journal of Money, Credit and Banking*.

Kurant, M., & Thiran, P. (2006). Layered complex networks. *Physical Review Letters*, *138701*(96). doi:10.1103/PhysRevLett.96.138701 PMID:16712049

Kyriakopoulos, F., Thurner, S., Puhr, C., & Schmitz, S. W. (2009). Network and eigenvalue analysis of financial transaction networks. *The European Physical Journal B*, *71*(4), 523–531. doi:10.1140/epjb/e2009-00255-7

Laine, T., Korpinen, K., & Hellqvist, M. (2013). Simulation Approaches to Risk, Efficiency, and Liquidity Usage in Payment Systems. In B. Alexandrova-Kabadjova, S. Martinez-Jaramillo, A. Garcia-Almanza, & E. Tsang (Eds.), *Simulation in Computational Finance and Economics: Tools and Emerging Applications* (pp. 69–83). Hershey, PA: Business Science Reference; doi:10.4018/978-1-4666-2011-7.ch004

Laine, T., Nummelin, T., & Snellman, H. (2011). *Combining liquidity usage and interest rates on overnight loans: an oversight indicator*. Bank of Finland Publications.

Lannoo, K., & Valiante, D. (2009). Integrating Europe's Back Office: 10 Years of Turning in Circles. Retrieved from http://papers.ssrn.com/abstract=1416108

Lannoo, K., & Levin, M. (2002, January). The Securities Settlement Industry in the EU: Structure, Costs and the Way Forward. *CEPS Reports in Finance and Banking No.*, *26*, 1.

Lasaosa, A., & Tudela, M. (2007). Risks and efficiency gains of a tiered structure in large-value payments: a simulation approach (pp. 149–182). In H. Leinonen (Ed.), Simulation studies of liquidity needs, risks and efficiency in payment networks. Helsinki: Scientific Monographs.

Laverde, M., & Gutiérrez, J. (2012). *Cómo caracterizar entidades sistémicas?: medidas de Impacto Sistémico para Colombia (Temas de Estabilidad Financiera, No.65)*. Bogotá, Colombia: Banco de la República.

Lazarow, A. (2011), Lessons from International Central Counterparties: Benchmarking and Analysis. Bank of Canada Discussion Paper 2011-4

Ledrut, E. (2007). How can banks control their exposure to a failing participant? (pp. 227–252). In H. Leinonen (Ed.), Simulation studies of liquidity needs, risks and efficiency in payment networks. Helsinki: Scientific Monographs.

Lee, R. (2011). *Running the World's Markets. The Governance of Financial Infrastructure.*

Lee, K.-M., Kim, J. Y., Lee, S., & Goh, K.-I. (2014). Multiplex networks. In G. D'Agostino & A. Scala (Eds.), *Networks of networks: the last frontier of complexity* (pp. 53–72). Cham, Switzerland: Springer. doi:10.1007/978-3-319-03518-5_3

Leinonen, H., & Soramäki, K. (1999). Optimizing liquidity usage and settlement speed in payment systems. Bank of Finland Publications. Retrieved from http://www.suomenpankki.fi/fi/julkaisut/tutkimukset/keskustelualoitteet/Pages/dp1999_16.aspx

Leinonen, H., & Soramäki, K. (2003). Simulating interbank payment and securities settlement mechanisms with the BoF-PSS2 simulator. Bank of Finland Publications. Retrieved from http://www.suomenpankki.fi/fi/julkaisut/tutkimukset/keskustelualoitteet/Documents/0323.pdf

Leinonen, H., & Soramäki, K. (2005). Optimising Liquidity Usage and Settlement Speed in Payment Systems (pp. 117–151). In H. Leinonen (Ed.), Liquidity, risks and speed in payment and settlement systems: a simulation approach. Helsinki: Suomen Pankki.

Leinonen, H., & Soramäki, K. (2005). Optimising liquidity usage and settlement speed in payment systems. In H. Leinonen (Ed.), *Liquidity, risks and speed in payment and settlement systems - a simulation approach* (pp. 115-148). *Proceedings from the Bank of Finland Payment and Settlement System Seminars 2005.*

Leinonen, H. (2005). *Liquidity, risks and speed in payment and settlement systems – a simulation approach.Proceedings from the Bank of Finland Payment and Settlement System Seminars 2003*-2004. Bank of Finland.

Leinonen, H. (2007). *Simulation studies of liquidity needs, risks and efficiency in payment networks.Proceedings from the Bank of Finland Payment and Settlement System Seminars 2005*-2006. Bank of Finland.

León, C., & Pérez, J. (2014). Assessing financial market infrastructures' systemic importance with authority and hub centrality. *Journal of Financial Market Infrastructures*, *2*(3), 67–87.

León, C., Berndsen, R. J., & Renneboog, L. (2014). *Financial Stability and Interacting Networks of Financial Institutions and Market Infrastructures* (European Banking Center Discussion Paper Series No.2014-11). Tilburg: Tilburg University.

León, C., Berndsen, R., & Renneboog, L. (2014). Financial Stability and Interacting Networks of Financial Institutions and Market Infrastructures. *CentER Discussionpaper Series*, 69.

León, C., Machado, C., Cepeda, F., & Sarmiento, M. (2010). Systemic risk in large value payments systems in Colombia: a network topology and payments simulation approach (pp. 267–314). In M. Hellqvist & T. Laine (Ed.), Diagnostics for the financial markets–computational studies of payment system. Helsinki: Scientific Monographs.

León, C., & Berndsen, R. J. (2014). Rethinking financial stability: Challenges arising from financial networks' modular scale-free architecture. *Journal of Financial Stability*, *15*, 241–256. doi:10.1016/j.jfs.2014.10.006

León, C., & Pérez, J. (2014). Assessing financial market infrastructures' systemic importance with authority and hub centrality. *Journal of Financial Market Infrastructures.*, *3*(2), 67–87.

Levels. A& Capel, J. (2012, Fall). Is collateral becoming scarce? Evidence for the euro area. *Journal of Financial Market Infrastructures*, 1(1), 29-53.

Levine, R. (2005). Finance and growth: Theory, evidence, and mechanisms. In P. Aghion & S. Durlauf (Eds.), *The Handbook of Economic Growth*. Amsterdam: North Holland.

Lichtenstein, S., Fischhoff, B., & Phillips, L. D. (1982). Calibration of probabilities: The state of the art to 1980 (pp.306-334). In Kahneman D., Slovic P., Tversky A. (Eds.), *Judgment under uncertainty: Heuristics and biases.*

Lindenlaub, D., Burhop, C., & Scholtyseck, S. (Eds.). (2014). *Schlüsselereignisse der deutschen Bankengeschichte.* Stuttgart: Franz Steiner Verlag.

Links between Security Settlement Systems. (2014). European Central Bank. Retrieved from http://www.ecb.europa.eu/paym/coll/coll/ssslinks/html/index.en.html

Lovin, H. (2010). Systemically important participants in the ReGIS payment system (pp. 219–234). In M. Hellqvist & T. Laine (Ed.), Diagnostics for the financial markets–computational studies of payment system. Helsinki: Scientific Monographs.

Lovin, H., & Pineta, A. (2010). Operational risk in ReGIS – a systemically important payment system (pp. 315–340). In M. Hellqvist & T. Laine (Ed.), Diagnostics for the financial markets–computational studies of payment system. Helsinki: Scientific Monographs.

Luoto, J. (in press). An adaptive sequential Monte Carlo sampler for DSGE models. *Bank of Finland Publications.*

Macroeconomic impact assessment of OTC derivatives regulatory reforms BIS- MAGD. (2013). Bank for International Settlements and the Macroeconomic Assessment Group on Derivatives.

Madigan, P. (2014, June 19). Banks track US-facing business to avoid swap dealer tag. *Risk Magazine.* Retrieved from http://www.risk.net/risk-magazine/feature/2350345/banks-track-us-facing-business-to-avoid-swap-dealer-tag

Maijoor, S. (2014, May 7). Keynote *Speech. The reform of financial markets: halfway there.* Proceedings of AFME European Post-Trade Conference, London.

Making over-the counter-derivatives safer: the role of central counterparties. (April, 2010). *International Monetary Fund.*

Making Over-the-Counter Derivatives Safer: The Role of Central Counterparties. (2010, April). Global Financial Stability Report, International Monetary Fund (IMF).

Mancini, L., Ranaldo, A., & Wrampelmeyer, J. (2014). The Euro interbank repo market. *Swiss Finance Institute Research Paper,* 13-71.

Manning, M., Erlend, N., & Schanz, J. (Eds, 2009). The Economics of Large-Value Payments and Settlement: Theory and Policy Issues for Central Banks. Oxford: Oxford University Press.

Manning, M., Nier, E., & Schanz, J. (Eds.). (2009). *The economics of large-value payments and settlement: theory and policy issues for central banks.* Oxford University Press.

Manning, M., Nier, E., & Schanz, J. (Eds.). (2009). *The economics of large-value payments and settlement: Theory and policy issues for central banks.* Oxford: University Press.

Markose, S. (2012). *Systemic Risk from Global Financial Derivatives: A Network Analysis of Contagion and Its Mitigation with Super-Spreader Tax.* IMF Working Paper, 12/282

Markose, S. M., Giansante, S., & Rais Shaghaghi, A. (2012). Too interconnected to fail financial network of US CDS market: Topological fragility and systemic risk. *Journal of Economic Behavior & Organization, 83*(3), 627–646. doi:10.1016/j.jebo.2012.05.016

Martí, J. R. (2014). Multisystem simulation: analysis of critical infrastructures for disaster response. In G. D'Agostino & A. Scala (Eds.), *Networks of networks: the last frontier of complexity* (pp. 255–278). Cham, Switzerland: Springer. doi:10.1007/978-3-319-03518-5_12

Martin, A. & McAndrews, J. (2008). *An Economic Analysis of Liquidity-saving Mechanisms. Federal Reserve Bank of New York Economic Policy Review*, 14(2) Special Issue: The Economics of Payments, 25–39.

Martin, A., & McAndrew, J. (2008, September). An Economic Analysis of Liquidity-Saving Mechanisms: *FRBNY. Economic Policy Review.*

Martinez-Jaramillo, S. & Molina-Borboa, J.L., Bravo-Benitez, B. (2014). The Role of Financial Market Infrastructures in Financial Stability: An overview. *In this volume.*

Martínez-Jaramillo, S., Alexandrova-Kabadjova, B., Bravo-Benítez, B., & Solórzano-Margain, J. P. (2012). *An empirical study of the Mexican banking system's network and its implications for systemic risk* (Working Papers No.2012-17), México: Banco de México.

Martinez-Jaramillo, S., Alexandrova-Kabadjova, B., Bravo-Benitez, B., & Solórzano-Margain, J. P. (2014). An empirical study of the Mexican banking system's network and its implications for systemic risk. *Journal of Economic Dynamics & Control*, *40*, 242–265. doi:10.1016/j.jedc.2014.01.009

Martínez-Jaramillo, S., Pérez, O. P., Embriz, F. A., & Dey, F. L. G. (2010). Systemic risk, financial contagion and financial fragility. *Journal of Economic Dynamics & Control*, *34*(11), 2358–2374. doi:10.1016/j.jedc.2010.06.004

Massarenti, M., Petriconi, S., Lindner, J. (2012). Intraday patterns and Timing of T2 Interbank payments. *Journal of Financial Market Infrastructures*, 1/2, 3-23.

Massoud, N., Saunders, A., & Scholnick, B. (2011). The cost of being late? The case of credit card penalty fees. *Journal of Financial Stability*, *7*(2), 49–59. doi:10.1016/j.jfs.2009.12.001

May, R. M., Levin, S. A., & Sugihara, G. (2008). Ecology for bankers. *Nature*, *451*(7181), 893–895. doi:10.1038/451893a PMID:18288170

McAndrews, J., & Rajan, S. (2000). The timing and funding of Fedwire funds transfers. *Economic Policy Review*, *6*(2), 17–32.

McDonald, J. B. (1984). Some generalized functions for the size distribution of income. *Econometrica*, *52*(3), 647–665. doi:10.2307/1913469

McLafferty, J., & Denbee, E. (2013). Liquidity Saving in CHAPS: A Simulation Study. In B. Alexandrova-Kabadjova, S. Martinez-Jaramillo, A. Garcia-Almanza, & E. Tsang (Eds.), *Simulation in Computational Finance and Economics: Tools and Emerging Applications* (pp. 120–142). Hershey, PA: Business Science Reference; doi:10.4018/978-1-4666-2011-7.ch007

McVanel, D. (2007). The impact of unanticipated defaults in Canada's Large Value Transfer System (pp. 253–282). In H. Leinonen (Ed.), Simulation studies of liquidity needs, risks and efficiency in payment networks. Helsinki: Scientific Monographs.

Memorandum of cooperation related to the supervision of cross-border covered entities. (2014, March 10). U.S. Commodity Futures Trading Commission & Financial Services Agency of Japan. Retrieved from http://www.cftc.gov/ucm/groups/public/@internationalaffairs/documents/file/cftc-jfsamoc031014.pdf

Memorandum of understanding concerning cooperation and the exchange of information related to the supervision of cross-border covered entities. (2014, March 25). *U.S. Commodity Futures Trading Commission, Alberta Securities Commission, British Columbia Securities Commission, Ontario Securities Commission, & Autorite des marches financiers.* Retrieved from http://www.cftc.gov/ucm/groups/public/@internationalaffairs/documents/file/asc-bcsc-osc-amfmou032514.pdf

Mercier and Sauer. (2013). Optimal central securities depository reshaping toward TARGET2-Securities. *Journal of Financial Market Infrastructures*, *2*(2), 3–51.

Michie, R. (2006). *The global securities market: a history*. Oxford University Press. doi:10.1093/acprof:oso/9780199280612.001.0001

Milne, A. (2007a). Competition and the rationalization of European securities clearing and settlement. In D. G. Mayes & G. E. Wood (Eds.), The Structure of Financial Regulation (p. 370–). Taylor & Francis (Routledge). doi:10.4324/9780203962312.ch12

Milne, A. (2009). The Fall of the House of Credit (p. 380). Cambridge, UK: Cambridge University Press. Retrieved from http://www.cambridge.org/gb/knowledge/isbn/item2428039/?site_locale=en_GB doi:10.1017/CBO9780511596643

Milne, A. (2005). *Standard setting and competition in securities settlement (No. 23-2005)*. Helsinki: Bank of Finland.

Milne, A. (2007b). The industrial organization of post-trade clearing and settlement. *Journal of Banking & Finance*, *31*(10), 2945–2961. doi:10.1016/j.jbankfin.2007.03.002

Milne, A. (2012). OTC central counterparty clearing: Myths and reality. *Journal of Risk Management in Financial Institutions*, *5*(3), 335–346.

Mollenkamp, C., Podkul, C., & Toonkel, J. (2012, January). Persistent trade failure problem gets partial fix. *Reuters*. Retrieved from http://www.ft.com/cms/s/0/97ff6658-d87b-11e0-8f0a-00144feabdc0.html#axzz3EifgnBQU

Monitoring indicators for intraday liquidity management [Consultative document]. (2012). Basel Committee on Banking Supervision, Bank for International Settlements.

Monitoring indicators for intraday liquidity management. (2012, July). *Bank for International Settlements*. Retrieved from http://www.bis.org/publ/bcbs225.pdf

Monitoring tools for intraday liquidity management. (2013). Basel Committee on Banking Supervision, Bank for International Settlements.

Montagna, M., & Kok, C. (2013). *Multi-layer interbank model for assessing systemic risk* (Kiel Working Papers No.1873). Kiel, Germany, Kiel Institute for the World Economy.

Morris, V. B., & Goldstein, S. Z. (2010). *The Life Cycle of a Security*. Lighbulb Press. Retrieved from http://www.dtcc.com/~/media/Files/Downloads/Settlement-Asset-Services/Underwriting/LCoaS.pdf

Moser, J. (1998). Contracting Innovations and the Evolution of Clearing and Settlement Methods at Futures Exchanges, *Federal Reserve Bank of Chicago Working Paper Series*, No. 1998-26

Moser, J. T. (1998). Contracting innovations and the evolution of clearing and settlement methods at futures exchanges. Federal Reserve Bank of Chicago working paper, No. WP-1998-26.

Moser, J. T. (1998). Contracting Innovations and the Evolution of Clearing and Settlement Methods at Futures Exchanges. *Federal Reserve Bank of Chicago Working Papers Series Research Department* (WP-98-26).

Moskow, M. H. (2006, April 4). Public policy and central counterparty clearing. Proceedings of Issues Related to Central Counterparty Clearing. Frankfurt, Germany.

Murphy, D. (2013). *OTC Derivatives: Bilateral Trading and Central Clearing*. Hampshire, UK: Palgrave Macmillan.

Murphy, D. (2013). *OTC Derivatives: Bilateral Trading and Central Clearing: An Introduction to Regulatory Policy, Market Impact and Systemic Risk*. Palgrave Macmillan. doi:10.1057/9781137293862

Nakajima, M. (2008). Global Trends of Payment Systems and the Next-Generation RTGS Project in Japan. In T. Kubota (Ed.), Cyberlaw for Global E-Business: Finance, Payment, and Dispute Resolution (pp. 109–127). Hershey, PA: IGI Global. doi:10.4018/978-1-59904-828-4.ch006

Nakajima, M. (2011). Payment System Technologies and Functions: Innovations and Development. Hershey, PA: IGI Global. doi:10.4018/978-1-61520-645-2

Nakajima, M. (2012, February-March). *The Evolution of Payment Systems: The European Financial Review* (pp. 8–9).

Nakajima, M., & Shukuwa, J. (2013). *All about Payment Systems* (3rd ed.) [in Japanese]. Tokyo, Japan: Toyo Keizai Inc.

NASDAQ. (n.d.). Historical Market Data. Retrieved from http://www.nasdaqomx.com/transactions/markets/nlx/marketdata/historic-market-data

New developments in clearing and settlement arrangements for OTC derivatives. (2007, March). Committee on Payment and Settlement Systems. Retrieved from http://www.bis.org/publ/cpss77.pdf

Newman, M. E. J. (2010). *Networks: an Introduction*. Oxford: Oxford University Press. doi:10.1093/acprof:oso/9780199206650.001.0001

Newman, M. E. J., Barabási, A.-L., & Watts, D. J. (2006). *The structure and dynamics of networks*. Princeton: Princeton University Press.

Nicaud (2012) *Payment systems, design, governance and oversight, edited by Bruce J. Summers*, Central banking Publications, London

Norman, B. (2010, *May*). Liquidity Saving in Real-Time Gross Settlement Systems — An Overview. *Bank of England Financial Stability Paper No.7.*

Norman, B., Shaw, R., & Speight, G. (2011). *The history of interbank settlement arrangements: exploring central banks' role in the payment system.* Bank of England Working Paper 412.

Norman, B. (2010).*Liquidity saving in real-time gross settlement systems – an overview. Bank of England Financial Stability Paper, 7,*1–11. Bank of England Publications.

Norman, P. (2007). *Plumbers and Visionaries: Securities Settlement and Europe's Financial Market*. Chichester: John Wiley & Sons.

Norman, P. (2008). *Plumbers and Visionaries*. Securities Settlement and Europe's Financial Market.

Norman, P. (2011). *The Risk Controllers. Central Counterparty Clearing in Globalised Financial Markets*. UK: John Wiley and Sons.

Norman, P. (2011). *The Risk Controllers: Central Counterparty Clearing in Globalised Financial Markets*. Chichester: John Wiley & Sons.

Norman, P. (2012). *The Risk Controllers*. Central Counterparty Clearing in Globalised Financial Markets.

North, M. (2009). *Kleine Geschichte des Geldes: Vom Mittelalter bis heute*. München: C.H. Beck.

Oehmke, M., & Zawadowski, A. (2012). *The Anatomy of the CDS Market* [Working Paper].

Oleschak, R., & Nellen, T. (2010). Does SIC need a heart pacemaker? (pp. 341–378). In M. Hellqvist & T. Laine (Ed.), Diagnostics for the financial markets–computational studies of payment system. Helsinki: Scientific Monographs.

Oleschak, R., & Nellen, T. (2013, *October*). Does SIC need a heart pacemaker? *Swiss National Bank Working Papers.*

Oliver, R., & Weiner, S. E. (2010). The Role of Central Banks in Retail Payments: The Central Bank as Operator. In *The Changing Retail Payments Landscape: What Role For Central Banks?* (pp. 199–216). Kansas City: The Federal Reserve Bank of Kansas City.

Ossolinski, C., Lam, T., & Emery, D. (2014). *The Changing Way We Pay: Trends in Consumer Payments.* Reserve Bank of Australia Research Discussion Paper, RDP2014-5.

OTC Derivatives Market Reforms Eighth Progress Report on Implementation. (2014, November 7). *Financial Stability Board.* Retrieved from http://www.financialstabilityboard.org/2014/11/eighth-progress-report-on-implementation-of-otc-derivatives-market-reforms/

Overview of Progress in the Implementation of the G20 Recommendations for Strengthening Financial Stability. Report of the Financial Stability Board to G20 Leaders. (2012, June 19). *Financial Stability Board.* Retrieved from http://www.financialstabilityboard.org/publications/r_120619a.pdf

Oxera (2011) *Monitoring prices, costs and volumes of trading and post-trading services, report prepared for the European Commission DG internal market and services*, Oxford and Brussels. Available: http://ec.europa.eu/internal_market/financial-markets/docs/clearing/2011_oxera_study_en.pdf

Oxera (2011). Monitoring Prices, Costs and Volumes of Trading and Post-trading Services, Report prepared for the European Commission DG Internal Market and Services, May.

Padget, J. F., & Powell, W. W. (2012). The Problem of Emergence. In J. F. Padget & W. W. Powell (Eds.), *The Emergence of Organizations and Markets* (pp. 2–29). Princeton: Princeton University Press.

Pahwa, S., Youssed, M., & Scoglio, C. (2014). Electrical networks: an introduction. In G. D'Agostino & A. Scala (Eds.), *Networks of networks: the last frontier of complexity* (pp. 163–186). Cham, Switzerland: Springer. doi:10.1007/978-3-319-03518-5_8

Papadimitriou, C. H. (1994). *Computational Complexity*. Addison Wesley.

Payment and Settlement Systems Report 2009 . (2010). Bank of Japan.

Payment and Settlement Systems Report 2012-2013 . (2013). Bank of Japan.

Payment Systems in Denmark, Chapter 2: Payment Systems in a Historical Perspective. (2005). Danmarks Nationalbank. København: Danmarks Nationalbank.

Payment Systems Worldwide: A Snapshot. (2011World Bank - Financial Infrastructure Series.

Payment, clearing and settlement systems in the CPSS countries, Volume 1. Committee on Payment and Settlement Systems. (2011, September). Basel, Switzerland: Bank for International Settlements.

Peltonen, T. A., Scheicher, M., & Vuillemey, G. (2013). *The network structure of the CDS market and its determinants.* ECB Working Paper, 1583

Pericoli, M., & Sbracia, M. (2003). A Primer on Financial Contagion. *Journal of Economic Surveys. Wiley Blackwell, 17*(4), 571–608.

Petterson, J. (2005). Simulation of liquidity levels and delays in the Swedish RIX system (pp. 218–228). In H. Leinonen (Ed.), Liquidity, risks and speed in payment and settlement systems: a simulation approach. Helsinki: Suomen Pankki.

Pirrong, C. (2005). Bund for Glory, or, It's a Long Way to Tip a Market, University of Houston Department of Finance, 8 March.

Pirrong, C. (2011). The Economics of Central Clearing: Theory and Practice, *ISDA Discussion Paper Series*, No. 1, May

Pirrong, C. (2011, May). The Economics of Central Clearing: Theory and Practice. ISDA Discussion Paper.

Pirrong, C. (2012). Clearing and Collateral Mandates: A New Liquidity Trap? *Journal of Applied Corporate Finance*, *24*(1), 67–73. doi:10.1111/j.1745-6622.2012.00366.x

Pirrong, C. (2013). Financial Exchanges. *Competition and Vertical Integration in Financial Exchanges Competition Policy International*, *7*(2), 90–102.

Powell, J (2014). A Financial System Perspective on Central Clearing of Derivatives, Speech, Board of Governors of the Federal Reserve System, November.

Principles for financial market infrastructures – consultative report. (2011, March). *Bank for International Settlements*. Retrieved from http://www.bis.org/publ/cpss94.pdf

Principles for financial market infrastructures. (2012, April). *Committee on Payment and Settlement Systems and the Technical Committee of the International Organization of Securities Commission.* Retrieved from http://www.bis.org/publ/cpss101a.pdf

Principles for financial market infrastructures. (2012a). CPSS-IOSCO. Bank for International Settlements.

Principles for Financial Market Infrastructures. (2012Committee on Payment & Settlement Systems. Basel, Switzerland: Bank for International Settlements.

Principles for financial market infrastructures. (2012BIS. Basel, Switzerland. *CPPS-IOSCO*, *5-9*, 13.

Principles for financial market infrastructures: Disclosure framework and Assessment methodology. (2012b). CPSS-IOSCO. Bank for International Settlements.

Principles for the Supervision of Banks' Foreign Establishments. (1983, May). *Basel Committee on Banking Supervision*. Retrieved from http://www.bis.org/publ/bcbsc312.pdf

Pröpper, M., Lelyveld, I., & Heijmans, R. (2008). *Towards a network description of interbank payment flows* (DNB Working Paper, No.177). Amsterdam: De Nederlandsche Bank (DNB).

Pröpper, M., Van Lelyveld, I., & Heijmans, R. (2013). Network Dynamics of TOP Payments Measuring free riding in large-value payment systems: The case of TARGET2. *The Journal of Financial Market Infrastructures*, *1*(3), 3–29.

Quinn, S., & Roberds, W. (2005). The Big Problem of Large Bills: The Bank of Amsterdam and the Origins of Central Banking. *Federal Reserve Bank of Atlanta Working Paper,* 16.

Quinn, S., & Roberds, W. (2006). An Economic Explanation of the Early Bank of Amsterdam, Debasement, Bills of Exchange, and the Emergence of the First Central Bank. *Federal Reserve Bank of Atlanta Working Paper,* 13.

RBA (2014). *Submission to the Financial System Inquiry*, March.

Real-Time Gross Settlement Systems Report . (1997, March). Bank for International Settlements.

Real-time gross settlement systems. (1997, March). Committee on Payment and Settlement Systems. Basel, Switzerland: Bank for International Settlements.

Recommendations for securities settlement systems. (2001BIS. Basel, Switzerland: CPSS-IOSCO.

Recovery and resolution of financial market infrastructures. (2012, July). Committee on Payment and Settlement Systems and the Board of the International Organization of Securities Commission. Retrieved from http://www.bis.org/cpmi/publ/d103.pdf

Recovery and Resolution Planning: Making the Key Attributes Requirements Operational. (2012, November). *Financial Stability Board.*

Rehlon, A. (2013). Central counterparties: What are they, why do they matter and how does the Bank supervise them? *Quarterly Bulletin*, Q2-2013.

Rehlon, A., & Nixon, D. (2013). Central counterparties: What are they, why do they matter and how does the Bank supervise them? Bank of England. *Quarterly Bulletin, 2013*, Q2.

Rempel, M. (2014). *Improving Overnight Loan Identification in Payments Systems.* Bank of Canada Working Paper 2014-25.

Renault, F. (2010). Concentration Risk and the Optimal Number of Central Counterparties for a Single Asset, *Banque de France Financial Stability Review*, No. 14, July, 169–176

Renault, F., & Pecceu, J. (2007). From PNS to TARGET2: the cost of FIFO in RTGS payment systems (pp. 41–86). In H. Leinonen (Ed.), Simulation studies of liquidity needs, risks and efficiency in payment networks. Helsinki: Scientific Monographs.

Renault, F., & Pecceu, J. B. (2007). From PNS to TARGET2: the cost of FIFO in RTGS payment system. In H. Leinonen (Ed.), *Simulation studies of liquidity needs, risks and efficiency in payment networks* (pp. 43-85). Bank of Finland Publications.

Renault, F., Beyeler, W. E., Glass, R. J., Soramäki, K., & Bech, M. L. (2007, November). *Congestion and Cascades in Coupled Payment Systems.* Paper presented at the joint European Central Bank-Bank of England conference on Payments and Monetary and Financial Stability, Frankfurt, Germany.

Report of the OTC Derivatives Regulators Group (ODRG) on Cross-Border Implementation Issues. (2014). OTC Derivatives Regulators Group. Retrieved from http://www.esma.europa.eu/system/files/2014-03-odrg_odrg_report_to_the_g20_march_2014.pdf

Revised good practice principles for supervisory colleges. (2014, January). *Basel Committee on Banking Supervision.* Retrieved from http://www.bis.org/publ/bcbs276.pdf

Riksbank. (2002). Central counterparty clearing for the securities market. Financial Stability Report 2.

Ripatti, K. (2004). Central counterparty clearing: constructing a framework for evaluation of risks and benefits. *Bank of Finland discussion papers.*

Rochet, J.-C., & Tirole, J. (2002). Cooperation among competitors: Some economics of payment card associations. *The Rand Journal of Economics*, *33*(4), 549–570. doi:10.2307/3087474

Rochet, J.-C., & Tirole, J. (2003). Platform Competition in Two-Sided Markets. *Journal of the European Economic Association*, *1*(4), 990–1029. doi:10.1162/154247603322493212

Rochet, J.-C., & Tirole, J. (2011). Must-take cards: Merchant discounts and avoided costs. *Journal of the European Economic Association*, *9*(3), 462–495. doi:10.1111/j.1542-4774.2011.01020.x

Rochet, J.-C., & Wright, J. (2010). Credit card interchange fees. *Journal of Banking & Finance*, *34*(8), 1788–1797. doi:10.1016/j.jbankfin.2010.02.026

Rome, E., Langeslag, P., & Usov, A. (2014). Federated modeling and simulation for critical infrastructure protection. In G. D'Agostino & A. Scala (Eds.), *Networks of networks: the last frontier of complexity* (pp. 225–253). Cham, Switzerland: Springer. doi:10.1007/978-3-319-03518-5_11

Rouchier, J., & Tanimura, E. (2012). When overconfident agents slow down collective learning. *Simulation, 88*(1), 33–49. doi:10.1177/0037549711428948

Rowady, E. Jr. (2010). *The Global Risk Transfer Market: Developments in OTC and Exchange-Traded Derivatives. Presentation*. TABB Group.

RTGS[plus]: the Bundesbank's New System for Individual Payments. (2000, June). *Deutsche Bundesbank Monthly Report.*

Russo, D. (2013, April). CPSS-IOSCO principles for financial market infrastructures: vectors of international convergence. European Central Bank. Banque de France. *Financial Stability Review, 17.*

Russo, D., (2013). CPSS-IOSCO Principles for financial market infrastructures: vectors of international convergence, Banque de France, *Financial Stability Review*, 17.

Russo, J. E., & Schoemaker, P. J. (1992). Managing overconfidence. *Sloan Management Review, 33*(2), 7–17. PMID:10120627

Rutz, R. D. (1989). Clearance, Payment, and Settlement Systems in the Futures, Options, and Stock Markets. *Board of Trade Clearing Corporation, Chicago, IL.*

Saade, A. (2010, September). *Estructura de red del Mercado Electrónico Colombiano (MEC) e identificación de agentes sistémicos según criterios de centralidad* (Reporte de Estabilidad Financiera). Bogotá, Colombia: Banco de la República.

Sandhusen, R. L. (2000). *Marketing*. Barron's Educational Series (3rd ed.).

Santos, T., & Schienkman, J. (2001). Competition Among Exchanges. *The Quarterly Journal of Economics, 116*(3), 1027–1061.

Schmidt, H. (2014). Die Entstehung der Deutschen Terminbörse 1988. In: Lindenlaub et al 414-440.

Schmiedel and Schönenberger. (2005) Integration of securities market infrastructures in the Euro Area. Occasional paper series ECB, Frankfurt, 20-21

Schmiedel, H., Kostova, G., & Ruttenberg, W. (2012). *The social and private costs of retail payment instruments. A European perspective.* ECB Occasional Paper Series, No. 137.

Schmitz, S. (2006, November). How payment systems affect monetary policy. Central Banking, 17, N 2.

Schmitz, S. W., & Puhr, C. (2007). Risk concentration, network structure and contagion in the Austrian Real Time Interbank Settlement System (pp. 183–226). In H. Leinonen (Ed.), Simulation studies of liquidity needs, risks and efficiency in payment networks. Helsinki: Scientific Monographs.

Schmitz, S. (2006). How payment systems affect monetary policy. *Central Banking, 17*(2), 65.

Schuh, S. D., Shy, O., & Stavins, J. (2010).*Who gains and who loses from credit card payments? Theory and calibrations*. FRB of Boston Public Policy Discussion Paper 10-3.

Schulz, C. (2011, February). *Liquidity requirements and payment delays. Participant type dependent preferences*. European Central Bank Working Paper Series No 1291.

Schweitzer, F., Fagiolo, G., Sornette, D., Vega-Redondo, F., Vespignani, A., & White, D. R. (2009). Economic networks: The new challenges. *Science, 325*, 422–425. doi:10.1126/science.1173644 PMID:19628858

SEC. (2011). *Impact of Recent SHO Rule Changes on Fails to Deliver* (p. 18). Retrieved from http://www.sec.gov/spotlight/shortsales/failsmemo042511.pdf

Second report on EU clearing and settlement arrangements. Directorate-General for Economic and Financial Affairs. (2003Giovannini Group. European Commission.

Securities trading, clearing, central counterparties and settlement in EU 25 – an overview of current arrangements. (2005, June). London School of Economics.

Serguieva, A. (2013, May). Systemic risk identification, modelling, analysis, and monitoring: An integrated approach, *Working Paper arXiv: general finance / computational engineering, finance and science*, 1310.6486, 1–19. Retrieved from http://arxiv.org/ftp/arxiv/papers/1310/1310.6486.pdf

Settlement Fails Report on Securities Settlement Systems (SSS) Measures To Ensure Timely Settlement (p. 9). (2011). ECB. Retrieved from https://www.ecb.europa.eu/pub/pdf/other/settlementfails042011en.pdf

Sheffield, H. (2014, July 7). Cross-border harmonisation threatened as MTF talks fall apart. *Global Capital*. Retrieved from http://www.globalcapital.com/article/m437mkgjc3p8/cross-border-harmonisation-threatened-as-mtf-talks-fall-apart

Shefrin, H., & Nicols, C. M. (2014). Credit card behavior, financial styles, and heuristics. *Journal of Business Research*, *67*(8), 1679–1687. doi:10.1016/j.jbusres.2014.02.014

Shefrin, H., & Thaler, R. H. (1988). The behavioral life-cycle hypothesis. *Economic Inquiry*, *26*(4), 609–643. doi:10.1111/j.1465-7295.1988.tb01520.x

Short selling. (2012). ESMA. Retrieved from http://www.esma.europa.eu/page/Short-selling

Singh, M. (2010). *Collateral, Netting and Systemic Risk in the OTC Derivatives Market*. Working Paper, International Monetary Fund.

Singh, M. (2011). *Velocity of Pledged Collateral: Analysis and Implications*. Working Paper, International Monetary Fund.

Single shared platform: user detailed functional specifications (Version 8.0). (2014). Deutsche Bundesbank, Banque de France and Banca d'Italia.

Skyrm, S. E. D. (2012). *The history of central counterparties*. Retrieved from http://scottskyrm.com/2012/11/the-history-of-central-counter-parties/

Soramäki, K. & Cook, S. (2013). SinkRank: an algorithm for identifying systemically important banks in payment systems. *Economics: The Open-Access, Open-Assessment E-Journal, 2013-28 (7)*.10.5018/economics-ejournal.ja.2013-28

Soramäki, K., Bech, M. L., Arnold, J., Glass, R. J. & Beyeler, W. E. (2006, March). The topology of interbank payment flows. *Federal Reserve Bank of New York Staff Reports*, 243.

Soramäki, K., Bech, M., Arnold, J., Glass, R., & Beyeler, W. (2006). *The Topology of Interbank Payment Flows*. Federal Reserve Bank of New York Staff Report No. 243.

Soramäki, K., Bech, M., Arnold, J., Glass, R., & Beyeler, W. (2006). *The topology of interbank payments flow* (Federal Reserve Bank of New York Staff Report No 243). New York: Federal Reserve Bank of New York.

Staff Guidance on Swaps Straight-Through Processing. (2013, September 26). U.S. Commodity and Futures Commission.

Stafford, P. (2013a). UK Gives Green Light to EuroCCP-EMCF Deal, *Financial Times*, 21 October.

Stafford, P. (2013b). EuroCCP cuts settlement feeds for UK and Irish Stocks, *Financial Times*, 12 August.

Stafford, P. (2014). LSE to Allow Customers to Clear Trades on EuroCCP, *Financial Times*, 21 May.

Standards of Risk Management Controls used by Central Counterparty Clearing Houses. (2001, November). European Association of CCP Clearing Houses.

Stango, V. (2003). Strategic responses to regulatory threat in the credit card market. *The Journal of Law & Economics*, *46*(2), 427–452. doi:10.1086/377291

Stango, V., & Zinman, J. (2009). What do consumers really pay on their checking and credit card accounts? Explicit, implicit, and avoidable costs. *The American Economic Review*, *99*(2), 424–429. doi:10.1257/aer.99.2.424

Steigerwald, R.S. (2014). *Financial Market Infrastructure: Selected References*. An Introduction to the Literature on Payment Systems, Trade Execution Facilities and Post-Trade Clearing and Settlement Systems. Federal Reserve Bank of Chicago, Financial Markets Group, mimeo.

Straffin, P. D. (1980). Algebra in geography: Eigenvectors of networks. *Mathematics Magazine*, *5*(5), 269–276. doi:10.2307/2689388

Strengthening Oversight and Regulation of Shadow Banking. (2013). FSB. *Policy Framework for Addressing Shadow Banking Risks in Securities Lending and Repos,* 20 -21.

Strogatz, S. (2003). *SYNC: how order emerges from chaos in the universe, nature and daily life*. New York: Hyperion.

Summers, B. (Ed.). (2012). *Payment Systems: Design, Governance and Oversight*. London: Central Banking Publications.

Supervisory framework for measuring and controlling large exposures - final standard. (2014BIS. Basel Committee on Banking Supervision.

SWIFT. (2012). *The SWIFT Index*. Mimeo.

T2S Framework Agreement (2012) Retrieved from http://www.ecb.europa.eu/paym/t2s/pdf/csd_FA/T2S_Framework_Agreement_Schedules.pdf??136c1c40cce184cf0474fcea50179129

T2S User Requirement Document 5.3 (2014) Retrieved from http://www.ecb.europa.eu/paym/t2s/pdf/urd_v5-03.pdf??c11cd4527ac7dc75c315924e60cc3277

T2S website: http://www.ecb.europa.eu/paym/t2s/html/index.en.html

Tafara, E., & Peterson, R. J. (2007). A Blueprint for Cross-Border Access to U.S. Investors: A New International Framework. *Harvard International Law Journal*, *48*(1), 32–68.

Target-2 Securities. (2014). ECB. Retrieved from http://www.ecb.europa.eu/paym/t2s/html/index.en.html

TARGET2 Single Shared Platform: User Detailed Functional Specifications. (2013). European Central Bank.

Taylor, A., & Higham, D. J. (2009). CONTEST: A controllable test matrix toolbox for MATLAB.[TOMS]. *ACM Transactions on Mathematical Software*, *35*(4), 26. doi:10.1145/1462173.1462175

TecHiLa Technologies. (2009). http://www.techila.fi/wp-content/uploads/2010/07/Tampere_University_of_Technology.pdf

Technical advice on third country equivalence under EMIR – US [Final report]. (2013, September 1). European Securities and Markets Authority. Retrieved from http://www.esma.europa.eu/system/files/2013-1157_technical_advice_on_third_country_regulatory_equivalence_under_emir_us.pdf

Telser, L. (1981). Margins and Futures Contracts. *Journal of Futures Markets*, *1*(2), 225–253.

Telyukova, I. A., & Wright, R. (2008). A model of money and credit, with application to the credit card debt puzzle. *The Review of Economic Studies*, *75*(2), 629–647. doi:10.1111/j.1467-937X.2008.00487.x

Thaler, R. H. (1999). Mental accounting matters. *Journal of Behavioral Decision Making*, *12*(3), 183–206. doi:10.1002/(SICI)1099-0771(199909)12:3<183::AID-BDM318>3.0.CO;2-F

The 2013 Federal Reserve Payments Study. (2014). Federal Reserve System.

The Bank of England's approach to the supervision of financial market infrastructures (2013, April). Bank of England.

The Code of Conduct on clearing and settlement: three years of experience, Financial Services Policy and Financial Markets, Brussels. ECOFIN. (2009). European Commission. Retrieved from http://ec.europa.eu/internal_market/financial-markets/docs/code/2009-11-06-code-report-ecofin_en.pdf

The Direct Costs of Clearing and Settlement: An EU-US Comparison. (2004). NERA Economic Consulting. London: Coproation of London. Retrieved from http://www.cityoflondon.gov.uk/business/economic-research-and-information/research-publications/Documents/2007-2000/direct-costs-of-clearing-and-settlement-executive-summary.pdf

The Global Association of Central Counterparties). (2009), The Value of Proposition of Central Counterparty Clearing Houses, Working Paper

The interdependencies of payment and settlement systems. (2008, June). *Bank for International Settlements*. Retrieved from http://www.bis.org/publ/cpss84.pdf

The Payment System. (2010European Central Bank.

The role of central bank money in payment systems. (2003). Committee on Payment and Settlement Systems.

The role of margin requirements and haircuts in procyclicality. (2010). CGFS. Retrieved from http://www.bis.org/publ/cgfs36.pdf

The SWIFT Index [Technical description]. (2012). SWIFT.

The TARGET2 simulator. (2013, December). *Target Newsletter*, 7. Retrieved from https://www.ecb.europa.eu/paym/t2/shared/pdf/newsletter/TARGET_Newsletter_issue_number_7.pdf

The Work of the Clearing and Settlement Advisory and Monitoring Experts' Group, Brussels. (2008). CESAME. Retrieved from http://ec.europa.eu/internal_market/financial-markets/docs/cesame/cesame_report_en.pdf

Thier, A. (2014). Die Gründung der Königlichen Giro- und Lehnbanco 1765. In: Lindenlaub et al, 63-78.

Tinkler, K. J. (1972). The physical interpretation of eigenfunctions of dichotomous matrices. *Transactions of the Institute of British Geographers*, *55*(55), 17–46. doi:10.2307/621721

Tölö, E., Jokivuolle, E., & Virén, M. (2014). *Do private signals of a bank's creditworthiness predict the bank's CDS price? Evidence from the Eurosystem's overnight loan rates*. Bank of Finland Research Discussion Paper No. 9.

TOM (The Order Machine) (n.d). Statistics. Retrieved from http://tommtf.eu/statistics/

Tsuchiya, S. (2013). The Effects of Settlement Methods on Liquidity Needs: Empirical Study based on Funds Transfer Data: *Bank of Japan Working Paper Series, No.13-E-2*

Tsuchiya, S. (2013). The effects of settlement methods on liquidity needs in Japan: An empirical study based on funds-transfer data from BOJ-NET. *Journal of Financial Market Infrastructures*, *1*(4), 109–131.

Tucker, P. (2013). Central Counterparties in Evolving Capital Markets: Safety, Recovery and Resolution *Banque de France Financial Stability Review*, No. 17, April, 179–184

Tucker, P. (2014, April 11). Are clearinghouses the new central banks? Proceedings of the Over-the-counter Symposium. Chicago, Il.

U.S. Commodity Futures Trading Commission. (2013, July 11). *Cross-Border Regulation of Swaps/Derivatives Discussions between the Commodity Futures Trading Commission and the European*

U.S. credit card abs performance may be nearing plateau [Press release] Fitch-Ratings. (2011, October 11). Retrieved from http://www.fitchratings.com/creditdesk/pressreleases/detail.cfm?prid=730344

UK Government (2014). *Consultation Outcome – Secondary Legislation for Non-Bank Resolution Regimes*, June

Union – A Path Forward. (n. d.). *Commodity Futures Trading Commission*. Retrieved from http://www.cftc.gov/PressRoom/PressReleases/pr6640-13

Verdier, M. (2011). Interchange fees in payment card systems: A survey of the literature. *Journal of Economic Surveys*, *25*(2), 273–297. doi:10.1111/j.1467-6419.2009.00607.x

Virtual currency schemes . (2012). European Central Bank.

Watts, D. J. (2003). *Small Worlds: The dynamics of networks between order and randomness*. Princeton University Press.

Wendt, F. (2006). Intraday Margining of Central Counterparties: EU Practice and Theoretical Evaluation of Benefits and Costs. *De Nederlandsche Bank Working Paper No. 107.*

Wendt, F. (2015). Central Counterparties: Addressing their Too Important to Fail Nature. *International Monetary Fund Working Paper 15/21.*

Williamson, O. E. (1981, November). The Economics of Organization: The Transaction Cost Approach. *American Journal of Sociology*, *87*(3), 548–577. doi:10.1086/227496

Wright, J. (2004). Determinants of optimal interchange fees in payment systems. *The Journal of Industrial Economics*, *52*(1), 1–26. doi:10.1111/j.0022-1821.2004.00214.x

Yang, S., Markoczy, L., & Qi, M. (2007). Unrealistic optimism in consumer credit card adoption. *Journal of Economic Psychology*, *28*(2), 170–185. doi:10.1016/j.joep.2006.05.006

Zhu, S. (2011). Is There a "Race to the Bottom" in Central Counterparties Competition? De Nederlandsche Bank Occasional Studies Vol 9 No 6.

Zinman, J. (2007). *Household borrowing high and lending low under no-arbitrage*. Darthmore College Working Papers.

About the Contributors

Martin Diehl is currently payment system analyst with the Deutsche Bundesbank. His analysis covers mainly TARGET2 and related issues. He is particularly interested in simulations, liquidity efficiency issues and topology of the payment system network. He is a trained economist (Diplom-Volkswirt and M.A. econ.) and philosopher and got his PH.D. from University Gießen, Germany. He joined Deutsche Bundesbank in 1998 as an economist. After five years as head of the speech writing group for the president he was seconded to the embassy in Beijing, serving as a representative of Deutsche Bundesbank to China. In 2008, he joined the department for payment and settlement systems in Deutsche Bundesbank.

Biliana Alexandrova-Kabadjova has been working at the Banco de México since 1997 and currently she is a payment systems analyst. She is a member of the Mexican National System of Researchers since 2009 and is a Visiting Fellow at the University of Essex. Her main contribution has been to build the most advanced model (in terms of complexity and realism) of the payment card market. Further, in relation to financial market infrastructures, she has developed a framework under which one can learn about how the intraday liquidity flows. Alexandrova-Kabadjova has published several refereed journal papers and book chapters, and has co-edited the books "Simulation in Computational Finance and Economics: Tools and emerging applications" and "Analyzing the Economics of Financial Market Infrastructures." She obtained her first degree with honors on Information Systems at the Instituto Tencologico y de Estudios Superiores de Monterrey, CCM in 1996. She received her Ph.D. in Computational Finance from the CCFEA from the University of Essex, UK in 2007. Her main research interests are in intraday liquidity, network analysis of market infrastructures and in agent-based computational economics.

Richar Heuver is a statistician in the payments division of the Dutch central bank since 1996. He was involved in the development of the data warehouse of the Dutch Large Value Payment System, closely monitoring statistics during the introduction of the cash euro in 2002. Afterward, he was more actively participating in the research on Large Value Payment Systems. His research focusses on stress scenario analysis, network topology, the interbank money market and identifying behavioural aspects and signs of liquidity problems with banks. Heuver graduated in physical education in 1985 and because of market prognoses started working for the central bank as a statistician in the Economics and Research Department. Since then he moved between several departments, always heavily involved in business intelligence and analysis of financial banking data.

Serafin Martinez-Jaramillo is a senior financial researcher at the financial stability general directorate at Banco de México. His research interests are: financial stability, systemic risk, financial networks, bankruptcy prediction and machine learning. He developed an agent-based financial market to study the link between agent behavior and the stylized facts in stock markets returns. Serafin has published book chapters, encyclopedia entries and papers in high impact international journals like: IEEE Transactions on Evolutionary Computation; the Journal of Economic Dynamics and Control, the Journal of Financial Stability and the International Journal of Intelligent Systems in Accounting, Finance and Management. He has also been member of the editorial committee of international conferences and reviewer of international journals like: IEEE Transactions on Evolutionary Computation, the Journal of Financial Stability, the Journal of Economic Dynamics and Control, Applied Intelligence. Serafin holds a PhD in Computational Finance from the University of Essex, where he is currently a visiting fellow. He has belonged to the Mexican National Researchers System since 2009.

***

Bernardo Bravo-Benitez holds a bachelor's degree in Actuarial Sciences by the National Autonomous University of Mexico (UNAM) and is a candidate for the Master of Science in Financial Engineering at Columbia University. He has worked as an analyst at the Payment Systems General Directorate of Banco de México for three years. Additionally, he has published papers in international journals: the Journal of Economic Dynamics and Control and Computational Economics. His research interests include: market risk, counterparty and credit risk, systemic risk and financial networks.

Anne-Katrin Brehm is working in Liquidity Management, Institutional Cash & Securities Services at Deutsche Bank AG Frankfurt. Prior to this, she worked in the Asset & Liability Management of Deutsche Bank AG in Singapore. She holds a bachelor's degree in International Management with spezialization in Finance by the International School of Management, Frankfurt am Main.

Louise Carter is a Manager in the Payments Policy Department at the Reserve Bank of Australia, with responsibility on the oversight of international clearing and settlement systems operating in Australia. She joined the Reserve Bank in 2005, and has worked on secondment at the Bank of England in the areas of CCP policy and OTC derivatives reform. She holds a Master's degree in Economics from the Australian National University.

Liliana Garcia-Ochoa is a planning analyst at the payment systems studies of Banco de México. She currently works on large value payment systems, retail payments and network analysis at Banco de México. Nowadays, she is working on applying evolutionary computation techniques to analize behaviour clustering of financial market infrastructures. Liliana holds an MSc in Computer Science from the Universidad Autónoma Metropolitana (UAM) and a MPP from the Centro de Investigación y Docencia Económicas (CIDE).

Christian Goerlach is the Head of Balance Sheet & Liquidity, Institutional Cash & Securities Services at Deutsche Bank AG. In this role, he leads a global team dealing with topics such as Liquidity-, Interest Rate- and Balance Sheet Management, Collateral Solutions, Funds Transfer Pricing and Intraday Liquidity Management. Previous positions include Asset & Liability Management, Treasury and Strategy.

Jennifer Hancock is a Senior Manager in the Payments Policy Department at the Reserve Bank of Australia, with the responsibility for leading its oversight of payment systems, intermediaries and the markets. She joined the RBA in 2002, with the majority of her career spent working in the Payments Policy Department. She has experience in regulation and oversight of retail and wholesale payment systems, as well as central counterparties and securities settlement systems. Her current responsibilities include contributing to international policy making and inter-agency efforts to ensure that Australia's regulatory framework for over-the-counter derivatives is consistent with best practice. Jennifer has previously co-authored two simulation studies of real-time gross settlement systems. She holds a Master's degree in Economics from the University of New South Wales.

Ronald Heijmans is a researcher and policy maker in the payments division at the De Nederlandsche Bank since 2006. The focus of his policy work is on legal aspects and statistics of the euro-area 'Large Value Payment System,' TARGET2. His research interest is in stress scenario analysis, network topology, the interbank money market, identifying behavioural aspects, signs of liquidity problems with banks and quantitative oversight. Heijmans obtained his PhD in Business and Economy from the University of Groningen in 2012 and graduated from the University of Leiden in 2001 with an MSc in astrophysics. From 2001 to 2006 he was a researcher for the Netherlands Organisation for Applied Scientific Research. His main research areas were stealth techniques for military vehicles and atmospheric modeling.

Alexandros Kaliontzoglou obtained his Diploma in Electrical and Computer Engineering in 2000 and his Ph.D. in Information Systems Security in 2006 from the National Technical University of Athens, Greece. He has extensive experience in the consultant and banking industries and has participated in several E.C. research projects in the fields of information systems security, e-business and e-government. He has authored several publications in the above areas. Since 2009, he has been working as an expert in information systems security for the Bank of Greece in the field of Payment Systems Oversight. His responsibilities focus on payment systems operational reliability assessment and payment instruments security and fraud monitoring. He is an information systems security expert for the SecurePay Forum ESCB initiative. His current research interests focus in payments pattern analysis.

Kasperi Korpinen is an Economist and project manager at the Bank of Finland's payments and securities settlement system simulator team under the Financial Stability and Statistics department. Formerly, he has worked for the global Accounting and Control Risk management functions of the Corporate Treasury of Nokia Corporation and the Monetary and Financial Statistics department of the Bank of Finland. He holds a Master's degree in economics and has pursued additional studies in computer sciences, mathematics, statistics and sociology. He has research experience with topics like interest rate formation of corporate bank loans and bank competition, liquidity need effects of Financial Market Infrastructures (FMI) mergers, liquidity risks and counterparty exposures of FMI participants and economic warning signal development and computational parallelization. Kasperi has strong experience in the development of large and complex applications: Risk monitoring and reporting systems, statistical production systems with signal monitoring and error detection and simulation based modelling systems.

Susan Kriete-Dodds graduated in Economics at the University of Paderborn. After working as an analyst at the Federal Statistical Office in Wiesbaden, she received her PhD at the University of Basel.

Carlos León is responsible for investigating and developing methodologies for comprehensively overseeing local market's financial institutions and infrastructures as the Research and Development Manager at the Central Bank of Colombia's Financial Infrastructure Oversight Department. He is currently focusing on the assessment of systemic importance and intraday liquidity risk, and on identifying the connective and hierarchical structure of financial networks. Present interests include network theory, fuzzy logic, fractal theory, portfolio optimization, risk management, and simulation methods. Prior working experience includes positions as a Researcher for the Central Bank of Colombia's Foreign Reserves Department and for the Operations and Market Development Department, and as Head of the Risk Management Group at Colombia's Ministry of Finance-Public Credit Directorate. He holds a M.Sc. in Banking and Finance from HEC-Université de Lausanne (Switzerland), a M.A. in International Economics and a B.A. in Finance and International Relations from Externado de Colombia University (Colombia). He is PhD from Tilburg University (The Netherlands).

Bradley Lonnen is working in Market Management, Institutional Cash & Securities Services at Deutsche Bank AG.

Jorge Cruz Lopez is a Principal Researcher in the Financial Markets Department and an Associate Coordinator of the Financial System Review (FSR) at the Bank of Canada. His research interests are asset pricing and financial risk management. His most recent work focuses on optimizing collateral systems, assessing the stability of central counterparties (CCPs), identifying systemic risks in derivative transactions and improving the allocation of reserve portfolios. As an Associate Coordinator of the FSR, he oversees and undertakes analytical work related to the assessment of systemic risks in Canada. Jorge holds a PhD in Finance from Simon Fraser University and has been a visiting scholar at HEC Paris in France and at Queensland University of Technology in Australia.

Mark Manning is Deputy Head of Payments Policy Department at the Reserve Bank of Australia, with responsibility for the Reserve Bank's oversight of payments, clearing and settlement systems and associated policy and research. He joined the Reserve Bank in 2008 on secondment from the Bank of England, returning in a permanent role at the start of 2012. Previously, he held a number of positions at the Bank of England in the Financial Stability Directorate, including in financial market infrastructure policy and research, prudential policy and market surveillance. Before entering central banking in 2002, Mark spent several years as a fund manager in the City of London, including spells at Goldman Sachs Asset Management and Kleinwort Benson Investment Management. Mark has published a number of articles and research papers on payments and financial market infrastructure issues, and is co-editor of a book entitled The Economics of Large-value Payments and Settlement: Theory and Policy Issues for Central Banks. He holds Masters Degrees in Economics and Finance from University College London and the London Business School, respectively.

Dietmar Maringer is a full professor at the Business and Economics Faculty at the University of Basel, Switzerland. His research interests include simulation techniques and methods from computational intelligence and evolutionary methods, applied to financial and economic problems, including market regulation, portfolio optimization, risk management, artificial markets, and high-frequency trading. He holds degrees in computing and finance from the Universities of Vienna, Austria, and Cambridge, UK.

Marco Massarenti's career in central banking started in 2010, working on payment statistics in the Directorate General Statistics. He then joined the Directorate General Payments and Market Infrastructures, where he conducted research on money markets using TARGET2 payments data. He finally joined the Directorate General Market Operations in 2013 working as a Market Operations Expert on operational activities and as project manager. His career also comprises two short work experiences at the Deutsche Bundesbank.

Alistair Milne is Professor of Financial Economics and Co-Director of the Centre for Post Crisis Finance, School of Business and Economics, Loughborough University; also Visiting Scholar, Monetary Policy and Research Department, Bank of Finland and current president of the International Banking, Economics and Finance Association (www.ibefa.org). He is the author of one of the most comprehensive books on the global financial crisis of 2007-2008 and has written more than 60 articles and book chapters on topics including bank capital management and regulation; economics and competition policy in payment and transactions systems; the role of banks in the macroeconomy; credit risk modelling; bankruptcy costs and corporate decisions; development finance; and real estate markets. He is regularly interviewed by UK and international media and invited to speak at industry and policy events, for example (Oct 2012, Sept 2013) at SIBOS the world's largest financial services conference on standard setting and (Oct 2011) on the subject of clearing and settlement networks to the chairman and members of the Federal Reserve Board Prior to joining Loughborough University he was for twelve and half years senior lecturer/ and reader at Cass Business School. Before this he was: an economic adviser to the financial intermediaries division, of the Bank of England; a lecturer in the Department of Economics, University of Surrey; a research fellow in the macroeconomic forecasting group at London Business School; an economist at HM Treasury; a research assistant at the Department of Economics, Birkbeck College; held an ODI fellowship to National Statistics Office, Zomba, Malawi; and taught for one year at a secondary school in Western Kenya. He holds a PhD from the London School of Economics and a BA/MA from King's College Cambridge.

José Luis Molina-Borboa is a financial researcher from Banco de México, where he has been using network and statistical models to study financial stability and measure systemic risk in Mexico since 2013. He holds a BSc. in Applied Mathematics from Instituto Tecnológico Autónomo de México (ITAM), having taken some courses at Université Paris-Dauphine. He has published in the Journal of Network Theory in Finance.

Alexander Mueller studied economics and political science in Freiburg (Germany) and Lille (France), graduating with a diploma in economics and a master's degree in political science. Since 2012, he has been working as an expert for payment system analysis in the Deutsche Bundesbank's division responsible for Strategy, Policy and Oversight in Payments and Securities Settlement. His responsibilities and current research activities are focused on simulation studies and the analysis of data derived from payment systems.

Masashi Nakajima is PhD in Economics and Professor of Faculty of Economics and Business Administration at Reitaku University, Japan. He had a long career at a central bank, i.e., the Bank of Japan (BOJ). During his career at the BOJ (1981-2006), he gained a wide range of experience as a central banker, holding senior positions in various departments. He also had experience working for the Bank for International Settlements (BIS) in 2003-2005. He distinguishes himself as a coauthor of "All about Payment Systems" (2013, 3rd edition, in Japanese) and "All about Securities Settlement Systems" (2008, 2nd edition, in Japanese), and an author of "Payment System Technologies and Functions" (2011, in English). These books cover a wide-range of payment and settlement system issues and are regarded as must-read books on the subject of payment and settlement systems. He is also the author of "All about SWIFT" (2009, in Japanese), which is the first book in the world in any language to give a comprehensive presentation of SWIFT that is the essential global provider of secure financial messaging services.

Jhonatan Pérez is responsible for monitoring the activity of local securities markets (corporate and sovereign fixed income, and equity) as the Specialized Professional for local markets at the Central Bank of Colombia's Financial Infrastructure Oversight Department. His work places an emphasis on supporting their legal framework from a central bank's macro-prudential perspective and on assessing systemic risk. Also, he undertakes research projects about issues related to the securities market and their architecture. Present interests include Central Securities Depository´s (CSD) business lines (clearing and settlement, custodian services, securities lending), risk management, network theory and simulation methods. Prior working experience includes positions as Futures Analyst at the Colombian Stock Exchange, as well as trainee at Central Bank of Colombia's Operations and Market Development Department. He holds a B.Sc. in Industrial Engineering from Universidad Industrial de Santander (Colombia) and specialized courses in network science (Michigan University) and financial markets structure (Yale University), among others.

Anna Pliquett joined the Deutsche Bundesbank twelve years ago as a bank examiner in the banking supervision. There she had the opportunity to follow the development of the Basel II framework and by conducting on-site inspections its implementation in German banks in practice as well. After six years in the banking supervision she moved to the central office of the Bundesbank and became actively involved in several work streams concerning exchanges, financial market infrastructures and financial stability. Her current division at the Bundesbank is responsible for payment and securities settlement systems. She is acting Head of Section of the oversight function of the Bundesbank concerning financial market infrastructures. Her main responsibilities include the monitoring and assessment of CCPs and policy work regarding CCPs, OTC derivatives and trade repositories. Prior her joining the German central bank she spent two years in the US and held the position of a compliance officer with a middle-sized broker-dealer. Her firm motivated her to join the CFA Institute, which lead to her receiving the CFA charter in 2006, already as a central banker in Germany. Before her time in the US, Anna earned an MBA in Economics from the former university of economic sciences in Budapest, Hungary, and a finance diploma from the University of Leipzig, Germany.

Luc Renneboog is Professor of Corporate Finance at Tilburg University and Director of Graduate Studies at the CentER for Economic Research; he is also visiting Professor at Cambridge University. Before joining Tilburg, Luc was at the Catholic University of Leuven and Oxford University. He was also a visiting professor at the London Business School, HEC Paris, Venice University, University Paris-Dauphine, University of Cardiff, and European University Institute (Florence). He has graduated from the University of Leuven with an MSc in commercial engineering and with a BA in philosophy, from the University of Chicago with an MBA, and from the London Business School with a PhD in Financial Economics. He is also a research member of CentER for Economic Research, TILEC (Tilburg Law and Economics Center) and ECGI (European Corporate Governance Institute, Brussels). His research interests are corporate governance, mergers and acquisitions, law and economics, ethical/socially responsible investing, and alternative investments (such as art, diamond markets). On these topics, he has published in the Journal of Finance, Management Science, American Economic Review, Journal of Financial Intermediation, Journal of Law and Economics, Journal of Corporate Finance, Strategic Management Journal, Journal of Banking and Finance, Cambridge Journal of Economics, Oxford Review of Economic Policy, and others.

Antoaneta Serguieva is Chair of the Computational Finance and Economics Technical Committee at the IEEE Computational Intelligence Society, and member of the Financial Computing and Analytics Group at University College London (UCL). She is Program Director for the UCL MSc Financial Computing, and Partnership Director at UCL for the partnership between the University of California (UC)-Berkeley's Haas School of Business and UCL Computer Science. Antoaneta has been a Visiting Fellow at the US Treasury Office of Financial Research, the Bank of England, and the Bank of Mexico. She has also been on sabbatical at UC-Berkeley, a Fellow at the New England Complex Systems Institute, and has recently joined the Centre for Computational Finance and Economic Agents at the University of Essex as a Visiting Fellow. Antoaneta holds an MEng in systems engineering, MBA in finance, PhD in computer science, and currently works on her PhD in applied mathematics focused on systemic risk, within the Financial Mathematics Research Group at King's College London. She has also supervised PhD students and four of them have already successfully completed their studies.

Aaron Unterman is Senior Legal Counsel in the Derivatives branch of the Ontario Securities Commission. He participates in the development of OTC derivatives policy and regulation through his involvement in the Canadian Securities Administrators OTC Derivatives Group, the OTC Derivatives Regulators Group, and the IOSCO Task Force on Derivatives. He is the author of a number of publications, including *Exporting Risk: Global Implications of the Securitization of U.S. Housing Debt* and *Innovative Destruction: Structured Finance and Credit Market Reform in the Bubble Era*; both of which were published in the University of California's Hastings Business Law Journal. Aaron is a former member of Osler, Hoskin & Harcourt LLP's Banking and Financial Services Group.

Index

T

V

www.ingramcontent.com/pod-product-compliance
Lightning Source LLC
LaVergne TN
LVHW060400300926
849162LV00006B/1312

* 9 7 8 1 4 6 6 6 8 7 4 5 5 *